Multilingual Individuals and Multilingual Societies

Hamburg Studies on Multilingualism (HSM)

Hamburg Studies on Multilingualism (HSM) publishes research from colloquia on linguistic aspects of multilingualism organized by the Research Center on Multilingualism at the University of Hamburg.

For an overview of all books published in this series, please see
http://benjamins.com/catalog/hsm

Editors

Christoph Gabriel
Kurt Braunmüller
Barbara Hänel-Faulhaber
Research Center on Multilingualism, University of Hamburg

Volume 13

Multilingual Individuals and Multilingual Societies
Edited by Kurt Braunmüller and Christoph Gabriel

Multilingual Individuals and Multilingual Societies

Edited by

Kurt Braunmüller
Christoph Gabriel
Hamburg University

John Benjamins Publishing Company
Amsterdam / Philadelphia

 The paper used in this publication meets the minimum requirements of the American National Standard for Information Sciences – Permanence of Paper for Printed Library Materials, ANSI z39.48-1984.

Library of Congress Cataloging-in-Publication Data

Multilingual individuals and multilingual societies / edited by Kurt Braunmüller, Christoph Gabriel.

p.   cm. (Hamburg Studies on Multilingualism, ISSN 1571-4934 ; v. 13)

Includes bibliographical references and index.

1. Multilingualism--Social aspects. 2. Languages in contact. 3. Sociolinguistics. I. Braunmüller, Kurt, 1948- II. Gabriel, Christoph.

P115.45M75   2012

306.44'6--dc23   2012020096

ISBN 978 90 272 1933 6   (Hb ; alk. paper)

ISBN 978 90 272 7349 9   (Eb)

John Benjamins Publishing Co. · P.O. Box 36224 · 1020 ME Amsterdam · The Netherlands
John Benjamins North America · P.O. Box 27519 · Philadelphia PA 19118-0519 · USA

The production of this series has been made possible
through financial support to the Research Center on Multilingualism
(Sonderforschungsbereich 538 "Mehrsprachigkeit")
by the Deutsche Forschungsgemeinschaft (DFG).

Table of contents

Foreword

Kurt Braunmüller and Christoph Gabriel
University of Hamburg, Germany

There can no longer be any doubt that the default modes of communication observed in large parts of the world are determined by both individual and societal multilingualism rather than by monolingualism. The contemporary reality of multilingual practices encompasses a vast array of facets ranging from diasystematic variation within one and the same language through different constellations of plurilingualism and involving the acquisition of more than one language from birth on to so-called receptive multilingualism (see Ten Thije & Zeevaert 2007). However, most current linguistic theories still consider the linguistic competence of a human being to be (primarily) monolingual by default, though likely in part due to the fact that describing and/or modeling a single and isolated linguistic system seems to be easier than investigating an individual's multilingual abilities and multifaceted linguistic competencies. Nevertheless, research focusing explicitly on the interaction between different languages contained within an individual's collective linguistic knowledge has grown continuously in importance during the last decades within both formal and functional frameworks. In the same way, one can observe a considerable increase in the number of studies devoted to the pluri-faceted constellations of societal multilingualism, addressing sociolinguistics, the sociology of language as well as language-pedagogical approaches (see Kramsch 2009 and Aronin & Singleton 2012, among others).

The 25 contributions assembled in this volume represent a selection from the more than 120 papers originally presented at the international conference "Multilingual Individuals and Multilingual Societies" (MIMS), organized by the *Sonderforschungsbereich "Mehrsprachigkeit"* (SFB 538, Collaborative Research Center on "Multilingualism", funded by the German Research Foundation 1999–2011) and held at the University of Hamburg in Germany from October 6–8, 2010. The aim of this conference was to present a panorama of contemporary research in multilingualism, thereby highlighting the three main areas of investigation the scholars in SFB 538 had focused on during the twelve years of successful work conducted since its foundation by its first chair, Jürgen M. Meisel, in 1999:

1. the acquisition of multilingualism,
2. historical aspects of multilingualism and variance, and
3. multilingual communication.

The investigation of the simultaneous and subsequent acquisition of more than one language had been a core interest of the SFB 538 from the very beginning (see Müller 2003, Lleó 2006, Rinke & Kupisch 2011, for example). Taking the so-called cognitive turn in linguistic theory as a starting point, the research performed within the individual projects focused mainly on multilingual acquisition beginning at birth (i.e. two languages, 2L1), although second language acquisition (SLA) and foreign language learning were also taken into account (i.e. L1 + L2 ... + L_n). A further point of interest addressed primarily during the last period of funding concerned the loss of linguistic competencies in individuals, the phenomenon known as language attrition that often occurs when speakers switch from their native language (sometimes incompletely acquired as a heritage language, see Polinsky & Kagan 2007, among others) to a dominant language for social reasons. One of the main research questions was the extent to which simultaneous acquisition processes influence each other, be it in either a positive or a negative way. Do linguistic systems develop more or less independently of one another (i.e. L1 | L2) or do they interact (i.e. L1 ↔ L2), and if so, how can this interaction be characterized?

Part I of the present volume thus concentrates on the question of **how languages are acquired and lost in multilingual settings** while focusing on first and second language acquisition, foreign language learning and language attrition. The languages investigated include Germanic languages such as German, Dutch, Swedish and English as well as languages from the Slavonic and Romance families, i.e. Russian and Polish on the one hand and French, Italian and Spanish on the other. Turkish is also taken into account as a non-Indo-European language that plays in crucial role in several Middle and Northern European countries as a result of migration-induced contact with the relevant official languages. The individual papers cover a vast variety of linguistic phenomena, among them morphology, syntax and morphosyntax (see the contributions by Manuela Schönenberger, Monika Rothweiler & Franziska Sterner; Nelleke Strik; Natasha Ringblom; Bernhard Brehmer & Monika Rothweiler; Cristina Pierantozzi; Antje Stöhr, Deniz Akpınar, Giulia Bianchi & Tanja Kupisch and Mihaela Pirvulescu, Ana Pérez-Leroux & Yves Roberge), segmental phonology (Aleksandra Żaba & Conxita Lleó) and discourse production (Natalia Gagarina). Two papers address special aspects of foreign language learning, both in an experimental context as is the case of Susanne Carroll's work on Anglophone learners of German as well as in an educational setting as in the article by Andrea Haenni Hoti & Sybille Heinzmann, who address the acquisition of L2 English and L3 French in Swiss primary schools. Finally, Julia Festman's contribution offers an overview of contemporary research in multilingualism from a neuro-psycholinguistic perspective with special reference to acquisition processes.

The second focus of the research performed in SFB 538 concerned multilingualism and linguistic variance as seen from an historical angle, i.e. contact-induced language variation and linguistic change as the result of multilingualism. The restructuring of parameters, grammatical replication or code copying, grammaticalization and the pragmatic bleaching of categories as the result of linguistic contact were some of the issues addressed here (see Braunmüller & Ferraresi 2003, Siemund & Kintana 2008 and Braunmüller & House 2009). Research on the phonological and particularly the prosodic aspects of language contact and change intensified steadily during the last two funding periods (see Gabriel & Lleó 2011). All research questions were fundamentally guided by the uniformitarian concept, which assumes that earlier linguistic behavior cannot have differed substantially from that of today's speakers. This allows for conclusions about linguistic situation of the past to be drawn based on observations made today, thereby linking diachronic investigation to research in language acquisition (see Lightfoot & Westergaard 2007, among others).

Part II of this volume thus represents a selection of papers dealing with the question of **how languages change in multilingual settings**, thereby addressing different aspects of contact-induced language variation and change. While the contributions of Martin Elsig and Steffen Höder explore language contact from an explicitly diachronic point of view and analyze data from Old French, Middle High German, Old Swedish and Medieval Latin, three additional articles are devoted to the investigation of more recent cases of language contact and explore the evolution of new contact varieties by adopting a rather micro-diachronic perspective on contact-induced linguistic change. The multilingual settings addressed here include the situation of Danish-Faroese bilingualism on the Faroese Islands (Caroline Heycock & Hjalmar Petersen), the contact between German and Hungarian in Rumania (Csilla-Anna Szabó) and the variety of Polish spoken by Polish-German bilinguals in Germany (Bernhard Brehmer & Agnieszka Czachór). The contribution by Svenja Kranich, Juliana House & Victor Becher also investigates linguistic change from a micro-diachronic standpoint and analyzes changing conventions in English-German translations. Finally, a group of four papers places special emphasis on the phonological reflexes of language contact, exploring not only primarily intonation (Sabine Zerbian; Rafèu Sichel-Bazin, Carolin Buthke & Trudel Meisenburg; Andrea Pešková, Ingo Feldhausen, Elena Kireva & Christoph Gabriel), but also segmental aspects (Ariadna Benet, Susana Cortés & Conxita Lleó). The languages addressed here include several Romance vernaculars such as Occitan, French, Italian, Spanish, and Catalan, as well as South African English in contact with several autochthonous languages.

Much of the research conducted within the scope of SFB 538 also focused on the multi-facetted forms of multilingual communication. While most activities during the first funding periods were devoted to the investigation of translation and interpreting processes as well as to receptive multilingualism and discourse production (see House & Rehbein 2004, Rehbein, Hohenstein & Pietsch 2007 and Kranich, Becher, Höder & House 2011), later research increasingly focused on multilingual practices and forms of their implementation (Meyer & Apfelbaum 2010), partly in close collaboration with partners from outside academia, e.g. from consulting businesses as well as healthcare and educational institutions of various kinds (see Bührig forthcoming).

A smaller bundle of three articles assembled in **Part III** represents the results from this line of investigation and is devoted to the analysis of language use in several linguistic contact settings. The papers by Kristin Bührig, Ortrun Kliche, Bernd Meyer & Birte Pawlak and Myfyr Prys, Margaret Deuchar & Gwerfyl Roberts deal with multilingual practices in the healthcare system, taking into account German in contact with several migrant languages, in particular Turkish and Portuguese, and the contact between English and Welsh, respectively, while the contribution by Chiara Vettori, Katrin Wisniewski & Andrea Abel takes a closer look at the German-Italian contact situation in South Tyrol.

Before ending this short foreword, we would like to express our gratitude to the many reviewers who generously offered their time and expertise to improve the quality of the contributions contained in this volume. Some of the reviewers are also authors or co-authors of papers included in this book, though most of them are not. They are listed in alphabetical order in the following: Tanja Anstatt (Bochum), Lluïsa Astruc (Cambridge), Petra Bernardini (Lund), Bernhard Bremer (Hamburg), Marcus Callies (Mainz), Patrick Carlin (Cardiff), Ursula Doleschal (Klagenfurt), Stig Eliasson (Mainz/ Uppsala), Cathrine Fabricius-Hansen (Oslo), Ingo Feldhausen (Frankfurt), Gisella Ferraresi (Bamberg), Caroline Féry (Frankfurt), Susann Fischer (Hamburg), Natalia Gagarina (Berlin), Angela Grimm (Frankfurt), Ulrike Gut (Münster), Gisela Håkansson (Lund), Éva Ház (Brussels), Gerd Hentschel (Oldenburg), Martin Hilpert (Freiburg), Janet Holmes (Wellington), Holger Hopp (Mannheim), Adelheid Hu (Luxembourg), Gerson Klumpp (Tartu), Klaus-Michael Köpcke (Münster), Bernd Kortmann (Freiburg), Marion Krause (Hamburg), Tanja Kupisch (Hamburg/Lund), Conxita Lleó (Hamburg), Erik Magnusson Petzell (Stockholm), Claudine Moulin (Trier), Erin O'Rourke (Alabama), Lisa S. Pearl (Irvine), Lukas Pietsch (Hamburg), Brechtje Post (Cambridge), Rajiv Rao (Madison), Hans Reich (Landau), Claudia Maria Riehl (Köln), Monika Rothweiler (Bremen), Helge Sandøy (Bergen), Monika Schmitt (Groningen), Katrin Schmitz (Wuppertal), Nils Skotara (Hamburg), Ilse Stangen (Hamburg), Renata Szczepaniak (Hamburg), Maite Taboada (Vancouver), Höskuldur Thráinsson (Reykjavík), Bertus van Rooy (North-West University, South Africa), Katrina Walsh (Hamburg), and Erika Werlen (Wuppertal). We finally wish to thank Liefka Würdemann, Jasmina Živković and Karoline Krüger (Hamburg) for their assistance in cross-checking the references.

References

Aronin, L. & D. Singleton. 2012. *Multilingualism* (IMPACTt: Studies in Language and Society 30). Amsterdam: John Benjamins.

Braunmüller, K. & G. Ferraresi, eds. 2003. *Aspects of Multilingualism in European Language History* (Hamburg Studies on Multilingualism 2). Amsterdam: John Benjamins.

Braunmüller, K. & J. House, eds. 2009. *Convergence and Divergence in Language Contact* (Hamburg Studies on Multilingualism 8). Amsterdam: John Benjamins.

Bührig, K., ed. Forthcoming. *Transferring Linguistic Know-how into Practice: Perspectives and Results* (Hamburg Studies on Multilingualism 15). Amsterdam: John Benjamins.

Gabriel, C. & C. Lleó, eds. 2011. *Intonational Phrasing in Romance and Germanic: Cross-linguistic and Bilingual Studies* (Hamburg Studies on Multilingualism 10). Amsterdam: John Benjamins.

House, J. & J. Rehbein, eds. 2004. *Multilingual Communication* (Hamburg Studies on Multilingualism 3). Amsterdam: John Benjamins.

Kramsch, C. 2009. *The Multilingual Subject: What Foreign Language Learners Say about their Experience and Why it Matters.* Oxford: OUP.

Kranich, S., V. Becher., S. Höder & J. House, eds. 2011. *Multilingual Discourse Production: Diachronic and Synchronic Perspectives* (Hamburg Studies on Multilingualism 12). Amsterdam: John Benjamins.

Lightfoot, D. & M. Westergaard. 2007. Language acquisition and language change: Interrelationships. *Language and Linguistics Compass* 1: 396–415.

Lleó, C. 2006. *Interfaces in Multilingualism: Acquisition and Representation* (Hamburg Studies on Multilingualism 4). Amsterdam: John Benjamins.

Meyer, B. & B. Apfelbaum, eds. 2010. *Multilingualism at Work: From Policies to Practices in Public, Medical and Business Settings* (Hamburg Studies on Multilingualism 9). Amsterdam: John Benjamins.

Müller, N., ed. 2003. *(In)vulnerable Domains in Multilingualism* (Hamburg Studies on Multilingualism 1). Amsterdam: John Benjamins.

Polinsky, M. & O. Kagan. 2007. Heritage languages: In the 'wild' and in the classroom. *Language and Linguistics Compass* 1: 368–395.

Rehbein, J., C. Hohenstein & L. Pietsch, eds. 2007. *Connectivity in Grammar and Discourse* (Hamburg Studies on Multilingualism 5). Amsterdam: John Benjamins.

Rinke, E. & T. Kupisch, eds. 2011. *The Development of Grammar: Language Acquisition and Diachronic Change. In Honour of Jürgen M. Meisel* (Hamburg Studies on Multilingualism 11). Amsterdam: John Benjamins.

Siemund, P. & N. Kintana. 2008. *Language Contact and Contact Languages* (Hamburg Studies on Multilingualism 7). Amsterdam: John Benjamins.

Ten Thije, J. D. & L. Zeevaert, eds. 2007. *Receptive Multilingualism: Linguistic Analyses, Language Policies and Didactic Concepts* (Hamburg Studies on Multilingualism 6). Amsterdam: John Benjamins.

PART I

How language is acquired and lost in multilingual settings

First and second language acquisition, foreign language learning and language attrition

Case marking in child L1 and early child L2 German*

Manuela Schönenberger[1], Monika Rothweiler[2]
and Franziska Sterner[2]
[1]University of Oldenburg, Germany; [2]University of Bremen, Germany

We examine case marking in spontaneous production data from four successive bilingual children and in experimental data from 21 successive bilingual and 14 monolingual children. A clear difference surfaces between spontaneous production data and experimental data. Based on the spontaneous production data, we conclude that the four successive bilingual children behave like the monolingual children studied by Eisenbeiss, Bartke & Clahsen (2006). They rarely produce structural case errors and often produce lexical case errors. But under experimental conditions, successive bilingual and monolingual children produce a large number of structural case errors, in particular with structural dative. Our experimental findings from the monolingual children are in stark contrast to those in Eisenbeiss et al., which are based on spontaneous production data only.

Keywords: German, Turkish, case errors, lexical case, structural case, child L1 acquisition, early child L2 acquisition

1. Introduction

In this paper we compare the acquisition of case in German by successive bilingual children with that by monolingual German children discussed in Eisenbeiss, Bartke & Clahsen (2006). Our intent is to investigate whether early L2 acquisition resembles L1 acquisition or whether it already shows similarities with adult L2 acquisition. According to Meisel (2009) domains of grammar are affected by maturational changes of the acquisition device around the age of 4. Meisel concludes from various studies that "although maturational changes affecting language development may happen at virtually every point of development, children proceed through periods during which sensitive phases for different grammatical phenomena cluster, thereby characterizing

---

*   We are grateful to two anonymous reviewers for very helpful and detailed comments.

particularly crucial periods" (2009: 10). Such critical periods occur around age 6 to 7, and around age 4. Since most of the successive bilingual children of our study started to be regularly exposed to German before the age of 4, we expect their acquisition of case in German to be comparable to that of monolingual children.

In Eisenbeiss et al.'s analysis the distinction between structural case and lexical case plays a crucial role. Based on spontaneous production data they observe that monolingual children do not have any difficulties with structural case, but that they do have difficulties with lexical case. In our analysis we use spontaneous production data from four successive bilingual children with L1 Turkish as well as experimental data from a larger group of children.[1] The experimental data include data from successive bilingual children with different L1s (Turkish, Russian, or Polish) and monolingual German children. Just like the monolingual children, the successive bilingual children produce more lexical than structural case errors in the spontaneous production data. However, in the experimental data, both the successive bilingual children, as well as the monolingual children, produce many structural case errors. We suggest that the consideration of both spontaneous and experimental data can provide a more complete picture.

Our paper is organized as follows. Section 2 introduces the German case system and the distinction between structural case and lexical case. Section 3 is based on Eisenbeiss et al. (2006). Section 3.1 provides a brief overview of the acquisition of case in German, the types of errors encountered, the explanations given by Eisenbeiss et al. to account for these errors, and a critical discussion of these explanations. In 3.2 the findings of their study are summarized and their criteria are described in more detail in Section 3.3. Sections 4 and 5 present our own study and outline our findings. Section 4 presents the results on case in the spontaneous production data from the four successive bilingual children with L1 Turkish. Section 5 describes the experiment used to obtain data from successive bilingual and monolingual children and summarizes the findings on case. Section 6 contains the discussion and Section 7 summarizes the conclusions.

2.   The German case system

2.1   Case forms in German

German distinguishes four cases: nominative, accusative, dative, and genitive. Case can surface on pronouns, on articles and article-like words, on attributive adjectives,

---

1.   The data from the successive bilingual children with L1 Turkish come from a project entitled 'Specific language impairment and early second language acquisition: differentiating deviations in morphosyntactic acquisition', directed by Monika Rothweiler. The project was part of the Collaborative Research Center 538 at the University of Hamburg, funded by the German Research Foundation (Deutsche Forschungsgemeinschaft, DFG). The authors gratefully acknowledge the support by the DFG.

and on a restricted class of nouns. In the examples in (1) there are two case assigners: finite I (INFL), which assigns nominative to the subject position, and the transitive verb *überholen* 'overtake', which assigns accusative to the object position. Case distinctions between the subject DP *der hinkende Hase* in (1a) and the object DP *den hinkenden Hasen* in (1b) are visible on the definite article, the attributive adjective, and the noun. No such case distinctions are visible in the DP *eine schnelle Schildkröte*, which receives accusative in (1a) and nominative in (1b).

(1)   a.   [Der hinkende Hase]$_{SUBJ}$ überholt [eine schnelle Schildkröte]$_{OBJ.}$
         the limping rabbit   overtakes   a   fast   turtle

       b.   [Eine schnelle Schildkröte]$_{SUBJ}$ überholt [*den*   hinkende*n*
         a   fast   turtle   overtakes the-ACC limping-ACC
         Hase*n*]$_{OBJ.}$
         rabbit-ACC

Genitive which can either be prenominal, as in *Omas Auto* 'granny's car', and which occurs frequently, or postnominal, as in *die Katze meiner Nachbarin* 'the cat of my neighbor', which is rare in spoken German, will not be discussed here.

Besides case, German has number (singular vs. plural) and three genders (masculine, feminine, and neuter). Tables 1a and 1b list the different case forms of the definite article and the personal pronouns. Since these case forms are suppletive, case, number,

Table 1a. Definite article

		NOM	ACC	DAT
SG	masculine	der	den	dem
	feminine	die	die	der
	neuter	das	das	dem
PL		die	die	den

Table 1b. Personal pronouns

			NOM	ACC	DAT
1st person	SG		ich	mich	mir
	PL		wir	uns	uns
2nd person	SG		du	dich	dir
	PL		ihr	euch	euch
3rd person	SG	masculine	er	ihn	ihm
		feminine	sie	sie	ihr
		neuter	es	es	ihm
	PL		sie	sie	ihnen

and gender cannot be teased apart in a given form. Moreover, all case forms are syncretic. For example, the article form *die* is ambiguous between [+feminine, +singular, +nominative], [+feminine, +singular, +accusative], [+plural, +nominative], and [+plural, +accusative]. The case forms that are unambiguous for a given gender and number are highlighted in the grey cells. In our discussion of case we shall use the following abbreviations in the tables and the examples: SG (singular), PL (plural), NOM (nominative), ACC (accusative), and DAT (dative).

2.2   Structural case vs. lexical case

For the analysis of the acquisition of case the distinction between structural case and lexical case plays an important role. Here only the cases that are relevant for child language are discussed. We follow Eisenbeiss et al. (2006) who consider as structural case nominative, accusative on complements of verbs and prepositions, and dative on indirect objects of ditransitive verbs. In the examples in (2) the DPs that receive structural case are italicized.

> (2) a. *Der*   *kleine Junge* schenkt *diesen*   *Goldfisch seiner*   *Oma.*
>   the-NOM little   boy   gives   this-ACC goldfish his-DAT granny
>   'The little boy will give this goldfish to his grandmother.'
>
>   b. *Ein*   *Frosch* springt schnell in *den*   *Teich.*
>   a-NOM frog   jumps   quickly in the-ACC pond
>   'A frog quickly jumps into the pond.'

Dative on objects of two-place predicates, on complements of prepositions, and on subjects with the theta-role experiencer are regarded as instances of lexical case. The DPs that receive lexical case are italicized in the examples in (3).

> (3) a. Das kleine Mädchen hilft *ihrem*   *Opa*   in *der*   *Garage.*
>   the little   girl   helps her-DAT grandpa in the-DAT garage
>   'The little girl helps her grandfather in the garage.'
>
>   b. *Mir*   graut davor.
>   me-DAT dread it
>   'I dread it.'

3.   The acquisition of case in German

3.1   An overview

In the two-word stage there are no case distinctions. The case system starts to develop after age 2 (Eisenbeiss et al. 2006). Accusative and dative appear in suppletive forms, in particular, in personal pronouns, before they start to appear as regular suffixes, as, for example, on indefinite determiners (see also Clahsen 1984, Meisel 1986, Tracy 1986). Case marking on nouns, as in (4), is acquired late. According to Eisenbeiss et al. this may be due to the fact that it is restricted to a small class of nouns and it is often omitted by native adult speakers.

(4) Er sieht den   Studenten   nicht.
     he sees the-ACC student-ACC not
     'He doesn't see the student.'

Eisenbeiss et al. note that the following three types of error are common in German child language:

– overgeneralization of structural case to contexts requiring lexical case (see 5a),
– omission of case suffixes on indefinite articles and article-words ending in *-ein* (see 5b),
– substitution of dative *-m* by accusative *-n* (see 5c).

(5) a. Ich winke dich.
         I   wave you-ACC

     a'. correct: Ich winke dir.
                  I   wave you-DAT
         'I am waving to you.'

     b. noch ein Fisch malen
         still a   fish draw
         'draw another fish'

     b'. correct: noch einen Fisch malen
                  still a-ACC fish draw

     c. Julia auf den   Bein sitzen
         Julia on the-ACC leg sit
         'sit on Julia's leg'

     c'. correct: Julia auf dem   Bein sitzen
                  Julia on the-DAT leg sit

They explain the occurrence of these three types of errors as follows. Children associate certain structural positions with certain cases, e.g. the object position with accusative case. This type of error is probably due to the fact that most verbs that take two arguments assign structural accusative to the internal argument. There are only a few verbs (e.g. *winken* 'wave', *danken* 'thank', *gehören* 'belong') that assign lexical dative to the internal argument.

For the omission of the case suffix in (5b) Eisenbeiss et al. provide a morphosyntactic explanation. Words like *ein* can have a strong form when they are used pronominally, but they have a weak form when they are used attributively, as shown by the contrast between (6a) and (6b). Children are assumed to overgeneralize the uninflected form to contexts in which this form is ungrammatical.

(6) a. Das ist einer.
         this is one

     b. Das ist ein Hund.
         this is a   dog

The substitution of *-m* by *-n* is assumed to be "due to the phonological similarity of these two forms rather than to a confusion between dative and accusative case" (Eisenbeiss et al. 2006: 11). Eisenbeiss et al. justify this assumption by pointing out that "the same children who substituted *-n* for *-m* supplied the correct dative markers *-r* for feminine singular and *-n* for plural nouns and did not overapply accusative forms in such cases" (Eisenbeiss et al. 2006: 11).

While we find the explanation for the first type of error plausible, the explanation for the omission of a case suffix seems less plausible. A distinction between spoken and written German should be made. As noted by Schönenberger (2011) native speakers rarely seem to use the accusative form *einen* in spoken German. Two adult speakers of German interacting with some of the successive bilingual children in our project more often used the reduced forms *ein* or *n* than *einen*, as shown in Table 2.

Thus these two speakers are much more likely to produce (7a) or (7b) than (7c). Whether the *n* in examples of the type in (7a) is lengthened could not be determined.

(7) a. Er hat ein Fisch gefangn.
         'He has caught a fish.'

     b. Er hat n Fisch gefangn.

     c. Er hat einen Fisch gefangn.

The form *einen* in (7c) is typical of written German. But while in written German there is no distinction between strong and weak inflection in the accusative and dative, such a distinction is made in spoken German.

As concerns substitution errors, a phonological account does not explain why substitution should be unidirectional, i.e. that *dem* is replaced by *den* but *den* is not replaced by *dem*. The similarity between the two forms is the same in both directions, thus a unidirectional error is not explained by this account. Furthermore, it is unclear whether substitution of *ihm* (him-DAT) by *ihn* (him-ACC), or vice versa, also occurs. These forms are phonologically as similar as *dem* and *den*. The authors do not mention

Table 2. *Einen* in spoken adult German (Schönenberger 2011)

	einen	ein	n
Vera	1	20	5
Silke	1	5	27

whether substitution only occurs in certain inflected words, or whether it also occurs in stem codas (*kämm* [kɛm] 'comb.1SG.PRESENT' vs. *kenn* [kɛn] 'know.1SG.PRESENT', *Kram* 'stuff' vs. *Kran* 'crane', etc.) which would be expected if substitution errors are based on phonological similarity between *m* and *n*, and which should then be unidirectional as well. But even if -*m* were replaced by -*n* in stem codas, an explanation for the unidirectionality covering these cases would be necessary.

3.2   The study by Eisenbeiss et al. (2006): Case marking by monolingual German children

Eisenbeiss et al. present and discuss spontaneous production data from 10 monolingual German children, five children with specific language impairment and five children without specific language impairment, and find no essential differences regarding case marking between these two groups of children. In the following, we concentrate on the data and results from the typically developing children.

Table 3 contains some information about the five typically developing children from whom data were used. The abbreviation MLU stands for 'mean length of utterance', which was calculated based on words (not morphemes). As can be seen from the table, the age ranges from 2;6 to 3;6, the MLU ranges from 2.1 to 4.2, and the number of analyzable case forms per child varies between 199 and 1644.

Table 4a summarizes the data concerning structural case. The second line is to be read as follows: there were 2619 contexts in which an unambiguous NOM case form was required and the children produced 2616 such forms, which amounts to 99.9% correct case marking in this context. As can be seen from the table, the children score very highly on all three structural cases.

Table 3. Information about monolingual child participants

Child	Age	MLU	recordings	analyzed case forms
Mathias	3;1–3;6	2.9–3.5	6	261
Carsten	3;6	4.2	1	775
Svenja	2;9–3;3	3.3–4.1	15	1644
Annelie	2;8–2;9	2.5–3.1	2	199
Leonie	2;6–2;11	2.1–3.1	7	322

Table 4a. Structural case in the monolingual German data

	children (n = 5)	
NOM	99.9%	(2616/2619)
ACC	99.0%	(298/301)
DAT	94.9%	(112/118)

Some examples in which the children produced a structural case error are given in (8). There were three examples in which the children used nominative instead of accusative, as in (8a), and six examples in which they are said to have used accusative instead of dative, as in (8b). Note that the case form *die* in (8b) is ambiguous between being nominative or accusative, and should therefore not be counted as an unambiguous overextension of accusative to a dative context. Interestingly, there were 31 examples in which the children used a PP instead of a DP to express the indirect object of a ditransitive verb, as in (9a). Sometimes the children also omitted the indirect object of a ditransitive verb, as in (9b). Considering indirect objects the authors note that "case-marking errors on indirect objects are extremely rare [and that] although some children experience difficulties expressing obligatory (third) arguments in target-like ways, this does not affect dative case marking in indirect object NPs" (Eisenbeiss et al. 2006: 21f).

(8) a. für jeder   eine   (Carsten)
         for each-NOM one

         correct: *jeden* instead of *jeder*
         '(There is) one for everybody.'

     b. Das sag ich die   Mama.   (Mathias)
         this tell I   the-NOM/ACC mommy

         correct: *der* instead of *die*
         'I will tell this to mommy.'   (Eisenbeiss et al. 2006: 20f)

(9) a. zu Ente geben   (Leonie)
         to duck give

         correct: *der* Ente geben
         '(I want to) give (that) to the duck.'

     b. Wir müssen das sente.   (Svenja)
         we   must   this give
         'We must give this (to somebody).'   (Eisenbeiss et al. 2006: 21)

The data on lexical case are summarized in Table 4b, in which case assignment by a verb (V) or a preposition (P) is listed separately. The percentages of correct case forms in these contexts are much lower. Examples of lexical case errors are shown in (10).

Table 4b. Lexical case in the monolingual German data

	children (n = 5)	
DAT (V)	64.3%	(18/28)
DAT (P)	68.9%	(93/135)

(10) a. Wer   das gehört?   (Svenja)
          who-NOM that belongs

          correct: *wem* instead of *wer*
          'Who does this belong to?'

      b. Ich bin kalt.   (Leonie)
          I   am   cold

          correct: *mir* instead of *ich*
          'I am cold.'   (Eisenbeiss et al. 2006: 23f)

To summarize, Eisenbeiss et al. distinguish between structural and lexical case. In their analysis they concentrate on unambiguous forms in utterances with a case assigner (cf. 3.3). Based on the spontaneous production data from five typically developing children they show that structural case does not pose a problem for these children, while lexical case does, independent of whether it is assigned by a verb or a preposition. The authors exclude substitution errors of e.g. *dem* by *den* from the counts. It is therefore unclear how often such substitution errors occurred (cf. 3.3).

3.3   The criteria used by Eisenbeiss et al. in their analysis of case

Since for our analysis of case we adopt the criteria of Eisenbeiss et al. in order to make a comparison between their data and ours, those criteria for analyzing the data will be presented in detail here. For clarity, we added the examples in (11) to (14). They counted case-marked forms according to the following conventions:

–   only unambiguous case forms are counted (see (11a) vs. (11b)),
–   only utterances in which the case assigner is overt are counted (see (12a) vs. (12b')),
–   all forms of indefinite articles, article-words, and pronouns that end in -*ein* in the base form and that are inflected in the same way, such as *ein* 'a', *mein* 'my', *kein* 'no', are not counted (see (13)),
–   substitutions of -*m* by -*n* are not counted, while correct productions of *dem* are counted (see (14)).

(11) a. Peter sieht *den*   hund.   (counted)
          Peter sees the-ACC dog

      b. Peter sieht *die*   maus.   (not counted)
          Peter sees the-NOM/ACC mouse

(12) a. Sie hilft *der*   Maus.   (counted)
          she helps the-DAT mouse

      b. Int.: Wem hilfst du?
                 'Whom do you help?'

      b'. child: *der*   Maus   (not counted)
                 the-DAT mouse

(13) a. Sie sieht *meinen* Hund.   (not counted)
          she sees my-ACC dog

      b. Sie sieht *meinen.*   (not counted)
          she sees mine

(14) a. Sie hilft *den*   Kind.   (not counted)
          she helps the-ACC child

      b. Sie hilft *dem*   Kind.   (counted)
          she helps the-DAT child

Some case forms that could have been included in their counts, such as substitution errors of e.g. *dem* by *den* were excluded from the counts. Since we consider controversial their account of these errors in terms of phonological similarity, in the analysis of our own data we provide counts in which such errors are excluded, as well as counts in which they are included.

4. Spontaneous production data from successive bilingual children with L1 Turkish

We analyzed spontaneous production data from four successive bilingual children, whose L1 is Turkish. Table 5 contains some information about these child participants. AO stands for 'age of onset', i.e. the age at which the children started to be exposed to German regularly, which is assumed to coincide with their age on entering a German kindergarten in Hamburg. ME stands for 'months of exposure' (to German).

Table 5. Information about child participants with L1 Turkish

child	AO	ME	MLU	recordings	analyzed case forms
Faruk	2;9	12–24	3.0–4.2	4	703
Eser	3;0	9–30,5	3.4–4.3	5	599
Gül	3;0	12–30,5	1.7–3.6	5	406
Fikret	4;2	8–29,5	2.1–3.4	8	632

Table 6a. Structural case in the early child L2 data

	children (n = 4)	
NOM	99.5%	(2059/2069)
ACC	93.0%	(146/157)
DAT	93.9%	(31/33)

Table 6b. Lexical case in the early child L2 data

	children (n = 4)	
DAT (V)	80.0%	(8/10)
DAT (P)	73.2%	(52/71)

To make a comparison between the successive bilingual children and the monolingual children in Eisenbeiss et al.'s study we used the same criteria as in Eisenbeiss et al. The data on structural case are summarized in Table 6a and those on lexical case are summarized in Table 6b.

In addition, there were 19 substitution errors in a dative context involving a prepositional case assigner (15 examples with *den* instead of *dem* and 4 examples with *ihn* instead of *ihm*). If these substitution errors were taken into account the percentage of correct case in DAT (P) would be even lower (57.8%).

Just like the monolingual children, the successive bilingual children perform much better on structural case than on lexical case, at least when lexical case is assigned by a preposition. Since we do not have enough data on lexical case assigned by verbs, we cannot determine whether lexical case assigned by verbs is also problematic.

5.   Experimental data from monolingual and successive bilingual children

We conducted an experiment to pursue the question whether children use PPs to express indirect objects in ditransitive verb constructions. We were also interested in case marking of the direct and indirect object. The original idea for this type of experiment goes back to Sonja Eisenbeiss (see Eisenbeiss, Bartke, Weyerts & Clahsen 1994). At the beginning of the experiment the experimenter introduced three finger puppets (varying in grammatical gender) to the child and told the child that it was each puppet's birthday and each was eager to be given presents. Several items which were possible presents were laid out in front of the child. She was asked to name each item in order to ensure she could recognize each one, and that it would be more natural for her to use the definite rather than the indefinite article later. We deliberately chose items that children are familiar with. The child was then asked to distribute the different items to the puppets and to talk about the action as she did so. The experimenter demonstrated how to proceed, by giving an item to a puppet and commenting on the action, as in (15). (For a more detailed description of the experiment and modifications of it, see Schönenberger, Sterner & Ruberg 2011a.)

(15)   Ich gebe dem   Schaf$_{DO}$ die   Brille$_{IO}$.
     I   give the-DAT sheep   the-NOM/ACC glasses
     'I'm giving the sheep the glasses.'

Table 7. Information about child participants[2]

Group	N children	N recordings	AO	Age	ME
L1 German	14	14		2;4–5;0	28–60
L1 Turkish	12	16	2;9–4;2	4;0–6;6	14–41
L1 Polish/Russian	9	13	2;10–3;9	4;7–6;0	13–37

Table 7 summarizes the relevant details of the children who participated. The successive bilingual children either spoke Turkish, Polish, or Russian as their L1. These languages have richer case systems than German, but they also use dative for the indirect object and accusative for the direct object in the construction we tried to elicit, as shown in (16).

(16) a. Gözlüğü$_{DO}$ koyuna$_{IO}$ hediye ediyorum.   Turkish
       glasses-ACC sheep-DAT present make-PROG-1SG
       'I'll give the glasses to the sheep.'

    b. Daruję   owcy$_{IO}$ okulary$_{DO}$.   Polish
       give-PRS.1SG sheep-DAT glasses-ACC.PL

    c. Darju   ovce$_{IO}$ očki$_{DO}$.   Russian
       give-PRS.1SG sheep-DAT glasses-ACC.PL

The children produced many case errors on the indirect object (see Schönenberger, Sterner & Ruberg 2011b). Some examples in which the indirect object is marked as non-dative are shown in (17). Note that the children also had problems with gender assignment. For example, one of the successive bilingual children assigned all three genders to the noun *Maus* 'mouse'. The monolingual children also produced gender errors (or inconsistent gender): the nouns *Tiger* 'tiger' and *Schlüssel* 'key' in (17b) are masculine not neuter.

(17) a. Ich schenke *die*   Maus   eine Blume.
       I   give   the-NOM/ACC mouse a   flower
                                         (Sergej, L1 Russian, ME 30)

       correct: Ich schenke der Maus eine Blume.
                 'I'll give the mouse a flower.'

    b. Ich schenke das   Slössel auch *das*   Tiger.
       I   give   the-NOM/ACC key   also the-NOM/ACC tiger
                                         (Rieke, L1 German, 3;10)

       correct: Ich schenke den Schlüssel auch dem Tiger.
                 'I'll also give the key to the tiger.'

---

2.   Four of the bilingual children in each group participated twice, with a gap of at least 5 months between sessions.

The form *der* is ambiguous between masculine nominative and feminine dative. Given that gender assignment was not always appropriate, the form *der* was classified as ambiguous in Tables 8a and 8b. In example (18a) *der* would be appropriate, but since the same child also used *den* in (18b), it is unclear whether this child construes *Maus* 'mouse' with feminine or with masculine. If there was some evidence that a child consistently construed a noun with feminine gender, *der* was analyzed as dative, and if a child consistently construed a feminine noun with masculine gender, *der* was analyzed as a case error.

(18) a. Ich möchte *der*   Maus   die Gabel und   der Messer schenken.
          I   would   the-DAT mouse the fork   and   the knife   give
                                                        (Juliane, L1 German, 3;9)

          correct: Ich möchte der Maus die Gabel und das Messer schenken.
                    'I'd like to give the mouse the fork and the knife.'

    b. möchte *den*   Maus   den   Ball schenken
        would   the-ACC mouse the-ACC ball give   (Juliane, L1 German, 3;9)

        correct: möchte der Maus den Ball schenken
                  '(I) would like to give the mouse the ball.'

The data on case marking of indirect objects are summarized in Table 8a. (n in the first row refers to the total number of indirect objects expressed as either Det N or as a pronoun.)[3] In contrast to Eisenbeiss et al. we also included utterances in which the case assigner is not present, as in (19). We included such examples because the construction we tried to elicit was always the same, thus the case assigner was either *schenken* or *geben*, both meaning *give*:

(19) Int. Wem schenkst du den Eimer?
           'Whom do you give the bucket?'

      child: die   Oma   (Fikret, L1 Turkish, ME15)
              the-NOM/ACC granny

Table 8a. Case marking on indirect object DPs (with and without overt case assigner) in child L1 and early child L2 German

	L1 German (n = 113)		L1 Turkish (n = 82)		L1 Russian/Polish (n = 92)	
DAT	36.3%	(41)	10.9%	(9)	25.0%	(23)
ambiguous	7.1%	(8)	10.9%	(9)	1.1%	(1)
Non-DAT	56.6%	(64)	78.0%	(64)	73.9%	(68)

3.   Overall the children rarely used pronouns to express the indirect object. There are 8 examples in the data from the L1 German children, 6 examples in the data from the L1 Turkish children, and 7 examples in the data from the L1 Russian/Polish children.

Table 8b. Case marking on indirect object DPs (with overt case assigner only) in child L1 and early child L2 German

	L1 German (n = 67)		L1 Turkish (n = 63)		L1 Russian/Polish (n = 71)	
DAT	47.8%	(32)	12.7%	(8)	22.5%	(16)
ambiguous	3.0%	(2)	6.3%	(4)	1.4%	(1)
Non-DAT	49.2%	(33)	81.0%	(51)	76.0%	(54)

There were many examples in which *dem* was substituted for by *den* and some in which *ihm* was substituted for by *ihn*. In total, there were 109 *dem-den* substitutions and 11 *ihm-ihn* substitutions. These are not included in Table 8a, although they are potential case errors. There were 40 substitution errors in the L1 German data, 37 in the L1 Turkish data, and 43 in the L1 Polish/Russian data. Had these examples been included in Table 8a, the error rate for each group of children would have been even higher. In our data many such substitution errors occurred, and inclusion rather than exclusion of these data can make a difference, as we will show in our discussion of accusative errors.

In Table 8b, only utterances with an indirect object and a case assigner are counted, in accordance with Eisenbeiss et al.'s criteria in Section 3.3. A comparison between Tables 8a and 8b reveals that the error rates change only slightly, independent of whether all utterances or only non-elliptical utterances with a case assigner are considered. That the monolingual children produce so many structural dative errors is in stark contrast to the findings in Eisenbeiss et al. In our experimental data, the error rate is almost 50% in examples with structural dative, whereas in the spontaneous data discussed by Eisenbeiss et al. it is less than 6%.

As well as indirect object DPs the successive bilingual children, and in particular the children with L1 Turkish, also used PPs instead of nominals, as shown in Figure 1. The monolingual children rarely did so. There were only three examples in their data. The differences between all three groups are highly significant (χ^2-test, p<.01). The label 'nominal' covers both DPs (Det N and pronouns) and bare Nouns.

There were 24 examples in which the successive bilingual children used a preposition that assigns dative case (generally *zu* 'to') and the complement was either a pronoun or a DP (Det N). The children used dative in three of these examples, and a non-dative form (*das/die*) in 13 examples. They also produced 8 substitution errors (*den/ihn*). In Eisenbeiss et al.'s account it is expected that the children produce errors in this context, since such prepositions are lexical case assigners.

Next we consider case on direct objects, which should be marked with accusative. There were some case errors in this context as well. The children sometimes used nominative instead of accusative, as in (20a). They also sometimes produced dative instead of accusative, as in (20b). It is unclear whether the latter type of error would be counted as such in Eisenbeiss et al. But given that they consider substitution of *dem* by *den* as the result of phonological similarity, the substitution of *den* by *dem* should be explained along the same lines.

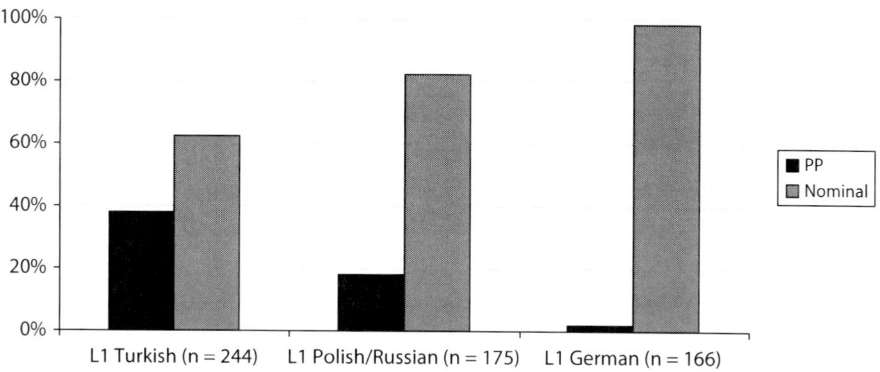

Figure 1. Realization of indirect objects as PP or as nominal (from Schönenberger et al. 2011b)

(20) a. Ich senke die   Maus *der*   Teller.
          I   give   the-NOM/ACC mouse the-NOM plate

$\qquad\qquad\qquad\qquad\qquad\qquad\qquad$ (Paulina, L1 German, 3;1)

        correct: Ich schenke der Maus den Teller.
                 'I'll give the mouse the plate.'

    b. *dem*   Auto geb ich zu Maus.   (Patryk, L1 Polish, ME 20)
       the-DAT car   give I   to mouse

       correct: Das Auto geb ich der Maus.
                 'The car, I'll give to the mouse.'

The data on case marking of direct objects are summarized in Table 9, in which accusative errors are subdivided into overextension of nominative (*der*) and overextension of dative (*dem*). All utterances were taken into account, independent of whether the case assigner was present or not. The German children more often produced *der* than *dem* errors, while the children with L1 Russian or Polish more often produced *dem* than *der* errors. If both types of errors are taken into account, the error rate increases slightly in the L1 German data and more than doubles in the L1 Russian/Polish data. The Turkish children performed best in this context. There were only two *der* errors and one *dem* error in their data. The fact that the monolingual children produced structural accusative errors is also in contrast to Eisenbeiss et al.'s finding.

Since the age range of the monolingual children was broad, ranging from 2;4 to 5;0, it is important to show that not only young children but also older children produced case errors in our experiment. In fact, the child who performed best (Rieke) is young (3;10), while the eldest child (Timm at age 5) performed very poorly on dative. Table 10 lists the number of correct and incorrect case forms per child. The number in brackets refers to substitution errors.

Table 9. Case marking on direct object DPs in child L1 and early child L2 German

	L1 German (n = 48)		L1 Turkish (n = 32)		L1 Russian/Polish (n = 44)	
ACC	36		29		33	
ACC error	8 (*der*) + 4 (*dem*)		2 (*der*) + 1 (*dem*)		4 (*der*) + 7 (*dem*)	
der	18.2%	(8/44)	6.5%	(2/31)	10.8%	(4/37)
der + dem	25.0%	(12/48)	9.4%	(3/32)	25.0%	(11/44)

Table 10. Distribution of correct and incorrect structural case forms in child L1 German

child	age	analyzed case forms	DAT	DAT error	ACC	ACC error
Lea	2;4	2 (+2)	1	1 (+2)	0	0
Bernd	2;7	5 (+2)	0	4 (+2)	1	0
Julian	2;10	7	3	4	0	0
Paulina	3;0	15 (+1)	1	7 (+1)	3	4
Erika	3;1	14 (+4)	2	9 (+4)	3	0
Laura	3;2	17 (+2)	0	14 (+2)	3	0
Martin	3;3	9 (+8)	0	3 (+8)	5	1
Petra	3;4	6 (+1)	0	6 (+1)	0	0
Rieke	3;10	15 (+1)	9	(+1)	6	0
Juliane	3;11	12 (+6)	6	1 (+6)	4	1
Martha	3;11	6 (+5)	2	4 (+5)	0	0
Jan	4;4	15 (+3)	8	3 (+1)	2	2 (+2)
Manuel	4;10	15 (+4)	8	2 (+2)	5	(+2)
Timm	5;0	11 (+5)	1	6 (+5)	4	0
Total	2;4–5;0	149 (+44)	41	64 (+40)	36	8 (+4)

6. Discussion

Based on spontaneous production data, Eisenbeiss et al. (2006) show that monolingual German children have no difficulties with structural case, but that they do with lexical case. We examined spontaneous production data from successive bilingual children and experimental data from successive bilingual and monolingual children. Based on the spontaneous production data, we conclude that the four successive bilingual children with L1 Turkish behave like the monolingual children studied by Eisenbeiss et al. They rarely produce structural case errors (less than 1% on nominative and less than 7% on non-nominative), but they do produce many lexical case errors (more than 20%). But under experimental conditions, successive bilingual and monolingual children produced a large number of structural case errors, in particular with structural dative (almost 50%). Our experimental findings from the monolingual children are in contrast to the findings in Eisenbeiss et al., which are based on spontaneous production data only.

Our study showed a clear difference between spontaneous production data and experimental data, which may be due to the fact that the experimental conditions were more demanding. The children were asked to produce a ditransitive verb construction, a construction they seem to avoid in spontaneous production. Moreover, the experiment was designed so that the children had to use non-pronominal DPs for the IO and the DO. An examination of the spontaneous data from the four successive bilingual children reveals that ditransitive verbs are used in only 12 examples. In only 8 of these are both objects produced, and the IO is always pronominal and the DO is generally expressed as *das* 'this'. Thus the results of the experimental task could be influenced by processing limitation effects, since the children were obliged to produce a construction they rarely use in spontaneous speech. Our experimental results also showed a clear contrast between structural dative and structural accusative. The former induced an error rate of almost 50% in the monolingual children and over 75% in the bilingual children, while the error rate for structural accusative was much lower. Surprisingly, the monolingual children produced as many accusative case errors as the children with L1 Polish or Russian, and they performed less well than the children with L1 Turkish. We have no explanation for this difference in performance.

In our analysis of case we applied the same criteria as Eisenbeiss et al. in order to make possible a comparison between the different data sets. We pointed out that their account of substitution errors in terms of phonological similarity is problematic, and noted that if substitution errors had been included in the analysis the number of errors with both structural dative and structural accusative would have been higher in our data. We would have benefited from knowing how often these errors occurred in Eisenbeiss et al.'s data, even if there were good reasons for excluding them from the counts. We suspect that inclusion of such errors would have reduced the contrast between structural and lexical case errors.

7. Conclusions

Based on an investigation of case in spontaneous and experimental data, we conclude that successive bilingual children with an early AO to L2 German (before age 4;2) behave very like monolingual German children in this domain of grammar. That there is no real contrast in performance between monolingual German children and successive bilingual children with L1 Turkish with an early AO has also been shown for the acquisition of Verb Second and finiteness marking by Rothweiler (2006) and for the acquisition of participle morphology by Sterner (2011). (But see Schönenberger 2011 for a contrast in the acquisition of articles between monolingual and successive bilingual children with L1 Turkish.)

Based on our data it is difficult to determine whether age of onset to German or amount of exposure plays a more important role in the bilingual children's performance. As can be seen from Table 5, two of the children, Gül and Fikret, have a similar MLU range and have been observed for a comparable amount of time, but they differ with respect to the AO. Gül was first exposed to German at age 3;0 and Fikret at age 4;2. Still, these two children behave very much alike in their performance on case. A comparision of their data in the last two recordings (at ME 27.5 and around ME 30) shows that both perform perfectly on nominative, and that they make few errors on accusative (Gül: 15/17 correct and Fikret: 22/24 correct) and structural dative (Gül: 2/3 correct and Fikret: 3/3 correct). But both children produce many errors on lexical dative (Gül: 4/11 correct and Fikret: 3/7 correct). Thus the difference in AO between these two children does not seem to have a big impact on their acquisition of case. There are two possible explanations why these children perform alike: either the acquisition of case happens before the end of the sensitive phase around age 4 and Fikret is still within that phase, or the acquisition of case is not affected by the sensitive phase around age 4. Following Meisel (2009), we regard the second explanation as less likely. However, a much closer analysis of different domains of grammar and with many more children would be required to test this very tentative conclusion.

References

Clahsen, H. 1984. Der Erwerb von Kasusmarkierungen in der deutschen Kindersprache. *Linguistische Berichte* 89: 1–31.

Eisenbeiss, S., S. Bartke & H. Clahsen. 2006. Structural and lexical case in child German: Evidence from language-impaired and typically developing children. *Language Acquisition* 13: 3–32.

Eisenbeiss, S., S. Bartke, H. Weyerts & H. Clahsen, eds. 1994. *Elizitationsverfahren in der Spracherwerbsforschung: Nominalphrasen, Kasus, Plural, Partizipien* (Theorie des Lexikons 57. Arbeiten des Sonderforschungsbereichs 282). Düsseldorf: Universität Düsseldorf.

Meisel, J. M. 1986. Word order and case marking in early child language. Evidence from simultaneous acquisition of two first languages: French and German. *Linguistics* 24: 123–183.

Meisel, J. M. 2009. Second language acquisition in early childhood. *Zeitschrift für Sprachwissenschaft* 28: 5–34.

Rothweiler, M. 2006. The acquisition of V2 and subordinate clauses in early successive acquisition of German. In *Interfaces in Multilingualism: Acquisition, Representation and Processing* (Hamburg Studies on Multilingualism 4), ed. C. Lleó, 91–113. Amsterdam: John Benjamins.

Schönenberger, M. 2011. Are difficulties with the prosodic representation the origin of prolonged article omission? In *Proceedings of the 11th Generative Approaches to Second Language Acquisition Conference (GALSA 2011)*, eds. J. Herschensohn & D. Tanner, 135–142. Somerville MA: Cascadilla Proceedings Project.

Schönenberger, M., F. Sterner & T. Ruberg. 2011a. *Indirect Objects and Dative Case in Child L1 and Child L2 German* (Arbeiten zur Mehrsprachigkeit 96). Hamburg: Universität Hamburg.

Schönenberger, M., F. Sterner & T. Ruberg. 2011b. The realization of indirect objects and dative case in German. In *Proceedings of the 11th Generative Approaches to Second Language Acquisition Conference (GALSA 2011)*, eds. J. Herschensohn & D. Tanner, 143–151. Somerville MA: Cascadilla Proceedings Project.

Sterner, F. 2011. German past participles in early successive language acquisition: Support for the dual mechanism model. Paper presented at the 11th Generative Approaches to Second Language Acquisition Conference (GASLA 2011), 25–27 March 2011, Seattle.

Tracy, R. 1986. The acquisition of case morphology in German. *Linguistics* 24: 47–78.

First exposure learners make use of top-down lexical knowledge when learning words[*]

Susanne E. Carroll
University of Calgary, Canada

Learning another language requires learning a new lexicon. Current second language acquisition theories make different predictions about the relative importance of L2 experience and L1 knowledge when learning new words. In a study of first exposure learners, clear effects of knowledge of L1 words were found. However, rapid learning after minimal exposure to continuous speech was also found, even when target words contained novel L2 sounds. Results show both the powerful role of L1 lexical knowledge on L2 word learning and the rapid rate at which sound forms are created and mapped to referents. This suggests that a more nuanced approach to discussion of frequency effects and transfer is needed.

Keywords: German, English, second language acquisition, input, word learning, segmentation, transfer

1. Experience and L1 knowledge in L2 word learning

Current second language acquisition theories attribute different degrees of importance to prior experience with the L2. They also attribute different roles to L1-knowledge. Among generativists, Schwartz & Sprouse (1994, 1996) assert that knowledge of the L1 lexicon is the starting point for L2 acquisition, along with L1 parameter-settings. In stark contrast, the Basic Variety model claims there are no L1 effects to be found at the

---

[*]   I gratefully acknowledge generous funding from the Social Sciences and Humanities Research Council of Canada through its general grants program (grant 410-2006-0323) and its Canada Research Chairs program (grant 950-202408), without which none of this research would have been possible. I thank my research assistants Danica MacDonald, who collected the data, Silke Weber, who recorded the stimuli, and Lindsay Hracs, who has kept the lab running smoothly for many months. I also thank the editors, Christoph Gabriel and Kurt Braunmüller, for the opportunity to present my research in this volume, and two anonymous reviewers whose criticisms and comments have made this a much better paper. Remaining deficiencies are my fault.

initial stage of L2 acquisition (Klein & Perdue 1997). Neither one of these models makes particular claims about input effects. The Basic Variety model assumes it plays a role in accounting for L2 development, while in the Schwartz & Sprouse model, as with all generativist theorizing, the role of input is downplayed because the learner's knowledge is greater than and more abstract than information that could be induced from it (Epstein, Flynn & Martohardjono 1996). The clearest claims about both L1 influence and input effects are to be found in the Competition Model and Construction Grammar usage-based proposals. This is because they are implemented in "bottom-up" feed-forward connectionist architectures. They predict strong across-the-board effects of L1 knowledge on L2 learning because knowledge of language is defined as heavily entrenched associative links between sounds and meanings (Bates & MacWhinney 1987, MacWhinney 2005: 57, Ellis 1998, 2002, 2003).[1] Since connections that have strong weights are easily activated, L2 speech ought to activate L1 lexical representations.[2] Initial connections between L2 sound forms and L2 lexical representations will nonetheless form on the basis of experience with L2 speech, but they will be weak and will lose out in competition to entrenched connections until such time that the weights in newly-formed connections increase enough to meet some threshold. Changing the weights in connections demands continued L2 listening experience and the belief is that this happens only incrementally (Ellis 1998, 2002, Mellow 2008).

Emergentists are committed to the premise that inputs are physically measurable, objective properties of stimuli (Bates & MacWhinney 1987). Consequently they predict transfer effects during pre-lexical processing (MacWhinney 2005). However, L1 entrenchment effects between sound forms and meanings are not consistent with evidence of rapid word learning at the beginning stage of L2 exposure (Osterhout, McLaughlin, Pitkänen, Frenck-Mestre & Molinaro 2006). An alternative hypothesis is that in learning any word, a learner must construct multiple representations, not just across levels of description (phonology, morpho-syntax, semantics) but *within* each level. Thus, a word might have multiple sound forms, with distinct types being processed as a consequence of different degrees of exposure to input. Learners might initially form L2 representations by segmenting from the speech stream acoustic exemplars. Such representations are rich in acoustic information and are stored in episodic memory (Palmeri, Goldinger & Pisoni 1993, Nygaard, Sommers & Pisoni 1994,

---

1.   MacWhinney (2005: 87) writes: "... the fact that L2 learning is so heavily influenced by transfer from L1 means that it would be impossible to construct a model of L2 learning that did not take into account the structure of the first language."

2.   Nothing in connectionist learning models requires that they represent lexical items. MacWhinney (2000) reviews a number of serious problems with models that have dispensed with lexical representations. His discussion brings out clearly that associations between sound forms (either phonetic tokens or phonological types) and meanings must be mediated by a lexical representation. In my discussion of connectionist and usage-based models, I will assume that they include lexical representations, an assumption that also facilitates comparisons between connectionism and algorithm-based learning models.

Goldinger, 1998). Through repeated exposure to specific exemplars in distinct phonetic contexts, more abstract properties such as timing slots (of consonants and vowels), syllables, and phonetic categories, might be computed (MacWhinney & Leinbach 1991). Independently, the acoustic exemplars could be associated to context referents through processing of visual input such as, say, pictures of people and objects. With greater exposure, more abstract representations of meaning might be derived. In this scenario, the learner's representations remain heavily contingent on experience. Consequently, such approaches predict considerable variation among learners based on the frequency of exposure to given words in specific contexts and to the same words in different contexts. They predict important differences among L2ers who have acquired their L2 in tutored contexts, largely through reading written texts and through learner-adjusted speech (Chaudron 1986, Håkansson 1986, 1987), and L2ers whose experience consists exclusively of exposure to speech.

2. Segmenting sound forms, recognizing words and making form-meaning correspondences

When speakers speak, they do not put pauses between their words. Speech is continuous, obscuring the boundaries between words. Nonetheless, when experienced listeners listen, they carve up speech into units of sounds, such as syllables, rhythmic units, and intonational phrases. This process is called *segmentation*. Segmentation roots word recognition in the speech signal. If words are complexes of representations, even learning the sound form of a word may present learning difficulties. Consider a learner who segments a form like ([staɹt]) *start* from the signal, he may or may not recognise *start* when it occurs in ([staɹ]) ([tɪd]) *started* (Dejean de la Bâtie & Bradley 1995, Christophe, Peperkamp, Pallier, Block, & Mehler 2004). Spotting words in larger words is something that proficient users of a language can do (Shillcock 1990, Dumay, Frauenfelder & Content 2002). They make use of phonological, lexical and syntactic information to recognize words (Mattys & Melhorn 2007). In contrast, in learning a first language, infants must segment the speech signal in the absence of such "top-down" knowledge. For example, infants being exposed to English do not know yet that no English word starts with the sequence *pf*. Such phonotactic knowledge will only emerge as the child builds a lexicon. By adulthood, the native English-listener can make use of this knowledge to segment words between the *p* and the *f* (Brent & Cartwright 1996, McQueen 1998). The native German-listener will have had quite different experience since common words like *Pfeffer* 'pepper' or *Kopf* 'head' reveal that German words can begin and end with *pf*. So segmentation at the initial stage of L1 learning must proceed differently than at the end-state. The infant will rely on recurrent and salient properties of the signal to carve it up into discrete sound units, including rhythm and intonation (Cutler 1994, Jusczyk 1997, Houston 2005).

Learning an L2 presents a situation in-between these two scenarios. On the one hand, on first exposure to another language, the child or adult L2er, like the pre-linguistic infant, has no discrete representations of sound units of the L2. She lacks L2 lexical representations and knowledge of L2 grammar. On the other hand, she brings to the learning task from the L1 much usable knowledge about linguistic units and linguistic structure. She knows, for example, that people can bear proper names and that these are nominal expressions. This kind of knowledge might guide inferential processes during early stages of L2 acquisition and provide information that goes beyond the perceptual salience of proper names in general (Bortfeld, Morgan, Golinkoff & Rathbun 2005). She knows the phonotactic constraints on L1 words. Knowledge of L1 phonotactic constraints has been shown to constrain L2 listening in fluent bilinguals (Avery & Best 1995, Hallé, Segui, Frauenfelder, & Meunier 1998, Tench 2003). When the L1 and the L2 exhibit the same constraints, L2ers presumably draw successfully on L1-knowledge. By hypothesis, if an Anglophone is learning French, where the sequence *pf* is also impossible as a word onset, he will correctly parse the *p* in one syllable and the *f* in the following syllable. What happens in learning German? Presumably some exposure to the novel sequence is required, but how much exposure is needed and under what circumstances is unclear. On the one hand, while L1 phonotactics have been shown to constrain statistical learning on first exposure, learners were still able to segment words beginning and ending with novel combinations (Finn & Hudson Kam 2008). This suggests that experience will result in target-like processing. However, Weber & Cutler (2006) demonstrate that L1 phonotactics continue to constrain L2 segmentation in highly proficient Dutch/English bilinguals. Altenberg (2005), in contrast, found effects of L1 knowledge of Spanish in a production task with intermediate and advanced learners, but not in perception.

Such differences might be due to many factors: to differences in the proficiency levels of the participants, to the language pairs involved (Dutch being in some respects more like English than Spanish); to the fact that the Spanish-speakers were living in an environment where English was the language of broader communication but the Dutch were not; or to differences in the tasks used. More studies that focus on these factors are needed. Another issue that merits attention is the fact that researchers differ in whether they are concerned with the investigation of processing based on extant representations or processing that results in the creation of *novel* representations. There is a fundamental difference between these two concerns that is critical to a coherent discussion of L2 acquisition (cf. Carroll 2001 for discussion). The former asks: How does the learner process speech once she has lexical representations? The latter asks: How does the learner form novel representations in the first place? Studies of learners at different stages of knowledge have traditionally been used to make inferences about the processes that led one knowledge state to turn into a more advanced state. By reducing the time gap between stages of learning, by controlling the input, and by describing it in depth, one can hope to shed real light on the processes that lead to the creation of novel representations. This is the logic behind the research discussed here.

Steady-state L2 users will differ considerably from one another in what they know about the L2 lexicon. While such variation in experience does not preclude studying L2 word learning (cf. Escudero, Hayes-Harb & Mitterer 2008), it requires using tasks that prevent top-down processing and these tasks may lack ecological validity. In other words, while perfectly suited for shedding light on details of speech processing in such knowledgeable listeners (see Weber & Cutler 2004, Cutler & Weber 2007), they are not ideal for drawing conclusions about how learners create novel representations in the first place.

3.   Why study first exposure learners?

By choosing participants who have no meaningful exposure to the L2, one can exclude the possibility that some of the learners have encoded representations of the target words through prior experience. By hypothesis, the learners have no L2 lexicon, no knowledge of the L2 sound system and no knowledge of the L2 grammar. Thus, one can exclude top-down processing that draws on L2 representations. This still leaves open the possibility that learners are drawing on L1 representations and L1-attuned processing strategies when analyzing the signal.

What do existing first exposure studies reveal about segmentation and form-meaning mappings?

Numerous studies of segmentation and statistical learning have been carried out that involve presenting adults with a continuous stream of synthesized C(onsonant) V(owel)-syllables from which prosodic cues to word boundaries have been removed. The hypothesis is that listeners will unconsciously compute transitional probabilities (TPs) between syllables and segment words at points of low probability (Saffran, Newport & Aslin 1996). Thus, if a synthesized string includes ... *beragabidumodalidu* ..., where *beraga*, *bidumo* and *dalidu* are all target "words", exposure will inform the learner that the TPs across *be*, *ra* and *ga* are very high and very low across *ga* and *bi*. When confronted with a word judgement task in which they have to compare sound tokens of target words to sound tokens of "partial words" created by re-aligning sylla-bles across points of higher transitional probability, e.g., ... *be ragabi dumoda lidu* ..., participants prefer the words (Saffran et al. 1996, see Folia, Uddén, De Vries, Forkstam, & Petersson 2010 for a recent review). Results show that segmentation of words under these conditions can occur with as little as two minutes of exposure (Endress & Bonatti 2007). In the absence of typical prosodic cues to word boundaries, this suggests that the computation of TPs plays a role in segmention. However, a weaker conclusion is motivated. Many of the studies used stimuli consisting exclusively of universal CV-syllables, with the consonants and vowels selected from the L1 repertoire. By transferring L1 knowledge at the syllable level, the learner ought to be able to prosodically parse such strings. This matters because perception of syllables is presumably a prerequisite for a statistical learning mechanism that counts the distribution of syllables in the input. If the input is, however, unintelligible, that is to say, the learner does not reliably hear syllables, then such a learning mechanism cannot perform. Unfortunately, learners must sometimes learn an L2 where the consonants and vowels are indeed different from those of the L1, and differences in phonetic repertoires are known to create perceptual difficulties for L2ers (Yamada & Tohkura 1992, Lively, Pisoni & Logan 1992, Pisoni & Lively 1995 among many others). Finally, Finn & Hudson Kam (2008: 480) point out that theories of processing and acquisition need to differentiate types of statistical regularities in the input. Transitional probabilities are statistical regularities that are specific to a given speech stream presented during an experiment and might not be stored in memory once a segmented unit has been processed (contrary to the assumptions of Exemplar Theory). In contrast, the statistical computations that are typically discussed in the literature on cue-based learning (and relevant to learning phonotactics) represent computations that must be stored in memory. As noted, Finn & Hudson Kam (2008) showed that constraints on the shape of English prosodic words robustly interfered with statistical learning.

Osterhout et al. (2006) demonstrated that English-speaking tutored learners of French were sensitive to the difference between real words and pseudo-words after only 14 hours of instruction. In an ERP study, they found that pseudo-words reliably elicited an N400 response, even though in a behavioural test, these learners did not reliably distinguish between the two types of words. The authors suggest that this effect may indicate that the learners had rapidly memorized the words, and reported a robust correlation between the N400 word/non-word effect and the frequency of the words in the learners' French textbook. Rapid segmentation and word-learning in a tutored context was also reported by Rast (2008, 2010), who studied native speakers of European French hearing Polish in a communicative language classroom. They were tested on sentence-repetition and translation tests after four and eight hours of instruction. Rast also examined effects of L1 phonological knowledge. Sentences of Polish were presented that contained words that were phonemically similar or not similar to French words.[3] Rast differentiated between "frequent" words (presented at

---

3. They were described as "phonologically transparent" or "not phonologically transparent". To define the phonologically transparent words, an independent group of 15 Francophone adults listened to Polish words and translated them into French. Answers were treated as correct translations if the listener identified a correct Polish root, e.g. *studentem* was translated as *étudiant, étude, étudient*. Translations such as *stupéfait, stupéfiant, soudain*, and "no response" were not accepted as correct. Some of these phonologically transparent words were clearly borrowings. Since Polish is a Slavic language and French is a Romance language, it is unlikely that these words are cognates as defined linguistically (see Carroll 1992 for discussion). In psycholinguistic studies of lexical processing, even nonce forms and words from artificial languages have been described as "cognates" (Van Hell & De Groot 1998, De Groot & Keijzer 2000). In such studies,

least 21 times) and words that occurred less often in the input. After four hours of instruction, learners were able to reliably repeat words from the Polish input but there was no difference between frequent and infrequent input. After eight hours of exposure, participants performed better on the frequent words.

Gullberg, Roberts, Dimroth, Veroude & Indefrey (2010) and Gullberg, Roberts & Dimroth (in press) point out that one should be cautious in generalizing to naturalistic learning contexts from studies of tutored learners. The students in the Osterhout et al. (2006) study were drilled on rules and had discrete orthographic representations of words to aid their word-learning. The French/Polish learners were exposed to auditory input only, but tutored learners are invariably exposed to "teacher talk" with its special adjustments in the use of questions, intonation and recasts to aid comprehension-in-context (Håkansson 1987). The Gullberg et al. studies were designed to study segmentation, frequency and gesture with stimuli that would capture the properties of a particular text-type, namely a televised weather report.[4] They used a word recognition task, a picture-sound form matching task, and a lexical decision task. "Frequent" words occurred eight times in a text consisting of 120 clauses, "infrequent" words occurred two times, with 292 word types presented in all. Several groups of Dutch native speakers listened to seven or 14 minutes of a Chinese-language videotape. Results showed that participants could rapidly segment words and map them to visual stimuli after seven minutes of exposure. Participants recognized Chinese words better if they were frequent and gesturally highlighted. However, the authors found differences in results that depended on the length of the words; participants were sensitive to distributional properties only with disyllabic words that occurred frequently. Gullberg et al. (in press) attribute this to general difficulties in processing sequences of monosyllables, but it might also indicate an L1-influenced preference for a minimal word of two syllables.

In these studies, participants were asked to watch the videotape without being told what they would see, or why. They also had no idea that they would be tested afterwards. These aspects of the design permit the authors to make strong claims about implicit learning since the participants could not have used encyclopaedic or social knowledge to perform on the various tasks. It does not follow, of course, that inferencing was excluded as the participants listened to the weather report. Given its stereotyped nature, and the fact that the researchers were counting on these properties to aid interpretation, we should conclude that learners probably were using inference to

---

what matters is that the sound form of one language activates a word of the other language. I shall simplify the discussion by referring to cognates in this way from this point.

4.   Thus, their choice of stimuli precluded interaction with the native speaker, a factor that many L2 researchers regard as a sine qua non of natural language learning (Gass 1997). Weather reports are also highly conventionalized text types. They draw on an extremely small set of vocabulary items, which are repeated again and again in simple sentence structures. These are just some of the reasons why weather reports were the first text type to be successfully employed in automatic machine translation. See Leplus, Langlais & Lapalme (2004).

bootstrap at least word meaning.[5] In short, this design too had its limitations, a fact that should encourage us to use a number of different designs to shed light on word learning at the initial state.

4.   Our studies

4.1   Methodology and stimuli

We have carried out a number of studies on L2 word learning using a paradigm that presents controlled auditory input. Learners were trained in two phases: participants were told that they would hear sequences of speech in German while looking at visual stimuli in the form of line drawings of people. They were told to learn the names of the individuals they saw. They then listened to single declarative sentences presented one after the other. As each sentence was heard, a different picture was presented on a computer screen. These were followed by 20 single questions and the same line drawings. The questions presented the listeners with a forced-choice between two options; examples are given below.[6] We were interested in studying if adults could accurately pick out the target name and map each name to the correct visual referents. By hypothesis, the task presupposes that the participants can segment the target name from continuous speech.

What is interesting about our paradigm, in comparison to those described above is that we are able to measure responses to inputs in terms of number of exposures, based on the learner's own behavioural responses. Crucially, we measure increased exposure, not in terms of an arbitrary period of time (7 minutes, 4 hours, 14 hours), but in terms of participants' performance on the task. In addition, we are the first to add a developmental aspect to the investigation of first exposure learners by testing participants approximately two weeks after initial training. We are thus able to answer the question: Do participants retain in long term memory representations of the words

---

5.   This should be obvious on the basis of a "thought experiment". Imagine that instead of talking about the sunrise and sunset while pointing to a picture of a sun on the weather map the speaker had recorded the following: "Don't you just love the colour yellow. Doesn't it just make you feel good when you see the sun come up." The whole point of using a weather report was to ensure the inference that the talk be about the objects on the map, rather than the decontextualized talk that typifies much of our language use.

6.   All stimuli were standardized, completely randomized, and the pace was experimenter controlled. The experiments were programmed in E-prime, a platform for computer-based experiments. Subjects were tested individually in the laboratory while seated comfortably at a computer terminal. They heard auditory stimuli through AKG k 171 studio-quality headphones. They had 2500 ms. to respond. Response keys were clearly marked on the keyboard with subjects pressing the F1 key if they thought the correct response was the first name in the NP conjunct, or the F12 key if they thought the correct response was the second name in the NP conjunct.

they were exposed to, especially after a hiatus with no input? Or, are the initial representations ephemeral and quickly disappear?

The design of the studies is presented in Table 1. I will present in detail the results from Study 2 – the cognate/non-cognate comparison. Cognate data from Studies 1 and 3 will be presented afterwards since they amount to replications of the cognate Exp. C with different groups of participants.

Table 2 presents an overview of the procedures used.

Although our task was less ecologically valid in some respects than that of Rast (2008), where interactions between the learners and a native speaker occurred, or Gullberg et al. (2010, in press), where the learners heard 7 minutes of continuous text, we did attempt to create stimuli that would be as natural as possible.[7] Proper names were chosen because they are very often among the first words that an L2er learns. The fact that we have found no published data dealing with proper names in L2 acquisition suggests that it is widely assumed that they will be easy to learn.[8] This

Table 1. The studies (*Order of the experiments was counter-balanced across subjects in each study, e.g. for half of the participants, Exp A < Exp B; for the other half Exp B < Exp A)

Study 1* L1 vs. L2 comparison	Exp. A: English first names in English sentences	Exp. B: German first names in German sentences (all names were cognate items)
Study 2* Cognate vs. non-cognate comparison	Exp. C: Same stimuli as Exp. B	Exp. D: German first names in German sentences (all names were non-cognate items)
Study 3* Length comparison	Exp. E: Same stimuli as Exp. B	Exp. F: German cognate and non-cognate first names + German last names in German sentences

---

7.   Gullberg et al. (2010, in press) report on the lexical properties of their stimuli but not on the phonetic or phonological properties. It is inconceivable the 7 minutes of continuous text equals 7 minutes of continuous speech. Pauses undoubtedly occurred in the stimuli, at the very least, at the ends of sentences. If so, our stimuli are perhaps more like those of the Gullberg et al. studies, with the difference that we have conducted phonetic analyses of our stimuli and can provide descriptions of the breaks in phonation, changes in fundamental frequency, syllable duration, and amplitude.

8.   Bortfeld at al. (2005) show that familiar names are highly salient for infants learning their L1. It seems reasonable to assume that familiar names will also be salient to L2ers. Eavesdropping on conversations in an unfamiliar language should convince the reader that familiar names of politicians, actors, or shopping malls will "pop out" from the rest of the L2 speech. Monaghan and Christiansen (2010) suggest that proper names, which may occur in the linguistic input without other linguistic context, once initially represented, may provide an easy route to segmenting stretches of speech lying in-between the name and the right edge of the utterance.

Table 2. Procedures used

Session 1

---

1. Ethical consent procedures were completed (subjects were provided with a general description of the purpose of the study).
2. Background questionnaire (questions related to language of the home, number of languages known, time spent outside of Canada, etc.)
3. Digital span task
4. Instructions in English (presented auditorily and in writing) along with practice items to familiarize subjects with the response method. Participants were told that they would hear sentences in German while looking at pictures of people, e.g, *Hier sehen Sie Reinhold.* 'Here you see Reinhold.' They were to learn the names of the people depicted. Participants were also told that they would hear questions asking them about the people depicted and were to press the F1 key if the correct response was the first word of two presented in a question, and to press the F12 key if the correct response was the second of two words presented in a question. E.g. *Sehen Sie hier Reinhold*$_{F1}$ *oder Reinhart* $_{F12}$? 'Do you see here Reinhold or Reinhart?' (Practice performed at computer console was self-paced.)
5. Training session (1 to a maximum of 10)
   Participants heard 20 statements and saw 20 different pictures. (Timing was experimenter-controlled). They then heard 20 questions and saw the same pictures again. (All stimuli were randomized; participants had 2500 msec. to respond.)
   At the end of each statement/question cycle, the accuracy score (Measure 1) of the participant appeared on the screen. If the participant scored 20/20, they proceeded to Test phase. If not, the training session was repeated until the participant got all items correct (Measure 2), or the experiment was terminated.
6. Test
   Participants saw a different picture of the same individuals.
   After each decision on the receptive task, participants pronounced their choice. Production data were recorded.

Session 2 (c. 2 weeks later)

---

7. Re-test1
   Participants saw the same pictures as in the Training sessions. The position of the names was reversed from that appearing in the Training and Test questions. Feedback was given if the participants made an error.
   After each decision on the receptive task, participants pronounced their choice. Production data were recorded.
8. Re-test2
   The pictures and questions of Re-test1 were used.
   After each decision on the receptive task, participants pronounced their choice. Production data were recorded.

---

assumption might turn out to be correct for various reasons, but it merits further investigation.[9]

The proper names chosen are typical German first names.[10] Cognate names were chosen because it was hypothesized that they might activate L1 names. Non-cognate names were chosen on the assumption that they would require the learners to create novel sound forms both phonetically and phonologically. In each experiment, 20 target names were embedded in one of four declarative sentence frames. Each frame is a natural way to introduce new information and includes deictic elements like *hier* 'here', *da* 'there', or *das* 'that' that referred to the pictures. Examples of both cognate items (C) and non-cognate (NC) items are shown in (1):

(1) a. Hier ist Agnes.   (C)
        [hiːʁeistʔagnəs]
        Here is Agnes.

    b. Da steht Claudia.   (C)
        [daʃteːtklaʊdia]
        There stands Claudia.

    c. Hier sehen Sie Lutz.   (NC)
        [hiːʁezeːənzilʊts]
        Here see you Lutz.

    d. Das ist Annegret.   (NC)
        [dasɪstʔanəgʁeːt]
        That is Annegret.

A single native speaker of Standard German produced all recordings. Sentences were between three and nine syllables long (mean = 5.4 in cognate sentences; mean = 5.1 in non-cognate sentences, t(19) = 0.6305, p = 0.53, n.s.). Each declarative sentence presented participants with an acoustically unique stimulus. After hearing all 20 declarative sentences, participants heard the corresponding questions to each presentational

---

9.   A reviewer suggested that proper names are not "real" words because they are not "meaningful". Proper names are, to the contrary, good words since they have prosodic structure, and belong to a grammatical class. In fact, proper names can be shown to occur in most of the syntactic contexts where common nouns occur (Jonasson 1994). Moreover, proper names have a meaning which is what permits them to refer and to combine with predicates in sentences like *Not every Susanne has blue eyes.* It is true, that expressions like *Susanne* in their naming function are neither predicates nor descriptions. As Katz (2001) puts it, proper names do not have "senses" which is why they do not license inferences from the particular properties of the INDIVIDUAL referred to other INDIVIDUALS who bear the same name. Not every person bearing the name *Susanne* has blue-eyes. Katz analyses their meaning as "the unique x who bears the name [...]" where "..." is either a sound form or an orthographic representation.

10.   Typical does not mean "fashionable". We did not use borrowings from English like *Kevin, Patrick* or *Peggy.*

frame with the target item embedded in a conjoined noun phrase. Target words occurred either as the first noun in the conjunct (in utterance-medial position) or as the second noun (in utterance-final position). These questions were also all acoustically unique. At no point did any of the subjects see written versions of the auditory inputs. See (2).

(2) a. Ist hier Dietmar oder Detlef?
         Is here Dietmar or   Detlef

     b. Steht da   Helga oder Heidrun?
         Stands there Helga or   Heidrun

     c. Sehen Sie hier Lutz oder Ludo?
         See   you here Lutz or   Ludo

     d. Ist das Annika oder Annegret?
         Is that Annika or   Annegret

The input on Measure 1 (accuracy on Training Trial 1) consisted of 40 distinct instances of speech. These 40 instances were repeated in subsequent training trials. A participant who learnt all 20 items on a single training trial would have been exposed to a particular declarative sentence exactly once. He would have been exposed to the corresponding questions once on Training Trial 1 and twice on Test. A participant who learnt all 20 items on 10 training trials would have been exposed to a particular declarative sentence 10 times and to the corresponding questions 11 times. This allows for a clear test of the prediction that segmentation and sound-form mappings occur incrementally and require repeated exposure to instances of speech in order to create appropriate associative connections. If processing at the phonetic level depends on L1-entrenched connections, we predict that segmentation of the words will be incremental and slow. Consequently, few or no learners should correctly respond to all 20 items on Training Trial 1 and we expect performance to improve significantly as more training trials are performed. We also predict relatively poor performance in Re-test 1. This is because two weeks later participants were presented with 20 new distinct acoustic exemplars for which no input-output mappings have been established. This is because we changed the positions of the target nouns.[11] Alternatively, if participants are analyzing L2 speech using abstract prosodic constituents such as syllables and feet, and if they are analyzing the input in terms of the phonetic categories of the L1, performance on Training Trial 1 might be very good, and frequency of exposures to the same instances of speech might not matter to forming sound-meaning mappings. On this scenario, performance on Re-test 1 should also be good since the learners will be able to segment a word even when it appears in a new

---

11. In other words, if the target was the first noun in the training and test questions, it became the second noun in the retest phase; if the target was the second noun during training and test, it became the first noun in the retest phase.

position in the input. Exposure might matter, however, to list learning. In other words, individual items might be readily segmented and mapped to referents depicted in the line drawings but learning all 20 items might require repeated exposure to fix the representations in long term memory. Finally, if learners use only the categories of the L1 to process the input, they should show no evidence of having represented unique L2 sounds in their production data. Instead, we should find L1 lexically-triggered pronunciations of the cognates and L1-accented pronunciations of the non-cognates.

4.2   Participants

Participants in all studies were English-speaking students from the University of Calgary who were paid a small fee for their participation. To qualify for the first exposure experiments, participants had to indicate on our background questionnaire that they had no prior knowledge of German, and had not been systematically exposed to German at home or elsewhere. We began with 33 participants in Study 2, 10 of who were not able to learn all 20 items in 10 training trials.[12] 23 participants performed the Test; 21 returned for the re-test phase of the study.

4.3   Results

Table 3 presents mean accuracy scores on the cognate and non-cognate items on Training Trial 1, Test, Re-test 1 and Re-test 2, as well as the mean number of trials to reach criterion.

Table 3. Study 2, cognate vs. non-cognate items

Word type	Training Trial 1	Test	Re-test 1	Re-test 2	# of Trials to criterion
Cognates	82.7%	95%	85.9%	93%	3.04
Non-cognates	70.6%	95%	79%	90%	5.56
Mean	81.1%	95%	82.5%	91.5%	4.3

---

12.   All of these participants were tested first on the non-cognate items. The mean accuracy score of those who did not finish the non-cognate experiment was .66 on Trial 1 versus .719 for those who did, t(31) = –1.30, p = 0.20, n.s. We submitted all of our participants to a digital span task prior to conducting the main experiments. A comparison of the digital span scores of the subjects who did not finish versus those who did showed no difference between the groups (4.13 vs. 4.1). I have no explanation for why 10 participants had trouble learning the non-cognate items, especially in the light of a later study which showed that participants could readily learn much longer names consisting of a first + last name, e.g. *Rainer Weisskopf* or *Gabrielle Blauhemd*.

One-sample means comparison tests revealed that performance on each measure was well above chance for each word type.[13] As Table 3 shows, participants had higher mean accuracy scores on the cognate words on Training Trial 1. A two-sample t-test on the difference of these means was significant, $t(55) = -4.09$, $p = 0.0001$. All stimuli had been presented in random order. Analyses of the responses according to the order of presentation of the stimuli in Training Trial 1 showed no correlation between accuracy and position of the item during the training trial. In other words, participants were as accurate in their responses on the first 5 items (before they would have been exposed repeatedly to the different frames) as they were on the last 5 items. Table 3 also shows that participants reached criterion faster on cognate than on non-cognate items. A paired t-test on the difference in the number of trials to criterion showed that this difference was significant, $t(22) = -5.61$, $p = 0.000$.

Table 3 shows that once all items were acquired, the type of word involved no longer made any difference. When re-tested two weeks later, however, participants selected the correct name when prompted by the question significantly better when it was a cognate name, $t(40) = 2.74$, $p = 0.009$. Once they had received feedback on the correct response, type of name again no longer had an effect on selection of the correct answer.

Table 4 shows the mean accuracy scores on each Training Trial as well as the number of individuals who scored 100% on each trial. As this table shows, participants reached criterion sooner on the cognate items; three participants learnt all items on Trial 1, almost half had learnt all items in two trials, and more than two-thirds had learnt all cognate items in three trials; by the end of Trial 5, only one participant had not learnt all items. In contrast, acquisition of the list of non-cognate items increased incrementally.

Table 4. Performance on the training trials

	Cognates Mean	# of 100% scores	Non-cognates Mean	# of 100% scores
Trial 1	82.7%	3	70.6%	0
Trial 2	92.3%	7	79.8%	1
Trial 3	93.5%	6	85.3%	4
Trial 4	95%	4	86.7%	1
Trial 5	97.5%	3	88.8%	5
Trial 6	90%	0 (N = 1)	91.1%	4
Trial 7	95%	0 (N = 1)	93.3%	5
Trial 8	100%	1	91.1%	1
Trial 9	–	–	92.5%	2
Trial 10	–	–	92.5%	–(N = 10)

13.   For cognates – Training Trial 1: $t(23) = 36.89$, $p = 0.000$; Test: $t(23) = 78.40$, $p = 0.000$; Re-test 1: $t(20) = 50.59$, $p = 0.000$; Re-test 2: $t(20) = 62.55$, $p = 0.000$. For non-cognates – Training Trial 1: $t(32) = 30.97$, $p = 0.000$; Test: $t(22) = 74.49$, $p = 0.000$; Re-test 1: $t(20) = 35.26$, $p = 0.000$; Re-test 2: $t(20) = 49.27$, $p = 0.000$.

Table 5. Cognate comparisons (Studies 1–3)

Study	Training Trial 1	Test	Re-test 1	Re-test 2	# of Trials to criterion
1	85.6%	96%	87.9%	93.6%	3.21
	(N = 25)	(N = 23)	(N = 22)	(N = 22)	
2	82.7%	95%	85.9%	93%	3.04
	(N = 33)	(N = 23)	(N = 21)	(N = 21)	
3	78.3%	95.7%	87.7%	96.3%	3.88
	(N = 26)	(N = 26)	(N = 22)	(N = 22)	
Mean	82.2%	95.6%	87.1%	94.3%	3.37

Table 5 present the results of the cognate stimuli from all three studies, and shows that the results are robust across three different groups of Anglophones.

To sum up the accuracy results, recall that our participants had no representations of either the German cognates or the non-cognates. Nevertheless, participants were segmenting both kinds of target words after only two exposures to the words in distinct acoustic inputs. In addition, we found robust effects of prior lexical knowledge in that our participants had higher scores on Training Trial 1 and Retest 1 on cognate items. Frequency of the input seemed to affect the ability to correctly associate a long list of 20 items to the appropriate pictures but not the ability to correctly map specific words to their pictures.

Response latencies were calculated from the onset of the stimulus to the offset.[14] Data are presented for correct responses only. Figure 1 shows that responses were

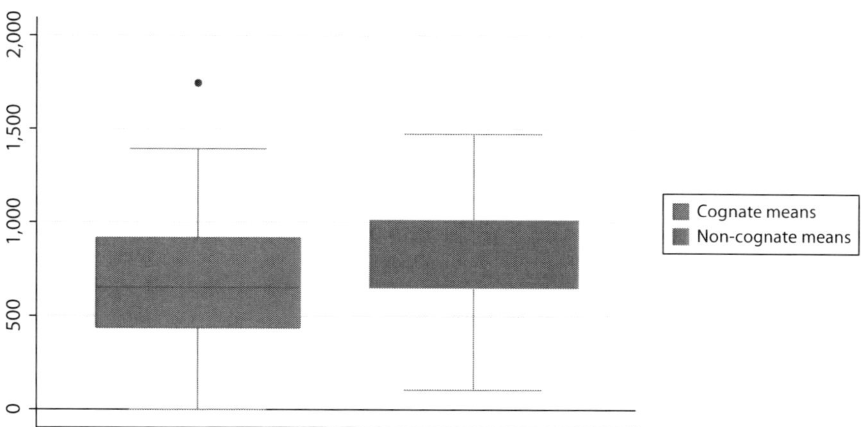

Figure 1. Response latencies from Study 2

---

14. Calculating latencies from the beginning of the stimulus to the end resulted in a negative value whenever the respondent pushed the key immediately after NP1, which they frequently did when NP1 was the correct response.

much faster on cognate items (681.7 ms, N = 90) than on non-cognate items (818.33, N = 98). This difference was significant, t(186) = –2.94, p = 0.003. The latency data provide strong evidence that the cognate stimuli were activating L1 lexical entries.[15]

Finally, although space limitations preclude detailed discussion of the production data (see Carroll 2010b), the analysis of transcriptions from Study 2 revealed that

Table 6. Qualitative and quantitative analysis of production data (stressed syllables are capitalized)

	Name#	Word Type	Ssyl l	Error type	Wksyll 1	Error type	Wksyll 2	Error type	Wksyll 3
1	KAI	NC	100.0%		–				
2	HEIke	NC	100.0%		94.7%				
3	HEIdrun	NC	100.0%		42.1%				
4	DIETmar	NC	100.0%		77.3%	Vowel + R			
5	aNIta	C	100.0%		50.0%	Vowel	70.80%		
6	reGIna	NC	100.0%		50.0%	R	100%		
7	caroLIna	C	95.8%	Vowel	0.0%	Vowel	0%	R	100%
8	JoHAnna	C	95.8%		91.7%	Onset	100%		
9	JOsef	C	95.5%		36.4%	Vowel, Coda			
10	Eberhardt	NC	95.5%		31.8%	Vowel + R			
11	geSIne	NC	95.2%		95.2%		100%		
12	SENta	NC	90.0%		100.0%				
13	BEnno	NC	86.4%	Vowel	100.0%				
14	FEMke	NC	81.8%	Vowel	95.5%				
15	Eva	C	73.9%	Vowel	52.2%	Vowel, Onset			
16	CLAUdia	C	66.7%	Vowel	100.0%		100%		
17	GEorg	C	66.7%	Vowel	58.3%	Vowel, Coda, R			
18	SÖNke	NC	58.8%	Vowel	100.0%				
19	HArald	C	58.3%		12.5%	Vowel, Coda			

15.   It must be emphasized that the fact that our subjects were responding with [ˈbɛno] *Benno* when they heard this non-cognate word does not show that *Benno* failed to activate English *Ben*, *Bennie*, *Benji* etc. Given the results here and in Rast (2008) it is highly likely that all L2 words that are similar enough to L1 words will activate those words. However, *Benno* is presumably not "similar enough" to *Bennie* for the speaker to say [ˈbɛni]. What phonetic and phonological properties make a word similar or not similar enough is a crucial question in the study of cognates.

participants were very good at repeating the target words. However, they were much more target-like on the non-cognate items than on the cognate items. See Table 6.

Lessened accuracy in pronouncing the German cognate words was due to the fact that they were often pronounced like the corresponding English words. Still some participants attempted to produce some aspect of the cognate-items input. So [jozɛf] *Josef* was not pronounced with an English affricate [dʒ], and [eːfa] *Eva* was not pronounced as [iːv] *Eve* but with [f] and the vowel [e]. Of course, the non-cognate items were produced with English-influenced gestures too, however, there was considerable variation observed and some participants were remarkably target-like on the (non-L1) mid front rounded vowels of *Sönke* and *Jörg* [œ] which would be inexplicable if the subjects had not encoded correct acoustic detail for these items. Thus, pronunciation of these words showed that learners were drawing on different types of sound representations – a representation that preserves information from the signal, as well as representations that encode English-only sounds.

5.   Discussion and conclusions

Learning another language entails learning a new lexicon. Words can be seen as a triplex of autonomous representations (Jackendoff 2002a, 2002b). In particular, we may surmise that the learner must segment sound forms from the speech signal, learn the morpho-syntactic properties of a word (its grammatical class, person, number, or gender features, its transitivity, etc.), and its semantic properties (its sense and its referent in a particular context). There is good reason to assume that acquiring all of these properties will demand considerable experience with the L2. Listening to an L2 is known to be more difficult for L2 learners and fluent bilinguals than for native speakers. Even advanced L2ers misparse words when listening to continuous speech (Voss 1977); they are disadvantaged when listening to the L2 in noise (Florentine 1985, Takata & Nabelek 1990, Hardison 1996, inter alia); they have difficulty adjusting to less familiar accents (Major, Fitzmaurice, Bunta & Balasubramanian 2002). Emergentist theories of second language acquisition predict such findings because they predict strong L1 transfer effects even during pre-lexical processing. Such effects might arise because L1 representations are impeding analysis of the input, or the simultaneous activation of both L1 and L2 representations might lead to difficulties in integrating information from multiple sources. The fact that our learners were able to encode for both receptive and production purposes the non-cognate words suggests that entrenchment at pre-lexical levels of processing is not an absolute barrier to segmentation and word learning. These results are consistent with the findings of other studies of first exposure learners (Osterhout et al. 2006, Finn & Hudson Kam 2008, Rast 2008, 2010, Gullberg et al. 2010, in press). We have succeeded in narrowing down even further the amount of experience the L2 requires: not much.

Our study provides clear evidence of L1-based lexical effects when first exposure learners are listening to a second language. These results are consistent with strong transfer theories, including not only connectionist models but also the Full Transfer/Full Access theory of Schwartz & Sprouse (1994, 1996). Nevertheless, the fact that some first exposure learners produced cognate words with input-based sounds (such as [eːfa] and not [iːv] 'Eve') shows that L1-lexical activation is not deterministically connected to the learners' pronunciation. As well, the fact that at least some learners attempted to pronounce novel sounds in the non-cognate words in a target-like way suggests that these participants have encoded a rich phonetic representation that preserves information from the signal, as exemplar-based theories predict. Because our learners had no prior exposure to German, we can reject as an account of such learner behaviours the hypothesis that some of the learners had already acquired these German names.

Our subjects performed well above chance on our task even on the first training trial, after only two exposures to the proper names. The mean score on the non-cognate items was 70.6%, substantially above the mean scores of 55% reported by Gullberg et al. (in press) after one exposure to the weather report and 60% after two exposures, but comparable to means of 68% reported for two-syllable items that were frequent. This is encouraging and suggests that our stimuli and task are capturing similar learning effects. However, because our paradigm allows us to directly measure the effects of cumulative exposure, we can say that hearing more of the same input had little effect on the processing of individual utterances in the input and that learners can rapidly memorize segmented stimuli (phonetic tokens) on far less input than had previously been supposed (Osterhout et al. 2006). This still leaves open the question of how much exposure is needed to learn a more abstract representation of the sound form of a word which would be needed to recognize the same word when pronounced by different talkers or by speakers with different accents.

Our data show not only that our participants can associate the sound forms of the words with a meaning (a referent), they can do so when the visual cues to the referent change and after a two-week period with no input at all. This is consistent with the findings of Gullberg et al. (2010, in press) and runs counter to an idea expressed in Osterhout et al. (2006: 224) that first exposure learners first learn a sound form and only subsequently, given more experience with L2 input, derive a meaning. Such findings show the necessity of basing claims about input effects on studies of input that are causally related to specific behavioural or other outcomes.

Our results strongly suggest that discussions of frequency in L2 acquisition should take account of the nature of the learning problem. It has been argued here that word-learning entails learning multiple representations that must ultimately be linked in memory as diverse instances of "the same word". Our results show that repeated exposure to the same input is not necessary to memorize a sound token. This is an interesting result in the light of studies of statistical learning in which the same stream of word sequences is presented again and again in a continuous loop (Saffran et al. 1996). It also adds greater precision to studies that have similar findings but measured exposure in terms of minutes or hours of time. If our interpretation of the data is correct, it follows that repetition of the same tokens will not be useful to a learning mechanism that is sensitive to *changes* in syllable sequences in the input. This is presumably part of the story as to why beginner L2ers segment recurrent strings of words as if they were a single phonetic or phonological unit (Wong Fillmore 1976, Wray 2002, Carroll 2010a). It might well be involved in explaining why our task is so easy in comparison to, e.g., listening to a weather report. One could make the case, as one reviewer did, that it is "obvious" that our task is easy because the stimuli make use of recurrent words. But, as noted, this fact is probably not relevant. Rather, it may be the case that the task is easy because the input can be readily parsed into feet. If our first exposure learners indeed represented the signal in terms of abstract L1-specific metrical categories such as feet and prosodic words (Cutler 1994), than they could have parsed the stimuli into sequences of one or two prosodic words before the utterance-medial targets and two prosodic words after, e.g. [dɛsɪst] ... [odɐ] ... *das ist* ... *oder* ... where the "..." stand in for the proper names. See Carroll (2011) for just such an analysis of the input. However, it must be emphasized that if first exposure learners imposed feet and prosodic words onto the first utterances they heard, this is a significant finding and not something to be presupposed.

Cutler & Shanley (2010: 1844) suggest that listening to L2 speech is "inordinately hard" and may require targeted training. Our study suggests that this is not necessarily so. When the L1 and the L2 are similar in terms of their repertoires of phonetic categories, their abstract phonological categories, and how those categories are instantiated in lexical items (the cognates), there are clear processing advantages for the first exposure learner. However, even when the L1 and the L2 differ in their consonants and vowels, their syllable structures, their stress patterns, and their use of tones (as is the case in the Dutch/Mandarin Chinese study of Gullberg et al. 2010, in press, or the Polish/French studies of Rast 2008, 2010), learners can still create discrete representations of sound tokens on the basis of minimal exposure.

To conclude, not all aspects of L2 learning require repeated exposure to the same inputs and not all aspects of L2 learning are slow and incremental. This is good news indeed because it shows that commonly held beliefs of many L2 learners (and possibly even SLA researchers) that listening to an L2 is hard may underestimate their true initial capacities. Controlled input studies with first exposure learners offer a feasible approach to the investigation of initial processing capacities, and are already shedding interesting light on what the learner can do with the input she receives.

References

Altenberg, E. P. 2005. The perception of word boundaries in a second language. *Second Language Research* 21: 325–358.

Avery, R. A. & C. T. Best. 1995. Phonological and phonotactic influences on perception of two non-native vowel contrasts. *Journal of the Acoustical Society of America* 97: 33–62.

Bates, E. & B. MacWhinney. 1987. Competition, variation, and language learning. In *Mechanisms of Language Acquisition*, ed. B. MacWhinney, 157–193. Hillsdale NJ: Lawrence Erlbaum Associates.

Bortfeld, H., J.Morgan, R. M. Golinkoff & K. Rathbun. 2005. Mommy and me: Familiar names help launch babies in speech-stream segmentation. *Psychological Science* 16: 298–304.

Brent, M. R. & T. A. Cartwright. 1996. Distributional regularity and lexical access. *Journal of Psycholinguistic Research* 26: 363–375.

Carroll, S. E. 1992. On cognates. *Second Language Research* 82: 93–119.

Carroll, S. E. 2001. *Input and Evidence: The Raw Material of Second Language Acquisition* (Language Acquisition and Language Disorders 25). Amsterdam: John Benjamins.

Carroll, S. E. 2010a. Explaining how learners extract 'formulae' from L2 input. *Language, Interaction and Acquisition/Langage, Interaction et Acquisition* 1: 229–250.

Carroll, S. E. 2010b. Exploring the locus of transfer in the L2 pronunciation of novel words. Paper presented at the Annual Meeting of the Canadian Linguistic Association, Concordia University, Montréal, Canada, 31 May 2010.

Carroll, S. E. 2011. What properties of input influence word learning on first exposure. Paper presented at Eurosla 21, Stockholm University, 8–10 September 2011.

Chaudron, C. 1986. The role of simplified input in classroom language. In *Learning, Teaching and Communication in the Foreign Language Classroom*, ed. G. Kaspar, 99–110, Aarhus: Aarhus University Press.

Christophe, A., S. Peperkamp, C. Pallier, E. Block & J. Mehler. 2004. Phonological phrase boundaries constrain lexical access: Adult data. *Journal of Memory and Language* 51: 523–547.

Cutler, A. 1994. Segmentation problems, rhythmic solutions. *Lingua* 92: 81–104.

Cutler, A. & J. Shanley. 2010. Validation of a training method for L2 continuous-speech segmentation. In *Proceedings of the 11th Annual Conference of the International Speech Communication Association (Interspeech 2010)*, 26–30 September 2010, 1844–1847, Makuhari, Chiba, Japan.

Cutler, A. & A. Weber. 2007. Listening experience and phonetic-to-lexical mapping in L2. In *Proceedings of the 16th International Congress of Phonetic Science (ICPhS 2007)*, eds. J. Trouvain & W. J. Barry, 43–48. Saarbrücken: Universität des Saarlandes.

De Groot, A. M. B. & R. Keijzer. 2000. What is hard to learn is easy to forget: The roles of word concreteness, cognate status, and word frequency in foreign-language vocabulary learning and forgetting. *Language Learning* 50: 1–56.

Dejean de la Bâtie, B. & D. C. Bradley. 1995. Resolving word boundaries in spoken French: Native and non-native strategies. *Applied Psycholinguistics* 16: 59–81.

Dumay, N., U. H. Frauenfelder & A. Content. 2002. The role of the syllable in lexical segmentation in French: Word-spotting data. *Brain and Language* 81: 144–161.

Ellis, N. C. 1998. Emergentism, connectionism and language learning. *Language Learning* 48: 631–664.

Ellis, N. C. 2002. Frequency effects in language processing: A review with implications for theories of implicit and explicit language acquisition. *Studies in Second Language Acquisition* 24: 143–188.

Ellis, N. C. 2003. Constructions, chunking, and connectionism: The emergence of second language structure. In *The Handbook of Second Language Acquisition*, eds. C. J. Doughty & M. H. Long, 63–103. Oxford: Blackwell.

Endress, A. & L. L. Bonatti. 2007. Rapid learning of syllable classes from a perceptually continuous speech stream. *Cognition* 105: 247–299.

Epstein, S. D., S. Flynn & G. Martohardjono. 1996. Second language acquisition: Theoretical and experimental issues in contemporary research. *Behavioral and Brain Sciences* 19: 677–758.

Escudero, P., R. Hayes-Harb & H. Mitterer. 2008. Novel second-language words and asymmetric lexical access. *Journal of Phonetics* 36: 345–360.

Finn, A. & C. L. Hudson Kam. 2008. The curse of knowledge: First language knowledge impairs adult learners' use of novel statistics for word segmentation. *Cognition* 108: 477–499.

Florentine, M. 1985. Speech perception in noise by fluent, non-native listeners. *Proceedings of Inter-Noise 1985*, 1021–1024.

Folia, V., J. Uddén, M. de Vries, C. Forkstam & K. M. Petersson. 2010. Artificial language learning in adults and children. *Language Learning* 60: 188–220.

Gass, S. M. 1997. *Input, Interaction and the Second Language Learner*. Mahwah NJ: Lawrence Erlbaum Associates.

Goldinger, S. D. 1998. Echoes of echoes? An episodic theory of lexical access. *Psychological Review* 105: 251–279.

Gullberg, M., L. Roberts & C. Dimroth. In press. What word-level knowledge can adult learners acquire after minimal exposure to a new language? *International Review of Applied Linguistics*.

Gullberg, M., L. Roberts, C. Dimroth, K. Veroude & P. Indefrey. 2010. Adult language learning after minimal exposure to an unknown natural language. *Language Learning* 60: 5–24.

Håkansson, G. 1986. Quantitative aspects of teacher talk. In *Learning, Teaching and Communication in the Foreign Language Classroom*, ed. G. Kaspar, 83–98. Aarhus: Aarhus University Press.

Håkansson, G. 1987. *Teacher Talk: How Teachers Modify their Speech when Addressing Learners of Swedish as a Second Language*. Lund: Lund University Press.

Hallé, P. A., J. A. Segui, U. Frauenfelder & C. Meunier. 1998. The processing of illegal consonants clusters: A case of perceptual assimilation? *Experimental Psychology: Human Perception and Performance* 24: 1–17.

Hardison, D. M. 1996. Bi-modal speech perception by native and non-native speakers of English: Factors influencing the McGurk effect. *Language Learning* 46: 3–73.

Houston, D. M. 2005. Speech perception in infants. In *The Handbook of Speech Perception*, eds. D. B. Pisoni & R. E. Remez, 417–448. Malden MA: Blackwell.

Jackendoff, R. 2002a. *Foundations of Language, Brain, Meaning, Grammar, Evolution*. Oxford: OUP.

Jackendoff, R. 2002b. What's in the lexicon? In *Storage and Computation in the Language Faculty*, eds. S. Nooteboom, F. Weerman & F. Wijnen, 23–58. Dordrecht: Kluwer.

Jonasson, K. 1994. *Le nom propre: Constructions et interprétations*. Louvain-la-Neuve: Éditions Duculot.

Jusczyk, P. W. 1997. *The Discovery of Spoken Language*. Cambridge MA: The MIT Press.

Katz, J. J. 2001. The end of Millianism: Multiple bearers, improper names and compositional meaning. *Journal of Philosophy* 98: 137–166.

Klein, W. & C. Perdue. 1997. The basic variety (or: Couldn't natural languages be much simpler?) *Second Language Research* 13: 301–347.

Leplus, T., P. Langlais & G. Lapalme. 2004. Weather report translation using a translation memory. In *Machine Translation: From Real Users to Research. Proceedings of the 6th Conference of the Association for Machine Translation in the Americas, AMTA 2004, Washington, DC,*

USA, September/October 2004, eds. R. E. Frederking & K. B. Taylor, 154–163. Berlin: Springer.

Lively, S. E., D. B. Pisoni & J. S. Logan. 1992. Some effects of training Japanese listeners to identify English /r/ and /l/. In *Speech Perception, Production and Linguistic Structure*, eds. Y. Tohkura, E. Vatikiotis-Bateson & Y. Sagisaka, 175–196. Amsterdam: IOS Press.

MacWhinney, B. 2000. Lexicalist connectionism. In *Models of Language Acquisition: Inductive and Deductive Approaches*, eds. P. Broeder & J. Murre, 9–32. Oxford: OUP.

MacWhinney, B. 2005. New directions in the Competition Model. In *Beyond Nature-nurture: Essays in Honor of Elizabeth Bates*, eds. M. Tomasello & D. I. Slobin, 81–110. Mahwah NJ: Lawrence Erlbaum Associates.

MacWhinney, B. & J. Leinbach. 1991. Implementations are not conceptualisations: Revising the verb learning model. *Cognition* 40: 121–157.

Major, R. C., S. F. Fitzmaurice, F. Bunta & C. Balasubramanian. 2002. The effects of non-native accents on listening comprehension: Implications for ESL assessment. *TESOL Quarterly* 36: 173–190.

Mattys, S. L. & J. F. Melhorn 2007. Sentential, lexical, and acoustic effects on the perception of word boundaries. *Journal of the Acoustical Society of America* 122: 554–567.

McQueen, J. M. 1998. Segmentation of continuous speech using phonotactics. *Journal of Memory and Language* 39: 21–46.

Mellow, D. 2008. Emergentist approaches to teaching and measurement: It's about time. Paper presented at the Annual meeting of the Canadian Association of Applied Linguistics, University of British Columbia, Vancouver, BC, 4 June 2008.

Monaghan, P. & M. H. Christiansen. 2010. Words in puddles of sound: Modelling psycholinguistic effects in speech segmentation. *Journal of Child Language* 37: 545–564.

Nygaard, L. C., M. S. Sommers & D. B. Pisoni. 1994. Speech perception as a talker-contingent process. *Psychological Science* 5: 42–46.

Osterhout, L., J. McLaughlin, I. Pitkänen, C. Frenck-Mestre & N. Molinaro. 2006. Novice learners, longitudinal designs, and event-related potentials: A means for exploring the neurocognition of second-language processing. *Language Learning* 56: 199–230.

Palmeri, T. J., S. D. Goldinger & D. B. Pisoni. 1993. Episodic encoding of voice attributes and recognition memory for spoken words. *Journal of Experimental Psychology: Learning, Memory and Cognition* 19: 1–20.

Pisoni, D. B. & S. E. Lively. 1995. Variability and invariance in speech perception. A new look at some old problems in perceptual learning. In *Speech Perception and Linguistic Experience: Theoretical and Methodological Issues in Cross-language Speech Research*, ed. W. Strange, 433–459. Timonium: York Press.

Rast, R. 2008. *Foreign Language Input: Initial Processing*. Clevedon: Multilingual Matters.

Rast, R. 2010. The role of linguistic input in the first hours of adult language learning. *Language Learning* 60: 64–84.

Saffran, J. R., E. L. Newport & R. N. Aslin. 1996. Word segmentation: The role of distributional cues. *Journal of Memory and Language* 35: 606–621.

Schwartz, B. D. & R. Sprouse. 1994. Word order and nominative case in non-native language acquisition: A longitudinal study of (L1 Turkish) German interlanguage. In *Language Acquisition Studies in Generative Grammar: Papers in Honor of Kenneth Wexler from the 1991 GLOW Workshops* (Language Acquisition and Language Disorders 8), eds. T. Hoekstra & B. D. Schwartz, 317–368. Amsterdam: John Benjamins.

Schwartz, B. D. & R. Sprouse. 1996. L2 cognitive states and the Full Transfer/Full Access model. *Second Language Research* 12: 40–72.

Shillcock, R. 1990. Speech segmentation and the generation of lexical hypotheses. In *Cognitive Models of Speech Processing: Psycholinguistic and Computational Perspectives*, ed. G. T. M. Altmann, 24–49. Cambridge MA: The MIT Press.

Takata, Y. & A. K. Nabelek. 1990. English consonant recognition in noise and in reverberation by Japanese and American listeners. *Journal of the Acoustical Society of America* 88: 663–666.

Tench, P. 2003. Non-native speakers' misperception of English vowels and consonants: Evidence from Korean adults in the UK. *International Review of Applied Linguistics in Language Teaching (IRAL)* 41: 145–173.

Van Hell, J. & A. M. B. de Groot. 1998. Conceptual representation in bilingual memory: Effects of concreteness and cognate status in word association. *Bilingualism: Language and Cognition* 1: 193–211.

Voss, B. 1977. *Hesitation Phenomena as Sources of Perceptual Errors for Non-native Speakers* (Applied and interdisciplinary papers, Series B 25). Trier: L.A.U.T.

Weber, A. & A. Cutler. 2004. Lexical competition in non-native spoken-word recognition. *Journal of Memory and Language* 50: 1–25.

Weber, A. & A. Cutler. 2006. First-language phonotactics in second language listening. *Journal of the Acoustical Society of America* 119: 597–607.

Wong Fillmore, L. 1976. *The Second Time Around: Cognitive and Social Strategies in Second Language Acquisition*. PhD dissertation, Stanford University.

Wray, A. 2002. *Formulaic Language and the Lexicon*. Cambridge: CUP.

Yamada, R. A. & Y. Tohkura. 1992. Perception of American English /r/ and /l/ by native speakers of Japanese. In *Speech Perception, Production and Linguistic Structure*, eds. Y. Tohkura, E. Vatikiotis-Bateson & Y. Sagisaka, 155–174. Amsterdam: IOS Press.

Wh-questions in Dutch

Bilingual and trilingual acquisition compared*

Nelleke Strik
Dalhousie University, Canada

This study investigates cross-linguistic influence in Dutch *wh*-questions in bilingual Dutch-French and trilingual Dutch-French-Italian acquisition. Five and seven year-old bilingual and trilingual children as well as monolingual children and adult controls (N = 49) participated in an elicited production task. In addition to target-like *wh*-fronted questions with subject-verb inversion, the majority of responses, the multilingual children produced two qualitatively different structures: *wh*-in-situ questions and *wh*-fronted questions without inversion. These structures are argued to result from transfer from French, and in the case of non-inversion with the *wh*-word *why* in the trilingual group from transfer from Italian. It is proposed that a theory of transfer based on derivational complexity can best account for these data.

Keywords: Dutch, French, Italian, *wh*-questions, multilingual acquisition, cross-linguistic influence, derivational complexity, structural overlap

1. Introduction

It is generally assumed that children who acquire two languages simultaneously early on in life develop two autonomous grammatical systems (cf. Meisel 1989, 2007, De Houwer 1990, among others). This does not mean that no interaction between the languages

* I would like to thank V. Moscati, M. Orioni, A.T. Pérez-Leroux, P. Reale, E. Segnini, the audience of the *International Conference on Multilingual Individuals and Multilingual Societies* (Hamburg, October 2010) and the members of the *Groupe Langage* of the François Rabelais University in Tours for useful comments and discussion. I am grateful to I. Paupert of the *Institut Néerlandais* in Paris and S. Starkenburg of the *Schoter Duijn* elementary school in Den Helder for their assistance in organizing the study, and to all the children and their parents as well as the adults for their participation. The research reported in this article benefitted from the support of SSHRC grant 410–09–2026, "The Acquisition of Object Clitics by Children Learning French as Their First or Second Language".

occurs at all, but rather cross-linguistic influence appears to be restricted (cf. Paradis & Genesee 1996 and Müller 2003, among others). In order to investigate the issue of cross-linguistic influence, I present data from *wh*-questions in two groups of multilingual Dutch children. I compare a group of bilingual Dutch-French to a group of trilingual Dutch-French-Italian children, all of whom live in France. Monolingual Dutch children and adults served as controls. *Wh*-questions in such a combination of languages offer an interesting domain to study cross-linguistic influence, because of the differences in interrogative structures. Dutch has a single grammatical *wh*-construction: *wh*-fronting with subject-verb inversion. In French, on the contrary, a large variety of *wh*-constructions are attested, including *wh*-in-situ and *wh*-fronting with or without inversion. In Italian, inversion is obligatory with all *wh*-words, except *perché* ('why'). Moreover, Italian is a pro-drop language: the subject is not always overtly expressed. In the present study, I discuss various approaches to cross-linguistic influence based on the notion of structural overlap and propose a new approach based on derivational complexity (cf. Strik & Pérez-Leroux 2011). The main question is to test whether, by virtue of cross-linguistic influence, new word orders can be introduced in the *wh*-questions of bilingual and trilingual children (i.e., transfer of these structures from one language to another). I hypothesize that this is indeed possible, provided these structures are less complex than the target structure in the language under study. As for trilingual children the aim is to examine whether the presence of a third language leads to additional multilingual effects.

2.   Cross-linguistic influence in multilingual acquisition

A common view in the study of bilingual development is that bilingual children may show quantitative but no qualitative differences compared to their monolingual peers (cf. Hulk & Müller 2000, Meisel 2007, among others). That is, bilingual children may produce different rates of a given grammatical structure, but they go through the same developmental stages as monolingual children. With respect to cross-linguistic influence, several models have been proposed to predict in which domains this can be expected. On the one hand, cross-linguistic influence can be constrained by language-external conditions, such as dominance from one language over the other or the frequency of a given structure in the source language. On the other, it can be constrained by language-internal or grammatical conditions, such as structural compatibility or domain-specific vulnerabilities.

Structural compatibility or overlap is a key notion in the hypothesis proposed by Hulk & Müller (2000). This approach predicts cross-linguistic influence under two conditions. First, when there is structural ambiguity, that is, only if language A has a syntactic construction which may be analyzed in more than one way and language B contains evidence for one of those two possible analyses. Second, the constructions have to involve the interface between syntax and pragmatics. Debate remains on the question of whether cross-linguistic influence is restricted to the syntax-pragmatics interface or other interfaces (see Pérez-Leroux 2011 for a critical review). Yip & Matthews (2009) refine the notion of structural overlap and propose to situate it at the level of surface strings. According to these authors, surface overlap exists between two languages, A and B, when language A allows one option and language B allows two, one of which is isomorphic to the option allowed in language A. In other words, not only the presence of a given structure in two languages, but also the basic word order in both languages must be considered.

Recently, it has been argued that derivational complexity is another grammatical condition that determines cross-linguistic influence (cf. Strik & Pérez-Leroux 2011). According to the Derivational Complexity Hypothesis as formulated in Jakubowicz (2011) for example, constructions requiring less computation, as measured by the number of overt movement operations, emerge before those requiring more computation. Strik & Pérez-Leroux (2011) propose that qualitatively different structures can be introduced from one language into the other in bilingual acquisition, when these structures represent a computational step in the derivation of the target structure.

In the field of multilingualism, relatively few studies focus on trilingual language acquisition, but Barnes (2006) and Wang (2008), for instance, offer a careful overview. Although trilingual acquisition shares a lot of features with bilingual acquisition and is generally studied in the same framework, it has been argued that trilingual competence is different (Hoffmann 2001). Without entering into this debate, the relevant point for the present study is that the mere presence of a third language creates a different situation compared to bilingual acquisition; more precisely, an additional potential source of cross-linguistic influence.

3.   *Wh*-questions in Dutch, French and Italian

3.1   Syntax of *wh*-questions in Dutch, French and Italian

In Dutch questions, the *wh*-word must be fronted. *Wh*-in-situ occurs only in echo-questions, as in other *wh*-fronting languages. Subject-verb inversion is obligatory, since Dutch is a V2 language (cf. Den Besten 1977, Zwart 1997):

(1)   Wie   zie   je?
      Who   see-2SG   you
      'Who do you see?'

Crucially, the V2 property concerns main clauses. In embedded clauses in Dutch, the verb remains in sentence-final position (after the object) and the subject directly follows the *wh*-word.

In French, substantive variation exists in *wh*-constructions. The *wh*-word can appear either fronted or in-situ (see (2a) versus (2b, c)). In questions with *wh*-fronting, the verb can either be inverted (i.e., moved) or uninverted (see (2b vs. c)).

(2) a. Tu vois   qui?
         you see-2SG who

     b. Qui tu   vois?
         who you see-2SG

     c. Qui vois-tu?
         who see-2SG you
         'Who do you see?'

Moreover, the fronted *wh*-word can appear with *est-ce que* or in a cleft construction. Questions with subject-verb inversion are rare or even non-existent in colloquial French, whereas uninverted *wh*-fronted and *wh*-in-situ questions are common (cf. Riegel, Pellat & Rioul 1994, Vinet 2001, Coveney 2002, among others). Embedded clauses exhibit the same word order as matrix clauses.

In Italian, *wh*-fronting is also obligatory. The same holds for inversion, if there is an overt subject, since Italian is a pro-drop language (see (3a), the equivalent of (1) and (2), and (3b)). However, with the *wh*-word *perché* ('why') inversion is facultative (cf. Rizzi 2001) (see (3c)).

(3) a. Chi vedi?
         who see-2SG
         'Who do you see?'

     b. Cosa vede   Anna?
         what see-3SG Anna
         'What does Anna see?'

     c. Perché Gianni filma   Anna?
         why   John   film-3SG Anna
         'Why does John film Anna?'

Contrary to Dutch and French, inversion also appears in embedded clauses in Italian. Uninverted embedded clauses are possible with a subjunctive verb and marginal with an indicative verb (Guasti 1996). The different options in *wh*-constructions in Dutch, French and Italian are given in Table 1.

Table 1. Syntax of *wh*-constructions in Dutch, French and Italian

	Dutch	**French**	**Italian**
Wh-fronting	obligatory	optional	obligatory
Wh-in-situ	echo	true questions, echo	echo
Inversion	obligatory	optional *(no inversion in colloquial French)*	obligatory *(null subjects; with 'why' inversion not obligatory)*
Embedded *wh*	no inversion	no inversion	inversion *(no inversion possible with subjunctive, marginal with indicative)*

3.2   Monolingual acquisition of *wh*-questions in Dutch, French and Italian

Few studies are available focusing solely on the acquisition of *wh*-questions in Dutch. With respect to the position of the *wh*-word, no *wh*-in-situ questions are reported in Dutch first language acquisition and no evidence is present for a *wh*-in-situ stage in this language (Van Kampen 1997, Strik 2008). Yet, omission of the *wh*-word is common (Van Kampen 1997). The V2 property (i.e., inversion) is acquired early, before age 2;06 (cf. Ruhland, Wijnen & Van Geert 1995).

Much more research has been done on the acquisition of *wh*-questions in French. As for the position of the *wh*-word, previous studies show a mixed picture. Studies on spontaneous data show that most children acquire *wh*-in-situ before *wh*-fronted questions (Plunkett 1999, Hamann 2000, 2006). However, the child Philippe is different (Hulk 1996). For instance, in Hamann (2006), in 80–90% of the questions the *wh*-word was in-situ for 2 year-old children. Elicited production data show a lower proportion of *wh*-in-situ questions: up to 50% for 3-year-old children in Strik (2007) and lower rates in other studies and for older children (Hulk & Zuckerman 2000, Hamann 2006, Strik 2007, 2008, Prévost, Tuller, Scheidnes, Ferré & Haiden 2010). A more homogeneous picture emerges for the position of the finite verb. Questions with inversion are almost non-existent in the production of young children, in both spontaneous and experimental data. Rates are not higher than 5% for 3 to 6 year-old children (Plunkett 1999, Hulk 1996, Hamann 2000, 2006, Hulk & Zuckerman 2000, Strik 2007, 2008). Prévost et al. (2010) report a higher rate, approximately 20%, of inverted *wh*-questions for 6-year-olds. Overall, the most frequent pattern in the speech of French children seems to be *wh*-fronting without inversion.

In the acquisition of questions in Italian, spontaneous data reveal that, as in Dutch, no *wh*-in-situ questions are produced and inversion is acquired early on (Guasti 1996, 2000, 2002). Guasti (1996) shows that in an elicited production task of *wh*-questions with 3 and 4 year-old children, the majority of responses had a null subject (about 70%). In both spontaneous and elicited production data, a few *wh*-questions without inversion were found. Crucially, in all these questions the *wh*-word was *why*, and these structures were thus consistent with the adult grammar.

3.3   Multilingual acquisition of *wh*-questions

In multilingual acquisition, a key question is whether there can be influence from one language on another. With respect to *wh*-questions, my goal is to determine whether transfer of *wh*-constructions can occur. Several cases of transfer are attested in the literature. Yip & Matthews (2000, 2007, 2009) reported transfer of *wh*-in-situ from Cantonese, an in-situ language, to English, a language with obligatory *wh*-fronting. Six English-Cantonese simultaneous bilingual children (ages 1;03–4;06) produced *wh*-in-situ questions in English. Proportions ranged from 13.3% to 92.3% for *what*-questions. Some sporadic cases of transfer of *wh*-fronting to Cantonese are also attested (Yip &

Matthews 2007). Soriente (2007) reports cases of transfer of *wh*-in-situ to Italian, an obligatory fronting language, from Indonesian, an optional in-situ language. Yip & Matthews (2000) and Soriente (2007) explain the transfer of *wh*-in-situ by dominance of the *wh*-in-situ language. Yip & Matthews (2009) refer to the notion of structural overlap (see Section 2). They note that echo questions in English may provide evidence for this structure as being an option, allowing for the overextension to non-echo questions. No transfer of *wh*-in-situ has been found in the Korean-English and Japanese-English children in Park (2008) and Mishina-Mori (2005). Bonnesen (2005), who studies the acquisition of the left periphery by two French-German bilinguals growing up in Germany (ages 1;06–6;0), does not report any instance of transfer of the French in-situ option to German, a *wh*-fronting language like Dutch.

As for inversion, few or no errors related to the position of the verb are found in the English-Dutch, French-German and Italian-Indonesian children in De Houwer (1990), Bonnesen (2005) and Soriente (2007). Austin, Blume & Sánchez (2009) studied Spanish-English bilingual children. They found a few cases of non-inversion in Spanish, a phenomenon unattested in Spanish monolinguals (Pérez-Leroux & Dalious 1998), yet reported in monolingual English acquisition (Thornton 2008 among others).

To my knowledge, Barnes (2006) provides the only study on trilingual development of *wh*-questions. In the longitudinal data of an English-Basque-Spanish child living in Spain (aged 2;0 to 3;06), a number of uninverted questions were found in English (exact counts are not given). Some were with the *wh*-word *why*, but non-inversion also occurred with other *wh*-words. As in Italian, inversion is not obligatory with *why* in Spanish. Questions without inversion, however, also show up in monolingual acquisition in English, primarily with *why* (Thornton 2008). Therefore, the uninverted questions cannot (only) be attributed to transfer from Spanish.

4. Study

4.1 Hypotheses

The present study aims to investigate whether qualitative differences can appear in Dutch *wh*-questions produced by Dutch-French(-Italian) children. In Table 2, the various *wh*-constructions in Dutch, French and Italian are presented and classified by the order of *wh*-word, subject (S) and verb (V).

The structural overlap approach (cf. Hulk & Müller 2000, Yip & Matthews 2009) can predict transfer of the *wh*-in-situ construction from French to Dutch. Echo *wh*-in-situ questions appear in Dutch and may provide evidence for this construction as being an option. However, in Dutch matrix questions a relevant surface analogue of *wh*-fronting without inversion does not exist. Therefore, the surface overlap approach would not directly predict the transfer of uninverted questions from French. Note,

Table 2. Word order of matrix *wh*-questions in Dutch, French and Italian

	Wh-in-situ	*Wh*-fronting
Dutch	S-V-*wh* (echo)	*wh*-V-S (only possibility)
French	S-V-*wh* (true questions and echo)	*wh*(-esk/cleft)-S-V *wh*-V-S (low frequency)
Italian	S-V-*wh* (echo)	*wh*-V(-S) (only possibility, except *why*)

however, that the *wh*-S order appears in embedded questions in Dutch, but the word order in embedded questions is SOV and not SVO, as is the case in matrix questions. For the derivational complexity approach (cf. Strik & Pérez-Leroux 2011), transfer of both *wh*-in-situ and non-inversion is possible, because both constructions involve less syntactic operations than the target construction with inversion. I propose to adopt the following hypotheses, and extend them to multilingual acquisition:

(4) Derivational complexity as a condition for bilingual transfer:
    a. Qualitatively different structures can be introduced from one language into the other under restricted conditions.
    b. Derivational complexity is a condition for transfer: less complex structures are more likely to be transferred.
    c. A new structure coming from Language A can enter Language B if it represents a computational step in the derivation of the functional analogue in Language B; the converse should not be possible.

(Strik & Pérez-Leroux 2011: 192)

For trilingual children, the situation is more complex, because two languages can be the source of transfer. Different scenarios are possible:

1. From a general perspective, the fact that trilinguals speak three languages might result in less input and a lower performance in each of the languages. In that case, the trilinguals will have more difficulties than the bilinguals. However, note that with respect to the use of Dutch, for both trilinguals and bilinguals, the Dutch input comes primarily from one parent in the household, which gives rise to a very similar situation for both groups.
2. Cross-linguistic influence might occur mostly from the majority language; French in the case of the present study. From this perspective, Italian will play a minor role, and trilinguals will behave the same as bilinguals.
3. Cross-linguistic influence might occur from the two other languages. If influence from Italian plays a role, the trilinguals will have less difficulties than the bilinguals with Dutch *wh*-questions, because in Italian, like in Dutch, inversion is obligatory with most *wh*-words and acquired early, and *wh*-in-situ is not attested.

4.2   Participants

Participants were 16 bilingual Dutch-French children and three trilingual Dutch-French-Italian children. The bilingual children had one Dutch and one French parent and the trilingual children one Dutch and one Italian parent. For all children French was the language of the community: they were living in France (Paris) and attended French schools. Only the bilingual children also spoke French at home, with one of their parents. The bilingual children were divided into two subgroups of eight children each: a younger group (Bi-5) with children in kindergarten, and an older group (Bi-7) with children in elementary school. The trilingual children (Tri-5) were age-matched with the younger bilinguals. Sixteen monolingual Dutch children (Mo-5), age-matched with the younger bilingual and the trilingual children, and 14 monolingual Dutch adults (Mo-ad) served as control groups. All children showed typical language and psychological development. The age range, mean age and standard deviation (SD) of the groups are presented in Table 3.

Table 4 shows information about the use of Dutch for the bilingual and trilingual children, based on parental reports. Factors considered include which parent spoke Dutch, the frequency of the use of Dutch at home, whether siblings in the household spoke Dutch together, and the frequency of travel to the Netherlands.

No considerable differences are found, except that the older bilinguals use slightly less Dutch at home than the younger bilinguals and the trilinguals.

Table 3. Participants

Group	Age		
	range	Mean	SD
Bi-5 (n = 8)	4;03–6;04	5;02	0;11
Bi-7 (n = 8)	6;05–7;11	7;02	0;06
Tri-5 (n = 3)	4;10–5;08	5;01	0;06
Mo-5 (n = 16)	4;07–5;08	5;01	0;05
Mo-ad (n = 14)	24–43	32	5;05

Table 4. Use of Dutch for bilingual and trilingual children

	Dutch parent		Level of home use of Dutch		Dutch with siblings		Travel to NL	
	Father	Mother	Daily	Often	No	Yes	Often	Occasionally
Bi-5	2	6	6	2	4	4	3	5
Bi-7	3	5	4	4	6	2	3	5
Tri-5	1	2	2	1	1	2	3	0

4.3   Experimental task

A picture task was used to elicit different types of *wh*-questions.[1] The task contained 10 (animate) subject *wh*-questions (not included in the results), 10 animate object *wh*-questions, 10 inanimate object *wh*-questions and 16 adjunct *wh*-questions (5 with the *wh*-word *where*, 5 with *how* and 6 with *why*), in a randomized order. The order was the same for all participants. For each question, two versions of the same picture were present. In the first version, one visible character was displayed, but the part depicting the subject, object or adjunct was hidden behind a white spot. The child was invited to ask the visible character a question concerning the missing element. After s/he asked the question, the second version of the picture, revealing the hidden part, was shown. Example (5) illustrates an animate object question.

(5)   De giraffe verft iets, maar we zien niet wat. Vraag het hem maar.
      'The giraffe is painting something but we don't see what. Ask him.'
      Expected response: *Wat verf je?* ('What are you painting?')

4.4   Results

Responses produced by the children were classified according to their structure. Target responses consist of complete *wh*-questions of the type introduced by the experimenter. Other responses are yes/no questions, irrelevant or incomplete *wh*-questions or unintelligible utterances. Target responses were further classified into three types: *wh*-fronted questions with inversion, the grammatical option in Dutch (*wh*-V-S), uninverted *wh*-fronted (*wh*-S-V) and *wh*-in-situ (S-V-*wh*) questions (see (6), (7) and (8) respectively). Since the distinction between *wh*-fronting and *wh*-in-situ and that between inversion and absence of inversion do not appear in subject *wh*-questions, these questions have not been included in the analyses.

(6)   Giraffe wat   verf   je?   (*wh*-V-S)   (Mo-5:1, 4;07)
      Giraffe what paint-2sg you
      'Giraffe, what are you painting?'

(7)   Waarom je   huilt?   (*wh*-S-V)   (Tri-5:2, 4;10)
      why   you cry-2sg
      'Why are you crying?'

(8)   Jij doe   wat giraffe?   (S-V-*wh*)   (Bi-5:4, 4;06)
      you do-2sg what giraffe
      'Giraffe who are you doing?'[2]

---

1.   The task was adapted from a task in French, developed by C. Jakubowicz and colleagues, and includes images made available by N. Friedmann from a Hebrew task.

2.   Note that the child uses the verb form *doe*, while the second person singular form should be *doet*, when no inversion occurs (see also Footnote 3).

Table 5. Mean proportions and SDs (in parentheses) of response types for object and adjunct questions per group

Group	Construction			
	wh-V-S	*wh*-S-V	S-V-*wh*	Other
Bi-5 (n = 8)	0.63 (0.4)	0.12 (0.12)	0.06 (0.13)	0.19 (0.23)
Bi-7 (n = 8)	0.91 (0.1)	0.02 (0.03)	0	0.07 (0.07)
Tri-5 (n = 3)	0.94 (0.1)	0.06 (0.1)	0	0
Mo-5 (n = 16)	0.94 (0.05)	0	0	0.06 (0.05)
Mo-ad (n = 14)	0.99 (0.03)	0	0	0.01 (0.03)

In Table 5, responses for object and adjunct *wh*-questions are presented.

The overall rate of target responses was high: about 80% of the responses in the younger bilingual group and more than 90% in all other groups. Grammatical questions with *wh*-fronting and inversion formed the majority.[3] However, rates of inverted questions were lower in particularly the younger bilingual group, because a small number of uninverted and *wh*-in-situ questions were produced in this group, as well as in the older bilingual and the trilingual group. The trilingual children produced more questions with inversion than both bilingual groups, although the difference from the older bilinguals is negligible. They perform equally well as the monolingual children. The younger bilinguals were significantly different from monolingual children for proportions of *wh*-fronting with inversion, but they were not significantly different from older bilingual children (see Strik & Pérez-Leroux 2011 for more details). Furthermore, older bilinguals were not different from the monolingual children and adults. Monolingual 5-year olds were also significantly different from adult controls. Due to sample size, I did not conduct statistical analyses for the trilingual children.

Considering individual responses, uninverted and *wh*-in-situ questions occurred only in a subset of the bilingual and trilingual children. Non-inversion responses were produced by five out of eight of the 5-year-old bilinguals, three out of eight of the 7-year-old bilinguals and one out three of the trilinguals. Interestingly, five out of six of the uninverted responses in the trilingual group were with the *wh*-word *waarom* ('why'), which does not require inversion in Italian (see (7) above). However, most of the uninverted responses in the bilingual groups (29 out of 36) were also with *waarom*. All *wh*-in-situ responses were produced by three of the younger bilingual children. For one of them it was the main response type. All of these children also produced uninverted structures.

---

3. However, a significant number of responses with inversion contained agreement errors in verbal inflection, especially in the bilingual groups. In the case of animate object *wh*-questions these questions became ambiguous with subject *wh*-questions.

5.   Discussion and conclusions

The results of the present study revealed that the bilingual and trilingual children produced mostly questions with *wh*-fronting and inversion, the target construction in Dutch. However, the younger bilingual children were significantly different from the monolingual children and adults with respect to the use of inversion. In addition to *wh*-fronting with inversion, two other structures were found in the bilingual and trilingual children: *wh*-fronted questions without inversion and *wh*-in-situ questions. *Wh*-fronting without inversion was more prevalent than *wh*-in-situ, and the latter was produced only by the younger bilingual children. Although these structures constituted a modest portion of the responses, they were produced by eight out of 16 bilingual children and one out of three trilingual children. Since there is no evidence for either a *wh*-in-situ stage or a non-inversion stage in Dutch, these patterns are qualitatively different from monolingual Dutch acquisition and result from cross-linguistic influence. These results are compatible with previous data showing transfer from the *wh*-in-situ construction to a *wh*-fronting language as described in Yip & Matthews (2000, 2007, 2009). They differ, however, from Bonnesen (2005), who did not find evidence for transfer of *wh*-in-situ from French to German.

It turned out to be the case that qualitative differences (with respect to monolingual development) can appear in the *wh*-questions of multilingual children. Yet, the production of qualitatively different structures is restricted and needs to be explained. Recall that the surface overlap hypothesis as adopted by Yip & Matthews (2009) can predict transfer from the *wh*-in-situ construction but not from non-inversion. Note that it is important to take into consideration the whole underlying structure of both matrix and embedded clauses, in order to define the context in which structural overlap can appear. Otherwise, embedded questions could provide the source of surface overlap, because inversion is not possible in embedded questions in Dutch and the *wh*-S sequence is attested there. I proposed to adopt the hypothesis put forth by Strik & Pérez-Leroux (2011), which suggests that derivational complexity is a condition for grammatical transfer. Both *wh*-in-situ and *wh*-fronting without inversion are less complex than the target structure in Dutch, *wh*-fronting with inversion. In the former, movement of neither the *wh*-word nor the verb takes place, and in the latter, furthermore, movement of the *wh*-word occurs, yet not of the verb. These constructions represent computational steps in the derivation of *wh*-fronting with inversion, where both the *wh*-word and the verb are moved. In the case of non-inversion with *why*-questions in the trilingual group, not only does transfer of a less complex structure occur, but this phenomenon also shows sensitivity to the properties of the *wh*-word *why* in Italian, which does not require inversion in the adult language. However, for the bilingual Dutch-French children, non-inversion was also the most prevalent with the *wh*-word *why*. I speculate the special tendency with *why* in the multilingual children might be due to the specific status of *why* in different languages (cf. Rizzi 2001).

The trilingual children produced more target questions with *wh*-fronting and inversion than the bilinguals of the same age and even than the older bilinguals. They were similar to the monolinguals. With respect to the different scenarios of trilingual acquisition, it can be concluded that the first scenario, where more difficulties occur for trilinguals than for bilinguals because of the presence of a third language, does not hold. The second scenario, according to which cross-linguistic influence occurs mostly from the majority language, French, does not seem to be confirmed either. No transfer of the *wh*-in-situ construction from French is attested. The only instance of transfer in the trilingual group is the *wh*-fronting without inversion construction, mostly with the *wh*-word *why*, as is grammatical in adult Italian. Therefore, the third scenario, according to which Italian has a facilitating effect on the acquisition of Dutch *wh*-questions, appears to be the most plausible. In any case, the trilingual children do not show more difficulties with *wh*-questions in Dutch than the bilingual children. From a descriptive perspective, two of the trilingual children (the ones with a Dutch mother and having daily use of Dutch at home, who happen to be the children displaying no transfer) probably received more input in Dutch than some of the bilingual children (who did not have daily use of Dutch at home). More trilingual data are needed to reach firmer conclusions and, the question, in particular, of the amount of input trilingual and bilingual children receive requires further investigation.

The transfer of *wh*-in-situ and non-inversion in multilingual Dutch is represented in the following model:

(9)   Qualitative effects in multilingual acquisition:

Language A (French)		**Language B** (Dutch)		**Language C** (Italian)	
X		X		X	
Y	→	Y	←	Y'	
Z	→	Z			*(under restricted conditions)*

(X: *wh*-V-S, Y: *wh*-S-V, Y': *wh*-S-V (*why*), Z: S-V-*wh*)

In this model transfer of new structures, *wh*-fronting without inversion (*wh*-S-V) and *wh*-in-situ (S-V-*wh*), occurs from language A, French, with multiple options to language B, Dutch, with one structural option. In the case of trilingual acquisition, influence from language C, Italian, gives rise to introduction of a sub-structure of *wh*-fronting without inversion in Dutch.

To conclude, the data presented in this paper support a restrictive theory of transfer. Derivational complexity is a possible factor in transfer. Derivationally less complex structures can appear not only as intermediate steps in the development of monolingual children, but also if triggered by contact between the grammars of multilingual children. Overall, the trilingual children are not at a disadvantage compared to their bilingual peers.

References

Austin, J., M. Blume & L. Sánchez. Submitted. Morphosyntactic attrition in the L1 of Spanish-English bilingual children. *Hispania*.

Barnes, J. 2006. *Early Trilingualism: A Focus on Questions*. Clevedon: Multilingual Matters.

Bonnesen, M. 2005. *Der Erwerb der linken Satzperipherie bei Französisch/Deutsch bilingual aufwachsenden Kindern*. PhD dissertation, University of Hamburg. <http://ediss.sub.uni-hamburg.de/volltexte/2005/2585/pdf/Dissertationgesamt.pdf> (17 February 2012).

Coveney, A. 2002. *Variability in Spoken French: A Sociolinguistic Study of Interrogation and Negation*. Bristol: Elm Bank.

De Houwer, A. 1990. *The Acquisition of Two Languages from Birth: A Case Study*. Cambridge: CUP.

Den Besten, H. 1977. On the interaction of root transformation and lexical delitive rules. In *On the Formal Syntax of the Westgermania* (Linguistik Aktuell/Linguistics Today 3), ed. W. Abraham, 47–131. Amsterdam: John Benjamins.

Guasti, M. T. 1996. Acquisition of Italian interrogatives. In *Generative Perspectives on Language Acquisition* (Language Acquisition and Language Disorders 14), ed. H. Clahsen, 241–269. Amsterdam: John Benjamins.

Guasti, M. T. 2000. An excursion into interrogatives in early English and Italian. In *The Acquisition of Syntax*, eds. M. A. Friedemann & L. Rizzi, 105–128. London: Longman.

Guasti, M. T. 2002. *Language Acquisition. The Growth of Grammar*. Cambridge MA: The MIT Press.

Hamann, C. 2000. The acquisition of constituent questions and the requirements of interpretation. In *The Acquisition of Syntax*, eds. M. A. Friedemann & L. Rizzi, 170–201. London: Longman.

Hamann, C. 2006. Speculations about early syntax: The production of *wh*-questions by normally developing French children and French children with SLI. *Catalan Journal of Linguistics* 5: 143–189.

Hoffmann, C. 2001. Towards a description of trilingual competence. *International Journal of Bilingualism* 5: 1–17.

Hulk, A. 1996. The syntax of *wh*-questions in child French. In *Connecting Children's Language and Linguistic Theory* (Amsterdam Series in Child Language Development 5), eds. W. Philip & F. Wijnen, 129–172. Amsterdam: University of Amsterdam.

Hulk, A. & N. Müller. 2000. Bilingual first language acquisition at the interface between syntax and pragmatics. *Bilingualism: Language and Cognition* 3: 227–244.

Hulk, A. & S. Zuckerman. 2000. The interaction between input and economy: Acquiring optionality in French *wh*-questions. In *BUCLD 24: Proceedings of the 24th Annual Boston University Conference on Language Development*, eds. S. C. Howell, S. A. Fish & T. Keith-Lucas, 438–449. Somerville MA: Cascadilla Press.

Jakubowicz, C. 2011. Measuring derivational complexity: New evidence from typically-developing and SLI learners of L1-French. *Lingua* 121: 339–351.

Meisel, J. M. 1989. Early differentiation of language in bilingual children. In *Bilingualism across the Lifespan: Aspects of Acquisition, Maturity and Loss*, eds. K. Hyltenstam & L. Obler, 13–40. Cambridge: CUP.

Meisel, J. M. 2007. On autonomous syntactic development in multiple first language acquisition. In *BUCLD 31: Proceedings of the 31st Annual Boston University Conference on Language*

Development, eds. H. Caunt-Nulton, S. Kulatilake & I. Woo, 26–45. Somerville MA: Cascadilla Press.

Mishina-Mori, S. 2005. Autonomous and interdependent development of two language systems in Japanese/English simultaneous bilinguals: Evidence from question formation. *First Language* 25: 291–315.

Müller, N. ed. 2003. *(In)vulnerable Domains in Multilingualism* (Hamburg Studies on Multilingualism 1). Amsterdam: John Benjamins.

Paradis, J. & F. Genesee. 1996. Syntactic acquisition in bilingual children: Autonomous or interdependent? *Studies in Second Language Acquisition* 18: 1–15.

Park, S. 2008. *The Acquisition of* Wh-*questions by Korean-English Bilingual Children: The Role of Crosslinguistic Influence*. MA thesis, Purdue University.

Pérez-Leroux, A. T. 2011. What I don't understand about interfaces. *Linguistic Approaches to Bilingualism* 1: 71–73.

Pérez-Leroux, A. T. & J. Dalious. 1998. The acquisition of Spanish interrogative inversion. *Hispanic Linguistics* 10: 84–114.

Plunkett, B. 1999. Targeting complex structure in French questions. In *BUCLD 23: Proceedings of the 23rd Annual Boston University Conference on Language Development*, eds. A. Greenhill, H. Littlefield & C. Tano, 764–775. Somerville MA: Cascadilla Press.

Prévost, P., L. Tuller., M. Scheidnes., S. Ferré & M. Haiden. 2010. Computational complexity effects in the acquisition of *wh*-questions in child L2 French. In *New Directions in Language Acquisition: Romance Languages in the Generative Perspective*, eds. P. Guijarres-Fuentes & L. Domínguez, 251–279. Newcastle: Cambridge Scholars.

Riegel, M., J. C. Pellat & R. Rioul. 1994. *Grammaire méthodique du français*. Paris: Presses Universitaires de France.

Rizzi, L. 2001. On the position "Int(errogative)" in the left periphery of the clause. In *Current Studies in Italian Syntax*, eds. G. Cinque & G. Salvi, 287–296. Oxford: OUP.

Ruhland, R., F. Wijnen & P. van Geert. 1995. An exploration into the application of dynamic systems modelling to language acquisition. In *Approaches to Parameter Setting* (Amsterdam Series in Child Language Development 40), eds. M. Verrips & F. N. K. Wijnen, 107–134. Amsterdam: University of Amsterdam.

Soriente, A. 2007. Cross-linguistic and cognitive aspects in the acquisition of WH-questions in an Italian-Indonesian bilingual child. In *Cognitive Aspects of Bilingualism*, eds. I. Kesckes & L. Albertazzi, 325–362. Dordrecht: Springer.

Strik, N. 2007. L'acquisition des phrases interrogatives chez les enfants francophones. *Psychologie Française* 52: 27–39.

Strik, N. 2008. Syntaxe et acquisition des phrases interrogatives en français et en néerlandais: une étude contrastive. PhD dissertation, University of Paris 8 (Vincennes/Saint-Denis).

Strik, N. & A. T. Pérez-Leroux. 2011. *Jij doe wat girafe?* Wh-movement and inversion in Dutch-French bilingual children. *Linguistic Approaches to Bilingualism* 1: 175–205.

Thornton, R. 2008. *Why continuity. Natural Language and Linguistic Theory* 26: 107–146.

Van Kampen, J. 1997. *First Steps in* Wh-*movement*. Delft: Eburon.

Vinet, M. T. 2001. *D'un français à un autre: La syntaxe de la microvariation*. Saint-Laurent, Québec: Fides.

Wang, X. 2008. *Growing up with Three Languages: Birth to Eleven*. Clevedon: Multilingual Matters.

Yip, V. & S. Matthews. 2000. Syntactic transfer in a Cantonese-English bilingual child. *Bilingualism: Language and Cognition* 3: 193–208.

Yip, V. & S. Matthews. 2007. *The Bilingual Child: Early Development and Language Contact.* Cambridge: CUP.

Yip, V. & S. Matthews. 2009. Conditions on cross-linguistic influence in bilingual acquisition: The case of *wh*-interrogatives. Paper presented at the 7th International Symposium on Bilingualism, Utrecht, Netherlands, 8–11 July 2009.

Zwart, J. W. 1997. *The Morphosyntax of Verb Movement: A Minimalist Approach to Dutch Syntax.* Dordrecht: Kluwer.

The emergence of a new variety of Russian in a language contact situation

The case of a Russian-Swedish bilingual child*

Natasha Ringblom
Stockholm University, Sweden

Simultaneous acquisition of two mother tongues is usually not discussed in terms of language contact. This might reflect the fact that the two languages are believed to develop independently of each other, which is known as The Autonomous Development Hypothesis that implies that bilingual children behave like monolinguals in each of their languages. Given this claim, a child who acquires two mother tongues simultaneously is expected to develop similarly to monolingual children of the respective languages. In this paper we attempt to test this claim on the acquisition of negation by a Russian-Swedish bilingual child and to show that the languages may not develop as independently from each other as was previously assumed. Rather, they develop in permanent interaction, where especially the weaker language ($L1_{weak}$) is influenced by a stronger one ($L1_{strong}$), which lead to the development of a totally new variety of Russian in this contact situation.

Keywords: Russian, Swedish, Bilingual First Language Acquisition, language contact, negation

1. Background

BFLA (<u>B</u>ilingual <u>F</u>irst <u>L</u>anguage <u>A</u>cquisition, see Meisel 1989, De Houwer 1990) and contact linguistics are two closely related fields that have developed largely in isolation from each other. Following Schumann (1987), Andersen (1983), DeGraff (1999), Yip & Matthews (2007), this work is an attempt to bring both of them together since the issues they deal with are closely related. Winford (2003: 11) distinguishes three kinds

---

* I would like to thank Marilyn Vihman, Stephen Matthews and two anonymous reviewers for the helpful comments on this article. I would also like to acknowledge the support of Wallenberg foundation in conducting this research and Cara Kellersmith for improving my English.

of contact situations: (1) those involving language *maintenance* – preservation of a language from one generation to the next, (2) those involving language *shift* – the partial or total abandonment of a group's native language in favour of the acquisition of another language and (3) those that lead to the creation of *new contact languages* – the languages involving restructuring and mixture of elements from several languages. This division, however, is not straight-forward. Following discussion in Winford (2003: 11), many contact situations cannot be assigned clearly to one or another of these categories. Often there is an inter-play between them.

Research traditions on bilingual children are usually divided into three "distinct areas" (Okita 2002: 28) where societal bilingualism is related to language contact while simultaneous language acquisition is not (ibid). This is surprising since language contact may be considered at the individual level as well (Weinreich 1953). The simultaneous acquisition of two mother tongues is normally not discussed in terms of language contact. Instead, the development of two languages is treated separately. This might reflect the fact that the two languages are believed to develop independently of each other, which is known as The Separate Development Hypothesis (De Houwer 1990, Meisel 1989, Paradis & Genesee 1996). Given this claim, a child who acquires two mother tongues simultaneously – in our case Russian and Swedish – is expected to develop similarly to monolingual Russian children in Russian and similarly to monolingual Swedish children in Swedish.

In this paper I attempt to test this claim on the acquisition of negation by the Russian-Swedish bilingual child Julia and to show that the languages may not develop as independently from each other as was previously assumed (see also Vihman 1985, Deuchar & Quay 2000 who also took a different perspective). Rather, the two languages develop in *constant interaction* (see Yip & Matthews 2007), where especially the weaker language ($L1_{weak}$) is influenced by a stronger one ($L1_{strong}$), which might lead to the development of a totally new variety of Russian.[1]

1.1   The subject of the study

The subject of the study is the author's daughter Julia, who was born and raised in Stockholm to a Russian mother and a Swedish father and is the third child in the family. Since birth, she has been addressed in either Russian or in Swedish. The parents tried to follow the one-person – one-language strategy (Ronjat 1913). However, after the child entered a Swedish day care at the age of 1 year 7 months, she gradually became Swedish dominant since the amount of Swedish input she received was much greater than Russian.

The mother was the primary source of the Russian language; yet, the Russian grandmother came and visited the family every year and used to stay for several

---

1.   Cf. discussion in Polinsky (2006) who examines American Russian – a reduced variety of Russian, spoken by immigrants who learned Russian as L1 and then moved to America and switched to English as their primary language.

months. Julia was also exposed to Russian during one month long visits to the Crimea. The data (80 audio and video tapes both in Swedish and Russian contexts, 6 diaries) were collected between the ages of 1 year 4 months and 5 years in different socio-linguistic settings and transcribed at regular intervals[2]. All non-target-like forms were singled out and analyzed separately.

1.2   Why negation?

Negation is a universal category that has important pragmatic functions and occurs early and frequently in children's production. Moreover, negation interacts with other grammatical categories and its placement can tell us about the functional architecture of syntactic representations in a child's grammar (Bonacker 1999: 156). Thus, other grammatical structures will be affected since they appear in a close interplay with negation.

Negation is also interesting from a *typological* point of view since it represents one of a few categories that seem to be more difficult to acquire in Swedish, at least from a morphological perspective, which is due to formally diverging realizations of negation (*inte, ej, [aldrig]* and *o-* in word formation). Thus, Julia's case proves particularly interesting since the child had to acquire both languages simultaneously.

1.3   The functions of negation

There are several typologies of negation found in the child language literature. One of the most famous one is the typology of Bloom (1970: 173):

–   non-existence
–   rejection
–   denial

Yet, other functions have also been proposed (Pea 1980, Murašova & Semušina 2007):

–   prohibition
–   self-prohibition (children telling themselves not to do something, for instance immediately before touching a forbidden object or at the moment of touching it)
–   possibility of making something (inability, helplessness)
–   desirability
–   reproach
–   protest

The following will provide a short survey of analysis-relevant issues on how negation is expressed in Russian and Swedish.

---

2.   Mini discs recordings of Julia's earliest vocalizations are available from the period of 1 month old.

1.4   Negation in Russian

The most common way to form and express negation in Russian is by using *ne* and *net*, where in general the proclitic *ne-* means 'not' and the particle *net* 'no'. The negative element always precedes the main verb and usually does not need to be combined with an auxiliary or modal verb form. When sentential negation is required, *ne-* precedes the finite verb and a strict adjacency is required between the two elements. In Russian, unlike Swedish, double negation is the norm: if the verb in a phrase is negative, all indefinite pronouns in that clause should be marked as negative.

In order to denote non-specificness of a DO (direct object) of a negated verb in Russian, the genitive case is usually used (see Adamec 1973/1977 and Timberlake 1986 for further discussion on the topic). It appears in complements of verbs that are in the scope of sentential negation, in cases where the complement has no identifiable referent in the world. Genitive of negation (GEN$_{Neg}$) may cause specific problems in acquisition of Russian, especially Russian as a foreign or a second language. Although inflectional morphology provides some difficulties even for monolingual Russian children, it is often mastered before the age of three (Cejtlin 2009, Gagarina 2008, Gvozdev 1949/2005). Thus, by the age of three, a Russian child is expected to comprehend the main morphological rules and be able to use them in his/her own sentences. Yet, complete acquisition of Russian morphology takes much longer (see Babyonyshev 1993, Gagarina & Voeikova 2009) and is often not acquired before the age of seven (Slobin 1966). It has not yet been established that Russian follows the same developmental time span in the situation of bilingualism due to specific challenges that bilingual situation presents (both intra-linguistic and extra-linguistic).

The following periods have been suggested in the acquisition of grammar (Gagarina 2008: 60–65)[3].

1.   *Pre-morphological period*[4]
–   Holophrase: 1;03 – 1;08
–   Telegraphic utterances: sentences containing more than one word (usually two): 1;08 – 1;10

2.   *The period of comprehending morphology as a system*
–   the formation of first morphological forms: 1;10 – 2;01
–   the use of inflexions for showing syntactic relations between the words (conjunctions and prepositions are not yet used for denoting grammatical relations in the sentence): 2;01 – 2;03
–   the period of using functional words for marking syntactic relations between the words: from 2; 3 to 3;0

---

3.   This classification is based on the monolingual acquisition of Russian.
4.   See Cejtlin (1989), Dressler (1997).

3. *The comprehending of morphological norm*
–   The complete acquisition of all types of declension and conjugation: from 3;0 to 7;0

1.5   Negation in Swedish

The main means of expressing negation in Swedish are: *inte, ej, aldrig*. Swedish employs negated auxiliaries such as *ska* <u>*inte*</u> ('will <u>not</u>'), *kan* <u>*inte*</u> ('can<u>not</u>'), *vill* <u>*inte*</u> ('do <u>not</u> want') etc. However, there are some indefinite pronouns with merged negation: <u>*ingenting*</u> 'nothing', <u>*ingen*</u> 'noone', <u>*inget*</u> 'nothing', which may cause problems in language acquisition because these forms are no longer overtly transparent: <u>*inte*</u> + *någon/nån* > <u>*ingen*</u>; <u>*inte*</u> + *något/nåt* > <u>*inget*</u>. The basic word order in Swedish negation is S V (Neg) O; i.e. V2. The position of negation morpheme *inte* is thus [–finite]/pre-V.

In Swedish the child has to learn that the position of sentence's adverbs may change its place depending on sentence structure, in main clauses <u>after</u> the finite verb, in subordinated clauses <u>before</u> the finite verb. The topic position of early child negation (e.g. *inte röra* 'do<u>n't</u> touch') can be considered equivalent to its function: it denies the contents of the following proposition.

2.   Negation in Julia's data

2.1   Pre-verbal negation: Gestures

The first case of understanding negation was noted at the age of 7 months. Julia understood prohibition and warning such as 'no' in both languages, which is in line with TD (<u>T</u>ypically <u>D</u>eveloping) monolingual children. Yet, since this study focuses on *production*, only Julia's productive forms will be discussed.

The first gesture *good bye* appeared at the age of 10 month. Later she usually accompanied it with whispering *-ka* (Russian for *poka* 'bye'). The child's gestures usually were very transparent and not language specific: disagreement was expressed by negative shaking of the head, disappearance of the object by spreading hands (usually promoted by the grown-ups in Julia's surroundings, accompanying it with *borta* (Sw. 'gone!') or *netu* (Rus. 'not').

Gestures did not disappear with the emergence of words since this way of expressing was present in both the speech and verbal production of the adults who were around the child. Particular gestures were often associated with certain interlocutors and were sometimes "person-specific" (just like many words later on): for instance, Julia made a sign of a cross only to her mother and sisters when they left the house and never to anyone else (since only these three people were accompanied with that sign by their grandmother when they left the house).

2.2   Verbal negation

2.2.1   *Pre-morphological period*

The first case of production of negation was at the age of 9 months, when the child pronounced *as'* (expression of disapproval; baby talk for 'don't do it') when rolling toilet paper (which was of course not allowed)[5]. At 1;2, Julia for the first time reacted to the fact that her mother was absent. When asked where the mother was, the child said: *Bota!* (Sw. *borta!* 'all gone!', with a retroflex [ʈ]). Just a month later, at 1;3, Julia said the word *nä* in the function of REFUSAL, when her mother tried to give her a second portion of porridge. Before that the child would express refusal with the help of gestures (for instance by shaking her head). Perhaps this function was very important for Julia since she was often offered more food than she could eat and more activities than she was capable of doing. The use of negation was thus motivated by necessity to express communicative intentions.

According to Bloom (1970), one of the first functions of negation is non-existence, which is also true in Julia's data. However, Julia's material also shows that even other functions can also take the primary position in her lexicon, which is in line with intentionality model (Bloom & Tinker 2001) that emphasizes motivation of the child in acquiring language and expressing her thoughts. However, while non-existence was expressed by the Swedish word *borta* ('all gone'), REFUSAL and DENIAL were rendered by the more trans-linguistic[6] lexical item *nä* [7].

The fact that the first proto-word was the word *nä* was not a coincidence since it could be used in both Russian and Swedish contexts. In Julia's speech *nä* could be used with a prolonged vowel, which emphasized her desire for not doing something:

(1)   MOM: Ska vi sova?
            'Shall we sleep?'
     JUL: Nää!
            'Nää'[8] **(1;8)**

At around 1;4 Julia started using holophrases[9] in the context of negation[10] (single word utterances that stand for the whole proposition): the chunk <u>ne</u> *mogu* ('can<u>not</u>',

---

5.   The word appeared frequently in the mother's CDS (<u>C</u>hild <u>D</u>irected <u>S</u>peech).

6.   I consider 'nä' to be a translinguistic term since it is very close phonologically to the Russian 'ne'.

7.   The child said *pta* (*borta* '[lit.] away', but here 'all gone') both in Russian and in Swedish contexts.

8.   The same can be said about the proto-words *ni, u* or *m*, that Julia used very often.

9.   The term HOLOPHRASE will be used about the children's early single word utterances (which generally signify that children may intend a whole proposition be a single word).

10.   The first holophrastic utterance was noted at 1;2 when the child said *pal'* 'fell down' on the toothbrush that fell down. Thus, the holophrastic utterances in the context of negation appeared a couple of months later.

pronounced as *nmagu*). The negation particle *ne* was attributed a modal reading here and was used with very broad semantics: the phrase could mean both 'do not want, will not', and 'cannot'. By the age of 1;7 the child had the following means for expressing negation: *net* (Rus. 'no'), *no, nej* (Sw. 'no'), *borta* (Sw. 'all gone'), *nä, niiii* (different expressions for 'no'), *blä* ('disquisting'). Most of these words were not used interchangeably but had their specific functions, where *borta* 'all gone' was only used to express non-existence and disappearance of the object; *blä* 'disquisting' when something did not taste well, *niii, no* and *näää* when she did not want to do something, *nej* and *net* ('no') were mostly used in answering questions (for instance when I asked her in the morning whether she wanted to have some porridge the child said *nej* meaning 'I do not want [that/it]'). These words were used to reject something or indicate that something was absent.

At around 1;8 other words appeared: *Nid'ja!* (*nel'z'ja* 'not allowed') and *nikak* ('it does not go/work!'). In order to emphasize not wanting even more, Julia would sometimes express negation in both languages – probably because of the double input from her environment or because similar strategies were noted in her interlocutors. The general impression was that Julia's first proto-words belonged to some unified system with a set of unified phonemes not yet differentiated into Russian or Swedish and that could be used in both linguistic contexts depending on the meaning that the child wanted to express.

2.2.1.1 *Telegraphic utterances*

Before Julia discovered morphological markers and started creating her own forms, there was a period of "telegraphic speech"[11] (Brown 1973), which is a common phenomenon across different languages. At the age of 1;7 Julia started actively using the two word combinations. She cried angrily *neja godasaka!* (here: *riskakor*) 'no, rice cookies' when her mother tried to take them away from the table. The child started combining the words she knew into longer sequences in order to express some idea: *Den-daj! Eje!* ('give me! That one!' (feminine; and stretching her hand at the same time; sc. give me the sunflower seed). Some other documented two word utterances at 1;7 were: *pappa komma* 'daddy come'; *dumma pappa* 'silly daddy'; *mamma, titta, mamma!* (when she saw a video camera 'mom, I want to look at the film with me'). While at 1;7, the two-word utterances were still very rare and few, by 1;8 the child started using them all the time: *A gunga?* – 'shall we swing?'; *Podi pat'!* (*idi spat'* 'go to bed'); *Idi, mama!* 'go away, mom!'; *Titta! Nosik!* 'Look! Nose!'; *Titta! Kolla! Vot'!* 'Look (Sw.), Look (Sw. synonym of *titta*); 'here' (Rus.).

---

11. An early form of sentence use consisting of only a few essential words (Papalia, Wendkos Olds & Duskin Feldman 2007).

(2)   JUL: moloko netu![12]
            'milk no' (pointing at the milk package that was empty).
            The child started looking at the package and said to herself: *bo-ta!*
            (*borta* 'away') (**1;8**)

It is interesting to note that while the first phrase was addressed to the mother, the second one was meant for Julia herself. When the mother heard it, she repeated after Julia both in Swedish and in Russian: *Borta! Netu!* 'Gone!' (Sw.) – 'Gone' (Rus.).

Julia's first negative sentences consisting of more than one word appeared at the age of 1;8 and included sentence external negation: *Nej dansa!* 'No, dance!'[13]' The negation here is marked by putting a negative element (a general negator *nej* used at that time), outside the nuclear utterance: *dansa*; NEC[dansa]). By this way the child marks that she does not want to dance but would rather sit and paint in her book. Earlier Julia would usually have pronounced *nej* ('no') as a one-word utterance.

By 1;10 even three word utterances started to appear more and more often: *Mama! Ja sju (choču) pit'!* ('Mom, I want to drink'[14]). At 1;10, Julia also started using copula in negative utterance (also with the function of disappearance): *Tomten är borta!* '[The] Santa Clause is gone!' (**1;11**). By this time, Russian and Swedish words were already used in separated contexts (at least when possible, i.e. when the child knew the Russian alternative):

(3)   MOM: Budem pisat'?
            'Shall we pee?'
      JUL: Né, né budé, budé!
            'No, will not, will not!' (**1;10**)
      SUS: Är Susie dum?
            'Is Susie stupid?'
      JUL: Nej
            'No.' (**1;11**)

By the age of 2, Julia used many phrases consisting of three words in Swedish with varying word order (since some phrases were chunks, not analyzed by the child into separate parts): *vill* <u>*inte*</u> *kyckling* ('do <u>not</u> want chicken'), *Julia vill* <u>*inte*</u> ('Julia does <u>not</u> want'); <u>*inte*</u> *hjälpa dig* ('<u>not</u> help you'). During this stage nominal and verbal inflexions were

---

12.   The correct form would be *moloka netu*, where *molok*a is the genitive form (= genititive/accusative syncretism in direct objects after negated verbs).

13.   Klima & Bellugi (1966, 1969, 1973) investigated the data of three American children and proposed different stages of acquisition of clausal negation. The first stage is sentence-external negation: "*no/not* + nucleus" or "nucleus + *no*". The authors stated that there is no clear evidence that the child even understands that the negative is embedded in the auxiliary of adult speech (Klima & Bellugi 1973: 341–342).

14.   This is one of the first examples of combining a subject and a predicate, which paves the way to the first syntax.

absent. A similar tendency was noted in Russian as well: *net guljat'* ('<u>no</u> go out'); *net spat'* ('<u>no</u> sleep')[15]; *ne bok* ('that is <u>not</u> the book that I mean'); *net mama bada* ('mommy should <u>not</u> bathe') etc. Any prepositions were also absent: *kissa pottan* ('pee pot'; **2;0**):

   (4)   JUL: Mama, Julia netu! (= u Julii netu)
                 NOM + netu (= 'Julia's chips are over') (**2;1**)

Modals and auxiliaries with adjacent negation are treated as unanalyzed negative modals by the child during this developmental period: *vill inte* 'do <u>not</u> want' (Sw.). Thus, the phrases as *vill inte mamma kaka* ('mommy does <u>not</u> want a cake') are considered normal for this developmental stage (viz. 2 years)[16].

The negators used at that time were Swedish *nej* (Sw. 'no') and Russian *net* ('no'). While *nej* was used in a more general sense, *net* tended to be used to reject something that the child did not want:

   (5)   MOM: Julia, pojdem guljat'?
          JUL: Net guljat'[17]
                 'No go out.' (The negation has its site outside the nuclear sentence (**2;0**)

2.2.1.2 *Morphological period: From frozen forms to linguistic innovations*

From 1;10 to 2;1 the child is said to enter a new developmental period – that of comprehending morphology as a system (see Gagarina 2008). At around 2 years, most Russian children are capable of constructing forms with correct case and number and many of these forms are used with corresponding prepositions or fillers (Cejtlin 2000). By the age of three the children productively use morphological forms on their own with the help of information they receive from input (Cejtlin 2009, Gagarina 2008).

At 2;0 Julia started using forms that seemed to be created on her own by using both languages simultaneously and became progressively more creative with every month: *bollik, bisjki* (a combination of a Swedish root plus the suffix used for diminutives in Russian), *zubborste* (Russian root "zub" from *zubnaja ščetka* and Swedish borste (brush) from *tandborste* 'toothbrush')[18]. At around 2;5 Julia discovers word order and plays with the pragmatical effect achieved by changing it: *mamma inte doma; inte mamma doma; nej, mamma inte hemma!* ('mom is <u>not</u> at home'); *bajsade*

---

15.   Zhenja Gvozdev, the son and main informant of N.A. Gvozdev, also used to say *net kormi* ('<u>no</u> feed', Gvozdev 1949/2005). The use of infinitives could also be explained in terms of the Optional Infinitive stage proposed by Wexler and colleagues in the acquisition of Western European languages.

16.   For further discussion see Bellugi (1967) and Leopold (1939–1949).

17.   Julia produced the equivalent non-negated auxiliaries both in Russian and Swedish only later and only then was she able to analyze these chunks into "auxiliary+ NEG".

18.   These forms were found in Russian context.

bebis (VS; the correct word order in Swedish would be: [*the*] *baby pooped*: SV); *Susie ljubjat ... ljubjat Susie* (when she heard her mother's phase *vse ljubjat Susie* 'everyone loves Susie').

Swedish *inte* (that is of course never used as a regular means for expressing negation in standard Russian) is consistently used by the child in both languages making other ways of expressing negation periphery: *inte nu, mamma!* <u>*Inte*</u> *ščas (colloquial för «sejčas»)* 'not now, mommy, not now' (2;5); *mamma, <u>inte</u> pyjamas åka dit* (Rus. *Mama, <u>ne</u> v pižame exatj tuda = <u>ne</u> ed' tuda v pižame)* 'mom, do<u>n't</u> go there in pyjamas!' (2;5) (compare: *ne* + verb in Russian); *Jag också vill <u>inte</u>*[19] ('I also do <u>not</u> want' said in Russian context)[20]: *netu batterier* '<u>no</u> batteries' (2;9); *Kisi netu*[21] *följa mig!* 'Cat <u>no</u> follow me!' (2;9); *netu nagellack* '<u>N</u>o nailpolish' (2;9); *Vi ska gå upp och åka pulka på snö där uppe. Tut <u>netu</u> snö!* 'We can go up there and go by sledge on the snow up there! There is <u>no</u> snow here!' (2;11).

When speaking Russian, Julia seems to translate the Swedish *inte* ('not') and uses it in the meaning of 'there is no', often before nouns (while Sw. 'inte' was used before verbs even in Russian; *netu* is used instead of *ne*). The child, as before, brings it outside the affirmative utterance: *<u>Netu</u> Juli bol'no* ('<u>no</u> Julia pain') (2;5); *mama, <u>netu</u> kupal'nik mokryj* ('Mom, <u>no</u> swimming suit wet – mom, the swimming suit is not wet anymore'); *<u>netu</u> pisala v štaniški* ('<u>no</u> pee in my pants') (2;6)[22]. There were, of course, the cases when the child moved the negative element inside the sentence: *Vika <u>netu</u> spit* ('Vica <u>not</u> sleep').

Inte corresponds to Russian *ne* and is used even in otherwise Russian sentences: *inte est' Julinu grušu* ('do <u>not</u> eat Julia's pear') (2;4); *Ručka <u>inte</u> mokryj*[23] ('the pencil is <u>not</u> wet') (2;5).

---

19. The child has not acquired the correct idiomatic Swedish expression yet, which is *heller <u>inte</u>*, which means that *också* has to be replaced by *heller* when negated ('not either'). Alternatively it can be transfer of a Russian *tože* 'also'.

20. One might get an impression that at the age of 2;5 Julia is still not able to separate between her two languages since she is inserting elements from one language into the other. However, not only was she able to differentiate between Russian and Swedish at this moment but she also forbid her mother to speak Swedish: *mamma, <u>inte</u> ryska!* (which, in this particular context, meant *eto <u>ne</u> po-russki!* 'This is not Russian!'). There are several other examples in Julia's data illustrating the child's sensitivity to correct language use:

GRAND: Liten båt! 'little boat'
JUL: Eto ne po-russki! Po-russki lodka!
              'That [is] not in Russian! In Russian lodka!' (2;6)

21. The Russian word *netu* becomes a sort of loan translation of Swedish *inte*.

22. In monolingual Russian children's speech, the negator usually stands either at the beginning or the end of the sentence.

23. Masculine instead of feminine.

(6) MOM: Julen'ka, poechali k vraču
            'Julia, let's go to the doctor'
     JUL: <u>Inte</u> nu, mamma! <u>Inte</u> *ščas*! (colloquial)
            '<u>Not</u> now (Sw.), mom; <u>not</u> now (Rus.)' (2;6)

At around two and a half years, Julia became aware of the fact that *inte* ('not') was a Swedish word and more often tried to replace it with Russian *netu* that seemed to be a loan translation of a Swedish *inte* when talking to her mother:

(7) JUL: Snigel <u>inte</u> dum!
            '[The] snail is <u>not</u> stupid!
            /And then translating to her mother/
            Snigel <u>netu</u> plochoj
            '[The] snail (Sw.) not bad.' (2;5)

A new stage in Julia's linguistic behaviour began when she started constructing her own sentences and the word *inte* became the general negator and took over the meanings that were previously expressed by other means: *inte mama na lekcii* ('there is no mommy at the seminar') (2;4). The negative element *inte* here ('not, don't') is placed outside the nuclear utterance *mama na lekcii* ('mommy at the seminar'), even though at the age of 2;4 the child more and more often used constructions with *inte* ('not') in the middle of the sentence: *ruchka <u>inte</u> mokryj*[24] ('pencil <u>no</u> wet') (2;4); *Mama net očki* ('mom <u>no</u> glasses' 2;3). Here the child moves negation from the beginning of the sentence to the middle of the sentence, which is also an important step in language construction. However, Julia still does not use prepositions in negation and nominative case is used instead of genitive after negation. In the phrases that the child heard often, the correct case was used: *mama, <u>netu</u> počty!* 'Mom, no post (2;3).

At 3, Julia was still using *netu* instead of *ne*: *Ja <u>netu</u> malen'kaja* ('I <u>no</u> little!'). The correct particles were only used during prefabs/calques like *ne choču* ('do <u>not</u> want') and *ne choču muzika!* ('Do <u>not</u> want music (NOM)' (3;0). *Netu* ('there is <u>no</u>') was also used in imperative: *netu släcka!* ('<u>No</u> switch off!' (3;1). The child tried to emphasize urgency or importance.

Inte has remained the general negator (even in Russian) until 2;5 when Julia went to Crimea with her family and when *inte* became more and more replaced by the Russian *netu: Netu Julii bol'no!* 'No Julia pain!'; *Mama, <u>netu</u> kupal'nik!* 'Mom, the swimming suit <u>no</u> wet!'; *Vica <u>netu</u> spit* 'Vica <u>no</u> sleep' *babuška, <u>netu</u> nožka!* (NOM) 'Granny, <u>no</u> leg!' *Ja <u>netu</u> pisala v štaniški!* 'I <u>no</u> pee in my pants';u menja *<u>netu</u> plastyr'* (NOM) 'By me <u>no</u> ploster' (2,5).

While in Crimea (2;6), the child also started using other negators, such as *<u>nel'zja</u>* ('<u>not</u> allowed') and *net* ('no') as synonyms for *netu* ('there is <u>no</u>'), *<u>nikogda</u>* ('<u>never</u>'):

---

24. Masculine instead of feminine.

nel'zja mame v[25] *pižame* ('not allowed mamma in pyjamas') which was said by the child when her mother sat down at the table in pyjamas and wanted to eat breakfast). The words *nel'zja* and *netu* have been in free distribution (just like many other 'synonymous' words until the child learned to discover the difference between them): *Vike netu trogat' etu. Susie nel'zja trogat'. Babuška trogat'.* 'Vica no touch it. Susie not allowed to touch. Grandmother touch.' (2,6). *Etu net gorjačaja, mama! Kormit'!* 'This not hot. Feed!' (sc. 'The food is not hot anymore! Feed me!'; 2;6). The words *net* and *netu* have also slowly lost their function as GENERAL NEGATORS and were used in their main function: the function of NON-EXISTENCE of something: *Susie uroki, ja net uroki. Juli net uroki* 'Susie lessons. I no lessons. Julia no lessons' (2;6). *Netu* was frequently used instead of conditional *Čtobi ne* ('in order not to'): Eto komary netu kusali? 'This is for mosquitoes not to bite?' and in imperatives: mama, netu staj! (= ne čitaj) 'Mom, do not read!' (2,6). The abundant input in the Crimea had a definitive impact on Julia's early grammar development.

After another month in the Crimea, by 2;6, the child almost replaced *netu* by *net*: *Net mucha* (NOM) 'No fly' (2;6); *Ja net ubit' babočku* 'I not kill butterfly'; *Net stuli (stula)* (an attempt to form GEN$_{Neg}$) 'No chair'; *Èto net gorjačij, mama? Eto tože net gorjačij?* 'It is not wet, mom? This one also not wet?' *Ja netu pit' kofe. Ja pi ... p'ju čaj!* [26] 'I no drink coffee. I der ... drink tea!' (2;6).

By 2;9 Julia became creative even in producing verbal innovations:

(8)   MOM: Julia, idi budi Susie!
           'Julia, go and wake up Susie!'

      JUL: Mama, Susie ne vstavaets'ja! (innovation)
           'Mom, Susie [is] not uppgotten (sc. will not get up)!' (2;9)

At 2;6 the child started producing short sentences with at least some bound morphemes and or/closed class grammatical words. This period was also very productive in Julia's speech when she created her own forms that often consisted of the elements from both languages. Julia created her own innovations both in Russian and in Swedish:

(9)   JUL: Mama, daj grušu!
           'Mom, give me a pear.'   (ACC)

      MOM: Julia uže s"ela grušu?
           'Has Julia already eaten her pear?'

      JUL: Da. Vkusnaja gruša. Netu gruša[27].   (NOM)
           'Yes, good pear. No pear.'
           (NOM instead of GEN after negation)

---

25.   Note even the emergence of prepositions in the child's speech, which marks a new period.

26.   Self-correction.

27.   This "innovation" is due to the fact that the child has not yet acquired the genitive of negation in Russian (the use of genitive case after negated transitive verbs in Russian).

MOM: <u>Netu</u> gruši, da?
    '<u>No</u> pear (GEN), right?'

JUL: <u>Netu</u>.
    '<u>No</u>' (2;2)

DAD: Vad gör pappa?
    'What does dad do?'

JUL: Åker bilen (definite form of the noun: <u>bil</u>+*en*)[28]
    'Go/es [by] the car.' (2;4).

Net and *ne* were used interchangeably in many phrases. The phrase *ne nado* ('do<u>n</u>'t') appears and is sometimes used interchangeably with *netu* (in the meaning of <u>ne</u>): *netu pisat' mamu* '<u>no</u> pee mom'; *ne nado pisat' mamu!*[29] 'do<u>n</u>'t pee (on) mom!'

The use of NOM instead of GEN after NEG is a typical mistake both in Julia's speech and in the speech of Russian monolingual children. Although in monolingual children this innovation disappears rather early, in Julia's speech the form was used well beyond the age of 5. This reflects the fact that Julia did not get enough input in order to construct correct forms. She was exposed to Swedish in pre-school between eight o'clock to four o'clock five days a week, which inevitable resulted in Swedish dominance. The child created her own forms in Russian under constant influence of Swedish. As a result, her Swedish became better every day, and she continued developing in accordance with monolingual Swedish norms. Her Russian, however, followed a somewhat different pattern. At 4;3 the child understood that something had to be done about genitive of negation and that the use of NOM after NEG was not correct and started using even more un-Russian-like construction *ne est'* ('there is <u>no</u>') instead of *ne* ('no'; which, to our opinion, was the calque of Swedish *har <u>inte</u>* in Russian)[30]. After *ne est'* ('there is no') the use of NOM was more legitimate according to the child: *U menja <u>ne</u> est' mëd* ('I do not have honey'); *U tebja <u>ne</u> est' čaj* ('you do <u>not</u> have tea') etc. This was a logical progression from Julia's perspective since the original construction (without negation) is formed by placing a noun after *est'*: *U menja est' mëd* ('I have honey'); *U tebja estj čaj* ('You have tea'). This calque was used by Julia frequently and for a longer duration than normal since Swedish became her dominant language.

3.   Discussion

Julia's linguistic development seems to follow the same developmental stages (so-called "linguistic milestones") that are found in monolingual children. During the first stages of the VERBAL PERIOD the child seemed to have a common proto-language with

---

28.   The correct expression would have been a set phrase: *åker bil* – 'goes by car'

29.   Said about a kitten who was sitting on the mother's lap.

30.   It should be noted that the form *net* ('no') historically emerges from *ne est'* ('<u>not</u> exist').

non-language specific proto-words from both languages to express the functions of impossibility, irritation, discomfort, forbid etc. The first case of producing negation in this proto-language was at the age of 9 months. At the age of 1;2 Julia for the first time reacted to the fact that her mother was absent (NON EXISTENCE). At the age of 1;3, Julia said the word *nä* in the function of REFUSAL. Although NON-EXISTENCE was expressed by the Swedish word *borta*, REFUSAL and DENIAL were rendered by the trans-linguistic lexical item *nä*.

During the whole PRE-MORPHOLOGICAL PERIOD (1;3–1;8), Julia tended to use one common negator in both languages in the function of REJECTION and DENIAL: *nä*, since this term was understandable in both languages and satisfied the communicative needs of the child at that stage of development. In the function of NON-EXISTENCE only the Swedish word *borta* 'all gone' was used until the Russian word *netu* appeared. When something was untasty, the child said *blä*. The word *nej* was used as the answer to a question, and, most often, to reject a proposition. *Nej* was also used with visitors who came to the family, Swedish relatives, and even with her mother. *Naja* (1;7) was a light form of rejection when the child knew that someone was playing with her.

The Russian phrases <u>*nikak*</u> 'does <u>not</u> go', <u>*ne*</u> *mogu* 'I can<u>not</u>' were often used interchangeably in Julia's speech. The meaning of <u>*ne*</u> *mogu* was broader than in its original sense (which stayed for several years), while the word <u>*nikak*</u> was mostly used in its literal meaning 'does <u>not</u> go'. At the end of pre-morphological period (1;10) the child became aware of the presence of two different linguistic varieties in her surroundings. Around 2, Julia started using forms that seemed to be created on her own by using both languages simultaneously. While before 2 years old the child was placing negation outside the nuclear utterance, and did not analyze chunks (*vill <u>inte</u> mamma kaka* = 'mom does <u>not</u> want a cake'), at around 2;3 the child started moving NEG. from the beginnig to the middle of the sentence: *mama <u>net</u> očki* ('mom <u>no</u> glasses'). By the age of 3, Julia still used *netu* ('no') as a general negator in Russian: *ja <u>netu</u> malen'kaja* ('I <u>no</u> little').

Some researchers state that there is no systematic influence between the two developing languages (Paradis & Genesee 1996, De Houwer 1990; Meisel 1989). However, Schlyter (1993), while investigating Swedish-French bilingual children, found errors they were not typical for monolingual children, yet, typical for second language learners. She compared the development of a weaker language with second language acquisition.

The results of the present study indicate that Julia's SWEDISH developed according to the monolingual norms, yet her RUSSIAN exhibited several features that are not present in the monolingual data of Russian children. In order to live up to the grammatical and communicative needs when using the weaker language and trying to solve the arising problems, the child created her own innovations. Categories that were not considered mandatory were often dropped in Russian or expressed by analytical constructions that fulfilled an equivalent function.

Seen from a monolingual and normative perspective, Julia's Russian seems to undergo structural alternations and replacements like

–   *simplification:* Eto komary <u>netu</u> kusali? 'This is for mosquitoes <u>not</u> to bite?'
–   *forming of analytical constructions:* Ja <u>ne</u> budu uechat' (3,5) 'I will <u>not</u> go'. Ja <u>ne</u> budu s″est' (4;5)[31] 'I will not eat.' U menja <u>ne</u> est' mëd (= u menja <u>net</u> mëda) (**4;2**) 'I do <u>not</u> have honey'.
–   *Transfer (code mixing?):* Eto <u>ne</u> flickans hund. Eto kto-tos ('*-s*' from *någon* Sw) *annans* 'This is <u>not</u> the girl's dog. It is someone else'; *med* grjaznye nožki (Rus: s grjaznymi nogami 'with dirty legs'). *Med* na*s* (s nami = Sw: *oss* 'we') 'with us'; on*s* (Rus on + Sw *hans*) 'his'.

Even though Julia learned to use some prepositions, auxiliaries, past tense forms, some DELAY was noticed in the acquisition of Russian morphology (or rather – she has not fully acquired some aspects of it). By the age of 3;5 a typically developing Russian child is expected to have comprehended the main morphological rules. Julia's data show various examples of a reduced case system (the nominative was used instead of the prepositional, the genitive and the dative), or wrong gender, violations in agreement rules; proper names were not inflected etc., thus showing more characteristics of Russian as a *second* language, an L2, rather than an L1 (cf. also the discussion in Cejtlin 2009).

Despite this deficiency, Julia was keen of speaking Russian and was using it in all domains. She easily initiated conversations in Russian and quickly replied when asked a question. She allowed grown-ups to correct her but did not like such corrections since she considered Russian to be 'her' language that she had the right to speak the way she wanted (cf. Protassova & Rodina 2005). At the age of 6 Julia and her older sister Susie declared *U nas svoj russkij!* 'we have our own Russian!'.

4. Conclusion

In the acquisition of negation Julia moved from (A) gestures via (B) interjections to (C) Modifier-Propositional-Chunks and later to creating (D) [simple] grammatical constructions. At this stage the child seemed to have a (E) common grammatical system that later would develop into (F) more complex constructions and (G) two separate grammatical systems. It appears that the complex morphological rules in Russian cannot develop without ample input, since several morphological categories were either set randomly by the child or not set at all. Language dominance is viewed as a major determinant for language contact phenomenon to occur.

It seems possible that if the child does not get an ample amount of input in the weaker language before the Critical Period (i.e. from 0 up to about 4 years, according to Meisel 2007) is over, she will not develop a full native command of it and develop

---

31. Even though forming future analytical constructions is not common for monolingual Russian children, some such cases were noted, yet, in much younger monolingual Russian children (from the discussion at the conference «Ontolingvistika – nauka XXI veka», St. Petersburg, May 4 – 6, 2011).

structures which are *more typical for L2 than for L1-acquisition*. Morphology may be a *vulnerable domain* in this respect since the very complex morphological rules in Russian cannot develop without abundant input. As a consequence, Julia acquired one stronger language, Swedish ($L1_{strong}$), and another language, a weaker language, Russian ($L1_{weak}$).

The linguistic variant under analysis has proven to be neither maintenance as a whole (since maintenance implies only changes by small degrees, see Winford 2003), nor a shift (since the child is actively bilingual) nor a NEW contact language but rather a new variety of Russian language that was actively created BY the child in a language contact situation with the help of the input she got from her environment (see also Tomasello 2003). Julia created her own innovations in order to live up to the grammatical and communicative needs when using the weaker language and trying to solve the arising problems.

It is believed that the self-created linguistic forms/innovations found in this study may be more typical of BFLA children exposed to Russian and Swedish simultaneously than it was previously assumed. It has been shown that such patterns are possible in cases of unbalanced bilingual development. The innovations and structural replacements do not only seem to depend on ambient languages, their structural complexity and influence on each other; the quality and quantity of input seems to influence the child's proficiency as well.

As this study has shown, cross-linguistic influence is inevitable in the situations of language contact when one language shows dominance over the other. Perhaps the critical question is whether all the 'deviations' are the result of language contact and Swedish dominance or whether some of them are developmental errors. It is hoped that the article will encourage researchers to pay closer attention to the kind of language a child is developing in a contact situation, not only if s/he is developing any.

References

Adamec, P. 1973/1977. *Очерк функционально-трансформационного синтаксиса современного русского языка* (*Očerk funkcional'no-transformacionnogo sintaksisa sovremennogo russkogo jazyka* 'Sketch of the functional non-transformational syntax of the modern Russian language'). Volume I: Однобазовые предложения (Odnobazovye predloženija 'Simple sentences'). Reprint of the 1st edn (Praha: SPN, 1973). Frankfurt: Slavisches Seminar der Universität Frankfurt, 1977.

Andersen, R. W. 1983. *Pidginization and Creolization as Language Acquisition*. Rowley MA: Newbury House.

Babyonyshev, M. 1993. The acquisition of Russian case. In *Papers on Case and Agreement II* (MIT Working Papers in Linguistics 19), ed. C. Phillips, 1–44. Cambridge MA: The MIT Press.

Bellugi, U. 1967. *The Acquisition of Negation*. PhD dissertation, Harvard University.

Bloom, L. 1970. *Language Development: Form and Function in Emerging Grammars*. Cambridge MA: The MIT Press.

Bloom, L. & E. Tinker. 2001. *The Intentionality Model and Language Acquisition.* Boston MA: Blackwell.

Bonacker, U. 1999. *Icelandic plus English: Language Differentiation and Functional Categories in a Successively Bilingual Child.* PhD dissertation, University of Durham.

Brown, R. 1973. *A First Language: The Early Stages.* Cambridge, MA: Harvard University Press.

Cejtlin, S. N. 1989. *Детская речь: Инновации формообразования и словообразования* (*Detskaja reč': Innovazii formoobrazovanija i slovoobrazovanija* 'Child language: Inflectional and derivational innovations'). PhD dissertation, Herzen State Pedagogical University Leningrad.

Cejtlin, S. N. 2000. *Язык и ребёнок: Лингвистика детской речи* (*Jazyk i rebjonok: Lingvistika detskoj reči* 'Language and the child: The linguistics of child language'). Moscow: Vlados.

Cejtlin, S. N. 2009. *Очерки по словообразованию и формообразованию в детской речи* (*Očerki po slovoobrazovaniju i formoobrazovaniju v detskoj reči* 'Essays on word formation and derivation in child language'). Moscow: Znak.

De Houwer, A. 1990. *The Acquisition of Two Languages from Birth: A Case Study.* Cambridge: CUP.

DeGraff, M. 1999. Creolization, language change, and language acquisition: A prolegomenon. In *Language Creation and Language Change: Creolization, Diachrony, and Development*, ed. M. DeGraff, 1–46. Cambridge MA: The MIT Press.

Deuchar, M. & S. Quay. 2000. *Bilingual Acquisition: Theoretical Implications of a Case Study.* Oxford: OUP.

Dressler, W. U. 1997. Introduction. In *Pre- and Protomorphology in Language Acquisition*, ed. K. Dziubalska-Kolaczyk, 7–14. Poznań: Nakom.

Gagarina, N. 2008. *Становление грамматических категорий русского глагола в детской речи* (*Stanovlenije grammatičeskih kategorij russkogo glagola v detskoj reči* 'First language acquisition of verb categories in Russian'). St. Petersburg: Nauka.

Gagarina, N. & M. Voeikova. 2009. The acquisition of case and number in Russian. In *Crosslinguistic Approaches to the Acquisition of Case and Number*, eds. U. Stephany & M. Voeikova, 179–215. Berlin: Mouton de Gruyter.

Gvozdev, A. N. 1949/2005. *От первых слов до первого класса: Дневник научных наблюдений* (*Ot pervyh slov do pervogo klassa: Dnevnik naučnyh nabludenij* 'From the first words to the first grade: A diary of scientific observations'). Moscow: Komkniga.

Klima, E. & U. Bellugi. 1966. Syntactic regularities in the speech of children. In *Psycholinguistic Papers*, eds. J. Lyons & R. J. Wales, 183–208. Edinburgh: EUP.

Klima, E. & U. Bellugi. 1969. Syntactic regularities in the speech of children. In *Modern Studies in English: Readings in Transformational Grammar*, eds. D. A. Reibel & S. A. Schane, 448–466. Englewood Cliffs NJ: Prentice-Hall.

Klima, E. & U. Bellugi. 1973. Syntactic regularities in the speech of children. In *Studies of Child Language Development*, eds. C. A. Ferguson & D. I. Slobin, 333–353. New York NY: Holt, Rinehart & Winston.

Leopold, W. 1939–1949. *Speech Development of a Bilingual Child: A Linguist's Record,* Vols I–IV. Evaston IL: Northwestern University Press.

Meisel, J. M. 1989. Early differentiation of language in bilingual children. In *Bilingualism across the Lifespan: Aspects of Acquisition, Maturity and Loss*, eds. K. Hyltenstam & L. Obler, 13–40. Cambridge: CUP.

Meisel, J. M. 2007. The weaker language in early child bilingualism: Acquiring a first language as a second language? *Applied Psycholinguistics* 28: 495–514.

Murašova, O. V. & V. A. Semušina. 2007. Отрицание в детской речи (Otrizanije v detskoj reči 'Negation in child language'). In *Семантические категории в детской речи* (*Semantičeskije kategorii v detskoj reči* 'Semantic categories in child language'), ed. S. N. Cejtlin, 138–160. St. Petersburg: Nestor-Istoria.

Okita, T. 2002. *Invisible Work. Bilingualism, Language Choice and Childrearing in Intermarried Families* (IMPACT: Studies in Language and Society 12). Amsterdam: John Benjamins.

Papalia, D., S. Wendkos Olds & R. Duskin Feldman. 2007. *Human Development*. Boston MA: McGraw-Hill.

Paradis, J. & F. Genesee. 1996. Syntactic acquisition in bilingual children: Autonomous or interdependent? *Studies in Second Language Acquisition* 18: 1–15.

Pea, R. D. 1980. The development of negation in early child language. In *The Social Foundations of Language and Thought: Essays in Honour of Jerome S. Brunner*, ed. D. R. Olson, 156–186. New York NY: Norton.

Polinsky, M. 2006. Incomplete acquisition: American Russian. *Journal of Slavic Linguistics* 14: 191–262.

Protassova, E. & N. Rodina. 2005. *Многоязычие в детском возрасте* (*Mnogojazyčije v detskom vozraste* 'Multilingualism in childhood'). St. Petersburg: Zlatoust.

Ronjat, J. 1913. *Le développement du langage observé chez un enfant bilingue*. Paris: Champion.

Schlyter, S. 1993. The weak language in bilingual Swedish-French children. In *Progression and Regression in Language*, eds. K. Hyltenstam & A. Viberg, 289–308. Cambridge. CUP.

Schumann, J. H. 1987. *The Pidginization Process: A Model for Second Language Acquisition*. Rowley MA: Newbury House.

Slobin, D. I. ed. 1966. *The Cross-linguistic Study of Language Acquisition*, Vol. 1: *The Data*. Hillsdale NJ: Lawrence Erlbaum Associates.

Timberlake, A. 1986. On hierarchies and the genitive of negation. In *Case in Slavic*, eds. R. Brecht & M. Levine, 338–360. Columbus OH: Slavica.

Tomasello, M. 2003. *Constructing a Language: A Usage-based Theory of Language Acquisition*. Cambridge MA: Harvard University Press.

Vihman, M. M. 1985. Language differentiation by the bilingual infant. *Journal of Child Language* 12: 297–324.

Weinreich, U. 1953. *Languages in Contact: Findings and Problems*. New York NY: Linguistics Circle of New York.

Winford, D. 2003. *An Introduction to Contact Linguistics*. Malden MA: Blackwell.

Yip, V. & S. Matthews. 2007. *The Bilingual Child: Early Development and Language Contact*. Cambridge: CUP.

The acquisition of gender agreement marking in Polish

A study of bilingual Polish-German-speaking children*

[1]Bernhard Brehmer and [2]Monika Rothweiler
[1]University of Hamburg, Germany; [2]University of Bremen, Germany

This study investigates the acquisition of gender agreement marking in Polish noun phrases. It thus sheds light on the general acquisition of noun gender in Polish which, in most cases, can be predicted by the *auslaut* of the noun. Whether a child knows the gender of a given noun is indicated by his/her ability to produce gender marked attributive adjectives. To test this ability we elicited attributive adjectives in a group of 34 Polish-German children from age 2;11 to 6;5 with Polish as L1. We tested contexts with typically and atypically marked nouns, as well as with nonce words. With respect to correct markings, error rates and error types, we checked whether the children relied on the morphophonological clues of a given noun and/or whether they use a default strategy. Furthermore, we investigated the development of gender agreement marking. Our results show that (1) even at age six the development of gender agreement/marking is not yet completed, (2) the children use morphophonological as well as semantic clues to identify the gender of a given noun, and (3) the children over-apply feminine and masculine markings.

Keywords: Polish, German, gender assignment, gender agreement, bilingual language acquisition, morphophonological clues

---

*   The research presented here was supported by the University of Hamburg and through grants by the *Deutsche Forschungsgemeinschaft* (DFG, 'German Research Foundation') to the authors for research projects at the *Collaborative Research Center on Multilingualism* at the University of Hamburg (SFB 538 'Multilingualism', 2002–2011, projects E4 and H8). Furthermore, the authors would like to express their gratitude to the two anonymous reviewers for their helpful suggestions and comments on earlier drafts of the paper.

1.   Introduction

This study aims to determine how bilingual children acquire gender in Polish. Polish has three basic classes of grammatical gender in the singular (masculine, feminine and neuter). Typically, the gender of a noun is indicated via the nouns' *auslaut* and marked by agreement with attributive elements in noun phrases, but also with predicative elements (see Section 2).[1] All of these agreeing elements have unambiguous agreement markers for the three genders. The identification of whether a child knows the gender of a given noun is therefore bound to his/her ability to produce gender marked attributes (or other associated targets) together with or without the corresponding noun.

Our paper concentrates on the acquisition of gender marking on attributive adjectives with respect to nouns that have typical or atypical *auslaut* structures in the nominative singular which suggest a certain gender. We investigated a group of children growing up in Germany with Polish as their first language. These children live in immigrant families who speak Polish as their L1, and they acquire German as an early L2 or simultaneously with Polish. The study is based on data of two elicitation tasks and investigates correct markings, error rates and error types in children from age 2;11 to 6;5 thus describing the development of gender marking up to school age.

2.   Gender classes, gender agreement and gender assignment in Polish

The topic of how many gender classes should be distinguished in Polish is debated very controversially among Polish linguists. For limitations of space, we will not discuss the different proposals here[2] but adopt the five gender distinctions first proposed by Mańczak (1956) and now widely acknowledged in standard grammars of Polish (see, e.g., Grzegorczykowa, Laskowski & Wróbel 1998). The underlying concept of this classification is that grammatical gender manifests itself in agreement classes, i.e. nouns are categorized with regard to gender according to the forms that are taken by associated elements which are syntactically related to the noun. Thus the classification of nouns by gender is realized by way of their agreement. If the agreement of attributes is decisive for the distinction of gender classes, the picture for Polish gets complicated by the fact that the semantic factors of animacy (feature ±animate) and virility (feature ±human) of the noun referent have to be taken into account. Whereas in the nominative singular only three gender classes can be distinguished (masculine – feminine – neuter), the class of masculine nouns has to be split up in three classes (masculine virile, masculine animate/non-virile, masculine

---

1.   Agreement in noun phrases is often also referred to as concord (e.g. Hawkins & Franceschina 2004). However, we will stick to the traditional term agreement throughout the entire paper.

2.   For an overview of the existing approaches to gender classification in Polish linguistics, see, e.g., Stefańczyk (2007: 17–20) or Weiss (1991, 1993).

inanimate) in accusative singular and plural contexts. In the plural, only two gender classes can be distinguished (masculine virile and the remainder). However, for the purpose of the present paper, the subdivision of the masculine nouns will be neglected since in our experimental tasks the children were forced to use the selected items in the nominative singular. In what follows, we will therefore only distinguish between the three basic gender classes: masculine, feminine and neuter.[3] Thus the general gender system of Polish as investigated here is comparable to the system of German (the L2 of our children) which equally distinguishes between these three gender classes in the singular.

Another structural parallel between Polish and German consists in the fact that gender is marked for certain word classes by agreement within the noun phrase (attributive agreement of adjectives, participles, some types of numerals and pronouns, in German also articles). However, in Polish gender is also marked by predicate agreement (mainly on finite verb forms which include the l-participle or passive participle and predicative adjectives).

A further crucial difference between the two gender systems is the fact that Polish offers more formal clues about the noun which can be used to tentatively determine its grammatical gender, whereas in German the system of gender assignment to nouns is much less transparent. In Polish, gender assignment is, on the whole, governed by the interaction of morphophonological (especially the *auslaut* structure of the noun in the nominative singular), morphological (declensional class) and semantic factors (sex of the referent). The morphophonological clues, however, play a particularly important role in gender assignment of nouns in Polish. Thus Polish nouns can be identified as belonging to a certain gender class largely by the word final sounds in the nominative singular (see Table 1):

Table 1. Association of word-final sounds with gender in Polish

	Masculine	Feminine	Neuter
Auslaut structure	(hard) consonant	- /a/	- /o/ - /e/
Examples	*mał-y pies* 'little dog' *mał-y but* 'little shoe'	*mał-a kobieta* 'little woman' *mał-a gwiazda* 'little star'	*mał-e okno* 'little window' *mał-e pole* 'little field'

---

3.   It has been argued that the traditional threefold division reflects the initial stance of the gender acquisition process since it is more salient and global in the sense that every noun can be attributed to one of these three classes, whereas only the masculine nouns are affected by the additional classes in the five gender division (see Krajewski 2005).

Thus nouns ending in a consonant are prototypically masculine, nouns ending in -*a* are typically feminine and nouns in -*o* and -*e* are normally neuter. As is shown in the table, attributive modifiers signal gender by their inflectional endings -*y* for masculine, -*a* for feminine, -*e* for neuter singular. However, the "rules" described here are not deterministic. There are exceptions to them, which are due to the interference of semantic and/or morphological factors. Thus there is a small class of masculines ending in -*a*, which denote mainly male persons or professions (e.g. *mężczyzna* 'man', *dentysta* 'dentist'). More problematic are, however, nouns ending in palatal or historically palatal consonants: Depending on the declensional class they belong to, they are either masculine (e.g. *gość* 'guest') or feminine (*kość* 'bone', *mysz* 'mouse'). Other "atypical" gender assignments are comparatively infrequent (e.g. feminines ending in -*i* such as *pani* 'Mrs' or neuter borrowings from Latin ending in -*um* like *muzeum* 'museum'). Thus, on the whole, gender assignment in Polish is highly predictable by the phonological shape of the noun in the nominative singular.

3. State of the art

3.1   The acquisition of gender in Polish

The acquisition of gender in Polish is far from having been studied in detail: the results available do not provide a clear picture. According to Olma (2007: 88), Polish children start to distinguish between three genders already at the age of 2 quite consistently, but animacy and virility as semantic factors that lead to a further distinction of masculine nouns in the accusative singular and to gender distinctions in the plural (see Section 2) do pose a problem for them during the whole preschool period. However, Olma's observations are based on the data of only one child. The most comprehensive account of the acquisition of grammatical gender in Polish is offered by Smoczyńska (1985: 644ff) who uses data of several Polish children and data from diary studies. She states that Polish children have acquired gender distinctions before the age of 2, the main reason for this claim being the observation that they acquire the declensional patterns of nouns (which are based on gender distinctions) surprisingly early and nearly without errors. The hypothesis that distinct gender classes are already available to the children from the onset of the acquisition of the declensional system is also supported by Krajewski (2005). However, if gender classes are defined as agreement classes, as was outlined in Section 2, the question of when children have acquired the gender system of Polish cannot be answered solely on the basis of the correct distinction of declensional paradigms. In our opinion, one must also take into account the correctness of gender markings on agreeing elements as an important indicator for the successful acquisition of gender.[4] Furthermore, it remains unclear as to whether the statements of

---

4.   Smoczyńska (1985: 645) claims that "... the occurrence of inappropriate gender agreement is limited to a very short period when adjectives, past-tense forms, or pronouns begin to appear,

Smoczyńska (1985) and Krajewski (2005) refer to the system in its entirety or only to the *prototypical* cases where the word-final sounds correctly indicate the gender of the respective nouns. There is no detailed information available describing when and how children master gender marking/agreement also in noun phrases with atypical nouns. The fact that the picture looks different with these nouns can be inferred from the observation made by Smoczyńska (1985: 625f) that children have problems in acquiring the declensional pattern for feminine nouns ending in a (historically) palatal consonant (type *mysz* 'mouse' mentioned in Section 2). She traces their problems back to the clash that these nouns occur in the input with modifiers and verb forms that indicate the feminine gender, although the absence of an inflectional affix in the nominative singular suggests masculine gender. According to Smoczyńska's observations, children then tend to either avoid these nouns, treat them as masculines, or provide them with the feminine ending -*a* (**mysz-a*) and treat them as regular feminine nouns. Even children over 4;0 have problems in applying the correct declensional pattern for these nouns.

3.2   The acquisition of gender in bilingual children

Empirical case studies on bilingual acquisition of gender assignment and gender agreement have suggested that the development of gender in bilingual language acquisition closely resembles its acquisition in monolingual contexts (e.g. Idiazabal 1995, Müller 1990, 1994, 2000, Möhring 2001). According to these authors, gender is acquired and mastered rather early (as in monolingual L1 acquisition). Furthermore, they claim that bilingual children develop each gender system independently and that no clear signs of crosslinguistic influences between the two gender systems in contact are noticeable.

Whereas the bulk of the research on gender acquisition by bilingual children is more concerned with gender acquisition in the L2 (or second L1), Dieser (2009) investigates the acquisition of grammatical gender both in the L1 Russian and in the second L1/L2 German of her bilingual subjects. Since the gender system of Russian is, in many respects, comparable to Polish, her results are of interest to the purpose of the present study. Based on longitudinal, cross-sectional and experimental data of Russian-German bilingual children which are compared to data from monolingual Russian children and early as well as late L2-learners of Russian, she shows that the strategies implied for determining the gender of Russian nouns are essentially the same for all three groups and that cross-linguistic effects play apparently no role in gender acquisition of Russian nouns. Gender assignment follows mainly formal clues,

---

and it should be attributed to the lack of knowledge of possible differentiation of these forms rather than of that concerning noun gender." Agreement errors may (at least at the beginning) indeed indicate problems with agreement marking on adjectives and other elements, but they may also reflect general problems of determining noun gender.

i.e. the morphophonological structures of the *auslaut* of the given noun. For very early phases of the acquisitional process, they even sometimes overrule semantic clues (i.e. the sex of the referent). Gender marking is highly consistent and nearly error-free for typical masculine and feminine nouns where the gender can be correctly predicted by the *auslaut* structure (this applies to real words as well as tested nonce words). The three investigated groups show no significant differences in error rates for these nouns. The acquisition of neuter, which is generally acquired later than masculine and feminine (mostly after the age of 4 or 5) in Russian, seems more problematic due to the fact that (i) neuter represents the most infrequent gender class for nouns, (ii) the neutralization of the phonological difference between /o/ and /a/ in favour of /a/ makes neuter nouns ending in unstressed *-o* indistinguishable from feminines ending in *-a*, and (iii) the declensional pattern of neuter nouns is identical for most of the cases with the declensional pattern of masculines (Dieser 2009: 48)[5]. Atypical nouns (e.g. feminine nouns ending in sibilants or soft consonants, which form comparable cases to Polish *mysz* 'mouse') cause most of the problems in gender acquisition. For bilingual children, error rates are significantly higher than for monolingual children and they reach ultimate attainment considerably later (by age 10–14, or even later, in contrast to age 7 in monolinguals) (Dieser 2009: 163). Dieser explains these differences by claiming that the gender of these nouns is acquired by item-based rote learning. Therefore, bilingual children and second language learners with their reduced input in the L1/L2 have more problems in coping with gender assignment to these nouns than monolinguals do. According to Dieser, this item-based learning view is corroborated by the fact that there are considerable differences in the speed of acquiring correct gender marking between different items that belong to these atypical nouns.

Thus the main goals of the present study are to check (1) whether the *auslaut* structure of the nouns plays a similarly important role for our bilingual children in selecting the gender of agreeing elements and (2) whether the hierarchy that Dieser established for Russian with regard to the course of gender acquisition in her bilingual subjects (1. typical masculine/ feminine nouns > 2. typical neuter nouns > 3. atypical nouns) holds for our Polish speaking bilingual children as well.[6]

---

5.   However, typical neuter real and nonce nouns ending in stressed /o/ and /e/ behaved like typical masculines and feminines in Dieser's experimental data, i.e. they do not pose more problems to monolingual and bilingual children than the typical masculine and feminine ones. When neuter nouns ending in unstressed /o/ and /e/ were included in the analysis, the bilingual children performed significantly worse than the monolingual controls (Dieser 2009: 152ff).

6.   For the purpose of the present paper, we will concentrate on the data of bilingual children only. Their comparison with data from a control group of Polish monolingual children of the same age range will be the topic of a separate study.

4.   Design of the present study

4.1   Participants

To address the question of how gender marking is acquired in Polish, we collected data from 34 children who live in Germany and have Polish as (one of) their L1. Most of the children were born in families where both parents are L1 speakers of Polish. In two couples one parent grew up as a Polish-German bilingual, in four more families one parent is a L1 speaker of German.[7] All children attend(ed) a German kindergarten. The data were collected in Hamburg and consist of elicited speech samples concentrating on the production of gender agreement marking on adjectives in noun phrases (see 4.2).

Most of the 34 children were tested twice, the time-span between first and second testing being between 4,5 and 9 months. Thus the corpus of the present study consists of a total of 59 test samples for children aged from 2;11 to 6;5. The test sessions were carried out with each child separately in a quiet room, mostly in the kindergarten, but sometimes also at the child's home, and were videotaped.

Table 2 gives an overview of the tested subjects. The children are divided into six age groups according to their age at each testing. The table indicates the group sizes, the age ranges, the mean age of each group and the respective standard deviations.

4.2   Methods

4.2.1   *Material*
In order to test the acquisition of gender categorization of nouns, we had to develop a test that would stimulate the children to produce a target marked by gender and syntactically bound to the noun, e.g. a determiner phrase. Since the main purpose of our paper consists in checking whether the children use formal clues in order to assign a certain gender to a given noun, the sample of test items includes real nouns whose

Table 2. Participants of the present study

participants	group 1	group 2	group 3	group 4	group 5	group 6
N	9	11	18	9	8	4
age range	2;11–3;10	4;1–4;5	4;6–4;11	5;0–5;4	5;6–5;11	6;0–6;5
mean age in	42,2,	50,8,	56,7,	61,9,	68,4,	74,5,
months, sd	sd 3,8	sd 1,4	sd 1,7	sd 1,5	sd 1,5	sd 2,4

---

7.   With regard to the results, the children from the families where one parent has German as a (second) L1 did not differ from the other children. For this reason they will not be treated separately in the analysis of the data.

auslaut structure correctly predicts their gender ("typical nouns") as well as real nouns whose *auslaut* structures suggest a gender different from the correct one ("atypical nouns").[8] In order to check the impact of item-based rote learning on gender marking in typical nouns, we added nonce words which follow the phonotactic regularities of Polish and whose *auslaut* structure predicts a certain gender when the prototypical morphophonological rule is applied to them. Table 3 presents the selected test items and their distribution among the different gender classes.

Since we also wanted to control for the influence of item-based rote learning, we had to check how familiar the children were with the test items. Therefore, we first played a memory game with the children that functioned as a naming task[9]. The children had to name the items that were displayed on the memory cards. Items that the children

Table 3. Overview of test items

Gender class	Real nouns		Nonce words
MASC – typical	*but* 'shoe'	*telefon* 'telephone'	*hoszer*
	kwiat 'flower'	*widelec* 'fork'	*niwes*
	słoń 'elephant'		
MASC – atypical	*astronauta* 'astronaut' / *kierowca* 'driver'[10]		
FEM – typical	*gwiazda* 'star'	*świnia* 'pig'	*wepa*
	krowa 'cow'		
FEM – atypical	*kość* 'bone'	*sól* 'salt'	
	mysz 'mouse'		
NEUT – typical[11]	*jabłko* 'apple'	*serce* 'heart'	*pęco*
	jajko 'egg'	*słońce* 'sun'	

8. An important factor for selecting the test items was whether it was possible to display them on a picture so that they could be identified by the children as easily as possible. This was a challenging task especially for the atypical nouns since, e.g., the overwhelming majority of atypical feminine nouns in Polish denote abstract entities like *miłość* 'love'. This is the reason why this group includes a mass noun *sól* 'salt', whereas the other groups are composed of animate and inanimate concrete nouns. However, *sól* was depicted with a picture showing a salt shaker, and the children apparently identified the mass noun directly with the object, so we would assume that for the children this categorical difference is not salient.

9. The nonce words were not included in this task but rather introduced during the elicitation tests described below. In introducing the nonce words, the test supervisor offered an explanation for which purpose the alleged referent of the word is used.

10. Since *astronauta* was problematic for our children in the naming task, we changed the item to *kierowca* for later tested subjects. Thus every subject had only one example of atypical masculines in his/her sample.

11. Atypical neuter nouns represent clear peripheral cases in the Polish noun system and were thus not included in our sample of items.

could not name spontaneously were introduced by the test supervisor and the children had to reproduce them at least once. The results of this naming test revealed that the children a) knew between 70% and 90% of the nouns, and that b) this was the case even for the youngest children in the sample.

4.2.2 *Elicitation tasks*

For prompting our children to use NPs that contain the selected test items together with a modifier (mainly an attributive adjective) we adapted two elicitation tasks that were designed by Ruberg (2010) for testing gender markings of German nouns. In order to prevent our subjects from getting bored by testing all 20 selected items (see Table 3) with one task, we decided to split our items into two groups and use two tasks. Both tasks operated in essentially the same way: the items were presented in pairs that showed a feature contrast between the two representations of the item (mainly differences regarding the color or the size of the illustrations of the item). In the first task, the test supervisor used a hand puppet that depicted a warlock. The child was told to tell the warlock which of the two representations of the item should disappear. Thus, the children were involved in the wizardry of making things disappear and had to name the feature of the representation of the item that they wanted to disappear ('blue egg', 'white egg' etc.). The second test was designed as a puzzle play. Each item was depicted on two puzzle pieces which had a different size. For each piece the child had to seek a fitting gap on a thin board. To make the task easier each gap had a picture of the item needed to fill the gap, thus guiding the child where to fix the different pieces. The child had to ask the test supervisor to give him/her the pieces he/she needed in order to fill the gaps. Therefore, the child had to name the item and the corresponding feature ('big pig', 'small pig' etc.).

4.2.3 *Preconditions and predictions*

In order to correctly produce adjectives that agree with the tested nouns with regard to gender, the children have to know that (i) gender is a classificatory category for nouns; (ii) Polish has a three gender system in the nominative singular; (iii) gender can be typically predicted by the morphophonological form of the *auslaut* of a noun; (iv) agreement has to be marked within a noun phrase, i.e. on the attributive adjective; and (v) Polish has unambiguous adjectival agreement morphemes for masculine, feminine and neuter in the nominative singular, which partly differ from the noun *auslaut* markers. As long as children do not know these three adjectival markers, gender agreement marking will be incomplete, and we have no possibility to examine whether the children have identified the gender classification and the morphophonological rules of gender indices (*auslaut*) on nouns. However, it turned out that all children except one[12] already used the three different adjectival markers.

---

12. One child of group 1 did not produce any neuter adjectives but rather only masculine and feminine forms.

4.2.4   *Data evaluation and statistics*

The test data were analyzed with respect to correctness, error rates and error types. First, we ran a correlation analysis of age and correctness for the total group of all children (see 5.1). To analyze the data with respect to different error types and/or to different word classes and gender types statistically, we used the non-parametric Wilcoxon Test (see 5.2, 5.3).

5.   Results

5.1   Correlation of age and correctness

The main results show that the correctness rates improve with age (Pearson's $r = 0,243$, $p = .064$). However, even six-year-olds did not perform at ceiling (see Figure 1). One main unexpected response with some of the atypical nouns was the manipulation of the *auslaut* in a way that it fits with the gender of the noun. One option was the use of diminutive forms: for example, the item *mysz* (‚mouse') is a feminine noun with an *auslaut* structure that suggests masculine gender. Many of the children used a correctly marked feminine noun phrase, but with the (correct) diminutive noun *myszka* (‚little mouse'), which shows a typical feminine *auslaut*. Such cases were also reported from monolingual Polish children (Smoczyńska 1985: 625). Smoczyńska explains this tendency with the high frequency of diminutives in Polish baby-talk register. However, in our corpus we find comparable cases of noun *auslaut* manipulations that support the explanation that this strategy is applied by the children to make the supposed gender of the noun more transparent. Thus some children produced (incorrect) *kierowiec* with an *auslaut* typically suggesting masculine gender instead of *kierowca*[13] or *kostka* with -*a* for feminines instead of *kość* ('bone')[14] and some more forms. Thus the children produce a form indicating masculine gender by a morphophonological process (the deletion of -*a*) or they produce a form indicating feminine gender by applying a morphological process (the suffixation of -*ka*).[15] The children's manipulation of the nominal endings suggests that they know the correct gender of the noun and the

---

13.   Similar cases occur in the acquisition of gender in Russian (see Dieser 2009: 47).

14.   According to Smoczyńska (1985: 626), monolingual Polish children do not use *kostka* as a more transparent alternative to *kość* since *kostka* has a different meaning ('knuckle', 'cube'). In our elicitation task, however, the response *kostka* refers to the picture of a bone.

15.   It might be the case that for some of the children *myszka* is the only noun they know for ‚mouse'. These cases should then be counted as correct answers to a typical feminine noun. However, it is not possible to separate these responses from manipulated forms, and there is evidence in our data that point to the fact that manipulation does play a role for some children: (1) In accordance with Smoczyńska (1985), sometimes also *mysza* occurs in our data, a form which is clearly in line with our suggestion that the children manipulate atypical nouns so that the form fits to the gender class of the noun. (2) Since we also got quite a lot of *mysz* responses,

morphophonological clues for gender class identification in Polish. By changing the *auslaut*, they try to produce unambiguous forms. There are only very few cases of manipulation of an *auslaut* which lead to gender errors (see Figure 1).

If the correctly manipulated forms are added to the number of correct forms, the correlation with age becomes more significant (Pearson's r = 0,300, p = .021). This significant correlation indicates that the children's knowledge about gender, morphophonological clues of nouns and gender agreement in the NP is increasing with age. Nevertheless, the fact that even in the group of the four oldest children the correctness rate only reaches 76.3%, indicates that the acquisition of gender and gender agreement is not yet complete when children enter school.

5.2   Correctness of gender markings with typical, atypical and nonce nouns

The analysis of correctness of agreement marking on adjectives in noun phrases with typical, atypical and nonce nouns reveals no development with age within individual noun categories. It does reveal, however, relevant differences with respect to the noun categories (see Table 4). The correctness scores with atypical nouns include instances with correct markings on adjectives referring to test nouns in their normative as well as in a manipulated form, as described in Section 5.1.

Agreement marking in neuter contexts seems to be especially problematic: correctness scores are low with typical nouns, and correct agreement only reaches 0% to 25% in neuter contexts with nonce nouns (less than in atypical feminine or masculine contexts). In contrast to this, correct agreement in feminine and masculine contexts with nonce words is quite high, from 70% to 92%.

Table 4. Correctness by noun categories

Correctness	group 1	group 2	group 3	group 4	group 5	group 6
MASC – typical	82%	95%	98%	96%	88%	100%
FEM – typical	78%	91%	96%	96%	92%	92%
NEUT – typical	64%	59%	75%	72%	72%	63%
MASC – atypical	44%	45%	72%	67%	50%	50%
FEM – atypical	30%	36%	57%	56%	46%	50%
nonce	56%	46%	57%	67%	53%	75%
nonce	70%	58%	72%	86%	71%	92%
MASC and FEM						
nonce NEUT	11%	9%	11%	11%	0%	25%

---

a generalization like "all Polish children know only the diminutive form *myszka* which therefore has to be treated as a typical feminine noun" is certainly not correct.

Table 5. Correctness by noun categories – statistical differences

statistically significant differences	typical masc and fem	typical neut	nonce masc and fem	atypical masc	atypical fem	nonce neut
NEUT – typical	$Z = 2.20$, $p < .05$	###	+++	+++	+++	+++
nonce MASC and FEM	$Z = 2.20$, $p < .05$	ns	###	+++	+++	+++
MASC – atypical	$Z = 2.20$, $p < .05$	$Z = 2.20$, $p < .05$	$Z = 2.03$, $p < .05$	###	+++	+++
FEM – atypical	$Z = 2.20$, $p < .05$	$Z = 2.20$, $p < .05$	$Z = 2.20$, $p < .05$	$Z = 2.03$, $p < .05$	###	+++
nonce NEUT	$Z = 2.20$, $p < .05$	$Z = 2.20$, $p < .05$	$Z = 2.20$, $p < .05$	$Z = 2.20$, $p < .05$	$Z = 2.20$, $p < .05$	###

The results of the in-group comparisons of different noun groups can be summarized by the following hierarchy which depicts the decrease in the correctness scores for the individual noun groups: typMasc/typFem < typNeut = nonce masc/fem < (atypMasc) < atypFem < nonce Neut. The word category 'atypical masculine' is put into brackets since the results rely on one item only, which was replaced during the study, so the item was not the same for all children (see Footnote 10). Since the correctness rates for masculine and feminine nonce words are very similar (no significant difference), they were calculated as one category, in contrast to neuter nonce nouns.

The correctness rates for agreement marking in contexts with typical masculine and feminine nouns do not differ statistically from each other. However, they differ significantly from the correctness rates in all other contexts. Table 5 shows in detail where statistically significant differences between the investigated contexts occur. The difference is always in favor of the more left-cited word category in the head row, i.e. the head row follows the above-mentioned hierarchy.

Thus, at this stage of the analysis, we can conclude the following:

1. Agreement of adjectives in contexts with typical masculine and feminine nouns is almost at ceiling, at least from age four onwards. Typical feminine and masculine nouns generate an unambiguous context for correct gender agreement, the children know the correct gender of these nouns or they use the morphophonological clues.
2. Agreement in neuter contexts is less perfect than in feminine and masculine contexts.
3. Agreement with atypical masculine nouns is much better than with atypical feminine nouns. This might be caused by the fact that the atypical masculine nouns 'astronaut' and 'driver' are semantically transparent and stereotypically refer to male persons. Thus the semantic clues override the misleading morphophonological clues.

4. Agreement with atypical nouns is most problematic if there are no semantic clues for the correct gender, i.e. in the feminine contexts.
5. Agreement in contexts with masculine and feminine nonce words is lower than with typical masculine and feminine nouns (as low as with typical neuter nouns).
6. Agreement in contexts with neuter nonce words is especially low supporting the observation that agreement with nouns of the neuter class causes problems.

If children followed the morphophonological clues (only) we would expect no agreement errors in contexts with typical nouns and nonce words. This prediction only holds for typical masculine and feminine nouns, not for neuter nouns or nonce nouns. Furthermore, we would expect many agreement errors with atypical nouns; this prediction is confirmed. Taken together, we have to explain the high error rates in neuter contexts.

5.3   Error analyses

More specific error analyses were run on the basis of the six age groups. As Figure 1 reveals, the percentage of remaining errors (= rest, e.g. no answers, use of deictic forms) decreases over age, which indicates that older children are better at coping with the experimental task.

There are two error types to be analyzed in detail: the consistent and the inconsistent agreement errors. A response was calculated as a consistent error if the child produced only one type of agreement error referring to a given test item, once or several times. A response was calculated as an inconsistent error if the child produced two or

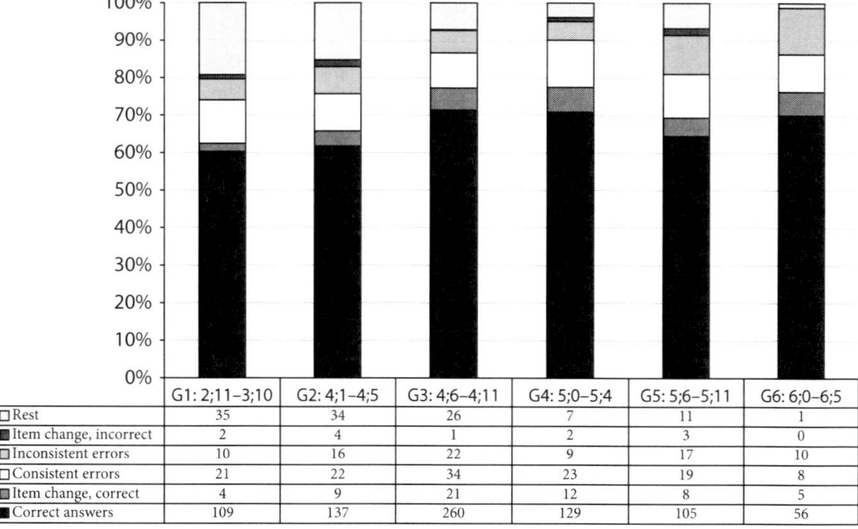

	G1: 2;11–3;10	G2: 4;1–4;5	G3: 4;6–4;11	G4: 5;0–5;4	G5: 5;6–5;11	G6: 6;0–6;5
☐ Rest	35	34	26	7	11	1
▣ Item change, incorrect	2	4	1	2	3	0
☐ Inconsistent errors	10	16	22	9	17	10
☐ Consistent errors	21	22	34	23	19	8
▦ Item change, correct	4	9	21	12	8	5
■ Correct answers	109	137	260	129	105	56

Figure 1. Amount of errors and error types

Table 6. Consistent and inconsistent errors (100% = correct and incorrect responses)

participants	group 1	group 2	group 3	group 4	group 5	group 6
consistent errors	11.60%	9.90%	9.30%	12.60%	11.70%	10%
inconsistent errors	5.50%	7.20%	6.00%	4.90%	10.40%	12.50%

more different agreement markings on adjectives referring to a given test item. As Table 6 reveals, the relative amount of consistent errors remains constant over time, while the relative amount of inconsistent errors increases with age (see also Figure 1).

5.3.1   *Consistent errors*

Consistent errors are misapplications of masculine markings to feminine and neuter contexts, and misapplications of feminine markings to masculine and neuter contexts. Only one misapplication of a neuter form was produced.[16] Most of these cases occur with atypical nouns and with nonce nouns. With typical nouns, there are only 12 consistent errors (see Table 7).

In atypical nouns, consistent errors always consisted of masculine agreement used with feminine nouns, and the use of feminine agreement with masculine nouns. These errors seem to be caused by the morphophonological clues of the nouns which mislead the children. As already mentioned in the previous section, the errors with masculine nouns are less than with feminine nouns, possibly because of the semantic male clues in the masculine nouns.

The nonce nouns and the typical nouns are the relevant test cases in order to check whether consistent agreement errors reveal a default gender marking. Table 7 gives an overview of over-applications of feminine and masculine agreement markings on adjectives (separately for contexts with typical nouns and with nonce nouns). The opportunities for making agreement errors in contexts with typical nouns are seven for masculine (four neuter and three feminine noun contexts), nine for feminine (four neuter and five masculine noun contexts), and eight for neuter markings (three feminine and five masculine noun contexts). The respective numbers for nonce nouns are: two for masculine (one feminine and one neuter contexts), three for feminine (two masculine and one neuter contexts), and three for neuter markings (one feminine and two masculine contexts). Altogether, there are 16 test contexts: 9 non-masculine contexts, 12 non-feminine contexts, and 11 non-neuter contexts.

The most frequent over-applied marking is the masculine marking: masculine agreement is over-applied in 47 cases (12 with typical nouns, 35 with nonce nouns), while feminine agreement is over-applied in 15 cases (3 with typical nouns, 12 with nonce nouns). The difference is significant: for nonce words only ($Z = 1.997$, $p < .05$), and for over-applications in nonce word and in typical noun contexts

---

16.   There is only one case of a neuter over-application to the feminine noun *gwiazda* ('star') by a child of group 1.

Table 7. Over-application of masculine and feminine agreement markings

Shifts	group 1	group 2	group 3	group 4	group 5	group 6	sum
typ feminine → masc	1	0	0	1	0	0	2
typ neuter → masc	0	2	2	2	3	1	10
typ masculine → fem	0	0	0	0	0	0	0
typ neuter → fem	0	2	1	0	0	0	3
nonce feminine → masc	2	3	3	3	1	0	12
nonce neuter → masc	5	4	6	5	3	0	23
nonce masculine → fem	1	1	2	1	1	0	6
nonce neuter → fem	0	0	4	0	1	1	6

($Z = 2.02$, $p < .05$). So, although the opportunities to misapply masculine markings are not dominant, masculine over-applications are prominent and occur about three times more often than feminine over-applications, while neuter over-applications are (almost) non-existent (see Footnote 16). Furthermore, Table 7 reveals that over-applications in typical noun contexts occur almost only in contexts with neuter nouns (13 of 15). The same applies to nonce nouns, since over-applications occur most often in neuter contexts (29 of 47).

The calculation of overgeneralization rates for feminine and masculine agreement marking is presented in Table 8. (All correct and consistent incorrect masculine agreement markings (typical and nonce nouns) = 100%, or all correct and consistent incorrect feminine agreement markings (typical and nonce nouns) = 100%.)
For the statistics we skipped the data of group 6 since only 4 children belong to this group, and over-applications of masculine and feminine forms occur only once. The difference between masculine and feminine overgeneralizations is marginally significant ($Z = 1.753$, $p = .08$).

Table 8. Overgeneralization rates of masculine and feminine agreement markings

	group 1	group 2	group 3	group 4	group 5	group 6	sum
Overgen. of masculine	13.8%	12%	9.6%	15.5%	12.7%	3.4%	11.4%
Overgen. of feminine	3.6%	7.9%	9.7%	3%	7.1%	6.7%	7%

Since the amount of over-applications of feminine forms to neuter and masculine contexts is quite high, we looked at the individual level: do individual children over-apply both masculine and feminine gender, or do children over-apply only one gender? Only in the latter case does over-application indicate the use of a default form. Concentrating first on nonce nouns alone, the analysis reveals no over-applications in 24 of the 59 test sets and just one instance of over-application in 23 test sets (14 masc and 9 fem). Thus in 12 test sets, the children produced more than one over-application. In 11 of these sets, the over-applications were consistent: 10 sets with masculine over-applications, and only one set with feminine. Adding the over-applications in contexts with typical nouns, the picture remains very similar: no over-applications in 20 test sets, and only one instance of over-application in 23 test sets. So the children produced more than one over-application in only 16 test sets. In 14 of these sets, the over-applications were consistent: 12 sets with masculine over-applications, and only two sets with feminine. This result strongly indicates that children who choose a default gender prefer the masculine, and that the inconsistent over-application of two genders is rare.

Since the overgeneralization of the masculine form is dominant, we analyze this as a default gender used by the children whenever they do not know the gender class of a given noun and/or when they do not rely on morphophonological or semantic clues. A similar overgeneralization of the masculine gender for children over age 3;0 has been reported for Russian (Dieser 2009: 46). While nouns with a typical *auslaut* structure for masculine or feminine nouns are often identified as masculine or feminine nouns and agreement markings are correctly supplied to the corresponding adjectives, the children are more uncertain about the neuter class. So it is this group where they resort to a default strategy most often.

5.3.2   *Inconsistent errors*

The picture that has emerged so far is supported by a descriptive analysis of the inconsistent errors. In almost all inconsistent responses, the children produced two gender options, in only one response a child applied all three gender markings. Altogether the children produced 84 instances of inconsistent responses, but only in five cases did none of the two gender markings fit to the given noun. Thus in most cases (= 94%) the children could not decide between the correct form and another possibility. All in all, 90 non-agreeing markings occur, 21 of them in contexts with atypical nouns (3 of them neuter markings). Most of the remaining 69 non-agreeing forms are feminine or masculine markings (34 masculine and 30 feminine), only five neuter markings occur in feminine or masculine contexts with typical or nonce nouns. The over-application of masculine forms then is dominant but only numerically, there is no statistical significant difference here.

The increase of inconsistent errors with age does not necessarily indicate an increase of problems with gender assignment. Given that, in almost all cases, the children switch between the correct and a false gender marking, these responses may also result from an approximation to the correct gender identification (see Table 6).

Another interesting observation is that 33 of all 84 cases of inconsistent responses occur in noun phrases with typical neuter nouns, i.e. although these four nouns only represent 20% of the test items, 39,3% of inconsistent errors occur here (even 50% (5 of 10) of the inconsistent errors in the oldest group). This provides further support for the neuter class and/or neuter agreement being problematic in Polish gender acquisition.

6.   General discussion and conclusion

The results of the present study can be summarized in five points:

1.   Children know the correct gender of many typical nouns, especially of masculine and feminine nouns, and they are able to apply the correct gender marking on the corresponding adjectives. The gender information of the noun might be rote learned or derived from the morphophonological clues which are salient to masculine and feminine nouns. If the children relied on morphophonological clues only, the correctness scores in contexts with typical nouns should equal those in contexts with nonce words. Since these scores are lower, however, we conclude that the children might not rely on the *auslaut* information alone, but also on rote learned gender information. This result is in contrast to the findings of Dieser (2009) for the acquisition of gender in Russian. Dieser finds that gender marking is nearly error-free for typical nouns and for nonce words if the gender can be correctly predicted by the *auslaut* structure (mainly in feminine and masculine forms). She claims that item-based rote learning of the gender information was limited to atypical nouns, and that children mainly relied on morphophonological clues for gender assignment.
     Furthermore, the use of manipulated forms for atypical nouns is in line with the assumption that the children have rote learned the respective gender information. The gender of atypical nouns cannot be derived from morphophonological gender clues. But the children know these clues and add them to atypical nouns, in some cases creating new forms with correctly agreeing adjectives, or they rely on these clues and produce agreement errors.
2.   Neuter nouns and neuter agreement seem to be a problem for the children. First, even in noun phrases with typical neuter nouns, the correctness rates are quite low. Second, correct agreement in neuter contexts with nonce nouns is very low. Third, the neuter marking is not over-applied to feminine and masculine contexts. Problems with neuter gender are also reported by Dieser (2009) for the acquisition of gender in Russian. Dieser explains this result with the low frequency of neuter nouns in general as well as with the neutralization of the phonological opposition between unstressed /o/ and /a/ in Russian. For Polish, neuter represents the most infrequent of the three gender classes, too (only less than 10% of all nouns, see

Stefańczyk 2007: 48). However, other factors come into play as well: Although the morphophonological *auslaut* options for neuter nouns are clearly distinguished from masculine and feminine endings due to the absence of qualitative vowel reduction in unstressed syllables in Polish, the typical neuter forms are less clear than the feminine and masculine forms: with nouns, there are two options, namely *-e* and *-o,* to indicate neuter gender, but only *-e* for adjectives (see Table 1). Furthermore, *-e* also functions as a marker of the nominative plural for some groups of masculine and feminine nouns and as the marker of nominative plural for all adjectives co-occurring with non-masculine virile nouns. So, in contrast to the *auslaut* structures of masculine and feminine nouns, there is no unambiguity for the neuter endings. Neuter *-e* for attributive elements is, therefore, less suited to over-application, and especially *-e* for nouns provides the child with less clear information about the noun gender.

3.   Semantic clues are of importance as well, in the Polish system and for the children. The atypical masculine nouns in our tests are semantically transparent, and stereotypically refer to male persons. In these cases, the children seem to rely on the semantic clues and disregard the misleading morphophonological clues.

4.   The fact that the children do not over-apply all attributive gender markings to the same extent provides evidence for a default strategy. The form most often over-applied is the masculine form. It is the best candidate for a default inflection since masculine is the most frequent gender in Polish (see Stefańczyk 2007: 48).
      This result is partly in line with the findings of Hawkins & Franceschina (2004). They suggest that gender assignment on the basis of formal properties of nouns is acquired first, and that it applies at a lexical level. They propose that setting a default form as a second step indicates that morphophonological properties of nouns become less relevant over time and that gender agreement involves a syntactic operation. Our data do not clearly support a two-stage development beginning with a lexically based morphophonological-clue strategy only, followed by a syntactically based default strategy clearly later in development. In our data, both strategies apply during the complete time of observation. More data of children younger than those of our study are needed to test whether an earlier stage without the use of default forms can be found. If so, this stage would be much earlier in acquisition than Hawkins & Franceschina (2004) propose.

5.   The results reveal that gender acquisition in Polish-German bilingual children is a long-lasting process. The persistent gender errors reveal that the acquisition of gender and gender agreement is not complete before the children enter school.

We therefore conclude that, for bilingual Polish-German children, the acquisition of gender assignment and gender agreement in Polish is not accomplished in early childhood. This result is in contrast to what Olma (2007) and Smoczyńska (1985) suggest for monolingual children. The errors occurring with gender agreement markings in noun phrases in our data may be caused by a) the children's ignorance (or problematic retrieval) of the gender feature of a given noun, and/or b) the ignorance of agreement requirements within a noun phrase. Since the correctness rates are high for the typical nouns, we assume that option b) is least likely for explaining our data. In all contexts with ambiguous gender information, i.e. with conflicts between declensional class and morphophonological clues, or in contexts where only morphophonological clues can serve to identify the gender of a given noun (i.e. in the case of nonce words), or with neuter nouns, children choose a strategy out of a variety of possible strategies: they rely on semantic clues if provided, they use morphophonological clues, especially in feminine and masculine contexts, or they apply a default form.

References

Dieser, E. 2009. *Genuserwerb im Russischen und Deutschen: Korpusgestützte Studie zu ein- und zweisprachigen Kindern und Erwachsenen*. München: Otto Sagner.

Grzegorczykowa, R., R. Laskowski & H. Wróbel. 1998. *Gramatyka współczesnego języka polskiego: Morfologia*. Warszawa: PWN.

Hawkins, R. & F. Franceschina. 2004. Explaining the acquisition and non-acquisition of determiner-noun gender concord in French and Spanish. In *The Acquisition of French in Different Contexts* (Language Acquisition and Language Disorders 32), eds. P. Prévost & J. Paradis, 175–205. Amsterdam: John Benjamins.

Idiazabal, I. 1995. First stages in the acquisition of noun phrase determiners by a Basque-Spanish bilingual child. In *Spanish in Four Continents: Studies in Language Contact and Bilingualism*, ed. C. Silva-Corvalán, 261–278. Washington DC: Georgetown University Press.

Krajewski, G. 2005. The role of grammatical gender in the acquisition of noun inflection in Polish. *Psychology of Language and Communication* 9: 75–84.

Mańczak, W. 1956. Ile jest rodzajów w języku polskim? *Język Polski* 36: 116–121.

Möhring, A. 2001. The acquisition of French by German pre-school children: An empirical investigation of gender assignment and gender agreement. In *EUROSLA Yearbook* 1, eds. S. Foster-Cohen & A. Nizegorodcew, 171–193. Amsterdam: John Benjamins.

Müller, N. 1990. Developing two gender assignment systems simultaneously. In *Two First Languages: Early Grammatical Development in Bilingual Children*, ed. J. M. Meisel, 193–234. Dordrecht: Foris.

Müller, N. 1994. Gender and number agreement within DP. In *Bilingual First Language Acquisition: French and German Grammatical Development* (Language Acquisition and Language Disorders 7), ed. J. M. Meisel, 53–88. Amsterdam: John Benjamins.

Müller, N. 2000. Gender and number in acquisition. In *Gender in Grammar and Cognition*, eds. B. Unterbeck, M. Rissanen, T. Nevalainen & M. Saari, 351–400. Berlin: Mouton de Gruyter.

Olma, M. 2007. Rozwój niektórych kategorii fleksyjnych rzeczownika i czasownika u dziecka w wieku do 5 lat (Cz. I. Fleksja imienna). *Poradnik językowy* 8: 80–92.

Ruberg, T. 2010. Grammatical gender in L1 and child L2 acquisition of German – the role of morphophonological patterns. Paper presented at the International Conference on Multilingual Individuals and Multilingual Societies (MIMS), University of Hamburg, Hamburg, Germany, 6–8 October 2010.

Smoczyńska, M. 1985. The acquisition of Polish. In *The Crosslinguistic Study of Language Acquisition*, Vol. I: *The Data*, ed. D. I. Slobin, 595–686. Hillsdale NJ: Lawrence Erlbaum Associates.

Stefańczyk, W. T. 2007. *Kategoria rodzaju i przypadka polskiego rzeczownika: Próba synchronicznej analizy morfologicznej.* Kraków: Wydawnictwo Uniwersytetu Jagiellońskiego.

Weiss, D. 1991. Sexus distinctions in Polish and Russian. In *Words are Physicians for an Ailing Mind*, eds. M. Grochowski & D. Weiss, 449–466. München: Otto Sagner.

Weiss, D. 1993. How many sexes are there? Reflections on natural and grammatical gender in contemporary Polish and Russian. In *Studies in Polish Morphology and Syntax*, eds. G. Hentschel & R. Laskowski, 71–105. München: Otto Sagner.

Discourse cohesion in the elicited narratives of early Russian-German sequential bilinguals*

Natalia Gagarina
ZAS Berlin, Germany

This study examines aspects of discourse cohesion in the elicited narratives of early Russian-German sequential bilinguals at age four to six and compares them to the narratives of monolingual Russian-speaking children at the same age as well as to a group of monolingual adults. This examination quantitatively and qualitatively inspects two groups of devices that establish referential and relational cohesion: (anaphoric) pronouns and connectives. The results show that bilinguals of all age groups produce longer utterances and use more word tokens per story in comparison to monolinguals. The younger group of bilinguals demonstrates higher rates of the use of referential and relational cohesive devices. Moreover, in bilingual children the extension of the use of cohesive devices from the local level to the level of more general discourse organization is more pronounced than in monolinguals. This finding is explained as a bilingual advantage over monolinguals reflecting the sensitivity of bilinguals to establishing cohesive ties in discourse. Thus, the results of this study expand evidence showing that advantages of bilinguals over monolinguals in some areas of language and cognitive competence.

Keywords: Russian, German, elicited narratives, early sequential bilinguals, discourse, coherence

---

*   The bilingual data come from the German-Israeli Consortium "Migration and Social Integration" (<http://www.migration.uni-jena.de/>, 8 June 2012) funded by the Bundesministerium für Bildung und Forschung (BMBF). The project *Language Acquisition as a Window to Social Integration among Russian Language Minority Children in Germany and Israel* of this Consortium (Grant No. 01UW0702B) carried out between ZAS, Berlin (PI Natalia Gagarina), and Bar-Ilan University, Tel Aviv (PIs Sharon Armon-Lotem and Joel Walters), dealt with input, language proficiency, social identity and integration of bilingual children between 4 and 6 years old.

1. Introduction

Elicited narratives as a data source provide a researcher with a wide range of linguistic phenomena for investigation. These include phenomena dealing with the more general features of coherent discourse organization belonging to the macrostructural level or specific grammatical and lexical features/categories within/across sentences or word level which belong to the microstructural level. The present contribution deals with the latter, microstructural, level of discourse organization, and examines means of referential and relational discourse cohesion. In particular, the study addresses quantitative and qualitative use of anaphoric pronouns and connectives (conjunctions as a clause-linking tool are the object of investigation) – devices which play a major role in establishing discourse cohesion (cf. Halliday & Hasan 1976). Under cohesion I understand here "the use of explicit linguistic devices to signal relations between sentences and parts of texts" (Connor 1996: 83). These linguistic devices, both lexical and grammatical, establish relationships across sentences and clauses.

The elicited narratives studied here come from the picture stories of bilingual Russian-German children whose home-language is Russian. Regular contact with German began for these children with their admission to kindergarten at age one to three. This group of bilinguals can be defined either as simultaneous or as early successive: a consensus is far from being in sight. Some researchers define children as simultaneous bilinguals, i.e. learners of two first languages, if they acquire these two languages directly from birth (De Houwer 1990, 1996), or if the onset of second language learning falls within the so-called *critical phase*, which is within the first two years (Tracy & Gawlitzek-Maiwald 2000), three years (Montrul 2008), or four years (Genesee 1989, Genesee & Nikoladis 2007), depending on the researcher. Others argue that early successive bilinguals, i.e. child second language learners, start second language contact/learning within the period between four and eight years (Meisel 2009), or four and six years (Montrul 2008), or three and six years (Paradis 2008). Since the issue of defining the type of bilingualism is beyond the scope of the present article, I restrict myself to labeling the investigated population, whose German learning began between the first and third year of life, as early successive bilinguals. These bilingual children didn't acquire prosodic and functional characteristics of the language at an early preverbal age as monolingual German-speaking children do, so that their bilingual acquisition cannot be considered identical to the monolingual L1 acquisition path and timing of German given the impact of early acquired perceptual knowledge on the later development of language (Höhle, Bijeljac-Babic, Herold, Weissenborn & Nazzi 2009, Höhle, Van de Vijver & Weissenborn 2006, Höhle & Weissenborn 2000, 2003).

Although the essentials of the influence of early bilingualism on children's cognitive and linguistic development are not yet fully understood, the growing body of studies on various aspects of bilingualism show advantages of bilingual children in certain areas of linguistic knowledge, such as, to name just a few, working memory (Yang,

Yang, Ceci & Wang 2005, Bialystok, Craik, Grady, Chau, Ishii, Gunji & Pantev 2005), conversational understanding (Siegal, Surian, Matsuo, Geraci, Iozzi, Okumura & Itakura 2010), pragmatics (Siegal, Matsuo & Pond 2007), and metalinguistic abilities (Bialystok 2004).

1.1   Discourse cohesion and coherence in narratives

Cohesive means in narratives participate in establishing discourse coherence and tying parts of discourse elements together into a meaningful whole; discourse coherence functions as "operational goals without whose attainment other discourse goals may be blocked" (De Beaugrande & Dressler 1996: 11), in which case successful communication will fail. Thus, discourse cohesion and coherence are agreed to be "the cornerstone of comprehension" (Graesser, McNamara & Louwerse 2003: 82). Halliday & Hasan (1976) suggest five types of cohesive means in English, namely reference, ellipsis, substitution, lexical cohesion and conjunctions. These devices can be grouped into those establishing the referential ties (the first four types) and those establishing the relational ties (the final type).

In recent decades, cohesive means of establishing referential linking as part of discourse research have been the subject of intensive investigation within various approaches in theoretical linguistics (Ariel 1990, Givón 1992, Strube & Hahn 1999, Van Hoek, Kibrik & Noordman 1999, Kibrik 2000, Ariel 2001, Kehler 2001, Grüning & Kibrik 2005, Benz & Kühnlein 2008) as well as in psycholinguistics and language acquisition research (e.g. Liles 1985, Bamberg 1987, 1994, McCabe & Rollins 1994, Miranda, McCabe & Bliss 1998, Gutiérrez-Clellen 2002). Researchers agree that referential cohesion is based on repeated reference to the same entity throughout discourse. While this repeated reference exhibits language-specific features in its expression (e.g. various types of NPs, pronominals, etc.), the underlying structure of discourse coherence obeys more universal rules of organization. These hierarchically organized rules define the choice of referring expressions (various linguistic devices) according to the principles of relative accessibility of a referent (Ariel 1990, 2004), so that linguistic devices denoting the repeated reference to the same entity change throughout a discourse. For example, while the first mentions of the main protagonists in the picture story (see appendix) are usually NPs and the subsequent mentions are pronouns, English exploits either indefinite or definite NPs and the pronoun it, and Russian uses a bare NP and the pronouns s/he. In particular, one of the main protagonists can be referred to in English as *a raven, the raven, it* and in Russian as *voron* 'raven' and *on* 'he' throughout the story; see example (1):

> (1)   Tam #[1] vorona   ili eshche kto-to,   ili voron.
>   there   crow-NOM.SG or else   somebody or raven-NOM.SG
>   'There is a crow there or somebody else, or a raven.'

---

1.   The sign # stands for a pause in spontaneous speech production.

> On uvidel   rybu   i   chaj   ili
> he see-PFV.PST.M fish-ACC.SG and tea-ACC.SG or
> kruzhku,   i   potom voron
> cup-ACC.SG and then   raven-NOM.SG
> vzjal   rybu,   poletel   na derevo.
> took-PFV.PST.M fish-ACC.SG fly-PFV.PST.M on tree-ACC.SG
> 'It saw a fish and tea or a cup, and then the raven took the fish and flew onto the tree.'

Research on (narrative) discourse in language acquisition discusses the age and pace of the development of pronominal and nominal referential devices as well as other devices that establish an intact discourse. The majority of these studies deal with monolingual language acquisition and provide contradictory evidence regarding, for example, the age of acquisition: on the one hand, in normally developing children discourse is considered to be one of the most prominent domains of later language development (Verhoeven 1993, see also Karmiloff-Smith 1980, Griffith, Ripich & Dastoli 1986, Ripich & Griffith 1988, Adams 2002); on the other hand, evidence of correct referencing has been found in children as young as three and four years old (Bamberg 1987, Bliss, McCabe & Miranda 1998, Hickmann 2003, Gülzow & Gagarina 2007a).

Fewer studies have dealt with the use of connective devices in children's discourse, although they are "crucial to the construction of a coherent integrated representation of a text, because they are used to provide explicit cues to the dependent relations between events and to establish structural coherence" (Cain 2003: 337). In her study on the production and comprehension of coherent and cohesive stories, Cain (2003) found out that monolingual English-speaking children age 6 to 8 more frequently use connectives in more coherent stories (see Cain & Oakhill 1996). Other studies of monolingual English-speaking children have documented a development of the use of interclausal connectives from age 5 to 10 (Shapiro & Hudson 1991, Stenning & Michell 1985).

Relatively little is known about the construction of cohesive discourse in bilingual children. Previous studies have concentrated on the investigation of one discourse *dimension*, dealing with the use of overt/null pronouns or the types/rates of pronominalization in general, or have examined a variety of discourse features (comprehensive multidimensional approach; Bliss et al. 1998, Miranda et al. 1998, Serratrice 2007a, 2007b, Gagarina 2008a, Sorace, Serratrice, Filiaci & Baldo 2009). In a study on Spanish-Italian bilinguals, Sorace et al. (2009) found that in contexts of referent maintenance in Italian, bilingual children use more superfluous overt pronouns than monolingual children. Serratrice (2007a, 2007b) found that English-Italian and Spanish-Italian bilinguals overuse overt subject pronouns in a broad range of contexts. She argues for the structural priming effect, which is applied to the pronouns: "In terms of the cross-structural priming of pronouns, if reference maintenance is structurally encoded by an overt pronoun virtually 100% of the time in English, the language in which the bilingual child receives quantitatively more input, it is likely that in Italian too overt pronouns will have an increased likelihood of being treated as pragmatically appropriate forms for reference maintenance" (Serratrice 2007b: 193). Taking into account the implications of the research on discourse in bilingual children, this contribution aims at the examination of two main devices responsible for establishing referentially and relationally cohesive discourse – pronouns and connectives. The first research question addresses a more general narrative characteristic: What are the differences, if any, in the length and MLUw (Mean Length of Utterance in words) of the mono- vs. bilinguals' narratives? The second question is more specific: How do monolingual and bilingual children diverge in their use of cohesive devices, such as pronouns and connectives and do these cohesive devices correlate to the number of utterances with verbs? Bilingual children are predicted to outperform monolingual children in the use of referential and relational cohesive devices, which might be due to two processes involved in the construction of a discourse: pronouns might be frequently used by bilinguals as a compensation for deficiencies in their vocabulary, and the high use of connectives may enable children to establish a local cohesion between propositions, to which bilinguals are sensitive.

1.2   Some facts about the acquisition of Russian

Studies on the monolingual acquisition of Russian have their origin in the pioneering and seminal study of Gvozdev, who kept a diary of the speech development of his son and thoroughly described the development of the lexicon and grammar on the basis of this diary (Gvozdev 1949). His and subsequent studies have shown that Russian-speaking children speedily acquire non-syncretic verb morphology but need more time to learn noun inflection, although they have already acquired both by age three (Babyonyshev 1993, Kiebzak-Mandera 2000, Gagarina 2003, 2008b, Gagarina & Voeikova 2009).

Referencing in discourse, however, presents a different situation. As previous analyses have shown, Russian-speaking monolingual children are much closer to the adult distribution of pronominals and noun phrases, even in the youngest age group, in comparison to German-speaking monolingual children. From age two and a half a steady approximation trend towards the adult proportions of cohesive referential devices in narrative discourse has been observed (Gülzow & Gagarina 2007a). This early acquisition of the correct use of anaphoric pronouns in narratives is explained by a more transparent form-function mapping within the system of pronouns in Russian as compared to German. As one dimension of discourse cohesion, the rate and type of anaphoric pronominalization in the narrative discourse of Russian-German five-year-old bilingual children was investigated by Gagarina (2008a). The results show that the German narratives of consecutive bilinguals demonstrate a lower pronominalization rate as compared to monolingual German-speaking children's narratives and to their own Russian narratives. Language-specific organization of the pronominal systems as well as language-specific structural features, such as pro-drop, are argued to have an impact on this pronominalization rate in discourse.

A number of recent studies have dealt with the attrition of Russian in bilingual children. Although these studies don't address discourse cohesion directly, their results are of relevance for the present contribution. It is known that the lexicon of bilingual children is poorer in comparison with that of monolingual children (Meng 2001, Cobo-Lewis, Pearson, Eilers & Umbel 2002, Windsor & Kohnert 2004, Klassert, Gagarina & Kauschke 2009, Hoff, Core, Place, Rumiche, Señor & Parra 2012) and that verbs are more robust than nouns in the less dominant or weakening language (see evidence for L1 Russian in Polinsky 2005 and Klassert 2011). While in monolingual children vocabulary steadily develops up to school age and beyond, bilingual children show a loss of already acquired grammatical features and lexical verbs; instead, the light verbs increase with age (see evidence for L1 Russian in Gagarina 2011). In the data investigated here, such a situation might cause poorer verb production, which, in its turn, might lead to less cohesion in narrative discourse and to a high amount of code-switching, interferences, verb errors, etc. On the other hand, a higher level of intact discourse in the narratives may be an effect of bilingualism itself – bilingual children have been shown to have advantages in cognitive and linguistic abilities essential for discourse organization (see the references on page 2).

2.   Method

For this study, the elicited narratives – the so-called Fox Story (Gülzow & Gagarina 2007a, see Appendix) and the Cat Story (Hickmann 2003: 344) – of 60 Russian-German early sequential bilinguals age four to six, of 36 Russian-speaking age-matched monolinguals, and of a control group of monolingual Russian-speaking adults were analyzed (see Table 1). The group of the bilingual population was kept as homogeneous as possible: all the children are first generation immigrants; both parents speak Russian as their mother tongue at home. The onset of regular exposure to German coincided with the admission to kindergarten between age one and three years. All children had had at least one year of exposure to German. Thirteen six-year-old children participated in bilingual programs where they (a) were taught both in Russian and in German in a bilingual school or (b) received support in Russian in after-school courses.

Table 1. Participants in the study and their ages

	Number of participants		Mean age in months (Standard Deviation (SD))	
	Monolinguals	Bilinguals	Monolinguals	Bilinguals
4 year olds	12	20	54 (4.0)	54 (3.1)
5 year olds	12	20	66 (2.1)	67 (2.7)
6 year olds	12	20	74 (1.6)	78 (3.8)
Adults	20			
Total	56	60		

All participants in the study underwent the same experimental procedure during which their narratives were elicited: first, they were shown the six individual pictures of one of the stories, which were placed in the correct sequence in a single, horizontal row in front of the participant. The experimenter allowed the participant to look at the pictures for a minute or two to get the gist of the story. Then the pictures were taken away and were placed anew in a two-picture sequence, so that the participant could see only two pictures in a row step-by-step while s/he was telling the story: picture 1 was placed in front of the participant with the request to start telling the story. When the participant stopped narrating, picture 1 was moved to the left and picture 2 was placed on top of picture 1; then picture 3 was placed next to the stack containing pictures 1 and 2, etc., so that the participants always saw two pictures in order to be able to 'keep track' of the story. The experimenter refrained from asking questions like *What's this?* in order not to provoke naming. Instead, the experimenter encouraged the participants to narrate by asking questions like *What's happening now?* and *How does the story continue?*

The narratives were transcribed according to the CHAT regulations (MacWhinney 2000). Morphological tagging was conducted with a special program developed for Russian spontaneous speech, MORCOMM (Gagarina, Voeikova & Gruzincev 2002), and additional manual coding of the reference coherence was carried out for all main tiers.

3.   Results and discussion

The results will be presented in two steps. In the first step, a general characterization of the elicited narratives, i.e. the length of the narrative in utterances and the MLU in words (MLUw), is given. In the second step, the main set of results is presented: the proportion of the use of anaphoric personal pronouns and connectives (the conjunction word class only in the investigation here) and the contexts of their use.

Table 2 gives a general overview of the length of the stories, measured in the number of utterances and MLUw. Segmenting oral language samples into utterances, turns, etc. and the precise definition of the borders of an utterance create difficulties for those working with spontaneous data. While some suggestions for language segmentation deal with a so-called communication unit, a somewhat shorter segment of oral speech consisting of an independent clause with its modifiers (for a definition see Loban 1976 and Hughes, McGillivray & Schmidek 1997), for this study a measure of dividing spontaneous speech into utterances based on intonational patterns and the length of a pause according to Brown (1973) was used. This way of defining utterance borders was more appropriate because the participants' stories were elicited by means of separate pictures (compiling a story) and the speech was delimited according to a single picture.

As depicted in Table 2, bilingual children decrease the length of their stories from age 4 to 5, while monolingual children increase the length of their stories from 10.75 utterances at age 4 to more than 17 utterances at age 6, so that the difference between

Table 2. An overview of the general narrative features

Age (in years)	Length of story in utterances		MLU in words	
	Bilinguals (SD)	Monolinguals (SD)	Bilinguals (Overall Tokens)	Monolinguals (Overall Tokens)
4	14.05 (5.29)	10.75 (2.24)	5.640 (1596)	4.755 (600)
5	11.85 (4.62)	14.41 (4.21)	4.058 (1584)	5.134 (874)
6	11.95 (3.45)	17.75 (5.98)	6.843[2] (1567)	5.298 (1101)
adults		10.89		6.508 (1772)

bilingual and monolingual children becomes more considerable and reaches a significant level with 6-year-olds (Mann-Whitney-U = 47.000; p = 0.004). The standard deviation decreases in the bilingual group towards 6-year-old children, whereas in the monolingual children it increases.

The MLUw steadily increases in monolingual children, although the sentences are longer in 4- and 6-year-old bilingual children and the overall number of tokens is generally higher in all groups of bilingual children in comparison with monolingual children. Although in monolinguals the number of tokens per story increases from 600 words at age 4 to 1101 words at age 6, this latter number is still lower than in all groups of bilingual children, who use – at all ages – more than 1500 words in their stories. In sum, bilingual children produce elicited narrative with fewer utterances, but these utterances are longer (i.e. contain more tokens per story). This might have various causes: some children might have longer insertions of code-switching elements or have problems in utterance termination and in correct segmentation during narrative production; other children may possess advanced narrative abilities, given that more than half of the 6-year-old bilingual children attended educational programs supporting their L1 Russian. Compare the two sentences of a bilingual child in example (2) and the three short sentences of a monolingual child in example (3).

> (2) I   vot ona sidit,   smotrit,
>   and here she sit-IPFV.PRS.3SG look-IPFV.PRS.3SG
>   kuda zhe   poletish'@*error*[3], chtob
>   where PART fly-PFV.FUT.2SG   in-order-to

---

2.   The MLUw in one outlier, the bilingual child *112, is 3.500. The number in the main table is given without this outlier; the inclusion of the MLUw of this child results in a mean of 5.172.

3.   The child uses the erroneous form *poletish'* (fly-PFV.FUT.2S) instead of the required infinitive *poletet'*.

detkam   kushat'   prinesti.   (*028, bil, 6;6)[4]
child-DAT.PL.DIM eat-IPFV.INF bring-PFV.INF
'And it is sitting, looking where to fly in order to bring children to eat.'

I   vot koshka   na   derevo &pole[5] &po # &hm,
and PART cat-NOM.SG on   tree-ACC.SG
polezla   i   sxvatila   detej.
climb-PFV.PST.F and grab-PFV.PST.F children-ACC.PL
'And now, the cat climbed on the tree and grabbed the children.'

(3) Ptica   xotela   vzjat'   rybu.
     bird-NOM.SG want-IPFV.PST.F take-PFV.INF fish-ACC.SG
     '(The) bird wanted to take the fish.'
     I vzjala.
     and take-PFV.PST.F
     'And took (it).'

     Potom zalezla   na derevo.   (*070, monol, 6;3)
     then   climb-PFV.PST.F on tree-ACC.SG
     'Then it climbed on the tree.'

Example (2) of the bilingual child is representative in the sense that although this child exhibits some disfluency in the narrative production, her sentences are longer and contain more complex elements establishing a coherent discourse: the connectives *chtob* 'in order to' and *i vot* 'and so'. The girl attempts to use the proper verb 'polezla' by uttering *&pole &po,* interrupting herself, inserting a pause # and a discourse filler *hm,* and then finally coming to the proper verb form.

The next analysis presents the use of connectives (see Figure 1) and examines the correlation between verb utterances and the production of coordinating and subordinating structures. Since verbs are considered to be one of the triggering factors for the production of full (and complex) sentences, this type of correlation is a further important indicator of the development of narrative discourse competence. While in bilingual children a significant correlation (Spearman = 0.368*, p = 0.012) was found between the increase in the use of utterances with lexical verbs and of connectives, in monolingual children this correlation is highly significant (Spearman = 0.367**, p = 0.007).

Connectives join parts of discourse/text on a relational cohesion level and don't represent one word class *per se*, but include prepositional phrases and the word classes of conjunctions, particles, and adverbs. For the present study (a) the connectives belonging to the class of coordinating conjunctions: *i* 'and', *a* 'and/but', *no* 'but' and their 'derivations' *i/a potom,* 'and then', *i vot* 'and here then' (Tribushinina, Gagarina & Valcheva forthcoming), and (b) the connectives establishing subordinating relations:

---

4.   6;6 defines the age of the child and means 6 years and 6 months.

5.   The sign & in front of a word means that this word is not calculated as part of a sentence and is not tagged with morphological categories.

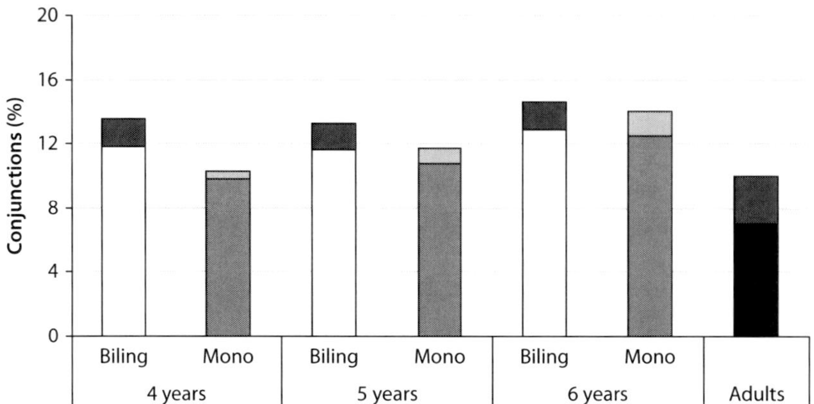

Figure 1. Conjunctions (connectives) out of all tokens. Upper parts of the bars: connectives as subordinating conjunctions; lower colored parts of the bars: connectives as coordinating conjunctions

chtoby 'so that', *esli* 'if', *kogda* 'when', *kuda* 'where', *potomu (chto)* 'because', etc., were considered.

As Figure 1 demonstrates, the two groups of children use the coordinating conjunctions from early on, and in monolingual children its amount even increases with age. While the difference in the use of coordinating conjunctions between the children and the adults is not significant at the beginning, it reaches a level of high significance with 6-year-olds (Mann-Whitney-U = 58.00; $p < 0.05$). Such use of coordinating connectives can be explained by the growing awareness of children of coherent discourse, so that they develop a strategy to help them connect the parts of the story/ utterances they produce: *and the bird flies, and it saw the fox, and it jumped*, or *it saw the bird and then it took, and then the dog came, and then it ran away* (cf. Bamberg 1987 on the fact that children at age six reach adult performance in narrative discourse). The bilingual children at all ages use more coordinating conjunctions overall than their monolingual peers. A more detailed look at the group of coordinating connectives reveals that the clear majority of them is *i* 'and': 65% for bilinguals and 51% for monolinguals. This overuse is due to the non-target children's production. Examples 2 to 5 give a taste of the frequent use of *i* 'and' (also *i potom* 'and then'), which begins a large number of clauses. The overused *i* 'and' is a typical device to establish a tie to subsequent propositions and to keep the discourse moving as in examples 4 and 5. It might also function as a marker of topicalization of an action, as in example 3 *hotela vzjat' rybu. I vzjala* 'wanted to take the fish. And took'.

The use of subordinating conjunctions in all groups of children is lower than in adults, though bilinguals of all ages produce a higher number of these conjunctions than monolinguals. This poor, but not surprising, production might have its roots in their frequency in adult speech and the functional domain they cover. The subordinating conjunctions are very infrequent in the adult narratives, less than 4% of all tokens. Since frequency has been shown by numerous studies to have an impact on child language acquisition (Tomasello 2003, Bybee 2007, Gülzow & Gagarina 2007b), this might partially explain the findings. Not only do children seldom hear subordinating conjunctions, but they also have to master their more complicated functional domain, since this type of conjunction doesn't express purely additive or linear sequential relations, but deals with more complex semantic relations such as causality, which belong to the domain of later language acquisition (Bloom, Laheya, Hooda, Liftera & Fiessa 1980, Peterson & McCabe 1987).

The final analysis provides an overview of the pronominalization rate as one of the cohesive devices in discourse. Figure 2 indicates that bilingual children overuse anaphoric personal pronouns in the two early groups (Mann-Whitney-U = 65.00; p < 0.05) and slowly approach the adult measures, while monolingual children already use the target number of pronouns by age three (this latter finding for monolingual children has been discussed in detail in Gülzow & Gagarina 2007a).

A closer look at the contexts in which bilingual children produce pronouns reveals that children adopt the tactic of *repeated structures:* once the child compiles a structure, he applies it several times in his storytelling, as in example (4). During such repetition the topic maintenance in discourse might be impaired.

(4) Potom ona, &hm, sidela,   sidela.
     then   she   sit-IPVF.PST.F sit-IPFV.PST.F
     'Then it was sitting, sitting.'

     i   potom ona, &hm, lezla,   lezla.   (*011, bil, 4;3)
     and then   she   climb-IPFV.PST.F climb-IPFV.PST.F
     'And then it was climbing, climbing.

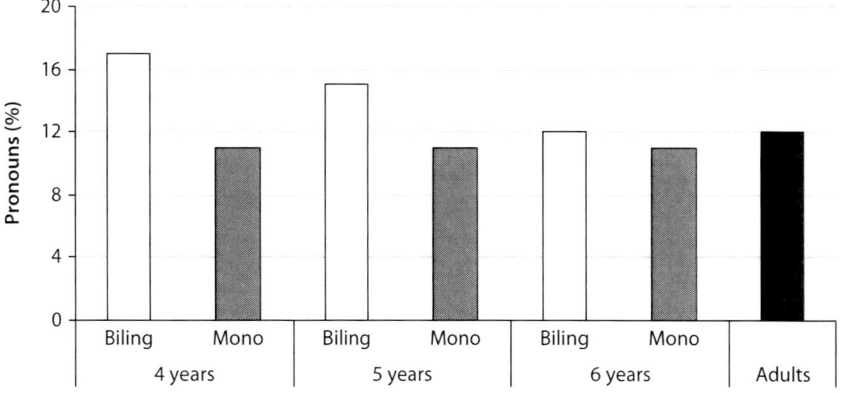

Figure 2. Pronouns out of all tokens

Another explanation of the overuse of pronouns might be rooted in the bilingual lexicon problems: as was mentioned above, numerous studies have demonstrated that bilingual children exhibit poorer verb vocabulary than monolingual children. It may be the case that as a consequence of such poor lexical skills, bilingual children use pronouns; their lexical abilities increase towards the older group, so that the bilinguals augment the number of NPs. Finally, the influence of non-pro-drop German is seen in the too frequent use of overt subject pronouns in sentences in which zero pronouns are admitted in Russian. In example (5) the child uses the repetition of the structure *i ona ego* + *Verb* 'and she it + Verb':

(5) I   ona ego vzjala   v rot,
     and she him take-PFV.PST.F in mouth-ACC.SG
     i   ona ego xotela   otnesti   obratno   (*022, bil, 4;9).
     and she him want-IPFV.PST.F bring-PFV.INF back
     'And it (the bird) took it (the fish) into the mouth and wanted to bring it back.'

A closer look at the type of anaphoric pronominalization (Table 3) shows that, in comparison with the other groups, the youngest group of bilingual children most frequently (a) uses pronominal anaphors referring to the subject, 57.1%, and (b) establishes cohesion on the local discourse level, i.e. uses anaphors referring to an antecedent in a previous proposition, 38.6% (for the definition of a proposition or a communication unit, see Hughes et al. 1997).

Bilingual children develop the ability to use referential cohesive devices with age: towards the group of 5-year-olds the number of anaphors connecting two neighboring propositions decreases by approx. 30% and the means of longer-distance cohesion (two to five propositions backwards) develop. Monolingual children don't show crucial changes in their abilities to referentially connect distant propositions: in the two older groups, around 32% of pronominal anaphors refer to an antecedent in a previous proposition.

Table 3. Pronouns: all pronouns referring to the subject (% of tokens out of all pronoun tokens) and all anaphoric pronouns referring to an antecedent in a previous proposition (% of tokens out of all pronoun tokens)

	Subject pronouns		Anaphors referring to an antecedent in a previous proposition	
	Bilinguals	Monolinguals	Bilinguals	Monolinguals
4-year-olds	57.1	18.9	38.6	27.0
5-year-olds	39.2	33.7	29.7	32.7
6-year-olds	45.8	33.9	30.7	32.3
Adults		35.5		69.5

A note on code-switching should be added. The narratives were elicited in a strict one-language-modus and the experimenter was a native speaker of either language in order to decrease the number of instances of code-switching: in all the bilingual data, the amount of code-switching comes to 89 instances, which is 0.8% of all tokens. The clear majority of this code-switching is found in referring to the main protagonists of the story: German *Hund* 'dog' for *sobaka*, *Katze* 'cat' for *koshka*, *Vogel* 'bird' for *prica*, *Schwanz* 'tail' for *hvost*; in the youngest group, for example, code-switching in these nouns constitutes 83% of all instances of code-switching.

4. Conclusion

To recapitulate, the present contribution quantitatively and qualitatively inspected two cohesive devices participating in the establishment of referential and relational discourse coherence: anaphoric pronouns and connectives. The empirical material for this study consisted of the elicited narratives of Russian-German bilinguals age four to six, which were compared with the narratives of Russian-speaking adults and mono-lingual children in the same age range. The results show that the youngest and the oldest groups of bilingual children produced longer utterances than their monolingual peers and used more word tokens per story, although the length of their stories (measured in the overall number of utterances) was smaller. Furthermore, as far as the use of referential and relational cohesive devices in the narratives is concerned, the youngest group of bilingual children used them considerably more often than the monolingual children at all ages. The qualitative analyses of relational devices showed that bilingual children, already in the youngest group, outperform monolinguals in their use of subordinating conjunctions: they produce more diverse conjunctions and apply them to a greater variety of linguistic structures. This finding may be explained as reflecting the sensitivity of bilinguals to establishing cohesive ties in discourse. Since bilingual children, although having been shown to have more restricted vocabulary resources, use more devices to link sentences and propositions in discourse; they can be seen as being more proficient in matters of microstructural discourse organization and more sensitive to the means of discourse coherence. This extends the areas in which bilingual children have already been shown to have advantages over monolin-guals (see Section 1), such as: working memory (Yang et al. 2005, Bialystok et al. 2005), pragmatics (Siegal et al. 2007), metalinguistic abilities (Bialystok 2001, 2004), conver-sational understanding (Siegal et al. 2010), and attentional and executive control pro-cesses (Carlson & Meltzoff 2008).

The use of referential devices provides somewhat more controversial results. While the youngest bilingual children use pronouns referring to the subject more often than monolinguals, this situation becomes more comparable in the two older groups. The youngest bilingual children show the highest proportion of pronominal anaphors which refer to an antecedent in a previous proposition, thus showing the early mastering of the use of cohesive devices on a microlevel of discourse structure. In sum, the findings of this study add to the areas of language and cognitive competence in which bilingual children have been shown to have advantages over monolinguals (Diamond 2010) and bring evidence of earlier abilities of these children to connect parts of discourse in a meaningful text by the referential and relational devices at their disposal.

Hopefully, further studies might resolve the controversy regarding the advantages vs. disadvantages of bilingualism that are currently the topic of discussion. On the one hand, research has shown that bilinguals "develop a specific type of cognitive benefit during infancy, and bilingualism offers some protection against symptoms of Alzheimer's dementia in old people" (Diamond 2010: 332); on the other hand, the public discussion often points to the disadvantages of many bilingual children with migration backgrounds.

Appendix

The Fox Story

References

Adams, C. 2002. Practitioner review: The assessment of language pragmatics. *Journal of Child Psychology and Psychiatry* 43: 973–987.

Ariel, M. 1990. *Accessing Noun Phrase Antecedents*. London: Routledge.

Ariel, M. 2001. Accessibility theory: An overview. In *Text Representation: Linguistic and Psycholinguistics Aspects* (Human Cognitive Processing 8), eds. T. Sanders, J. Schilperoord & W. Spooren, 29–87. Amsterdam: John Benjamins.

Ariel, M. 2004. Accessibility marking: Discourse functions, discourse profiles, and processing cues. *Discourse Processes* 37: 91–116.

Babyonyshev, M. 1993. The acquisition of Russian case. In *Papers on Case and Agreement* II (MIT Working Papers in Linguistics 19), ed. C. Phillips, 1–44. Cambridge MA: MIT.

Bamberg, M. G. 1987. *The Acquisition of Narratives*. Berlin: Mouton de Gruyter.

Bamberg, M. G. 1994. Development of linguistic forms: German. In *Relating Events in Narrative: A Crosslinguistic Developmental Study*, eds. R. A. Berman & D. I. Slobin, 189–237. Hillsdale NJ: Lawrence Erlbaum Associates.

Benz, A. & P. Kühnlein, eds. 2008. *Constraints in Discourse* (Pragmatics & Beyond New Series 172). Amsterdam: John Benjamins.

Bialystok, E. 2001. Metalinguistic aspects of bilingual processing. *Annual Review of Applied Linguistics* 21: 169–181.

Bialystok, E. 2004. The impact of bilingualism on language and literacy development. In *Handbook of Bilingualism*, eds. T. K. Bhatia & W. C. Ritchie, 577–601. Oxford: Blackwell.

Bialystok, E., F. I. M. Craik, C. Grady, W. Chau, R. Ishii, A. Gunji & C. Pantev. 2005. Effect of bilingualism on cognitive control in the Simon task: Evidence from MEG. *NeuroImage* 24: 40–49.

Bliss, L. S., A. McCabe & A. E. Miranda. 1998. Narrative assessment profile: Discourse analysis for school-age children. *Journal of Communication Disorders* 31: 347–363.

Bloom, L., M. Laheya, L. Hooda, K. Liftera & K. Fiessa. 1980. Complex sentences: Acquisition of syntactic connectives and the semantic relations they encode. *Journal of Child Language* 7: 235–261.

Brown, R. 1973. *A First Language: The Early Stages*. Cambridge MA: Harvard University Press.

Bybee, J. 2007. *Frequency of Use and the Organization of Language*. Oxford: OUP.

Cain, K. 2003. Text comprehension and its relation to coherence and cohesion in children's fictional narratives. *British Journal of Developmental Psychology* 21: 335–351.

Cain, K. & J. Oakhill. 1996. The nature of the relationship between comprehension skill and the ability to tell a story. *British Journal of Developmental Psychology* 14: 187–201.

Carlson, S. M. & A. N. Meltzoff. 2008. Bilingual experience and executive functioning in young children. *Developmental Science* 11: 282–298.

Cobo-Lewis, A., B. Z. Pearson, R. E. Eilers & V. C. Umbel. 2002. Effects of bilingualism and bilingual education on oral and written English skills: A multifactor study of standardized test outcomes. In *Language and Literacy in Bilingual Children*, eds. D. K. Oller & R. E. Eilers, 43–63. Clevedon: Multilingual Matters.

Connor, U. R. 1996. *Contrastive Rhetoric: Cross-cultural Aspects of Second Language Writing*. Cambridge: CUP.

De Beaugrande, R. & W. U. Dressler. 1996. *Introduction to Text Linguistics*. London: Longman.

De Houwer, A. 1990. *The Acquisition of Two Languages from Birth: A Case Study*. Cambridge: CUP.

De Houwer, A. 1996. Bilingual language acquisition. In *The Handbook of Child Language*, eds. P. Fletcher & B. MacWhinney, 219–250. Oxford: Blackwell.

Diamond, J. 2010. The benefits of multilingualism. *Science* 330: 332–333.

Gagarina, N. 2003. The early verb development and demarcation of stages in three Russian-speaking children. In *Development of Verb Inflection in First Language Acquisition: A Cross-linguistic Perspective*, eds. D. Bittner, W. U. Dressler & M. Kilani-Schoch, 131–169. Berlin: Mouton de Gruyter.

Gagarina, N. 2008a. Anaphoric pronominal reference in Russian and German narratives: Bilingual and monolingual settings. *Zeitschrift für Slawistik* 53: 326–338.

Gagarina, N. 2008b. *Становление грамматических категорий русского глагола в детской речи (Stanovlenije grammatičeskih kategorij russkogo glagola v detskoj reči* 'First language acquisition of verb categories in Russian'). St. Petersburg: Nauka.

Gagarina, N. 2011. Acquisition and loss of L1 in a Russian-German bilingual child: A case study. In *Путь в язык: Одноязычие и двуязычие (Put' v jazyk: Odnojazyčije i dvujazyčije* 'The path to language: Mono- and bilingualism'), ed. S. N. Cejtlin, 137–163. Moscow: Jazyki slavjanskih kul'tur.

Gagarina, N. & M. Voeikova. 2009. The acquisition of case and number in Russian. In *Cross-linguistic Approaches to the Acquisition of Case and Number*, eds. U. Stephany & M. Voeikova, 179–215. Berlin: Mouton de Gruyter.

Gagarina, N., M. Voeikova & S. Gruzincev. 2002. New version of morphological coding for the speech production of Russian children (in the framework of CHILDES). In *Investigations into Formal Slavic linguistics: Contributions of the Fourth European Conference on Formal Description of Slavic Languages*, eds. P. Kosta, J. Blaszczak, J. Frazek, L. Geist & M. Zygis, 243–258. Frankfurt: Peter Lang.

Genesee, F. 1989. Early bilingual development: One language or two? *Journal of Child Language* 16: 161–179.

Genesee, F. & E. Nikoladis. 2007. Bilingual first language acquisition. In *Handbook of Language Development*, eds. E. Hoff & M. Shatz, 324–342. Oxford: Blackwell.

Givón, T. 1992. The grammar of referential coherence as mental processing instructions. *Linguistics* 30: 5–55.

Graesser, A., D. McNamara & M. Louwerse. 2003. What do readers need to learn in order to process coherence relations in narrative and expository text? In *Rethinking Reading Comprehension*, eds. A. P. Sweet & C. E. Snow, 82–98. New York NY: Guilford.

Griffith, P., D. Ripich & S. Dastoli. 1986. Story structure, cohesion, and propositions in story recalls by learning disabled and nondisabled children. *Journal of Psycholinguistic Research* 15: 539–555.

Grüning, A. & A. A. Kibrik. 2005. Modelling referential choice in discourse: A cognitive calculative approach and a neural networks approach. In *Anaphora Processing: Linguistic, Cognitive and Computational Modelling*, eds. A. Branco, T. McEnery & R. Mitkov, 163–198. Amsterdam: John Benjamins.

Gülzow, I. & N. Gagarina. 2007a. Noun phrases, pronouns and anaphoric reference in young children narratives. In *Intersentential Pronominal Reference in Child and Adult Language: Proceedings of the Conference on Intersentential Pronominal Reference in Child and Adult Language (ZAS Papers in Linguistics 48)*, eds. D. Bittner & N. Gagarina, 203–223. Berlin: ZAS.

Gülzow, I. & N. Gagarina. 2007b. Introduction. In *Frequency Effects in Language Acquisition,* eds. I. Gülzow & N. Gagarina, 1–11. Berlin: Mouton de Gruyter.

Gutiérrez-Clellen, V. F. 2002. Narratives in two languages: Assessing performance of bilingual children. *Language and Education* 13: 175–197.

Gvozdev, A. N. 1949. *Формирование у ребёнка грамматического строя русского языка* (*Formirovanije u rebjonka grammatičeskogo stroja russkogo jazyka* 'The construction of the grammatical system by a Russian speaking child'). Moscow: Akademija Pedagogicheskih Nauk RSFSR.

Halliday, M. A. K. & R. Hasan. 1976. *Cohesion in English*. London: Longman.

Hickmann, M. 2003. *Children's Discourse: Person, Space, and Time across Languages*. Cambridge: CUP.

Hoff, E., C. Core, S. Place, R. Rumiche, M. Señor & M. Parra. 2012. Dual language exposure and early bilingual development. *Journal of Child Language* 39: 1–27.

Höhle, B., R. Bijeljac-Babic, B. Herold, J. Weissenborn & T. Nazzi. 2009. Language specific prosodic preferences during the first half year of life: Evidence from German and French infants. *Infant Behavior and Development* 32: 262–274.

Höhle, B., R. van de Vijver & J. Weissenborn. 2006. Word processing at 19 months at its relation to language performance at 30 months: A retrospective analysis of data from German learning children. *Advances in Speech and Language Pathology* 8: 356–363.

Höhle, B. & J. Weissenborn. 2000. Lauter Laute? Lautsegmente und Silben in der Sprachperzeption und im Spracherwerb. In *Deutsche Grammatik in Theorie und Praxis*, eds. R. Thieroff, M. Tamrat, N. Fuhrhop & O. Teuber, 1–11. Tübingen: Niemeyer.

Höhle, B. & J. Weissenborn. 2003. German-learning infants' ability to detect unstressed closed-class elements in continuous speech. *Developmental Science* 6: 122–127.

Hughes, D., L. McGillivray & M. Schmidek. 1997. *Guide to Narrative Language: Procedures for Assessment*. Eau Claire WI: Thinking Publications.

Karmiloff-Smith, A. 1980. *Psychological Processes Underlying Pronominalization and Non-Pronominalization in Children's Connected Discourse*. Chicago IL: Chicago Linguistic Society.

Kehler, A. 2001. *Coherence, Reference, and the Theory of Grammar*. Stanford CA: CSLI.

Kibrik, A. A. 2000. Cognitive discourse analysis: Some results. In *Cognition in Language Use: Selected Papers from the 7th International Pragmatics Conference*, ed. E. Németh, 164–180. Antwerp: International Pragmatics Association.

Kiebzak-Mandera, D. 2000. Formation of the verb system in Russian children. *Psychology of Language and Communication* 4: 27–46.

Klassert, A. 2011. *Lexikalische Fähigkeiten bilingualer Kinder mit Migrationshintergrund: Eine Studie zum Benennen von Nomen und Verben im Russischen und Deutschen*. PhD dissertation, Philipps University of Marburg.

Klassert, A., N. Gagarina & C. Kauschke. 2009. Lexikalische Fähigkeiten bilingualer Kinder. In *Schwerpunktthema: Ein Kopf – zwei Sprachen: Mehrsprachigkeit in Forschung und Therapie. Tagungsband zum 2. Herbsttreffen Patholinguistik* (Spektrum Patholinguistik 2), eds. J. Heide, S. Hanne, O.-C. Brandt, T. Fritzsche & M. Wahl, 113–119. Potsdam: Universitätsverlag.

Liles, B. Z. 1985. Cohesion in the narratives of normal and language-disordered children. *Journal of Speech and Hearing Research* 28: 123–133.

Loban, W. 1976. *Language Development: Kindergarten through Grade Twelve* (NCTE research report 18). Urbana IL: National Council of Teachers of English.

MacWhinney, B. 2000. *The CHILDES Project: Tools for Analyzing Talk*. Mahwah NJ: Lawrence Erlbaum Associates.

McCabe, A. & P. Rollins. 1994. Assessment of preschool narrative skills: Prerequisite for literacy. *American Journal of Speech and Language Pathology* 4: 45–56.

Meisel, J. M. 2009. Second language acquisition in early childhood. *Zeitschrift für Sprachwissenschaft* 28: 5–34.

Meng, K. 2001. *Russlanddeutsche Sprachbiografien: Untersuchung zur sprachlichen Integration von Aussiedlerfamilien.* Tübingen: Narr.

Miranda, A. E., A. McCabe & L. S. Bliss. 1998. Jumping around and leaving things out: A profile of the narrative abilities of children with specific language impairment. *Applied Psycholinguistics* 19: 647–667.

Montrul, S. 2008. *Incomplete Acquisition in Bilingualism: Re-examining the Age Factor* (Studies in Bilingualism 39). Amsterdam: John Benjamins.

Paradis, J. 2008. Are simultaneous and early sequential bilingual acquisition fundamentally different? Paper presented at Models of Interaction in Bilinguals, University of Wales, Bangor, UK, 25 October 2008.

Peterson, C. & A. McCabe. 1987. The connective 'and': Do older children use it less as they learn other connectives? *Journal of Child Language* 14: 375–381.

Polinsky, M. 2005. Word class distinctions in an incomplete grammar. In *Perspectives on Language and Language Development*, eds. D. D. Ravid & H. B.-Z. Shyldkrot, 419–436. Dordrecht: Springer.

Ripich, D. & P. Griffith. 1988. Narrative abilities of children with learning disabilities and non-disabled children: Story structure, cohesion, and propositions. *Journal of Learning Disabilities* 21: 165–173.

Serratrice, L. 2007a. Cross-linguistic influence in the interpretation of anaphoric and cataphoric pronouns in English-Italian bilingual children. *Bilingualism: Language and Cognition* 10: 225–238.

Serratrice, L. 2007b. Null and overt subjects at the syntax-discourse interface: Evidence from monolingual and bilingual acquisition. In *The Acquisition of Romance Languages: Selected Papers from The Romance Turn* II, eds. S. Baauw, J. van Kampen & M. Pinto, 181–200. Utrecht: LOT.

Shapiro, L. R. & J. A. Hudson. 1991. Tell me a make-believe story: Coherence and cohesion in young children's picture-elicited narratives. *Developmental Psychology* 27: 960–974.

Siegal, M., A. Matsuo & C. Pond. 2007. Bilingualism and cognitive development: Evidence from scalar implicatures. In *Proceedings of the Eighth Tokyo Conference on Psycholinguistics (TCP 2007)*, ed. Y. Otsu, 265–280. Tokio: Hituzi.

Siegal, M., L. Surian, A. Matsuo, A. Geraci, L. Iozzi, Y. Okumura & S. Itakura. 2010. Bilingualism accentuates children's conversational understanding. *PlosOne.* <http://www.plosone.org/article/info:doi%2F10.1371%2Fjournal.pone.0009004> (10 February 2012).

Sorace, A., L. Serratrice, F. Filiaci & M. Baldo. 2009. Discourse conditions on subject pronoun realization: Testing the linguistic intuitions of older bilingual children. *Lingua* 119: 460–477.

Stenning, K. & L. Michell. 1985. Learning how to tell a good story: The development of content and language in children's telling of one tale. *Discourse Processes* 8: 261–279.

Strube, M. & U. Hahn. 1999. Functional centering: Grounding referential coherence in information structure. *Computational Linguistics* 25: 309–344.

Tomasello, M. 2003. *Constructing a Language: A Usage-based Theory of Language Acquisition.* Cambridge MA: Harvard University Press.

Tracy, R. & I. Gawlitzek-Maiwald. 2000. Bilingualismus in der frühen Kindheit. In *Sprachentwicklung*, ed. H. Grimm, 495–536. Göttingen: Hogrefe.

Tribushinina, E., N. Gagarina & E. Valcheva. Forthcoming. Acquisition of additive connectives by Russian-German bilinguals: A usage-based approach. In *Usage-based Approaches to Language Acquisition and Language Teaching* (Studies on Language Acquisition), eds. J. Evers-Vermeul, L. Raiser & E. Tribushinina. Berlin: Mouton de Gruyter.

Van Hoek, K., A. A. Kibrik & L. Noordman, eds. 1999. *Discourse Studies in Cognitive Linguistics* (Current Issues in Linguistic Theory 176). Amsterdam: John Benjamins.

Verhoeven, L. 1993. Acquisition of narrative skills in a bilingual context. In *Current Issues in European Second Language Acquisition Research*, eds. B. Kettemann & W. Wieden, 307–323. Tübingen: Narr.

Windsor, J. & K. Kohnert. 2004. In search for common ground. Part I: Lexical performance by linguistically diverse learners. *Journal of Speech, Language and Hearing Research* 47: 877–890.

Yang, H., S. Yang, S. J. Ceci & Q. Wang. 2005. Effects of bilinguals' controlled-attention on working memory and recognition. In *Proceedings of the 4th International Symposium on Bilingualism*, eds. J. Cohen, K. T. McAlister, K. Rolstad & J. MacSwan, 2401–2404. Somerville MA: Cascadilla Press.

German segments in the speech
of German-Spanish bilingual children[*]

Aleksandra Żaba and Conxita Lleó
University of Hamburg, Germany

The production of segments in a first language (L1) has been reported to be different in bilingual children as compared with monolingual children. Often, consonants involve a delay in the bilinguals' data (see, e.g., Lleó & Rakow 2006), whereas vowels are usually not associated with any delay (see Kehoe 2002). The present work shows new data that suggest that consonants, in this case the ones involved in the German voicing contrast (which is neutralized in final position), contribute to a delay in bilingual acquisition. A vowel, specifically, German underlying schwa, did not cause any delay. In fact, target-like production of schwa seems to have been subject to acceleration in the case of the bilinguals.

Keywords: German, Spanish, bilingual acquisition, voicing contrast, final devoicing, phonotactics, voicing into closure, underlying schwa, markedness, frequency

1. Introduction

Previous research on language acquisition suggests various differences in the way bilingual vs. monolingual children acquire the segments of a first language (L1) (see, e.g., Kehoe 2002, Kehoe, Lleó & Rakow 2004, Lleó & Rakow 2005, and Lleó & Rakow 2006 for production; Pallier, Bosch & Sebastián-Gallés 1997 and Ramon-Casas, Swingley, Bosch & Sebastián-Gallés 2009 for perception). For example, in a study by Lleó & Rakow (2006), German-Spanish bilingual children aged 2;0 to 2;3 did not assimilate the place of articulation of coda nasals within words to the same degree as monolinguals did, and across words bilinguals hardly did any assimilation, whereas

* The monolingual data used for the analyses contained herein stem from the project PAIDUS and the bilingual data from the project TPE3 of the Research Center on Multilingualism at the University of Hamburg. The present study has been carried out within the Research Center on Multilingualism, supported by the *Deutsche Forschungsgemeinschaft* (German Research Foundation), to which we extend our thanks for financial support.

monolinguals assimilated target-like at about 90%. Also German long vowels show a delay of several months in the production of speech in the German-Spanish bilingual condition (Kehoe 2002). And consonants in coda position in Spanish are acquired earlier by German-Spanish bilingual children than by monolingual Spanish children (Lleó, Kuchenbrandt, Kehoe & Trujillo 2003).

Production patterns in bilingual L1 acquisition may be accounted for by the relative markedness levels of segments (as well as by their relative complexity, i.e., sounds involving allophony and/or allomorphy, considered to be complex, may be delayed). In general, unmarked structures have been associated with early acquisition, and marked ones with late acquisition. This effect of markedness seems especially prominent in bilingual populations. As an example, Kehoe, Trujillo & Lleó (2001) found that German-Spanish bilingual children lagged behind monolingual German children in their production of voice onset time (VOT), attributed to the fact that both German and Spanish contain marked VOT values: German has positive VOT values (and aspiration) in its voiceless stops, while Spanish voiced stops are characterized by prevoicing. See also Lleó (2002) for the prosodic domain. Marked structures thus may incur a delay in bilingual acquisition, in particular if only one of the two languages of the bilingual offers evidence for their acquisition. Although markedness may be a source of delay, high frequency may compensate, as in the case of the acceleration of coda production in Spanish in German-Spanish bilinguals (Lleó et al. 2003), codas being present in both languages and being extremely frequent in German.

The present article reports on data that provide further insight into the production of German consonantal and vocalic segments by German-Spanish bilingual and monolingual German children. The segments in focus are a) stops involved in the German voicing contrast, which is neutralized in syllable-final position, and b) German schwa.

The main questions we asked are whether German-Spanish bilingual children produce the stops involved in the German voicing contrast and their concomitant unmarked final voiceless, as well as posttonic (underlying) schwa at the same time as, later, or earlier than monolingual German children. Spanish does not impose a neutralization of the voicing contrast in final position. Also, Spanish does not have central vowels such as schwa. It was therefore interesting to focus on children acquiring both German and a language with different voicing values for stops in final position and without schwa, and to investigate when these bilingual children produced the respective sounds target-like. Further, our goal was to shed light on whether relative markedness would roughly correspond to relative learnability, in that unmarked segments would be acquired early, while marked ones would be acquired late(r), in particular in the case of the bilingual children. Specifically, final voiceless may not incur a delay in the bilinguals due to its low markedness, in spite of the fact that there is no systematic final devoicing in Spanish. Further, schwa may be produced later by the bilinguals. This prediction is based on the special phonological status of schwa, in that it lacks specification (on the prosodic or the segmental levels; see Kager 1989, Van Oostendorp 1998, 2000 and Section 3.1), a fact that in Kehoe & Lleó's (2003) study was associated with a delay in the production of schwa by monolingual children (relative to other sounds).

2. The German voicing contrast

2.1   Theoretical description and acquisition

In German, obstruents contrast in voicing initially (e.g. *Bein* [bajn] and *Pein* [pʰajn]), and medially (e.g. *Bundes* [bundəs] and *buntes* [buntəs]), but not finally, where only voiceless obstruents occur (e.g. *Bund* [bunt] and *bunt* [bunt]). That is, in final position, the contrast is neutralized. This restriction can be described as a process of final devoicing, in which an underlyingly voiced obstruent becomes voiceless in syllable final position, or by the traditional notion of phonotactics: in final position, only voiceless obstruents are permitted. In, e.g., Optimality Theory terms, such situations are expressed as the outranking of the markedness constraints that militate against voicing in codas over the faithfulness constraints that protect voicing (Hayes 2004); i.e., voiced obstruents in final position are marked.

In Spanish, the contrast between voiceless (unaspirated) and voiced appears mainly in word-initial position, and word-medially after a nasal; otherwise, voiced stops in most word-medial positions are produced as spirants [β, ð, ɣ]. In final position, German only allows voiceless stops, often produced as aspirated, too. Spanish has a preference for open syllables (72% of all syllables are open, according to Delattre 1965: 42), the voiced coronal /d/ being the only stop in word final position; medially the three places of articulation, labial, coronal and dorsal, are allowed. The inventory of Spanish coda stops in word-final position is thus /d/, and the inventory of fricatives /s, θ/. The underlyingly voiced stop /d/ in word-final coda is only produced as such in highly formal contexts, and it receives various realizations. It either undergoes deletion, is produced as a voiced or voiceless interdental fricative, or as a voiceless stop. The most frequent voiceless obstruent in the coda is /s/. We thus see that Spanish, although it does have a medial contrast and mostly voiceless obstruents in final position, does not enforce final devoicing or the corresponding phonotactic restriction as systematically as German does. German-Spanish bilingual children need to acquire the German voicing contrast and neutralization, with evidence for it only in one of their two languages (German), plus they must acquire the voicing contrast of Spanish. Based on these two facts, it is possible that bilinguals are delayed in their target-like production of the German voicing system.

Moreover, in the position of syllable coda, voiceless obstruents are considered relatively unmarked and voiced obstruents relatively marked (Jakobson 1941/1968). Among the reasons adduced for markedness is that maintaining voicing in codas is difficult for aerodynamic reasons (see, e.g., Chomsky & Halle 1968, Westbury & Keating 1986). There is a great deal of literature on L1 acquisition and second language (L2) learning suggesting that structures that are unmarked are produced early in acquisition,

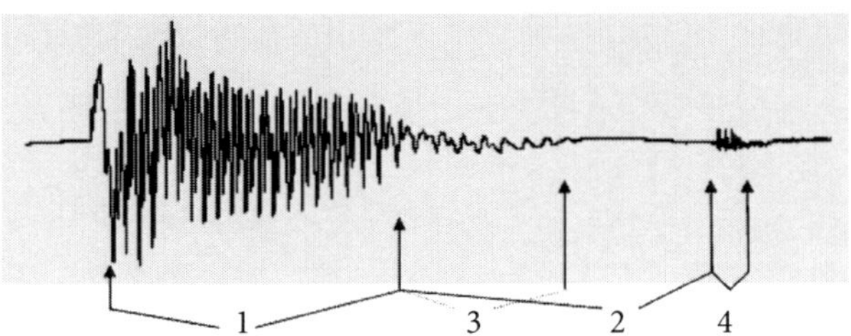

Figure 1. Waveform of stop (partially devoiced), preceded by a vowel (from Smith et al. 2009)

whereas marked structures are produced late (see, e.g., Jakobson 1941/1968, Montes Giraldo 1971, Ferguson & Farwell 1975, Macken 1978, Hawkins 1987, Levelt 1994, Pater 1997 for L1 acquisition; and Eckman 1977, Anderson 1987, Benson 1988, and many others for L2 learning). Unmarkedness may cause bilinguals to produce the German contrast and to only produce voiceless in final position, i.e., to not be delayed in their production of the medial contrast and final voiceless.

2.2   The study

In the present article, we investigate whether the medial contrast and the phonotactic restriction on voicing in final position is produced target-like earlier than, later than, or at the same time by German-Spanish bilinguals as by monolingual German children. Voicing in medial and final positions was operationalized as proportion voicing into closure (ViC) (following Smith, Hayes-Harb, Bruss & Harker 2009) and calculated as the percentage of glottal pulsing out of a given stop closure, both of which were measured with Praat (Boersma & Weenink 1992ff). Figure 1 illustrates this method. The vowel is represented in 1, the closure of the stop in 2, ViC in 3, and the duration of the consonant release is represented in 4. For the present study, 2 and 3 were measured, and the percent of 3 out of 2 was calculated. That is, proportion ViC was calculated as a percentage of the closure duration.

2.2.1   *Participants*
Our study measured the production of the voicing contrast (in medial position) and final devoicing in the recordings of the spontaneous speech of 4 German-Spanish bilingual children from the corpus of project TPE3 at the Research Center on Multilingualism at the University of Hamburg (aliases: Jens, Manuel, Nils, and Simon). The results were compared to the production of 4 monolingual German children from the corpus of project PAIDUS at the same Research Center (aliases: Britta, Johannes, Marion, and Thomas). The ages investigated were 1;5–3;0, divided into two age phases: 1;5–2;2 and 2;3–3;0.

All bilingual children had Spanish-speaking mothers and German-speaking fathers. The main care person during the first two years of life for these children was the mother.

The parents of Jens and Simon followed the *une personne, une langue* rule by addressing the child in his/her respective language, while the parents of Nils and Manuel mixed German and Spanish. Most parents communicated with each other using German, only Simon's parents reported sometimes communicating in Spanish with each other. But they also reported that Simon met weekly with his German grandparents for one day and talked with them in German. Jens and Simon first attended a bilingual German-Spanish day care center at 3;0, i.e., later than the time periods relevant for the present article. Nils started attending a day care center already as early as age 1;5. The language of communication there was German exclusively. Manuel did not attend any day care center.

Children were audio- and video-recorded at their homes in unstructured play situations interacting with one of the parents and a researcher. Recordings took place fortnightly from the beginning of word production (ages 1;0 to 1;3) until approximately ages 2;6–3;0, and monthly thereafter. The bilinguals were recorded by two separate research teams, a German- and a Spanish-speaking team. During German sessions, only German words were spoken, and only the native German parent could be present. Spanish sessions were kept in Spanish, and only the native Spanish parent could participate. Subsequently to the recordings, data from all sessions were glossed and transcribed phonetically. Only the German sessions, ages 1;5–3;0, were of relevance for the present study.

Language dominance was determined by comparing the mean length of utterance or MLU (calculated in terms of words) in a recording session carried out in one language with the MLU of a recording session conducted in the other language (MLU has been shown to be a valid measure for language proficiency in, e.g., Eisenberg, McGovern Fersko & Lundgren 2001). If at a certain age, the MLU of the Spanish utterances and that of the German utterances were similar, the child could be said to be a balanced bilingual. For example, around age 3;0, Jens' MLU was comparable across the two sessions (3.07 in the German, and 2.62 in the Spanish session). The MLU of Manuel was 4.33 in the German and 3.24 in the Spanish session, and that of Simon was 3.07 in the German session, and 3.20 in the Spanish session. Nils produced an MLU of 4.00 in the German, and 2.40 in the Spanish session. To sum up, all children could be considered balanced bilinguals, with a slight German dominance in the case of Jens and Manuel, and a stronger German dominance in the case of Nils. These dominance profiles will be addressed further in the discussion (see Section 2.3).

2.2.2 *Data and methods*

The focus was on medial voiced vs. voiceless stops (to investigate the medial contrast), and on medial voiced vs. final underlyingly voiced and voiceless (henceforth, final voiceless) stops (to address final devoicing/phonotactics). Words were mostly 1- and 2-syllable words with a labial, coronal, or dorsal stop (medial or final). Examples of words include: *hab* '(I) have', *geben* 'to give', *Lied* 'song', *baden* 'to bathe', *Zug* 'train', *Züge* 'trains'. In the case of the bilinguals, we analyzed 167 words with medial (54 underlyingly voiced and 12 voiceless stops during phase 1, i.e., ages 1;5–2;2, and 70 underlyingly voiced and 31 voiceless stops during phase 2, i.e., ages 2;3–3;0) stops and 59 words with final stops (25 during phase 1 and 34 during phase 2). In the case of the monolinguals, 90 words with medial stops (14 underlyingly voiced and 28 voiceless stops during phase 1 and 22 underlyingly voiced and 26 voiceless stops during phase 2) and 54 words with final stops (31 during phase 1 and 23 during phase 2) were analyzed.

2.2.3 *Results for the medial contrast*

If one averages across the monolingual children's data, proportion ViC is significantly higher in the monolingual production of medial voiced stops (97.21) than in their production of medial voiceless stops (77.54) at ages 1;5–2;2, $z = -2.890$, $p = .007$, as well as at 2;3–3;0 (80.95 for medial voiced and 63.19 for final voiceless), $z = -2.024$, $p = .043$. This corresponds to the individual results, shown in Table 1: monolingual children exhibited a target-like trend in medial position during both age periods, with higher values for medial voiced than medial voiceless, although the difference only reached significance in the case of one of the monolinguals (Britta), at age 1;5–2;2.

If one averages across the bilingual children's data, the results indicate that these children did not produce a contrast at 1;5–2;2, with both target voiced (58.56) and target voiceless stops (73.92) showing low proportion ViC values, and a non-target like trend, which is non-significant ($z = -1.652$, $p = .099$). The trend is correct at age 2;3–3;0 (73.96 for voiced and 63.32 for final), but it does not reach significance ($z = -1.529$, $p = .126$). Again, this group result is similar to the individual results in Table 1, and shows a non-target-like trend: proportions ViC were higher for target voiceless and lower for target voiced for bilinguals age 1;5–2;2. At age 2;3–3;0, bilinguals Manuel and Simon were the only ones with significantly higher values for medial voiced than for medial voiceless, whereas the other two bilinguals kept the previous trend with higher values for voiceless (see Table 2 for statistical results).

Table 1. Proportion ViC (i.e., length of glottal pulsing out of length of closure duration) in medial contrast and final voiceless in 4 monolingual (mono) and 4 bilingual (bil) children[1]

			Mono *Britta*	*Mono* *Joh*	*Mono* *Mar*	*Mono* *Thom*	*Bil* *Jens*	*Bil* *Man*	*Bil* *Nils*	*Bil* *Simon*
1;5–2;2	*Med*	*Vcd*	**100**	100	97.80	93	41	43.67	**31.11**	71.26
		Vcl	**52.13**	85.14	79.67	91.9	100	No data	**64.43**	84
2;3–3;0	*Med*	*Vcd*	72.7	80.67	100	85	66.7	**72.38**	52.93	**86.72**
		Vcl	55.55	59.17	71.40	80	81.63	**45.50**	53	**66.60**
1;5–2;2	*Fin*	*Vcl*	**59.71**	**57.38**	No data	76.45	50	75.50	**61.57**	No data
2;3–3;0	*Fin*	*Vcl*	**30.71**	42	No data	70.67	60.80	53.09	58.31	No data

---

1.   Boldface indicates where a contrast was significant (or marginally significant) according to nonparametric (Mann-Whitney) tests.

Table 2. Mann-Whitney U-test results, based on the proportion ViC values displayed in Table 1[2]

		Mono Britta	*Mono Joh*	*Mono Mar*	*Mono Thom*	*Bil Jens*	*Bil Man*	*Bil Nils*	*Bil Simon*
				Medial voiced vs. medial voiceless					
1;5–2;2	z	−2.095	−1.262	−1.537	−.330	−1.549	N/A	−1.974	−.947
	p	**.044**	.383	.250	.839	.222	N/A	.055	.394
2;3–3;0	z	−1.340	−1.248	−1.342	−.274	−1.098	−2.347	−.106	−2.094
	p	.197	.240	.413	.800	.315	**.017**	.945	.064
				Medial voiced vs. final voiceless					
1;5–2;2	z	−2.058	−2.074	N/A	−.664	.0001	−1.732	−2.171	N/A
	p	.056	**.039**	N/A	.571	.99	.200	**.032**	N/A
2;3–3;0	z	−2.670	−2.587	N/A	.0001	.077	−1.565	−.627	N/A
	p	**.007**	**.009**	N/A	.99	.097	.134	.555	N/A

2.2.4   *Results for final voiceless*

As regards the comparison between medial voiced and final voiceless, if one averages across the data, voicing is significantly longer in medial than in final position during the first (97.21 for medial and 64.68 for final), $z = -3.596$, $p = .000$, and the second age phase (80.95 for medial and 42.30 for final), $z = -4.013$, $p = .000$, of the monolingual children. This is in line with Tables 1 and 2, where all monolinguals showed a target-like trend, with higher values medially than finally. The differences were significant for monolinguals Britta and Johannes at both ages. When the devoicing results are averaged across the bilinguals, the trend is not target-like during the first phase (58.56 medial vs. 61.76 final; no significance: $z = -.470$, $p = .638$), but it is correct at phase 2 (73.96 medial vs. 57.35 final) with a significant difference: $z = -2.271$, $p = .023$. With regard to the individual results for devoicing (Table 1 in Section 2.2.3), the same non-target-like trend of producing target medial voiced with values more appropriate for voiceless was followed by bilinguals Jens, Manuel, and Nils at age 1;5–2;2. At age 2;3–3;0, bilinguals Jens and Manuel produced more voicing for medial voiced than for final voiceless, although these results did not reach significance. Bilingual Nils kept the previous trend, and bilingual Simon, again, did not produce final voiceless.

2.3   Discussion

Altogether, the unmarked final voiceless stops are produced by monolingual German children target-like at around the same time as these children produce the voicing

---

2.   Again, 'N/A' refers to cases in which no comparisons were possible, due to a lack of data in one of the groups of sounds; boldface indicates where a contrast was significant (or marginally significant).

contrast in medial position. The fact that monolingual children already perceive the contrasts and the phonotactics of their native language early, sometimes as early as at age 8–10 months (e.g. Werker & Tees 1984, Werker & Lalonde 1988, Jusczyk, Friederici, Wessels, Svenkerud & Jusczyk 1993, Friederici & Wessels 1993, Jusczyk, Luce & Charles-Luce 1994), together with the relatively low markedness of final voiceless, seem to play an important role in explaining the pattern in the monolingual children's early onset of target-like production in the present study.

It appears to be the case, though, that the medial contrast between voiced and voiceless manifested by means of ViC is not yet acquired by bilingual children at age 2;3–3;0, based on the group results. The individual results also show that none of the bilingual children produced any statistically significant difference (with a correct trend) between target medial voiced and voiceless stops at age 1;5–2;2, whereas two children produced a statistically significant difference at 2;3–3;0. These two children were Manuel and Simon, who differed with regard to their language balance (recall that Manuel was slightly German dominant; see Section 2.2.1). This suggests that language balance measured in terms of MLU did not seem to have any influence on the production of voicing in these bilinguals. With respect to the question whether final stops were voiceless (or devoiced) in final position, they did show low ViC values, although a significant difference with medial voiced stops did not appear at age 1;5–2;2, but only at age 2;3–3;0. Considered individually, none of the bilinguals produced a statistically significant difference between medial voiced and final voiceless (with more voicing in medial than in final position). Again, the fact that some of the children were slightly German-dominant did not seem to play a role here.

However, the lack of contrast does not seem to originate in a lack of devoicing, as the final stops produced by bilinguals do have low voicing values, implying that they are voiceless. The lack of contrast seems rather to stem from the target voiced stops in medial position, which, as produced by the bilinguals, show very low values, actually corresponding more to voiceless than to voiced stops. It is plausible to assume that bilinguals may be delayed in the acquisition of voiced stops as compared with monolinguals. After all, voiced obstruents are more marked than voiceless ones, and in the bilingual context some cases of delayed acquisition have been often reported, based on markedness. In many cases, just a slight delay has been found, covering only a few months. For instance, Kehoe (2002) reports a delay of about six months in the acquisition/production of long vowels in German, and thus of the contrast between long vs. short vowels in German-Spanish bilinguals. In the present case, the delay experienced by the bilinguals in the production of the voiced counterparts of stops also leads to a lack of contrast, between medial voiced and medial voiceless, and between medial voiced and final voiceless. The reason for this slight delay would thus be the markedness of voiced stops vs. voiceless ones, its effect augmented by the facts that Spanish does not impose final devoicing in the way German does and that the voicing systems of German and Spanish differ (see Section 2.1), bilingual children thus having to acquire two different voicing systems. It seems as if bilinguals kept the initial grammar (with markedness being highly ranked) longer than monolinguals, which results in low voicing values in the voiced stops of the bilinguals, as well as a lack of contrast.

3.   German schwa

3.1   Theoretical description and acquisition

We focus on the so-called underlying schwa, as, e.g., in the second/unstressed syllable of German words such as *Robbe* 'seal' or the first syllable (also unstressed) of *genug* 'enough'. Much research exists on the theoretical status of schwa (e.g. Wiese 1986, Kager 1989, Féry 1995, Hammond 1997, Van Oostendorp 1998, 2000). In moraic theories, schwa is considered non-moraic and unsyllabified throughout the early stages of syllable formation (e.g. Kager 1989). In projection theory (Van Oostendorp 2000), schwa is unspecified for Place. In phonetic terms, schwa is neutral and deviating from peripheric vowels. It is regarded as placeless (Van Oostendorp 2000), because it is often influenced by acoustic and articulatory properties of neighboring consonants. E.g., Koopmans-van Beinum (1994) states that schwa has a lot of variation in F2 values due to the influence of surrounding consonants (see, e.g., also Browman & Goldstein 1992). Often, schwa has lower amplitude than other, full vowels as well as a shorter duration, which is mostly the case in non-final position (see also Lindblom 1963).

Schwa occurs in several of the West Germanic languages, e.g., in Dutch, English, and German (Delattre 1965, Kehoe & Lleó 2003). In Dutch, 30% of the vowels produced are schwas (Levelt 2008). Schwa is also the Dutch epenthetic vowel. Beside the Germanic languages, however, not many languages contain the sound. Only 20% of the languages involved in the UCLA phonological segment inventory (UPSID) database (based on 317 languages) have schwa in their inventory. The remaining 80% only allow for full vowels. In languages that do contain schwa, the sound only occurs in certain positions. As an example, schwa cannot form the head of a foot in most languages, which means that it can only occur in unstressed positions (Levelt 2008). Schwa has been described as underspecified on either the segmental (Kager 1989) or the prosodic levels (Van Oostendorp 1998, 2000). Some posit the constraint NON-HEAD-SCHWA (Cohn & McCarthy 1998), which militates against schwa in stressed syllables. And, e.g., in the view of projection theory (Van Oostendorp 1998, 2000), the constraint PROJECT (syllable, V) blocks underlying schwa from emerging as the constraint requires syllable heads to have vocalic features (while schwa is underspecified for such features).

In spite of the fact that schwa has been extensively addressed in the theoretical literature, not much research has focused on the acquisition of schwa in young children (except for, e.g., Kehoe & Lleó 2003 for German monolingual acquisition, Levelt 2000 and 2008 for Dutch monolingual acquisition). According to Levelt (2000), Dutch children begin producing schwa target-like around age 2;0–3;0. Kehoe & Lleó's (2003) study suggests that German children produce German schwa at approximately 2;6–3;0.

Both time periods are rather late, considering that babies lose sensitivity to vowel contrasts irrelevant to their native language phonology around age 6 months (consonants around age 8 months). That is, babies are influenced by the phonological categories of their native language around that age already. Before schwa is produced target-like, it is often augmented to a full short or a full long vowel in the children's production.

The present research followed up on the study by Kehoe & Lleó (2003) to investigate when and how children start producing schwa, by looking at the production of schwa using a new group of children, namely German-Spanish bilingual children. Spanish lacks central vowels such as schwa, and schwa may be acquired even later by children, who, in addition to a language that contains schwa acquire a language without schwa. Furthermore, due to the fact that schwa is underspecified, be it on the prosodic (e.g. Kager 1989) or the segmental levels (Van Oostendorp 1998, 2000), it differs from other vowels and is therefore possibly difficult for children to acquire. This corresponds to the findings of, e.g., Kehoe & Lleó (2003) who found that monolingual children produce other sounds, e.g. syllabic consonants, better/earlier than schwa. In the case of schwa, children need to learn a mismatch between the prosodic and segmental domain, making it difficult to acquire the sound.

The fact that schwa may be somewhat difficult to acquire, coupled with the fact that bilingual children have evidence for schwa only in one of their two languages leads us to assume that there will be a delay in the production of schwa in the bilinguals relative to the monolinguals.

3.2   The study

3.2.1   *Participants*
The participants were three German-Spanish bilingual children from the corpus of project TPE3 (aliases: Jens, Simon, and Manuel). The focus was on ages 1;10–3;0, which were divided into three phases for the purpose of analysis (1;10–2;1, 2;2–2;6 and 2;7–3;0). In addition, for comparison, we will mention the results of four monolingual German children from Hamburg, which are taken from the 2003 study by Kehoe & Lleó. The corpus description, as well as the description of the linguistic background for the bilinguals is as in the study on final voiceless (see Section 2.2.1).

3.2.2   *Data and methods*
For the present analysis, we looked at spontaneous utterances taken from phonetic transcripts from corpus TPE3. Transcripts had been prepared by experienced phoneticians. The words that were analyzed were trochees, i.e., two syllable words with a stressed syllable followed by an unstressed one. Examples include *Katze* 'cat' and *Robbe* 'seal'. We analyzed 238 words with target schwa uttered by the child Jens (143 during phase 1, 24 in phase 2, and 71 in phase 3), 354 produced by Simon (90 during phase 1, 157 in phase 2, 107 in phase 3), and 385 by Manuel (68 in phase 1, 103 in phase 2, 214 in phase 3).

Table 3. Percent target-like production of schwa in 3 bilingual (bil) and 4 monolingual (mono) children (approximated means for monolinguals calculated based on results in Lleó & Kehoe 2003)[3]

Phase (age)	Bil Jens	Bil Simon	Bil Manuel	Mono
1 (1;10–2;1)	59 ($z = -2.347$, $p = .019$)	16 ($z = -6.522$, $p = .000$)	35 ($z = -1.572$, $p = .116$)	0
2 (2;2–2;6)	14 ($z = -2.115$, $p = .034$)	44 ($z = -.457$, $p = .648$)	**73** ($z = -5.058$, $p = .000$)	0
3 (2;7–3;0)	20 ($z = -6.016$, $p = .000$)	**58** ($z = -3.004$, $p = .003$)	**90** ($z = -9.618$, $p = .000$)	23

3.2.3 *Results*

Table 3 lays out the percentages of target-like schwa production. Other sounds frequently produced for schwa, not mentioned in the table, are full vowels (e.g. [e] or [ɛ]). We do not include them in the description, as the goal here is to highlight the production of target-like schwa.

As seen in Table 3, the percentages of schwas produced target-like were high in the case of the bilinguals, whereas substitutions by other sounds were not numerous. The number of schwa produced target-like was lower in the case of the monolinguals. Overall, the bilinguals produced more target-like schwas than the monolinguals; only the bilingual Jens produced fewer target-like schwas during phase 3 than the monolinguals. That is, the fact that only one of the two languages acquired by the bilinguals has schwa did not contribute to a delay in the onset of target-like production of schwa. In fact, there seems to be an acceleration in the target-like production of schwa in the bilinguals relative to the monolinguals.

3.3   Discussion

Why did the monolingual children produce schwa target-like relatively late, whereas the bilinguals were not delayed, in spite of the fact that native language contrasts tend to be acquired early by monolingual children (e.g. Werker & Tees 1984; Werker & Lalonde 1988, Jusczyk et al. 1993, Friederici & Wessels 1993)? It is possible that schwa is, in general, a sound that is difficult to acquire. Phonological theories of schwa (see Section 3.1, above) consider schwa to be underspecified on one or more levels: according to the no mora theory, schwa is weightless and lacks a prosodic position; according to the projection theory, schwa lacks articulatory features. Hence, in this

---

3.   Boldface indicates where schwa was significantly more frequent than a full vowel produced for target schwa, based on Mann-Whitney U-tests; cases in which there is no boldface in spite of a statistical result refer to significantly more frequent full vowels than schwas.

respect, schwa is different from other sounds. Children need to learn this difference, and this may be what creates a delay in the acquisition of the sound. In the case of German-Spanish bilinguals, the acquisition of schwa may be aided by some aspect of their bilingualism.

As one (admittedly rather speculative) possibility, German-Spanish bilinguals receive training for schwa based on the many polysyllables in their input (frequent in Spanish), which contain various unstressed syllables. Hearing these syllables may strengthen the bilinguals' awareness of unstressed syllables in German, as well as that of schwa (often occurring in unstressed syllables in German), leading to the bilinguals producing schwa target-like earlier than in the case of the monolinguals. The latter group of children lack the extra input of unstressed syllables from Spanish.

As a further possibility, consider that Spanish has a vocalic system of five cardinal vowels, without vowel reduction in unstressed position. On the background of these unreduced cardinal vowels of Spanish (plus the 14 vowels of German), schwa may become rather salient to the bilingual child, as it has been argued that the perception abilities of the bilingual child may be enhanced in the vocalic spectrum, i.e., that their experience in the vocalic field is boosted by the input of two different vocalic systems. It has often been shown that consonants and vowels are acquired differently in early childhood, vowels being acquired earlier than consonants.

4.   General discussion

The present research addressed the production of consonantal and vocalic segments in German by a group of German-Spanish bilinguals, and compared their productions with the ones of German monolinguals. Whereas, as expected, the German voicing contrast in stops (and its unmarked neutralization in final position) was acquired early by German monolinguals, bilinguals were delayed, which was in particular reflected in the low voicing values of their voiced stops. The delay in the bilinguals was probably due to the markedness associated with voiced obstruents. In the case of schwa, the monolinguals were, unexpectedly, delayed relative to the bilinguals, an effect that may have at its root a positive influence of German-Spanish bilingualism on schwa: German-Spanish children may benefit in their acquisition of schwa from their acquaintance with frequent unstressed vowels in Spanish, given that the Spanish child lexicon contains many polysyllables. As an alternative, schwa, being a non-peripheral vowel, may be a salient sound for German-Spanish bilinguals for the reason that Spanish has only a cardinal vowel system; this saliency may contribute to the mastery of schwa production in the bilinguals relative to the monolinguals.

These results are in line with previous research, where most cases of delay in bilingual acquisition had to do with consonants (see, e.g., Kehoe, Lleó & Rakow 2004 on VOT, Lleó & Rakow 2005 on spirants, Lleó & Rakow 2006 on nasals). The only vowel property that has been shown to involve delay in bilingual acquisition is (the marked) vowel length (see Kehoe 2002). The fact that children encounter more difficulties with consonants may in many cases be related to the fact (well-known in phonetics) that consonants are more complex events than vowels. In general, vowels have been shown to be acquired before consonants by monolingual children. However, in the case of the present study, schwa seems to pose a challenge to monolingual acquisition. This may be based on the special phonological status of schwa (see Section 3.1), making it more difficult to acquire than other vowels. Similar results (suggesting that schwa is difficult to learn) were obtained by Kehoe & Lleó (2003), who show that schwa is produced later target-like by German monolingual children than, e.g., syllabic consonants. In spite of the special status of schwa, the bilinguals in the present study were not delayed, in fact, a slight acceleration took place. The reason may be that German-Spanish bilinguals are perhaps able to train their perception (and to generalize this knowledge to benefit their production) of the unstressed vowel schwa, thanks to the positive additive influence of their other language (Spanish) having many unstressed syllables and a cardinal vowel system (which may render schwa salient to the bilingual children.

To conclude, the present work has presented new data that suggest that consonants, in this case the ones involved in the German voicing contrast (which is neutralized in final position), contribute to a delay in bilingual acquisition. German underlying schwa did not cause any delay, on the contrary. This is in line with previous work that showed that (a) the production of segments in a L1 is different in bilingual children as compared with monolinguals, and that, specifically, (b) consonants involve a delay in the bilinguals' data (see, e.g., Lleó & Rakow 2006), whereas vowels are usually not associated with any delay (see Kehoe 2002).

References

Anderson, J. 1987. The markedness differential hypothesis and syllable structure difficulty. In *Interlanguage Phonology: The Acquisition of a Second Language Sound System*, eds. G. Ioup & S. H. Weinberger, 279–291. Cambridge MA: Newbury House.

Benson, B. 1988. Universal preference for the open syllable as an independent process in interlanguage phonology. *Language Learning* 38: 221–242.

Boersma, P. & D. Weenink. 1992ff. *Praat: Doing Phonetics by Computer* (Computer program). <http://www.praat.org>

Browman, C. & L. Goldstein. 1992. Targetless schwa: An articulatory analysis. In *Papers in Laboratory Analysis*, II: *Gesture, Segment, Prosody*, eds. G. Doherty, R. Ladd, M. Beckman & J. Kingston, 26–56. Cambridge: CUP.

Chomsky, N. & M. Halle. 1968. *The Sound Pattern of English*. New York NY: Harper & Row.

Cohn, A. & J. McCarthy. 1998. Alignment and parallelism in Indonesian phonology. *Working Papers of the Cornell Phonetics Laboratory* 12: 53–137.

Delattre, P. 1965. *Comparing the Phonetic Features of English, French, German, and Spanish*. Heidelberg: Groos.

Eckman, F. 1977. Markedness and the contrastive analysis hypothesis. *Language Learning* 27: 315–330.

Eisenberg, S. L., T. McGovern Fersko & C. Lundgren. 2001. The use of MLU for identifying language impairment in preschool children: A review. *American Journal of Speech Language-Pathology* 10: 323–342.

Ferguson, C. A. & C. B. Farwell. 1975. Words and sounds in early language acquisition. *Language* 5: 439–491.

Féry, C. 1995. *Alignment, Syllable, and Metrical Structure in German* (SfS-Report-02-95). Tübingen: Seminar für Sprachwissenschaft.

Friederici, A. D. & J. M. I. Wessels. 1993. Phonotactic knowledge of word boundaries and its use in infant speech perception. *Perception & Psychophysics* 54: 287–295.

Hammond, M. 1997. Vowel quantity and syllabification in English. *Language* 73: 1–17.

Hawkins, J. A. 1987. Implicational universals as predictors of language acquisition. *Linguistics* 25: 453–473.

Hayes, B. 2004. Phonological acquisition in Optimality Theory: The early stages. In *Constraints in Phonological Acquisition*, eds. R. Kager, J. Pater & W. Zonneveld, 158–203. Cambridge: CUP.

Jakobson, R. 1941/1968. *Child Language, Aphasia, and Phonological Universals* (translated by A. R. Kuler). The Hague: Mouton, 1968. (*Kindersprache, Aphasie und allgemeine Lautgesetze.* Uppsala: Almqvist & Wiksell, 1941).

Jusczyk, P. W., A. D. Friederici, J. M. I. Wessels, V. Y. Svenkerud & A. M. Jusczyk. 1993. Infants' sensitivity to the sound patterns of native language words. *Journal of Memory and Language* 32: 402–420.

Jusczyk, P. W., P. A. Luce & J. Charles-Luce. 1994. Infants' sensitivity to phonotactic patterns in the native language. *Journal of Memory and Language* 33: 630–645.

Kager, R. 1989. *A Metrical Theory of Stress and Destressing in English and Dutch.* Dordrecht: Foris.

Kehoe, M. 2002. Developing vowel systems as a window to bilingual phonology. *International Journal of Bilingualism* 6: 315–334.

Kehoe, M. & C. Lleó. 2003. A phonological analysis of schwa in German first language acquisition. *Canadian Journal of Linguistics* 48: 289–327.

Kehoe, M., C. Lleó & M. Rakow. 2004. Voice Onset Time in bilingual German-Spanish children. *Bilingualism: Language and Cognition* 7: 71–88.

Kehoe, M., C. Trujillo & C. Lleó. 2001. Bilingual phonological acquisition: An analysis of syllable structure and VOT. In *Proceedings of the Colloquium on Structure, Acquisition and Change of Grammars: Phonological and Syntactic Aspects* (Arbeiten zur Mehrsprachigkeit 27), eds. K. F. Cantone & M.-O. Hinzelin, 38–54. Hamburg: Universität Hamburg.

Koopmans-van Beinum, F. 1994. What's in a schwa? Durational and spectroanalysis of natural continuous speech and diphones in Dutch. *Phonetica* 51: 68–79.

Levelt, C. C. 1994. *On the Acquisition of Place.* The Hague: HAG.

Levelt, C. C. 2000. Schwa-schma: The development of /ə/ in Dutch child language. Paper presented at the 16th IATL Conference, Tel Aviv University, Tel Aviv, Israel, 12 April 2000.

Levelt, C. C. 2008. Phonology and phonetics in the development of schwa in Dutch child language. *Lingua* 118: 1344–1361.

Lindblom, B. 1963. Spectrographic study of vowel reduction. *Journal of the Acoustical Society of America* 35: 1773–1781.

Lleó, C. 2002. The role of markedness in the acquisition of complex prosodic structures by German-Spanish bilinguals. *International Journal of Bilingualism* 6: 291–313.

Lleó, C., I. Kuchenbrandt, M. Kehoe & C. Trujillo. 2003. Syllable final consonants in Spanish and German monolingual and bilingual acquisition. In *(In)vulnerable Domains in Multilingualism* (Hamburg Studies on Multilingualism 1), ed. N. Müller, 191–220. Amsterdam: John Benjamins.

Lleó, C. & M. Rakow. 2005. Markedness effects in voiced stop spirantization in bilingual German-Spanish children. In *Proceedings of the 4th International Symposium on Bilingualism (ISB4)*, eds. J. Cohen, K. T. McAlister, K. Rolstad & J. MacSwan, 1353–1371. Somerville MA: Cascadilla Press.

Lleó, C. & M. Rakow. 2006. Nasalassimilation und prosodische Hierarchie im monolingualen und bilingualen Erwerb des Spanischen und des Deutschen. In *Phonetik und Nordistik: Festschrift für Magnús Pétursson zum 65. Geburtstag*, eds. C. El Mogharbel & K. Himstedt, 95–117. Frankfurt: Theo Hector.

Macken, M. 1978. Permitted complexity in phonological development: One child's acquisition of Spanish consonants. *Lingua* 44: 219–253.

Montes Giraldo, J. J. 1971. Acerca de la apropiación por el niño del sistema fonológico español. *Thesaurus* 26: 322–346.

Pallier, C., L. Bosch, & N. Sebastián-Gallés. 1997. A limit on behavioral plasticity in speech perception. *Cognition* 64: B9-B17.

Pater, J. 1997. Minimal violation and phonological development. *Language Acquisition* 6: 201–253.

Ramon-Casas, M., D. Swingley, L. Bosch & N. Sebastián-Gallés. 2009. Vowel categorization during word recognition in bilingual toddlers. *Cognitive Psychology* 59: 96–121.

Smith, B. L., R. Hayes-Harb, M. Bruss & A. Harker. 2009. Production and perception of voicing and devoicing in similar German and English word pairs by native speakers of German. *Journal of Phonetics* 37: 257–275.

Van Oostendorp, M. 1998. Schwa in phonological theory. *GLOT International* 3: 3–9.

Van Oostendorp, M. 2000. *Phonological Projection: A Theory of Feature Content and Prosodic Structure*. Berlin: Mouton de Gruyter.

Werker, J. F. & C. E. Lalonde. 1988. Cross-language speech perception: Initial capabilities and development change. *Developmental Psychology* 24: 672–683.

Werker, J. F. & R. C. Tees. 1984. Cross-language speech perception: Evidence for perceptual reorganization during the first year of life. *Infant Behavior and Development* 7: 49–63.

Westbury, J. R. & P. A. Keating. 1986. On the naturalness of stop consonant voicing. *Journal of Linguistics* 22: 145–166.

Wiese, R. 1986. Schwa and the structure of words in German. *Linguistics* 24: 695–724.

Agreement within early mixed DP

What mixed agreement can tell us about the bilingual language faculty[*]

Cristina Pierantozzi
University of Urbino, Italy

The aim of this paper is to investigate whether code-mixing can help us understand the architecture of the (Bilingual) Language Faculty, by comparing the predictions about mixed DPs made by the Bi-Lexical Model (MacSwan 1999) and the Distributed Morphology (Halle & Marantz 1994). The empirical basis consists of the naturalist data of two bilingual children acquiring Italian/German and Italian/Spanish, since birth. The data shows an interesting asymmetry in the frequency of the types of mixed agreement with the determiners of the two languages.

Keywords: Italian, German, Spanish, code switching, early mixed DP, mixed agreement, Distributed Morphology, Bilingual Language Faculty

1. Introduction

The ongoing debate about mixed DPs in adult (Jake, Myers-Scotton & Gross 2002, MacSwan 2005, Herring, Deuchar, Couto & Quintanilla 2010) and infant bilingual speakers (Cantone & Müller 2008, Liceras, Fernández Fuertes, Perales, Pérez-Tattam & Spradlin 2008, Radford, Kupisch, Köppe & Azzarro 2007) highlights the need to re-think about the notion of the "grammaticality" of a mixed sentence in connection with the interplay among internal and external factors. At the heart of the discussion we can

---

[*]   This paper reports the results of my PhD Dissertation granted at the University of Urbino. I would like to thank the audience of the MIMS conference, the children interviewed and their parents for participating at the project. I am very grateful to many people for their comments and suggestions; my supervisor Caterina Donati, Jürgen M. Meisel, Tanja Kupisch, Gloria Cocchi, Giuliana Giusti, Regina Köppe, Matthias Bonnesen, Barbara Miertsch, Anne-Kathrin Riedel, Esther Rinke, Susanne Rieckborn, Aldona Sopata, Claudia Stöber and Imme Kuchenbrandt. All remaining errors are mine.

find the conflicting predictions made by the feature-checking approach to code-mixing (MacSwan 1999, 2005) with respect to the published data.[1]

According to the feature-checking approach, the grammatical restrictions of code-mixing are imposed by the same principles at work in monolingual speech. Differently from a monolingual speaker, a bilingual can simply select lexical items from two separate Lexicons and produce them with the corresponding phonological components. As in monolingual speech, it is the checking process that assures the well-formedness (i.e. grammaticality) of the clause by means of the deletion and the evaluation of the un-interpretable features. Therefore, in a mixed DP the feature-checking approach predicts that "The switched noun determines the gender of the determiner" (Cantone 2007: 85).

If one of the two languages in contact is a genderless language, different predictions are made about the grammaticality of the mixed DP (see MacSwan 1999, 2005, Radford et al. 2007) depending on the classification of the gender feature in N as ±interpretable. The strongest prediction bans the switching between D and N in this language pair (Radford et al. 2007). The following examples of the insertion typology (Muysken 2000) from English/Spanish data should thus be ill-formed, because the uninterpretable gender feature in N in (1) and in D in (2) survives to the checking process:

(1)   she got to the$_{\text{SG/PL}}$ *manguera*$_{\text{F.SG}}$
      'She got to the hose.'   (Spanish/English; Herring et al. 2010: 569)

(2)   Veo las$_{\text{F.PL}}$ *houses*$_{\text{PL}}$
      'I see the houses.'   (Spanish/English; Muysken 2000: 23)

If the gender feature in N is considered as interpretable as in Chomsky (1995), only the mixed DP in (1) should be well-formed, because the English D does not have the uninterpretable gender feature triggering the checking process (MacSwan 1999). Under this account, the default gender (i.e. the unmarked gender: masculine for Spanish) is expected in (2). The predictions contrast both with the published data. In the English/Spanish data of adult bilinguals reported in Jake et al. (2002), the 70% of the 230 English NPs occur with an inflected Spanish determiner as in (2). The same strong preference for this pattern is found in early mixed DPs of Spanish/English and French/English bilingual children (see Liceras, Spradlin & Fernández Fuertes 2005, Liceras et al. 2008, Pierantozzi, Donati, Bontempi & Gasperoni 2006).

---

1.   The feature-checking approach is the current generative approach to code-switching. The generative theory is a formal theory about language, according to which language is an innate faculty consisting of a finite set of universal principles and parameters. The feature-checking process and the distinction between interpretable and uninterpretable features represent the formalization of a basic assumption within the Minimalist Program: the need of the syntax to respect interfaces conditions: Logical Form (LF) and Phonological Form (PF). Uninterpretable features must be checked and deleted before spell-out.

In order to account for the high frequency of the pattern in (2) with respect to that in (1) two different hypotheses have been developed. The former, advanced by Moro (2001), resorts to recent theoretical developments of the Minimalist Program, more precisely to the definition of the Agree operation as a "'one fell swoop' operation" (Chomsky 2000: 124). Given the fact that, in (2), D (the probe) has a complete set of phi-features, the pattern in (2) becomes grammatical because D should be able to delete and valuate its own features as a unit. However, it is unclear what enables the valuation of the gender feature in D because the English noun (the goal) is genderless. Moreover, in (2) D receives the feminine gender of the Spanish equivalent noun "casa" (i.e. the analogical gender; see Poplack, Pousada & Sankoff 1982). If the latter has not been selected how does the checking process work?

A plausible answer to this question is to claim that the phonological content of the selected words is late inserted, as claimed by the Distributed Morphology theory (henceforth DM; see Halle & Marantz 1994, Harley & Noyer 1999). In this paper I will provide evidences for the second hypothesis (see Liceras et al. 2005, 2008 for a similar proposal), supported by the pattern of mixed agreement recorded in the data of two bilingual children living in Italy and acquiring German and Spanish respectively.

The paper is organized as follows: in Section 2 I will discuss the DM approach to the Bilingual Language Faculty. In Section 3, I will present the data and the configuration of the Language Dominance of the two bilingual children. In Section 4, I will verify the level of competence reached by the children in the monolingual DPs by looking at the rates of mismatch in agreement. In Section 5 I will present the results concerning the mixed DPs. In Section 6 conclusions will be drawn.

2. The Distributed Morphology approach

The DM framework is a generative theory about the morphology/syntax interface. It departs from the current prominent Lexicalist Hypothesis by rejecting the notion of a generative Lexicon. The bundles of features stored and assembled in the Lexicon are replaced with three static Lists accessible by the grammar at different points of the derivation, see Figure 1.

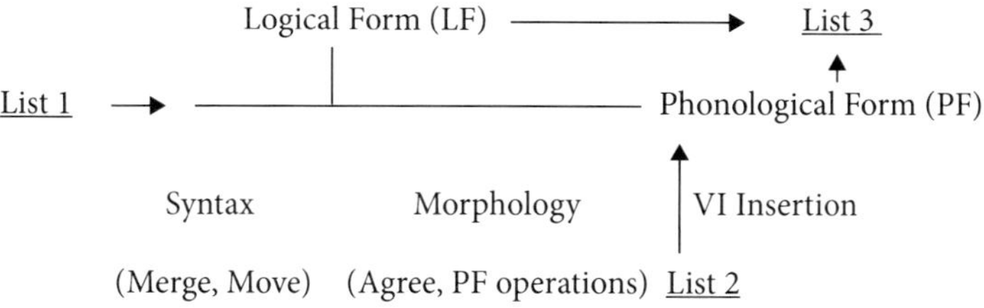

Figure 1. The architecture of Distributed Morphology (DM)

Syntax is the only generative module. It selects and assembles the syntactic primitives hosted in List 1 into more complex objects (words and phrases). The syntactic primitives consist of syntactic-semantic features without any phonological content. This bundle of features comes in two types: lexical morphemes (l-m: roots) and formal morphemes (f-m: functional morphemes). Before spell-out, the morphological component, placed along the PF branch, modifies in a limited way the abstract syntactic structure by applying PF operations. Only after the operations the abstract structure, consisting only of interpretable and valued terminal nodes, receives its phonological content: the Vocabulary Items (VI) hosted in List 2. The insertion of the VI is subjected to the restrictions of the Subset Principle (Halle 1997).

The basic requirement for the insertion of VI is that the feature specification of the terminal node must match the feature specification of VI. In this case the insertion is local. However, in some cases this one to one correspondence is not met, because a) the language does not overtly realize the feature of the terminal node (i.e. Syncretism), or b) more than one VI with the same feature specification (i.e. Allomorphy) compete for insertion under the same terminal node. The Subset Principle deals with these cases by allowing, in the former case, the insertion of a VI having a subset of the features specified in the abstract node, and by choosing, in the latter case, the most specified VI. The choice is made on the basis of non-local relations: the feature specifications of adjacent terminal nodes. A good example illustrating the VI insertion of allomorphs is the formation of plural nouns in English (see Embick & Noyer 2007: 7f).

The Subset Principle applies to the insertion of the VI of the f-m. Whether the roots are late inserted or may compete for insertion is an open question (see Embick & Noyer 2007, Harley & Noyer 1999, Siddiqi 2006). In this paper I will assume, with Harley & Noyer (1999), that roots are late inserted without competition and, with Pfau (2009), that the terminal nodes of the roots are equipped with a non-compositional meaning. On the definition of gender feature, I will follow the DM account provided by Kramer (2009). More precisely I will assume that the gender feature is a valued feature that may be classified as ±interpretable on the basis of its position along the abstract structure of the DP. In particular, it is an interpretable gender in the little head n (biological gender), while it is an uninterpretable feature in the root (grammatical gender).

In the Bilingual Competence, List 1 and List 2 must be doubled, because they represent the source of the cross-linguistic variation[2]. List 1 contains the syntactic-semantic parameters, and List 2 their morpho-phonological realizations. As in MacSwan's (1999) Bi-Lexical Model, code-mixing stems from the operation Select. In contrast to

---

2.   List 3, also know as Encyclopedia, contains the non-linguistic knowledge about the extra-linguistic referents of words. According to Marantz (1997) this List is the locus of the "special meanings" (i.e. idioms). Because of its extra-linguistic nature I will not discuss this List in this section and I will speculate that in the Bilingual Competence there is only one List 3.

MacSwan's model, however, selection may involve two different stages of the derivation: a) the beginning, if the selection involves the two Lists 1 (the morphosyntactic level, henceforth MS) and b) the final one, when the grammar accesses the List 2 in order to pronounce the clause.

Consider a language pair such as Italian/English. Here in the mixed DPs in (3–4) below, the functional heads (f–m) are selected from the List 1 of one language of the two languages: the Italian List 1 in (3) and the English List 1 in (4). Given the uniform selection at MS level, D and N agree: at point of the spell-out, the terminal nodes consist of interpretable and valued features:

(3) MS level: $[_{D}$ ~~uφ~~: SG, F $[_{NUM}$ φ: SG $[_{n}$ [√N ~~uφ~~: F]]]]
     VI level: la [SG, F]   house

(4) MS level: $[_{D}$ ~~uφ~~: SG $[_{NUM}$ φ: SG $[_{n}$ [√N]]]]
     VI level: the [SG]   casa

The VI insertion of D is deterministic: if the English and Italian definite articles competed for insertion, only the feminine form *la* would match the feature specification of the abstract node D in (3). The same holds for the VI insertion of the English D in (4). In short, in (3–4) the mixing arises from the VI insertion of the roots, because roots do not compete for insertion and therefore a root from any of the two languages may be chosen.

In language pairs having both the gender feature, such as Italian and Spanish or Italian and German, the picture becomes more complex. In this case, without any further cues (i.e. the adjective position in Italian/German languages pair) it is difficult to establish from which List 1 the D has been selected[3]. For example, the N *sea* has a different gender in Italian and Spanish: it is masculine in Italian (*mare*) and feminine in Spanish (*mar*). The mixed DPs *el mare* and *il mar* ('the sea') in (5) may be the output of different combinations, that is: a) the uniform selection from the Italian List 1 and b) the mixed selection from the two Lists 1, in particular the selection of the D from Spanish and the root from Italian. In both cases, at PF, the terminal nodes will have the same feature specification:

(5) MS level: $[_{D}$ ~~uφ~~: SG, M $[_{NUM}$ φ: SG $[_{n}$ [√N ~~uφ~~: M]]]]
     VI level: a. el [SG, M]   mare
                 b. il [SG, M]   mar

At PF, the VI of the Italian and Spanish D may be inserted, because both match the feature specification of D. The same abstract structure seems to generate two different types of mixed agreement: the agreement with the equivalent N in (5a) and the agreement with the selected N in (5b).

---

3.   The problem of the visibility of the language with respect to the selection from List 1 is not trivial. However, we may speculate that in languages pairs such Italian/Spanish there is no need to double the parameters having the same value. The two Lists 1 may share a subgroup of syntactic-semantic features, for example determiners.

The DM approach to code-mixing seems thus to be able to derive all the patterns of mixed DPs discussed in the previous section, but it is prone to problems concerning the visibility of Lists combinations and, may over-generate. However, we may suppose that external factors will dictate further restrictions by cutting an array of the patterns generated by the Bilingual Language Faculty. Possible candidates may be: 1) the Bilingual Mode (Grosjean 2001), 2) the Language Dominance and 3) the Bilingual Setting.

Before to proof whether the bilingual children under investigation will prefer one pattern of mixed DP over the other, it is important to assess the configuration of their Language Dominance.

3.   The data: Two Italian bilingual children

The following data are original data collected at the University of Urbino under the direction of Caterina Donati. They consist of longitudinal data of two bilingual children living in Italy: the boy – Leucò (2;4.27–3;4.03) – is acquiring German, and the girl – Lucia (1;06.25–2;07.24) – is acquiring Spanish[4]. Both children have been raised bilingual since birth through the "one-parent-one language" educational strategy and they both went to the Italian kindergarten at the age of 3. In both cases, Italian is the language of the father as well as the primary language at home. The children have been audio-recorded at home by an Italian speaker and by their mothers in different and conjunct sessions. The corpora differ with respect to the number of recording in each language. Unfortunately, most of the recordings concerning the Italian/Spanish girl were conducted by the Italian speaker[5]

The two children are basically balanced. In contrast to Leucò, Lucia shows however a slight dominance in Italian: see Figures 2–3 reporting the MLU (word) values[6].

The fact that these children are not strongly unbalanced bilingual does not allow us to verify the role of the language dominance in the frequency of the type of mixed agreement recorded in the mixed DPs. Any asymmetry in the distribution of the latter should then be ascribed only to internal factors.

---

4.   The age range of the two corpora differs because the two children began to talk at different times: see MLU values in Figures 2 and 3.

5.   For reasons of space I cannot report the tables of the two corpora (see Pieranozzi 2008). In order to indicate the language of the child's interlocutor I will label the graphs by using a capital letter beside the age of the child at the time of the recording: I for Italian, G for German, S for Spanish and B for those recording where both languages have been used.

6.   The judgement is supported by the results concerning other indices employed in order to define the language dominance, more precisely: the Upper Bound and the Type Token Ration based on the noun and on verb (see Pierantozzi 2008).

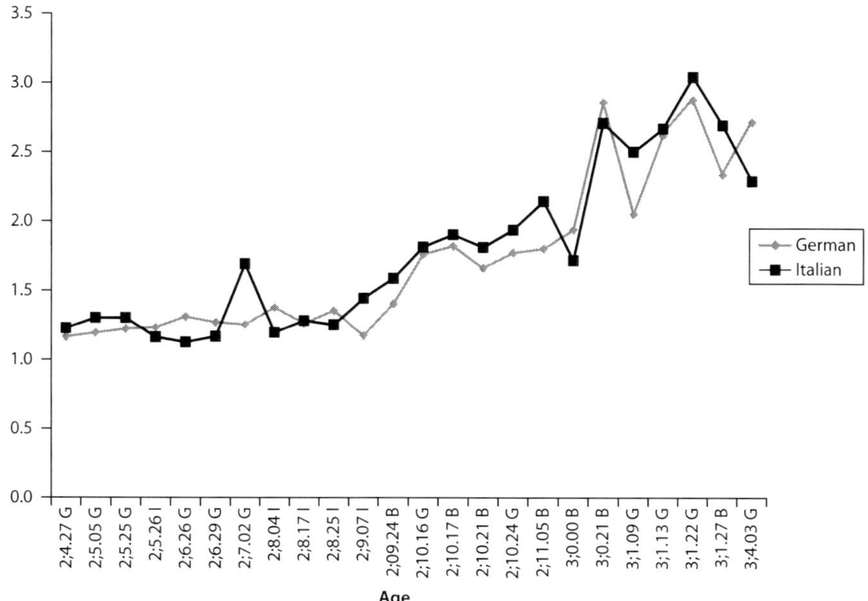

Figure 2. Leucò's MLU (word)

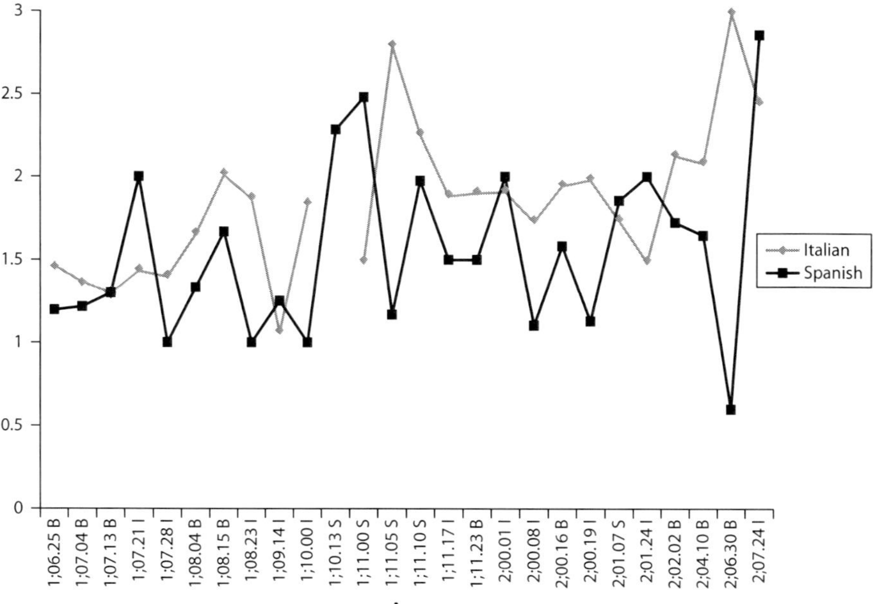

Figure 3. Lucia's MLU (word)

4. Cross-linguistic influence: Testing the level of competence in monolingual DPs

In this section I will verify the development of the competence in agreement reached by our children in monolingual DPs, and I will compare the results with the published literature on bilingual and monolingual children.

In Bilingual First Language Acquisition there is a vast consensus about the Differentiation Hypothesis, while there is still disagreement on the factors driving the directionality of cross-linguistic influences. The strongest Hypothesis claims that a less/more complex syntactic domain in one language will exercise a positive/negative influence over the other language. A central question is then how to define the complexity of a syntactic domain.

According to Kupisch (2006), it is important to take into account all linguistic levels, their interfaces with syntax and the child's sensibility to them at the different stages of language development. On the basis of these criteria, the DP domain results to be less complex to acquire in Romance languages than in German. In Romance Languages such as Italian and Spanish, bare nouns are in fact less frequent than in German. Moreover, the morphological realization of the number and gender features in D is more transparent than in German. In German, on the contrary, D displays a high degree of syncretism. The German D discerns three genders (masculine, feminine and neuter) and realizes overtly the case feature.

The lower complexity of the DP domain in Romance languages is also suggested by the data of monolingual children. Indeed, in the data of children acquiring a Romance language the functional category D emerges earlier than in German children and it displays a higher rate of gender agreement accuracy[7].

In Figure 4 below I will report the results pertaining the rates of mismatch in agreement attested in Leuco[8].

In Leucò's data, the first occurrence of D is recorded in Italian at the age 2;04.27, and in German at the age of 2;05.05. D became productive in Italian at the age of 2;05.26, while in German only at the age of 2;09.24[9].

As can be observed, the two languages develop asymmetrically but mirroring the development of Italian and German monolingual children. The rate of mismatches in German is always higher than in Italian, where the rate is lower than the 15%. This rate

---

7.   See Pizzuto & Caselli (1992) for data on Italian children, Pérez & Pereira (1991) for data on Spanish children and Eisenbeiss (2000) for data on German children.

8.   The figures of this section report the data of the recordings, which contain more than 5 tokens. In the counting I included only the determiners displaying overt agreement given the agreement rules of the languages under investigation.

9.   I have considered D to be productive if the child is able to use two different forms of D with at least 3 different nouns. I have also included proto-articles.

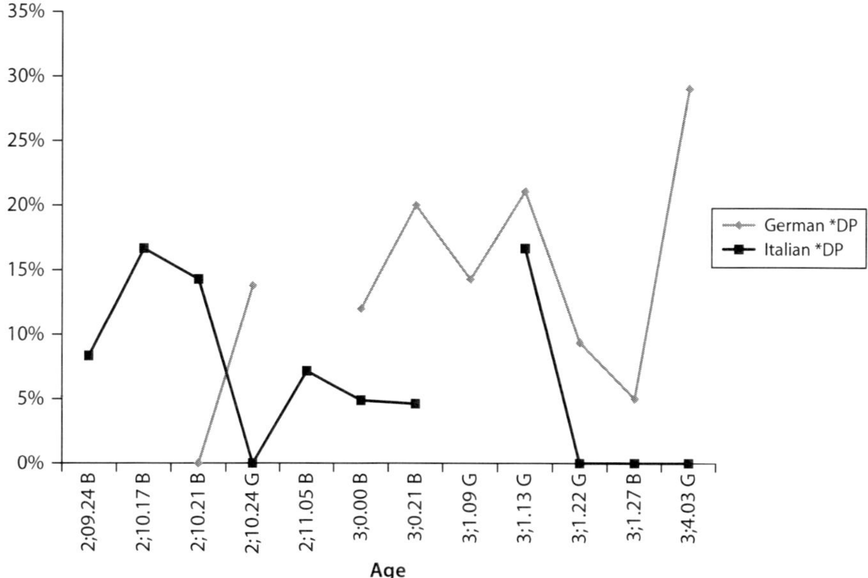

Figure 4. Leucò's rates of mismatches in gender, number and case agreement

is however higher than the one attested in monolingual children and may be interpreted as a negative influence of German. In German, on the contrary, the rates of mismatches reaches the 22% at the age of 2;11.5 and it is even 26% at the age of 3;4.03.

The mismatches attested in Italian may be grouped into three types: 1) mismatches with the indefinite article, 2) mismatches with nouns ending in -*e* and 3) mismatches in number agreement where N is inflected in the plural and the D left in the singular form. This latter type of mismatch is also attested in German. In the German DP the mismatches generally involve the definite article *die* and neuter nouns merged with the definite form *der*. The type of mismatches attested in Italian and German monolingual DPs does not differ from those produced by monolingual and bilingual children (see Cantone 1999, Kupisch, Müller & Cantone 2002 and references quoted therein).

In Lucia's data, the first occurrence of D is attested at the age of 1;08.04 in Italian and at the age of 1;06.05 in Spanish. Lucia came to use D productively at the age of 1;08.24 in Italian and at the age of 1;10.13 in Spanish. In contrast to Leucò, Lucia has a very high accuracy of agreement in both languages: see Figure 5 below. I found only 4 mismatches in the data, the typologies of which are in line with those found in the

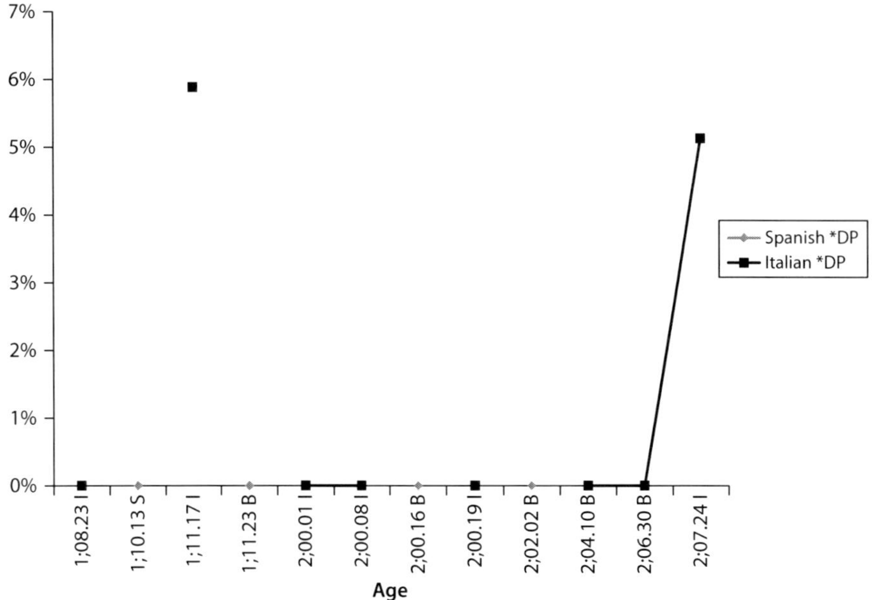

Figure 5. Lucia's rate of mismatches in gender and number agreement

Italian data for Leucò. In Lucia's corpus, however, there are no mismatches with the indefinite article either in Spanish or in Italian[10]:

Overall, as concerns monolingual DPs, the development of the competence in agreement mirrors the development observed in monolingual children. In fact, the Italian/German child has a lower competence in German than in Italian and the mismatches found in the data do not differ from a qualitative point of view from those reported in the literature.

5.   Mixed DPs: Types of mixed agreement

Several studies on early bilingualism claim that early mixing is governed by the same principles at work in adult code-mixing (Cantone 2007, Cantone & Müller 2008, and the references quoted therein). In contrast to adult bilingual code-mixing, however, early mixing reflects the state of the two developing grammars. According to Meisel

---

10.   The forms of the indefinite singular articles *un* and *una* and the definite singular articles *la* are the same in Italian and Spanish. Therefore in the counting they have been classified as Italian or Spanish on the basis of the language of the child's interlocutor. In the mixed sentence, however, they have been excluded, because it is difficult to establish to which language they belong. In a mixed clause such as *no questa è la mia cama* ('no that is my bed'), attested in Lucia data at age of 2;07.24, there is no way to establish if the child is using an Italian or Spanish D.

(1994), the grammatical constraints may be observed as soon as the functional categories emerge in the two languages. This relation is corroborated by the data.

Accordingly, the two bilingual Italian children under analysis begin to switch the language between D and N as soon as the functional category D is attested in monolingual sentences. The first occurrence of mixed DP mirrors the developmental stage in monolingual DPs. Indeed, in an early stage proto-articles are very frequent in mixed as well as in monolingual DPs[11]. The frequency of mixed DPs increases as soon as D becomes productive in the two grammars.

In the Figures 6–7 I will report the type of mixed agreement attested in Leucò's mixed DP with respectively an Italian and a German D. The instances of feature sharing consists of instances where the Ns have the same gender in the two languages, or the gender is simply not detectable because of the syncretism of the German D or the final vowel of the Italian D is elided. As can be observed in most of the mixed DPs, the selected N and the equivalent N share the gender feature, as in (6):

(6)   a.   la$_{F.SG}$ tasche$_{F.SG}$ (*borsa*$_{F.SG}$ 'the bag' Leucò 3;0.21)

       b.   die$_{F/M/N.PL}$ giochi$_{M.PL}$ (*spielzeug* 'the games' Leucò 3;1.22)

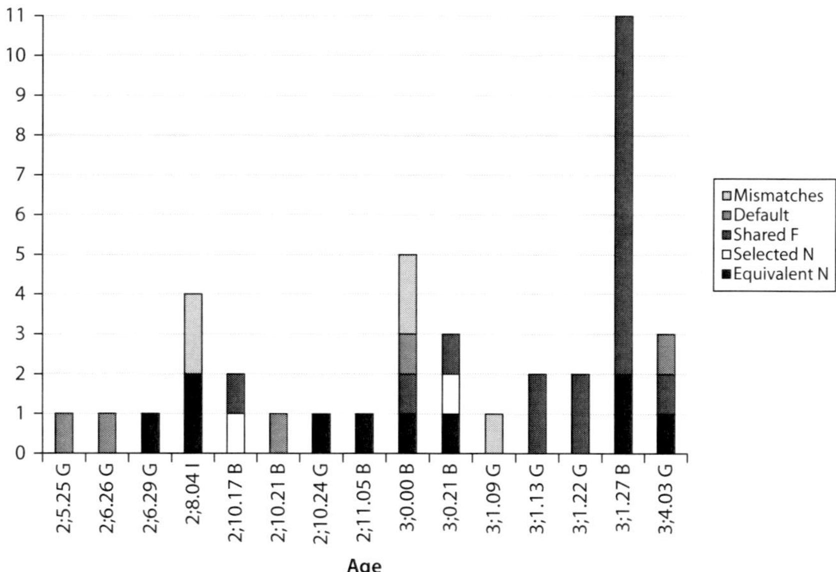

Figure 6. Type of mixed agreement with the Italian D

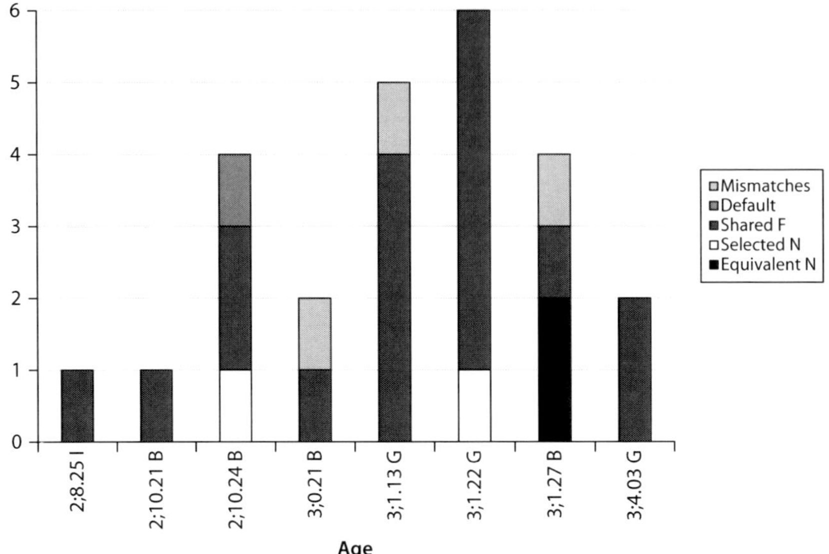

Figure 7. Type of mixed agreement with the German D

This type of mixed agreement does not help us understand how the feature checking works in mixed DPs. In (6a) the child does not to have to choose between the gender of the selected N or the equivalent, while in (6b) the plural forms do not display the gender feature. In the data there are 23/88 (28%) mixed DPs with the N of a different gender in the two languages: one of them do not agree with D (7a), one occurs with the default gender (7b) and 3 display mismatches in number agreement, but D carries the gender of the equivalent N (7.c):

(7)   a.   quelle$_{F.PL}$ augen$_{N.PL}$ (*occhio*$_{M.PL}$ 'the eyes' Leucò 3;01.09)

b.   il$_{M.SG}$ bein$_{N.SG}$ (*gamba*$_{F.PL}$ 'the leg' Leucò 3;04.03)

c.   le$_{F.PL}$ licht$_{N.SG}$ (*luce*$_{F.SG}$ 'the lights' Leucò 2;08.04)

In 5 of the 23 mixed DPs, D displays the gender of the selected N (8a), while in the other 14 (74%) mixed DPs the gender is provided by the equivalent: 6 of these 14 contain an Italian D and a German neuter N (8b).

(8)   a.   eine$_{F.SG}$ casa$_{F.SG}$ (*haus*$_{N.SG}$ 'a house' Leucò 2;10.24)

b.   la$_{F.SG}$ wasser$_{N.SG}$ (*acqua*$_{F.SG}$ 'the water' x2 Leucò 2;11.05

If we compare the patterns of mixed DPs reported in Figures 6 and 7 above, an interesting asymmetry emerges. The mixed agreement of the equivalent is more frequent with the Italian D, and is attested from a very early stage. There are instead only two instances of this type of mixed agreement with the German D, such as the mixed DP in (9) recorded in the last recording at the age of 3;04.03.

(9)   ein$_{\text{M/N.SG}}$ blaues$_{\text{N.SG}}$ biberon$_{\text{M.SG}}$ (*Fläschchen*$_{\text{N.SG}}$ x2 Leucò 3;1.27)
'a blue baby's bottle'

In Lucia's data, I found 28 mixed DPs. In 13 of them the gender of the selected N is the same as the equivalent, while in 7 of them the choice of the gender is not visible because the final vowel of the Italian D is elided (10).

(10)   l'avion$_{\text{M.SG}}$ (*aereo*$_{\text{M.SG}}$ x2 'the airplane' Lucia 2;00.19)

There are then only 8 mixed DPs with the Ns having a different gender in Italian and Spanish: 5 agree with the analogical gender (63%; 11a), while 3 with the selected N (37%; 11b).

(11)   a.   le$_{\text{F.PL}}$ zapatos$_{\text{M.PL}}$ (*scarpe*$_{\text{F.PL}}$ 'the shoes' Lucia 2;00.01)

      b.   el$_{\text{M.SG}}$ mare$_{\text{M.SG}}$ (*mar*$_{\text{F.SG}}$ 'the sea' Lucia 1;11.17)

As in Leucò's data, the pattern in (11a) is distributed asymmetrically, and is attested only in the mixed DPs with the Italian D. In Leucò's data the asymmetry may be seen as a consequence of the different degree of the competence in agreement reached in Italian and German. However, this account cannot explain the absence of the agreement with the equivalent gender with the Spanish D, because Lucia has a high level of competence in both languages. The unexpected asymmetry may be ascribed to the dominance of Italian. According to Bernardini & Schlyter (2004), it is indeed the stronger language that provides the functional categories in early mixing. However, Lucia is not strongly unbalanced. The unexpected asymmetry may be also the consequence of a) the methodology in collecting her data, and b) the need to exclude all definite and indefinite feminine articles (see note 10). In other words it could be that the agreement with the equivalent is simply not detectable if the D is feminine. In order to verify the role of the language dominance and the impact of the methodology in the frequency of the types of mixed agreement more data of Italian/Spanish balanced and unbalanced bilingual children are needed.

6.   Conclusion

Overall the results are in line with the data reported in Radford et al. (2007): the two Italian bilingual children are able to realize agreement in the mixed DP by resorting to the gender of the selected N as well as to the gender of the equivalent. In the data of the Italian/Spanish girl the two types of mixed agreement are equally frequent. In the data of the Italia/German child the agreement with the equivalent noun is the most frequent one. Both children strongly prefer the latter in mixed DPs having an Italian D.

In the case of the Italian/German child this strong preference may be a consequence of the different degree of competence in agreement reached by the child in the monolingual DPs. The lower competence in agreement in German will block the agreement with the equivalent because the child has trouble with the gender of the German Equivalent N. Put differently the opacity of the gender feature of the German N encourages the agreement with its Italian equivalent. In the data of the Italian/ Spanish girl, however, the attested asymmetry is surprising and more data are needed.

The data of the Italian/German child contrasts, however, with the data of four Italian/German bilingual children reported in Cantone & Müller (2008). According to the authors, the agreement with the selected N is the most frequent pattern. A possible explanation for this contrast may be the primary language of the environment: the bilingual children analyzed by Cantone & Müller (2008) in fact, live in German.

Given that, the Language Faculty should be flexible enough in order to generate both types of mixed agreement. The fact that a high degree of competence in agreement is the basic requirement to use both types of mixed DP provides an evidence for their grammaticality. An account of code-mixing based on the DM approach seems to be flexible enough in deriving all the patterns of mixed DPs. However, this is worked out only on the basis of the DP domain and it may over-generate. Future research will tell us whether a DM model of the Bilingual Language Faculty is supported by patterns attested in other syntactic domains and language pairs.

References

Bernardini, P. & S. Schlyter. 2004. Growing syntactic structure and code-mixing in the weaker language: The Ivy Hypothesis. *Bilingualism: Language and Cognition* 7: 49–69.

Bottari, P., P. Cipriani & A. M. Chilosi. 1993/1994. Protosyntactic devices in the acquisition of Italian free morphology. *Language Acquisition* 3: 327–369.

Cantone, K. F. 1999. *Das Genus im Italienischen und Deutschen: Empirische Untersuchung zum bilingualen Erstspracherwerb*. MA thesis, University of Hamburg.

Cantone, K. F. 2007. *Code-switching in Bilingual Children*. Springer: Dordrecht.

Cantone, K. F. & N. Müller. 2008. *Un nase* or *una nase*? What gender marking within switched DPs reveals about the architecture of the bilingual language faculty. *Lingua* 118: 810–826.

Chomsky, N. 1995. *The Minimalist Program*. Cambridge MA: The MIT Press.

Chomsky, N. 2000. Minimalist inquiries: The framework. In *Step by step: Essays on Minimalist Syntax in Honor of Howard Lasnik*, eds. R. Martin, D. Michaels & J. Uriagereka, 89–155. Cambridge MA: The MIT Press.

Eisenbeiss, S. 2000. The acquisition of the DP in German child language. In *Acquisition of Syntax: Issues in Comparative Developmental Linguistics*, eds. M. A. Friedemann & L. Rizzi, 26–62. London: Longman.

Embick, D. & R. Noyer. 2007. Distributed Morphology and the syntax/morphology interface. In *The Oxford Handbook of Linguistic Interfaces*, eds. R. Ramchand & C. Reiss, 289–324. Oxford: OUP.

Grosjean, F. 2001. The bilingual's language modes. In *One Mind, Two Languages: Bilingual Language Processing*, ed. J. L. Nicol, 1–22. Malden MA: Blackwell.

Halle, M. 1997. Distributed Morphology: Impoverishment and fission. In *Papers at the Interface* (MIT Working Papers in Linguistics 30), eds. B. Bruening, Y. Kang & M. McGinnis, 425–449. Cambridge: MIT.

Halle, M. & A. Marantz. 1994. Some key features of Distributed Morphology. In *Papers on Phonology and Morphology* (MIT Working Papers in Linguistics 21), eds. A. Carnie & H. Harley, 275–288. Cambridge: MIT.

Harley, H. & R. Noyer. 1999. Distributed Morphology. *GLOT International* 4: 3–9.

Herring, J. R., M. Deuchar, M. C. P. Couto & M. Quintanilla. 2010. 'I show the madre': Evaluating the predictions about codeswitched determiner-noun sequence using Spanish-English and Welsh-English data. *International Journal of Bilingual Education and Bilingualism* 13: 553–573.

Jake, J., C. Myers-Scotton & S. Gross. 2002. Making a minimalist approach to codeswitching work: Adding the matrix language. *Bilingualism: Language and Cognition* 5: 69–91.

Kramer, R. 2009. *Definite Markers, Phi-features and Agreement: A Morphosyntactic Investigation of the Amharic DP*. PhD dissertation, University of California, Santa Cruz.

Kupisch, T. 2006. *The Acquisition of Determiners in Bilingual German-Italian and German-French Children*. Munich: Lincom.

Kupisch, T., N. Müller & K. F. Cantone. 2002. Gender in monolingual and bilingual first language acquisition: Comparing Italian and French. *Lingue e linguaggio* 1: 107–149.

Liceras, J. M., R. Fernández Fuertes, S. Perales, R. Pérez-Tattam & K. T. Spradlin. 2008. Gender and gender agreement in bilingual native and non-native grammars: A view from child and adult functional-lexical mixings. *Lingua* 118: 827–851.

Liceras, J. M., K. T. Spradlin & R. Fernández Fuertes. 2005. Bilingual early functional-lexical mixing and the activation of formal features. *International Journal of Bilingualism* 9: 227–253.

MacSwan, J. 1999. *A Minimalist Approach to Intra-sentential Code-switching*. New York NY: Garland.

MacSwan, J. 2005. Codeswitching and generative grammar: A critique of the MLF model and some remarks on "modified minimalism". *Bilingualism: Language and Cognition* 8: 1–22.

Marantz, A. 1997. No escape from syntax: Don't try morphological analysis in the privacy of your own lexicon. In *Proceedings of the 21st Annual Penn Linguistics Colloquium* (Penn Working Papers in Linguistics 4, 2), eds. A. Dimitriadis, L. Siegel, C. Surek-Clark & A. Williams, 201–225. Philadelphia PA: University of Pennsylvania.

Meisel, J. M. 1994. Code-switching in young bilingual children: The acquisition of grammatical constraints. *Studies in Second Language Acquisition* 16: 413–439.

Moro, M. 2001. The semantic interpretation and syntactic distribution of determiner phrases in Spanish/English codeswitching. Paper presented at the 3rd International Symposium on Biligualism (ISB3), Bristol, UK, 17–24 April 2001.

Muysken, P. 2000. *Bilingual Speech: A Typology of Code-mixing*. Cambridge: CUP.

Pérez-Pereira, M. 1991. The acquisition of gender: What Spanish children tell us. *Journal of Child Language* 18: 571–590.

Pfau, R. 2009. *Grammar as Processor: A Distributed Morphology Approach to Spontaneous Speech Errors* (Linguistik Aktuell/Linguistics Today 137). Amsterdam: John Benjamins.

Pierantozzi, C. 2008. *La relazione di accordo all'interno del DP misto nel bilinguismo infantile*. PhD dissertation, University of Urbino.

Pierantozzi, C., C. Donati, L. Bontempi & L. Gasperoni. 2006. The puzzle of mixed agreement in early code mixing. In *Language Acquisition and Development: Proceedings of the 2005 GALA Conference*, ed. A. Belletti, 454–466. Newcastle: Cambridge Scholars.

Pizzuto, E. & M. Caselli. 1992. The acquisition of Italian morphology: Implications for models of language development. *Journal of Child Language* 19: 491–557.

Poplack, S., A. Pousada & D. Sankoff. 1982. Competing influences on gender assignment: Variable process, stable outcome. *Lingua* 57: 1–28.

Radford, A., T. Kupisch, R. Köppe & G. Azzarro. 2007. Concord, convergence and accommodation in bilingual children. *Bilingualism: Language and Cognition* 10: 239–256.

Siddiqi, D. 2006. *Minimize Exponence: Economy Effects on a Model of the Morphosyntactic Component of the Grammar*. PhD dissertation, University of Arizona.

Gender marking in L2 learners and Italian-German bilinguals with German as the weaker language*

Antje Stöhr, Deniz Akpınar, Giulia Bianchi and Tanja Kupisch
University of Hamburg, Germany

This paper explores mastery of grammatical gender in German as weaker and dominant language by Italian-German adult simultaneous bilingual speakers as well as highly proficient L2 learners of German with Italian as their L1. Data show that in both bilinguals and L2ers deviances from the target predominantly occur in gender assignment, whereas errors of agreement are infrequent in both groups, indicating that deficiency affects the lexical level rather than morphosyntax. Ceiling performance of the bilingual speakers in German as dominant language suggests that native-like attainment is possible in simultaneous bilingual acquisition but only under the condition that early Age of Onset (AoO) coincides with sufficient input.

Keywords: German, Italian, bilingual language acquisition, second language acquisition, attrition, incomplete acquisition, gender assignment, gender agreement

1. Introduction

A growing number of studies comparing adult bilingual speakers (2L1ers) and second language learners (L2ers) in the last two decades has shown both similarities and differences among these two types of populations (e.g. Au, Knightly, Jun & Oh 2002, Håkansson 1995, Lipski 1993, Montrul 2008, Montrul, Foote & Perpiñán 2008). These

---

* These data were collected as part of the Research Project E11. The project was funded by the German Science Foundation (Deutsche Forschungsgemeinschaft, DFG) as part of the Collaborative Research Center on Multilingualism (Sonderforschungsbereich 538 "Mehrsprachigkeit") hosted by the University of Hamburg. It was directed by Tanja Kupisch and started in June 2009 with Dagmar Barton, Giulia Bianchi and Ilse Stangen as research assistants. We wish to thank two anonymous reviewers for their valuable comments on an earlier version of this paper.

have been shown to depend on several factors, such as level of proficiency of the target language (see Montrul 2005), amount and quality of input in adulthood and modality of acquisition (i.e. written vs. spoken, Montrul et al. 2008). Furthermore, different modules of the grammar seem to be affected to a different extent in bilingual and L2 acquisition. While phenomena at the syntax-discourse interface are subject to a high degree of instability in both modalities of acquisition, syntax proper seems to be more immune to language attrition (see Sorace 2011 for an overview).

Comparing bilingual speakers and L2 learners on grammatical gender allows us to investigate the two populations with respect to lexical and syntactic knowledge and determine the role of Age of Onset (AoO). Previous studies on gender marking have shown that both adult bilingual speakers and L2 learners deviate from the target (i.e. Rogers 1987, Dewaele & Véronique 2001, Franceschina 2001, 2005, Montrul et al. 2008) even if attaining native knowledge seems to be possible in L2 acquistion (White, Valenzuela, Kozlowska-MacGregor & Leung 2004). Under debate is still whether the source of the problem is lexical or syntactic (Carroll 1989, Franceschina 2005, Grüter, Lew-Williams & Fernald 2011) and whether AoO is the crucial factor to the achievement of native knowledge.

Our study will address the following questions:

1. Is early Age of Onset a sufficient condition to attain and maintain native-like competence?
2. What are the similarities and differences between simultaneous bilingual speakers in their weaker language and L2 learners?
3. Does attrition affect gender in the weaker language? If it does, are lexicon and morpho-syntax affected to the same extent?
4. What is the role of the other language (here, Italian) with respect to the speakers' accuracy on gender in German?

2. Gender in German

2.1   Gender assignment in German

German has three genders: masculine (M), feminine (F) and neuter (N). According to Bauch (1971) 50% of German nouns are masculine, while 30% are feminine and 20% neuter. Gender assignment in German follows semantic, morphological and phonological rules. In most cases, the gender of animate nouns reflects the natural sex of its referent, as in the case of *die Frau* 'the woman' and *der Mann* 'the man' (Mills 1986: 23ff), which are feminine and masculine, respectively. There are only a few exceptions to the natural gender rule, such as *das Mädchen* 'the girl', which is neuter although referring to a feminine entity. Beside the natural gender rule, there are 15 other semantic rules in German (Köpcke 1982: 71ff, Köpcke & Zubin 1983, 1984). For example, names of alcoholic beverages are generally masculine, e.g. *der Schnaps* 'the schnaps', and names of numbers are generally feminine, e.g. *die Sieben* 'the seven'.

Gender assignment in German also follows morphological and phonological rules. For example, the derivational suffix *-ung* is associated with feminine gender, e.g. *die Bedeutung* 'the meaning', and nouns ending in *-chen* are typically neuter, e.g. *das Hühnchen* 'the chicken' (diminutive). Once phonological rules are taken into account, a correlation has been shown to exist between syllabicity and gender, as well as between gender and either the initial or the final sound of the word (Altman & Raetting 1973, Köpcke 1982). For example, words ending in [ɛt] are associated with neuter, e.g. *das Bett* 'the bed', bisyllabic nouns ending in [ə] are assigned feminine, e.g. *die Kerze* 'the candle', and words ending in [ts] are generally masculine, e.g. *der Pilz* 'the mushroom'. Even if some regularities have been shown to exist for gender assignment in German, the picture is far from being clear, because (i) the number of rules is high, (ii) there are exceptions to these rules, and (iii) formal and semantic rules sometimes contradict one another.

2.2   Gender agreement in German

While nouns have gender as an inherent property, elements other than nouns receive gender through agreement with the head. German marks gender on determiners and adjectives. Three different inflectional paradigms exist in German: weak, mixed, and strong. Here, we will focus on the weak and the mixed paradigms[1], which differ in type of determiner and morphology of the adjective.

In the weak (definite) paradigm, the article is marked for gender. The adjective does not indicate gender distinctions in nominative case:

(1) a. der   schöne   Mann   (nominative case)
         the-M handsome man-M

     b. die   schöne   Frau   (nominative case)
         the-F beautiful woman-F

     c. das   schöne   Mädchen   (nominative case)
         the-N beautiful girl-N

In the accusative case, the adjective shows a different inflection only if the noun is masculine.

(2) a. den   schönen   Mann   (accusative case)
         the-M handsome-M man-M

     b. die   schöne   Frau   (accusative case)
         the-F beautiful woman-F

---

1.   The strong paradigm is found when there is no preceding determiner – a condition we have not included in our study.

   c. das   schöne   Mädchen   (accusative case)
       the-N beautiful girl-N

In the mixed paradigm, adjectives in the nominative and accusative cases change their endings depending on the gender of the noun (see examples 3). Only DPs in the masculine paradigm mark the distinction between nominative and accusative case. Unlike definite articles, indefinite neuter and masculine articles are homophonous in nominative case.

(3) a. ein schöner   Mann   (nominative case)
       a-M handsome-M man-M

     b. einen schönen   Mann   (accusative case)
       a-M   handsome-M man-M

     c. eine schöne   Frau   (nominative and accusative case)
       a-F   beautiful-F woman-F

     d. ein schönes   Mädchen   (nominative and accusative case)
       a-N beautiful-N girl-N

The examples in (3) illustrate the interaction between gender and case. In the nominative and accusative cases, all articles (except for nominative neuter and masculine) and all adjective endings are unambiguously marked for gender. By contrast, in both weak and mixed paradigms, adjectives in genitive and dative cases, as well as in the plural are inflected in *-en* (e.g. masculine *des schönen Mannes/der schönen Frau* 'of a beautiful man/woman', *dem schönen Mann/der schönen Frau* 'to the beautiful man/woman', *der schönen Männer/der schönen Frauen* 'of the beautiful men/women', *den schönen Männern/den schönen Frauen* 'to the beautiful men/women'). In other words, the adjectives do not mark gender distinctions here.

To sum up, gender agreement in the German DP shows a complex interaction with definiteness and case.

3. Gender in Italian

3.1 Gender assignment in Italian

In contrast to German, Italian has only two genders: masculine and feminine. Similar to German, gender assignment in Italian follows both semantic and morpho-phonological rules (Chini 1995). In Italian, more than 70% of all singular nouns end in [a] or [o], e.g. *casa* 'house' and *libro* 'book'. Those ending in *-a* are feminine and those ending in *-o* are masculine. There is a third relatively large group of nouns ending in [e], which can be either feminine or masculine (e.g. *neve* 'snow' is feminine but *mare* 'sea' is masculine). However, some of them exhibit morpho-phonological cues that are associated with gender. For example, words ending in *-one* (e.g. *pallone* 'ball') are usually associated with masculine and those ending in *-trice* (*lavatrice* 'washing machine') are generally feminine. As in German, the natural gender rule also applies. Furthermore, certain semantic classes are associated with one particular gender. For example, names of fruit are typically feminine (e.g. *mela* 'apple') and those of trees are generally masculine (e.g. *melo* 'apple tree'). In general, in comparison to German, the gender of most Italian nouns is easily predictable based on a few unambiguous formal cues, even though exceptions are attested for Italian as well.

3.2   Gender agreement in Italian

In Italian, determiners and adjectives agree in gender with the head noun they are associated with. In contrast to German, gender agreement within the Italian DP does not vary depending on the definiteness of the noun phrase. Furthermore, gender agreement is not a function of case in Italian, since morphological case shows neither on determiners nor on adjectives in this language. Examples of gender agreement with masculine and feminine nouns with definite and indefinite determiners are provided in (4a) through (4d):

(4)   a.   il   ragazzo bello
          the-M boy-M   handsome-M

      b.   un   ragazzo bello
          a-M boy-M   handsome-M

      c.   la   ragazza bella
          the-F girl-F   beautiful-F

      d.   una ragazza bella
          a-F girl-F   beautiful-F

4.   Previous research on the acquisition of gender in monolingual and bilingual acquisition

It has been commonly observed that monolingual children acquire gender relatively early in German and Italian. Children are sensitive to formal and semantic regularities taking them as cues for assignment. For L2 learners, by contrast, it has often been argued that the inherent gender feature of the noun category cannot be acquired (if the L1 lacks it), although L2ers may attain native-like performance through meta-linguistic knowledge and explicit learning (e.g. Carroll 1989).

While some researchers have postulated that semantic rules take precedence over formal rules in gender assignment (e.g. Corbett 1991), others have recently claimed that it depends on the language and the strength of individual cues which type of rule is prominent (Rodina & Westergaard forthcoming). Many acquisition studies have reported that phonological cues are prevalent during the early stages of acquisition (e.g. Karmiloff-Smith 1979 for French; Levy 1983 for Hebrew; Szagun, Stumper, Sondag & Franik 2007 for German; Chini 1995 for Italian; Rodina & Westergaard forthcoming for Russian). However, some studies suggest that in languages where formal and semantic rules are equally prominent for gender assignment, the two may be acquired simultaneously (Mills 1986, Müller 1990). Rodina & Westergaard (forthcoming) have convincingly shown for Russian that children are highly sensitive to fine distinctions in syntax and morphology and use detailed input information to make inferences about nominal gender rather than using particular cues regardless of the noun class.

Mills (1986) investigated longitudinal data from three German-speaking children, showing sporadic use of gender marked articles from around 2;0 and regular use from age 2;4 with indefinite articles being used more frequently than definite ones. Error rates drop below 10% by age 3;0. Definite articles tend to be unproblematic, although overuse of the feminine definite article *die* has occasionally been reported. Mills also observed that nouns ending in [ə] were always used with the correct gender, even when requiring masculine gender (e.g. *der Hase* 'the hare', *der Löwe* 'the lion'), indicating that overgeneralization of phonological cues is not necessarily found with very frequent items.

Szagun et al. (2007) investigated 21 monolingual children acquiring German, making similar observations: Error rates drop well below 10% by age 3;0 and children made more errors with nouns that do not conform to phonological rules than with nouns that do. Bilingual children have also been shown to acquire gender by age three, and they are sensitive to phonological and semantic rules (e.g. Müller 1990 for children acquiring German simultaneously with a Romance language).

For our study, these findings imply that if we find incomplete mastery of gender in 2L1ers, it is more likely due to attrition than incomplete acquisition because gender is acquired very early and because our subjects had exposure to both languages from birth.

5.   Our study

We investigated knowledge of gender assignment and gender agreement in 20 Italian-German bilinguals, with German as their weaker or stronger language and compared them with 19 Italian advanced L2 learners of German. Our participants performed an Acceptability Judgment Task (henceforth AJT) and an Elicited Production Task (henceforth EPT).

5.1   Participants

Three groups of subjects participated in our study: a. early German-Italian bilinguals (2L1) who grew up in Italy, b. early German-Italian bilinguals (2L1) who grew up in Germany, c. Italian L2 learners of German.

Table 1. Overview of subjects

	2L1ers (German weak)	2L1ers (German strong)	L2-German
Number	8	11	19
AoO (mean AoO)	0	0	11 or later (19.2)
Age range	18–45	18–45	18–45
Mean age	27	29.2	31.3
Cloze test Italian	84%	64%	83%
Cloze test German	58%	80%	55%

For the 2L1ers, language dominance was assessed based on three criteria: a. country of residence during childhood, b. self-assessment, c. proficiency in a cloze test. For the 2L1ers who grew up in Germany, German was the stronger language, for the 2L1ers who grew up in Italy, German was the weaker language even if some of them lived in Germany when we tested them. Italian remained the stronger language of the L2ers, even if some of them had been living in Germany for a long time. All bilinguals were raised in bi-national families and their parents followed the one person–one language strategy. The preconditions for the L2ers to participate were that their first contact with the L2 was after age 11 and that their level of German was advanced. Participants were recruited in Italy and in Germany, for both 2L1ers and L2ers, and they were between 18 and 45 years old. Table 1 provides an overview of the three groups of participants.

5.2   Acceptability Judgment Task (AJT)

The AJT contained a total of 36 items containing nouns selected according to semantic, morphological[2], and phonological assignment rules as well as exceptions to these rules. Stimuli were evenly distributed among these assignment rules and roughly among the three genders and controlled for transfer from Italian. Half of the items were grammatical and half of them ungrammatical. Items were presented in a different random order at each run. An overview of the items is provided in Table 2 below.[3]

Participants had to judge sentences that included definite DPs testing for gender assignment and agreement. More precisely, they were instructed to read as well as to listen to each sentence and repeat the sentence if they found it sounded correct or make changes if they found it sounded incorrect. Participants were given three times the length of the stimulus to repeat or correct it. Stimuli were presented both visually and auditorily because it had been argued previously that bilinguals in their weaker

---

2.   Note that we also tested assignment in compound nouns. Assignment in compounds follows morphological rules, but we will present them separately in the results section.

3.   The AJT also tested other phenomena than gender, but these will not be reported here.

Table 2. Overview of criteria for selection of items with examples (based on Köpcke (1982: 71ff), Mills (1986: 30), Szagun et al. (2007: 447f)

	Semantic	Morphological	Phonological
Masculine	weather terms	-ling	[ts]
n = 14	*Regen* 'rain'	*Pfifferling* 'chanterelle'	*Satz* 'sentence'
Feminine	fruits	-ung	[ə]
n = 14	*Pflaume* 'plum'	*Zeitung* 'newspaper'	*Ratte* 'rat'
Neuter	chemical elements	-chen	[ɛt]
n = 8	*Uran* 'uranium'	*Törtchen* 'tartlet'	*Bett* 'bed'

language may have disadvantages in written tasks (see Montrul et al. 2008: 506f for difference between heritage and L2 learners in written and spoken tasks).

5.3 Elicited Production Task (EPT)

The EPT elicited gender assignment and agreement in the weak and mixed paradigm within the German DP. It elicited eighteen DPs. The nouns were balanced across the three genders, and the distribution of stimuli with respect to assignment regularities was similar to the AJT except that no exceptions were included. Some fillers testing memory capacity of our participants were inserted.

In the EPT, the participants were first presented with two objects (e.g. two pianos) that differed in one feature (e.g. their color) and were asked to describe each of them using a word that describes "how the object is". An example of question and answer is provided in (5).

(5) a. Was siehst du?
      'What do you see?'

   b. ein$_N$ schwarzes$_N$ Klavier$_N$ und ein$_N$ braunes$_N$ Klavier$_N$
      'a black piano and a brown piano'

In the case participants were uncertain about a noun or did not use the target noun (e.g. *Keybord* instead of *Klavier*), the experimenter provided the target noun without revealing the gender (e.g. *What you see is called "Klavier"*). After seeing the two objects for the first time, the participants were presented with only one of the two objects they had previously seen and were asked to indicate what is missing. An example of question and answer is provided in (6).

(6) a. Was fehlt jetzt?
      'What is missing now?'

   b. das$_N$ schwarze$_N$ Klavier$_N$
      'the black piano'

5.4   Data analysis

In analyzing the data, we included in the counts of assignment (either correct or incorrect) only those items that were consistently assigned the same gender.[4] Such a case is exemplified in (7), where the neuter noun *Klavier* 'piano' was assigned masculine gender in both the indefinite and the definite condition. In case of non-consistent assignment, e.g. if the noun was assigned a different gender in the definite and the indefinite condition, as in (8), we excluded the items from the assignment counts (see Montrul et al. 2008 and Meisel 2009 for similar procedures). Normally, the article was taken as an indicator of the assigned gender. In the indefinite condition, where masculine and neuter articles are homophonous, we also took the adjective into account.[5]

(7)   a.   *ein   schwarzer   Klavier
           a-M/N black-M   piano-N

    b.   *der   schwarze   Klavier
           the-M   black-M/F/N piano-N

(8)   a.   *ein   brauner   Meerschweinchen
           a-M/N brown-M   guinea pig-N

    b.   das   braune   Meerschweinchen
           the-N   brown-M/F/N guinea pig-N

We also excluded from the counts nouns whose final sound or sounds were mispronounced, e.g. *Gurkel* instead of *Gurke* 'cucumber'. As for gender agreement, we counted as errors all items in which either the article or the adjective did show incorrect agreement, as shown in (9).

(9)   a.   *ein   runde   Pfanne
           a-M/N round-F pan-F

    b.   *das   gefülltes   Brötchen
           the-N   filled-N   roll-N

---

4.   In both the AJT and in the EPT each noun occurred or was elicited twice: In the AJT, once in combination with an attributive adjective and once in combination with a predicative adjective; in the EPT, once in an indefinite DP and once in a definite one.

5.   An anonymous reviewer notes that taking the endings of adjectives into consideration (with regard to gender assignment) goes beyond gender assignment – which is what is being analyzed here – and enters the realm of gender agreement. S/he is concerned whether it is methodologically licit to count adjective agreement as if it were gender assignment. We agree with the reviewer that we cannot be sure whether the adjective reflects agreement or assignment. However, the same point could be raised with respect to the article. Like the adjective, the article receives gender through agreement with the noun. Although it has been more common in the literature to take the article as an indicator of assignment, it is equally unjustified. Note also, that there were very few cases in which our participants dropped the article, so that a different procedure would not have changed the results considerably.

6. Results

6.1   Gender assignment

The overall results for assignment in the two experiments combined show that gender assignment was affected similarly in the groups of the 2L1 speakers in their weaker language and the L2ers, with mean values of 88.1% for the former group and 80.9% for the latter. By contrast, 2L1ers with German as their stronger language performed at ceiling (97.4%).

A closer look at the AJT and the EPT separately (see Figure 1) reveals that accuracy of the three groups of speakers on gender assignment differed in the two experiments.

Repeated-measures ANOVAs shows that both the bilingual speakers in their weaker language and the L2ers are more accurate in the EPT than in the AJT ($F(1, 18)$ = 19.395, $p < 0.001$ for L2ers; $F(1, 7) = 9.281$, $p = 0.019$ for the 2L1ers). Opposed to this trend, accuracy in the bilingual group with German as the stronger language is significantly higher in the AJT than in the EPT, $F(1, 10) = 6.962$, $p = 0.025$.

We suspect that our 2L1ers with German as their weaker language and the L2ers had more problems with gender assignment in the AJT than in the EPT because the EPT elicited no nouns exhibiting exceptions to assignment rules (and such nouns turned out to provide most difficulties, see Figure 2).

A one-way ANOVA finds a significant effect for semantically determined assignment (in the joint results of the AJT and EPT) between the three groups, $F(2, 35) = 12.459$, $p < 0.001$. Bonferroni ($p = 0.011$) and Tuckey ($p < 0.001$) post-hoc tests show that 2L1ers with German as their stronger language were significantly better than the other two groups. The same effect holds for morphological rule assignment. The 2L1ers with German as the stronger language outperformed the other two groups,

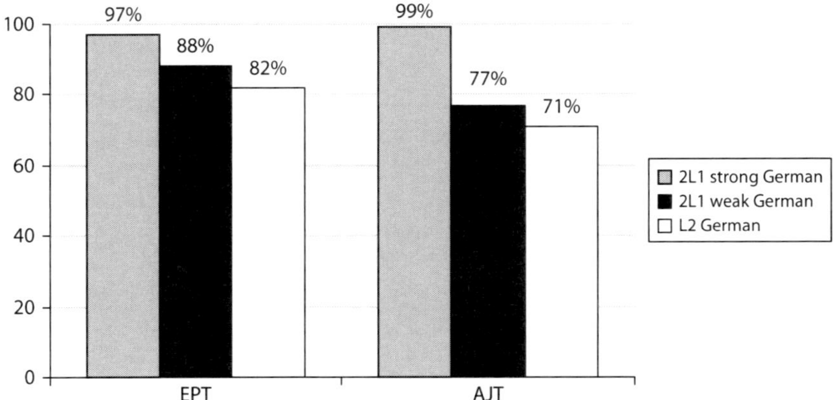

Figure 1. Accuracy in (%) in gender assignment in the AJT and the EPT

$F(2, 35) = 16.431$, $p < 0.001$. Bonferroni and Tuckey post-hoc tests (both $p < 0.001$) confirm this. The L2 group was also significantly less accurate with phonologically-based assignment than the other two groups, $F(2, 35) = 15.374$, $p < 0.001$, as confirmed by Bonferroni and Tuckey post-hoc tests ($p < 0.005$). Results for rule exceptions show the clearest difference between groups. The 2L1ers with German as stronger language outperform the other two groups, $F(2, 35) = 32.829$, $p < 0.001$, as confirmed by Bonferroni and Tuckey post-hoc tests ($p < 0.001$).

Interestingly, phonological items are those where all groups are most accurate. Recall that phonological rules are also among the first to be acquired in L1 German (Mills 1986, Szagun et al. 2007).

Since Italian is also a gendered language, we investigated the role of language influence in gender assignment, i.e. the question whether our subjects were more likely to choose the correct gender for a German noun if its translation equivalent in Italian had the same gender. Data on accuracy with respect to lexical transfer are provided in Figure 3.

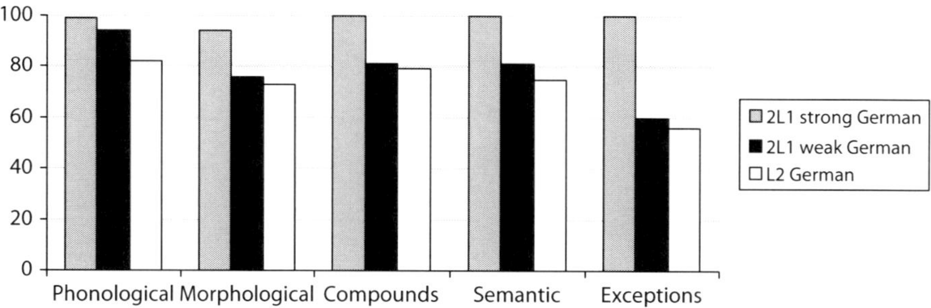

Figure 2. Accuracy (in %) in gender assignment in the five types of words (AJT and EPT)

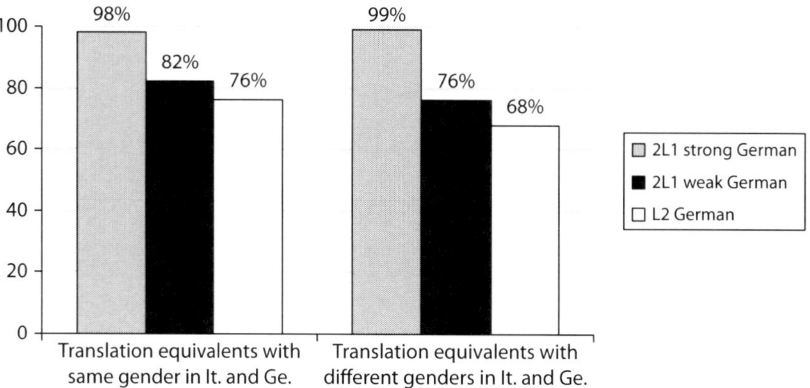

Figure 3. Gender assignment and lexical transfer

Multiple repeated-measures ANOVAs show a significant effect among the groups with respect to language transfer. One repeated-measures ANOVA found that participants in the L2 group assigned gender more accurately to nouns with matching gender in German and Italian than to nouns with different genders in the two languages, F(1, 18) = 6.987, p = 0.017. The opposite effect holds for the 2L1ers with German as the stronger language, $F(1, 10) = 6.404$, $p = 0.03$. Unlike in the other two groups, no effect for transfer was found in the 2L1ers with German as weaker language, $F(1, 7) = 1.822$, $p = 0.219$. Summarizing, the L2ers were significantly better in gender assignment when the German and Italian noun equivalents matched in gender, while this did not hold for the 2L1ers. It should be noted though, that even with nouns that have different genders in German and Italian, all subjects perform well above chance. Therefore, success in gender assignment cannot be attributed to language influence alone.

6.2 Gender agreement

All groups performed 100% accurately with respect to gender agreement in the AJT, in which only definite DPs (i.e. those representing the weak paradigm) were tested. They were less accurate in the EPT, where they were faced with the weak and mixed paradigm. Figure 4 compares the results for agreement across tests and conditions.

The L2 group was significantly more accurate with definite than with indefinite DPs in the EPT, $F(1, 18) = 8.733$, $p = 0.008$. For the 2L1ers with German as the stronger language a repeated-measures ANOVA failed to find a significant effect between definite and indefinite DPs, $F(1, 9) = 0.248$, $p = 0.630$. For the 2L1ers with German as the weaker language, no significant difference between the two conditions could be found either, $F(1, 7) = 0.180$, $p = 0.684$.

The question arises as to what makes the mixed, indefinite paradigm more difficult for L2 learners. Possibly, they have problems retrieving the correct morphological form of the adjective. The most frequent type of error is represented by cases like $ein_{M/N}$ $singende_{F?}$ $Spatz_{M}$ 'a singing sparrow', $ein_{M/N}$ $giftige_{F?}$ $Pilz_{M}$ 'a poisenous mushroom',

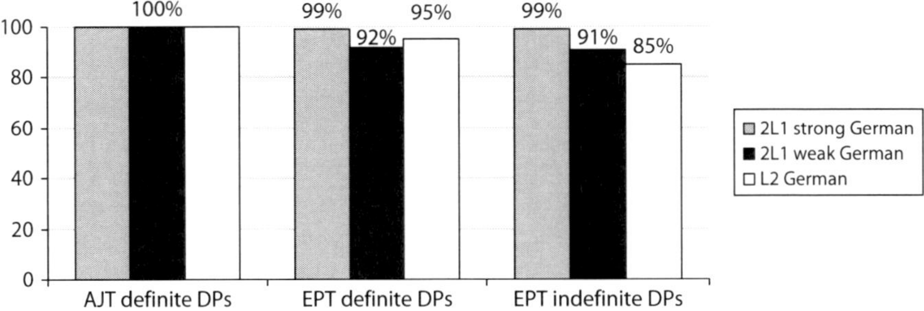

Figure 4. Gender agreement across conditions

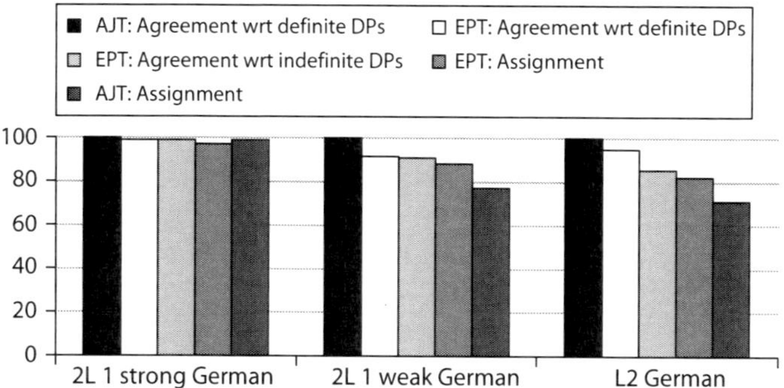

Figure 5. Gender agreement vs. assignment

$ein_{M/N}$ *männliche*$_{F?}$ *Stinktier*$_N$ 'a male skunk', where the adjective looks as if it had been marked for feminine gender, while, at the same time, having the morphological shape required by most adjectives in the weak paradigm in nominative and accusative cases. It therefore appears more plausible to assume that this form represents some kind of default. In fact, with feminine nouns less adjective errors were found; it was more typical that an inappropriate article had been chosen (e.g. $ein_{M/N}$ *quadratische*$_F$ *Bratpfanne*$_F$ 'a rectangular pan'). The facts suggest that agreement in the weak paradigm is most vulnerable in L2 acquisition. This does not imply that agreement per se is problematic. Rather, L2ers may have problems retrieving the correct form in production choosing a default form instead. The default form occurs in both the weak and mixed paradigm and has a relatively high token-frequency.

Comparing agreement and assignment (Figure 5), there are no differences for the bilinguals with German as their stronger language, as they perform target-like across the board. The 2L1ers with German as their weaker language and the L2ers were more successful in agreement than in assignment. Moreover, their data witness problems in the same domains, albeit with different quantities.

7. Conclusions

Our study addressed four questions. The first was whether early age of onset is sufficient to attain and maintain native-like competence. Our data provided evidence that this is not the case, as only bilingual speakers with German as their stronger language (who grew up in Germany) showed ceiling effects across the board, while bilingual speakers with German as their weaker language (who grew up in Italy) did not. Note, however, that among both the L2ers and the 2L1ers with German as weaker language, there were noticeable individual differences with some participants showing ceiling performance, while others seem to have acquired the systems (or lexicons, as we propose further below) incompletely.

Our second question concerned similarities and differences between bilingual speakers in their weaker language and L2ers. For assignment, we found that bilinguals with German as their weaker language and L2ers had problems with the same type of items, specifically those that do not follow assignment rules. Moreover, they performed best when assignment rules were phonologically driven. This could be taken to indicate that the acquisition of phonologically driven assignment rules (and assignment rules more generally) is not subject to differences in the age of onset. In agreement too, data from L2ers and 2L1ers with German as the weaker language witness problems in the same domain, namely in the mixed paradigm tested in the EPT (although the differences between weak and mixed paradigm were not significant for the bilinguals). To sum up, the study has demonstrated qualitative similarities between 2L1ers in their weaker language and L2ers of German (i.e. the same error-pattern), while showing quantitative differences (i.e. in the amount of errors).

The third question we raised was whether lexicon and morpho-syntax are vulnerable to the same extent. It was shown that assignment was error-prone, while there were only occasional errors in agreement. This leads us to conclude that morpho-syntax is not vulnerable to incomplete acquisition or attrition, unlike the lexicon. Interestingly, the same held true for L2 learners (in line with Grüter et al. 2011).

Finally, we investigated the role of transfer from Italian with respect to the speakers' accuracy on gender marking in German. Only the L2ers were significantly better in gender assignment when German and Italian noun equivalents matched in gender than when they did not. However, even the L2ers performed well above chance with nouns having different genders in German and Italian. Therefore, these results suggest that successful acquisition of gender assignment cannot be attributed to lexical transfer alone.

References

Altman, G. & V. Raettig. 1973. Genus und Wortauslaut im Deutschen. *Zeitschrift für Phonetik, Sprachwissenschaft und Kommunikationsforschung* 26: 297–303.

Au, T., L. Knightly, S. Jun & J. Oh. 2002. Overhearing a language during childhood. *Psychological Science* 13: 238–243.

Bauch, H. J. 1971. Zum Informationsgehalt der Kategorie des Genus im Deutschen, Englischen und Polnischen. *Wissenschaftliche Zeitschrift der Universität Rostock* 20: 411–419.

Carroll, S. E. 1989. Second language acquisition and the computational paradigm. *Language Learning* 3: 535–594.

Chini, M. 1995. *Genere grammaticale e acquisizione: Aspetti della morfologia nominale dell'italiano L2*. Milano: Franco Angeli.

Corbett, G. 1991. *Gender*. Cambridge: CUP.

Dewaele, J. M. & D. Véronique. 2001. Gender assignment and gender agreement in advanced French interlanguage: A cross-sectional study. *Bilingualism: Language and Cognition* 4: 275–297.

Franceschina, F. 2001. Morphological or syntactic deficits in near-native speakers? An assessment of some current proposals. *Second Language Research* 17: 213–247.

Franceschina, F. 2005. *Fossilized Second Language Grammars: The Acquisition of Grammatical Gender* (Language Acquisition and Language Disorders 38). Amsterdam: John Benjamins.

Grüter, T., C. Lew-Williams & A. Fernald. 2011. Grammatical gender in L2: Where is the problem? In *BUCLD 35: Proceedings of the 35th Annual Boston University Conference on Language Development*, eds. N. Danis, K. Mesh & H. Sung, 246–258. Somerville MA: Cascadilla Press.

Håkansson, G. 1995. Syntax and morphology in language attrition: A study of five bilingual expatriate Swedes. *International Journal of Applied Linguistics* 5: 153–171.

Karmiloff-Smith, A. 1979. *A Functional Approach to Child Language*. Cambridge: CUP.

Köpcke, K. M. 1982. *Untersuchungen zum Genusystem der deutschen Gegenwartssprache*. Tübingen: Niemeyer.

Köpcke, K. M. & D. Zubin. 1983. Die kognitive Organisation der Genuszuweisung zu den einsilbigen Nomen der deutschen Gegenwartsprache. *Zeitschrift für germanistische Linguistik* 11: 166–182.

Köpcke, K. M. & D. Zubin. 1984. Sechs Prinzipien für die Genuszuweisung im Deutschen: Ein Beitrag zur natürlichen Klassifikation. *Linguistische Berichte* 93: 26–50.

Levy, Y. 1983. It's frogs all the way down. *Cognition* 15: 75–93.

Lipski, J. 1993. Creoloid phenomena in the Spanish of transitional bilinguals. In *Spanish in the United States: Linguistic Contact and Diversity*, eds. A. Roca & J. Lipki, 155–182. Berlin: Mouton de Gruyter.

Meisel, J. M. 2009. Second language acquisition in early childhood. *Zeitschrift für Sprachwissenschaft* 28: 5–34.

Mills, A. E. 1986. *The Acquisition of Gender: A Study of English and German*. Berlin: Springer.

Montrul, S. 2005. Second language acquisition and first language loss in adult early bilinguals: Exploring some differences and similarities. *Second Language Research* 21: 199–249.

Montrul, S. 2008. *Incomplete Acquisition in Bilingualism: Re-examining the Age Factor* (Studies in Bilingualism 39). Amsterdam: John Benjamins.

Montrul, S., R. Foote & S. Perpiñán. 2008. Gender agreement in adult second language learners and Spanish heritage speakers: The effect of age and context of acquisition. *Language Learning* 58: 503–553.

Müller, N. 1990. Developing two gender assignment systems simultaneously. In *Two First Languages: Early Grammatical Development in Bilingual Children* (Language Acquisition and Language Disorders 7), ed. J. M. Meisel, 193–234. Amsterdam: John Benjamins.

Rodina, Y. & M. Westergaard. Forthcoming. Cues and input frequency in the acquisition of grammatical gender in Russian. *Journal of Child Language*.

Rogers, M. 1987. Learners' difficulties with grammatical gender in German as a foreign language. *Applied Linguistics* 8: 48–74.

Sorace, A. 2011. Pinning down the concept of "interface" in bilingualism. *Linguistic Approaches to Bilingualism* 1: 1–33.

Szagun, G., B. Stumper., N. Sondag & M. Franik. 2007. The acquisition of gender marking by young German-speaking children: Evidence for learning guided by phonological regularities. *Journal of Child Language* 34: 445–471.

White, L., E. Valenzuela, M. Kozlowska-MacGregor & Y.-K. I. Leung. 2004. Gender and number agreement in nonnative Spanish. *Applied Psycholinguistics* 25: 105–133.

Appendix

Items in the Acceptability Judgment Task

a. *Grammatical Items*

Die alte Kiefer im Garten meiner Eltern ist fast fünf Meter hoch.

Die heiße Kürbissuppe schmeckt heute besonders gut.

Die köstliche Pfifferlingsoße ist selbstgemacht.

Die schlimme Herzkrankheit meiner Tante muss von einem Arzt behandelt werden.

Die schmutzige Ratte ist aus der Kanalisation gekommen.

Die starke Abneigung gegen Spinnen macht mich ganz verrückt.

Die strahlende Sonne ist das Zentrum unseres Planetensystems.

Die ständige Gier der Menschen gehört zu den 7 Todsünden.

Der enorme Reichtum meiner Eltern ermöglicht mir ein gutes Leben.

Der kommerzielle Uranabbau ist sehr umstritten.

Der leckere Pfifferling ist in meinem Garten gewachsen.

Der mittelmäßige Sprung des Sportlers reichte nicht für eine Medaille.

Der trockene Wein aus Italien schmeckte gut zum Essen.

Der wachsende Kommerz ist das Ziel vieler Geschäftsleute.

Das ausgeliehene Anatomiebuch ist verschwunden.

Das knarrende Scharnier muss gefettet werden.

Das leckere Törtchen kostet zwei Euro.

Das radioaktive Uran wird für die Atomkraft genutzt.

b. *Ungrammatical Items*

Das diesjährige Meisterschaft im Tennis findet in Hamburg statt.

Das hohe Reling verhindert, dass jemand ins Wasser fällt.

Das neue Törtchenform ist sehr praktisch beim Backen.

Der letzte Pflaume ist für dich.

Der menschliche Anatomie wird seit der Antike erforscht.

Der traditionelle Weinprobe hat mir sehr gut gefallen.

Das gelbe Schwefel stinkt wie verdorbene Eier.

Das hübsche Bierdeckel ist für die Sammlung meines Opas.

Das lästige Schädling muss aus meinem Haus verschwinden.

Die gewonnene Meisterschaftspokal steht im Clubhaus.

Die lange Satz ist schwer zu verstehen.

Die leckere Käse ist heute im Angebot.

Die riesige Kürbis im Garten ist perfekt für Halloween.

Die ständige Regen geht mir auf die Nerven.

Der gesunde Herz schlägt ungefähr 70 mal pro Minute.

Der helle Grün steht dir wirklich gut.

Der verbreitete Christentum ist die größte Weltreligion.

Die amerikanische Bier aus Chicago schmeckt wie Wasser.

II. Items in the Elicited Production Task

eine verdorbene Banane/die verdorbene Banane
eine runde Pfanne/die runde Pfanne
eine günstige(re) Zeitung/die günstige(re) Zeitung
eine krumme Gurke/die krumme Gurke
eine kleine Tanne/die kleine Tanne
eine warme Heizung/die warme Heizung
ein lilaner Schmetterling/der lila(ne) Schmetterling
ein spanischer Sekt/der spanische Sekt
ein schlafender Mond/der schlafende Mond
ein rennender Frischling/der rennende Frischling
ein singender Spatz/der singende Spatz
ein giftiger Pilz/der giftige Pilz
ein belegtes Brötchen/das belegte Brötchen
ein schwarzes Bett/das schwarze Bett
ein braunes Meerschweinchen/das braune Meerschweinchen
ein menschliches Skelett/das menschliche Skelett
ein braunes Klavier/das braune Klavier
ein weibliches Stinktier/das weibliche Stinktier

A bidirectional study of object omissions
in French-English bilinguals[*]

Mihaela Pirvulescu, Ana T. Pérez-Leroux and Yves Roberge
University of Toronto, Canada

A common assumption in the field of bilingual acquisition is that while bilinguals might have separate language representations, the languages can also influence one another. Previous studies on object (clitic) omission consider a combination of null argument and non-null argument languages, and results vary. The debate concerns whether or not cross-linguistic effects exist in this domain. This paper reports data from bilingual French-English children on an elicited production task. The goal of the paper is to determine if we can observe a bilingual effect in the domain of object clitic omission which cannot be attributed to cross-linguistic influence. We conclude that such effects exist and we propose to attribute them to the retention of a default null object representation.

Keywords: French, English, cross-linguistic influence, clitics, object omission, bilingual effects

1. Introduction

Under what conditions does cross-linguistic influence in bilingual language development occur? Crucial issues in this research domain include the causes, the directionality, and the potential role of language external factors such as language balance and the quality and quantity of the input. Proposed language-internal restrictions on cross-linguistic influence include grammatical domains (the interface syntax-pragmatics) and language typology (Müller, Hulk & Jakubowicz 1999, Hulk & Müller 2000, Yip & Matthews 2000, among others). Inherent in the ongoing discussions is the idea that the

* We would like to thank Isabel Belzil, Jürgen Meisel, Johanne Paradis, Nelleke Strik, Danielle Thomas, the audience at the conference Multilingual Individuals and Multilingual Societies, Hamburg 2010, and two anonymous reviewers for their insightful comments. This work was partially funded by Social Sciences and Humanities Research Council of Canada (410–05–0239 and 410–09–2026).

input itself has some bearing: since the bilingual child is exposed to two languages, the input is problematic to a certain extent. Some authors propose that the problem resides in surface ambiguity but the proposals differ in how the learning mechanism resolves this ambiguity in bilingual context: by temporarily relying on default structures reinforced by the other language (Hulk & Müller 2000, Müller & Hulk 2001) or by using fixed linguistic chunks from the target language conjoined in a non-target, non-analyzed linear string (Döpke 2000). The crucial idea is that input is problematic insofar as it concerns grammatical areas involving cross-linguistic contrasts; for example null objects being available or prohibited, *wh*-words being allowed *in situ* or having to move in interrogatives, etc. Input as a measurable factor underlying language dominance was also proposed as a determinant of cross-linguistic influence (Grosjean 1982, Yip & Matthews 2000, Bernardini & Schlyter 2004).

While it is very likely that one language can directly influence the other, we consider here other possible types of developmental effects arising from bilingual input. More specifically, we investigate whether a bilingual effect can exist if we can factor out cross-linguistic influence. We explore this question by studying object omission in simultaneous bilingual children. Previous work has identified increased patterns of object omissions in bilingual children, but data has originated primarily from combinations of topic-drop (German, Dutch) or null argument (Chinese) languages and non-null argument languages (French, Italian, English). In this article we investigate whether a bilingual effect in object omissions can occur when object pronouns are obligatory in both languages; we use French and English. Previous studies have shown that monolingual children in both languages have an early stage of pronominal omission, but of different duration (Pérez-Leroux, Pirvulescu & Roberge 2008).

2.   Background

2.1   General assumptions about bilingual development

A common assumption in the study of cross-linguistic influence is the hypothesis of language differentiation (Meisel 1986, Genesee 1989, Paradis 2000). At the same time, it is acknowledged that while bilinguals might have separate bilingual representations, the languages can influence one another (Paradis 2001, Lleó, Kuchenbrandt, Kehoe & Trujillo 2003, Kupisch 2006, Nicoladis 2002). Cross-linguistic influence in bilingual children can either lead to quantitative differences with respect to monolingual development (i.e., different rates of production, resulting in acceleration or delay; see Pérez-Leroux, Cuza & Thomas 2011, Kupisch 2007, Bernardini & Schlyter 2004, Gawlitzek-Maiwald & Tracy 1996, among others) or to qualitative differences (i.e., transfer, the introduction of certain structures from one language into the other; see Yip & Matthews 2000, Döpke 2000, among others). Cross-linguistic influence is not random but restricted, and a key question is to define under which circumstances (i.e., in which language combinations and in which grammatical domains) it can occur. Key characteristics gathered from previous research so far are domain specificity, language typology and unidirectionality.

2.2   Previous studies of object omission in bilingual development

Previous studies on object omission in bilingual children consider combinations of topic-drop or null argument languages and non-null argument languages. Several research papers by Müller and colleagues have shown that for the phenomenon of object drop and object preposing the Germanic language (German or Dutch) influences the Romance language (French or Italian) and not vice-versa (Van der Linden & Hulk 1996, Müller & Hulk 2000, Müller et al. 1999, Hulk 2000, Hulk & Müller 2000, Müller & Hulk 2001). These studies analyzed spontaneous speech from children between early 2 and 3 years of age. Their proposal is that cross-linguistic influence happens generally when two conditions are met: 1) the affected property is at the interface between pragmatics and syntax (the C-domain in their case); 2) there is structural overlap between the two languages. In the specific case of object omission, the two conditions are met, according to the authors. First, object omission (or object drop) in initial grammars can be characterized universally as empty topics licensed via a default discourse licensing strategy. Second, a combination of languages, such as German and French, presents the necessary structural overlap: the default discourse-based strategy (discourse licensing of empty objects) is present in both languages in the early grammar; however, in French, the input can be ambiguous between discourse-licensing strategy and morphological licensing. For example, a construction such as (1) could reinforce the discourse-licensing strategy (Hulk & Müller 2000: 230; *ec* stands for 'empty category'):

(1)   Ça   j'ai   vu *ec*
     that I = have seen
     'I have seen that.'

The construction with an object clitic, while a cue pointing to a morphological licensing strategy, could also be ambiguous because of the preverbal position of the clitic, as in (2):

(2)   Marie le voit *ec*
     Marie him = sees
     'Mary sees him.'

This results in 'indirect' influence, where the discourse-based licensing strategy is reinforced in French (or Italian) by the input from the topic-drop language (German or Dutch). This indirect influence manifests as a quantitative difference with respect to monolinguals: bilingual children omit objects at a higher rate and for a longer time in French (or Italian) than monolingual francophone or italophone children. For monolingual French children, some naturalistic data show the omissions are between 11 and 20%; resolution time of omissions is late 2 year olds in these studies (see Jakubowicz, Müller, Riemer & Rigaut 1997, Van der Velde, Jakobowicz & Rigaut 2002, Müller & Hulk 2001). However, subsequent work taking in consideration only the clitic context shows that omissions can be as high as 60% in spontaneous speech (Pirvulescu 2006). For bilingual children object omission in French can be as high as 100% and by late 3 year-old they still omit around 25% of the objects (Müller & Hulk 2001).

Considering two typologically distant and genetically unrelated languages, Cantonese and English, Yip & Matthews (2000, 2005) analyze a naturalistic corpus of two Cantonese-English bilingual children (2 to 3 years of age) and find evidence for licensing of null objects in child English, which they attribute to cross-linguistic influence from Cantonese[1]. They consider cross-linguistic influence in this domain to be both quantitative (higher rate of null objects in English for bilinguals compared to monolingual English) and qualitative (transfer of a syntactic structure – the null topic – from Cantonese into English). The directionality of transfer appears to be due to language dominance, with non-target structures found more prevalent in English (non-dominant language) when Cantonese is the dominant language. Another proposed factor, echoing findings in the studies discussed above, is input ambiguity. The fact that some verbs in English can appear without an object makes the English input consistent with the postulation of null objects. This is why, the authors hypothesize, illicit null objects can still remain in the English of bilingual children as old as 6 years of age, while they disappear much earlier in monolingual Anglophones: by age 3 in spontaneous corpora, by age 4 in experimental setting; see Ingham (1993), Hyams & Wexler (1993), Huang (1999) for spontaneous corpora; Pérez-Leroux et al. (2008) for experimental data.

The studies reviewed above have different takes concerning the bilingual vs. monolingual acquisition of direct objects: Müller and colleagues assume continuity between monolingual and bilingual development with respect to the initial representation and the role played by the input. However, the work by Yip and Matthews suggests that bilingual and monolingual children take different acquisitional paths. Both studies argue for a form of cross-linguistic influence and both proposals take the Chinese-like null topic representation as the common structure in both languages of the bilinguals:

(3)   [Topic]$_i$ eat x$_i$ (where the topic is specific)

The null object is a variable and a Chinese-like recoverability mechanism is in place, where the null object is recovered from the discourse through an empty IP-adjoined

---

1.   Another work treating two typologically unrelated languages is Blais, Oshima-Takane, Genesee & Hirakawa (2010); the authors did not find any influence from Japanese (which allows null arguments) onto French in the domain of object omission; however, the children were older (mean age 5;08) which might mean that they already resolved the null object language setting.

topic. Müller and colleagues propose that this initial representation in early grammar is a default universal structure. According to this proposal, the change from a Chinese-type grammar to a French-type grammar is triggered by the lexical instantiation of the CP domain, which makes the null object illicit in the adjoined IP position. Quantity and quality of the input regulates the resolution of the illicit null objects in non-null object languages: for bilinguals, evidence for the null object representation is more pervasive when one of the languages is a topic-drop or a null object language. In this case, illicit null objects will be higher and will remain for a longer period in bilingual than in monolingual acquisition. For Yip and Matthews, English bilinguals, unlike English monolinguals, assume the structure in (3) under influence from Cantonese.

For both types of analysis, a bilingual effect is obtained only when one of the languages of the bilingual child allows null objects. The clear prediction that these studies make is that a bilingual child acquiring two languages that do not allow null objects (such as English and French, for example) should not exhibit more object omissions in their Romance language as compared with monolinguals. We are testing this prediction in the current study. In addition, we consider that studies of interactions between two languages that are different with respect to the grammatical property investigated run the risk of confounding two possible sources of bilingual effects: those due to the grammatical differences (unidirectional cross-linguistic influence) and those due to the mere exposure to two languages (general bilingual effect). In the study by Pérez-Leroux, Pirvulescu & Roberge (2009), children acquiring French (aged 3;0–4;2, N = 34) in a monolingual context and a French/English bilingual context differ in the amount of omissions: francophone children (identified as monolinguals by their parents) growing up in an Anglophone environment had almost twice as many object omissions as the francophone monolingual children from Montreal. English exposure (although, presumably, mostly passive) played a role in the domain of object omission.

In order to tease apart the two sources, unidirectional cross-linguistic influence vs. bilingual effect, we focus on two non-referential null object languages: English and French. In this language pair, grammatical difference is not an issue in the particular domain under study, as we will argue below in our discussion of object omission from the perspective of a typology of null objects.

3.   Object omission and microvariation

Work on object omission must take into account the variety of null object constructions in adult grammars, and the initial UG-given representation(s) that mediate attainment of these constructions. For our purposes, it is essential to establish a general distinction between two constructions with unexpressed direct object complements that can be argued to involve syntactic representations with null objects. A first type of null object is found with transitive verbs used intransitively, with an implicit interpretation of the missing object. We adopt Hale & Keyser's (2002) approach, namely that the semantic interpretation of the non-referential object is not accidental and follows from its syntactic representation as a null bare noun akin to a cognate object standing in a selectional semantic relation with the verb as shown in (4); see Cummins & Roberge (2005). Examples in (5), based on Gillon (2006), show the selectional link between verb and null object.

(4)

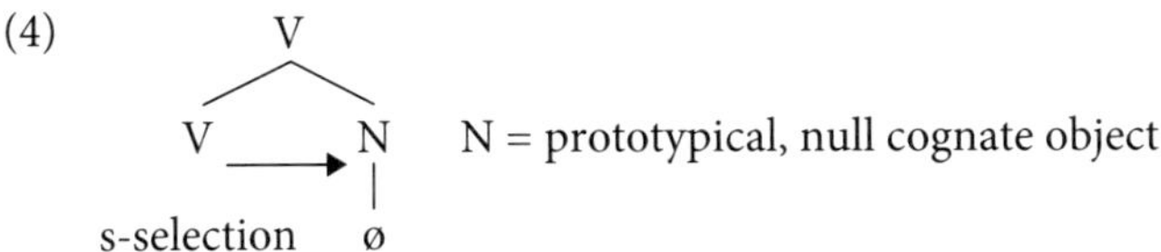

(5)   a.   Bill read/ate __ this afternoon.   (='stuff')
            → quantificational (i.e. generic, indefinite)
       b.   Hilary always leaves __ early.   (='places')
            → quantificational
       c.   Hilary left __ at noon.   (='there')
            → ambiphoric (co-text or deictic)
       d.   John always washes __ before going to bed.   (='himself')
            → reflexive
       e.   Hilary and John met __ at noon for lunch.   (='each other')
            → reciprocal

A second type of null object is referential (or anaphoric) and can be licensed in various language-specific ways. In the case of discourse-oriented languages, such as Mandarin Chinese or Japanese, where pronouns are rare, a null object can refer freely to a previously established discourse antecedent through a null topic in the left periphery; see Huang (1982, 1984).

(6)   Mandarin; Huang (1982: 355)
       Q: Lisi, shei kanjian-le __?
            Lisi who see-PFV
            'As for Lisi, who saw (him)?'

       A: Zhangsan shuo ni   kanjian-le __.
            Zhangsan say   you see-PFV
            'Zhangsan said that you saw (him).'

Similar null objects are present in languages with pronominal systems. In some cases, such as Portuguese, anaphoric discourse linked null objects coexist with accusative clitics. Raposo (1986) argues that there is free variation in Portuguese between null objects and accusative clitics. Similarly, in Polish there are referential null objects with contextual determined antecedent, as shown in (7). Finally, referential null objects can also be found in some languages with developed systems of morphological V-obj agreement, such as Pashto, as in (8).

(7) Polish

> A: Czy podlalas   moja palme?
>
>   if   water-PST-2SG my   palm
>
>   'Did you water my palm?'
>
> B: Podlalam   *ec*/ja.
>
>   water-PST-1SG ec/it
>
>   'I watered (it).'   (Kowaluk 1999: 137; *ec* stands for 'empty categsory')

(8) Pashto

> a. ma maṇa wə-xwar-a
>
>   I   apple Prf-eat-3FSG
>
>   'I ate the apple.'
>
> b. ma *e* wə-xwar-a
>
>   I   Prf-eat-3fsg
>
>   'I ate it.'   (Huang 1984: 535–536; *e* stands for 'empty category')

This non-exhaustive list of cross-linguistic null object possibilities is meant to illustrate the variety that can potentially be found in the input any child is exposed to. It could be that the target language has a fairly restricted set of null object constructions, as in English for instance, or a more developed system, as in Portuguese. In terms of language acquisition, this variety underscores the need for children's initial grammar to be sufficiently flexible to accommodate the range of possibilities. We hypothesize that the minimal structure in (4) is used by children as an all-purpose, semantically unrestricted representation for all null object contexts and that the acquisition process refines the lexical and syntactic representation of this N, resulting in more restrictive representations reflecting the null object constructions found in the target grammar; see Pérez-Leroux et al. (2008). More specifically, our hypothesis implies that the representation in (4) applies as an initial default representation and serves as the basis for the development of referential null object constructions. If this is the case, it should hold for both monolingual and bilingual acquisition.[2] More importantly for our purposes, the variety of null object constructions highlights the fact that the study of bilingual development involving such drastically different languages as Japanese and English, Pashto and English, or Portuguese and French with richly different syntactic null object representations, may obscure what is really going on in terms of interactions. Given our objective to minimize potential cross-linguistic influences in order to determine whether or not there is still a bilingual effect, such pairs are not ideal. Minimally different languages such as French and English allow a more fine-grained study, as we can examine whether there is still a bilingual effect despite the similarities. Most recent studies agree on the following description of the two languages at play, although

---

2. The details of how this can be achieved developmentally go beyond the scope of this paper but interactions between morphological agreement, cliticization, binding-theoretic concepts, movement, and empty categories are necessarily at play.

they do not necessarily agree on the kind of analysis needed to account for the facts; see Lambrecht & Lemoine (1996, 2005), Cummins & Roberge (2005), Larjavaara (2000) and references cited. In both languages, most transitive verbs can appear without an overt object; the null object is of the non-referential type (9)–(10). Even verb types that resist this alternation can be found in intransitive frames in corpora, as in (11)–(12).

(9)   Look; the cow's eating the grass! vs. the cow's eating__!
(10)   Regarde; la vache mange l'herbe. vs. la vache mange__!
(11)   There are those who annihilate__ with violence – who devour __.
(12)   *Manger! je suis garant qu'il dévore__.*
       (Beaumarchais, *Le mariage de Figaro*)

In both languages, transitive and unergative verbs differ in their frequency of occurrence in the two frames. French and English, for the most part, disallow discourse-linked referential null objects of the Portuguese or Japanese type. Examples in (13)–(14) are only grammatical with non-referential reading of the null object. For a referential reading, both languages require an overt pronoun, as shown in (15)–(16). However, as represented in (17), accusative clitic pronouns in French are affixed to the verb (or auxiliary) and the construction includes a null pronominal in the canonical object position.

(13)   * John read this book and I read__ too.
(14)   * Jean a lu ce livre et j'ai lu__ aussi.
(15)   John read this book and I read it too.
(16)   Jean a lu ce livre et je l'ai lu aussi.
(17)   ... je l'ai lu *pro* aussi.

The advantage of studying the English-French pair is that the difference between the two languages reduces to the existence of (accusative) clitics in French but not in English. But inasmuch as *pro* has all the properties of a pronoun, there is no reason to argue that the two languages differ in terms of the presence or absence of referential null objects. Both French and English use pronouns to refer back to a linguistic antecedent. In French, this pronoun is a *pro*, whose features correspond to those of the clitic. In English it is a strong pronoun. The clitic vs. strong pronoun distinction would only be considered relevant in the grammatical domain under study here if it could be shown: 1) that the existence of an accusative clitic system in French is responsible for the availability of a referential null object construction without *pro* in this language; and/or 2) if it could be shown that in the process of acquiring French as an L1, children systematically omit accusative clitics. Concerning the first point, Lambrecht & Lemoine (1996, 2005), Cummins & Roberge (2005) and Larjavaara (2000), among others, argue that there exists a referential null object construction in

French. However, the exact nature of this construction remains unclear; Grüter (2009) puts it this way:

> ... there appears to be converging evidence that referential null objects are indeed attested in French, although their exact distribution is only poorly understood at this point. Although earlier studies proposed that referential null objects were confined to a closed (albeit large) class of transitive verbs ..., more recent work assumes the null instantiation of referential direct objects to be a fully productive, though strongly stigmatized, option in contemporary French, constrained by pragmatic, discursive, and stylistic factors (Grüter 2009: 217).

Available corpus studies so far are scarce; Pirvulescu (2006) analyzes omissions in the clitic-context in child-directed speech and finds 9.4% omissions; omissions peak at 70–80% for children under 2;5 in the same context. Schmitz & Müller (2008), also analyzing child-directed speech, find around 10% omissions in the object position in general. The results from experimental studies (Pérez-Leroux et al. 2008) show that in a context unambiguously eliciting accusative clitics (i.e., a referential object), the adults results give 81% clitics, 18% DP, and only 1% null referential objects. For the sake of comparison, the 3 year-old children's results are 13% clitics, 51% DPs, and 35% null referential objects. We conclude that the existence of a marked referential null object construction in French is not likely to be a factor in the current study. As for the second point, L1 French acquisition studies clearly show that children, when they omit accusative clitics, do so optionally: in the same (clitic) contexts, attested child answers are omissions, or DPs or pronominal clitics (Müller, Crysmann & Kaiser 1996, Jakubowicz et al. 1997, Pirvulescu 2006, Pérez-Leroux et al. 2008).

Returning to the acquisition context, since children have acquired the French accusative clitic system, there is no reason to believe that one language should have an influence on the other with respect to object omission. The English input should not lead to an increase in non-target like null objects in French. Let us now consider other potential hypotheses.

Hypothesis and prediction: The bilingual effect

We assume the child starts with an unrestricted null object; thus, some features of the experience must aid the child in making inferences about the proper range of meanings of null objects in order to arrive at the target grammar. To be more specific, previous studies of monolingual children show that null object constructions present an inherent ambiguity in that the adult use of transitive verbs can often appear in a context with a potential available antecedent, obscuring the difference between referential vs. generic interpretation (Pérez-Leroux et al. 2008). Therefore, the issue of input ambiguity is relevant for both monolingual and bilingual acquisition. We propose that in both modes of acquisition, the child will cope with the ambiguity in the same way: by retaining the default representation. Moreover, it has been proposed that in monolingual acquisition the frequency in the input of a grammatical property correlates with the timing of the acquisition of the property (Yang 2002). The bilingual acquisition context represents, from this point of view, a case where, especially for balanced bilinguals, there is equally reduced input in each language with respect to monolingual acquisition of the respective languages (Paradis & Genesee 1996). If the bilingual input is both more ambiguous (variation at the same time within and across languages) and less robust then it is bound to provide conflicting learning data affecting the reweighting algorithm and lead to a delay in grammar selection. We therefore expect a bilingual effect independent of the two languages of a bilingual child and we present two competing hypotheses:

Hypothesis 1: Bilingual Continuity Hypothesis: dual input is compatible with a larger array of grammars from the hypothesis space and, in the case of objects, will lead to longer retention of the default representation (i.e. object omission). We expect more omissions in French of bilingual children's French than in French monolinguals even when the other language of bilinguals is not a null argument language.

Hypothesis 2: Cross-linguistic influence: unidirectional influence happens from one language to another when there is language overlap. This is to be expected, for the domain of object omission, in the case of a null argument (Chinese, Japanese) or topic drop (German, Dutch) and non-null argument language (French) but not when both languages are non-null argument languages (such as French and English). Since one of the languages in this study is English, we expect no significant omissions in the French of bilingual children when compared to French monolinguals.[3] A boosting effect on pronouns in French could be expected.

4. Method

4.1   Participants

Twenty-nine bilingual children and 30 monolingual Francophone children (who served as controls and were from the Montreal area) between the ages of 3 and 5 participated in the study. Children were separated into age groups, as summarized in Table 1. This follows previous elicitation studies on monolingual Francophones, where 3 year-olds are shown to be in an omission stage (see Pérez-Leroux et al. 2008).

---

3.   Cross-linguistic influence might show as influence of the pronominal system of English (strong pronoun, canonical position) on the pronominal clitic system of French (weak pronoun, non-canonical position). However, so far it has mostly been shown that bilingual children do not make such placement errors, and that these are typical of adult L2-learners (Granfeldt & Schlyter 2004 and references therein). But see Hulk (2000) where the author finds some placement errors with clitics, which are attributed to influence from Dutch.

Table 1. Bilingual and monolingual age groups

	French Monolinguals			Bilinguals		
	N	Age range	Mean (SD)	N	Age range	Mean (SD)
3 year-olds	9	3;0–4;0	3;06.6 (4.8 mo)	9	3;01–3;10	3;05.5 (3.2)
4 year-olds	12	4;02–4;11	4;06.8 (3.5 mo)	11	4;01–4;11	4;05.6 (3.4)
5 year-olds	9	5;0–5;07	5;03.4 (2.2 mo)	9	5;02–6;01	5;06.3 (3.5)

In studying this population we sought to examine whether in a simultaneous balanced bilingual population, French-speaking children would show alterations in the timetable of development. A factorial ANOVA with age as dependent variable and age group and bilingual status as factors showed that there were no significant differences in age for bilinguals and monolinguals (F(1,53) = .079, p = .77), nor an interaction of bilingual status across age groups (F(2,53) = 1.99, p = .14). These results confirm that the groups were well matched for age.

4.2   Language input assessment

We employed a language questionnaire based on an adapted language history questionnaire by Paradis, Nicoladis & Crago (2007). This instrument measures language exposure (based on who spends how much time with the child and the language spoken; language spoken at school; extra-curricular – TV and friends) and length of exposure (the total amount of exposure over the years). We chose balanced bilinguals based on a measure calculated from parental evaluation of child fluency (completely fluent/quite fluent/somewhat fluent/not fluent), following Paradis et al. (2007). We focused our recruitment on balanced bilinguals, to ensure that there was a strong opportunity for a bilingual effect to be detected if there was one, but at the same time, that any effects could not be attributed to French being the weak language (i.e. language dominance effects).

4.3   Experimental design

French and English versions of a Picture Elicitation Task were used, with order of language counter-balanced across participants. The sessions were administered by two testers: one native French speaker and one native English speaker. Eight optionally transitive verbs were used with different events for the same verb in each language (i.e., different pictures): eat, drink, cut, read, hit, push, tickle, lick and the French equivalents *manger, boire, couper, lire, frapper, pousser, chatouiller, lécher.* The verbs were in a semi-randomized order for each language (different orderings of verbs for French and English versions of task). Four verbs were used with animate objects and four with inanimate objects. For French, four objects were masculine and four feminine. For each language, there was one training item and four distracters for a total of 13 items per elicitation task. An example of the elicitation task is provided in the following.

(18)   Animate Story
       What is the mean boy doing to the dog?/Qu'est-ce que le garçon méchant fait au chien?
       Target: He is hitting it.   Il le frappe.
                                                 he it = hit-PRS.3SG
       Null Object: He is hitting ___.   Il frappe.
                                                 he hit-PRS.3SG

(19)   Inanimate Story
       What is the boy doing with the juice?/Qu'est-ce que le garçon fait avec le jus?
       Target: He is drinking it.   Il le boit.
                                                 he it = drinks-PRS.3SG
       Null Object: He is drinking ___.   Il boit ___.
                                                 he drinks-PRS.3SG

4.4   Results

Responses were coded according to the status of the direct object, as in (20). The comparison with monolinguals was carried out for French, to observe whether there is a bilingual effect in this language. Mean proportions for each type of response are presented in Table 2 for both French and English of bilinguals and in Table 3 for French monolinguals.

(20)   a.   pronominal answer: Elle le pousse./She is pushing it.
       b.   DP answer: Il boit le lait./He is drinking milk.
       c.   null answer   Il mange ___./He is eating ___.
       d.   other: non-responses, non-relevant responses and responses not using the target verbs

Table 2. Responses in French and English for bilingual children

	Age group	Null Mean (SD)	DP Mean (SD)	Pronoun Mean (SD)	Other Mean (SD)
French	3 year-olds	.79 (.22)	.02 (.04)	.12 (.15)	.07 (.11)
	4 year-olds	.53 (.37)	.10 (.20)	.31 (.35)	.05 (.11)
	5 year-olds	.46 (.32)	.13 (.16)	.39 (.25)	.02 (.06)
English	3 year-olds	.71 (.27)	.07 (.09)	.22 (.31)	0
	4 year-olds	.46 (.40)	.13 (.23)	.39 (.32)	0
	5 year-olds	.36 (.36)	.09 (.15)	.55 (.40)	0

Table 3. Responses in French for French monolinguals

Age group	Null Mean (SD)	DP Mean (SD)	Pronoun Mean (SD)	Other Mean (SD)
3 year-olds	.49 (.25)	.06 (.13)	.43 (.23)	.02 (.05)
4 year-olds	.38 (.28)	.15 (.16)	.41 (.28)	.06 (.08)
5 year-olds	.37 (.25)	.03 (.06)	.56 (.21)	.04 (.06)

Table 2 shows that there were considerable omissions in both languages. For the purpose of this study we will concentrate on results on French bilinguals and monolinguals. We considered whether there is an effect of age on object clitic omissions, as in previous studies on monolingual children. We were also interested in comparing bilinguals with monolinguals with respect to the omissions in French to see whether there is a bilingual effect in this language. To answer these questions, we conducted an age by group factorial ANOVA on the proportion of null responses in the clitic elicitation task for both bilinguals and monolinguals. The analysis showed a significant effect of bilingual status, (F(1,53) = 5.979, p = .018) and significant effect of age (F(2,53 = 3.452, p = .039). The interaction between age and bilingual status was not significant (F(2,53) = .022, p = .367). We thus observe that younger children in both groups (bilinguals and monolinguals) produce higher rates of null object responses than older children, and bilinguals consistently give more null object responses than monolinguals, so that the developmental patterns seemed comparable but delayed. Lack of interaction between age and bilingual status shows that resolution of null objects occurs later in bilinguals, but at the same rate.

Finally, we evaluated the impact on omissions of external variables in French such as language exposure, length of exposure and parental ratings. Language exposure and length of exposure correlated to each other and to parental rating. Language exposure was highly correlated with length of exposure (r = .553, p = .002). Parental ratings were correlated to language exposure (r = .711, p < .000). This indicates that parental reports of fluencies were consistent with their characterization of linguistic environment of the child. However, none of these external variables show a correlation to the proportion of omissions.

To sum up, in this population of child bilinguals who were selected both for their language history (consistent and sustained exposure to both languages before age 3), and their fluency (fluent enough to speak in both languages), variability in parental assessment or external conditions do not correlate with the magnitude of the bilingual effect observed in terms of object omissions[4]. The results are similar with those found

---

4.   This general absence of association between external and syntactic variables can be due to issues of statistical power (sample size), or sample selection (as we concentrated on a rather homogeneous self-selected sample of successful bilinguals rather than the whole spectrum of the population). It can also be attributed to the design of the questionnaire, which may not be sensitive or reliable enough to pinpoint the relevant factors in the language context.

in previous studies for monolingual acquisition by francophone children (see Pérez-Leroux et al. 2008); however in the case of French bilinguals the rate of omission is higher and while the pace of change is similar to monolinguals, bilingual children resolve the omission later.

5. Discussion

The results show that there is a bilingual effect in our population: while there is comparable development between bilinguals and monolinguals, bilinguals omit more and their development is protracted. We did not find signs of English influence on French: the presence of English in the input does not lead to higher production of pronouns in French. To the contrary, we found more omissions in the French of bilinguals than in monolinguals. This is unexpected under Hypothesis 2 but predicted by Hypothesis 1.

These results show that bilingualism itself seems to be the source of the effect and not the particular combination of languages. This is in line with some previous studies on the acquisition of pronominal subjects also showing that regardless of whether the bilinguals' other language is a null subject language (Spanish) or not (English), the process of anaphora resolution in Italian is affected (see Sorace, Serratrice, Filiaci & Baldo 2009 and Serratrice, Sorace, Filiaci & Baldo 2009, both with older bilingual children). The authors propose interface difficulties coupled with differences in processing between bilingual and monolingual speakers, i.e. that bilinguals are less efficient than monolinguals in the integration of multiple sources of information.

We advocate for a different type of explanation based on the retention of the default null object representation and on the nature of bilingual input. Considering the null object possibilities across languages presented in Section 3, we propose that the common denominator between all languages is the construction in (4). Assuming that null objects are part of the universal initial representation in the grammar of a child, we propose that the first developmental step from this default initial setting in UG to other target constructions is a referential use of the construction. This renders possible object omission in pronominal contexts in French (and English), languages that otherwise do not allow null objects in this particular context. As such, there is no (relevant) difference between a monolingual and a bilingual child, since despite the number of languages a child is exposed to simultaneously, s/he only has one UG to guide the development within the hypothesis space.

However, in the process of acquisition, the child makes the transition from the default N to the proper range of null objects according to the language(s) s/he is exposed to. Features of the linguistic environment guide the child in making inferences about the proper types of null objects. Therefore, while the UG is the same no matter the language, the process by which the child arrives at the proper null object typology must be radically different in the case of exposure to one versus two (or more) languages. The schemas below attempt to illustrate this view. Let us assume language X

(Lx) is uniquely present in the input. Then Lx becomes the target. The Lx input interacts with UG in a certain manner (grammar selection $x\rightarrow$) resulting in the grammar of Lx (Gx). Lx is the child's language.

(21) $Lx \rightarrow UG_{\ x\rightarrow} \rightarrow Gx$

If the uniquely available input is language Y, the same occurs but there is (obviously) a different grammar selection ($y\rightarrow$).

(22) $Ly \rightarrow UG_{\ y\rightarrow} \rightarrow Gy$

Hypothesis 1 is based on the proposal that, in a bilingual environment, while both Lx and Ly are present in the input and the acquisition result is two grammars (Gx and Gy), the process of grammar selection is neither the coexistence of $x\rightarrow$ and $y\rightarrow$ nor the backgrounding of $x\rightarrow$ by $y\rightarrow$ (or vice-versa) but rather a selection that proceeds differently from $x\rightarrow$ or $y\rightarrow$. We use b (for bilingual) to illustrate this:

(23) $Ly + Lx \rightarrow UG_{\ b\rightarrow} \rightarrow Gx + Gy$

The input a bilingual child is faced with is less robust and potentially more ambiguous than in monolingual acquisition (the bilingual child is exposed to language variation within and across languages). By definition then, a bilingual child is exposed to less input in each of her languages. One can assume that the relevant amount of data (in the learnability sense of Yang 2002) is reduced. Therefore, the statistical footprint of a particular grammar takes longer to detect and the UG default is retained for a longer time. Crucially, we wish to emphasize that the delay observed is not due to cross-linguistic influence. This may also hold for typological different languages, such as German and French. More generally, it may be the case that the delay in the domain of object omission previously identified in the literature is not due at all to cross-linguistic influence.

It is very important to emphasize that, for the present time, this proposal applies only to the acquisition of the constructions explored in this paper. More specifically, we are not proposing that one language can never influence the development of another in individuals in a bilingual context. Rather our proposal is fully domain-specific (the domain of null object possibilities) because this is a domain in which the default UG representation in combination with the variety of target possibilities MUST apply in the same manner, whether there is one, two, or many languages present in the input. The bilingual effect is thus simply a longer reliance on the default representation.

References

Bernardini, P. & S. Schlyter. 2004. Growing syntactic structures and code-mixing in the weaker language: The Ivy Hypothesis. *Bilingualism: Language and Cognition* 7: 49–69.

Blais, M.J., Y. Oshima-Takane, F. Genesee & M. Hirakawa. 2010. Crosslinguistic influence on argument realization in Japanese-French bilinguals. In *BUCLD 35: Proceedings of the 34th Annual Boston University Conference on Language Development*, eds. K. Franich, K. M. Iserman & L. L. Keil, 34–45. Somerville MA: Cascadilla Press.

Cummins, S. & Y. Roberge. 2005. A modular account of null objects in French. *Syntax* 8: 44–64.

Döpke, S. 2000. Generation of and retraction from cross-linguistically motivated structures in bilingual first language acquisition. *Bilingualism: Language and Cognition* 3: 209–226.

Gawlitzek-Maiwald, I. & R. Tracy. 1996. Bilingual bootstrapping. *Linguistics* 34: 901–926.

Genesee, F. 1989. Early bilingual development: One language or two? *Journal of Child Language* 16: 161–179.

Gillon, B. 2006. *English relational words: Context sensitivity and implicit arguments.* Ms, McGill University, Montreal.

Granfeldt, J. & S. Schlyter. 2004. Cliticisation in the acquisition of French L1 and L2. In *The Acquisition of French in Different Contexts* (Language Acquisition and Language Disorders 32), eds. P. Prévost & J. Paradis, 333–370. Amsterdam: John Benjamins.

Grosjean, F. 1982. *Life with Two Languages: An Introduction to Bilingualism.* Cambridge MA: Harvard University Press.

Grüter, T. 2009. A unified account of object clitics and referential null objects in French. *Syntax* 12: 215–241.

Hale, K. & S. J. Keyser. 2002. *Prolegomenon to a Theory of Argument Structure.* Cambridge MA: The MIT Press.

Huang, C.-T. J. 1982. *Logical Relations in Chinese and the Theory of Grammar.* PhD dissertation, MIT.

Huang, C. T. J. 1984. On the distribution and reference of empty pronouns. *Linguistic Inquiry* 15: 531–574.

Huang, P. Y. 1999. *The Development of Null Arguments in a Cantonese-English Bilingual Child.* MA thesis, Chinese University of Hong Kong.

Hulk, A. 2000. L'acquisition des pronoms clitiques français par un enfant bilingue français-néerlandais. *The Canadian Journal of Linguistics* 45: 97–118.

Hulk, A. & N. Müller. 2000. Bilingual first language acquisition at the interface between syntax and pragmatics. *Bilingualism: Language and Cognition* 3: 227–244.

Hyams, N. & K. Wexler. 1993. On the grammatical basis of null subjects in child language. *Linguistic Inquiry* 24: 421–459.

Ingham, R. 1993. Input and learnability: Direct-object omissibility in English. *Language Acquisition* 3: 95–120.

Jakubowicz, C., N. Müller, B. Riemer & C. Rigaut. 1997. The case of subject and object omissions in French and German. *BUCLD 21: Proceedings of the 21st Annual Boston University Conference on Language Development*, eds. E. Hughes, M. Hughes & A. Greenhill, 331–342. Somerville MA: Cascadilla Press.

Kowaluk, A. 1999. Null objects in Polish: Pronouns and determiners in second language acquisition. *Working Papers in English and Applied Linguistics* 6: 135–152.

Kupisch, T. 2006. The emergence of article forms and functions in a German-Italian bilingual child. In *Interfaces in Multilingualism: Acquisition, Representation and Processing* (Hamburg Studies on Multilingualism 4), ed. C. Lleó, 45–109. Amsterdam: John Benjamins.

Kupisch, T. 2007. Determiners in bilingual German-Italian children: What they tell us about the relation between language influence and language dominance. *Bilingualism: Language and Cognition* 10: 57–78.

Lambrecht, K. & K. Lemoine. 1996. Vers une grammaire des compléments zéro en français parlé. In *Absence de marques et représentation de l'absence*, eds. G. Deléchelle & M. Fryd, 279–309. Rennes: Presses Universitaires de Rennes.

Lambrecht, K. & K. Lemoine. 2005. Definite null objects in (spoken) French: A construction-grammar account. In *Grammatical Constructions: Back to the Roots* (Constructional Approaches to Language 4), eds. M. Fried & H. C. Boas, 13–55. Amsterdam: John Benjamins.

Larjavaara, M. 2000. *Présence ou absence de l'objet: Limites du possible en français contemporain*. Helsinki: Academia Scientiarum Fennica.

Lleó, C., I. Kuchenbrandt, M. Kehoe & C. Trujillo. 2003. Syllable final consonants in Spanish and German monolingual and bilingual acquisition. In *(In)Vulnerable Domains in Language Acquisition* (Hamburg Studies on Multilingualism 1), ed. N. Müller, 191–220. Amsterdam: John Benjamins.

Meisel, J. M. 1986. Word order and case marking in early child language. Evidence from simultaneous acquisition of two first languages: French and German. *Linguistics* 24: 123–183.

Müller, N., B. Crysmann & G. A. Kaiser. 1996. Interactions between the acquisition of French object drop and the development of the C-system. *Language Acquisition* 5: 35–63.

Müller, N. & A. Hulk. 2000. Crosslinguistic influence in bilingual children: Object omission and root infinitives. In *BUCLD 24: Proceedings of the 24th Annual Boston University Conference on Language Development*, eds. S. C. Howell, S. A. Fish & T. Keith-Lucas, 546–557. Somerville MA: Cascadilla Press.

Müller, N. & A. Hulk. 2001. Crosslinguistic influence in bilingual language acquisition: Italian and French as recipient languages. *Bilingualism: Language and Cognition* 4: 1–21.

Müller, N., A. Hulk & C. Jakubowicz. 1999. Object omissions in bilingual children: Evidence for crosslinguistic influence. In *BUCLD 23: Proceedings of the 23rd Annual Boston University Conference on Language Development*, eds. A. Greenhill, H. Littlefield & C. Tano, 482–494. Somerville MA: Cascadilla Press.

Nicoladis, E. 2002. What's the difference between 'toilet paper' and 'paper toilet'? French-English bilingual children's crosslinguistic transfer in compound nouns. *Journal of Child Language* 29: 1–20.

Paradis, J. 2000. Beyond one system of two: Degrees of separation between the languages of French-English bilingual children. In *Cross-linguistic Structures in Simultaneous Bilingualism* (Studies in Bilinigualism 21), ed. S. Döpke, 175–200. Amsterdam: John Benjamins.

Paradis, J. 2001. Do bilingual two year olds have separate phonological systems? *International Journal of Bilingualism* 5: 19–38.

Paradis, J. & F. Genesee. 1996. Syntactic acquisition in bilingual children: Autonomous or interdependent? *Studies in Second Language Acquisition* 18: 1–25.

Paradis, J., E. Nicoladis & M. Crago. 2007. French-English bilingual children's acquisition of the past tense. In *BUCLD 31: Proceedings of the 31st Annual Boston University Conference on Language Development*, eds. H. Caunt-Nulton, S. Kulatilake & I. Woo, 497–507. Somerville MA: Cascadilla Press.

Pérez-Leroux, A. T., A. Cuza & D. Thomas. 2011. Clitic placement in Spanish/English bilingual children. *Bilingualism: Language and Cognition* 14: 221–232.

Pérez-Leroux, A. T., M. Pirvulescu & Y. Roberge. 2008. Null objects in child language: Syntax and the lexicon. *Lingua* 118: 370–398.

Pérez-Leroux, A. T., M. Pirvulescu & Y. Roberge. 2009. Bilingualism as a window into language faculty: The acquisition of objects in French-speaking children in bilingual and monolingual contexts. *Bilingualism: Language and Cognition* 12: 97–112.

Pirvulescu, M. 2006. Theoretical implications of clitic omission in early French: Spontaneous vs. elicited production. *Catalan Journal of Linguistics* 5: 221–236.

Raposo, E. 1986. On the null object in European Portuguese. In *Studies in Romance Linguistics*, eds. O. Jaeggli & C. Silva-Corvalán, 373–390. Dordrecht: Foris.

Schmitz, K. & N. Müller. 2008. Strong and clitic pronouns in monolingual and bilingual acquisition of French and Italian. *Bilingualism: Language and Cognition* 11: 19–41.

Serratrice, L., A. Sorace, F. Filiaci & M. Baldo. 2009. Bilingual children's sensitivity to specificity and genericity: Evidence from metalinguistic awareness. *Bilingualism: Language and Cognition* 12: 1–19.

Sorace, A., L. Serratrice, F. Filiaci & M. Baldo. 2009. Discourse conditions on subject pronoun realization: Testing the linguistic intuitions of older bilingual children. *Lingua* 119: 460–477.

Van der Linden, E. H. & A. Hulk. 1996. Language differentiation in a French-Dutch bilingual child. In *EUROSLA 6: A Selection of Papers* (Toegepaste Taalwetenschap in Artikelen 55), eds. E. Kellerman, B. Weltens & T. Bongaerts, 89–103. Amsterdam: VU Uitgeverij.

Van der Velde, M., C. Jakubowicz & C. Rigaut. 2002. The acquisition of determiner phrase and pronominal clitics by three French-speaking children. In *The Process of Language Acquisition: Proceedings of the 1999 GALA Conference*, ed. I. Lasser, 115–132. Frankfurt: Peter Lang.

Yang, C. 2002. *Knowledge and Learning in Natural Language*. Oxford: OUP.

Yip, V. & S. Matthews. 2000. Syntactic transfer in a Cantonese-English bilingual child. *Bilingualism: Language and Cognition* 3: 193–208.

Yip, V. & S. Matthews. 2005. Dual input and learnability: Null objects in Cantonese-English bilingual children. In *Proceedings of the 4th International Symposium on Bilingualism (ISB4)*, eds. J. Cohen, K. T. McAlister, K. Rolstad & J. MacSwan, 2421–2431. Somerville MA: Cascadilla Press.

Foreign language reforms in Swiss primary schools

Potentials and limitations*

Andrea Haenni Hoti and Sybille Heinzmann
University of Lucerne, Switzerland

In German-speaking Central Switzerland, French used to be the only foreign language (FL) taught in primary schools (from grade five onwards). Some cantons have now implemented a program including English as the first FL (L2) to be learnt at school (from grade three onwards), followed by French as the second FL (L3) (from grade five onwards). To examine the impact of this school reform, children of both programs were compared with respect to their French competencies (N = 893). After one year of French instruction, students with previous English (L2) instruction exhibited higher skills in French (L3) listening and reading than students without previous English (L2) instruction. One year later, however, the initial advantage of the more experienced learners had disappeared. The results argue for a more coordinated instruction of the different FLs taught at school that takes the existing experiences of the students into account.

Keywords: English, French, third language acquisition, foreign language acquisition, school reforms, primary schools

1.　Introduction of a second foreign language into Swiss primary schools

In 2004, the Swiss Conference of Cantonal Ministers of Education issued a new series of guidelines for foreign language (henceforth FL) instruction throughout Switzerland (see EDK 2004). One of the recommended innovations was to introduce instruction of a second FL in primary schools (grades 1 to 6). While one of the FLs taught at primary

---

* 　This contribution is based on a journal article (see Haenni Hoti, Heinzmann, Müller, Wicki, Oliveira & Werlen 2011), but contains additional results which could not be presented in the above-mentioned journal article. We would like to thank the two anonymous reviewers for their constructive feedback and suggestions on our paper.

schools should be a national language, the other should be either English or another national language. This specification aims at taking into account both the political and cultural significance of the four national languages (German, French, Italian, Rhaeto-Romanic) on a national level, as well as the increasing importance of English as a lingua franca on an international level.

In most German-speaking cantons of Central Switzerland the primary school children now learn English (L2) from 3rd grade onwards and French (L3) from 5th grade onwards (two to three lessons per subject a week). Since the cantons, in which the present study was conducted, have implemented this school reform at different rates, a comparison of both educational programs, the old model with French instruction only and the new model with instruction in two FLs (English and French) was carried out to gain insights into the effectiveness of both programs and the impact of English instruction on the acquisition of French.

For the sake of simplicity and perspicuity we will follow the institutional perspective when using the terms first language (L1), second language (L2) and third language (L3) in the following. In the school system of Central Switzerland High German[1] is officially the local language of instruction (L1). In the new model English is the first FL at school and, hence, the second language (L2) and French is the second FL at school and, accordingly, the third language (L3). From the point of view of the individual children and their individual language biographies the situation may look different: In the case of children growing up bi- or multilingual High German may already be the second, third, or even fourth language that they learn.

The starting point of this study is the idea that the same language, French in our case, is learnt more efficiently as an L3 (new model) than as an L2 (old model) because students with previous FL learning experience in English can use their FL skills as a resource when learning French.

2.   Theoretical background of the study

The assumption that previously learnt languages facilitate subsequent language learning is based on the theoretical tenets of Third Language Acquisition (henceforth TLA). Learners of an L3 can draw upon their mother tongue(s) as well as their first FL (L2) as resources in the process of TLA (see Jessner 2008: 39). Therefore, it can be assumed that – under favourable conditions – learners of an L3 will learn the given language more successfully and also qualitatively differently from learners who learn the same

---

1.   In the diaglossic context in which this study was carried out this is to say that the majority of the children who grow up speaking Swiss German at home are taught in a language variety (High German) that is not their home language. Nevertheless, in light of the close linguistic relatedness of Swiss German and High German it seems justified to regard Swiss German as a dialectal variety of German and the students' L1 rather than the first foreign language (L2) learnt at school.

language as an L2 as they have more opportunities for language comparisons (see Marx & Hufeisen 2004: 145).

This assumption is partly backed up and partly refuted by empirical studies on the effects of bilingualism on TLA in different countries. According to Cenoz (2003: 74) a facilitating effect of bilingualism on TLA can be observed in studies that examine the L2-L3 transfer of general receptive or productive skills rather than of specific linguistic subskills, as L2 language proficiency does not seem to affect all aspects of TLA in the same way. Furthermore, a facilitating effect generally emerges in studies where the languages investigated are taught at school and benefit from the institutional support of the school system. In such a context additive bilingualism or more precisely biliteracy is fostered among the students. In a Swiss study by Brohy (2001) German-Rumantsch bilinguals were compared to German-speaking monolinguals with respect to their general ability in French. Students learning French as their L3 showed significantly higher performance in French than students learning French as their first FL (L2). Similarly, several studies conducted in the Basque Country and in Catalonia examined the acquisition of English as an L3 by students who are bilingual either in Spanish and Basque or Spanish and Catalan (see Cenoz 1991, Lasagabaster 1997, Muñoz 2000, Sagasta Errasti 2003 and Sanz 2000). In a large variety of oral and written tests the bilingual students outperformed the monolingual Spanish-speaking students with respect to their English proficiency which led the authors to conclude that (additive) bilingual learners are at an advantage in L3 acquisition.

Similar to the studies reported above, the focus of our study will be on the general language proficiency of the learners. It examines the effect of bilingualism (German (L1) and English (L2)) on learners' L3 French skills (listening and reading) in a setting where all three languages benefit from the institutional support of the school system.

More mixed results are reported from studies involving groups of bilingual immigrants whose non-dominant mother tongue(s) are in most cases not fostered by the public school system. In a study carried out by Sanders & Meijers (1995) in the Netherlands no differences were found between Turkish- or Arabic-Dutch bilingual learners and monolingual Dutch learners with respect to their English skills (grammatical judgement, spontaneous language use, word comprehension and word recognition). These findings are partly backed up by another Dutch study (see Schoonen, Van Gelderen, De Glopper, Hulstijn, Simis, Snellings & Stevenson 2002, Van Gelderen, Schoonen, De Glopper, Hulstijn, Snellings, Simis & Stevenson 2003). In the German KESS 4 study (see Bos & Pietsch 2006: 213), which investigated the English competencies of 4th graders in Hamburg, children who have one parent that was born abroad were found to perform equally well on an English listening test as children whose parents were both born in Germany, while children whose parents were both born abroad were found to score significantly lower. In the additional data collection of the German EBAFLS[2] (see Rauch, Jurecka & Hesse 2010) study, which was also carried out in Hamburg and specifically

---

2.   European Bank of Anchor Items for Foreign Language Skills.

looked at the language competencies of Turkish students, no significant differences were found between Turkish and German 9th grade students in relation to their English reading skills. These results are in line with the interpretation of Cenoz & Hoffmann (2003: 3) that a positive effect of bilingualism on TLA might not be found in studies conducted with immigrants and in so-called 'subtractive contexts' where the development of literacy in the students' home language is neglected by the school system and where, accordingly, their level of bilingualism might not be sufficient to exert a measurable facilitating effect on TLA. The idea that literacy development in the home language plays a crucial role is also found in Canadian studies on French immersion programs. The available evidence indicates that immigrant English as a second language (ESL) students enrolled in French immersion programs perform as well in French as their Anglophone classmates, but they may perform even better if they have already developed literacy skills in their home language when joining French immersion programs (see Hurd 1993 and Swain, Lapkin, Rowen & Hart 1990).

On the other hand, the position of Cenoz and Hoffmann outlined above is questioned by the findings of the German DESI study (see Klieme 2006). In this study the English listening, reading, text reconstruction and creative writing skills as well as the language awareness of about 11'000 ninth graders (with a subsample taking part in an oral test) were assessed along with their German competencies. Despite being conducted in a public school context which can be described as 'subtractive' insofar as support for the immigrants' non-dominant home languages is generally nonexistent, a positive effect of bilingualism on TLA was found as immigrant students outperformed their peers with regard to their English (L3) skills. The authors of the study conclude that learning English is easier for students who have already learnt German as a second language. Under comparable conditions in terms of social background, general cognitive abilities, gender, and schooling, growing up in a multilingual family is associated with a head start in English (see Klieme 2006: 5). Even students with an exclusively non-German language background demonstrated a higher achievement in English than the monolingual German-speakers. Apparently, a positive and facilitating impact of bilingualism on TLA can also be observed in the case of immigrant children learning in a subtractive school context.

The results of an Iranian study also suggest that bilingual learners are at an advantage when learning an L3 even if the school and society at large do not foster biliteracy (see Modirkhamene 2006: 290). Modirkhamene investigated the English (L2 or L3) reading competencies of monolingual Persian speakers and bilingual Persian-Turkish speakers with comparable socioeconomic and educational background who were learning English in a language course at university. The study was carried out in the northwest of the Iran in an environment where literacy in Turkish is not officially fostered at school. The bivariate analysis revealed that bilingual learners for whom English was their L3 had significantly better reading skills than monolingual learners for whom English was their L2.

Although the focus of our study is not on immigrant or minority children, we will include the language background of the students in the analysis in order to examine if additional home language resources (besides bilingualism in German and English) have a positive effect on the acquisition of French.

3.   Methodology

3.1   Participants

The study has a longitudinal design comprising a random sample of two groups of students following two different educational models of FL learning (N = 893).

Group 1 (N = 542): children with the new model learning English from 3rd grade onwards and French from 5th grade onwards.

Group 2 (N = 351): children with the old model without English instruction learning only French from 5th grade onwards.

The gender distribution of the sample is even with 51% girls and 49% boys. The average age of the students as reported by themselves was 12;1 years in 6th grade. As far as their national identification is concerned 78% of the students indicated in the student questionnaire that they were Swiss, 11% indicated that they feel affiliated to at least two countries (one of them being Switzerland) and 11% indicated being foreigners. Eighty-five percent of the students in this analysis only speak one language at home. Of these the vast majority speak Swiss German at home. Fifteen percent of the children speak more than one language (variety) at home including the following languages next to Swiss German or High German: Albanian, Serbian/Croatian, Portuguese, Italian, Turkish, Bosnian, Tamil, Aramean, Dutch, Thai, Macedonian, Rhaeto-Romanic, Spanish, Flemish, Polish, Arabic, Vietnamese, Hindi or Japanese.

3.2   Data collection process

The English listening and reading skills of the first group were assessed in grades 3, 4 and 5. In sixth grade, only English reading skills were assessed. The French listening and reading skills were assessed in both groups within the framework of the third and fourth data collections (5th and 6th grade). Equally assessed in both groups were German reading skills in grades 3, 4 and 6.[3] Apart from the achievement tests, the study involved a student questionnaire that was filled in by all students.

---

3.   Furthermore, the oral interaction skills in both FLs were assed in a subsample of four students per school class (see Haenni Hoti, Heinzmann & Müller 2009). Because of the selectivity of this subsample we will abstain from a comparison of the two groups of students with regard to their oral interaction skills. The FL writing skills of the students were not included in the study as writing does not feature prominently in the FL primary school curriculum in grades 3 and 4 and because it would have exceeded the available resources.

3.3   Instruments

3.3.1   *English and French listening and reading skills*

The construction of our tasks was inspired by a variety of studies conducted with young learners, material developed for and offered by national and international testing institutions as well as a number of course books (see Lenz & Studer 2007, OCR 2005–2007, University of Cambridge ESOL Examinations 2003/2004/2007). The difficulty and the thematic content of the tasks were adapted to the study plans and course books for English and French. Wherever possible, calibrated tasks that can be assigned to the levels of the Common European Framework of Reference for Languages (CEFR) were used (see Lenz & Studer 2007).

For these paper and pencil tests an ample variety of task formats was aimed at. Furthermore, care was taken to ensure that different text genres and topics were incorporated. The majority of the tasks required an understanding of individual words and sentences that provide specific pieces of information. Some tasks also required a more global understanding and interpretation of the texts as for example when students were required to indicate the main statement or the genre of a text or when they were asked to infer character traits of a person from the information provided in the text. The tasks did not narrowly focus on individual aspects of linguistic competence. Rather, the children had to mobilize a large array of general and communicative language competencies (including sociolinguistic and pragmatic competencies[4]) to successfully solve the tasks.

Scales measuring English and French reading and listening skills were constructed based on Item Response Theory (see Hartig 2007). The English listening scales (grades 3–5) comprise between 19 and 30 items in each test version and the English reading scales (grades 3–6) between 18 and 25 items. The French listening scales (grades 5 and 6) comprise between 19 and 22 items and the French reading scales (grades 5 and 6) 23 items. Rasch analysis was conducted by means of the program Winsteps 3.67.0 (see Linacre 2008). The items appear to measure single constructs and exhibit good reliabilities, coefficients for all scales ranging between .96 and .99. Person reliability coefficients were lower, ranging between .40 and .77, indicating ceiling effects. In summary, the psychometric properties of the scales appear reasonably good, although a few more difficult items would have improved the scales.

3.3.2   *German (L1) reading skills*

For the measurement of the reading skills in German two tests were used in 3rd grade that were developed within the framework of an assessment in the canton of Zurich

---

4.   These featured most prominently in the oral interaction tasks where sociolinguistic and pragmatic competencies can be most easily observed. This is also evident in the CEFR descriptors for these competencies (see Europarat 2001: 122, 124–125, 129). But it needs to be pointed out that very few descriptors are available for lower levels of sociolinguistic and pragmatic competence (A1, A2).

(see Moser, Keller & Tresch 2003). The first test consisted of a literary text with 14 multiple choice questions. In the second test the students had to read a short story and then identify eight underlined words (persons and objects) in a corresponding picture. In 4th grade, a reading comprehension test of the Progress in International Reading Literacy Study (PIRLS or IGLU in German) was used (see Bos, Lankes, Prenzel, Schwippert, Valtin & Walther 2003, Mullis, Martin, González & Kennedy 2003). This test consisted of 11 open and closed questions revolving around a story. In 6th grade a reading test which was developed for competence testing in 6th grade classes in Sachsen (Sächsisches Bildungsinstitut 2007/2008) was used. It consisted of 10 closed questions about a literary text. As only a rough assessment of the L1 competencies of the students was required the German reading comprehension scales were not created on the basis of item response theory but by calculating sum scores on the basis of the number of correct answers.

3.3.3   *The student questionnaire*

Besides a number of demographic variables (gender, age, nationality, length of residency in Switzerland, number of languages spoken at home, (Swiss-)German (L1) spoken at home, literacy of the household), the student questionnaire encompassed questions about the following topics: metacognitive, cognitive and social learning strategies, motivation, self-concept as a learner of English/French, feelings of being overburdened and fear of making mistakes, attitudes towards TL speakers and countries and parental assistance with learning English and French.

The use of learning strategies by the students was assessed by means of items that are based on Oxford's (1990) Strategy Inventory for Language Learning (SILL). The students were asked how often they employ certain learning strategies while learning French. The items targeting students' strategy use yielded five different scales. The metacognitive strategies scale (6 items, $\alpha = .65$) entails participation of the learners in terms of planning and evaluating their learning. The three cognitive learning strategies scales (2–3 items each, $\alpha = .47$ to 73) encompass strategies of interlingual transfer between L2 and L3, of dealing with spoken and written texts and of concentration while learning French. Social learning strategies (3 items, $\alpha = .47$) involve getting assistance from other people if necessary or providing assistance oneself. The total amount of variance explained by these five scales is 53%. The questionnaire items regarding the use of learning strategies were answered on a four-point answer scale ranging from 'frequently' to 'never'.

The items probing into the learners' language learning motivation are based on instruments used in research carried out by Dörnyei, Csizér & Németh (2006) and Gardner (1985) and were answered on a four-point scale ranging from 'totally true' to 'not at all true'. The corresponding scale subsumes aspects of intrinsic (enjoying hearing and speaking the French language) and extrinsic motivation (learning French in order to be able to communicate with people from all over the word and in order to be able to understand French song texts, computer games and internet contributions) (8 items, $\alpha = .76$, explained variance 37%).

The items used to assess the self-concept of the students are based on the instruments used in Stöckli's (2004) and Schaer & Bader's (2005) studies in the primary school context. The self-concept scale probes into the students' self-evaluation of their French competence, their perception of the ease of learning and their expectancy for success (3 items, α = .74, explained variance 66%). Again the items were answered on a four-point scale from 'totally true' to 'not at all true'.

The students were also asked about their feelings of being overburdened and their fear of making mistakes during French classes (4 items, α = .72, explained variance 55%) as well as about their attitudes towards French speakers and countries (4 items, α = .80, explained variance 63%). These items too, draw on previous instruments used by Dörnyei et al. (2006), Gardner (1985) and Stöckli (2004). The corresponding answer scale consisted of four categories ranging from 'totally true' to 'not at all true'.

Parental assistance was assessed by two single items. Students were asked how often their father and mother helped them with learning French at home.

All the scales of the student questionnaire were generated on the basis of factor analysis with SPSS 14.0. The screen plot criterion was used to guide the decision as to the number of factors to be extracted. For the learning strategies scales only a rotation technique was necessary. Varimax rotation was used for the generation of these scales.

3.4   Data analysis

Multiple regression models were used to compare the French skills (listening and reading) of both groups of learners (with and without previous English instruction) while controlling for a large number of other variables which might influence the scores on the achievement tests in French: gender, age, cantonal affiliation, nationality, length of residency in Switzerland, number of family languages, (Swiss-)German spoken at home, literacy of the household, type of study plan (regular or special curriculum), metacognitive, cognitive and social learning strategies, motivation, self-concept as a learner of French, feelings of being overburdened and fear of making mistakes, attitudes towards French speakers and countries, parental assistance with learning French and German reading skills. As our sample consists of classes and students within classes there is a multilevel structure in the data. Students in the same class tend to be more similar to each other than students across different classes because of their shared learning environment. To take this into account mixed effects models were fitted using the lme4 package in the statistical program R 2.8.1., written by Bates (2005).[5]

---

5.   A top-down strategy as recommended by Diggle, Heagerty, Kung-Yee & Zeger (2002) was applied for the model selection process. We started with the full model containing all available explanatory variables. Based on the Akaike information criterion (AIC) interactions were checked and clearly unnecessary variables were dropped. In multilevel modelling, a simple equivalent to the R-square used in multiple regression analysis does not exist. Analogue measures to R-squared have been proposed, but are not widely used. Goodness of fit measures, such as AIC are considered instead (see Bates 2005, Faraway 2006 and Snijders & Bosker 1999).

4. Results

4.1 French listening in grades 5 and 6

Table 1 below lists those factors which were included in the final and best-fitting model to explain the French listening skills in 5th grade. P-values are not included in Table 1 (or any of the following tables) because they can be quite misleading (see Footnote 5). Cantonal affiliation clearly affects achievement in the French listening test: the students learning French as an L2 (canton Lucerne), who did not have any English instruction, performed significantly worse in the French listening test than the students with English instruction who are learning French as an L3 (cantons Obwalden, Zug and Schwyz). It seems, consequently, that previous and additional English instruction has a positive effect on the acquisition of listening skills in French. Furthermore, the age of the learners plays a role. Learners who were twelve years-old or older in 5th grade scored significantly lower in the French listening test than learners who were younger than eleven years-old (see Table 1). We can only speculate about the reason for this.

Table 1. Factors influencing students' French listening comprehension scores (5th grade)

	Regression coefficient[6]	Standard error
Intercept[7]	1.05	.16
Canton of Zug	.03	.18
Canton of Schwyz	.21	.18
Canton of Lucerne	−.51	.13
Group of 11- and 11½-year-olds	−.15	.14
Group of ≥ 12-year-olds	−.35	.15
Two and more languages spoken in the family	.21	.10
Children with special curriculum	−.35	.15
Between 51 and 100 books at home	.04	.08
Over 100 books at home	.15	.08
Feelings of being overburdened and fear of making mistakes	−.10	.05
Self-concept as a learner of French	.21	.06
German (L1) reading skills in grade 4	.42	.14

(n = 758; ICC = 0.13)

---

6. The (unstandardized) regression coefficient estimates to what extent a student of the group in question differs from the reference student according to the intercept.

7. The intercept corresponds to the mean score of the reference student who is less than 11 years-old, goes to school in the canton of Obwalden, is socialized monolingually, does not follow a special curriculum, has at most 50 books at home and has an average value on the feelings of being overburdened, self-concept and German reading scales.

It is possible that the group of older learners consists of children who have been later enrolled into the school system or who had to repeat a school year before grade 3.

The listening skills in French are also affected by the number of languages spoken at home (see Table 1). Children who speak more than one language at home, performed significantly better than children who are socialized in a monolingual family. What is crucial is not whether High German and Swiss German are spoken at home but whether more than one language is being spoken in the family. As could be expected, weaker children with a special curriculum who follow a reduced educational program in at least one school subject exhibit significantly lower French listening skills than their peers. The educational background of the household in which the children live is also important. Children of families with ample literacy resources as measured by the number of books at home (more than 100 books) demonstrated significantly higher listening skills after one year of French instruction than children of families with limited educational resources (less than 51 books). Learners' well-being in the French classes is also related to the performance in the French listening test. The more students feel overtaxed and are afraid of making mistakes the lower their scores are. In contrast, the scores get better with increasingly positive self-concepts of the students as learners of French. In other words the easier they perceive learning French to be, the more positive their perception of their own competence in French and the higher their expectation to succeed the better they performed in the French listening test in 5th grade. Last but not least the children's scores in the German (L1) reading test in 4th grade turned out to be a significant predictor of their performance in the French listening test in 5th grade. The better the children's reading skills in German (L1), the better their listening skills in French. The German reading comprehension, the self-concept of the learners and the cantonal affiliation are the most powerful predictors in this model (see Table 1). In addition to the fixed effects discussed above, there is also a significant random class effect with an estimated intraclass correlation coefficient (ICC) of 0.13. Class effects, therefore, explain 13% of the variability in French listening comprehension. How well a student performed in the French listening test is, consequently, also dependent on which class he or she is in. What exactly leads to these class differences (group dynamics, teacher personality, quality of instruction, school environment) cannot be clarified here.

Table 2 below lists those factors which were included in the final and best-fitting model to explain the French listening skills in 6th grade.

A look at the table will show that cantonal affiliation and by implication group affiliation no longer plays a role as soon as a series of other variables and class effects are taken into account. Consequently, the group who is learning French as an L3 no longer performs significantly better than the group who is learning French as an L2. Children who speak more than one language at home also do not perform significantly better than the monolingual children anymore.

In sum, one year later the advantage of the more experienced learners (both those with FL learning experience in English and those with additional home languages) has disappeared.

Table 2. Factors influencing students' French listening comprehension scores (6th grade)

	Regression coefficient	Standard error
Intercept	1.53	.04
Group of under 12-year-olds	.04	.07
Group of ≥ 13-year-olds	−.11	.06
Between 0 and 10 books at home	−.15	.12
Between 11 and 50 books at home	−.19	.06
Between 51 and 100 books at home	−.04	.05
Self-concept as a learner of French	.17	.03
German (L1) reading skills in grade 6	.09	.02

(n = 859; ICC = 0.07)

The dominant explanatory factors in this model are the self-concept of the learners and their German (L1) reading skills (see Table 2): The easier the 6th graders perceive learning French to be, the more positive their perception of their own competence in French and the higher their expectation to succeed the better they performed in the French listening test in 6th grade. The better their performance in the German reading test the better their listening skills in French. Furthermore, the age of the learners and the literacy resources of their family also contribute to the explanation of their French listening skills in 6th grade, just as they did in 5th grade. Learners who were thirteen years-old or older in 6th grade scored significantly lower in the French listening test than younger learners. Children of families with comparatively few literacy resources (less than 51 books at home) demonstrated significantly lower listening skills after two years of French instruction than children of families with more ample educational resources (more than 100 books at home). As was the case in 5th grade, a significant random class effect was found. The estimated intraclass correlation coefficient (ICC) in 6th grade is 0.07.

4.2   French reading in grades 5 and 6

The analysis with regard to the French reading skills yields a similar picture as the one we saw regarding the listening skills. The model in Table 3 illustrates which factors make a statistically significant contribution to the prediction of the French reading skills in 5th grade. Cantonal affiliation is a relevant variable. Learners with previous and additional English instruction did significantly better in the French reading test than learners without previous knowledge in a FL. Besides cantonal affiliation, gender is relevant in that boys did significantly worse in the French reading test than girls. The group of twelve year-olds or older children and the group of children with a special curriculum also scored significantly lower. On the other hand, better reading skills go hand in hand with a more positive self-concept as a learner of French. Furthermore,

Table 3. Factors influencing students' French reading comprehension scores (5th grade)

	Regression coefficient	Standard error
Intercept	.94	.15
Group 2 (Canton of Lucerne)	−.25	.12
Gender (boys)	−.13	.06
Group of 11- and 11½-year-olds	−.20	.13
Group of ≥ 12-year-olds	−.42	.14
Children with special curriculum	−.54	.16
Self-concept as a learner of French	.39	.05
German (L1) reading skills in grade 4	1.16	.14

(n = 778; ICC = .14)

the learners' reading skills in the local language of instruction exert a significant influence as was the case for French listening skills. The better the students' German (L1) reading skills in 4th grade, the better their reading skills in French in 5th grade. The dominant variables in this model with most explanatory power are the 5th graders' self-concept as learners of French and the German (L1) reading skills (see Table 3).

Apart from the individual factors listed above, class affiliation is an important factor, just as it was for French listening. Class affiliation explains 14% of the variability in French reading skills in 5th grade.

Once again, cantonal or group affiliation no longer represents a significant explanatory variable in 6th grade as soon as the class effects are taken into account (see Table 4). Just as for the French listening skills, the advantage of the more experienced learners (those with English instruction) disappears from 5th to 6th grade. Students with previous and additional English instruction neither perform better nor worse in the French reading test in 6th grade than students without English instruction who learn French as their first FL (L2).

The dominant explanatory variables of the French reading skills in 6th grade are the self-concept as learners of French and German (L1) reading skills (see Table 4). The more positive the learners' self-concept and the better their reading skills in the local language of instruction the better their reading skills in French. Furthermore, as could be expected, weaker learners with a special curriculum who follow a reduced educational program in at least one school subject exhibit significantly lower French reading skills than their peers in 6th grade.

In addition, the age of the learners once again plays a role. This time it is not the group of thirteen year-olds and older learners that significantly differs from the others but the group of under 12-year-olds. Students who are under 12 years old in 6th grade and, hence, younger than their average peers score significantly higher in the French reading test than their older peers. In addition, one item which was used to assess

Table 4. Factors influencing students' French reading comprehension scores (6th grade)

	Regression coefficient	Standard error
Intercept	1.87	.07
Group of under 12-year-olds	.23	.10
Group of ≥ 13-year-olds	−.05	.08
Sometimes using a German word when speaking French	−.16	.07
Often using a German word when speaking French	−.32	.08
Children with special curriculum	−.55	.12
Self-concept as a learner of French	.44	.05
German (L1) reading skills in grade 6	.46	.03

(n = 857; ICC = 0.14)

learning strategies appears as an explanatory variable. Children who indicated that they sometimes or often use a German word if they do not know the corresponding word in French performed significantly worse in the French reading test than children who indicated that they do this rarely or never. This communication strategy seems to be used mainly as a compensation for missing target language resources. This might explain why it figures as an indicator of a lower French reading competence in 6th grade. The significant class effect explains 14% of the variability in French reading comprehension in 6th grade.

5.   Discussion and conclusion

The comparison of students with and without English instruction in grade 5 revealed that students who have had English instruction display higher skills in French (listening and reading) than students who have had no English instruction. Consequently, after one school year, children who learn French as a second FL (L3) are more successful than children who learn French as their first FL (L2). That is to say that besides German reading competencies, English listening and reading competencies have an additional facilitating effect on the acquisition of French. This corroborates findings of previous studies carried out in Spain and Switzerland where a positive effect of bilingualism on TLA was found in a context where the languages examined benefitted from the institutional support of the school system and where general language skills of the students were measured (see Brohy 2001, Cenoz 1991, Lasagabaster 1997, Muñoz 2000, Sagasta Errasti 2003 and Sanz 2000). Apart from this, children with a bi- and multilingual family background are at an advantage compared to monolingually raised children when learning French, at least as far as their listening skills are concerned. Apparently, immigrant minority languages can also constitute important sources for language comparisons and for the formulation and testing of hypotheses about the functioning of the TL in the process of learning French, even in a so called 'subtractive' school context and even if they are not closely linguistically related as is the case for the majority of the immigrant languages involved in our study. This result is consistent with the findings of the German DESI-study, where bilingual immigrant children showed higher skills in the first FL learnt at school (English) than monolingually raised German speakers (see Klieme 2006: 5). That an advantage of immigrant children does not clearly emerge in the case of reading skills in French in grade 5 might be attributable to a learning environment where the literacy skills of immigrant children in their non-dominant mother tongue(s) are not fostered in school (see Cenoz & Hoffmann 2003).

One year later in grade 6 the comparison of the two groups of learners yields a different picture, however. The initial advantage of the more experienced learners (both those with previous English instruction and those with additional home languages) have disappeared and children with and without English instruction and children with and without additional home languages perform equally well in the listening and reading tests in French (L3). It may be that the disappearance of the initial advantage of the more experienced learners is attributable to classroom practices which do not explicitly use and activate the learners' previously acquired linguistic resources and learning experiences during French classes. Hence, the results argue for a more coordinated instruction of the different FLs taught at school that takes the existing experiences and language skills of the students into account (including languages of immigrants) and builds upon them. The results of our study suggest that, while the primary school children learn an additional FL with the new model in which English is learnt from 3rd grade and French from 5th grade onwards, they do not seem to learn French more efficiently in the long run than the children with the old model. It seems that the acquisition of French only profits from (previous) English instruction at the initial stage. Apparently, the potential of the new educational model where two FLs are taught in primary school cannot be fully exploited as long as FL instruction continues to be little coordinated and segregated according to the different target languages and as long as a monolingual habitus (see Gogolin 1994) prevails with regard to the treatment of immigrant languages.

References

Bates, D. 2005. Fitting linear mixed models. *R-News* 5: 27–30.
Bos, W., E. M. Lankes, M. Prenzel, K. Schwippert, R. Valtin & G. Walther. 2003. *Erste Ergebnisse aus IGLU: Schülerleistungen am Ende der vierten Jahrgangsstufe im internationalen Vergleich.* Münster: Waxmann.

Bos, W. & M. Pietsch. 2006. *KESS 4 – Kompetenzen und Einstellungen von Schülerinnen und Schülern am Ende der Jahrgangsstufe 4 in Hamburger Grundschulen* (Hamburger Schriften zur Qualität im Bildungswesen 1). Münster: Waxmann.

Brohy, C. 2001. Generic and/or specific advantages of bilingualism in a dynamic plurilingual situation: The case of French as official L3 in the school of Samedan (Switzerland). *International Journal of Bilingual Education and Bilingualism* 4: 38–49.

Cenoz, J. 1991. *Enseñanza-aprendizaje inglés como L2 o L3*. Leioa: Universidad del País Vasco.

Cenoz, J. 2003. The additive effect of bilingualism on third language acquisition: A review. *International Journal of Bilingualism* 7: 71–87.

Cenoz, J. & C. Hoffmann. 2003. Acquiring a third language: What role does bilingualism play? *International Journal of Bilingualism* 7: 1–5.

Diggle, P., P. Heagerty, L. Kung-Yee & S. Zeger. 2002. *Analysis of Longitudinal Data*, 2nd edn. Oxford: OUP.

Dörnyei, Z., K. Csizér & N. Németh. 2006. *Motivation, Language Attitudes and Globalisation: A Hungarian Perspective*. Clevedon: Multilingual Matters.

EDK (Swiss Conference of Cantonal Ministers of Education), ed. 2004. *Sprachenunterricht in der obligatorischen Schule: Strategie der EDK und Arbeitsplan für die gesamtschweizerische Koordination*. Bern: EDK.

Europarat. 2001. *Gemeinsamer europäischer Referenzrahmen für Sprachen: Lernen, lehren, beurteilen*. Berlin: Langenscheidt. <http://www.goethe.de/referenzrahmen> (6 June 2012).

Faraway, J. J. 2006. *Extending the Linear Model with R: Generalized Linear, Mixed Effects and Nonparametric Regression Models*. Boca Raton FL: Chapman & Hall.

Gardner, R. C. 1985. *Social Psychology and Second Language Learning: The Role of Attitudes and Motivation*. London: Arnold.

Gogolin, I. 1994. *Der monolinguale Habitus der multilingualen Schule*. Münster: Waxmann.

Haenni Hoti, A., S. Heinzmann & M. Müller. 2009. "I can you help?": Assessing speaking skills and interaction strategies of young learners. In *The Age Factor and Early Language Learning*, ed. M. Nikolov, 119–140. Berlin: Mouton de Gruyter.

Haenni Hoti, A., S. Heinzmann, M. Müller, W. Wicki, M. Oliveira & E. Werlen. 2011. Introducing a second foreign language in Swiss primary schools: The effect of L2 listening and reading skills on L3 acquisition. *International Journal of Multilingualism* 8: 98–116.

Hartig, J. 2007. Skalierung und Definition von Kompetenzniveaus. In *Sprachliche Kompetenzen: Konzepte und Messung. DESI-Ergebnisse Band 1*, eds. B. Beck & E. Klieme, 83–99. Weinheim: Beltz.

Hurd, M. 1993. Minority language children and French immersion: Additive multilingualism or subtractive semi-lingualism? *Canadian Modern Language Review* 49: 514–525.

Jessner, U. 2008. State-of-the-art article. Teaching third languages: Findings, trends and challenges. *Language Teaching* 41: 15–56.

Klieme, E. 2006. *Zusammenfassung zentraler Ergebnisse der DESI-Studie*. <http://www.dipf.de/de/projekte/pdf/biqua/DESI_Ausgewaehlte_Ergebnisse.pdf> (6 June 2012).

Lasagabaster, D. 1997. *Creatividad y conciencia metalingüística: Incidencia en el aprendizaje del inglés como L3*. PhD dissertation, University of the Basque Country.

Lenz, P. & T. Studer. 2007. *Lingualevel: Instrumente zur Evaluation von Fremdsprachenkompetenzen 5. bis 9. Schuljahr*. eds. Bildungsdirektoren-Konferenz Zentralschweiz (BKZ), Nordwestschweizerische Erziehungsdirektoren-Konferenz (NW-EDK) und Erziehungsdirektoren-Konferenz der Ostschweizer Kantone und des Fürstentums Liechtenstein (EDKOst). Bern: BLMV.

Linacre, J. M. 2008. *Winsteps Rasch Measurement Computer Program* (Version 3.67.0). Chicago IL: Winsteps.com.

Marx, N. & B. Hufeisen. 2004. Critical overview of research on third language acquisition and multilingualism published in the German language. *International Journal of Multilingualism* 1: 141–154.

Modirkhamene, S. 2006. The reading achievement of third language versus second language learners of English in relation to the interdependence hypothesis. *International Journal of Multilingualism* 3: 280–295.

Moser, U., F. Keller & S. Tresch. 2003. *Schullaufbahn und Leistung: Bildungsverlauf und Lernerfolg von Zürcher Schülerinnen und Schülern am Ende der 3. Volksschulklasse*. Bern: hep.

Mullis, I. V. S., M. O. Martin, E. J. González & A. M. Kennedy. 2003. *PIRLS 2001 International Report: IEA's Study of Reading Literacy Achievement in Primary Schools*. Chestnut Hill MA: Boston College. <http://timss.bc.edu/pirls2001i/PIRLS2001_Pubs_IR.html> (6 June 2012).

Muñoz, C. 2000. Bilingualism and trilingualism in school students in Catalonia. In *English in Europe: The Acquisition of a Third Language*, eds. J. Cenoz & U. Jessner, 157–178. Clevedon: Multilingual Matters.

OCR (Oxford, Cambridge and RSA Examinations). 2005–2007. *Asset Languages: External Assessment Sample Tasks*. Cambridge: OCR. <http://www.assetlanguages.org.uk> (6 June 2012).

Oxford, R. L. 1990. *Language Learning Strategies: What Every Teacher Should Know*. New York NY: Newbury House.

Rauch, D. P., A. Jurecka & H. G. Hesse. 2010. Für den Drittspracherwerb zählt auch die Lesekompetenz in der Herkunftssprache: Untersuchung der Türkisch-, Deutsch- und Englisch-Lesekompetenz bei Deutsch-Türkisch bilingualen Schülern. In *Migration, Identität, Sprache und Bildungserfolg* (Zeitschrift für Pädagogik, Beiheft 55), eds. C. Allemann-Ghionda, P. Stanat, K. Göbel & C. Röhner, 78–100. Weinheim: Beltz.

Sächsisches Bildungsinstitut. 2007/2008. *Kompetenztest Deutsch (6. Jahrgangsstufe)*. Radebeul: Sächsisches Bildungsinstitut.

Sagasta Errasti, M. P. 2003. Acquiring writing skills in a third language: The positive effects of bilingualism. *International Journal of Bilingualism* 7: 27–42.

Sanders, M. & G. Meijers. 1995. English as L3 in the elementary school. *ITL: Review of Applied Linguistics* 107: 59–78.

Sanz, C. 2000. Bilingual education enhances third language acquisition: Evidence from Catalonia. *Applied Psycholinguistics* 21: 23–44.

Schaer, U. & U. Bader. 2005. *Evaluation Englisch in den 6. Klassen Appenzell Innerrhoden 2005*. Appenzell Innerrhoden: Fachhochschule Nordwestschweiz, Pädagogische Hochschule.

Schoonen, R., A. van Gelderen, K. de Glopper, J. Hulstijn, A. Simis, P. Snellings & M. Stevenson. 2002. Linguistic knowledge, metacognitive knowledge and retrieval speed in L1, L2 and EFL writing. In *New Directions for Research in L2 Writing*, eds. S. Randsdell & M.-L. Barbier, 101–122. Dordrecht: Kluwer.

Snijders, T. & R. Bosker. 1999. *Multilevel Analysis: An Introduction to Basic and Advanced Multilevel Modeling*. London: Sage.

Stöckli, G. 2004. *Motivation im Fremdsprachenunterricht: Eine theoriegeleitete empirische Untersuchung in 5. und 6. Primarschulklassen im Unterricht in Englisch und Französisch*. Aarau: Sauerländer.

Swain, M., S. Lapkin, N. Rowen & D. Hart. 1990. The role of mother tongue literacy in third language learning. *Vox* 4: 111–121.

University of Cambridge ESOL Examinations. 2003/2004/2007. *Cambridge Young Learners English Tests: Sample Papers*. Cambridge: University of Cambridge.
Van Gelderen, A., R. Schoonen, K. de Glopper, J. Hulstijn, P. Snellings, A. Simis & M. Stevenson. 2003. Roles of linguistic knowledge, metacognitive knowledge and processing speed in L3, L2 and L1 reading comprehension: A structural equation modeling approach. *International Journal of Bilingualism* 7: 7–25.

"Multilingual brains"

Individual differences in multilinguals – a neuro-psycholinguistic perspective[*]

Julia Festman
University of Potsdam, Germany

Individual differences in multilinguals are considered as group-specific behavior and processing. For this review paper, we selected two lines of research to look into more specifically. In the first research project, two groups of multilinguals (early and late trilinguals) are compared on a sentence processing task using fMRI. Findings showed the specific differences in processing due to age of onset. The second project compared two groups of healthy bilinguals differing in their susceptibility to switch unintentionally between two languages. A variety of tasks and different methods (including psycholinguistics and electroencephalography) allowed isolating the key factor distinguishing both groups: cognitive control (assessed by executive functions tasks). The non-switcher group was more efficient, faster and more correct, whereas the switchers showed difficulties of language control and cognitive control, in particular being more distracted by irrelevant information.

Keywords: multilingualism, language acquisition, language learning, individual speakers, brain imaging, electrophysiology, executive control

---

[*]   This article is based on the papers presented at a workshop on 'Multilingual brains', organized by Susanne M. Reiterer and the author and held within the scope of the *International Conference on Multilingual Individuals and Multilingual Societies* (Hamburg, October 2010). The workshop was generously supported by the Jung Stiftung für Wissenschaft und Forschung (Hamburg), Brain Products (Gilching), De Gruyter (Berlin) and the Collaborative Research Center "The construction of meaning" (Sonderforschungsbereich 833 "Bedeutungskonstitution" (Tübingen). The author is very grateful to the German Research Foundation (Deutsche Forschungsgemeinschaft, DFG) who provided the financial support for this entire line of research (FE 941/1–1) and to T.F. Münte and A. Rodriguez-Fornells for support on the entire research project. Furthermore, the author thanks the anonymous reviewer for suggestions on an earlier version of this manuscript.

1.   Contemporary research on multilingualism with a focus on individual differences and the brain

This review paper focuses on contemporary research in multilingualism at the neuro-psycholinguistic level. We will first provide a rough overview of current research trends before examining in detail two comprehensive research projects, the first by Elise Wattendorf using functional magnetic resonance imaging (fMRI) (Section 2) and the second by Julia Festman using psycholinguistic language tasks, neuropsychological testing and electrophysiology (Section 3). In the last section, we will summarize the key findings of both research projects and stress the necessity for methodological advances as well as the need to incorporate an individual-differences point of view.

Comparisons of monolingual and bilingual speakers informed us about the difference it makes to learn one language only compared to the acquisition of a second, early or late. The picture, these days, turned out to be more complex. Therefore, we will mainly summarize two research projects on individual differences within groups of multilinguals. Contemporary research in the field of multilingualism incorporates the view on processes of the brain. Recent research looked (a) at learning induced changes of the brain e.g. with regard to phonetics (Golestani, Price & Scott 2011). Manuela Macedonia revealed in her line of study that foreign language learning would profit from a more embodied teaching approach, i.e. enactment, defined as performing representative gestures during encoding in order to enhance memory encoding and facilitate retrieval (Macedonia, Muller & Friederici 2010, Macedonia & Knösche 2011, Macedonia, Muller & Friederici 2011). (b) Another focus is on comparisons of multilingual speakers to other multilinguals, which is methodologically a crucial step forward and will thus be in the center of this review. In a study by Elise Wattendorf, brain activation of early versus late multilinguals was compared. Julia Festman contrasted two groups of late bilinguals in terms of behavior (language, cognition and intelligence) as well as electrophysiological patterns (Festman, Rodríguez-Fornells & Münte 2010, Festman 2012). Such comparisons challenge the previous approach of comparing a monolingual to a bilingual group, an approach which dominated the research so far. (c) The variability of brain function or brain activation is taken into consideration when attempting to systemize it. For example, Chantel S. Prat and colleagues suggest a thorough look at individual capabilities e.g. in Prat & Just (2008), whereas Susanne M. Reiterer and colleagues pursued an in-depth investigation of language talent/language aptitude, see Dogil & Reiterer (2009). This is to name just a few of the contemporary examples.

Until now, individual differences in multilingual language acquisition have been largely neglected or even ignored, although already far back in history some individuals (polyglots and hyper-polyglots) demonstrate extraordinary language abilities in the acquisition of all or some of the subsystems of language (e.g. phonological, semantic, lexical, morphological, syntactic domain). However, maybe due to the technical advances in imaging techniques (for example, fMRI; Electro- and Magneto-encephalography, EEG + MEG), and due to growing interdisciplinarity within the "cognitive sciences", individual differences in multilingual language acquisition and use, or put differently, "multilingual brains", recently started to attract more and more attention.

Although studies were conducted on multilingual participants, not all of them were strictly speaking "multilinguals". The information provided and used in order to create groups (e.g. proficiency level, types of proficiency assessment, etc.) as well as participant descriptions and the findings could not entirely satisfy many researchers who had tried to characterize multilinguals on many levels based on information from language acquisition history, language backgrounds, current language use, language proficiency tests, etc. An extremely comprehensive and very useful methodological outline has been put forward by Grosjean (1998) regarding the study of bilinguals. To give just one example, multilinguals are not necessarily bilinguals, but much of the imaging literature uses bilinguals as an umbrella term for speakers of more than one language, often ignoring the fact that more than two languages might be mastered, even at a very high level of proficiency. The strong impact the knowledge of a third language has on language processing is thereby not taken into consideration. Festman (2009) extended Green's (1986) theory of language processing of two languages to three languages and suggested that the active use of three languages involves the inhibition of two currently unused languages in order for the third, the current language of production to be ready for use. This additional need to inhibit not only one but two languages requires much mental resources and demands very strong language control abilities for production in a strictly monolingual mode. How demanding trilingualism is, can be different for the individual speaker, depending on a number of factors, such as individual cognitive abilities which shape language processing, the level of language proficiency of each language, the frequency and recency of using these three languages, the speech situation (e.g. formality, feeling at ease, stress, etc.), as well as the requirements in connection with the language output.

In this review paper we attempt to provide insights into recent work of two researchers who are working on Bi- and Multilingualism within the framework of a neuroscientific background, focusing on the comparison of multilinguals with other multilinguals. This comparison allows both a big step forward in understanding the impact of control abilities on language control (i.e., the use of a certain language according to environmental circumstances) as well as a thorough consideration of methodological advances in research dealing with individual differences in multilingualism.

2. Comparisons of early and late multilinguals (fMRI-study): Wattendorf

In this section the part of the work of Elise Wattendorf, which is related to this topic, will be presented. Wattendorf, Festman, Westermann, Keil, Zappatore, Francheschini, Lüdi, Radue, Münte, Rager & Nitsch (submitted) investigated sentence processing in multilinguals by comparing early and late multilingual speakers. The impact of age of acquisition on the manner of cerebral representation of multiple languages is a key issue in the imaging literature. For a comprehensive review see Wattendorf & Festman (2008).

The Swiss research group followed an earlier approach by Kim, Relkin, Lee & Hirsch (1997) who contrasted early (during infancy) and late (L2 acquisition after puberty) bilinguals during sentence production and found overlapping activations for L1 and L2 in early bilinguals and spatially segregated activations in late bilinguals. The study by Mahendra, Plate, Magloire, Milman & Trouard (2003) is yet another example comparing early (before age 6) with late (after age 6) bilinguals on language production (words and sentences). They found higher activation in anterior and posterior language areas during word and sentence production in L1 and L2 of early bilinguals. Both studies indicate that early bilingualism leads to functional plasticity. Additionally, a study by Mechelli, Crinion, Noppeney, O'Doherty, Ashburner, Frackowiak & Price (2004) revealed that early bilingualism leads to structural plasticity: when comparing early (age <5) versus late (age 10–15) bilinguals using voxel-based morphometry (VBM), higher grey matter density was found in early bilinguals in the inferior parietal lobe. To conclude, the early bilingual brain differs from the late bilingual brain during sentence production but not during language perception tasks (e.g. Hasegawa, Carpenter & Just 2002), and it concerns processing of the first (L1) and second (L2) acquired language. Differences were mainly observed in left prefrontal regions.

In order to determine the representation of additional languages (L3) related to the effect of age of acquisition (early versus late), Wattendorf and colleagues set out for a study on sentence processing while also extending the scope of brain imaging to possible changes in other brain regions. Methodologically they aimed at comparing language-related activity between corresponding languages of early and late bilinguals. The group (4 female) of early multilinguals was comprised of eight speakers who had acquired L1 and L2 before age 3, but L3 after age 9. The group of late multilinguals (8 speakers) had learned L1 before age 3, but L2 and L3 after age 9. Independent of the age of acquisition, all 16 subjects showed "mastery" in their L1 and L2 (level C1 in the CERF) and "efficient proficiency" in their L3 (level C2) on a proficiency self-evaluation test. The language task during the scanning session consisted of a narration (30 sec) to a person familiar to the participant about their activities of the day before the day of scanning at a certain time point (morning, afternoon, night). The task was administered several times in each session, since the participant had to use a certain language for the task (L1, L2 or L3), according to instructions. To be able to determine the language-related activity, a baseline condition was used: every 30 seconds, the language task was interrupted, and participants were asked to tap their forefinger following an auditory cue (e.g. describe morning activity in L1, finger tapping, describe afternoon activity in L2, finger tapping, describe evening activity in L3, etc.). Wattendorf and colleagues used a conjunction analysis to determine the pattern of activity within every subject between two runs. To sum up, she incorporated different methodological approaches in her study: she used sentence production as a more complex language production task, asked her participants to follow task requirements in three languages, and "double-checked" the task-related and language-specific brain activation by conducting the same experiment in two runs (i.e. brain activation is measured on two different days using fMRI, and only the specific activation that is found on both testing sessions was used as the final result).

Results showed regional differences in neuronal activities between both groups. Late multilinguals revealed a higher activation in the Posterior Superior Temporal Gyrus (pSTG) than early multilinguals in all comparisons. The latter, however, showed higher activation in the prefrontal cortex, the striatum and the parieto-occipital junction. These three areas are usually interpreted as areas related to control functions of the brain (e.g. Abutalebi & Green 2007): the prefrontal cortex selects between competing responses and inhibits previously salient information, the striatum orchestrates multiple parallel excitatory and inhibitory connections, information processing, and sequencing, and plays a key role in cognitive flexibility. Finally, the parieto-occipital junction maintains a mental representation, and is involved in working memory. With regard to bilingual language control, the prefrontal cortex is related to control of language interference and language switching by means of inhibition of the non-target language (Rodríguez-Fornells, Van der Lugt, Rotte, Britti, Heinze & Münte 2005, Hernandez, Martínez & Kohnert 2000). In the same context, the striatum was found to be involved in parallel information processing during semantic priming in the non-target language and during translation (Crinion, Turner, Grogan, Hanakawa, Noppeney, Devlin, Aso, Urayama, Fukuyama, Stockton, Usui, Green & Price 2006, Price, Green & Von Studnitz 1999), and the parieto-occipital junction when language switching was required. It is involved in holding online phonological information (Price et al. 1999).

To sum up, early bilingualism influences brain activity in prefrontal regions, the basal ganglia and the parieto-occipital junction. Language control and cognitive control involve prefrontal regions, the basal ganglia and the parieto-occipital junction. The effect of early bilingualism on language control, such as revealed during translation, inhibition, priming and switching tasks is still largely unknown. Early bilingualism influences cognitive control, but which brain regions are involved is still not precisely known.

3.   Comparisons of "switcher"-bilinguals with "non-switcher"-bilinguals: Festman

In collaboration with Thomas Münte (Lübeck) and Antoni Rodríguez-Fornells (Barcelona), Julia Festman set out to realize a study on switching behaviour and control abilities of 29 Russian-German late bilinguals. The underlying assumption of this research project was that not all bilinguals behave the same when it comes to switching between languages. While some switch frequently, others don't. Festman took a widely ranging approach to study the possible relation between switching behaviour and control abilities.

3.1   Background information

According to a language history questionnaire, 28 participants spoke Russian as their first language (L1) and German as L2 (for one participant German was L1 and Russian L2). Most participants were late bilinguals, exposed to German at an average of 11.4 years (SD = 6.1). They had been living in Germany for an average of 9 years (SD = 4.03), and were on average 15.5 years old (SD = 6.5) upon arrival to Germany. All participants were living in Magdeburg, Germany, at the time of testing, and were regularly exposed to German and Russian. Most participants were students at the university (n = 16), others were still in high school (n = 9), or had already finished their university studies (n = 4).

Self-ratings of language proficiency of the two investigated languages as well as other language knowledge were collected (see Festman et al. 2010). Participants rated their current proficiency in four language skills (speaking, comprehension, writing and reading) for all of their acquired languages on a 4-point scale (1 = poor, 4 = perfect). On average, their rating indicated good (with a trend to perfect) language proficiency both in Russian and German.

3.2   Creating groups: Bilingual picture naming task

A bilingual picture naming task (see Festman et al. 2010) based on an alternating runs paradigm served as an objective measure for language proficiency. Participants were asked to name 240 pictures as fast and as accurately as possible (trying neither to make errors nor to correct themselves). Every picture was displayed on a computer screen for 1500ms. Participants were informed that the language in which a given picture had to be named was determined by the color of a frame (red or green), which appeared 300ms prior to the picture. They were instructed that the sequence of switching between the two languages was completely regular. Two consecutive pictures required a response in German, and the next two in Russian, and so on (GG RR GG RR).

This task is much more complex and difficult for bilinguals compared to monolinguals: due to parallel activation of words from both languages, bilinguals have to consciously suppress non-target language words, which usually pop up during lexical search and retrieval. Moreover, the task demands vary depending on the proficiency level in both languages. In sum, in a bilingual setting, this task measures not only language proficiency in the sense of lexical competence. In particular it provides an indication of the speaker's ability to prevent cross-language interference.

This bilingual picture naming task was used to create two groups of bilinguals. Language interference was used as the critical measure for group assignment. Errors of interference were scored when the correct name was uttered in the non-target language. Using Ward's method, participants were grouped into 2 clusters on the basis of these errors, "switchers" (n = 15, 9 women, 10 to 20 errors or interference) and "non-switchers" (n = 14, 12 women, 1 to 8), with switchers being those speakers who switch unintentionally and frequently while non-switchers don't.

3.3   Bilingual Interview

We used a bilingual interview to assess whether this switcher vs. non-switcher group distinction based on the naming paradigm results might hold up as well under more natural circumstances (see Festman 2012). In the interview, the same participants had to respond to a number of questions predefined prior to the interview. Two research assistants (one a native speaker of German, the other of Russian) acted as interviewers strictly following the question outline. Six topics were presented, each for five minutes in one target language. The interviewers took turns after 5 minutes. Thereby, the language of the interview changed (e.g. 5 minutes conversation in German about the current work situation, then 5 minutes in Russian about the family life). As a result, the switchers produced significantly more errors of cross-language interference in both languages than the non-switchers. Group differences were highly significant for both languages. Speech production, however, did not differ in any other aspect, e.g., fluency, syntactic complexity, grammatical correctness or word-finding difficulties. Thus what distinguished both groups most is their in/ability to prevent errors of cross-language interference in monolingual settings, i.e., when a specific target language is required.

3.4   Bilingual verbal fluency

We collected additional information on word production under conditions of memory retrieval and language control (see Festman 2012). In a verbal fluency task, participants were asked to produce words of a certain language, German or Russian, for 1 minute at a time, belonging to a certain category (e.g. animals) or starting with a certain letter (e.g. *s*). Results revealed that both groups did not differ in language proficiency (no significant differences between switchers and non-switchers as well as between German and Russian on any of the 8 subtests) but better language control abilities of non-switchers (less errors of cross-language interference) while the error production apart from these errors was the same.

3.5   Language modes

A second questionnaire (reported in Festman 2012) was used to determine whether differences in language control behaviour could be explained by differences in language mode (following Grosjean's 1982 concept of language mode): non-switchers might have a tendency to use and prefer only one language (monolingual mode) while switchers usually use and prefer both (bilinguals mode). Information was collected on switch behaviour, language attitude and attitude towards switching, language speaking environment and use of language mode. We did not obtain any group-specific language use patterns in any of our investigated domains. Non-switchers were not more frequently in a monolingual mode, and switchers were not mainly in a bilingual mode.

Language mode did not reveal itself as the key factor to determine language control differences apparent as cross-language interference. Differences we did find with the help of the questionnaire were that non-switchers showed more self-awareness regarding switching as well as a better consideration of and adaptation to the communicative partner's language knowledge (Festman 2012).

All data put together revealed no differences in language proficiency between speakers who switch frequently ("switchers") and those who do not ("non-switchers").

3.6   Executive control tasks

In a novel approach we further investigated our two groups of bilinguals, distinguished by their susceptibility to produce cross-language interference, asking whether bilinguals with strong language control abilities ("non-switchers") have an advantage in executive functions (e.g. inhibition of irrelevant information, problem solving, planning efficiency, generative fluency and self-monitoring) compared to those bilinguals showing weaker language control abilities ("switchers"). In a series of neuropsychological tasks both groups were compared with regard to executive control functions. The use of these tasks was motivated by Green's (1986) idea that cross-language interference is a sign for a failure of control over both languages. If the non-target language is not sufficiently inhibited, it can override the initial language choice and at the lexical level the word belonging to the non-target language will be produced instead of the word in the target language.

Four executive function tasks (Tower of Hanoi, Go/Nogo, Divided Attention, and Ruff Figural Fluency Test) were administered. These tasks will be described now in more detail (see Festman et al. 2010).

Tower of Hanoi (TOH)
A computerized version (version 1.5) of the TOH puzzle was used. The participants, seated in front of a computer screen, faced the display of three pegs of the same height, with the left peg having three discs piled on it. They were instructed that the goal was to move all the discs from the left to the right peg by clicking and dragging a disc with the mouse button. Only one disc could be moved at a time, and be placed either on an empty peg or on top of a larger disc. Every rule violation was punished with error points. Participants were asked to complete the task as quickly as possible by using the smallest number of moves, with the least possible error points. Solving this test involves several aspects of executive functions: problem solving, planning ahead, working memory, and inhibition.

For the analyses, two measures were used. As an indicator for the ability to solve a problem, we compared the number of moves between the two groups, reasoning that even if subjects did not plan ahead their moves, as it was previously assumed, they had to remember the end-goal of the task and had been asked to perform their moves as quickly as possible. – At this point, we would like to share a performance detail being aware that it is purely an observation: after instruction some subjects would sit still and stare at the screen for a few seconds before using the mouse in order to execute their moves speedily, while others would start immediately and perform in a trial-and-error-like fashion. It could be that, in contrast to the latter participants, the former did indeed construct a plan how to solve the problem. – The error points were meant to indicate inhibition abilities in accordance with specific rules.

Go/Nogo paradigm
A classical Go/Nogo paradigm involves different types of stimuli to which the response has to be inhibited ("Nogo") or not inhibited ("Go"). In our version of the paradigm, overall five different stimuli (pattern) were presented, and a go-response had to be executed for two stimulus patterns (pushing a mouse button), but upon presentation of any of the other three patterns, the response had to be inhibited ("Nogo", withholding pushing the mouse button).

In a Go/Nogo task the ability to deliberately inhibit dominant, automatic responses when necessary can be measured. Five different stimulus patterns were presented. Since a go response was required only on two, and a nogo response on three of the five different stimuli patterns, working memory was involved (the stimuli had to be remembered and whether it was a go or nogo stimulus). Out of a total of 100 trials 40 were "go"-stimuli. Each of the patterns was presented in random order in the center of a black screen for 1000 ms.

Divided Attention
A visual and an auditory task were presented simultaneously (i.e., attention has to be divided between both tasks). In the visual task, the participant was presented with a 4 x 4 matrix of white crosses and dots on black background on a computer screen. The participant had to identify whether four crosses form a square at any point within the matrix (target stimulus). In the test, overall 100 white stimulus pictures were displayed on a black screen, each for 2000 ms, and then replaced by the next stimulus picture. In the auditory task, two different sine-wave tones were presented to the participant wearing head phones. The participant listened to the sequence of tones and had to identify tone repetitions (target stimulus); otherwise, the tones alternated regularly, every 1000ms. 200 auditory stimuli were presented. Participants were required to respond to visual and auditory targets as quickly and correctly as possible by button press. This dual task situation necessitates the adequate allocation of attentional resources to each of the two tasks and thus probes executive aspects of attention.

Ruff Figural Fluency Test (RFFT)
This paper-and-pencil test assesses generative fluency, another aspect of executive functioning. It requires the production of novel designs. Successful task performance requires fluent and flexible thinking, i.e., the formulation and use of production strategies (e.g. enumeration, rotation). In order to avoid repetition of responses it also

involves self-monitoring, i.e. avoidance of repetition of previously generated responses, while observing the generation rule. More specifically, the RFFT consists of five subtests, each of which contains a different stimulus pattern made up of five dots. Every subtest (1 minute) is administered on a separate sheet of paper, each with 35 identical stimulus patterns presented in a 5 x 7 matrix. For the analysis, the number of produced unique patterns as well as the number of repeated patterns (perseverations) was scored.

Our results were clear-cut. The non-switcher group demonstrated a better performance on the Tower of Hanoi and Ruff Figural Fluency task, faster reaction time in a Go/noGo and Divided Attention task, and produced significantly fewer errors in the Tower of Hanoi, Go/noGo, and Divided Attention tasks when compared to the "switchers". This demonstrates a strong link between language control abilities and executive control abilities in this group of late bilinguals. Previously, this connection has been established by brain imaging studies (e.g. Hernandez et al. 2000). We were the first to show this link on behavioral grounds.

3.7   Subtests of the WAIS-R (German adaptation HAWIE-R, Tewes 1991)

In order to determine the impact of intelligence on the group behavior, we administered the Wechsler Adult Intelligence Scale (four subtests of the German version of the WAIS). The subtests "Information", "Similarities", "Picture Completion", and "Block Design" were selected. The first two are part of the Verbal IQ test scale, whereas the latter two are used to analyze non-verbal capabilities (Performance IQ test scale).

The Information subtest examines the participant's general knowledge. It focuses on the capability to understand simple information. The experiment asks short test questions (e.g. 'Who wrote *Hamlet?*'), and the participant should respond immediately.

The Similarities subtest is meant to assess logical reasoning, in particular abstraction and conceptualization. The experimenter presented verbally item pairs (e.g. *banana* and *orange*; *library* and *zoo*), and the abstract similarity amongst them has to be identified (solution: fruit; a place to store something).

The Picture Completion task assesses aspects of visual perception. Participants are presented with line drawings and have to identify a missing feature, e.g. the missing knob of a door. Task execution involves the ability to differentiate between important and unimportant details.

The Block Design test is supposed to reflect the participant's abilities of visual construction and of solving problems. The participant is required to organize blocks according to patterns on cards.

We observed that non-switchers performed significantly better on the two Verbal subtests (Information and Similarity), but not on the two selected Performance subtests (Picture Completion, Block Design).

3.8   More on control abilities

Language proficiency as well as age at onset, number of acquired languages, language mode, attitudes, intelligence, etc. had been excluded as explanatory factors for the observed group-specific behaviour. Since executive control was found to have a great impact on interindividual differences in these two groups of late bilinguals, we further investigated the groups' control abilities. In another paper (Festman & Münte 2012) we described group performance on an adapted version of the Wisconsin Card Sorting Test (WCST) and a standard Eriksen-Flanker task.

In the WCST, at the start of each trial, four cards were presented in one line in the center of a computer screen. Response buttons were assigned in the following way: The number key "1" should be used for the first card (depicting one red triangle), "2" for the second card (two green stars), "3" for the third card (three yellow crosses), and "4" for the forth card (four blue circles). Below this display, one larger card (e.g. one blue star) was shown which had to be sorted according to a certain rule and was presented until response (button press of one of the four number keys) was given. The participant had to choose between three rules: color (red, yellow, green, blue), number (1–4), and shape (circle, star, triangle, cross). The rule to be applied changed unpredictably after 5–7 trials (e.g. from "sort according to color" to "sort according to shape"). Two different feedback signs ("smileys" ☺ or ☹) followed each response (1000ms after response, duration 1000ms) and provided guidance. A new card to be sorted was presented at 1400ms after feedback. The necessity to change the rule was indicated by a "change-rule-sound". In case of rule change, participants had to find the correct new rule by trial-and-error.

The WCST showed that non-switchers outperformed switchers in speed and accuracy, and were better at finding and applying the correct rule.

In the flanker task, an array of five white letters is presented shortly on a black background on the computer screen. The participant has to indicate with a button press (right or left forefinger) which of the two letters, H or S, is presented in the middle of the letter line (central task). The flanking letters provide either congruent (HHHHH or SSSSS) or incongruent (SSHSS or HHSHH) information. The flanking letters (i.e., additional visual information to the central task) can facilitate (→ congruent) or complicate (→ incongruent) the response decision. These two conditions were used as a measure of response conflict, since responses tend to be slower for incongruent than for congruent trials. The difference between the two conditions ("conflict effect") is commonly used to reveal the time needed to resolve the conflict between the target letter and the flanking letters.

We observed that on the flanker task, non-switchers performed faster and better than the switchers on incongruent trials, while they responded as well as the switchers on congruent trials. This shows that switchers are not overall worse performers rather that they differ from non-switchers on very specific aspects. Moreover, non-switchers had a higher correction rate following an error what points at stronger self-monitoring abilities of this group.

During the flanker task, we also recorded EEGs from the scalp of each of the 29 participants. Therefore, tin electrodes were mounted in an electro cap. One particular EEG-component is of great relevance here: the error-related negativity (ERN, Gehring, Goss, Coles, Meyer & Donchin 1993). This component starts usually just after the time of response. It is a negative going waveform commonly observed for error trials and is interpreted as an indication of the amount of response conflict. We found a significant difference between the two groups also with regard to their EEG: the non-switchers showed a significantly smaller ERN compared to the switchers, indicating that they probably have less response conflict. In the flanker task, this could be interpreted as the non-switchers being less distracted from the flanking letters than the switchers.

In sum, the non-switcher group consistently performed better and faster, seemed to be less distracted from non-target languages as well as other, currently irrelevant stimulus information (other rules in the card sorting test, flanking letters in the flanker task), demonstrated better self-monitoring abilities, and better efficiency to deal with conflict. Compared to switchers, the non-switcher group showed superior executive subfunctions which we interpret in terms of a general information processing advantage (given the number of different tasks assessed so far).

4. Conclusion

Individual differences of multilinguals have been observed in age of onset, proficiency level in different language skills and language components (e.g. lexicon, syntax, etc.), aptitude, exposure/experience, manner of acquisition, etc. Researchers recently attempted to go beyond the linguistic scope and to assess individual differences at a more cognitive, neuro-psycholinguistic level. Two research projects have been presented in this paper. Wattendorf investigated the impact of age of acquisition on multilingual sentence processing in terms of brain functioning. Festman extended the concept of switching and not switching to a general behavioral level and to the underlying executive functions, using a variety of methods, including psycholinguistics and electroencephalography. A so far unexplored area of individual differences was determined: the particular need for an efficient system of executive control to be able to inhibit the currently unused language.

Both research projects incorporated methodological advances in research dealing with individual differences in multilingualism. Wattendorf assessed production in three languages and excluded coincidental brain activation by asking participants to perform on the same task a second time on another day. By linking both task performances together, consistent brain activation could be analyzed. Festman worked with the same group of participants in this longitudinal study and put together a number of findings from a variety of tasks and methods yielding a complex and in-depth picture of group-specific behavior.

Multilinguals are far from being a homogenous group. But as the findings of the reported research projects has shown, they are also not only heterogeneous. Otherwise, research would have to turn to single case studies. But what we understand is that clustering groups became more difficult the more critical factors are known to influence language in general and multilingualism in particular. We still should keep on clustering multilingual individuals into groups (else task-related performance becomes statistically difficult to analyze, and the findings become limited in their power), but clustering needs to be done more carefully. This review paper in particular points at the considerable impact cognitive control has on multilingual processing. Cognitive control should be considered as a criterion according to which bilinguals could be subdivided into homogenous groups at the level of processing.

We believe that good neuroscientific studies on "multilingual brains" need to take into account current findings on individual differences of multilinguals and best include researchers on multilingualism for example to give advice regarding the different crucial factors to be considered in subject selection/clustering and stimulus material as well as contribute to the theoretical implications of the findings for multilingualism from a linguistic point of view. Thus, this paper is written both for researchers on multilingualism as well as for brain scientist interested in how the brain processes multiple languages. There is much more need to further the understanding of the workings of two research groups, linguists and brain scientists. One particular aspect is to unify the terminology and concepts as well as definitions, such as "bilingual" and "multilingual". This paper aimed at providing linguists and brain scientists with the basic concept of, the research related to as well as the strong impact cognitive control has on the processing of multiple languages: it rules it all.

References

Abutalebi, J. & D. W. Green. 2007. Bilingual language production: The neurocognition of language representation and control. *Journal of Neurolinguistics* 20: 242–275.

Crinion, J., R. Turner, A. Grogan, T. Hanakawa, U. Noppeney, J. T. Devlin, T. Aso, S. Urayama, H. Fukuyama, K. Stockton, K. Usui, D. W. Green & C. J. Price. 2006. Language control in the bilingual brain. *Science* 312: 1537–1540.

Dogil, G. & S. M. Reiterer, eds. 2009. *Language Talent and Brain Activity*. Berlin: Mouton de Gruyter.

Festman, J. 2009. *Three Languages in Mind*. Saarbrücken: VDM.

Festman, J. 2012. Language control of late bilinguals. *Bilingualism: Language and Cognition* 15, 580–593.

Festman, J. & T. F. M. Münte. 2012. Cognitive control in Russian-German bilinguals. *Frontiers in Psychology* 3, 1–7.

Festman, J., A. Rodríguez-Fornells & T. F. M. Münte. 2010. Individual differences in control of language interference in late bilinguals are mainly related to general executive abilities. *Behavioral and Brain Functions* 6. <http://www.behavioralandbrainfunctions.com/content/6/1/5> (6 June 2012).

Gehring, W. J., B. Goss, M. G. H. Coles, D. E. Meyer & E. Donchin. 1993. A neural system for error detection and compensation. *Psychological Science* 4: 385–390.

Golestani, N., C. J. Price & S. K. Scott. 2011. Born with an ear for dialects? Structural plasticity in the 'expert' phonetician brain. *The Journal of Neuroscience* 31: 4213–4220.

Green, D. W. 1986. Control, activation, and resource: A framework and a model for the control of speech in bilinguals. *Brain and Language* 27: 210–223.

Grosjean, F. 1982. *Life with Two Languages: An Introduction to Bilingualism.* Cambridge MA: Harvard University Press.

Grosjean, F. 1998. Studying bilinguals: Methodological and conceptual issues. *Bilingualism: Language and Cognition* 1: 131–149.

Hasegawa, M., P. A. Carpenter & M. A. Just. 2002. An fMRI study of bilingual sentence comprehension and workload. *NeuroImage* 15: 647–660.

Hernandez, A. E., A. Martínez & K. Kohnert. 2000. In search for the language switch: An fMRI study of picture naming in Spanish-English bilinguals. *Brain and Language* 73: 421–431.

Kim, K. H. S., N. R. Relkin, K. M. Lee & J. Hirsch. 1997. Distinct cortical areas associated with native and second language. *Nature* 388: 171–174.

Macedonia, M. & T. R. Knösche. 2011. Body in mind: How gestures empower foreign language learning. *Mind, Brain, and Education* 5: 196–211.

Macedonia, M., K. Muller & A. D. Friederici. 2010. Neural correlates of high performance in foreign language vocabulary learning. *Mind, Brain, and Education* 4: 125–134.

Macedonia, M., K. Muller & A. D. Friederici. 2011. The impact of iconic gestures on foreign language word learning and its neural substrate. *Human Brain Mapping* 32: 982–998.

Mahendra, N., E. Plate, J. Magloire, L. Milman & T. P. Trouard. 2003. fMRI variability and the localization of languages in the bilingual brain. *NeuroReport* 14: 1225–1228.

Mechelli, A., J. T. Crinion, U. Noppeney, J. O'Doherty, J. Ashburner, R. S. Frackowiak & C. J. Price. 2004. Structural plasticity in the bilingual brain: Proficiency in a second language and age at acquisition affect grey-matter density. *Nature* 431: 757.

Prat, C. S. & M. Just. 2008. Brain bases of individual differences in cognition. *Psychological Science Agenda* 22. <http://www.apa.org/science/about/psa/2008/05/prat.aspx> (6 June 2012).

Price, C. J., D. W. Green & R. von Studnitz. 1999. A functional imaging study of translation and language switching. *Brain* 122: 2221–2235.

Rodríguez-Fornells, A., A. van der Lugt, M. Rotte, B. Britti, H. J. Heinze & T. F. M. Münte. 2005. Second language interferes with word production in fluent bilinguals: Brain potential and functional imaging evidence. *Journal of Cognitive Neuroscience* 17: 422–433.

Wattendorf, E. & J. Festman. 2008. Images of the multilinguals brain: The effect of age of second language acquisition. *Annual Review of Applied Linguistics* 28: 3–24.

Wattendorf, E., J. Festman, B. Westermann, U. Keil, D. Zappatore, R. Francheschini, G. Lüdi, E. W. Radue, T. Münte, G. Rager & C. Nitsch. Submitted. Early bilingualism influences early and subsequently later acquired languages in cortical regions representing control functions.

PART II

How language changes in multilingual settings

Contact-induced language variation and change

Subject-verb inversion in 13th century German and French

A comparative view*

Martin Elsig
Goethe University of Frankfurt, Germany

The present study examines whether subject-verb inversion in Old French is similarly conditioned to its counterpart in Middle High German. In the generative literature, inversion in Old French has often been ascribed to a verb second (V2) property, possibly as a result of language contact with Germanic. Using corpus data from the 13th century, this study compared the most and the least favorable contexts for inversion in Old French and Middle High German. A variable rule analysis of the data reveals some important differences between the two languages. This challenges the view that inversion in Old French is generated by the same grammatical system as inversion in V2 languages.

Keywords: Old French, Middle High German, subject-verb inversion, verb second, variable rule analysis

1. Introduction

The aim of this study is to investigate whether 13th century Old French (OF) and Middle High German (MHG) have an identical underlying grammatical system with regard to subject-verb inversion (INV). INV in OF is widely held to be the reflex of an underlying verb second (V2) grammar, very much like modern Germanic. In fact,

*   This study is part of the research project "Multilingualism as cause and effect of language change", directed by Jürgen M. Meisel and Esther Rinke. This project was among the last 15 to be funded by the German Science Foundation (Deutsche Forschungsgemeinschaft, DFG) within the Collaborative Research Center on Multilingualism (Sonderforschungsbereich 538 "Mehrsprachigkeit"), established at the University of Hamburg between 1999 and 2011. I wish to thank the project directors, Jürgen M. Meisel and Esther Rinke, for many fruitful discussions. This paper has benefited a lot from the comments of Rocío Pérez-Tattam and of two anonymous reviewers. All remaining errors are, of course, my own.

language contact with Germanic has often been held responsible for this apparent V2 property of OF (Mutz 2009: 61, Posner 1996: 53, Thomason & Kaufman 1988: 128, Von Wartburg 1958: 66, 104). Mathieu (2009: 345) states that "[t]his influence of Germanic on what was to become French may have been through contact, first through the invasion of Gaul by the Francs, and second, by the Normans in the North-West." In this study, French and German linguistic data are compared in order to verify this contact-based explanation of OF V2. For the purposes of comparability, the data have been extracted from texts of the same genre, geographical location and time period: written charters from the region between the rivers Rhine and Meuse dating back to the 13th century, when the OF V2 structure was supposedly at its apogee according to Côté (1995). This paper intends to contribute to a clarification of the question whether the internal grammar of speakers of OF can be qualified as Germanic in nature when it comes to the verb second property.

Subject-verb inversion is illustrated in (1) for MHG and in (2) for OF. In both examples, there is a direct object in first position, followed by the finite verb in second position and the subject immediately to the right of the finite verb.

(1) die   hant   ſie   von ime   enpfang-en.
     them[ACC.PL] AUX.3PL they[NOM.PL] from him[DAT.SG] receive-PTCP
     'They have received them from him.'   (MHG, I.274.280.35)

(2) (et) ceſte paiſ   ne   puet
     and this peace.treaty[ACC.SG] NEG can[PRS.3SG]
     on   fai-re   ſenſ   mo(n) acort
     one[NOM.SG] do-INF without my   consent
     'And one cannot sign this peace treaty without my con sent.'
                                       (OF, 70. – wIII481 – 1264 July 31)

INV in Germanic is intimately connected to the V2 property. According to the traditional generative analysis proposed by Den Besten (1983), the verb moves to C°. This movement is proposed to be triggered by a set of finiteness features in C°. The linear constraint, according to which only one constituent may precede the finite verb in matrix clauses, is accounted for by placing the initial XP in Spec,CP, the single preverbal position.[1] This XP may be the subject, resulting in canonical subject-verb order, or any other constituent, resulting in INV. Den Besten's account has the additional advantage of explaining the asymmetrical nature of most V2 languages, i.e. the absence of V-to-C movement in subordinate clauses. In embedded contexts, C° is occupied by the conjunction. As a consequence, verb movement into this position is blocked.[2]

---

1. Under a split CP analysis such as Rizzi's (1997), this account is not tenable. Various alternative explanations have been proposed since to account for this linear restriction (e.g. Meinunger 2006, Müller 2005, Zwart 2005).

2. The availability of V2 in subordinate clauses of symmetrical Germanic V2-languages such as Yiddish and Icelandic has been explained either in terms of a CP-recursion analysis or as a

Regarding the question of the historical point in time at which the V2 property became entrenched in German grammar, Axel (2007: Chapter 2) claims that Old High German already exhibited a regular asymmetrical V2 grammar. According to this author, the deviations from the V2 constraint, e.g. patterns of verb end, were exceptions that only occurred in a restricted class of contexts. In the period of MHG, the V2 grammar was well consolidated.

OF also exhibits a number of contexts in which the subject appears in postverbal position and which have been interpreted as evidence in favor of a V2 grammar (Roberts 1993, Vance 1997), in contrast to the modern varieties of French or of other Romance languages. The example in (2) illustrates one such context. However, a look at the data reveals that, contrary to Germanic, INV is by no means a uniform phenomenon in OF: A nominal subject may variably occur in a position preceding or following participles or infinitives. The former construction is known as simple INV, the latter as free INV (Roberts 1993), illustrated in examples (3) and (4).

(3) et   celi moitíe   doi-ent   li   cuens
    and this half[ACC.SG] must-PRS.3PL the count[NOM.SG]
    de bar deffus dis   et   fui hoir ten-ir
    of Bar above mention[PTCP] and his heirs hold-INF
    dou   conte de lucemb(our) en   fie ...
    of.the count of Luxembourg in   fief
    'And the aforementioned count of Bar and his heirs shall get this half as a
    fief ...'   (OF, 155. wIV403 1277 May 23)

(4) Et   pour ceft hommage at   donn-ei   Li
    and for   this duty   AUX.3SG give-PTCP the
    diz   henris   a moí ... deus
    aforemention[PTCP] Henry[NOM.SG] to me   two
    cens   liure-s   de treuecíens
    hundred pound-PL[ACC] of Trierese
    'And for this duty, the aforementioned H. has given to me ... two hundred
    pounds from Trier.'   (OF, 122. wIV199 1270 July 13)

Free INV as shown in (4) is a typical feature of modern Romance null subject languages. The exact structural position of the clause-final subject DP is a matter of debate in the literature. Some authors locate it *in situ*, i.e. in its argument position, Spec,*v*P (see, e.g., Alexiadou & Anagnostopoulou 1995, 1998, 2001, 2007, Barbosa 2001, 2009). This is supported by the observation that, in information-structural terms, the postverbal subject DP is the most informative part and is therefore

---

result of V2 at the IP-level (see Iatridou & Koch 1992, Vikner 1995 and the discussion in Hegarty 2005: 53ff, among many others).

focused.[3,4] In contrast, the cartographic approach (see Belletti 2004, 2005, Rizzi 2006) assumes that the subject moves into a low vP-peripheral focus projection (see Sheehan 2009: 231f for discussion).

Simple INV as shown in (3) is very similar to V2-constrained INV in Germanic languages (as exemplified in (1)). In the literature, it is the basis for positing V-to-C movement and hence a V2 grammar for OF (Adams 1987, Benincà 2006, Labelle 2007, Platzack 1995, Roberts 1993, Vance 1997).[5] However, this analysis does not explain why the linear constraint, according to which only one constituent can precede the finite verb in matrix clauses, applies much less regularly in OF than in Germanic languages. It does not explain why there are many contexts in which more than one constituent appears in preverbal position (see the discussion in Poletto 2002).

The focus of the research on the V2 property of OF, and, more generally, of Old Romance has shifted from the linear second position constraint to V-to-C movement as the single most important characteristic of V2 (see Benincà 2006, Labelle 2007), notwithstanding some evidence that V ≥ 3 matrix clauses in OF are incompatible with an underlying V2 grammar (see Fischer 2010: 147 and Kaiser 2002: 168, among others). More specifically, in V ≥ 3 clauses the finite verb can be preceded by more than one constituent, as shown in (5).

> (5) Et   ce   Rachat   elleſ   ont   faít
>   and this repurchase[ACC.SG] they[NOM.PL] AUX.3PL do[PTCP]

---

3.   I adopt a bipartite information-structural division of each clause into a topic-comment and a focus-background domain (see Dahl 1974). I follow Reinhart's (1981) notion of aboutness topic, according to which each sentence can only have one topic. The comment may contain material that is part of the common knowledge, i.e. the presupposition, shared by the author and the intended audience of the utterance. It also contains non-presupposed material. The presupposed part of the sentence, including the aboutness topic, constitutes the background of the sentence. The non-presupposed part is its focus, i.e. the most informative part of the sentence. While comment and background overlap, topic and focus are mutually exclusive (apart from contexts of contrast).

4.   The analysis according to which focused constituents remain *in situ*, that is, in their vP-internal argument position is based on Diesing's (1992) Mapping Hypothesis. According to this hypothesis, VP-internal material is mapped into the Nuclear Scope, while material from the IP is mapped into a restrictive clause. Within the Nuclear Scope, constituents receive a focus interpretation. Non-focused material, i.e. the information pertaining to the background, has to move out of the VP.

5.   Among the proponents of a V2 analysis of OF, there is no unanimity whether OF has a symmetrical or an asymmetrical V2 grammar: Lemieux & Dupuis (1995) argue for the former, Vance (1997) adopts the latter point of view. According to Côté (1995), early OF was a symmetrical V2 language that turned into an asymmetrical one by the time of late OF. Rinke & Meisel (2009) reject a V2 analysis of OF. They argue that OF subordinate clauses feature word order patterns that are not compatible either with a symmetrical or an asymmetrical V2 grammar. As this study focuses on matrix clauses only, I will not pursue this question any further.

par   mon Lauſ ...
through my   approval
'And they have done this repurchase with my approval ...'

(OFr, 35. – wIII220 – 1256 April)

According to Rinke & Meisel (2009) who argue against a V2 property of OF, INV in this language is an interface phenomenon between pragmatics and syntax. The authors propose that variable placement of the subject in preverbal or postverbal position is sensitive to the distribution of information-structural functions within the clause. More precisely, inverted subject DPs bear information focus or form part of a thetic or presentational sentence, whereas preverbal subjects are associated with a topic reading. This account is not contingent on a V-to-C movement analysis. Instead, it draws a parallel with modern Romance null subject languages. INV is structurally accounted for by assuming T° to be the final target of verb movement in declarative matrix clauses, while the subject DP remains *in situ*, i.e. in Spec,*v*P.

As mentioned earlier, this paper will explore whether the underlying grammar of OF can be qualified as Germanic with regard to V2. For this purpose, INV in OF will be compared with its counterpart in MHG in data extracted from texts from the relevant location and time period. Section 2 presents the methodology used to extract and compare the data. Section 3 discusses the data and Section 4 puts forward several conclusions that can be derived from this study.

2. Methodology

This study analyses data taken from the *Corpus of Old German Original Charters until the Year 1300* (based on Wilhelm, Newald, De Boor, Haacke & Kirschstein 1932–1986, electronically edited by Kurt Gärtner and Andrea Rapp)[6] and from the *Corpus of OF Charters, 1237 until 1281, Edition of the Charters of Countess Ermesinde (1226–1247) and of Count Henry V (1247–1281) of Luxembourg* (based on Wampach 1935–1955, electronically edited by Holtus, Overbeck & Völker 2003).[7]

---

6.   See <http://urts55.uni-trier.de/cgi-bin/iCorpus/CorpusIndex.tcl> (23 February 2012).

7.   See <http://www.rmnet.uni-trier.de/cgi-bin/RMnetIndex.tcl?hea=qf&for=qafranzu> (23 February 2012). These data were compiled, evaluated and prepared for linguistic analysis by "... the research project 'Westmitteldeutsche und ostfranzösische Urkunden- und Literatursprachen im 13. und 14. Jahrhundert ('Eastern Old French and Western Middle High German in the charters and the literature of the thirteenth and fourteenth centuries'), ... carried out at the universities of Trier and later on Göttingen within the framework of the Sonderforschungsbereich ('Interdisciplinary Research Unit') 235 'Zwischen Maas und Rhein. Beziehungen, Begegnungen und Konflikte in einem europäischen Kernraum' ('Between the Meuse and the Rhine: Relationships, contacts, and conflicts in a central area of Europe'). [Headed] by Günter

From a subsample of 112 OF charters and of 79 MHG charters, I extracted 452 OF and 435 MHG declarative matrix clauses. Since charters represent a highly formulaic text genre, I focused on those parts of the documents where the style is least constrained by textual conventions, viz. the context and the narratio in particular, excluding protocols and eschatocols. I only included matrix clauses with an overt subject, as it is not entirely clear whether null subjects in OF are located in preverbal or in postverbal position. The generalization, stated by Foulet (1928) and adopted by Adams (1987), Roberts (1993), and Vance (1997), that null subjects must be postverbal since they are restricted to contexts in which an overt subject would be postverbal, too, i.e. non-subject-initial matrix clauses, is, at best, a tendency rather than a rule. Considering that there is no context in OF which categorically triggers INV, it would not be accurate to infer a postverbal placement of the null subject in all non-subject-initial matrix clauses. Certain adverbs or adverbial clauses such as *neporquant* 'nevertheless', *certes* 'certainly' or *ja* 'never' rarely trigger INV when occurring clause-initially (see Vance 1997: 41f). Sentence (5) above provides another example in which INV does not take place, even though the clause is introduced by a direct object. This shows that INV is not a categorical but rather a context-dependent phenomenon in OF (see also Becker 2005, Elsig & Rinke 2007). Against this backdrop, Kaiser (2002: 133) decides to exclude subjectless clauses from his empirical study, a methodological decision I adopt here as well. The clauses were then coded according to whether the subject was inverted or not, and to the linear position of the finite verb vis-à-vis other constituents, i.e. V1 clauses, XV clauses as in (1) and (2), V ≥ 3 clauses as in (5), and clauses with canonical subject-verb order (SV).

On the basis of Rinke (2007) and Rinke & Meisel (2009), I selected four independent variables that potentially condition INV, (1) type of constituent(s) preceding the finite verb, (2) grammatical verb type, (3) nominal or pronominal nature of the subject, and (4) definiteness or indefiniteness. With regard to the first variable, INV in a V2 grammar should occur consistently with clause-initial non-subject constituents, regardless of their grammatical or pragmatic function. In a non-V2 grammar, on the other hand, INV might be restricted to certain lexical or functional contexts. With regard to the second variable, INV might occur in a non-V2 grammar preferentially with certain grammatical verb types, i.e. those whose subject is analyzed as an internal rather than an external argument. These verb types include unaccusatives, passives, reflexives and predicatives (see Marantz 1984, Perlmutter 1978 and Stowell 1978, among others)[8]. In contrast, INV in a V2 grammar should occur irrespective of verb type. The third and fourth variables, that is, the nominal or pronominal status of the subject and the definiteness of referential constituents should show a tendency to correlate quantitatively with the information-structural functions of topic and

---

Holtus (Göttingen) and Kurt Gärtner (Trier), this interdisciplinary research project was funded … by the Deutsche Forschungsgemeinschaft [between 1995 and 2001]" (Völker 2007: 208).

8.   Henceforth, the label 'unaccusatives' will be used as a cover term for these verb types.

focus (Rinke & Meisel 2009). Topics are known or inferable to the addressee of the message (Reinhart 1981: 61). Therefore, they might be realized more often as definite and/or pronominal constituents than as indefinite and/or nominal. A focused constituent, on the other hand, introduces information which the speaker or writer assumes not to be known by the addressee at the time of utterance. Indefinite constituents and nouns should be more frequent in this context. INV in a V2 grammar is expected to be much less sensitive to these information-structural functions than in a non-V2 grammar (Rinke & Meisel 2009).

The influence of these variables on INV was determined using a multiple logistic regression function implemented in GoldVarb X (Sankoff, Tagliamonte & Smith 2005). Factor weights (FW) indicate the probability that the variant in question, i.e. INV will be chosen as a result of the influence of each of the individual factors. High factor weights indicate a favoring effect and low factor weights a disfavoring effect.

3. Results

The comparison of word order patterns in the MHG and OF charters reveals a highly similar distribution: in both languages, V ≥ 3 clauses make up the bulk of the data, followed by XV clauses, SV clauses, and V1 declarative matrix clauses, in decreasing order of frequency.

However, this is not applicable to the distribution of INV vs. no INV. Specifically, the results in Figure 1 show that INV is prevalent in German V ≥ 3 clauses (74%, N = 140/190), whereas it is virtually non-existent in the French ones (1.3%, N = 3/235). In both languages, fronted subordinate clauses represent the most frequent context showing V ≥ 3.

In the German data, V ≥ 3 is by and large restricted to two contexts: conditional clauses and relative clauses, followed by a short resumptive element, either an adverb or a pronoun, as illustrated in (6a, b).

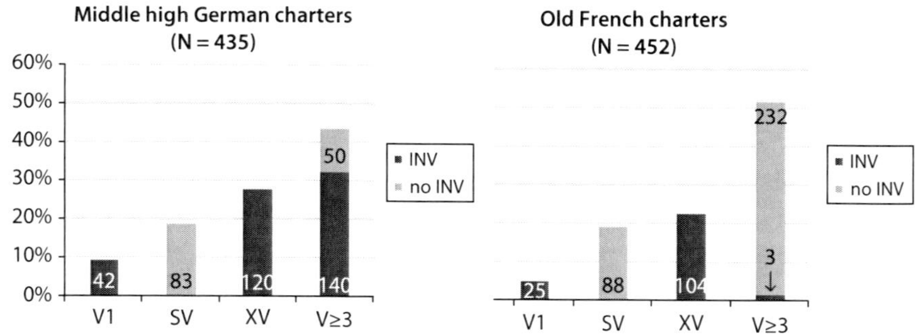

Figure 1. Distribution of word order variants in the MHG and OF charters

(6) a. Jſt   aber   dc   ſi   niht vberein
          is[PRS.3SG] however that they not   into.an.agreement
          mugent kummen, ſo ſul-nt   ſi
          might   enter   so shall-PRS.3PL they[NOM.PL]
          kieſ-en   ein obeman ...
          elect-INF a   conciliator[ACC.SG]
          'However, if they do not come to an agreement, they shall elect a con-
          ciliator ...'   (MHG, V.N64.045.10)

     b. vnde geſchih-it   in widir   dem
          and   happen-PRS.3SG in against the
          vridin   ...   dekein ſchade, den
          peace.treaty [DAT.SG] any   harm   it[ACC.SG]
          ſul-n   wir abe   tuon
          shall-PRS.3PL we [NOM.SG] remove
          'And if any harm happens to the peace treaty ..., we shall remove it.'
                                                                (MHG, V.N3.006.03)

Of a total of 190 German V ≥ 3 clauses, there are 132 cases of this type. In 47 cases, the subject precedes the verb, as in (7).

(7) welle-nt   aber   die Houeſezen   ir
     want-PRS.3PL however the residents [NOM.PL] their
     reht   an der Houeſtete vn an dem buwe
     right[ACC.SG] on the farm   and on the buildings
     duffe verkovff-en ſie   fvl-ent   ez
     upon sell-INF   they[NOM.PL] shall-PRS.3PL it[ACC.SG]
     von erſt biete-n   dem houeherren
     from first offer-INF to.the landlord[DAT.SG]
     'But if the residents want to sell their right on the farm and on the buildings
     thereupon, they shall offer it first to the landlord.'   (MHG, IV.3482.564.46)

In all these cases, the subject is a resumptive pronoun that refers back to a constituent within the preceding subordinate clause. These are instances of German Left Dislocation (see Frey 2004), in which the fronted constituent or adverbial clause can be analyzed as being external to the syntax of the matrix clause initiated by the resumptive element.

In the OF charters, constructions displaying V ≥ 3 are much more variable and are not restricted to certain contexts. In sharp contrast with the German data, INV occurs only in three out of 235 V ≥ 3 clauses. In most cases, fronted subordinate clauses do not trigger INV, irrespective of whether the subject is resumptive or not, and irrespective of whether it is pronominal or nominal, as shown in (8). This confirms the findings reported by Kaiser (2002: 154), who interprets these cases as triggers of a non-V2 grammar.

(8)   et   ſe il auen-oit   que por lo   dit
      and if it happen-IPFV.3SG that for the aforementioned
      Conte de lucenborc ...   Gagi-er   auen-iſt
      count of Luxemburg   remunerate-INF happen-SBJV.PST.3SG
      acunne meſcheance de mort ...   li   diz
      none   misfortune of death   the aforementioned
      coinſ   de lucenborc ne ſu har
      count[NOM.SG] of Luxemburg nor his heir
      n=an   porr-oient   rienſ   demand-er ...
      NEG=therefrom can-COND.PRS.3PL nothing[ACC.INDF] claim -INF
      'And if it happened that no deadly misfortune ... took place which could pre-
      vent the remuneration of the count of Luxemburg ..., neither the aforemen-
      tioned count of Luxemburg nor his heir could claim anything ...'
                                          (OFr, 167. wIV443 1278 April 28)

The French data show variation between INV and preverbal subjects after sentence-
initial objects and prepositional phrases, as shown in (9). In contrast, these contexts
categorically trigger INV in the German data.

(9)   et   pour touteſ ceſ   chozeſ deuant dit-eſ   le
      and for   all   these things before say-PTCP.F.PL the
      dit   conte   de lucembourc requíer-t ...
      aforementioned count[NOM.SG] of Luxemburg requires-PRS.3SG ...
      'And for all the aforementioned things, the aforesaid count of L. requires ... .'
                                          (OFr, 90. – wIV066 – 1268 March 3)

The comparison between German and French V ≥ 3 clauses shows that preverbal subjects after another sentence-initial constituent are more restricted in MHG than OF.
This is to be expected under the assumption that the V2 property has become firmly
entrenched in the grammar of MHG. OF, on the other hand, does not seem to show
the same kinds of restrictions.

Another difference between the languages concerns the position of the inverted
subject DP with regard to participles and infinitives. In the German data, the postverbal subject always precedes non-finite verbs (simple INV). However, the French data
shows variation in this respect. Free INV occurs in 39% of all matrix clauses with an
inverted subject DP (N = 24/61). Simple INV occurs in 23% of the cases (N = 14/61).
23 tokens (38%) are structurally ambiguous since they lack a non-finite verb. Free INV
is not characteristic of a V2 syntax. In fact, it is a typical feature of modern Romance
null subject languages. On the other hand, simple INV, as a typical property of V2
languages, has often been taken as a diagnostic in favor of the V2 character of OF. As
mentioned earlier, this is not uncontroversial (see Rinke & Meisel 2009: 106). Even if
one were to interpret its occurrence as supporting a V2 analysis of this language, its

rate of occurrence is rather low. Three quarters of all postverbal subject DPs in the data are compatible with a non-V2 grammar.

In the following section I will compare the OF and the MHG data with regard to the factors influencing pre- or postverbal placement of the subject in declarative matrix clauses.

3.1   Subject-verb inversion in MHG

The results summarized in Figure 1 show that INV in MHG occurs in the contexts of V1, XV and V $\geq$ 3 declarative matrix clauses. As mentioned earlier, I focus on four variables to determine their potential influence on the inversion or non-inversion of the subject: (1) type of sentence-initial constituent (in the context of XV and V $\geq$ 3 clauses), (2) grammatical verb type, (3) the subject's pronominal or nominal status, and (4) its definite or indefinite status. With regard to the first variable, INV is categorical after an initial object (N = 45) or prepositional phrase (N = 26). INV is almost categorical when the sentence starts with an adverb (N = 54/56). Table 1 below lists the factor groups and factors conditioning categorical and variable choice of INV in MHG.

The important range of the first factor group, together with the categoricity or near categoricity of INV with initial objects, PPs and adverbs, confirms that this factor group has the strongest influence on INV when compared to the other independent variables under consideration. Relative clauses disfavor INV because the subject often occurs as a resumptive pronoun in preverbal position (N = 17).

All other factor groups play a relatively minor though significant role as regards INV. If the finite verb is an auxiliary or modal, INV is favored. Furthermore, an indefinite or nominal subject is more likely to occur in postverbal position than a definite or pronominal subject.

3.2   Subject-verb inversion in OF

The results summarized in Figure 1 show an important difference between INV in the MHG and the OF charters. In the former, a sentence-initial non-subject constituent regularly triggers the inversion of the subject. Instances of V $\geq$ 3 (initial adverbial or relative clauses) occur in highly restricted contexts: only a resumptive element can occupy the position between the fronted subordinate clause and the finite matrix verb, a pattern indicative of German Left Dislocation. In the OF charters, however, INV is not necessarily triggered by the presence of a sentence-initial non-subject constituent. V $\geq$ 3 is productive and it is not restricted to the contexts observed in the German data (only three out of 235 V $\geq$ 3 clauses exhibit a postverbal subject). In contrast to the German data, in OF there is no single context in which INV is obligatory. The placement of the subject with regard to the finite verb is variable, even after initial objects, adverbs, and PPs.

Table 1. Variable rule analysis of INV in non-null subject declarative matrix clauses (MHG charters)

Middle High German	FW	%	N	Total N
Input value (INV)	.69	69.4%	302	435
Initial constituent				
Object	–	100%	45	45
PP	–	100%	26	26
Adverb	.84	96.4%	54	56
Adverbial clause	.45	80.3%	122	152
Relative clause	.12	43.3%	13	30
Range	72			
Verb type				
Auxiliary	.62	78.7%	48	61
Modal	.56	74.6%	170	228
Unaccusative	.36	61.6%	45	73
Transitive	.36	53.4%	39	73
Range	27			
Subject: (pro)nominal				
Nominal	.60	76.6%	108	141
Pronominal	.45	66.0%	194	294
Range	15			
Subject definiteness				
Indefinite	.75	87.7%	71	81
Definite	.44	65.3%	231	354
Range	32			

Table 2 summarizes the results of the variable rule analysis of non-null subject declarative matrix clauses in the OF charters.

The results show that sentence-initial objects and adverbs are very likely to trigger INV (see example in (10)), similarly to German. However, initial PPs allow for much more variation, although they still favor INV (compare (11) with (9)). The low factor weight of initial adverbial clauses indicates that preposed subordinate clauses disfavor INV in the postposed matrix clause. It confirms the observation that, by the mid–13th century, canonical subject-verb order has by and large replaced INV in these contexts (Ingham 2006: 36, see also Skårup 1975).

Table 2. Variable rule analysis of INV in non-null subject declarative matrix clauses (OF charters), verb type has been removed from the analysis

Old French	FW	%	N	Total N
Input value (INV)	.29	29.2%	132	452
Initial constituent				
Object	.98	89.6%	43	48
Adverb	.97	88.9%	16	18
PP	.78	46.5%	33	71
Adverbial clause	.13	3.5%	6	171
Relative clause	–	0%	0	3
Range	85			
Verb type				
Auxiliary		48.3%	43	89
Unergative		33.3%	1	3
Transitive		29.4%	37	126
Modal		27.9%	43	154
Unaccusative		10.0%	8	80
Range				
Subject: (pro)nominal				
Nominal	.59	32.6%	61	187
Pronominal	.44	26.8%	71	265
Range	15			
Definiteness				
Definite	[.51]	29.7%	129	434
Indefinite	[.20]	16.7%	3	18
Range				

(10)   Encore au-ons   no(us) rec-év   ...   Mil
       also   have-PRS.3PL we   [NOM.PL] receive-PTCP thousand
       li(vres)   de par(isis) ...
       pounds[ACC.PL] of Paris
       'We also have received a thousand Parisian pounds ...'
                                    (OFr, 67. – wIII474 – 1264 May 21)

(11)   Aus   autres demandes apres   di-t   le
       to.the other requests   thereafter say-PRS.3SG the
       co(n)te   de lucebourc ...
       count [NOM.SG] of Luxembourg
       'The Count of Luxembourg responds to the other following requests ...'
                                    (OFr, 91. – wIV070 – 1268 March-June)

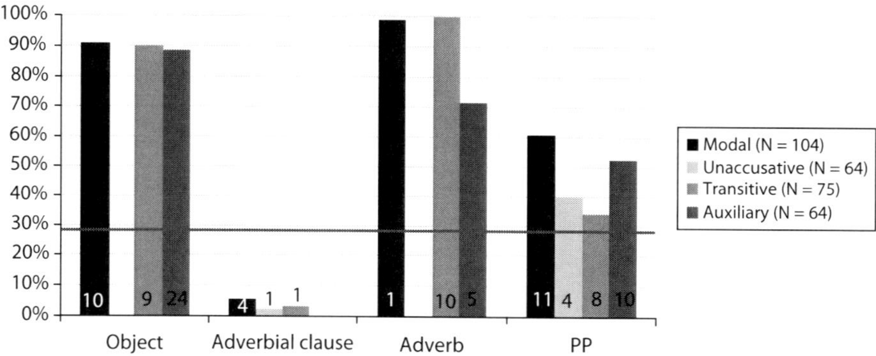

Figure 2. Rates of INV triggered by modal, unaccusative, transitive, and auxiliary verbs in the contexts of clause-initial objects, adverbial clauses, adverbs and PPs (cross-tabulation, Old French). Horizontal line: overall percentage of INV

In contrast with German, no consistent or independent effect of auxiliary and modal verbs could be observed in the French data, as shown in Figure 2.

The cross-tabulation in Figure 2 shows that it is not the verb type but rather the clause-initial constituent that conditions pre- or postverbal placement of the subject. Initial objects and adverbs favor INV, whereas preposed adverbial clauses disfavor INV, regardless of verb type. It is only with initial PPs that particular verb types show individual effects on INV, particularly in the case of modals and auxiliaries. In sum, no single verb type favors or disfavors INV consistently and independently of initial constituent type.

The nominal or pronominal character of the subject is the second (and the only remaining) significant factor group for INV. The results show that the French and German data pattern together in this respect: nominal subjects favor INV compared to pronominal subjects. The effect of subject definiteness is not significant, but this could be related to the scarcity of contexts where indefinite subjects are used in the French charters (4%, N = 18/452).

In summary, the most important difference between the German and the French charters with regard to INV becomes apparent when an adverbial subordinate clause precedes its associated matrix clause. Such fronting has a crucial effect on the preverbal field in German, but not in French. In German, short resumptive elements only appear in preverbal position. In contrast, French does not show any such restriction, and canonical subject-verb order is the predominant word order. Therefore, initial adverbial clauses strongly disfavor INV in the variable rule analysis, contrary to German. Sentence-initial PPs show variation between INV and no INV in French. In German, however, they categorically induce INV. As to verb type, whereas no consistent effect could be observed in the French data, German modal and auxiliary verbs clearly favor INV. Finally, both languages also show a number of commonalities. When the sentence starts with an object or an adverb, INV is favored in French as well as German. In the case of objects, INV is actually compulsory in German. Also, a nominal subject is significantly more likely to be inverted than a pronominal one. The favoring influence of indefiniteness could only be confirmed in the German data, as the French data does not contain that many contexts with indefinite subjects.

4. Discussion

This study reveals important differences between the MHG and the OF charters. Crucially, it shows that initial objects, PPs and adverbs induce INV almost categorically in German, which is consistent with a V2 grammar. In contrast, these contexts induce INV in French to a varying degree. This is expected if INV is pragmatically conditioned in OF, as opposed to structurally conditioned as in German.

Even though this study does not investigate the information-structural function of the subject, its results tie in with the approach outlined in Rinke & Meisel (2009) for OF. According to these authors, the preverbal domain is reserved for the topic (see also Marchello-Nizia 1999). If an adverb or a referential constituent occurs in this domain, it is very likely to instantiate the topic of the sentence. Assuming that sentences can have only one topic, the inverted subject is necessarily part of the comment. Following Rinke & Meisel (2009), the prediction would be that preverbal subjects in $V \geq 3$ clauses provide background information, while an inverted subject in OF either falls within the domain of the information focus or is part of the presupposed part of the comment. INV in German XV clauses, on the other hand, is a structural phenomenon. It derives from the realization of a non-subject constituent in preverbal position, irrespective of its information-structural status. That said, the finding that nominal and indefinite subjects favor INV in both languages shows that that the tendency to place the topic at the initial position and the focus towards the final position of the sentence applies cross-linguistically.

The study shows that the German data appear to deviate from a strict V2 constraint, most particularly in the context of fronted conditional or adverbial clauses. It should be noted, however, that the second position in these $V \geq 3$ constructions (i.e. the first position of the associated matrix clause) is occupied by short, resumptive elements such as pronouns and light adverbs in these contexts. No such restriction was observed in OF: here, the subject almost categorically occurs between the fronted subordinate clause and the finite verb. It is discourse-neutral, i.e. it either has topical properties or it is part of the presupposed background of the sentence. The question of whether the fronted subordinate clause occupies a high position in the left periphery of the matrix clause or whether it is external to the syntax of the matrix clause is not relevant for the purposes of this study. Suffice it to say that French word order patterns in this context can be explained by assuming that the subject occupies its regular position, Spec,TP, and that the finite verb is in T°, along the lines of Kaiser (2002) and

Rinke & Meisel (2009). In contrast, the resumptive element in second position in German V ≥ 3 clauses with an initial subordinate clause is never discourse-neutral. It is always a topic. If V-to-C movement is a constitutive property of the V2 constraint, this would appear to indicate movement of the verb and of the resumptive element into a designated topic projection within the left periphery.

As this study is a synchronic snapshot of thirteenth century language use, a potential contact-induced effect of Germanic on subject-verb inversion in OF, perhaps at an earlier time, cannot be excluded. The results show, however, that by the mid-thirteenth century, the speakers of OF and of MHG draw on different grammars for subject inversion.

References

Adams, M. 1987. From Old French to the theory of pro-drop. *Natural Language and Linguistic Theory* 5: 1–32.

Alexiadou, A. & E. Anagnostopoulou. 1995. SVO and EPP in null subject languages and Germanic. *FAS Papers in Linguistics* 4: 1–21.

Alexiadou, A. & E. Anagnostopoulou. 1998. Parametrizing AGR: Word order, V movement and EPP-checking. *Natural Language and Linguistic Theory* 16: 491–539.

Alexiadou, A. & E. Anagnostopoulou. 2001. The subject-in-situ generalization and the role of case in driving computations. *Linguistic Inquiry* 32: 193–231.

Alexiadou, A. & E. Anagnostopoulou. 2007. The subject-in-situ generalization revisited. In *Interfaces + Recursion = Language? Chomsky's Minimalism and the View from Syntax-semantics*, eds. H.-M. Gärtner & U. Sauerland, 107–148. Berlin: Mouton de Gruyter.

Axel, K. 2007. *Studies on Old High German Syntax* (Linguistik Aktuell/Linguistics Today 112). Amsterdam: John Benjamins.

Barbosa, P. 2001. On inversion in *wh*-questions in Romance. In *Subject Inversion in Romance and the Theory of Universal Grammar*, eds. A. C. J. Hulk & J.-Y. Pollock, 20–59. Oxford: OUP.

Barbosa, P. 2009. Two kinds of subject *pro*. *Studia Linguistica* 63: 2–58.

Becker, M. G. 2005. Le *Corpus d'Amsterdam* face à une vieille question: l'Ancien français est-il une langue V2? In *Romanistische Korpuslinguistik II: Korpora und diachrone Sprachwissenschaft*, eds. C. D. Pusch, J. Kabatek & W. Raible, 345–358. Tübingen: Narr.

Belletti, A. 2004. Aspects of the low IP area. In *The Structure of CP and IP*, ed. L. Rizzi, 16–51. Oxford: OUP.

Belletti, A. 2005. Extended doubling and the VP periphery. *Probus* 17: 1–35.

Benincà, P. 2006. A detailed map of the left periphery of medieval Romance. In *Crosslinguistic Research in Syntax and Semantics: Negation, Tense, and Clausal Architecture*, eds. R. Zanuttini, H. Campos, E. Herburger & P. Portner, 53–86. Washington DC: Georgetown University Press.

Côté, M.-H. 1995. Concurrence structurale, conditions d'appréhensibilité et changement syntaxique: La chute de la structure V2 en français. *Revue Canadienne de Linguistique* 40: 165–200.

Dahl, Ö. 1974. Topic-Comment structure revisited. In *Topic and Comment, Contextual Boundness and Focus*, ed. Ö. Dahl, 1–24. Hamburg: Buske.

Den Besten, H. 1983. On the interaction of root transformations and lexical deletive rules. In *On the Formal Syntax of the Westgermania. Papers from the 3rd Groningen Grammar Talks, Groningen, January 1981* (Linguistik Aktuell/Linguistics Today 3), ed. W. Abraham, 47–131. Amsterdam: John Benjamins.

Diesing, M. 1992. *Indefinites*. Cambridge MA: The MIT Press.

Elsig, M. & E. Rinke. 2007. Les adverbes et l'inversion en ancien français: Le Nouveau Corpus d'Amsterdam soumis à l'analyse linguistique. In *Le Nouveau Corpus d'Amsterdam: Actes de l'atelier de Lauterbad, 23–26 février 2006*, eds. P. Kunstmann & A. Stein. 159–180. Stuttgart: Steiner.

Fischer, S. 2010. *Word-Order Change as a Source of Grammaticalisation* (Linguistik Aktuell/ Linguistics Today 157). Amsterdam: John Benjamins.

Foulet, L. 1928. *Petite syntaxe de l'ancien francais*, 3ᵉ édn. Paris: Honoré Champion.

Frey, W. 2004. The grammar-pragmatics interface and the German prefield. *Sprache und Pragmatik* 52: 1–39.

Hegarty, M. 2005. *A Feature-based Syntax of Functional Categories: The Structure, Acquisition, and Specific Impairment of Functional Systems*. Berlin: Mouton de Gruyter.

Holtus, G., A. Overbeck & H. Völker. 2003. *Luxemburgische Skriptastudien: Edition und Untersuchung der altfranzösischen Urkunden Gräfin Ermesindes (1226–1247) und Graf Heinrichs V. (1247–1281) von Luxemburg*. Tübingen: Niemeyer.

Iatridou, S. & A. Koch. 1992. The licensing of CP recursion and its relevance to the Germanic verb-second phenomenon. *Working Papers in Scandinavian Syntax* 50: 1–24.

Ingham, R. 2006. Syntactic change in Anglo-Norman and continental French chronicles: Was there a 'middle' Anglo-Norman? *French Language Studies* 16: 25–49.

Kaiser, G. A. 2002. *Verbstellung und Verbstellungswandel in den romanischen Sprachen*. Tübingen: Niemeyer.

Labelle, M. 2007. Clausal architecture in early Old French. *Lingua* 117: 289–316.

Lemieux, M. & F. Dupuis. 1995. The locus of verb movement in non-asymmetric verb-second languages: The case of middle French. In *Clause Structure and Language Change*, eds. A. Battye & I. Roberts, 80–109. Oxford: OUP.

Marantz, A. P. 1984. *On the Nature of Grammatical Relations*. Cambridge MA: The MIT Press.

Marchello-Nizia, C. 1999. *Le français en diachronie: Douze siècles d'évolution*. Gap: Ophrys.

Mathieu, E. 2009. On the Germanic properties of Old French. In *Historical Syntax and Linguistic Theory*, eds. P. Crisma & G. Longobardi, 344–357. Oxford: OUP.

Meinunger, A. 2006. Interface restrictions on verb second. *The Linguistic Review* 23: 127–160.

Müller, S. 2005. Zur Analyse der scheinbar mehrfachen Vorfeldbesetzung. *Linguistische Berichte* 203: 297–330.

Mutz, K. 2009. Über das Französische und seine Wechselwirkungen mit dem Deutschen. In *Unsere sprachlichen Nachbarn in Europa*, ed. C. Stolz, 47–67. Bochum: Brockmeyer.

Perlmutter, D. M. 1978. Impersonal passives and the unaccusative hypothesis. In *Proceedings of the Fourth Annual Meeting of the Berkeley Linguistics Society*, eds. J. J. Jaeger, A. C. Woodbury, F. Ackerman, C. Chiarello, O. D. Gensler, J. Kingston, E. E. Sweetser, H. Thompson & K. W. Whitler, 157–189. Berkeley CA: Berkeley Linguistics Society.

Platzack, C. 1995. The loss of verb second in English and French. In *Clause Structure and Language Change*, eds. A. Battye & I. Roberts, 200–226. Oxford: OUP.

Poletto, C. 2002. The left-periphery of V2-Rhaetoromance dialects: A new perspective on V2 and V3. In *Syntactic Microvariation*, eds. S. Barbiers, L. Cornips & S. van der Kleij, 214–242.

Amsterdam: Meertens Institute. <http://www.meertens.knaw.nl/books/synmic> (23 February 2012).

Posner, R. 1996. *The Romance Languages*. Cambridge: CUP.

Reinhart, T. 1981. Pragmatics and linguistics: An analysis of sentence topics. *Philosophica* 27: 53–94.

Rinke, E. 2007. *Syntaktische Variation aus synchronischer und diachronischer Perspektive: Die Entwicklung der Wortstellung im Portugiesischen*. Frankfurt: Vervuert.

Rinke, E. & J. M. Meisel. 2009. Subject-inversion in Old French: Syntax and information structure. In *Proceedings of the Workshop "Null-subjects, Expletives, and Locatives in Romance"* (Arbeitspapiere des Fachbereichs Sprachwissenschaft 123), eds. G. A. Kaiser & E.-M. Remberger, 93–130. Konstanz: Universität Konstanz.

Rizzi, L. 1997. The fine structure of the left periphery. In *Elements of Grammar: A Handbook in Generative Grammar*, ed. L. Haegeman, 281–337. Dordrecht: Kluwer.

Rizzi, L. 2006. On the form of chains: Criteria positions and ECP effects. In *Wh-Movement: Moving on*, eds. L. L.-S. Cheng & N. Corver, 97–133. Cambridge MA: The MIT Press.

Roberts, I. 1993. *Verbs and Diachronic Syntax: A Comparative History of English and French*. Dordrecht: Kluwer.

Sankoff, D., S. Tagliamonte & E. Smith. 2005. *Goldvarb X: A Variable Rule Application for Macintosh and Windows* (Computer program). Toronto: Department of Linguistics, University of Toronto.

Sheehan, M. 2009. 'Free' inversion in Romance and the null subject parameter. In *Parametric Variation: Null Subjects in Minimalist Theory*, eds. T. Biberauer, A. Holmberg, I. Roberts & M. Sheehan, 231–262. Cambridge: CUP.

Skårup, P. 1975. *Les premières zones de la proposition en ancien français: Essai de syntaxe de position*. København: Akademisk Forlag.

Stowell, T. 1978. What was there before there was there. In *Proceedings of Chicago Linguistic Society 14*, eds. D. Farkas, W. M. Jacobsen & K. W. Todrys, 458–471. Chicago IL: Chicago Linguistic Society.

Thomason, S. G. & T. Kaufman. 1988. *Language Contact, Creolization, and Genetic Linguistics*. Berkeley CA: University of California Press.

Vance, B. 1997. *Syntactic Change in Medieval French: Verb-Second and Null-Subjects*. Dordrecht: Kluwer.

Vikner, S. 1995. *Verb Movement and Expletive Subjects in the Germanic Languages*. Oxford: OUP.

Völker, H. 2007. A 'practice of the variant' and the origins of the standard. Presentation of a variationist linguistics method for a corpus of Old French charters. *Journal of French Language Studies* 17: 207–223.

Von Wartburg, W. 1958. *Évolution et structure de la langue française*, 5e édn. Bern: Francke.

Wampach, H.-C. 1935–1955. *Urkunden- und Quellenbuch zur Geschichte der altluxemburgischen Territorien bis zur burgundischen Zeit* (10 Bände). Luxemburg: St. Paulus.

Wilhelm, F., R. Newald, H. de Boor, D. Haacke & B. Kirschstein, eds. 1932–1986. *Corpus der altdeutschen Originalurkunden bis zum Jahr 1300* (5 Bände). Lahr: Schauenburg.

Zwart, J.-W. 2005. Verb second as a function of Merge. In *The Function of Function Words and Functional Categories* (Linguistik Aktuell/Linguistis Today 78), eds. M. den Dikken & C. M. Tortora), 11–40. Amsterdam: John Benjamins.

Multilingual constructions

A diasystematic approach to common structures[*]

Steffen Höder
University of Münster, Germany

Language contact phenomena are often described with reference to their effect on the monolingual systems of the varieties involved, both in historical and in contact linguistics. This contribution argues that an essentially multilingual perspective on these phenomena is more adequate. Bilingual speakers in stable bilingual groups create a common system for all their languages, incorporating both interlingual links and language-unspecified elements along with language-specific structures. In a construction grammar analysis, such systems as well as changes within this type of system can be conceptualized as interlingual constructional networks, which are established, stored, and processed in exactly the same way as monolingual grammars.

Keywords: German, Danish, Old Swedish, Latin, multilingualism, diasystem, construction grammar

1.   Introduction

This contribution addresses a central theoretical problem in contact linguistics: is it reasonable to assume that the languages or varieties used by a multilingual speaker group remain distinct systems even in cases of intense and stable language contact, or is it more appropriate to assume one common system? While it is a standard assumption in sociolinguistic studies that in dialect contact situations the varieties involved represent one (variable) system, the case is less straightforward when it comes to different languages.

---

*   I wish to thank all the people who have been willing to discuss some of the topics of this paper with me, in particular Karoline Kühl, Kurt Braunmüller, Adele Goldberg, and Gabriele Diewald. Furthermore, my thanks are due to two anonymous reviewers for their insightful and helpful comments.

In the following sections, I will argue that links between language-specific elements constitute a system of overarching structures, based on the identification of elements that are perceived as equivalent by multilingual speakers. The common core of the system is used in multilingual language processing, but also facilitates innovations that lead to an increasing congruence of the respective languages. Furthermore, I sketch out how such a system can be modeled within a construction grammar (CxG) approach (Diasystematic Construction Grammar, DCxG). This is first illustrated by pairs of closely related languages and then by the case of Old Swedish and Medieval Latin, two distantly related but typologically relatively similar languages that were in contact in late medieval Sweden.

2.   Theoretical focus: Diasystems and multilingual constructions

2.1   Arguments for a multilingual analysis

In contact linguistic studies the focus is often placed on the result of language contact from the perspective of one of the languages involved, rather than on the mechanisms of contact itself. While studies on (present-day) multilingualism concentrate on speakers' communicative behavior (including both their individual linguistic repertoires and multilingual communicative strategies such as code-switching or borrowing and 'mistakes', i.e. interferences) and language processing, contact as a factor in language change is primarily invoked in retrospective explanations. The story usually told is that elements and structures are transferred from one language to another, get established (possibly accompanied by additional intralingual innovations triggered by the initial transfer), and are increasingly integrated into the structural, functional, semantic, and phonological systems of the recipient language.[1]

Such descriptions are, of course, correct in the sense that they account for the changes within the individual language systems. However, they are premised on a monolingual perspective on what are, essentially, multilingual situations. Multilingual phenomena are analyzed as the result of an interaction or, indeed, a conflict between distinct language systems that are conceived of as rather static, coherent, and monolithic, much in the tradition of the structuralist view of languages as *systèmes où tout se tient*. Implicitly, such a view seems to assume that multilinguals are purists to the extent that they (consciously or unconsciously) keep their different languages apart in both their cognition and their communication with others. This is, however, an unmotivated assumption. Multilingualism is far more prevalent than monolingualism, measured

---

1.   The terms and concepts used to describe and classify such phenomena are, of course, manifold. What I label transfer here, in a broad sense, includes what is called, for example, 'borrowing' by Thomason & Kaufman (1988) as well as Matras (2009), 'code-copying' by Johanson (2008), 'grammatical replication' by Heine & Kuteva (2005), or even 'convergence' in Myers-Scotton's (2002) model.

on a global and historical scale (Lüdi 1996: 234ff), and a multilingual communicative mode (Grosjean 2001) is the rule rather than the exception in multilingual speaker groups, i.e. a communicative mode in which more than one language is constantly used or activated in some way in the discourse (manifesting itself in *ad hoc* borrowings, frequent code-switches and the like, or multilingual communicative strategies such as accommodation, semi-communication, and similar phenomena). *Mono*lingual modes in multilingual groups, in contrast, are rather an effect of socio- or extralinguistic factors that prevent some or all kinds of multilingual phenomena.[2]

Psycholinguistic studies also emphasize that the linguistic knowledge of multilingual speakers (especially in multilingual groups) is not simply the sum of their individual monolingual competences, and that multilinguals are not 'multiple monolinguals'. Multilinguals process their languages in a way different from monolingual speakers, which suggests cognitive interaction between the languages at various levels (see, e.g., Grosjean 1989, 2008: 9ff).

If we assume that multilingualism is not only widespread but, in a way, a fundamental characteristic of the human language faculty,[3] then there is a need for a theoretical approach to multilingual language use which integrates this perspective into the grammatical description of multilingual speakers' linguistic knowledge, or at least a coherent description of the interrelations between the languages involved. This implies a multilingual system that captures both language-specific and multilingual structures as interdependent parts of *one* grammatical and lexical system.[4]

While theoretically motivated, such an approach is also relevant in, for instance, the investigation of code-switching or transfer phenomena in language contact situations. Standard code-switching models such as Myers-Scotton's (2002) Matrix Language Frame Model take considerable pains to ultimately determine the language of a particular sequence, morpheme, construction, or category within a given multilingual utterance, especially in order to figure out which of the languages at hand is dominant

---

2.   Obvious examples are lexical purism, which can have official status (as in Standard Icelandic, but less so in colloquial varieties), or particular constructions that are stigmatized in a specific variety (e.g. [*weil* 'because' + V2 CLAUSE] in written German, while being perfectly normal in the spoken language). In addition, a monolingual mode may be demanded in certain contexts, as in the schools of the Danish minority in Germany where pupils are required to use *either* Standard Danish *or* Standard German instead of the local, German-influenced variety of Danish or the multilingual mode common in everyday conversation (Kühl 2008: 261).

3.   It can be argued that the synchronic and diachronic variability of language, as well as the capability of all humans to cope with intralingual variation, indeed implies that multilingualism has the status of an 'essential universal', related to Coseriu's (1974) notion of 'historicity' (see Oesterreicher 2001).

4.   This is even more obvious if we accept that there is no straightforward distinction between multi*lingualism* and multi*lectalism*, i.e. the knowledge and use of different varieties (of one language) – mono*lectalism* does not exist, as not even a monolingual speaker's competence is restricted to only one variety of his/her language.

(the 'matrix language'). This approach relies, of course, on the possibility to distinguish different languages within an utterance (and, optimally, to divide the utterance into monolingual linear segments). However, the more similar two languages are, the less feasible such an assignment becomes. Examples demonstrating this difficulty abound in the contact linguistic literature; the following three cases of bilingual (Colloquial North) High German-Low German utterances may illustrate the point:

(1)   An *dat* Licht kann *de* Hausmeister nix   *ännern.*
      at   the light can   the caretaker   nothing change
      'The caretaker can't do anything about the light.'

(2)   Keinen Muckefuck,   richtigen Kaffe, *dat smeckt goot.*
      no   coffee substitute real   coffee that tastes   good
      'No coffee substitute, [but] real coffee, that tastes good.'

(3)   In Kiel mag Anna nich wohnen.
      in Kiel likes Anna not   live
      'Anna wouldn't like to live in Kiel.'

In these examples, the sequences in italics are unambiguously Low German, and the underlined words are unequivocally High German, whereas the remaining part of the utterances – in fact, the majority of words – is totally ambiguous (in (3), this is true for the whole utterance).

Yet, even this analysis still greatly exaggerates the proportion of unambiguously monolingual elements, since it is only based on the lexical surface, i.e. the language of the (lexical and grammatical) morphs. Most of the abstract semantic, morphological, syntactic, and in part even phonological structures that are also present in these utterances are in fact undistinguishable between the two languages. Research on the communicative behavior of multilinguals as well as studies in areal linguistics suggests that – provided two languages are used by the same speaker group in similar communicative contexts or domains – the most prominent idiosyncrasies of the two languages will be on the level of the lexical (or, indeed, phonological) surface.[5] Conversely, the number of actually deviating (not purely lexical) structures tends to be rather low.

It would, therefore, be more to the point not to focus on whether an element in a multilingual utterance belongs (or can be analyzed as belonging) to language A or B, but rather on whether it represents some *common* structure shared by A and B or an *idiosyncratic* feature of one of the languages. Such a perspective may be less compelling in contact situations in which the languages are less similar. But even contact languages without a (close) genetic relationship often share a lot rather abstract structural

---

5.   See Muysken's (2000: 122ff) discussion of 'congruent lexicalization', Aikhenvald's (2007: 28ff) observations on 'morpheme-per-morpheme intertranslatability' or Heine & Kuteva's (2005: 179f) remarks on 'exact structural equivalence'.

patterns, and these similarities or overlaps are not only constructible in theory, but indeed form part of a multilingual's knowledge (see Section 2.2).

2.2   Interlingual identification: Diasystematic links

The idea that shared structures are in some way accessible to and in fact utilised by multilingual speakers within their linguistic knowledge and language processing goes back to Weinreich's (1954: 390) useful notion of 'diasystem':

> A 'diasystem' can be constructed by the linguistic analyst out of any two systems which have partial similarities ... But this does not mean that it is always a scientist's construction only: a 'diasystem' is experienced in a very real way by bilingual (including 'bidialectal') speakers ...

This notion was, as is well known, developed as an attempt to introduce a structuralist approach into dialectology, and has mostly been applied to dialectal phonology (Weinreich's own examples were from Yiddish dialects): two dialects are said to be part of the same (phonological) diasystem if certain elements (e.g. phonemes) in dialect A regularly correspond to a set of elements in dialect B. However, the concept can easily be extended to also cover (a) other parts of the language system and (b) different languages in addition to different dialects.[6]

The basic process in establishing a 'real' diasystem, i.e. one that is embedded in speakers' cognition and language use, is *interlingual identification* (Weinreich 1964: 7f). Interlingual identification is based on similarity relations between different elements in different varieties, which are perceived as equivalents by multilingual speakers according to (often competing) structural, phonic, semantic, functional, pragmatic, or other criteria (see Section 3 for examples). Two elements or structures in two different varieties are thus not equivalent to each other by themselves, intrinsically or self-evidently. Rather, interlingual equivalence is to some degree arbitrary and always reflects a creative act of a multilingual community, even though it is partially motivated by one of several competing similarity relations. The result of a successful interlingual identification is an established diasystematic link between two different elements, i.e. a socially conventionalized mapping.[7]

---

6.   Weinreich's original proposal presupposed the existence of language-specific 'systems' in a strictly structuralist sense. For the purpose of the following discussion, this is, of course, not a necessary prerequisite.

7.   Evidence for social conventionalization comes, as an example, from phonological substitution rules in loanword integration. For example, French [ɑ̃ ɛ̃ ɔ̃ œ̃)] are regularly rendered as [aŋ ɛŋ ɔŋ œŋ] in (Colloquial North) High German (e.g. French *engagement* [ɑ̃gaʒmɑ̃] > NoHG *Engagement* [aŋgaʒə'maŋ] 'commitment'), based on phonetic similarity. In contrast, Standard German (StG) /eː/ is usually taken to correspond to Low German (LG) /ɛi̯/ rather than the phonetically more similar /e/ (as can be seen in mutual loanwords: StG *System* [zys'teːm] > LG

If we take a diasystematic link between two language-specific elements as constituting a more abstract item within an overarching system shared by the two languages, then we can assume the existence of 'dia-elements': a 'diaphoneme' would be the abstract unit of which two language-specific phonemes are variants (such as StG /aɪ̯/, Austrian Standard German /ɛɪ̯/), a 'diamorph' represents phonologically corresponding morphs conveying the same semantic information (e.g. StG *Haus* [haʊ̯s] 'house', LG *Huus* [hus]; cf. the terminology introduced by Haugen 1956: 46f), lexical 'diaconcepts' typify mutually translatable lexemes (Dan *by*, Swe *stad* 'town'), 'diasyntactic' items link different language-specific constructions that are functionally identical and structurally parallel to some extent (such as verb-initial polar questions in e.g. StG *bist du wach?* and Dan *er du vågen?* 'are you awake?'), and so forth.

Diasystematic links and dia-elements constitute a network through which two language systems used within a multilingual speaker group are interconnected. The degree to which two varieties in contact participate in the common diasystem depends, of course, on their typological similarity: closely related and typologically similar languages can more easily develop a high degree of diasystematicity – i.e. the common intersection of their systems is larger – than more distant languages, which retain a larger proportion of idiosyncrasies in their systems (Höder 2011, forthcoming).

2.3   A construction grammar perspective: Diasystematic Construction Grammar

Among contemporary grammatical frameworks, approaches from the construction grammar (CxG) 'family', such as Croft's (2001) typologically inspired Radical Construction Grammar or Goldberg's (1995, 2006) Cognitive Construction Grammar, can most convincingly adapt to the idea of a diasystematic component in the grammar, connecting more than one monolingual system. To my knowledge, only little work has been done up to now on language contact within a CxG approach (but see, as an example, Pietsch's 2010 work on contact-induced change in Irish English). However, the idea that constructions are the locus of contact-induced language change seems acceptable to many (see Heine & Kuteva 2005: 44), a view that is reinforced by the recent growing interest in CxG approaches to diachronic change in general (see, for instance, the contributions in Bergs & Diewald 2008).

Despite the existing theoretical variation among CxG approaches, they all agree on the following ideas:

Systeem [zɪsˈtɛɪ̯m] 'system'; LG *Reep* [rɛɪ̯p] > StG *Reep* [reːp] 'rope'); this mapping is based on the distribution of the respective vowels in cognates. Another hint at the existence of conventionalized correspondences is that they change over time: English /ʌ/ used to be treated as an equivalent of Standard German /ø/, while today it corresponds to /a/; this change is reflected in different renderings in earlier and more recent loanwords, e.g. English *pumps* [pʌmps] (shoes) > StG *Pumps* [pømps], but *punk* 'Punk' (music genre) [pʌŋk] > StG *Punk* [paŋk].

a. the whole grammar is organized as an inventory of constructions, i.e. form–meaning pairs, in a continuum involving everything from lexically filled constructions (such as words) via partially filled constructions (for example in inflectional paradigms) to maximally schematic ones (such as syntactic or prosodic patterns);
b. more schematic and more concrete constructions are connected through inheritance links, forming a network of interdependent elements;
c. speakers learn schematic constructions by categorizing them on the basis of the available input, resulting in an economic representation of their linguistic knowledge;
d. not all constructions are rule-based and productive, many are irregular in that they are not predictable from more abstract structures.

In other words, speakers organize their linguistic knowledge and, hence, the grammar of their varieties through abstraction and generalization processes: filled constructions that behave identically in some respect are taken to instantiate a single, more abstract construction. While this kind of usage-based grammatical organization is assumed to apply in all types of linguistic situations, and while CxG has been primarily applied to monolingual contexts, there is no *a priori* reason why such generalization and abstraction processes should be blocked by language boundaries in multilingual environments. On the contrary, it has to be expected that categorization as a cognitively economic process does include all languages (and dialects, of course) in any situation in which the available input is multilingual, too. Interlingual identification, therefore, *is* categorization in very much the prototypical CxG sense: similar constructions in two different languages are taken to instantiate a common 'diaconstruction'.

Consequently, Diasystematic Construction Grammar assumes that, within a multilingual system, some constructions are unspecified for language (such as abstract syntactic constructions and lexical concepts), while others (above all lexically and phonologically filled constructions) are language-specific. Language-specificity can be modeled as being part of the pragmatic meaning of a construction, which manifests itself in contextual restrictions of the type 'use language L_x in the pragmatic contexts $C_{x:1,2,3,\,\dots}$'. This is in line with the fact that multilingual groups tend to associate their respective varieties with different communicative functions, both in terms of large-scale polyglossia within a society and the specific criteria for language choice shared by, say, a bilingual family (as well as the criteria for the choice of a variety within *any* language community). The idea of a multilingual diasystem is thus fully compatible with a CxG perspective on the organization of grammar and grammatical knowledge.

Table 1 illustrates the relation between language-specific and unspecified constructions, involving different types and degrees of schematicity:[8]

---

8. Conventions: Meaning and form are arranged in separate lines. Lexical meanings are marked by inverted commas (e.g. 'town'), grammatical meanings by angle brackets (<polar question>). Pragmatic contexts are abbreviated by the corresponding glottonym in curly brackets ({Swe}). Square brackets ([...]) indicate the form of a construction, with schematic components

Table 1. Language-specific and unspecified constructions

	lexical diaconcept	diamorph	diasyntactic construction
contact languages	Danish, Swedish	Standard German, Low German	German, Danish
unspecified	'town' [_]	'house' [/h_s/]	<polar question> [FINITE$_1$ + ...]
language A	'town' {Dan} [*by*]	'house' {StG} [/haʊ̯s/]	–
language B	'town' {Swe} [*stad*]	'house' {LG} [/hus/]	–

Danish and Swedish, for example, share a common diaconcept ('town'), but this concept is expressed by different and non-cognate morphs (see column 1). The Standard German-Low German bilingual speakers have a common construction meaning 'house', which is partly phonologically filled (consonantal onset and coda), whereas the language-specific constructions only specify the stem vowel (which, in turn, is based on a diaphonemic construction that defines the respective vowels [aʊ̯] and [u] as language-specific variants; see column 2). Finally, German-Danish bilinguals can do without language-specific constructions for polar questions, as *one* schematic construction (specifying the verb-initial word order) is sufficient for both languages (see column 3).[9]

2.4   Towards interlingual congruence: Pro-diasystematic change

Diachronically, diasystematic links should be expected to lead to or at least facilitate increasing interlingual congruence in situations of stable and intense language contact, i.e. a higher proportion of common structures and a lesser proportion of idiosyncrasies. This is achieved through a regularization of interlingual correspondences. In DCxG terms, this 'pro-diasystematic' change implies an increase in the number of schematic constructions unspecified for language.

From the multilingual speakers' cognitive perspective, pro-diasystematic change involves a simplification of the common system, as a construction loses its language-specific contextual restriction and, thus, can become productive in the other language

---

in small capitals (e.g. SUBJ), lexically filled components in italics (*by*), phonologically filled parts between slashes (/hus/). An underscore (_) indicates an unspecified component. Numerical indexes represent the linear order of elements.

9.   In fact, all of the unspecified constructions given in Table 1 could in principle, given an appropriate multilingual context, apply to *any* of the mentioned languages (e.g. /h_s/ in Swedish *hus* [hʉːs], or the lexical concept 'town' in German *Stadt*, which of course is a cognate of the Swedish lexeme).

as well: a form in language B is predictable on the basis of (a) the form in language A and (b) its inheritance link to an unspecified diaconstruction.[10] Thus, pro-diasystematic change is not necessarily the same thing as transfer from language A to B, nor does it always coincide with constructional borrowing, as the two languages need not become more similar with respect to the concrete forms. In contrast, pro-diasystematic change can even result in interlingual *divergence* at the surface (for instance, the diaphonemic identification of StG /aɪ̯/ with LG /ɛɪ̯/ leads to the innovative form *Ee* /ɛɪ̯/ 'egg' in Low German, based on StG *Ei* /aɪ̯/, even though the traditional form in Low German is also *Ei*; see Höder 2011). It is crucial, though, that pro-diasystematicity is a factor relevant to the social selection rather than the initial emergence of innovative forms: a bilingual group will preferably accept pro-diasystematic innovations, but, of course, other innovations are not ruled out and may even be preferred if favored by system-external factors (as, for example, with emblematic idiosyncrasies used to express linguistic identity or group affiliation in bilingual contexts).

In the following section, I will discuss, from a diasystematic perspective, a language contact situation in which both contact-induced language change and diachronic stability occur.

3. Case study: Latin-Old Swedish contact

3.1 Background: Written Old Swedish

In medieval Sweden, Latin – the fossilized variety of Classical Latin used in ecclesiastical institutions – is the predominant written language, used mainly for administrative, religious, and literary purposes, while Old Swedish is used in the domains of everyday life as a non-standardized and primarily spoken language. From the 13th century onwards, however, Swedish is also used in written communication, a process starting out in a highly multilingual environment: the scribes are mainly Latin-Swedish bilingual clerics, organized in close-knit monastic communities, the texts are often translated from Latin sources, text types are adapted from Latin models, and Latin textual norms are used even when writing in Swedish, a process that opens the door for a wide range of contact-induced language change phenomena (see Wollin 1981/1983). The result is the emergence of a distinct, written variety of Late Old Swedish (ca. 1375–1526).[11]

Latin and Old Swedish represent rather distantly related branches of the Indo-European family and are, therefore, not very similar in the lexicon. Grammatically,

---

10. This type of multilingual simplification includes cases in which the monolingual systems of the individual languages get *more* complex due to the innovation (Dahl 2009; for examples, see Sections 3.2 and 3.3).

11. For a comprehensive discussion and analysis of syntactic innovations in written Old Swedish see Höder (2010).

however, their typological distance is rather low. This includes a relatively complex inflectional system in both languages, as the inherited system of Old Swedish is still quite intact around 1300, though slowly giving way to a more agglutinative system as found in Modern Swedish. However, there are discrepancies in different parts of the languages' morphology and syntax, in which a common system is impossible to construct. The following sections illustrate the diachronic development of different multilingual phenomena from a diasystematic point of view.

3.2   Category mapping in nominal inflection

Old Swedish and Latin nouns are inflected for three categories, viz. case, number, and gender. It is not surprising that bilingual speakers identify these categories interlingually, as can be inferred from code-switching phenomena in Old Swedish texts, in which Latin words and phrases are assigned a Swedish gender or syntactically integrated in (and inflected according to) Swedish constructions:

(4)   æst thu <u>helias</u>   som koma scal for   domadagh
      are you Elijah-NOM(Lat) who come shall before Doomsday
      'Are you Elijah, who will come before Doomsday?'   (SsS 95)

(5)   ey ær <u>helie</u>   <u>persona</u> min <u>persona</u>
      not is Elijah-GEN(Lat) person my person
      'Elijah's person is not my person.' (SsS 95)

(6)   scippadh*ir* ... til <u>confessorem</u>   <u>generalem</u>
      invested   to confessor-ACC.SG(Lat) general-ACC.SG.M(Lat)
      '[after he is] invested ... as general confessor'   (OCG 113)

The underlined forms illustrate bilingual case mapping: the name *helias* in (4) and (5) is marked as nominative or genitive by the corresponding Latin suffixes depending on the Swedish construction it occurs in (expressing a predicative complement or a possessor, respectively); in (6), the Latin accusative *confessorem generalem* is governed by the Swedish preposition *til*.[12] The loanword *persona* in (5), whether an *ad hoc* borrowing or already established, is assigned feminine gender (cf. the agreeing pronoun *min* 'my' [M/F]).

Interestingly, the interlingual identification of nominal inflectional categories is based on different similarity relations. Number is clearly mapped on a semantic basis, whereas gender assignment is partly based on semantic and partly on formal equivalences: the correspondence between gender and sex in nouns and proper names referring to humans (such as Lat *femina* ↔ OSw *kona*) suggests a functional equivalence even for (the majority of) nouns in which gender assignment is largely arbitrary; this equivalence is reinforced by formal similarities, especially in the feminine gender, as feminine nouns typically contain a suffix *-a* in both languages.

---

12.   In Early Old Swedish (like in Old Norse), *til* normally governed the genitive; in Late Old Swedish, however, the accusative was frequently used after this preposition.

Case is mapped on the basis of similar functions and distributions across syntactic constructions (such as the genitive in the possessive construction). As for the dative (OSw and Lat) and ablative (Lat), the mapping is more complex and in parts diffuse, the more so because dative and ablative are frequently homophonous in Latin, which makes an interlingual identification on the basis of formal similarity easily possible. As prepositional constructions in Latin never contain a dative, the ablative is used even after Old Swedish prepositions that usually take the dative case (such as *moth* 'against' in (7)), whereas the Latin dative is used in the ditransitive construction (e.g. *sancte birgitte*[13] in (8)).

(7) [han] wende   sik   <u>moth   seniore</u>
     [he]   turn-SBJV REFL against senior-ABL(Lat)
     '[he] shall turn to the senior [a church official]'   (OCG 113)

(8) Maria gwdz modher kwngør <u>sancte</u>   <u>birgitte</u>
     Mary God's mother tells   holy-DAT.F.SG(Lat) Birgitta-DAT.SG(Lat)
     'Mary, God's mother, tells Saint Birgitta'   (Bir 137)

Additional evidence comes from participial constructions, more precisely from *absolute participles* (see Ahlberg 1942, Höder 2010: 222ff). Absolute participles represent a marginal but productive construction in Written Old Swedish, modeled on – and used as an equivalent of – a functionally and structurally corresponding construction in Latin, the so-called 'ablative absolute'. In this construction, a verb takes a participial form in the ablative case, and the agent (with active participles) is also expressed as an ablative ([NOUN$_{ABL}$ + VERB$_{PTCP.ABL}$]). The Swedish construction follows the same pattern, except that participial forms are uninflected and the ablative is replaced by the dative case ([NOUN$_{DAT}$ + VERB$_{PTCP}$]):

(9) iach scriffwar ed*er* aff gwdelikom kærlek <u>gwdhy   tet</u> vetandhe
     I   write   you of divine   love   God-DAT it   knowing
     'I write to you out of divine love, with God knowing it.'   (Bir 146f)

The nominal inflectional categories (encoded morphologically in both languages) are thus treated by the bilingual speakers as representing language-specific variants of common, unspecified categories. The possessive construction [NOUN + NOUN$_{GEN}$], for example, is language-unspecific, as it can be filled by either Swedish or Latin nouns and genitives. The same holds for the ditransitive construction [VERB + NOUN$_{DAT}$ + NOUN$_{ACC}$]. The prepositional construction [PREP + NOUN$_{DAT}$] is exclusively Swedish but linked to the corresponding Latin construction [PREP + NOUN$_{ABL}$] via a more schematic diaconstruction [PREP + NOUN$_{DAT/ABL}$]. Similarly, schematic absolute participle constructions are language-unspecific ([NOUN$_{DAT/ABL}$ + VERB$_{PTCP}$]), but language-specific constructions are needed to account for the actual case marking.

---

13. The suffix *-e* is often used in Medieval Latin as a graphical variant of (Classical) *-ae*.

The interlingual mapping of the nominal inflectional categories is, from a diasystematic point of view, almost perfect in the sense of morpheme-based inter-translatability. Once established, it is thus a case of *stable diasystematicity* in a contact situation; no changes are observable during the Old Swedish period.[14]

In contrast to diasystematic stability as a result of a near-perfect congruence between two language systems, the existence of a fourth morphological category in Old Swedish causes *stable idiosyncrasy*: definiteness. Definiteness in Late Old Swedish is a complex category, applying to nominal constructions rather than nouns and expressed by different and in part optional markers (both determiners and adjectival/nominal suffixes), as is illustrated in (10):

(10)   Tha gømdhis   æn <u>then   gambla   laghen</u>
       then observed-PASS still DEF.M.SG old-SG.DEF law-DEF.M.SG
       'At that time the old law was still in effect.'   (Bir 166)

Latin did not have a formally or functionally similar category (even though demonstratives such as *iste* 'this', for instance, evidently imply definiteness).[15] Consequently, the Latin-Old Swedish bilinguals do not treat any Latin structures as equivalents to Swedish definiteness, neither in translating (definiteness markers are used depending on the [implicit] context) nor in code-switching (*ad hoc* borrowings from Latin are not marked for definiteness). Definiteness thus represents a language-specific construction. Latin nouns in Swedish nominal constructions are accordingly treated as unspecified for definiteness and, hence, occur both in definite and non-definite contexts, as illustrated in (11) by the form *confessore* used in a definite context:

(11)   abb*atisson*ne   wal   ra*n*zsake ...
       abbess-GEN.PL-DEF-GEN.PL election investigate-SBJV
       biscop*en*   m*ädh* <u>confessore</u>
       bishop-DEF.M.SG with   confessor-ABL(Lat)
       'The bishop shall investigate the abbesses' election together with the confessor.'
                                                                          (OCG 122)

Even this behavior is stable during the Old Swedish period, except when conventionalized loanwords are integrated morphologically, with Swedish suffixes being used in

---

14.   In the later development of Swedish, however, the interlingual mapping becomes less unambiguous and less stable (see Wollin 2007); a likely explanation is that other factors (such as phonologically based gender assignment) become more dominant as the relevance of bilingual diasystematicity decreases when the written language is no longer used exclusively by educated, bilingual speakers.

15.   The earliest written sources in Old Swedish deviate from the later norm in that definiteness is not obligatorily marked; this system is thus closer to Latin than the later one. However, by about 1400, definiteness seems to be fully established as a (mandatory) grammatical category in Written Old Swedish.

general (cf. the Swedish genitive suffix *-o* along with the definiteness marker *-nne* in *abbatissonne* in (11); the corresponding Latin genitive would be *abbatissae*).

3.3   Pronominal relative clauses

An example of *increasing diasystematicity* is the emergence of pronominal relative clauses in Old Swedish (for a detailed analysis see Höder 2010: 199ff, see also Lindblad 1943). In Early Old Swedish (prior to 1375), relative clauses with an antecedent are exclusively introduced by uninflected relative particles (such as *sum*; see example (12)) or gaps. Latin, on the other hand, has only pronominal relativizers (with full-fledged inflectional paradigms), mostly homophonous with interrogative determiners (e.g. the most frequent *qui*). However, Swedish and Latin relative clause constructions are easily identifiable as interlingual equivalents, based on their similar meaning (providing additional information about a given referent) and structural similarities (finite clauses, clause-initial relativizers, coreference with an antecedent).[16]

In Written Old Swedish (after 1375), bilingual speakers increasingly use inflected relative pronouns along with the inherited relativizers, predominantly the pronouns *hviliken* (originally an interrogative 'which'; see example (13)) and *þän* (otherwise demonstrative 'that'). The innovative relativizers are particularly frequent in appositive relative clauses, which also constitute an innovative functional relative clause type (as opposed to restrictive and generalizing relative clauses).

(12)   The preste <u>som</u> væl foresta sino   æmbete
      the priests REL well govern POSS.3SG.REFL-DAT office
      'The priests that administer their office well …'   (SsS 101)

(13)   … kærlekin <u>hwlkin</u>   høxth ær j   allom dygdom
      love-DEF REL-NOM.SG.M highest is in all   virtues
      '… love, which is the highest of all virtues'   (Bir 149)

The emergence of pronominal relativizers can be interpreted as an instance of grammatical replication (Höder 2010: 218ff), presumably reinforced by the increasingly common practice of formally equivalent translation from Latin sources (Kranich, Becher & Höder 2011) and the social prestige of that language.[17]

From a bilingual point of view, though, this process is at the same time a highly pro-diasystematic and thus a cognitively economic change. Before the innovation, bilingual speakers have to store and process language-specific relative clause constructions which are diasystematically linked, but only through very abstract, schematic, and

---

16. For a typological overview of possible relativization strategies beyond this type, see Lehmann (1984: 43ff and passim).

17. Quantitative analyses show that appositive relative clauses in Latin sources are usually rendered as pronominal relative clauses in Old Swedish translations (Höder 2010: 216f).

semantically unspecific diaconstructions, viz. a 'relative clause diaconstruction' (specifying the clause-initial position and clause-internal function of the relativizer) and a 'relativizer diaconstruction' (representing the grammatical concept of a lexically expressed relativizer). Anything else is language-specific, in particular the morphological properties of the relativizers (uninflected vs. marked for case, number, and gender):

Table 2. Old Swedish and Latin relative clause constructions (pre-change)

unspecified	{Old Swedish}	{Latin}
<relative clause> [REL$_1$ + ...]	<restrictive relative clause> [REL.PARTICLE$_1$ + ...]	<relative clause> [REL.PRON$_1$ + ...]
<relativizer> [_]	<relative particle> [_]	<relative pronoun> [INTERR.PRON$_1$ + CNG$_2$]

But with pronominal relativizers in Old Swedish, as a result of the innovation, bilingual speakers can construct relative clauses in both languages based on common constructions (reflecting the originally Latin model), including (a) relative clause constructions that allow for appositive clauses, (b) an exactly equivalent complex grammatical meaning of the pronominal relativizers (specifying case, number, and gender rather than just signaling relativization), and (c) even a lexical diaconstruction in the case of the relative/interrogative pronouns OSw *hviliken* and Lat *qui*, which correspond to each other in any clause type. The combined system can be summarized (in a somewhat idealized fashion) in the following way:[18]

Table 3. Old Swedish and Latin relative clause constructions (post-change)

unspecified	{Old Swedish}	{Latin}
	<relative clause> [REL.PARTICLE$_1$ + ...]	–
<relative clause> [REL.PRON$_1$ + ...]	–	–
<relative pronoun> [INTERR.PRON$_1$ + CNG$_2$]	–	–
'which (REL/INTERR)' [_]	'which (REL/INTERR)' [*hviliken*]	'which (REL/INTERR)' [*qui*]

---

18. The devil is the details that are not included in the table: hybrid relativizers (consisting of both a pronoun and a particle), frequency differences in the distribution of pronominal and non-pronominal relativizers across different texts, and suchlike (discussed in detail in Höder 2010: 203ff). Still, the overall picture can be captured neatly in a set of constructions such as the ones in Table 3.

As pronominal relativization does not replace the particle strategy, the idiosyncratic Swedish constructions are preserved but no longer obligatory; this is reflected in the language-unspecific pronominal relative clause construction as compared to the idiosyncratic non-pronominal relative clause construction in Old Swedish. This point illustrates nicely that the simplification of a multilingual system can lead to a complexification of a monolingual system. Old Swedish is becoming more complex: two alternative constructions (±pronominal) are possible in Written Old Swedish, whereas earlier only one construction (−pronominal) was possible. However, if we assume a bilingual system with language-specific and unspecified elements, the same development – i.e. the emergence of an alternative relativization strategy – is obviously a simplifying change.

4. Conclusion

Language contact involves, as a rule, long-term, stable, intense multilingualism, socially embedded in multilingual speaker groups. Consequently, all kinds of interlingual transfer and contact-induced change require, at some stage, a form of conventionalized multilingual communicative behavior and some kind of cognitive interaction between the languages. Therefore, I have advocated an essentially multilingual perspective on language contact in this contribution. Multilingual speaker groups know (though not necessarily consciously), utilize, and conventionalize diasystematic relations between their languages. They establish and expand regular correspondences, generalize and abstract on the basis of language-specific structures, and eventually organize their languages into a common system. Within a DCxG framework, this system, consisting both of diasystematic and idiosyncratic elements, can be modeled as an interlingual network of constructions with different degrees of schematicity.

Sources

Bir = Lindell, I. (ed). 2000. *Heliga Birgittas uppenbarelser bok 7 efter Cod. Ups. C 61* [Samlingar utgivna av Svenska fornskriftsällskapet 1.84]. Uppsala: Svenska fornskriftsällskapet.
OCG = "Ordning vid val af confessor generalis i Vadstena kloster", 1900–1916. In *Småstycken på forn svenska*. Volume 2, R. Geete (ed.), 109–124. Stockholm: Norstedt.
SsS = Andersson, R. (ed) 2006. *Sermones sacri Svecice. The sermon collection in Cod. AM 787 4°* [Samlingar utgivna av Svenska fornskriftsällskapet 1.86]. Uppsala: Svenska fornskriftsällskapet.

References

Ahlberg, M. 1942. *Presensparticipet i fornsvenskan: En syntaktisk studie.* Lund: Blom.

Aikhenvald, A. Y. 2007. Grammars in contact: A cross-linguistic perspective. In *Grammars in Contact: A Cross-linguistic Typology*, eds. A. Y. Aikhenvald & R. M. W. Dixon, 1–66. Oxford: OUP.

Bergs, A. & G. Diewald, eds. 2008. *Constructions and Language Change.* Berlin: Mouton de Gruyter.

Coseriu, E. 1974. *Synchronie, Diachronie und Geschichte: Das Problem des Sprachwandels.* München: Fink.

Croft, W. 2001. *Radical Construction Grammar: Syntactic Theory in Typological Perspective.* Oxford: OUP.

Dahl, Ö. 2009. Increases in complexity as a result of language contact. In *Convergence and Divergence in Language Contact Situations* (Hamburg Studies on Multilingualism 8), eds. K. Braunmüller & J. House, 41–52. Amsterdam: John Benjamins.

Goldberg, A. E. 1995. *Constructions: A Construction Grammar Approach to Argument Structure.* Chicago IL: University of Chicago Press.

Goldberg, A. E. 2006. *Constructions at Work: The Nature of Generalization in Language.* Oxford: OUP.

Grosjean, F. 1989. Neurolinguists, beware! The bilingual is not two monolinguals in one person. *Brain and Language* 36: 3–15.

Grosjean, F. 2001. The bilingual's language modes. In *One Mind, Two Languages: Bilingual Language Processing*, ed. J. L. Nicol, 1–22. Malden MA: Blackwell.

Grosjean, F. 2008. *Studying Bilinguals.* Oxford: OUP.

Haugen, E. 1956. *Bilingualism in the Americas: A Bibliography and Research Guide.* Tuscaloosa AL: University of Alabama Press.

Heine, B. & T. Kuteva. 2005. *Language Contact and Grammatical Change.* Cambridge: CUP.

Höder, S. 2010. *Sprachausbau im Sprachkontakt: Syntaktischer Wandel im Altschwedischen.* Heidelberg: Winter.

Höder, S. Forthcoming. Constructing diasystems: Grammatical organisation in bilingual groups. In *Language Contact and Change – Grammatical Structure Encounters the Fluidity of Language*, eds. T. Åfarli & B. Mæhlum. Amsterdam: John Benjamins.

Höder, S. 2011. Niederdeutsch und Norddeutsch: Ein Fall von Diasystematisierung. *Niederdeutsches Jahrbuch* 134, 113–136.

Johanson, L. 2008. Remodeling grammar: Copying, conventionalization, grammaticalization. In *Language Contact and Contact Languages* (Hamburg Studies on Multilingualism 7), eds. P. Siemund & N. Kintana, 61–79. Amsterdam: John Benjamins.

Kranich, S., V. Becher & S. Höder. 2011. A tentative typology of translation-induced language change. In *Multilingual Discourse Production*, eds. S. Kranich, V. Becher, S. Höder & J. House, 11–44. Amsterdam: John Benjamins.

Kühl, K. H. 2008. *Bilingualer Sprachgebrauch bei Jugendlichen im deutsch-dänischen Grenzland.* Hamburg: Kovač.

Lehmann, C. 1984. *Der Relativsatz: Typologie seiner Strukturen, Theorie seiner Funktionen, Kompendium seiner Grammatik.* Tübingen: Narr.

Lindblad, G. 1943. *Relativ satsfogning i de nordiska fornspråken* (Lundastudier i nordisk språkvetenskap A 1). Lund: Gleerup.

Lüdi, G. 1996. Mehrsprachigkeit. In *Kontaktlinguistik: Ein internationales Handbuch zeitgenössischer Forschung*, 1. Halbband, eds. H. Goebl, P. H. Nelde, Z. Starý & W. Wölck, 233–245. Berlin: Mouton de Gruyter.

Matras, Y. 2009. *Language Contact*. Cambridge: CUP.

Muysken, P. 2000. *Bilingual Speech: A Typology of Code-mixing*. Cambridge: CUP.

Myers-Scotton, C. 2002. *Contact Linguistics: Bilingual Encounters and Grammatical Outcomes*. Oxford: OUP.

Oesterreicher, W. 2001. Historizität – Sprachvariation, Sprachverschiedenheit, Sprachwandel. In *Language Typology and Language Universals*, Band 2, eds. M. Haspelmath, E. König, W. Oesterreicher & W. Raible, 1554–1595. Berlin: Mouton de Gruyter.

Pietsch, L. 2010. What has changed in Hiberno-English: Constructions and their role in contact-induced change. *Language Typology and Universals* 63: 118–145.

Thomason, S. G. & T. Kaufman. 1988. *Language Contact, Creolization, and Genetic Linguistics*. Berkeley CA: University of California Press.

Weinreich, U. 1954. Is a structural dialectology possible? *Word* 10: 388–400.

Weinreich, U. 1964. *Languages in Contact: Findings and Problems*. The Hague: Mouton.

Wollin, L. 1981/1983. *Svensk latinöversättning* (Samlingar utgivna av Svenska fornskriftsällskapet 1.74). Lund: Blom.

Wollin, L. 2007. 'Hoo haffuer honom lärdt then grammaticam?' Die Flexion lateinischer Lehnwörter im älteren Schwedisch. In *Hochdeutsch in Skandinavien III. III. Internationales Symposium, Greifswald, 24–25. Mai 2002* (Osloer Beiträge zur Germanistik 38), ed. C. Lindqvist, 33–50. Frankfurt: Peter Lang.

Pseudo-coordinations in Faroese[*]

Caroline Heycock[1] and Hjalmar P. Petersen[2]
[1]University of Edinburgh, UK; [2]University of the Faroe Islands, Tórshavn

In this article we describe the system of pseudo-coordinations in Faroese –
coordinations in the verbal system in which the second conjunct appears in
fact to be subordinated to the first – in the light of previous discussions of this
phenomenon in Scandinavian. We discuss pseudo-coordinations – mainly,
but not exclusively, with verbs of posture in the first conjunct – that have
an aspectual interpretation (e.g. *sit and ...*); and also pseudo-coordinations
where the second conjunct alternates with an infinitive clause (e.g. *try and ...*).
We conclude with an overview of the distribution of pseudo-coordinations
in Germanic, and offer some suggestions as to how they may have arisen
in Faroese.

Keywords: Faroese, Danish, syntactic change, word order, language contact,
pseudo-coordination, subordination, hendiadys, absentives

1. Introduction

In common with the Mainland Scandinavian languages, but unlike Icelandic (Josefsson
1991, Wiklund 1996), Faroese has a rich system of what have been termed pseudo-
coordinations, a term that in the Scandinavian context probably goes back to Teleman
(1974). In this article we will attempt to give a description of the phenomenon in modern Faroese (FA), to compare it with pseudo-coordination as it has been described and
analyzed in particular in Mainland Scandinavian, and to provide some speculations as
to the origins of the construction(s) within Faroese.

* We would like to thank Victoria Absalonsen, Zakaris Svabo Hansen, Jógvan í Lon Jacobsen
and Marius Staksberg for their help with examples and judgments; and two anonymous reviewers, whose comments on an initial version led to significant improvements. All errors of fact and
interpretation however remain the responsibility of the authors.

2. What are pseudo-coordinations?

The pseudo-coordination that we discuss here (sometimes also referred to in the literature as verbal/clausal hendiadys) has the apparent form of "ordinary" coordination in the verbal system, but with a number of distinct syntactic and semantic features. These will be discussed in more detail in the course of this article, but as a first summary we can take the following:

1. The tense/aspect of the verbs in the conjuncts (which we will refer to as V1 and V2) must match; in ordinary coordination this is not required.
2. The second conjunct never has an overt subject.
3. "Asymmetric" extraction is possible from the second conjunct, in apparent violation of Ross's (1967) Coordinate Structure Constraint.
4. The two conjuncts are not perceived as being informationally equivalent; the initial verb may be "bleached" of at least some aspect of its independent meaning. Thus, for example, a verb with a positional meaning like 'sit' or 'stand' as V1 no longer entails this bodily position but carries instead an aspectual meaning.

To illustrate: (1) below is potentially ambiguous between ordinary coordination and pseudo-coordination. The ordinary meaning entails that Jógvan is seated, and eating fish. Read as a pseudo-coordination, there is no entailment that Jógvan is actually sitting, just that he is engaged in the act of eating fish (the semantic bleaching of V1 mentioned in point 4 above).

(1) Jógvan   **situr**   **og etur**   fisk.   (FA)
Jógvan-NOM sit-PRS.3SG and eat-PRS.3SG fish-ACC
'Jógvan is sitting and eating fish' *or* 'Jógvan is eating fish.'

If we change the aspect of one of the conjuncts, as in (2a), the sentence remains grammatical; but as it is now unambiguously a case of ordinary coordination, it unambiguously entails that Jógvan is sitting. The same effect obtains if we give the second conjunct an overt subject, as in (2b). Conversely, extraction of a *wh*-phrase from the second conjunct, as in (2c), is only compatible with the pseudo-coordination reading, so this example does not have the entailment that Jógvan is sitting.

(2) a. Jógvan   **situr**   **og hevur**   **etið**   fisk.
Jógvan-NOM sit-PRS.3SG and have-PRS.3SG eaten-SUP fish-ACC
'Jógvan is sitting and has eaten fish.'

b. Jógvan   **situr**   **og hann**   **etur**   fisk.
Jógvan-NOM sit-PRS.3SG and he-NOM eat-PRS.3SG fish-ACC
'Jógvan is sitting and he is eating fish.'

c. **Hvat** situr   Jógvan   og etur   *e*?
what sit-PRS.3SG Jógvan-NOM and eat-PRS.3SG
'What is Jógvan eating?'

We can initially distinguish two main types of pseudo-coordination in Faroese. In the first type, the interpretation of the construction is principally aspectual. Thus the examples in (3) all express some type of progressive or durative aspect.[1] The first example is from the FADAC database, which consists of data from spoken FA (For more on the FADAC database, see Section 3 and Petersen 2010: 55ff).[2]

(3) a. Eg   **standi**   **og hugsi**   um   Lenu.
         I-NOM stand-PRS.1SG and think-PRS.1SG about Lena-ACC
         'I am thinking about Lena.'   (FADAC)

     b. ... hann hoyrir   í   útvarpinum,   at   ein bilur
         he-NOM hear-PRS.3SG in radio-DEF-DAT that a   car-NOM
         á   Eysturoynni   **liggur**   **og koyrir**   við
         on Eysturoy-DEF-DAT lie-PRS.3SG and drive-PRS.3SG with
         fullari ferð   á   skeivari síðu.
         full   speed-DAT on wrong   side-DAT
         'He hears on the radio that a car on Eysturoy is driving at full speed on the wrong side of the road.'
                      (heima.olivant.fo/~finnur/hahaha.htm; accessed 31 January 2011)

This is the type which Wiklund (1996) refers to as "Pseudocoordination A (PCA)." Pseudo-coordinations of this type are also found in all the Mainland Scandinavian languages (Danish, Swedish and Norwegian). This suggests a convergence area within the Scandinavian languages consisting of Mainland Scandinavian and Faroese (Petersen 2010: 116), an issue that we will return to in Section 5.

Pseudo-coordinations are also found in Afrikaans, English, Low German and North High German dialects (see Höder 2011).

(4) a. Ik   **bün**   bi **un feul.**   (Low German)
         I-NOM be–PRS.1SG at and wipe–PRS.1SG
         'I am wiping the floor.'   (Höder 2011: 177)

     b. Denn **geht**   er   bei **und repariert**   das.
         then go-PRS.3SG he-NOM at   and repair-PRS.3SG it-ACC
                                              (North High German (dialect))
         'Then he proceeds to repair it.'   (Höder 2011: 177)

---

1.   In this article we will gloss over the distinction between these two types of aspect. See Hesse (2009, 2011) for more detailed discussion of the aspectual interpretation of pseudo-coordinations in Faroese, and also Barnes & Weyhe (1994: 211) and Thráinsson, Petersen, Jacobsen & Hansen (2004: 74).

2.   From now on, all examples are in Faroese unless indicated otherwise.

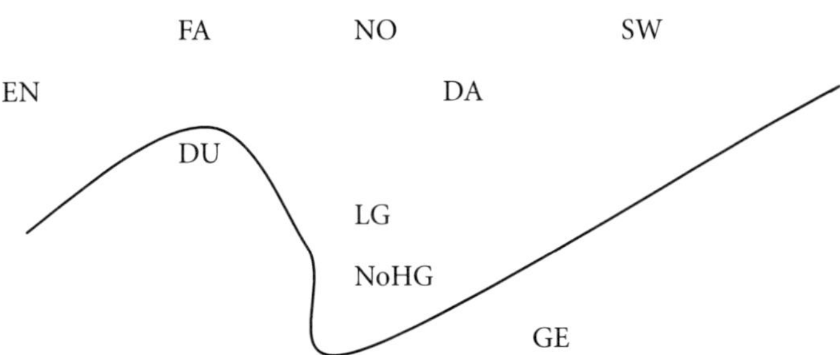

Figure 1. Pseudo-coordination in the Germanic languages

That is, while pseudo-coordinations are found in Faroese and the languages just mentioned, they are not found in standard German, Dutch[3] (Höder 2011), or Icelandic (Josefsson 1991, Wiklund 1996).

In contrast to this first type of pseudo-coordination, in the second type, which Wiklund (1996) refers to as "Pseudo-coordination B (PCB)" there is alternation with infinitival complementation.

> (5) a. **Royn**   **at selja**   húsini!
>   try-IMP.SG to sell-INF house-DEF-ACC-PL
>   'Try to sell the house!'
>
>   b. **Royn**   **og sel**   húsini!
>   try-IMP.SG and sell-IMP.SG house-DEF-ACC-PL
>   'Try and sell the house!'

As can be seen from the translation, English also has this type of coordination with *try* (see Hommerberg & Tottie 2007 and references therein). Within Scandinavian, Wiklund cites examples from spoken Swedish (although she says only that these are allowed by "speakers of some dialects") and seems to indicate that it is also possible in some Northern Norwegian dialects, but not in Danish, although her discussion is not entirely clear on this point (Wiklund 1996: 31ff).

Besides *pröva* 'try,' Wiklund cites Swedish *fortsätta* 'continue,' *börja* 'begin', *sluta* 'stop', *skynda sig* 'hurry', *se till* 'make sure', *komman ihåg* 'remember', *glömma* 'forget' and politeness phrases such as *vara snäll* 'be kind/please' and *vara så god* 'be so good/ help yourself' as verbs that can appear as V1 in PCB in Swedish.

---

3.   They are however found in Middle Dutch (Le Roux 1923, Roberge 1994, Robbers 1997, De Vos 2005).

3.   On the hunt for pseudo-coordination in Faroese

3.1   Sources

Our principal data come from the FADAC (Faroese-Danish Corpus) database at the Collaborative Research Center on Multilingualism (Sonderforschungsbereich 538 "Mehrsprachigkeit") at the University of Hamburg, with some supplement from the *Corpuseye* online tagged corpus, and the *Språkbanken* corpus.

The Faroese part of the FADAC database consists of informal interviews with a number of native Faroese speakers from three generations: 16–21, 40–50 and 70+. The speakers – divided between male and female – come from different dialect areas within the Faroe Islands. The data were originally collected for work on Faroese-Danish bilingualism but can obviously also be used for different research purposes, as is done here.

The *Corpuseye* corpus <http://corp.hum.sdu.dk/cqp.fo.html> (16 March 2012) consists of the text from issues of the newspaper *Sosialurin* from 2004 (approximately 112,000 words), and a selection of texts from the Faroese edition of Wikipedia (approximately 94,000 words). The texts are tagged for part-of-speech. The *Språkbanken* corpus <http:/spraakbanken.gu.se> (16 March 2012) consists of all the issues of the newspaper *Dimmalætting* from 1998; it does not have part-of-speech tagging.

We also searched through volumes I–IV of *FøroyaKvæði/Corpus carminum Faeroensium*, which is a collection of Faroese ballads. The language in these ballads represents older Faroese, although it is hard to date the language with any accuracy, as these ballads, first written down in the second half of the 18th and in the 19th century, are part of an oral tradition. We obtained the ballads in electronic format from *Føroy-amálsdeildin* (The Institute for Faroese, part of *Fróðskaparsetur*, the University of the Faroe Islands), Tórshavn. The total word count in volumes I–IV is 683,869.

Finally, as a supplement to this, we have used Google to search the internet, searching for e.g. *standi og* 'stand-PRS1SG' on Faroese websites (using the command "site:fo"). We have also where necessary constructed examples. Where Faroese examples and judgments are given without other attribution these are due to the Faroese-speaking author of this article, HPP, and other native speakers we have consulted.

A summary of the pseudo-coordinations that we found in the FADAC database, the two corpora, and *Føroyakvæði* is given in the Appendix.

	Young (16–20)	Mid (40–50)	Old (70+)
Male	8	10	8
Female	8	11	7

Figure 2. Faroese speakers in the FADAC database

3.2   Diagnostics

As the discussion in Section 2 suggests, while there are cases where we can determine whether a given coordination is a case of ordinary coordination or a pseudo-coordination, many examples that occur in texts or dialogues cannot be unequivocally assigned to one or the other type. Further, it has been argued in a study of pseudo-coordinations in English and Afrikaans by De Vos (2005) that as well as distinguishing between pseudo-coordinations that alternate with infinitive subordinations and those that do not, it is necessary to distinguish between subtypes within PCA which have distinct syntactic properties both inter- and intra-linguistically. In particular, De Vos argues that while both (6a) and (6b) below are pseudo-coordinations in English, they have different syntactic properties.[4]

(6)   a.   He went and bought a whole stack of books.
      b.   He went to the bookshop and bought a whole stack of books.

We discuss a number of the diagnostics most relevant for Faroese below.

3.2.1   *Non-inversibility of conjuncts*

It is a minimal (necessary, but not sufficient) condition for a coordination to qualify as a pseudo-coordination that the two conjuncts cannot appear in the inverse order without a significant change in meaning: (7a, b) are not equivalent. In contrast, ordinary coordination in at least some cases will allow the two conjuncts to appear in the opposite order, as shown in (8a, b).

(7)   a.   Hann   **situr**   og   **lesur.**
           he-NOM   sit-PRS.3SG   and   read-PRS.3SG
           'He is reading.'

      b.   Hann   **lesur**   og   **situr.**
           he-NOM   read-PRS.3SG   and   sit-PRS.3SG
           'He reads and sits.'

(8)   a.   Hann   **etur**   og   **drekkur.**
           He-NOM   eat-PRS.3SG   and   drink-PRS.3SG
           'He eats and drinks.'

      b.   Hann   **drekkur**   og   **etur.**
           he-NOM   drink-PRS.3SG   and   eat-PRS.3SG
           'He drinks and eats.'

---

4.   De Vos refers to the construction in (6a) as Contiguous Coordination (ConCo) and that in (6b) as Scene-setting Coordination (SceCo). On the other hand, writing about pseudo-coordination within Scandinavian, Hesse (2011: 148) is unequivocal in excluding any case with a locative adjunct in the first conjunct from the category of pseudo-coordination

There are of course cases of ordinary coordination where temporal ordering is implied, as in (9), so that there is a significant change of meaning when the conjuncts appear in the opposite order.

(9)   a.   She shot him and she was imprisoned.   ≠
       b.   She was imprisoned and she shot him.

Notice however that such cases involve actions that are read as occurring in sequence. In the case of Faroese pseudo-coordinations, the two conjuncts cannot be exchanged even though no temporal sequencing is implied.

3.2.2   *Extraction*

As mentioned earlier, pseudo-coordination allows for asymmetric extraction out of the second conjunct, in apparent violation of the coordinate structure constraint and the "Across-the-Board" [ATB] constraint (Ross 1967, Williams 1978). This contrasts with canonical cases of symmetric coordination. Extraction from a pseudo-coordination in Faroese was illustrated in (1, 2c) above, repeated here as (10a, b); the contrasting pattern with ordinary coordination is illustrated in (11).

(10)   a.   Jógvan   **situr**   **og etur**   fisk.
            Jógvan-NOM sit-PRS.3SG and eat-PRS.3SG fish-ACC
            'Jógvan is sitting and eating fish' *or* 'Jógvan is eating fish.'

       b.   Hvat **situr**   Jógvan   **og etur**   e?
            what sit-PRS.3SG Jógvan-NOM and eat-PRS.3SG
            'What is Jógvan eating?'

(11)   a.   Jógvan   **tosar**   **og etur**   fisk.
            Jógvan-NOM talk-PRS.3SG and eat-PRS.3SG fish-ACC
            'Jógvan is talking and eating fish'

       b.   *Hvat **tosar**   Jógvan   **og etur**   e?
            what talk-PRS.3SG Jógvan-NOM and eat-PRS.3SG
            Intended: 'What is Jógvan talking and eating?'

Not only arguments, but also adjuncts can be extracted; of course in the case of adjuncts it is more difficult to determine the extraction site, but (12) has an interpretation where what is being asked about is the carefulness of reading, not of sitting:[5]

(12)   Hvussu vandaliga **situr**   hann   (har)
       how   carefully sit-PRS.3SG he-NOM (there)
       og lesur   bókina?
       and read-PRS.3SG book-DEF-ACC
       'How carefully is he reading the book (there)?'

---

5.   For readers familiar with De Vos's work on pseudo-coordination in English and Afrikaans, it may be of interest that in Faroese it appears that the inclusion of a locative in the first conjunct does not block this type of extraction.

Again, as has been much discussed for English, there are a number of exceptions to these constraints on extraction, so this diagnostic must also be treated with caution (see Wiklund 1996, De Vos 2005).

3.2.3   *Negation, yes/no questions*

In aspectual pseudo-coordinations (PCA), negation appears in the first conjunct, but negates the whole complex:

(13) Jógvan   **situr**   **ikki og hyggur**
      Jógvan-NOM sit-PRS.3SG NEG   and look-PRS.3SG
      út   gjøgnum vindeygað
      out through window-DEF-ACC
      'Jógvan isn't looking out of the window'.

Compare the ordinary coordination, as illustrated in (14). If only the first verb appears before negation, the second verb does not fall within its scope.

(14) Jógvan   **dagdroymir**   **ikki og hyggur**
      Jógvan-NOM daydream-PRS.3SG NEG and look-PRS.3SG
      út   gjøgnum vindeygað
      out through window-DEF-ACC
      'Jógvan isn't daydreaming and/but (he) looks out of the window'.

Similarly, a yes/no question is formed, questioning the whole complex, by moving only the first verb in the pseudo-coordination to first position, as in (15a). Movement of both finite verbs is excluded, as illustrated in (15b).

(15) a. **Situr**   Jógvan   **og lesur?**
          sit-PRS.3SG Jógvan-NOM and read-PRS.3SG
          'Is Jógvan reading?'

      b. *****Situr**   **og lesur** Jógvan?
          sit-PRS.3SG and read-PRS.3SG Jógvan-NOM
          Intended: Is Jógvan reading?

In ordinary coordination, on the other hand, both options are possible:

(16) a. **Lesur**   Jógvan   **og skrivar?**
          read-PRS.3SG Jógvan-NOM and write-PRS.3SG
          'Does Jógvan read and write?'

      b. **Lesur**   **og skrivar**   Jógvan?
          read-PRS.3SG and write-PRS.3SG Jógvan-NOM
          'Does Jógvan read and write?'

3.2.4 *Presentational focus*

Faroese allows a "presentational focus" construction where the initial position is occupied by an expletive and the subject appears post-verbally. Thus alongside (17a) we find also (17b):

(17) a. Ein drongur lesur.
          a   boy-NOM read-PRS.3SG
          'A boy reads'

      b. Tað   lesur   ein drongur.
          it-NOM   read-PRS.3SG a   boy-NOM
          'There is a boy reading'.

As discussed extensively in Lødrup (2002) with respect to Norwegian, ordinary coordination cannot co-occur with this construction in Faroese in the way illustrated in (18); but pseudo-coordination can, as shown in (19):

(18) a. Ein drongur **lesur**   **og skrivar.**
          a   boy-NOM read-PRS.3SG and write-PRS.3SG
          'A boy reads and writes'.

      b. *__**Tað**__   **lesur**   ein drongur **og skrivar.**
          it-NOM read-PRS.3SG a   boy-NOM and write-PRS.3SG
          Intended: 'There is a boy reading and writing'.

(19) a. Ein drongur **situr**   **og skrivar.**
          a   boy-NOM sit-PRS.3SG and write-PRS.3SG
          'A boy is writing'.

      b. **Tað**   **situr**   ein drongur **og skrivar.**
          it-NOM sit-PRS.3SG a   boy-NOM and write-PRS.3SG
          'There is a boy writing'.

3.2.5 *Semantic bleaching of V1*

De Vos (2005) points out that in English, pseudo-comparatives with *go* as V1 and no intervening material between the verbs show no restrictions on the subject imposed by *go* itself; it is also clear that in this construction *go* has lost any meaning of change of location.

(20) a. It went and rained on us.

      b. He lay down, and in seconds he had gone and fallen asleep!

This semantic bleaching, and concomitant transparency to subject selection, can therefore be used as a diagnostic for the particular construction, and is one reason that De Vos (2005) distinguishes between two types of pseudo-coordination in English. This bleaching may be a matter of degree, however; Lødrup states that the locational verbs that participate in pseudo-comparatives in Norwegian retain at least some aspects of their "literal" meaning at the same time as expressing durative or progressive aspect (Lødrup 2002: 122, see also Hesse 2009, 2011). We return to semantic bleaching in Section 4.

3.2.6 *Failure of distributivity*

Presumably in consequence of the different semantic contribution of the two verbs in a pseudo-coordination, overt markers of distributivity like *both* cannot occur in pseudo-coordinations. Hence (21a), which in the absence of *bæði* (both) is most naturally read as a pseudo-coordination, contrasts with (21b), an ordinary coordination.

> (21)   a.   #Hon   **bæði situr**   og **bindur.**
>   she-NOM both sit-PRS.3SG and knit-PRS.3SG
>   Literally: She both sits and knits
>
>   b.   Hon   **bæði drekkur**   og **roykir.**
>   she-NOM both drinks-PRS.3SG and smokes-PRS.3SG
>   'She both drinks and smokes'.

4.   Characteristics of pseudo-coordination in Faroese

4.1   Pseudo-coordination with aspectual meaning (PCA)

Lødrup's (2002) paper is the most detailed recent discussion of pseudo-coordination in Scandinavian easily available, and so to put Faroese in the context of the mainland Scandinavian languages, we largely follow his grouping and order of presentation here.

4.1.1 *Positional verbs*

As in the other Scandinavian languages, Faroese makes use of positional verbs to express progressive/durative aspect (Henriksen 2000: 45). Consider for example (22a, b), and compare also the examples in (3a, b) above.[6]

> (22)   a.   ... ikki at tala   um, tá   tey   **liggja**
>   ... not to talk-INF about, when they-NOM lie-PRS.PL
>   **og koyra**   sunnudagskoyring ...
>   and drive-PRS.PL Sunday-driving-ACC
>   '... Not to mention when they are driving [their] Sunday trips'
>   (kvinna.fo. 16.01.09; accessed 21.10.10)
>
>   b.   Harra Gud   í himmalinum   situr,   teir
>   Lord   God-NOM in heaven-DEF-DAT sit-PRS.3SG they-NOM

---

6.   The sentence in (22b) is from the FADAC database. Here a man of the older generation talks about an old trawler. The sentence is difficult to translate; the lexical meaning of *tufla* is to 'walk clumsily'. The informant refers to the fact that the ship is old, and difficult to sail in the icy waters of Greenland.

liggja   og tufla   og tufla ...
lie-PRS.PL and stumble-PRS.PL and stumble-PRS.PL
'Good Lord(N) in heaven, they sail so clumsily.'   (FADAC)

An example like (22a) also shows that *liggja* is more bleached of its lexical meaning than Lødrup reports for the positional verbs in Norwegian pseudo-coordinations. *Liggja* does not retain its literal meaning here; it would be completely infelicitous to say in this context *tey liggja* 'they lie' of the participants in the action described.

Semantic bleaching is also very obvious in (23), from the FADAC database. The informant is not standing when she utters (23), on the contrary she is sitting down with her cup of coffee.

(23) Eg   **standi**   **og hugsi**   um   Lenu.
I-NOM stand-PRS.1SG and think-PRS.1SG about Lena-ACC
'I am thinking about Lena.'   (FADAC)

The verb *sita* 'to sit' when in a pseudo-coordination may retain at least some aspects of its lexical meaning. This is very clear in (24a), where the author says that she thinks that it is impolite that people who visit her just sit down and sent text messages. The meaning of *sita* 'to sit' in (24b) is also, if not totally bleached, then at least blurred, so to say. The sentence is about how people outside the capital are waiting for two more tunnels to be built. It is used figuratively, as it is not necessarily the case that these people are sitting while they wait for the government to make a decision.

(24) a.   ... at fólk,   sum eg   havi   á   vitjan
... that people-NOM that I-NOM have-PRS.1SG on visit-DAT
sita   **og sms'a.**
sit-PRS.PL and text message-PRS.PL
'... that visiting people are texting.'
(kvinna.fo 18.01.05; accessed 22 February 2011)

     b.   So, fyri at gleða   tey mongu fólkini,
so for to please-INF the many   people-DEF-ACC
ið   spent   **sita**   **og bíða**   eftir
that excitedly sit-PRS.PL and wait-PRS.PL for
avgerðini   um   holini   bæði ...
decision-DEF-DAT about tunnels-DEF-ACC both-ACC
'So, in order to please those people who excitedly sit and wait for the decision concerning the two tunnels ...'
(Planet.portal.fo 25.6.08; accessed 22 February2011)

According to Vannebo (2003: 166) pseudo-coordinations in group 1 express an aspectual meaning; FA does not differ from the Mainland Scandinavian languages in this, as *liggja og* 'lie and', *sita og* 'sit and' and *standa og* 'stand and' express progressive/durative aspect, while *ganga og* 'go and' expresses iterative aspect. On this, see Henriksen (2000: 45). The progressive/durative meaning is also expressed by *vera og* 'be and,' about which we will say more below. For a further discussion of the aspectual meaning of these constructions and how it arises, see Hesse (2009, 2011).

In addition to stative positional verbs, Lødrup (2002) discusses the use of verbs of assuming a position as pseudo-coordinations. We have however not found any clear example of this kind of case in the Faroese sources we have searched; (25) is a potential example, but it is not at all clear that there is any semantic bleaching of *seta seg* 'sit down.'

(25) Eg   trúgvi   neyvan at   eitt djór
      I-NOM believe-PRS.1SG hardly that an animal-NOM
      fer   at **seta seg   og   filosofera**
      go-PRS.3SG to sit-INF REFL and philosophize-INF
      um   moralir   og   etikkir.
      about morals-ACC and ethics-ACC
      'I hardly believe that an animal is going to sit down and philosophize about morals and ethics'.   (gaming.fo 7.2.10; accessed 24.02.11)

4.1.2   *Verbs of motion*

The Faroese verb of motion that most clearly occurs as V1 in pseudo-coordinations is *ganga* 'to go, to walk.' As discussed in (Henriksen 2000: 45), from which (26) is taken, *ganga* in a pseudo-coordination expresses iterative aspect, as indicated by the translation. (27) is a further example from an internet forum.

(26) Hann **gongur   og   argar**   fólk.
      he-NOM go-PRS.3SG and tease-PRS.3SG people-ACC
      'He is always teasing people'.   (Henriksen 2000: 45(5))

(27) Hvat skal   eg   gera ... havi eina sokallaða
      what shall-PRS.1SG I-NOM do-INF have a   so-called
      vinkonu   sum **gongur   og   lýgur**
      girlfriend-ACC that go-PRS.3SG and lie-PRS.3SG
      um   meg ... Hon   **gongur   og   sigur,**
      about me-ACC she-NOM go-PRS.3SG and say-PRS.3SG
      at   eg   havi   havt   ein annan ...
      that I-NOM have-PRS.1SG have-SUP another-ACC
      'What shall I do? I have a so-called girlfriend who keeps lying about me ... she keeps saying that I have had another'
                                       (kvinna.fo 8.8.08; accessed 20 February 2011)

4.1.3   *Vera (be)*

Two examples of the use of *vera* in pseudo-coordinations are given in (28):

(28) a. Teir **vóru**   **og drógu**   lunda.
          they be-PST.PL and draw-PST.PL puffins-ACC
          'They were catching puffins, by pulling them out of the holes/nests'
                                                        (Henriksen 2000: 45)

      b. ... táið eg   **var**   **og bygdi**
          ... when I-NOM be-PST.1SG and build-PST.1SG
          hospitalið   í   60-inum.
          hospital-DEF-ACC in sixties-DAT
          '... when I was [among the people] who built the hospital in the sixties'.
                                                        (FADAC)

Note that it is possible to include a locative adjunct in either the first or the second
conjunct (although the preference seems to be for the first):

(29) a. Hann   **er**   í   Danmark **og lesur**.
          he-NOM be-PRS.3SG in Denmark and study-PRS.3SG
          'He is studying in Denmark.'

      b. Hann   **er**   **og lesur**   í   Danmark.
          he-NOM be-PRS.3SG and study-PRS.3SG in Denmark
          'He is studying in Denmark.'

As noted earlier, Hesse (2011) asserts that if the first conjunct contains a locative adjunct, the coordination cannot be taken to be a pseudo-coordination. Note, however,
that (29a) does not seem to differ markedly in interpretation from (29b), and, further,
allows extraction – even of adjuncts – from the second conjunct:

(30) {Hvat/Hvussu seriøst}$_i$ **er**   hann   í   Danmark **og lesur** t_i?
      what/how   hard   be-PRS.3SG he-NOM in Denmark and study-PRS.3SG
      '{What/How hard} is he studying in Denmark?'

We therefore rather follow Lødrup in concluding that even if V1 is modified by a locative adjunct the whole construction can be a pseudo-coordination.

Bertinetto, Ebert & De Groot (2000), Ebert (2000) and Vogel (2007) have argued
that Faroese pseudo-comparatives with V1 *vera* 'be' are, or can be used as absentives.
This term seems to originate with De Groot (2000), who uses it to refer to the "grammatical expression of absence" (2000: 695). Lockwood points out that (31) would be a
typical sign on an office door (Lockwood 1977: 140), a context cited by De Groot as
typical for an absentive.

(31) **Eri**   **og fái**   mær   millummála.
      be-PRS.1SG and get-PRS.1SG me-DAT tea-ACC
      Verði   skjótur aftur.
      become-PRS.1SG soon   back.
      'Gone for tea. Will be back soon.'

Of course, the fact that *vera og* can be used in a context in which the referent of the subject is clearly absent does not mean that the construction itself *encodes* that meaning, it might only be compatible with it. More significant is that in a number of circumstances *vera og* cannot be used if the referent of the subject is co-present with the speaker. For example, in the context of a phone inquiry as to whether Rúnar has gone to work, Rúnar's wife can reply using *standa og mála* 'stands and paints', but not *er og mála* 'is and paints', if she is in the same room as Rúnar as she speaks; the latter would convey that Rúnar was somewhere else.

(32)   Nei, hann   {# **er**/   **stendur**}
       no   he-NOM   be-PRS.3SG / stand-PRS.3SG
       og málar   køkin
       and paint-PRS.3SG kitchen-DEF-ACC
       Intended: 'No, he is painting the kitchen.'

De Groot says of the absentive that it encodes the information that the referent of the subject is absent from the "deictic centre"; is involved in an activity; will be absent for a predictable time; and will return (De Groot 2000: 695, 697). Any characterization of Faroese in these terms will require a careful definition of how the "deictic centre" is determined, however. Thus, De Groot (2000) and Abraham (2008) claim that, by definition, absentives cannot be used of people who are in the presence of the speaker, and cannot be used of 1st person subjects in the present tense (with present rather than future meaning). But neither restriction holds absolutely of the use of *vera og* in Faroese. Thus a speaker can introduce herself as follows:

(33)   Halló. Eg   eiti   Caroline úr   Skotlandi.
       hello I-NOM name-PRS.1SG Caroline from Scotland-DAT.
       Eg   **eri**   **og vitji**   Hjalmar.
       I-NOM be-PRS.1SG and visit-PRS.1SG Hjalmar
       'Hi. I'm Caroline from Scotland. I'm visiting Hjalmar.

It seems that what licenses the use of *vera og* in this kind of situation is the lexical entailment of *vitja* 'visit' that the referent of the subject is absent from their usual home. Here however we do not have space to go into the semantics of the Faroese *vera og* construction in more detail, or to investigate whether or not uses like (33) above are also found for "absentives" in the other languages for which they have been proposed.

4.1.4   Taka 'take'

The occurrence of the verb 'take' in pseudo-coordination in Scandinavian is described in detail in Vannebo (2003). The example in (34a) is from Henriksen (2000: 45); (34b) is from colloquial speech, and (34c) is from the FADAC database, where a woman is explaining how they used to play hide-and-seek when they were children.

(34) a. Hann **tók** **og bardi** hann av.
he-NOM take-PST.3SG and beat-PST.3SG him-ACC off
'He beat him senseless'. (Henriksen 2000: 45)

b. Eg **taki** **og selji** bilin, vissi
I-NOM take-PRS.1SG and sell-PRS.1SG car-DEF-ACC if
eg ikki fái hatta arbeiðið
I-NOM NEG get that job-ACC
'I am going to sell the car, if I don't get that job'.

c. Altso mann **tekur** **og so rennur** undan.
you.see one-NOM take-PRS.3SG and so run-PRS.3SG away
'You see, one simply runs away'. (FADAC)

The aspectual meaning of the *taka* construction in the Mainland Scandinavian languages is connected with sudden initiation of the activity (Teleman, Hellberg & Andersson 1999: 907, Vannebo 2003: 173; this is also the case in FA, as shown in example (34c).

As a final note in this section, FA does not have any pseudo-coordinations corresponding to the "purely aspectual" Norwegian cases (Lødrup 2002): *drive på* 'carry on', *holde på* 'carry on' and *vere åt* 'be to.'

4.2 Pseudo-coordination that alternates with infinitival complementation

The most central exemplar of this type of pseudo-coordination in Faroese is *royna og* 'try and', as introduced above in (5b), repeated here as (35):

(35) **Royn** **og sel** húsini!
try-IMP.SG and sell-IMP.SG house-DEF-ACC
'Try and sell the house.'

Faroese has also borrowed another verb with a similar meaning from Danish, *prøva* 'try', The example in (36) is from the FADAC database:

(36) Hvat veitst tú um
what know-PRS.2SG you-NOM about
Sjálvstýrisflokkin? **Prøva** **og fortel!**
independence-party-DEF-ACC Try-IMP.SG and tell-IMP.SG
'What do you know about the Independence Party? Try and explain!'
(FADAC)

In contrast to the wide variety of cases discussed for Swedish in Section 2 above, in Faroese for example *halda áfram* 'continue', *byrja* 'start', and *steðga* 'stop' cannot function as the V1 in a pseudo-coordination, but rather must be followed by an infinitive:

(37)   Hann   **heldur áfram/byrjar/steðgar at lesa**   bókina.
      he-NOM continue/begin/stop-PRS.3SG to read-INF book-DEF-ACC
      'He {continues/begins/stops} {to read/reading} the book.'

It is certainly possible to find such verbs as in the first conjunct of a coordination, as in (38), but these are all read as "ordinary" coordinations. The activity that is stopped, continued or started is not necessarily the one denoted by the second verb – as would be the case if these were pseudo-coordinations – rather some other activity, understood from context, is stopped/continued/started.[7]

(38)   Hann   steðgar/ helduráfram/ byrjar   og
      he-NOM stop/   continue/   begin-PRS.3SG and
      lesur   bókina.
      read-PRS.3SG book-DEF-ACC
      'He stops/continues/begins and reads the book.'

In distinction to the aspectual type of pseudo-coordination, both *royna og* and *prøva og* appear to be limited to the imperative and the infinitive. See the examples in (35) and (36) above, and the following:[8]

(39)   a.   **Royn/prøva og   les**   bókina!
          try-IMP.SG   and read-IMP.SG book-DEF-ACC
          'Try and read the book!'

      b.   **Roynið/prøvið og   lesið**   bókina!
          try-IMP.PL   and read-IMP.PL book-DEF-ACC
          'Try and read the book!'

---

7.   For some speakers *halda uppat* 'stop' can be V1 in a PCB, although it appears not to be considered standard. An informant during fieldwork in the Faroes in 2008 volunteered that she had heard *Halt uppat og skríggja* 'Stop shouting (Literally: stop and shout) although she herself was dubious as to how "correct" it was. The Faroese author of this article does not use this construction, and we have not yet been able to find out whether, for those who do, it is subject to the same distributional constraints as we find for *royna/prøva*.

8.   Some speakers – perhaps a minority – marginally accept 3rd person plural verbs in the present, where the inflection is identical to the infinitive. For such speakers there is a contrast between (40) and (ia). The example in (ib) is from the internet:

(i)   a.   Tey   **royna/prøva og   lesa**   bókina.
         they-nom try-PRS.PL   and read-PRS.PL book-DEF-ACC
         'They try and read the book.'

      b.   Starvsfólk   og   avvarðandi   **royna**   **og   gera**
         workers-nom   and   relatives-NOM   try-PRS.PL   and do-PRS.PL
         sítt   allarbesta
         their   best
         'Workers and relatives try and do their best.'
         <www.tjodveldi.fo/forsida/tidindi.aspx?PID=36&NewsID=965> (7 April 2011)

   c. Tú mást   **royna/prøva og lesa**   bókina.
      You must-PRS.2SG try-INF   and read-INF book-DEF-ACC
      You must try and read the book.'

(40)   *Hann   **roynir/prøvar og lesur**   bókina.
       he-NOM try-PRS.3SG   and read-PRS.3SG book-DEF-ACC
       Intended: 'He tries to read the book.'

In English, the constraints on *try and* are parallel to those on *go* + verb and *come* + verb (You should go talk to him; Come talk to me!) in that in English the constraint appears to be purely (surface) morphological: both V1 and V2 have to be bare stem forms. This includes the imperative and the infinitive, but also any present tense form other than 3rd singular (Try and be patient! You should try and be patient. They generally try and be patient. *He tries and is patient. *I tried and was patient). It is striking that the constraints in Faroese are very similar – the cases that are excluded are those in which there is past tense morphology or person/number morphology that is distinct from the infinitive (see the footnote above for the questionable status of present tense plural forms). But in Faroese this generalization cannot be stated in terms of bare stem forms, since the plural imperative in Faroese shows distinct suffixal morphology, as illustrated in (39b), and the infinitive is not identical to the bare stem in verbs other than those of Class 1 (infinitive *at kalla* 'to call', imperative *kalla!* 'call!').

In these restrictions, the distribution of pseudo-coordinations with *royna* as V1 is different from Mainland Scandinavian; as reported in Wiklund (1996: 33), in Swedish at least *pröva* 'try' can occur in a pseudo-coordination in tensed and supine forms as well as in the imperative.[9]

As with the aspectual type of pseudo-coordination, this type also can be negated by negating the first verb:

(41) **Royn**   **ikki og sel**   húsini!
      try-IMP.SG NEG and sell-IMP.SG house-DEF-ACC
      'Don't try to sell the house!'

Strikingly, negation in this position can also easily be interpreted as taking scope only over the second verb. For example, the example in (42) can be interpreted with this narrow scope for negation, as shown by the translation:

(42) **Royn**   **ikki og blív**   ov sein!
      try-IMP.SG NEG and become-IMP.SG too late
      'Try not to be too late!'

---

9.   These restrictions in Faroese might suggest an effect of contact with English; however Björkman (2009) cites Modern Greek and Marsalese that show a similar phenomenon in the related 'go/come + verb' construction, so it seems that this kind of restriction may arise independently; this remains to be explored.

It is tempting to conclude from this that *og* must be within the second conjunct, possibly occupying the same position as the infinitive marker *at*, since it in general in FA the negative marker precedes *at* in infinitives. However, it has been noted (Hommerberg & Tottie 2007: 56) that *contra* the discussion in Horn (1989: 323), *try* can act as a 'Neg-Raiser.' That is, there are cases in English of a negation that is syntactically associated with *try* nevertheless semantically scoping only over the embedded verb. (43a, b) are two attested examples from Hommerberg & Tottie (2007).[10]

(43)   a.   I don't try and let things bother me.
       b.   Looking at her made him so sick, he didn't try to think about what he was doing.

Given the possibility that *royna* 'try' might also be a Neg-Raising verb, the negative marker *ikki* in (42) may be in the matrix even when interpreted with low scope, and hence does not allow us to conclude anything about the position of *og*. That this may be the explanation is suggested by the fact that negation may also follow the second verb, as in (44a). The order in (44b) is also possible; presumably this is to be linked to the emergence of negative imperatives with the order *Negation–Imperative* (see Petersen 2010).

(44)   a.   **Royn   og ger   ikki** nakað   býtt!
            try-IMP.SG and do-IMP.SG NEG anything-ACC stupid
            'Try not to do anything stupid!'

       b.   **Royn   og ikki ger**   nakað   býtt!
            try-IMP.SG and NEG do-IMP.SG anything-ACC stupid
            'Try not to do anything stupid!'

5.   The origin of pseudo-coordinations in FA, grammaticalization

Are the pseudo-coordinations we find in FA borrowed or the result of an internal change only? Vannebo (2003) expresses the opinion that the *ta* 'take'-constructions in Scandinavian are the result of an internal change, and that these started already at an early stage. Petersen (2010) briefly discusses pseudo-coordinations in FA, and he argues that as FA lacks the *vera að* 'be at' construction in IC, which expresses the progressive aspect, speakers have borrowed the pseudo-coordination construction from DA. This holds for at least the positional verbs *standa* 'stand', and *liggja* 'lie', and for *vera* 'be'. Danish *ganga* 'go', on the other hand, has a distant locative interpretation, different to the Faroese iterative interpretation of pseudo-coordinations with *ganga*.

---

10.   For the British-English speaking author of this article, however, these examples are completely unacceptable; Hommerberg & Tottie (2007) suggest that the spread of Neg-Raising to *try* may be a recent development.

Support for a northern convergence area is given in Höder (2011), where he shows that these constructions are found not only in NO, DA and SW, but also in Low German and non standard variants of High North German (see Figure 1 above). This suggests a spread that might have started with the Hansa, and we may thus tentatively conclude that at least the constructions in question in FA are borrowed from DA, especially since they are not found in IC and thus are not likely to have been inherited.

While we find potential instances of pseudo-coordination in the language of the ballads, we have not found any clear examples of semantic bleaching of the V1[11]. This means that the borrowed V1 + *og* + V2 construction may have been adapted to a pre-existing structure in Faroese: a case of syntactic borrowing with no word order change.

6. Conclusion

Pseudo-coordinations do not express two equal events, in contrast to "normal" coordinations. Instead, in one type we find semantic bleaching of the first verb, so that it functions more like an auxiliary; that is, it gives rise to an aspectual meaning (Vannebo 2003, Hesse 2009, 2011). Bleaching is of course one of the characteristics Heine & Kuteva (2005: 80) set up as an indicator of grammaticalization, that is, what they call desemanticization, or loss of meaning content.

In Faroese pseudo-coordinations, we find semantic bleaching with *standa* 'to stand', *sita* 'to sit', *liggja* 'to lie' and *ganga* 'to walk', *vera og* 'be and', *taka og* 'take and', but not with *koma og* 'come and', or *fara og* 'go and'. The latter two are not discussed in this article.

In this article we have discussed two different instances of pseudo-coordination in Faroese: one (PCA) in which the construction is used to convey a number of different aspectual meanings, and in which the initial verb is largely bleached of its original meaning, and one (PCB) in which the pseudo-coordination alternates with an infinitive-embedding construction – in this case the initial verb (typically *royna/prøva* 'try') does not undergo any change of meaning. We have speculated that at least the first of these types has been borrowed into Faroese from Danish, and that the use of the positional verbs and *vera* 'to be' has the same function in Faroese as the *vera að* progressive construction has in Icelandic. While we have described a number of the syntactic properties of these pseudo-coordinations, we have not here given a syntactic analysis: we hope to do so in future work.

---

11.   An example with *sita og* 'sit and' is from CCF 73 Aa; note that there is no evidence of semantic bleaching of *sita* 'to sit'.

(i)   Elvar   **situr**   **og klæðir**   seg,   eina morgun   stund
     Elvar-NOM   sit-PRS.3SG and dress-PRS.3SG   self-ACC,   one morning   hour-ACC
     'Elvar sits and dresses himself early one morning'.

References

Abraham, W. 2008. Absent arguments on the absentive: An exercise in silent syntax. Grammatical category or just pragmatic inference? *Sprachtypologie und Universalienforschung* 61: 358–374.

Barnes, M. & E. Weyhe. 1994. Faroese. In *The Germanic Languages,* eds. E. König & J. van der Auwera, 190–218. London: Routledge

Bertinetto, P. M., K. H. Ebert & C. de Groot. 2000. The progressive in Europe. In *Tense and Aspect in the Languages of Europe* (Eurotyp 6), ed. Ö. Dahl, 517–558. Berlin: Mouton de Gruyter.

Björkman, B. 2009. The syntax of syncretism. Talk given at the 20th Meeting of the North East Linguistic Society (NELS 20), MIT, Cambridge, MA, 13–15 November 2009.

De Groot, C. 2000. The absentive. In *Tense and Aspect in the Languages of Europe* (Eurotyp 6), ed. Ö. Dahl, 693–719. Berlin: Mouton de Gruyter.

De Vos, M. 2005. *The Syntax of Verbal Pseudo-coordination in English and Afrikaans.* PhD dissertation, University of Leiden.

Ebert, K. H. 2000. Progressive markers in Germanic languages. In *Tense and Aspect in the Languages of Europe* (Eurotyp 6), ed. Ö. Dahl, 605–639. Berlin: Mouton de Gruyter.

Heine, B. & T. Kuteva. 2005. *Language Contact and Grammatical Change.* Cambridge: CUP.

Henriksen, J. 2000. *Orðalagslæra.* Vestmanna: Sprotin.

Hesse, A. 2009. *Zur Grammatikalisierung der Pseudokoordination im Norwegischen und in den anderen skandinavischen Sprachen.* Tübingen: Francke.

Hesse, A. 2011. Zur Entwicklung der aspektuellen Bedeutung bei der skandinavischen Pseudokoordination. *NOWELE* 60/61: 147–169.

Höder, S. 2011. Dialect convergence across language boundaries: A challenge for areal linguistics. In *Language variation – European perspectives III: Selected papers from the 5th International Conference on Language Variation in Europe (ICLaVE 5), Copenhagen, June 2009,* eds. F. Gregersen, J. K. Parrott & P. Quist, 173–184. Amsterdam: John Benjamins.

Hommerberg, C. & G. Tottie. 2007. *Try to* and *try and*? Verb complementation in British English and American English. *ICAME* 31: 45–64.

Horn, L. 1989. *A Natural History of Negation.* Chicago IL: University of Chicago Press.

Josefsson, G. 1991. Pseudocoordination – a VP + VP coordination. *Working Papers in Scandinavian Syntax* 47: 130–156.

Le Roux, J. J. 1923. *Oor die Afrikaanse sintaksis.* Amsterdam: Swets and Zeitlinger.

Lockwood, W. B. 1977. *An Introduction to Modern Faroese.* Tórshavn: Føroya Skúlabókagrunnur.

Lødrup, H. 2002. The syntactic structures of Norwegian pseudocoordination. *Studia Linguistica* 56: 121–143.

Petersen, H. P. 2010. *The Dynamics of Faroese-Danish Language Contact.* Heidelberg: Winter.

Robbers, K. 1997. *Non-finite Verbal Complements in Afrikaans.* PhD dissertation, University of Amsterdam.

Roberge, P. 1994. On the origins of the Afrikaans verbal hendiadys. *Stellenbosch Papers in Linguistics* 28: 45–81.

Ross, H. 1967. *Constraints on Variables in Syntax.* PhD dissertation, MIT.

Teleman, U. 1974. *Manual för grammatisk beskrivning av talad och skriven svenska.* Lund: Studentlitteratur.

Teleman, U., S. Hellberg & E. Andersson. 1999. *Svenska Akademiens grammatik.* Stockholm: Svenska Akademien.

Thráinsson, H., H. P. Petersen, J. L. Jacobsen & Z. S. Hansen. 2004. *Faroese: An Overview and Reference Grammar*. Tórshavn: Føroya Fróðskaparfelag.

Vannebo, K. 2003. Ta og ro deg ned noen hakk: On pseudocoordinations with the verb *ta* 'take' in a grammaticalization perspective. *Nordic Journal of Linguistics* 26: 165–198.

Vogel, P. M. 2007. *Anna ist essen!* Neue Überlegungen zum Absentiv. In *Kopulaverben und Kopulasätze: Intersprachliche and Intrasprachliche Aspekte*, eds. L. Geist & B. Rothstein, 253–284. Tübingen: Niemeyer.

Wiklund, A. L. 1996. Pseudocoordination is subordination. *Working Papers in Scandinavian Syntax* 58: 29–53.

Williams, E. 1978. Across-the-board rule application. *Linguistic Inquiry* 9: 31–43.

Appendix

In the tables below we set out the numbers of examples of pseudo-coordinations that we found in the FADAC database, the two corpora that we consulted (*Corpuseye* and *Språkbanken*), and the ballads in volumes I–IV of *FøroyaKvæði/Corpus carminum Faeroensium*.

FADAC database

		Pres			Past		
		1p	2p	3p	1p	2p	3p
standa	Sg.	2		1			2
'to stand'	Pl.			3			2
sita	Sg.	1		1			2
'to sit	Pl.						3
liggja	Sg.						
'to lie'	Pl.			1			
ganga	Sg.					1	
'to walk'	Pl.					4	
vera	Sg.	2			1		
'to be'	Pl.						3
fara	Sg.						1
'to go'	Pl.						
koma	Sg.						
'to come'	Pl.						4

Corpuseye/Språkbanken

		Pres			Past		
		1p	2p	3p	1p	2p	3p
standa	Sg.			1			6
'to stand'	Pl.						3
sita	Sg.						1
'to sit'	Pl.			3			2
liggja	Sg.						2
'to lie'	Pl.						2
ganga	Sg.						
'to walk'	Pl.			1			
vera	Sg.						1
'to be'	Pl.						1

Ballads

		Pres			Past		
		1p	2p	3p	1p	2p	3p
standa	Sg.			7			6
'to stand'	Pl.						
sita	Sg.			2			
'to sit'	Pl.						
liggja	Sg.			1			
'to lie'	Pl.						
vera	Sg.						
'to be'	Pl.			1			

Toward a fused lect

Mixed German-Hungarian concessive conditionals in a German dialect in Romania[*]

Csilla-Anna Szabó
University of Gießen, Germany

This study investigates the use in the German dialect of Palota (Romania) of a mixed construction[1] consisting of the Hungarian generalizing particle *akár-* ('ever') and a German interrogative *wh*-pronoun, e.g. *wer, wann, wo* etc. which, following the Hungarian 'ever'-*wh*-compound pattern has emerged as a conjunction for the concessive conditional (Leuschner 2000) – a clause type that has a complex structure in Standard German but which is not common in German dialects. A qualitative analysis of the data (23 hours of informal conversations with 33 participants) reveals that there are no monolingual alternatives for concessive conditional conjunctions in the German dialect and that there is no variation of these forms, thus pointing to a grammaticalization process and supporting a movement along the continuum code-switching → language mixing → fused lects (Auer 1998b).

Keywords: German, Hungarian, fused lects, concessive conditional, bilingual conversation, grammaticalization, code-switching, code-mixing, congruent lexicalization

1. Introduction

German dialects often differ from Standard German (StG) not only in lexicon and phonology, but also in syntax. Regional varieties are in general distinguished by their

---

[*] I wish to thank Eric Anchimbe and two anonymous reviewers for helpful suggestions and critical remarks. I, of course, retain full responsibility for the way in which I have interpreted their comments. My sincere thanks to the speakers from the German speech community of Palota who agreed to share with me their conversations and lives.

1. The term *construction* will be used in this paper not in the sense it is used in the Construction Grammar.

less complex syntactic structure as compared to the standard variety. In previous studies on the syntactic structure of German dialects spoken in Germany but also of German dialects in language contact situations in South Eastern Europe (e.g. Post 1992, Wolf 1987), it has been suggested that subordinate clauses are less frequent than in the standard language. Also, these studies illustrated that in the dialects, subordinate clauses are less frequent than paratactic constructions. In the case of the German dialects of the Banat region south of Palota, the place of investigation, Wolf (1987: 239) found out that about 85% of all clauses represent main clauses and only 15% of them are subordinate clauses. This result may be traced back to the fact that in many cases the dialect uses a parataxis in place of subordinate clauses.

There are a number of subordinate clause types and conjunctions available in the standard language that are, however, absent in spoken dialects. Wolf (1987: 243) enumerates clauses with the German conjunctions *dass* ('that'), *eb* (StG *ob*, 'whether'), *weil* ('because'), *wie* (meaning StG *während*, 'while'), *wu* (StG *wo*, 'where'), *wann* (meaning both StG *wann* 'when' and *wenn* 'if') and *zeit* (StG *seit*, 'since') that are attested in the German dialects of the Banat region. Post (1992: 136) mentions that some sentence-level conjunctions (Maschler 1997, 2000) of Standard German such as *indessen, infolgedessen, insofern, zumal, nun, falls, obgleich, obwohl, obschon, ungeachtet, gleichwohl, wenngleich, wiewohl* are absent in the Palatinate German dialect. Most of them are conjunctions that mark relationships of time, concession, cause and condition. The absence of these conjunctions, however, does not mean that the dialect is not able to express these semantic relations. The dialect uses other resources, i.e. structures that have the same semantic properties and syntactic functions as the corresponding conjunctions.

In language contact situations, indigenous languages often use the contact languages as a resource for introducing new strategies of combining clauses unknown in the language before contact. These new structures express grammatical relations that are otherwise unlikely to be present within the recipient system, thus filling grammatical gaps (Matras 2000: 512–513).[2] This is also the case of the German dialect in Palota: being in a close contact with Hungarian as well as Romanian, and isolated geographically from other German speaking speech communities, this German dialect used Hungarian to achieve a concessive conditional construction with a mixed German-Hungarian conjunction as illustrated in the following excerpt from a conversation between three German-Hungarian bilinguals (two women and one man) which

---

2.   Szabó (2010: 404–412) discusses the frequent insertion of several Hungarian sentence-level conjunctions into the German dialect of Palota (North-West-Romania), such as the Hungarian adversative conjunction *hanem* (StG *sondern*, 'but'), the concessive conjunction *pedig* (StG *obwohl*, 'although'), the causal conjunction *mert* (StG *weil*, 'because'), the temporal conjunction *míg* (StG *bis*, 'until') as well as the mixed German-Hungarian modal conjunction *ahelyett dass* (StG *anstatt dass*, 'instead of'). The German equivalents of these conjunctions are used only in the cases of *mert* and *míg*. Thus, these findings support the movement toward a fused lect that is taking place in the speech community of Palota.

I recorded in Palota in 2003.[3] In this segment LJ, a German-dominant, German-Hungarian bilingual woman in her sixties, tries to describe to me, while having lunch in her kitchen, the status of the German dialect in the past:

(1) **ákerwu**   mer gange   sinn,
  wo auch immer wir gegangen sind
  'Wo wir auch immer waren, ...
  'Wherever we were, ...

  mir han   unser (.) sprouch gredt,
  wir haben unsere   Sprache geredet
  wir haben unsere Sprache gesprochen.'
  we spoke our language.'

There is a mixed German-Hungarian conjunction in Excerpt (1), consisting of the Hungarian generalizing particle *akár-*[4] (in the German dialect of Palota, it is pronounced as *áker-*),[5] meaning StG *auch immer* ('ever') and the German interrogative *wh*-pronoun *wu* (StG *wo*, 'where'). This mixed conjunction, *ákerwu*, introduces the so-called universal concessive conditional (UCC; Leuschner 1998, 2000, 2005). This type of subordinate clause that in Standard German has a very complex syntactic structure, involving a German *wh*-pronoun and generalizing particles like *auch* and/or *immer* '-ever' (Leuschner 1998, 2000, 2005), was not attested in the German dialects from which the mixed German dialect of Palota originates.[6] However, such mixed German-Hungarian UCC constructions seem to be common language contact phenomena in the so-called Danube Swabian dialects. Evidence can be found in the German dialects of present-day Hungary (e.g. Földes 2005), as well as in the Swabian dialects of the neighboring Sathmar region north (see Gehl 1994, Knecht 1999, 2001) and in the East-Franconian dialects of the Banat region south of Palota (see Hâncu, Irimescu, Ivănescu,

---

3.   Details of the corpus are presented in Section 3. Transcription basically follows GAT 2 (Selting, Auer, Barth-Weingarten, Bergmann, Bergmann, Birkner, Couper-Kuhlen, Deppermann, Gilles, Günthner, Hartung, Kern, Mertzlufft, Meyer, Morek, Oberzaucher, Peters, Quasthoff, Schütte, Stukenbrock & Uhmann 2009). Each line denotes an intonation unit and is usually followed in the second line by a German gloss. Since this gloss in most of the cases is not close enough to a German utterance, a third line will be added which provides a literal translation. The English version in line 4 of the transcription is a quasi-linear translation. Conjunctions with the Hungarian generalizing particle *akár-* are given in boldface. Other transcription conventions used are: "(.)" = brief pause; "(-)" = measured pause, ca. 0.2–0.5 sec.; ", ; ." = final pitch falling to low, falling slightly, rising slightly; ":" = elongation; "_" = latching.

4.   Etymologically, the particle *akár-* is related to the Hungarian conjunction *akár* (StG *ob*, 'whether, if') which derives from Hungarian *akar* (StG *wollen*, 'to want') (Földes 2005: 168).

5.   For further details concerning the phonological characteristics of the particle *akár-* in the German dialect of Palota as well as in other language contact situations see Section 4.

6.   For more details concerning the dialects of origin of the mixed German dialect of Palota see Section 2.

Kottler & Şandor in preparation). Furthermore, similar compounds are also present in other contact languages of Hungarian in the Carpathian Basin, such as in some Romani dialects, showing a great productivity of the compounds with the Hungarian generalizing particle *akár-* in all these contact languages: e.g. the form *akārkaj* (StG *wo auch immer* 'wherever') in Carpathian Romani (Rostás-Farkas & Karsai 2001: 15) or the form *akaršje* (StG *wer auch immer* 'whoever') in Bea Romani (Orsós & Kálmán 2009: 59).[7]

Thus, a grammaticalization process is taking place and a new bilingual grammar is emerging in the speech of these bi-/trilinguals with respect to the employment of mixed German-Hungarian UCC conjunctions. The present study seeks to investigate the pattern of this grammaticalization process. The overarching questions for the present study centre on how this bilingual conjunction and thus the new bilingual grammar evolved and what the path of grammaticalization in the emergence of this bilingual grammar is.

According to the classification of code-mixing by Muysken (2000), I suggest that the UCC conjunctions in the German mixed dialect of Palota are an example of borrowing through congruent lexicalization (Muysken 2000: 150–151) since the building pattern of the German-headed constructions is very similar to that of (monolingual) Hungarian compounds. These bilingual compounds with their specialized functions are the only resources available for the speakers, and there is no variation of these forms. The use of the mixed bilingual conjunctions in this type of clause is obligatory; it is part of the grammar of the mixed dialect and speakers have no other choice. In Auer's (1998b) terms, it seems to be the case of a fused lect.

Considering the three language alternation phenomena of code-switching (CS), language mixing (LM) and fused lects (FL), Auer (1998b) suggests that they form a continuum, in which code-switching, i.e. the ad hoc juxtaposition of two codes (languages) perceived and interpreted by participants as a locally meaningful event, is at one extreme, and fused lect, i.e. a stabilized mixed variety consisting of a reduction in variation and an increase in rule-governed, non-variable structural regularities, is at the other extreme of this continuum. The phenomenon of language mixing, i.e. the juxtaposition of two languages in a way that is meaningful to participants not in a local, but only in a more global sense, is located at some point in between these two polar extremes. Auer proposes tentatively "to see the continuum CS → LM → FL as a case of structural sedimentation which some might call 'grammaticalization'" (1998b: 1). Movement in the opposite direction along this continuum is prohibited (Auer 1998b: 22). In other words, Auer suggests that there is a movement from cases of code-switching to cases of fused lects, with the phenomenon of language mixing being an intermediate stage in this process.

With respect to the question, to what extent UCC conjunctions follow the path CS → LM → FL suggested by Auer (1998a, 1998b), I would like to argue that in this particular case, the movement along this continuum indeed proceeds in the code-switching → language mixing → fused lects direction. However, an initial

---

7.   I thank an anonymous reviewer for suggesting this point to me.

code-switching-stage can only be assumed, since there are no written historical documents about language usage in the speech community of Palota which would permit research into historical language contact and could demonstrate the existence of such a stage.

The paper is organized as follows: First, I give an overview of multilingualism in the speech community of Palota, focusing on the sociolinguistic and linguistic situation (Section 2). After presenting the data and the methodology in Section 3, I discuss the syntactic structure of the bilingual concessive conditional clause in the German dialect of Palota, comparing it with the syntactic structure of the Standard German and Hungarian equivalent, respectively (Section 4). Due to limitations of space, only a very limited number of examples will be discussed. In Section 5, I conclude that there are strong structural similarities with the Hungarian equivalents, the lexical material from two unrelated languages sharing a grammatical structure and thus leading to a new emergent bilingual grammar of a fused lect through grammaticalization.

2.   Multilingualism in the speech community of Palota

With a population of 566 people, the village of Palota is located at a distance of about 9 km from the Romanian-Hungarian border. It was founded in the 18th century under the reign of Joseph II. Most of the settlers came from the South-West of Germany; some further settlers came in a later period from the neighboring region of Arad and from the villages of present day Hungary. As a German settlement of the late 18th century however it has a rather isolated position in the region because it lies at a distance of about 100 km from both the nearest German community of the Sathmar region in the north and the German villages of the Arad region in the south. According to the 2002 census, Germans and German-speaking people now represent no more than about half of the population. The other half of the population is covered by members of the Hungarian and Romanian ethnic group.

From a sociolinguistic point of view, the most important thing happening in multilingual Palota today is a change in patterns of language choice (Szabó 2010). Due to its isolated geographical position, the historical-political events (Palota was from the second half of the 19th century until World War II alternately part of Hungary and Romania) and the macrosociological changes (deportation, expropriation of the houses with all the facilities, the loss of land property, mixed marriages, emigration), the German dialect of the community has become the subject of more than one language shift. The first shift from the German dialect to Hungarian started in the late 19th century and almost reached completion by the 1940s. The second shift was to Romanian. It started in the 1940s and became more accentuated after 1945. It has since been accelerated by recent social changes, e.g. changes in the school system with Romanian as the language of instruction, increase of mixed marriages, of commuters, children and young people working or studying outside the village, emigration, etc. The peculiarity of this multilingual situation is that the target language of the first shift in Romania, i.e. Hungarian, had become a minority language itself before the shift was able to reach completion, and the second shift now, i.e. to Romanian, runs parallel to the first, and is hence resulting in a multilingual situation.

There are mainly three languages that are used in the village: German, Hungarian and Romanian. However, German seems to be an inappropriate term for the variety spoken there. The languages that the settlers brought along were different German dialects according to the region they came from. Over time, these dialects evolved closer into one dialect mixture, which came into being as a linguistic habit, norm of a small community, but lacking any necessary resource for standardization. Although it is in fact a mixture of Palatinate and Moselle Franconian dialects (Gehl 2003: 39), German-speaking inhabitants of the village use to call it *Swabian* or simply *unser Sproch* ('our language') and they treat it as a separate language, distinguishing it clearly from Standard German, which is treated as a foreign language and which is not understood by mostly old people.

3.   Data and methodology

The data for this study are extracted from a corpus of approximately 23 hours of audio-recorded interviews that I collected in February 2003 and August-September 2004 as part of my fieldwork for a larger project (Szabó 2010). The project focuses on examining language shift and code-mixing in the multilingual speech community of Palota. Through a combination of ethnographic research, questionnaires and extensive interviews, I gathered different types of data to enable me study a range of topics, such as language use patterns, code-switching and code-mixing in different word classes. In the course of my research, I interviewed 33 speakers all of German descent, both men and women, who were born in Palota and who had lived in the village for their whole lives.[8] They range in age from 3 to 88 at the time of the fieldwork. According to the self-reported language choice patterns, all the speakers are German-dominant and most of them are fluent in the German dialect of the speech community, Hungarian and Romanian. Only elderly people are not familiar with Romanian.

The conversations took place in the homes of the participants, thus providing me with long sketches of informal discourse and quite natural data. They represent conversations usually between two to five participants who are family relatives, friends and neighbors. They deal with a wide range of topics such as everyday life in the village, family stories and affairs, narratives of personal experience in the past, views about ethnic and linguistic development in the village, the German dialect and its status and use, as well as memories of elderly people from the time of deportation into the forced labor camps of the Soviet Union.

---

8.   Personal details, such as place of birth, place of residence as well as ethnic filiation were self-reported by the participants in the questionnaires.

Of the 23 hours of interviews, only selected sections, in which speakers make use of language contact phenomena, such as code-switching or code-mixing, were transcribed and analyzed in detail following a transcription method based on GAT 2 (Selting et al. 2009). Although the language spoken by the participants is a dialectal variety of German, I do not use a phonetic transcription, since a dialectal-phonological analysis is not the subject of this study.

Due to the attested low frequency of subordinate clauses and conjunctions in spoken German dialects, the study does not aim to examine the employment of the UCC and its bilingual conjunction in the German dialect of Palota from a quantitative perspective, but rather from a qualitative one, that reveals a more detailed description of the grammaticalization process leading to a new, bilingual grammar of a fused lect. As there are no equivalent constructions for the concessive conditional in the German dialects, a comparison will be made with the Standard German corresponding constructions on the one hand, and with the Hungarian ones on the other hand. They serve as a building pattern for the bilingual constructions, thus leading to a functional parallelism across languages and yielding further support for the process of grammaticalization.

4. The universal concessive conditional in written/spoken Standard German and in the German dialect of Palota

In present-day written Standard German, the UCC consists of a German *wh*-pronoun and generalizing particles like *auch* and/or *immer* (corresponding to English '-ever'; see Leuschner 1998, 2000, 2005). In fact, it represents a conditional whose protasis states or implies a series of sufficient conditions, exhausting the spectrum of possibilities within a given parameter, for the truth of the apodosis (Leuschner 1998: 161). Thus, the meaning of the UCC comes about compositionally, the irrelevance of the actual protasis value to the truth of the apodosis being achieved by generalizing (*immer* '-ever'), additive (*auch*, corresponding to English 'also, too') or other particles focusing the *wh*-pronoun (Leuschner 1998: 162). This is a very complex construction with a wide range of different forms and a discontinuous structure (Leuschner 2000: 342).[9]

In the German dialect of Palota the role of the conjunction in the UCC is taken up by mixed German-Hungarian indefinite pronouns and indefinite adverbial pronouns consisting of the Hungarian generalizing particle *akár-* (corresponding to German *auch immer* 'ever') and a German interrogative *wh*-pronoun. These bilingual expressions are built according to the Hungarian 'ever'-*wh*-compound pattern.[10]

---

9. For a survey of the typology of concessive conditionals in general and the so-called universal concessive conditional in particular, see Leuschner (1998, 2000, 2005).

10. Taking into account the alternative constructions of the UCC in Standard German *Egal/ Gleichgültig/Gleich, w-* ... ('No matter, wh-') which is the result of a grammaticalization process (for a detailed description of the grammaticalization scale of these constructions see Leuschner

Table 1. Typology of mixed German-Hungarian UCC conjunctions in the German dialect of Palota

German dialect of Palota	Hungarian	Standard German	English translation
ákerwer	akárki	wer auch immer	'whoever'
ákerwas	akármi	was auch immer	'whatever'
ákerwu	akárhol	wo auch immer	'wherever'
ákerwuhin	akárhová	wohin auch immer	'wherever'
ákerwann	akármikor	wann auch immer	'whenever'
ákerwie	akárhogy	wie auch immer	'however'

The range of the forms of this mixed German-Hungarian UCC conjunction employed by the speakers as well as the Hungarian and Standard German equivalents can be seen in Table 1. The first two of them are substantival conjunctions with the German *wh*-pronouns *wer* ('who') and *was* ('what') and the rest constitutes adverbial conjunctions.

Phonologically, there is however one peculiarity: While the pronunciation of the generalizing particle is [ˈɔkaːr] in Standard Hungarian and [ˈakːaːr] in the German dialect of Hajós in the south of Hungary (Földes 2005: 167–171), the speakers of the German dialect in Palota pronounce it as [ˈakər] similar to the forms *åggerwånn* and *åggerwås* in the East-Franconian dialects spoken in Baumgarten in the neighboring Banat region (see Hâncu et al. in preparation).[11]

Excerpt (1) in Section 1 dealt with the adverbial UCC conjunction *ákerwu* ('wherever'). The following two excerpts show the employment of further mixed conjunctions of this type. Expressing her displeasure about the linguistic behavior of the Romanian population of the village who do not greet German people in German or in Hungarian, LJ, the speaker from Excerpt (1), employs the conjunction *ákerwann* ('whenever') in (2) below:

2005: 289–292), one might argue that, conversely, the German dialect rather seems to integrate the Hungarian particle *akár-* resulting into a mixed Hungarian-German conjunction. (I thank an anonymous reviewer for pointing this out.) However, exactly the great productivity of these mixed constructions not only in the German dialects in contact with Hungarian but also in other contact languages – as outlined in Section 1 – suggests that this is not the case here.

11.   With respect to the source of this divergent pronunciation of the Hungarian particle, I do not disagree with an anonymous referee's suggestion that this could be seen in the influence of different regional varieties of Hungarian on the Danube Swabian dialects in present-day Hungary and its neighboring countries, where pronunciations like [ˈɔkɔr], [ˈakar] in the Palóc dialect in the northern Hungarian county Nógrád or [ˈɔkar] in the region Érmellék north of Palota can be found (Lőrinczy et al. 1979: 181f). However, although Földes (2005: 168) mentions that the compounds with the particle *akár-* have been part of the communicative repertoire of the Germans in Hungary for a long period of time, there is not enough evidence for the assumption that this pronunciation was brought to Palota by the settlers who came at a later period to Palota from the northern Hungarian county Heves – the neighboring county of the Nógrád county in the south-east – or from the Arad region.

(2) weil **ákerwann**   i_ hnausgon   of die gass,
     weil wann auch immer ich hinausgegangen auf die Gasse
     'Denn immer wenn ich auf die Straße gehe, ...
     'Because, whenever I'm going on the street, ...

     niemal einmal grießen se   net   ungarisch.
     nicht   einmal grüßen sie nicht Ungarisch
     grüßen sie nicht einmal auf Ungarisch.'
     they are greeting not even in Hungarian.'

In Excerpt (3), TL, a woman in her sixties, talks about the linguistic behavior and education of her niece who lives in Bucharest and has a Romanian father. So, it is clear that the language used in the family is Romanian. She expresses sadness and anger over the unwillingness of her niece to learn German, because, as she argues, that would be to her benefit. In her talk, participant TL uses the adverbial concessive conditional conjunction *ákerwie* ('however'):

(3) há:t (-) **ákerwie**   ich gwollt han, net
     aber   wie auch immer ich gewollt habe nicht
     'Aber so sehr ich es auch wünschte, wollte sie nicht.'
     'But, however I wanted, she didn't want.'

The data also show some occurrences of the substantival conjunctions which, similar to their function as indefinite pronouns, can potentially be inflected. Thus, there are marked forms for *wer* in the accusative (*wen*), genitive (*wessen*) and dativ case (*wem*) and for *was* in the genitive (*wessen*) and dative case (*wem*). However, evidence from the corpus of Palota shows no such inflected forms. In Excerpt (4), LJ employs correctly the conjunction *ákerwer* ('whoever') in the nominative case, while speaking about the trilingual sale assistant from the village shop:

(4) un **ákerwer**   gange   is;
     und wer auch immer gegangen ist
     'Und wer auch immer zu ihr gekommen ist, ...
     'And whoever came to her, ...

     alles hat et gwisst,
     alles hat sie gewusst
     hat sie immer gewusst, ...
     she always knew ...

     wat et zu gen   so wann se schwobisch pockert han.
     was sie zu geben so wann sie schwäbisch verlangt haben
     was sie ihnen geben sollte, wenn sie auf Schwäbisch fragten.'
     what to give as they asked in Swabian.'

The corpus also demonstrates the employment of these mixed bilingual constructions as indefinite pronouns. However, an inflected form could not be attested here either. In

Excerpt (5), MO, a trilingual woman in her sixties, neighbor and a good friend of LJ from excerpts (1) and (2), gives voice to her fear of letting strangers, in particular gypsies in her house:

> (5)   hát   kannst du net   **ákerwer**   in de haus tien.
>   aber kannst du nicht irgendjemand in das Haus tun
>   'Du kannst aber nicht irgendjemanden ins Haus hineinlassen.'
>   'But you can not let anybody enter the house.'

In this excerpt, the form *ákerwer* is in the nominative case, although the correct grammatical form should be *ákerwen* in the accusative case.

To sum up, we have seen in the illustrations above that with regard to the UCC conjunction the German dialect of Palota tends to use grammatical constructions that are less complex as compared to those in the standard language. The German-Hungarian bilingual conjunctions constructed according to the Hungarian pattern are on the one hand less complex and on the other hand more economic and transparent than the analytical forms of Standard German, which consist of a *wh*-pronoun and the generalizing particles *auch* or/and *immer*. We can, therefore, say that this lack of complexity and its economic and transparent facets are the major motivation for this kind of bilingual behavior in the speech community of Palota.

Due to the less complex structure of this clause type in the German dialect of Palota, it is likely that, comparing it to the written and spoken Standard German UCC, there are also differences in the field structure. Moreover, it is quite possible that there is some similarity with the field structure of the Hungarian concessive conditional clause. In order to examine this aspect, I take first the concessive conditional clause in Excerpt (2) and analyze it while comparing it in Table 2 with constructed written as well as spoken Standard German forms:

Table 2. Field structure of UCC in Excerpt (2). The first line of the table represents the written, the second line the spoken clause in Standard German. The third line contains the clause in the German dialect of Palota.

Pre-front field	Front field	Left brace	Middle field	Right brace	End field
	Wann ich auch immer auf die Straße gehe	grüßen	Sie nicht einmal auf Ungarisch.		
Wann ich auch immer auf die Straße gehe	sie	grüßen	nicht einmal auf Ungarisch.		
ákerwann i_hnausgon of die gass	niemal einmal	grüßen	se net ungarisch		

A look at the field structure of the whole spoken Standard German clause shows the position of the UCC in front of the front field. This structure is possible, because, as Auer (1996: 295ff, 299ff) suggests, the syntax of the spoken German is more liberal as that of the written form, where there is a restriction that the front field, also called topic position, may be occupied by exactly one constituent. Thus, it shares the characteristic feature of all pre-front field structures, i.e. to project syntactically into the following space without defining one particular syntactic unit.

Examining the field structure of the UCC in Standard German (both written and spoken) we can see a structure as illustrated in Table 3. The example shows that the position of the generalizing particle is relocatable. The particles *auch* and *immer* can occur together or they can alternate, in some cases being used only the particle *auch* and in other cases only the particle *immer*.

In the German dialect of Palota (line 3 in Table 2), we can see that on the level of the whole clause there is no difference between it and the spoken Standard German construction, the UCC taking the position of the pre-front field. However, as Table 4 shows, the field structure of the UCC differs in some points from that of the spoken Standard German sentence: First, there are no generalizing particles with a variable position in the middle field, and second, the adverbial was moved from the middle field to the end of the clause in a position after the right brace; this is a characteristic feature of subordinate clauses in German dialects (Wolf 1987: 244).

The position of the finite verb in a subordinate clause, i.e. not at the very end of the clause is, however, not at all uniform in the German dialect of Palota, as exemplified in the UCC in Excerpt (3) where the finite verb takes the position of the right brace (see Table 5).

A look at the field structure of the constructed Hungarian UCC of Excerpt (2) in Table 6 reveals similar patterns of the concessive conditional in the German dialect of Palota and in Hungarian.

Table 3. Field structure of UCC in written and spoken Standard German
(GP = generalizing particle, S = subject)

	Left brace	Middle field				Right brace	
Front field	*wh*-pronoun	GP	S	GP	Adverbial	Verb	End field
–	Wann	auch immer	ich	–	auf die Straße	gehe	–
–	Wann	–	ich	auch immer	auf die Straße	gehe	–
–	Wann	immer	ich	–	auf die Straße	gehe	–

Table 4. Field structure of the UCC in the German dialect of Palota (GP = generalizing particle, S = subject)

Front field	Left brace *wh*-pronoun	Middle field GP	S	GP	Adverbial	Right brace Verb	End field
–	ákerwann	–	i	–	–	hnausgon	of die gass

Table 5. Field structure of UCC in Excerpt (3) (GP = generalizing particle, S = subject)

Front field	Left brace *wh*-pronoun	Middle field GP	S	GP	Adverbial	Right brace Verb	End field
–	ákerwie	–	ich	–	–	gwollt han	–

Table 6. Field structure of the UCC in Excerpt (2) in the German dialect of Palota and in Hungarian (GP = generalizing particle, S = subject)

Front field	Left brace *wh*-pronoun	Middle field GP	S	GP	Adverbial	Right brace Verb	End field
–	ákerwann	–	i	–	–	hnausgon	of die gass
–	akármikor	–	–	–	–	kimegyek	az utcára
–	akármikor	is	–	–	–	kimegyek	az utcára

Thus, in both varieties all positions for generalizing particles and adverbials of the middle field are empty. However, in Hungarian, like in Standard German, there is also a possibility to introduce the Hungarian particle *is* (StG *auch*, 'also, too') in the middle field of the clause.

5. Concluding remarks

A detailed examination of the material presented above has shown that the transfer of the Hungarian generalizing particle *akár-* fills a gap in the recipient language, the German dialect of Palota, by expressing a concessive conditional semantic relation that was non-existent in the language before contact. The close comparison of the structure of the conjunctions that introduce this subordinate clause type as well as the field structure in written and spoken Standard German, in the German dialect of Palota and in Hungarian has revealed strong similarities with the Hungarian equivalents. I would, therefore, like to suggest that in the case of the mixed bilingual conjunctions employed by the speakers a process of congruent lexicalization is at work, since the material comes from two different lexical inventories that share a grammatical structure (Muysken 2000: 3, 122).

Moreover, these mixed German-Hungarian constructions, although they can function as indefinite pronouns too, as we have seen in Section 4, have specialized in function, i.e. they are used to introduce a certain type of subordinate clause, hence pointing to a grammaticalization process into an emergent bilingual grammar. The fact that e.g. no structural contrast was observed between conjunctions and indefinite pronouns seems to support Maschler's (2000: 557) conclusion, according to which a separation via language alternation would prevent a full grammaticalization into a fused lect. She concludes further that "as long as codeswitching is a 'living strategy' for the bilingual ..., this operates as a force preventing full grammaticization into a fused lect" (Maschler 2000: 557). Since these mixed conjunctions are the only resources available for the speakers to express a concessive conditional semantic relationship, i.e. there are no monolingual German alternatives for them in the mixed German dialect of this speech community, and since there is no variation of these forms, not even of the compounds with the German interrogative pronouns *wer* and *was*, the use of the bilingual conjunctions in this type of clause is obligatory; it is part of the grammar of the mixed dialect and speakers have no other choice. The meaning and the functional specialization of the bilingual conjunctions, however, go back to the meaning and syntactic function of the structurally equivalent monolingual Hungarian conjunctions, thus supporting Maschler's claim that "there exist parallel pathways of grammaticization for discourse markers in various unrelated languages" (Maschler 2002: 271).

Returning to the typology by Auer (1998b), the German dialect of Palota seems to be likely to develop into a fused lect. As Auer (1998b: 15) suggests, "given the appropriate sociolinguistic context, there is a tendency in communities of speakers who code-mix to further constrain the possibilities of juxtaposing the two languages and to develop functional specializations". Since several cases of code-mixing were observed in the verbal phrase, noun phrase as well as by discourse markers, adverbials, particles and conjunctions (see Szabó 2010), I would like to suggest that in the case of the concessive conditional conjunction the movement along the continuum suggested by Auer does indeed proceed in the code-switching → language mixing → fused lects direction, although the existence of an initial code-switching-stage remains only an assumption, as there are no written historical documents about language usage in the speech community of Palota which would permit research into historical language contact. However, the mixed German-Hungarian concessive conditional conjunctions as well as indefinite pronouns seem to relate to the borrowing hierarchies suggested by Matras (2009: 161–162)[12]: (14c) "concessive, conditional, causal, purpose > other subordinators" and (13c) "indefinites > interrogatives > (other) deixis, anaphora". Matras (2009: 162) considers that the explanation for these hierarchies as well as the motivating factor for borrowings lies in "the potential clash between hearer-sided and

---

12. I thank an anonymous reviewer for suggesting this point to me.

speaker-sided attitudes and expectations, a consequent relative rise in interactional tension and intensity of the speaker-sided processing, and greater likelihood to lose control of the selection and inhibition mechanism". Taking this pragmatic perspective, it can be assumed that the mixed German-Hungarian concessive conditional conjunctions and indefinite pronouns might have originated in a stage of code-switching.

Thus, language mixing does not develop towards a loss but rather towards an increase of linguistic structure (Auer 1998b: 15). For the German-speaking inhabitants of the multilingual speech community examined here, it probably means a chance to continue using the German dialect that can express several semantic relations, even though it is a mixed language undergoing language shift still in progress towards Hungarian.

References

Auer, P. 1996. The pre-front field in spoken German and its relevance as a grammaticalization position. *Pragmatics* 6: 295–322.

Auer, P. 1998a. Introduction: Bilingual conversation revisited. In *Codeswitching in Conversation*, ed. P. Auer, 1–24. London: Routledge.

Auer, P. 1998b. From codeswitching via language mixing to fused lects: Toward a dynamic typology of bilingual speech. *Interaction and Linguistic Structures* 6: 1–28.

Földes, C. 2005. *Kontaktdeutsch: Zur Theorie eines Varietätentyps unter transkulturellen Bedingungen von Mehrsprachigkeit.* Tübingen: Narr.

Gehl, H. 1994. Deutsch-ungarische Sprachinterferenzen. In *Interferenzen in den Sprachen und Dialekten Südosteuropas*, eds. H. Gehl & M. Purdela-Sitaru, 161–211. Tübingen: Institut für Donauschwäbische Geschichte und Landeskunde.

Gehl, H. 2003. *Wörterbuch der donauschwäbischen Landwirtschaft.* Stuttgart: Steiner.

Hâncu, E., I. Irimescu, A. Ivănescu, P. Kottler & M. Şandor, eds. In preparation. *Wörterbuch der Banater deutschen Mundarten.*

Knecht, T. 1999. Lexikalische Interferenzen aus dem Rumänischen und Ungarischen in den schwäbischen Dialekten von Beschened und Petrifeld. In *Interethnische Beziehungen im rumänisch-ungarisch-ukrainischen Kontaktraum vom 18. Jahrhundert bis zur Gegenwart*, eds. H. Gehl & V. Ciubotă, 345–374. Satu Mare: Muzeului Sătmărean & Tübingen: Institut für Donauschwäbische Geschichte und Landeskunde.

Knecht, T. 2001. Lexikalische Interferenzen in den sathmarschwäbischen Dialekten der Gemeinden Bescheneed, Petrifeld und Terem. In *Dialekt – Lehnwörter – Namen. Sprachliche Studien über die Sathmarer Schwaben*, ed. H. Gehl, 53–114. Tübingen: Institut für Donauschwäbische Geschichte und Landeskunde.

Leuschner, T. 1998. At the boundaries of grammaticalization: What interrogatives are doing in concessive conditionals. In *The Limits of Grammaticalization* (Typological Studies in Language 37), eds. A. G. Ramat & P. J. Hopper, 159–187. Amsterdam: John Benjamins.

Leuschner, T. 2000. "..., *wo immer* es mir begegnet, ... – *wo* es *auch* sei". Zur Distribution von 'Irrelevanzpartikeln' in Nebensätzen mit *w- auch/immer. Deutsche Sprache* 28: 342–356.

Leuschner, T. 2005. Ob blond, ob braun, ich liebe alle Frau'n. Irrelevanzkonditionalen als grammatikalisierter Diskurs. In *Grammatikalisierung im Deutschen*, eds. T. Leuschner, T. Mortelmans & S. de Groodt, 279–307. Berlin: Mouton de Gruyter.

Lőrinczy, É. B., F. Hosszú, É. Balogh & L. Balogh, eds. 1979. *Új magyar tájszótár.* Band 1 A–D. Budapest: Akadémiai kiadó.

Maschler, Y. 1997. Emergent bilingual grammar: The case of contrast. *Journal of Pragmatics* 28: 279–313.

Maschler, Y. 2000. Toward fused lects: Discourse markers in Hebrew-English bilingual conversation twelve years later. *International Journal of Bilingualism* 4: 529–561.

Maschler, Y. 2002. On the grammaticization of *ke'ilu* 'like', lit. 'as if', in Hebrew talk-in-interaction. *Language in Society* 31: 243–276.

Matras, Y. 2000. Fusion and the cognitive basis for bilingual discourse markers. *International Journal of Bilingualism* 4: 505–528.

Matras, Y. 2009. *Language Contact.* Cambridge: CUP.

Muysken, P. 2000. *Bilingual Speech: A Typology of Code-mixing.* Cambridge: CUP.

Orsós, A. & L. Kálmán. 2009. *Beás nyelvtan.* Budapest: Tinta Könyvk.

Post, R. 1992. *Pfälzisch: Einführung in eine Sprachlandschaft.* Landau: Pfälzische Verlagsanstalt.

Rostás-Farkas, G. & E. Karsai. 2001. *Cigány-magyar, magyar-cigány szótár.* Budapest: Kossuth.

Selting, M., P. Auer, D. Barth-Weingarten, J. Bergmann, P. Bergmann, K. Birkner, E. Couper-Kuhlen, A. Deppermann, P. Gilles, S. Günthner, M. Hartung, F. Kern, C. Mertzlufft, C. Meyer, M. Morek, F. Oberzaucher, J. Peters, U. Quasthoff, W. Schütte, A. Stukenbrock & S. Uhmann. 2009. Gesprächsanalytisches Transkriptionssystem 2 (GAT 2). *Gesprächsforschung* 10: 353–402.

Szabó, C.-A. 2010. *Language Shift und Code-mixing: Deutsch-ungarisch-rumänischer Sprachkontakt in einer dörflichen Gemeinde in Nordwestrumänien.* Frankfurt: Peter Lang.

Wolf, J. 1987. *Banater deutsche Mundartenkunde.* Bukarest: Kriterion.

The formation and distribution of the analytic future tense in Polish-German bilinguals*

Bernhard Brehmer and Agnieszka Czachór
University of Hamburg, Germany

The paper deals with the formation and use of the two variants of the analytic future tense in Polish by Polish-German bilinguals. Two groups of Polish-German bilinguals were examined: (i) early bilinguals who were already born in Germany or came to Germany before entering school (= heritage speakers), (ii) late bilinguals who moved to Germany at least after finishing school in Poland. The data were taken from elicited narratives and an acceptability judgment task and were compared to data from a monolingual Polish control group. The analysis showed that the formal restrictions for composing the analytic future tense in Polish (i.e. selection of the imperfective aspect) are not really vulnerable to attrition in both bilingual groups. There are, however, differences in the distribution of the two forms of the analytic future tense. The early bilinguals tend to use the combination auxiliary + infinitive of the main verb more frequently since it (i) replicates the corresponding German pattern for the formation of the analytic future, and (ii) allows for not specifying certain grammatical features (e.g. gender), thus reducing the cognitive load for the speaker. The late bilinguals even prefer the combination auxiliary + l-participle to a higher degree than the controls. This could point to a desire to avoid the pattern that is extant in the surrounding language German, but also to a general preference for colloquial features due to reduced exposure to written forms of Standard Polish.

Keywords: Polish, German, bilingualism, contact-induced change, tense/aspect system, analytic future, heritage speakers, first generation immigrants

---

* The research presented here was supported by a grant from the German Science Foundation (Deutsche Forschungsgemeinschaft, DFG) for the project H8 "Current Polish-German Bilingualism in Germany" within the Collaborative Research Center on Multilingualism (Sonderforschungsbereich 538 "Mehrsprachigkeit") at the University of Hamburg. Furthermore, the authors would like to express their gratitude to Tomke Brüggemann for assistance in statistically testing the data and two anonymous reviewers for their valuable comments on earlier drafts of this paper.

1.   Introduction

One of the most remarkable traits of the Polish verbal system is the coexistence of three regular means for expressing the future tense[1]. Besides the formal and functional distinction between the perfective future and the imperfective future, which can be found in other North Slavic languages as well (see Section 2), the peculiarity of Polish consists in the duality of two analytic ways of expressing the future tense. Both variants are derived from the imperfective aspect and use the same auxiliary (the synthetic future form of *być* 'to be') but with a different form of the main verb: either the infinitive or the so called l-participle (see Section 3). Whereas the first analytic form with the infinitive is known from a lot of Indo-European languages (e.g. German, English or Russian), the latter continues the original form of the *futurum exactum* in Old Church Slavic (see Birnbaum 1958: 21f)[2]. However, as is claimed by most linguists (e.g. Mönke 1971: 91), both forms denote the simple future tense and are thus semantically equivalent as early as from the onset of the history of written Polish.

Our paper addresses the question how Polish-German bilingual speakers build and use the analytic future tense in their L1 Polish. Bearing in mind the fact that one of the two competing forms has a direct parallel in German (namely the form with the infinitive) we suppose that there might be cross-linguistic effects influencing the frequency and distribution of the two analytic ways of expressing future tense in Polish. For this purpose, we gathered data from two different groups of Polish-German bilinguals by eliciting spontaneous speech as well as using an acceptability judgment task (see Section 5). The data were compared to data from a monolingual Polish control group to reveal potential differences in the use of the analytic future tense by the three groups.

2.   Tense and aspect in Polish

As in all other North Slavic languages[3], tense and verbal aspect cannot be treated independently in Polish. Evidence from language acquisition supports this view since tense

---

1.   Apart from the three forms morphologically marked for future tense in Polish, it is also possible to use present tense forms to denote future events. However, the use of this *praesens propheticum* in Polish is clearly restricted to a limited set of contexts if compared to other languages, e.g. German (see Czochralski 1972: 275–277, Mönke 1971: 23–40).

2.   It is not clear whether the compound future form with the l-participle is really a direct formal continuation of the *futurum exactum* which can be found in Old Church Slavic texts. Mönke (1971: 93ff) argues for an independent development of the l-participle analytic future tense in Polish.

3.   In South Slavic languages, there is no comparable distinction between synthetic and analytic future forms: the future tense is expressed only via an analytical form where the main verb can be imperfective or perfective.

and aspect morphology emerge simultaneously in Polish (Smoczyńska 1985: 647). For the purpose of the present paper, the following quote from a grammar of Standard Polish concisely illustrating the relationship between tense and aspect will suffice:

> Any given Polish verb can be assigned to one of the two aspects, perfective or imperfective. In general, perfectives indicate that the verbal action represents a complete whole, rather than a continuing process or repetition. One of the possible meanings of perfective verbs has been referred to as "change of state" ..., as opposed to a continuing, unchanged state that uses the imperfective ... The imperfective can be used when no particular emphasis is being placed on whether the action was complete or incomplete, i.e. when that factor is irrelevant to the speaker ... In the present tense, there is no aspectual opposition. When imperfectives use the present tense series of endings ..., the meaning is that of present tense, but when perfectives use the very same endings, the meaning is that of a completed action in the future ... The imperfective creates its future by means of the auxiliary construction ... Outside of the present and future, both aspects have a regular opposition without the use of auxiliary verbs, that is, in such parts of the paradigm as the past tense, infinitive, imperative, past participles, and even the verbal noun (Feldstein 2001: 100).

From the point of view of morphology, perfective verbs are often (though not necessarily) marked by prefixes (e.g. *zrobić* 'to do $_{\text{PERFECTIVE}}$' vs. *robić* 'to do $_{\text{IMPERFECTIVE}}$') whereas imperfectivity is mostly indicated by special suffixes (e.g. *dostawać* 'to get $_{\text{IMPERFECTIVE}}$' vs. *dostać* 'to get $_{\text{PERFECTIVE}}$')[4] or the absence of prefixes.

3.   The formation of the future tense in Polish

As was already indicated in the quotation from Feldstein (2001) in Section 2, perfective and imperfective Polish verbs form the future tense in different ways. Perfective verbs convey future events when they are used with the same inflections that would denote present tense with their imperfective counterparts. Thus the perfective future is formed synthetically, e.g. *napiszę* 'I will write $_{\text{PF}}$', with {na} being the prefix indicating perfectivity, and {ę} being the inflection for first person singular (with perfective and imperfective verbs). Imperfective verbs, however, form the future analytically by using the inflected synthetic future form of the auxiliary *być* 'to be' plus the main verb which can occur in two forms: The first variant uses the infinitive (e.g. *będę pisać* 'I will write $_{\text{INF.IPF}}$'), whereas the second is built with the so called l-participle, since it historically represents an active past participle (e.g. *będę pisał* 'I will write $_{\text{PART.MASC.SING.IPF}}$'). The main functional difference between these two variants lies in the fact that the l-participle

---

4.   In what follows, we will use the abbreviations *pf.* for 'perfective' and *ipf.* for 'imperfective', respectively.

is inflected for grammatical gender and number. Thus, it contains more information about the subject than the competing form with the infinitive, where the inflected form of the auxiliary indicates person and number, but not gender.

The distribution of perfective and imperfective future forms is generally motivated by their aspectual distinctions, i.e. it is not a function of the future itself (see Czochralski 1972: 280ff or Wierzbicki 1999: 182ff). There has been, however, some discussion in the literature about the distribution of the two imperfective future forms, which will be summarized in the next section.

4.   The relationship between the two analytic future forms in Polish

Considerable attention has been paid to the diachronic development of the ratio between the frequencies of the two compound future forms in Polish texts (see Cyran 1961, Mönke 1971: 92ff, Zagrodnikowa 1972, Proeme 1991 or Pawlak 1997). It is generally acknowledged that both forms are present from the very onset of the occurrence of texts written in Polish in the 14th century. Until the middle of the 15th century, the infinitive form clearly prevails, but since then the participle form has steadily increased at the expense of the infinitive form (Cyran 1961). In texts from as early as the 16th century, the compound form with the participle quantitatively outweighs its alternative, at least in the singular, but from the 17th century also in the plural (Zagrodnikowa 1972: 351ff). However, according to Zagrodnikowa (1972: 355), there are some indications of a secondary expansion of the infinitive form in the 19th century. This expansion led, as Zagrodnikowa claims, also to a higher frequency of the infinitive form in some types of written Polish (mainly newspaper texts) in the middle of the 20th century. The preponderance of the infinitive in comparison to the participle form in newspaper texts of the 1980s and early 1990s is also attested to by Pawlak (1997: 142f). She concludes her investigation of the frequency of the two competing forms in different text genres by stating that the more colloquial the language use in the texts, the clearer is the preference for the participle form against the infinitive. The high frequency of the infinitive form in newspaper texts represents according to Pawlak (and already Zagrodnikowa 1972: 358) a tendency to replicate foreign patterns[5]. Furthermore, she claims that the official and ceremonial style of newspaper texts in late socialist Poland would favor the use of the infinitive (taking up an argument first proposed by Proeme 1991: 186). To sum up this line of argumentation, according to most of the researchers

---

5.   Pawlak (1997: 143) mentions English, German and Russian as possible sources, since all three languages have the same analytic pattern with the infinitive to express future tense. At least with regard to socialist times a replication of Russian patterns in newspaper texts seems plausible. Cyran (1961: 224) identifies puristic resistance against replicating German and Russian patterns as a possible motivating factor for the expansion of the participle form in the history of Polish.

the participle form is nowadays the preferred mode for expressing the analytic future tense in colloquial speech, whereas the infinitive is more frequently used only in some rather formal genres of written Polish.

Thus the difference between the two forms is seemingly due to their different stylistic values and not to semantic distinctions[6]. However, much effort has been invested in proving that the two forms do not alternate completely at random in Polish texts. One of the factors that have been identified as having an impact on the actual distribution of the two competing forms is the *word order* of the components[7]. Thus, according to Nitsch (1956: 194), the occurrence of the two forms depends on the word order of the auxiliary and the main verb form: Both forms can occur in normal word order, i.e. if the auxiliary precedes the main verb form (*będę pisać/pisał*), whereas in inverted order (called "szyk odwrotny" or "szyk przestawiony" = 'reversed order') only the infinitive form is possible (*pisać będę*, but not **pisał będę*, which is considered a regionally marked form and not acceptable for speakers of Standard Polish)[8]. This claim was corroborated by counts of the occurrence of the respective word order patterns in contemporary Polish prose by Proeme (1991: 194) and Pawlak (1997: 140).

Another factor which apparently has an influence on the distribution of the two forms is the *gender and number* of the subject. Nitsch (1956: 192) observed a firm pattern of distribution of the two forms in some Polish dialects which depended on the grammatical gender of the subject: For masculine subjects, the speakers used only the l-participle form, whereas female and neuter subjects were only or at least predominantly associated with the infinitive form. In plural contexts the trend was not as clear as in the singular, but the dialect speakers preferred the infinitive form in these instances. Nitsch (1956) tried to account for this distribution by pointing out the fact that the feminine, neuter and plural l-participle forms consist of an additional syllable in comparison to the form of the masculine l-participle and the infinitive (cf. feminine:

---

6.   Only Proeme (1991) tries to identify differences between the two compound forms on the semantic level. However, he admits that "the two forms cannot have different referential meanings – [they] can only present the situation in a slightly different way – shed a different light on it" (Proeme 1991: 200). According to him, the infinitive form, for instance, serves "to focus on the intention to do the thing mentioned rather than on the event mentioned itself" (Proeme 1991: 217).

7.   For an overview of the different accounts in Polish grammars on the supposed complementary distribution of the two forms with regard to the placement of auxiliary and main verb see Mönke (1971: 80ff) and Proeme (1991: 182ff).

8.   However, Nitsch (1956: 194) states that in reversed order the infinitive form sounds more natural only when it is accompanied by negation. Furthermore, he notes that in older grammars the word order auxiliary + infinitive was considered a *calque* of German and rejected by normative grammarians who therefore claimed (or rather prescribed) a complementary distribution between the two forms depending on the placement of auxiliary and main verb: *będę pisał* (AUX + l-participle), but *pisać będę* (infinitive + AUX).

będę pisał-a, neuter: *będzie pisał-o*, plural: *będą pisal-i/pisał-y* vs. masculine: *będę pisał* and infinitive: *będę pisać*). According to him, this preference for the shorter form seems to be the reason why the mentioned correlations were established (Nitsch 1956: 195).[9] Other linguists later tried to apply these observations to samples of written Standard Polish. It turned out that, for masculine singular subjects, the tendency to combine with the participle form can be established for Standard Polish as well. However, the interdependence between feminine and neuter subjects in the singular and a respective preference for the infinitive form is far less regular than in Nitsch's data on dialects (see, e.g., Mönke 1971: 99f, Proeme 1991: 198, Pawlak 1997: 140). With regard to plural forms, Proeme (1991: 198) states that for male personal subjects, there is a strong predominance to select the infinitive form (76% in his data), whereas with non-male personal subjects[10] the ratio resembles that of feminine and neuter singular subjects which is close to fifty-fifty[11].

Other factors that have been said to have an influence on the choice of one of the two compound future forms include syntactic restrictions: Modals or other verb types that are followed by an infinitive as a complement do normally select the l-participle form in order to avoid the clash of two infinitives: *będę musiał pisać* 'I will have to write' instead of *?będę musieć pisać* (Mönke 1971: 101)[12]. Furthermore, infinitive forms seem to be preferred in subordinate clauses and for phonological reasons with verbs that contain [w] (graphically represented as <ł>) in their stems, cf. *będę działać* 'I will function' instead of *?będę działał* (Mönke 1971: 102f).

---

9.   Pawlak (1997: 143) offers an alternative explanation: Since the infinitive form is not inflected for gender, she sees a parallel in the use of not inflected forms of titles or names of occupations when referring to female referents, e.g. *rozmawiam z doktor Nowak* 'I talk to doctor Nowak' (where absence of inflection indicates the female sex of Dr Nowak) instead of *rozmawiam z doktorem Nowakiem* (where Dr Nowak is male).

10.   Polish distinguishes between two genders in the plural: the male personal or virile gender (for animate male personal, i.e. virile referents) and the non-male personal gender (for the remaining semantic classes of referents).

11.   Proeme (1991: 199), however, underlines a high degree of idiolectal variation with regard to the correlation between the gender of the subject and the preference for one of the two competing forms of the compound future tense. This means that some of the Polish authors he investigated are highly reluctant to use the infinitive form in all genders and numbers, whereas others tend to use it even with masculine subjects in the singular.

12.   This restriction does not hold for Old Polish, but it is established in texts written after the 16th century (Mönke 1971: 105ff). Proeme (1991: 194f) states that this restriction does not apply for all modal verbs to the same degree: In his data, *chcieć* 'want', *musieć* 'must' and *móc* 'can' never occur with the infinitive compound future form, but *mieć* 'should' does, although not very frequently.

5. Study design and research questions

5.1 Participants of the study

The study reported here is part of a larger research project on language attrition among Polish speaking immigrants in Germany[13]. We focus on potential attrition in several grammatical domains (case, gender assignment, tense and aspect, word order etc.). The general aim of the project is to determine (i) which of the investigated domains are more vulnerable to attrition than others and (ii) which role German as the surrounding (and often already dominant) language of our informants plays in inducing grammatical change. For this purpose, we compare data from three different groups:

The subjects of the first group could be called heritage speakers of Polish since they consist of young adults who were born in Germany to Polish speaking families[14] or moved to Germany before the age of six, i.e. before entering school. Therefore, they acquired their L1 Polish only within the family and were never exposed to formal schooling in Polish. Contact with German started at least in kindergarten, i.e. from age three. Thus this group will be called early bilinguals (EB) throughout the paper.

The second group consists of informants who finished school in Poland and came to Germany after the age of 15. They have been living in Germany for an uninterrupted period of at least two years. In contrast to the first group, it can be assumed that they completely acquired their L1 Polish before the onset of the acquisition of German, which is clearly an L2 for them. Thus they could be classified as first generation speakers of Polish in Germany who might have undergone some attrition in their L1 Polish. They will be referred to as the late bilingual group (LB).

Data from these two groups were compared to a group of controls who were recorded in Warsaw. They never acquired German as a foreign language and never lived abroad for a longer period of time ($\geq$ one year). With regard to their sociolinguistic characteristics (e.g., age, sex, educational background etc.), they were selected to match the characteristics of the EB. For reasons of convenience we will call them "monolinguals" (ML). Table 1 gives an overview of the three subject groups.

---

13. Following Polinsky (1997: 370) we use 'attrition' as an umbrella term to denote any form of deviant grammar of our informants concerning their L1 Polish which results either from "forgetting the language system by a non-aphasic speaker (most commonly due to the influence of another dominant language, as in emigration)" [= attrition in a strict sense, see, e.g., Schmid 2008] or from a "process whereby a given grammar system undergoes a significant reduction (under conditions of immigration) when it is passed from one generation to the next, i.e. incomplete learning of the language system".

14. In order to keep this sample as homogeneous as possible, we included only people in the sample whose parents were both L1 speakers of Polish.

Table 1. Participants of the present study

Participants	Early bilinguals		Late bilinguals		Monolinguals	
N	30		30		30	
sex (male: female)	10	20	10	20	10	20
mean age	22,5		37,3		24,1	
mean age at first exposure to German	2,0		25,1		–	
mean exposure to German	20 years		12 years		–	

5.2   Data collection procedure

The data used for the present analysis are taken from two sources. First, we use semi-spontaneous speech data which were gathered through an elicited narrative. In order to make our informants use as many analytic imperfective future forms as possible, their task was to tell how they imagine life in the year 3000. To guarantee a comparable amount of data for all three groups, the test instructor ensured that every single narrative lasted for approximately five minutes. The narratives were recorded and then transcribed using the EXMARaLDA tools[15]. All instances of analytic future tense forms were coded according to the following criteria: aspect of the verb (ipf. vs. pf.); form of the main verb (infinitive vs. l-participle); person; number; gender of the subject.

For the second type of data we used a bimodal acceptability judgment task. The informants were presented with sentences in random order on a computer screen which they had to judge for their correctness. The test battery included altogether 32 sentences to test possible attrition effects regarding the tense-aspect-system of Polish, but only 14 were designed to describe future events. Half of them contained an analytic future tense form, so they will be our primary concern here[16]. This sample of 7 test items included sentences that corresponded to the norms of Standard Polish (n = 1) as well as sentences violating them (n = 6). The violations consisted of analytic forms that were derived from perfective verbs (n = 5, e.g. *będziemy zrobili* 'we will do $_{\text{PART.MASC-PERS.PL.PF}}$') as well as one analytic form where an auxiliary was combined with a synthetic perfective future form (*będę poleżę na plaży* 'I will lie $_{\text{1.SING.PF}}$ on the beach'). Therefore, the aim of this task was to check whether our bilingual subjects still recognize the formal rules underlying the formation of the analytic future forms in Polish (see Section 6.1. below). All sentences that were rejected by our informants were presented to them again at the end of the task and the informants were asked to give

---

15.   See <http://www.exmaralda.org> (8 June 2012).

16.   The other test items represented sentences with synthetic perfective future forms as well as sentences where present tense forms were used to convey future events. A separate study will deal with the judgment of these items in comparison with the results of the judgment on the analytic future forms, which is presented in this paper.

reasons for their decision. This procedure should make sure that they rejected the sentences precisely because of the wrong aspect.

5.3   Research questions and hypotheses

Since the future tense in German is expressed via analytic means that are identical to one of the analytic forms in Polish, namely the combination of the future form of the auxiliary *sein* 'to be' plus the infinitive of the main verb (e.g. *Ich werde schreiben* 'I will write'), we expect cross-linguistics effects to occur in the data of our bilingual subjects. More specifically, we will focus on three research questions in this paper:

RQ 1:   *Do our bilingual data provide evidence for L1 attrition with regard to the formation of the analytic future tense in Polish?*

Since aspect as a fully grammaticalized verbal category is missing in German, it might be the case that aspect is either not completely acquired by the informants of our EB group or vulnerable to loss in our LB group. If this is the case, the failure to distinguish between imperfective and perfective verbs should have consequences for the formation of the analytic future tense. Therefore, we would expect that our bilingual subjects show errors already on this formal level by using the analytic form with perfective verbs.

RQ 2a: *Are there differences regarding the relative frequency of the two compound future tense forms between our three groups?*

As the German analytic future form supports only one of the two competing patterns in Polish, we expect that the infinitive variant should be overrepresented in the bilingual data if compared to the controls. More specifically, we expect a gradual increase of the frequency of the infinitive form from the ML to the LB and finally to the EB group at the expense of the participle form. Given the fact that the participle form is said to clearly prevail in colloquial Polish (see Section 4), it should be the dominant (if not the only preferred) form in the oral narratives of our ML, whereas the German model should positively impact on the frequency of the infinitive form in our bilingual groups. This seems even more plausible regarding the fact that the variant with the infinitive represents a normatively approved form in Polish, i.e. it must not be considered a negative transfer from German by our bilingual informants. Therefore, the question arises whether this could really be called an instance of 'attrition' in its traditional sense (see Footnote 13). If we consider the main difference between the two analytic forms a stylistic one, we could claim that attrition in this special case manifests itself in a failure to recognize the stylistic values of the two competing forms. What is getting attrited, then, is rather the knowledge about possible variation than the knowledge of grammatical rules.

Additionally, another focus will be on the distribution of the two forms in our data:

RQ 2b: *Which of the factors discussed in Section 4 (i.e., word order, gender/number of the subject) influence the distribution of the two analytic forms in our data?*

If we are indeed witnessing the expansion of the infinitive form in our bilingual data, the question is which of the factors mentioned in Section 4 as regulating the distribution of the two forms is less decisive for our bilingual informants in choosing between the variants. Thus we assume that the variation between the two alternative forms should be more at random for our bilingual groups but depend on the influence of features like word order, gender or number of the subject etc. in our control group.

RQ 1 will be addressed on the basis of both available data sets (i.e. the elicited narratives as well as the acceptability judgment task), whereas the investigation of RQs 2a and 2b must rely, as a matter of fact, on the data taken from the elicited narratives alone.

6. Results

6.1 Verbal aspect and the formation of the analytic future tense (RQ 1)

This subsection deals with data regarding the formal restriction in Polish that the compound future tense can only be derived from imperfective verbs. Grammars of Standard Polish explicitly state that a violation of this rule clearly makes one sound like a non-native in Polish: "The auxiliary *będę* may not under any circumstances be combined with perfective verbs. Such a combination produces a serious grammatical error" (Swan 2002: 257).[17] The performance of our bilingual informants provides support for the claim that the restriction of the analytic future tense to imperfective verbs poses no problems for speakers who have acquired Polish as L1. Two pieces of evidence can be mentioned here: (i) Violations of this rule occur very infrequently in our data; (ii) they are restricted to one of the examined groups, namely the heritage speakers (EB). But even in the EB group they represent rather idiosyncratic cases of deviations from the norm as will be shown in the discussion of the errors found in the data of this group (a) in the acceptability judgment task and (b) in the oral narratives.

a. Among the six test sentences in our acceptability judgment task where the analytic future tense occurred with a perfective verb, only three were sporadically accepted by our informants of the EB group. But even with these three seemingly

---

17. Such errors, however, do occur in Polish child language, although they are restricted to the initial phases of the acquisition of the tense system in Polish and children frequently correct themselves after having used an analytic future form with a perfective verb (Smoczyńska 1985: 648). Furthermore, this tendency finds a parallel in the historical development of Polish: According to Mönke (1971: 72), perfective verbs occurred in analytic future tense constructions sporadically in Old Polish texts, but such constructions totally disappeared no later than in the 19th century.

"critical" test sentences the bulk of errors occurred in the data of rather few individuals. Thus, out of 90 judgments on these three sentences in the EB group (3 sentences x 30 informants), only 14 judgments turned out to be incorrect, which corresponds to a general correctness rate of 82%. Even for the sentence that produced the highest amount of judgment errors (n = 7, i.e. half of the incorrect judgments in the whole group), the correctness rate was still 77%. With regard to the individual level, two informants failed in rejecting all of the three "critical" sentences, another three subjects had problems in judging two of them. This could lead to the conclusion that the aspect system in Polish seemingly represents no vulnerable domain even for the EB group. However, a look at related formal rules regarding the use of imperfective verbs in Polish indicates that this is not the case. For reasons of comparison, we included six test sentences with the phasal verb *zaczynać/ zacząć* 'to start to do sth.' in our acceptability judgment task. This phasal verb (as well as other phasal verbs) can only be combined with an imperfective infinitive in Polish (irrespective of tense) because of its core semantic property of focusing on the beginning of an activity. Thus phasal verbs like *zaczynać/ zacząć* show the same categorical restriction with regard to aspect choice of the main verb[18] if compared to the analytic future tense. Therefore, we included five sentences in our acceptability judgment task where the phasal verb was followed by a perfective verb and one instance which showed the normative combination with an imperfective verb. As with the analytic future tense, errors occurred only in the acceptability data of the EB group, but this time they were much more frequent: All six test sentences (even the correct one!) posed problems for our informants, i.e. errors were rather evenly distributed among the test items. The general error rate reached 24% (n = 44). Acceptance rates for the test sentences that included a perfective verb varied from 33 to 20% per item. Thus the analytic future tense forms show a remarkably high degree of stability with regard to the bilinguals' knowledge of the underlying formal rules if compared to the analogical cases of the phasal verb *zaczynać/zacząć.*

b.   These results from the acceptability judgment task are mirrored by the data from the elicited narratives. Here, too, aspectual errors in forming the compound future tense occur very sporadically in the data and are restricted to the EB group. Altogether only five instances of aspectual errors (out of a total of 287 analytic future forms) were found in the data of three informants of the EB group. Two of them already showed problems in the acceptability judgment task with recognizing the formal rule of building the compound future tense in Polish.

A closer look at these errors reveals interesting details: The informants used or accepted perfective verbs as part of the analytic construction which are distinguished

---

18.   However, phasal verbs can only be combined with the infinitive of the main verb, never with the l-participle, as is the case with the analytic future tense.

from their imperfective counterparts only through the absence or alternation of a suffix, e.g.:

(1) Może   ludzie więcej czasu będą   spędzić   w domu.
     Perhaps people more time will-AUX.3PL spend-INF.PF in home.
     'Perhaps people will spend more time at home.'

Here, the perfective verb *spędzić* should be replaced by its imperfective partner *spędzać* to produce the correct form, the only difference being the suffix {i}/{a}. Nearly all other errors in both data sets represent comparable cases (cf. pairs like ipf. *dostawać* vs. pf. *dostać* 'to get', ipf. *zmieniać* vs. pf. *zmienić* 'to change', ipf. *przepisywać* vs. pf. *przepisać* 'to copy' etc.). No errors, however, occur with perfective verbs that are marked by a prefix (cf. pairs like ipf. *robić* vs. pf. *zrobić* 'to make', ipf. *czekać* vs. pf. *poczekać* 'to wait' etc.). This kind of marking of the aspectual distinction seems to be cognitively more salient for the heritage speaker group, thus preventing them to use or accept the respective forms as part of the analytic future construction. Consequently, the problems that our bilingual informants encounter seem to lie more in the correct identification of the imperfective aspect than in not knowing the formal rules underlying the formation of the analytic future tense in Polish.

6.2   Relative frequency of the two compound future forms in the data (RQ 2a)

The frequency of the two alternatives of the compound future tense was assessed on the basis of the data from the elicited narratives that our informants were asked to deliver on the topic of how they imagine life in the year 3000. Table 2 provides an overview of the frequency of occurrence of the two forms.

At first glance, it looks as though the hypothesis regarding the expected preference for the infinitive form by bilingual speakers (see Section 5.3.) is not confirmed by our data: the participle form prevails in all examined groups. Furthermore, no steady increase of the infinitive form can be attested to from the ML to the LB and EB data. Thus the infinitive is more common in the data from the controls than in the data from the late bilingual speakers, which contradicts our initial assumption that the MLs should almost exclusively use the participle form as the typical form in colloquial Polish. What confirms our initial assumptions, however, is the fact that the infinitive indeed shows the highest relative frequency in the EB group, and that there are differences in the

Table 2. Frequency of the two competing forms in the narratives

	Early Bilinguals		Late Bilinguals		Controls	
infinitive	131	45.6%	114	34.5%	115	40.2%
l-participle	156	54.4%	216	65.5%	171	59.8%
Σ	287	100%	330	100%	286	100%

ratio of the two forms between the three groups (in rough numbers: EB: 10% difference between infinitive and participle form, LB: 30%, ML: 20%). Another striking result of our analysis is the fact that even on the individual level there are no signs for replacing the participle form with the infinitive form in our bilingual speakers. 29 of the 30 tested heritage speakers (EBs) used more than one analytic future tense form in their narratives, but only two of them exclusively used one of the competing forms in their narratives.[19] As for the LB group, there were also only two informants who concentrated on participle forms, whereas the other informants used at least one infinitive form in their narratives. In the ML data, four out of 30 tested subjects refrained from using both forms: two stuck to the infinitive form only, the other two chose the participle form. So even on the individual level, there is no indication for an expansion of one form at the expense of the other in all three groups.

There is one restriction in the distribution of the two forms that is observed by all of our informants. As was mentioned in Section 4, the use of a main verb that is followed by an infinitive complement (e.g. modals like *musieć* 'to have to') normally blocks the choice of the compound future form with the infinitive in order to avoid the co-occurrence of two infinitives. In our data, this rule is violated only once (by a speaker from the EB group):

(2) [Ludzie] będą   musieć   się   tak zachowywać.
     [People] will-AUX.3PL must-INF.IPF REFL so behave-INF.IPF
     'People will have to behave so.'

In all other instances, the participle variant is used which makes it a rather obligatory form in these contexts. Thus we may argue that, with such verb types, there seems to be no choice between the infinitive and the l-participle. Following Proeme (1991: 194f), we therefore excluded these instances from our quantitative analysis in order to get a clearer picture of the distribution of the two forms in contexts where a real competition between the alternatives is at stake. With this modification, the quantitative distribution is shown in Table 3.

A non-parametric χ^2-test was employed to check whether the differences between the frequency of the two forms within each group are statistically significant and whether there are differences across the groups.

Table 3. Distribution of the two alternatives in potentially distinctive contexts

	Early Bilinguals		Late Bilinguals		Controls	
infinitive	130	52.6%	114	39.0%	115	44.4%
l-participle	116	47.4%	178	61.0%	144	55.6%
Σ	246	100%	292	100%	259	100%

---

19. One informant chose the participle form whereas the other used the infinitive form only.

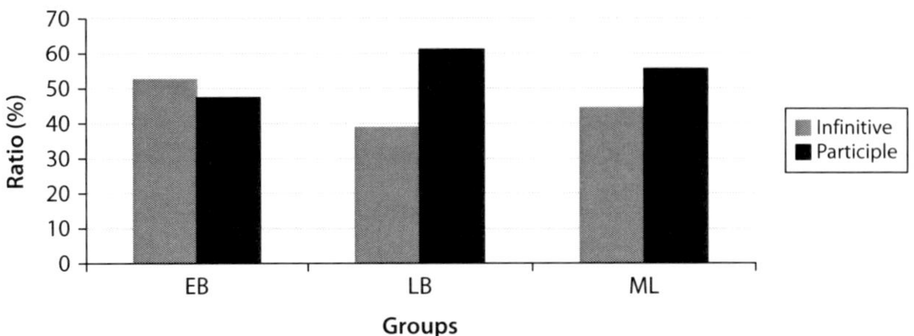

Figure 1. Distribution of the two variants in the three groups

The difference between the frequency of the infinitive and participle form is significant only for the LB group ($\chi^2 = 14.52$, df = 1, p < 0.001).[20] The EB group is the only group that prefers the infinitive form to the participle, which is in line with our initial prediction. However, they do not use the infinitive significantly more often than the other two groups.[21]

As far as the differences between the three investigated groups are concerned, the following results can be stated: There is a highly significant difference between the EB and the LB group with regard to the frequency of the participle form ($\chi^2 = 13.08$, df = 1, p < 0.001, EB↔LB). The ML group occupies an intermediate position on this scale since it does not differ significantly from both the EB and the LB group with regard to the frequency of the participle form.[22] Consequently, what we get is a steady increase of the difference between the participle and the infinitive form from the EB group to the ML and LB group. However, only the two groups EB and LB at the poles of this continuum differ significantly with regard to the quantitative distribution of the competing forms ($\chi^2 = 10.6$, df = 1, p < 0.01, EB/LB:).[23]

6.3   Impact of gender and number on the distribution of the two forms

In Section 4, different factors were introduced that, according to the literature, have an impact on the distribution of the alternative forms. One factor was the *word order* of the components. However, for the current study word order can be left aside since, in

---

20. Cf. χ^2-values for the difference between infinitive vs. participle forms in the other groups: $\chi^2 = 0,8$ (EB) and $\chi^2 = 3,25$ (ML)

21. Cf. χ^2-values for the difference regarding the frequency of the infinitive form in the three groups: $\chi^2 = 1,2$ (EB↔LB), $\chi^2 = 0,92$ (EB↔ML) and $\chi^2 = 0,02$ (LB↔ML).

22. Cf. χ^2-values for the difference regarding the frequency of the participle form in the other groups: $\chi^2 = 3.02$ (EB↔ML) and $\chi^2 = 3.59$ (LB↔ML).

23. Cf. χ^2-values for the difference regarding the distribution of the two forms between the other groups: $\chi^2 = 3.64$ (EB↔ML) and $\chi^2 = 1.74$ (LB↔ML)

Table 4. Frequency of the two forms with regard to gender and number of subject

	Early Bilinguals		Late Bilinguals		Controls	
	Infinitive	Participle	Infinitive	Participle	Infinitive	Participle
MASC	5 (12%)	37 (88%)	3 (5%)	56 (95%)	2 (4%)	55 (96%)
FEM	7 (47%)	8 (53%)	8 (38%)	13 (62%)	8 (40%)	12 (60%)
NEUTR	20 (44%)	25 (56%)	20 (37%)	34 (63%)	13 (35%)	24 (65%)
MP-PL[25]	76 (68%)	36 (32%)	70 (59%)	48 (41%)	71 (70%)	30 (30%)
NMP-PL	22 (69%)	10 (31%)	12 (31%)	27 (69%)	21 (48%)	23 (52%)

all examined narratives, only one instance of the so-called reversed order was found[25]. Thus reversed word order cannot account for the more frequent use of the infinitive in our EB and ML data.

Table 4 gives an overview of the distribution of the two forms with regard to gender and number of the subject.

There is a clear distinction between the singular and the plural. As far as the singular is concerned, it is evident that the data regarding the distribution of the two forms in the LB and ML group are nearly identical. The EB data show a certain, though not very robust trend in all genders towards a higher ratio of the infinitive form in the singular if compared to the two other groups. The differences between the two forms in the masculine are, to a high degree, significant (p < 0.001) for all three groups.[26] Thus our data corroborate the statements reported in Section 4 above concerning the preference for the participle form if the subject has masculine gender. Feminine and neuter subjects clearly behave differently, although they still trigger the participle form to a higher degree. Only in the EB group is the quantitative relationship between the two variants nearly balanced. However, the differences are not statistically significant. This holds for the relationship within the three groups[27] as well as when comparing the ratios across the groups.

In the plural the three groups behave differently. For male personal subjects, there is a clear tendency to prefer the infinitive form in the EB and ML group whereas in the LB group, the quantitative differences between the two forms are lowered. However,

---

24. MP-PL and NMP-PL stand for male personal (= virile) and non-male personal (= non-virile) gender which compose the gender distinction in the plural, see note 10. Thus MASC, FEM and NEUTR refer only to subjects in the singular.

25. It is interesting to note that, in this instance, it was the l-participle that occurred before the auxiliary, i.e. it represented a pattern that in recent empirical accounts is either not attested at all or characterized as an idiolectal peculiarity (see Proeme 1991: 194 or Pawlak 1997: 139f).

26. Cf. χ^2-values: $\chi^2 = 24.4$ (EB), $\chi^2 = 47.6$ (LB) and $\chi^2 = 46.6$ (ML).

27. Cf. χ^2-values: EB: $\chi^2 = 0,13$ (fem)/0,58 (neutr); LB: $\chi^2 = 1,24$ (fem)/3,64 (neutr); ML: $\chi^2 = 0,46$ (fem)/3,3 (neutr).

the differences are statistically significant for all three groups, although the significance reaches a lower level for the LB group ($\chi^2 = 4.11$, $p < 0.05$ as opposed to $\chi^2 = 14.29/16.65$, $p < 0.001$ for the EB/ML group, with $df = 1$ for all comparisons). These findings confirm the observation of Proeme (1991: 198) that contexts with male personal subjects represent a characteristic domain of the compound future form with the infinitive in contemporary Polish. With non-male personal subjects there is a significant polarity between the two bilingual groups: Whereas the EB group prefers the infinitive form to the same degree as with male personal subjects, the ratio is exactly reverse in the LB group. The differences between infinitive and participle forms are significant in both groups ($\chi^2 = 4.53$ (EB)/5.79 (LB), $df = 1$, $p < 0.05$). Thus both groups form a contrast to the ML controls, where the ratio is near to fifty-fifty ($\chi^2 = 0.11$, $df = 1$, not significant). We could, therefore, claim that it is the distribution with plural subjects that most clearly discriminates the three groups under focus: The EB group favors the infinitive form irrespectively of the gender of the plural subjects, whereas the ML group prefers the infinitive form only with male personal subjects. The LB group, however, uses the participle form in both contexts to a higher degree if compared to the EB and ML group (especially in the case of NMP subjects).

7. General discussion and conclusions

If we return to the hypotheses that were set out in Section 5.3, the analysis shows that some of the initial predictions are not confirmed by our data. Although errors on the level of the formation of the analytic future tense occur, they are restricted to the EB group and even there they can only be classified as rather individual problems in distinguishing between perfective and imperfective verbs. The underlying rule of the obligatory combination of the compound future tense with imperfective verbs remains unaffected by attrition in our heritage speaker group (EB), especially if compared to other related cases as the combinability of phasal verbs with imperfective infinitives.

As far as the ratio between the frequencies of the two competing analytic forms is concerned, the EB group indeed slightly prefers the infinitive to the participle variant, as was initially expected. However, the difference is not statistically significant. This result of the infinitive form showing a higher frequency than in the other groups could, of course, be related to the influence of German which indirectly supports this pattern due to the existence of an identical structure, i.e. the analytic future with an auxiliary *sein* 'to be' plus infinitive. However, the striking preference for the infinitive form in case of plural subjects in this group suggests another (additional) explanation: The selection of the infinitive form clearly reduces the cognitive load in speech processing since it allows the speaker to refrain from specifying grammatical features that must be expressed with the competing participle form, namely gender and number. As has been shown elsewhere (Czachór & Brehmer 2010), gender distinction and gender marking in the plural poses serious problems for our EB speakers, which is maybe due to the lack of a parallel distinction in German. In choosing the infinitive form, the bilingual speakers can thus avoid this challenging task without producing a grammatical error in their (weaker) L1 Polish. Thus the reduction of cognitive load in this domain may enable the speaker to invest more time in the planning of the following stretch of discourse. This would explain why the frequency of the infinitive is especially high for both genders in the plural whereas the distribution of the two forms in the singular, where gender distinction seems to be not problematic for our heritage speakers (Czachór & Brehmer 2010), closely resembles the ratios in the LB and ML group.

The LB group did not show a higher proportion of the infinitive form when compared to the monolingual controls. They actually stand out for their frequent use of the participle form which is even more dominant than in the ML group. Two explanations could account for this fact: (i) First, their preference for the structure that is missing in German could be due to a desire to not sound too "German-like" when speaking Polish. Although this may hardly be a conscious "puristic" attitude towards the infinitive form, the knowledge that an alternative exists for expressing the analytic future tense in Polish might subconsciously lead to a higher frequency in the use of the participle form. This in turn could offer an explanation why the EB group shows a high frequency of the participle forms, too. After all, it is the LB group (represented by their parents) which certainly provides the main input for the EB group in acquiring Polish. (ii) Second, the reduced exposure of the LB group to (especially written forms of) Standard Polish in Germany might lead to an overuse of the "colloquial" form of the analytic future tense as opposed to the infinitive form which is often characterized as having an official tinge in contemporary Polish (see Section 4). The ML group, on the other hand, may be more aware of stylistic differences of this kind, which allows them to recognize and actively use different registers. However, more empirical research on the distribution of the two forms in contemporary spoken (monolingual) Polish is needed before we can draw firmer conclusions about possible reasons for this difference between the LB and ML group.

References

Birnbaum, H. 1958. *Untersuchungen zu den Zukunftsumschreibungen mit dem Infinitiv im Altkirchenslavischen*. Stockholm: Almqvist & Wiksell.

Cyran, W. 1961. Dlaczego giną w języku polskim formy czasu przyszłego złożone z bezokolicznikiem? *Język Polski* 41: 223–224.

Czachór, A. & B. Brehmer. 2010. The restructuring of the Polish gender system by Polish-German bilinguals. Paper presented at the International Conference on Multilingual Individuals and Multilingual Societies (MIMS), University of Hamburg, Hamburg, Germany, 6–8 October 2010.

Czochralski, J. A. 1972. *Verbalaspekt und Tempussystem im Deutschen und Polnischen: Eine konfrontative Darstellung*. Warszawa: Wyd. Naukowe.

Feldstein, R. F. 2001. *A Concise Polish Grammar.* Durham, NC: SEELRC. <http://www.seelrc.org:8080/grammar/pdf/compgrammar_polish.pdf> (6 June 2012).

Mönke, H. 1971. *Das Futurum der polnischen Verba.* München: Otto Sagner.

Nitsch, K. 1956. Tajemnice polskiego czasu przyszłego złożonego. *Język Polski* 36: 190–196.

Pawlak, D. 1997. Użycie form analitycznych czasu przyszłego we współczesnej polszczyźnie. *Prace Filologiczne* 42: 135–144.

Polinsky, M. 1997. American Russian: Language loss meets language acquisition. In *Annual Workshop on Formal Approaches to Slavic Linguistics: The Cornell Meeting 1995* (Michigan Slavic Materials 39), eds. W. Browne, E. Dornisch, N. Kondrashova & D. Zec, 370–406. Ann Arbor MI: Michigan Slavic Publications.

Proeme, H. 1991. On the compound future tense in Polish. In *Studies in West Slavic and Baltic Linguistics*, ed. A. A. Barentsen, 181–271. Amsterdam: Rodopi.

Schmid, M. S. 2008. Defining language attrition. *Babylonia* 2/08: 9–12.

Smoczyńska, M. 1985. The acquisition of Polish. In *The Crosslinguistic Study of Language Acquisition*, Vol. 1: *The Data*, ed. D. I. Slobin, 595–686. Hillsdale NJ: Lawrence Erlbaum Associates.

Swan, O. E. 2002. *A Grammar of Contemporary Polish.* Bloomington IN: Slavica.

Wierzbicki, M. 1999. *Das Tempus- und Aspektsystem im Deutschen und Polnischen.* Heidelberg: Groos.

Zagrodnikowa, A. 1972. Rywalizacja dwu typów czasu przyszłego złożonego *będę pisał – będę pisać*: Próba interpretacji statystyczno-stylistycznej. *Język Polski* 52: 346–358.

Changing conventions in English-German translations of popular scientific texts[*]

Svenja Kranich, Juliane House and Viktor Becher
University of Hamburg, Germany

This contribution summarizes results of the project *Covert Translation*, where we investigated the influence of Anglophone communicative conventions on German via translation. Our hypothesis was that the prestige of English as a *lingua franca* and the growing number of translations from English into German leads to a decline in "cultural filtering", i.e. a diminishing tendency of translators to adapt conventional Anglophone norms to German norms. In this way, English-German translations may introduce linguistic variation to certain target language registers, with Anglophone usage norms also spreading to non-translated German texts. We will here review a number of project studies using a corpus consisting of (1.) English popular scientific texts, (2.) their translations into German, and (3.) comparable non-translated German texts. These studies show that English-German translations are characterized by a considerable degree of source language 'shining-through', which has, however, only in one case led to Anglophone communicative norms spreading to non-translated German texts. We conclude that, for the popular science genre, translation-induced influence of English on German is a marginal phenomenon.

Keywords: English, German, language change, communicative conventions, translation, source language interference

1. Introduction

Globalized and internationalized communication in many areas of contemporary life is today leading to an ever increasing demand for texts that are at the same time meant for members of different linguistic and cultural communities. Such texts are either produced simultaneously in these different communities as what has been called 'comparable texts', or they are translated 'covertly' (House 1977/1981, 1997), mostly from

---

[*]   We would like to thank two anonymous reviewers of this article for their constructive and insightful comments.

English, the dominant *lingua franca*. Comparable texts are texts on similar topics which, despite being produced in differing environments, belong to the same genre and essentially fulfill the same function. As opposed to an overt translation, where the original text is left unchanged as much as possible given the necessary switch into another language, a covert translation (House 1977/1981, 1997, 2010) is a translation in which the communicative purpose of the original is maintained via the use of a so-called 'cultural filter' used to adapt an original text to conventionalized expectation norms of the new target audience. In view of the importance of English as a global *lingua franca* in many influential domains of contemporary life, it is reasonable to assume that such cultural filtering in covert translation and comparable text production may now be in a process of change. This is the hypothesis we investigate in our project "Verdecktes Übersetzen – Covert Translation".[1]

The general assumption underlying the project is that the dominance of the English language in today's global communication leads to variation and change of indigenous communicative norms of German (and other languages) in both covert translations from English and comparable original texts such that an adaptation to Anglophone norms results. More concretely, we hypothesize that adaptations to Anglophone communicative norms can be located along dimensions of empirically established communicative preferences (see Section 3 below). An influence of English on German texts would manifest itself in quantitative and qualitative changes in the use of certain linguistic items and structures in German translations and comparable texts in genres where Anglophone dominance is particularly noticeable, such as in the areas of popular science or business.

In this paper, we present research from our project that has been carried out on the popular science genre. The article is structured as follows: In the next section, we present the project corpus of popular scientific texts. Section 3 introduces the reader to the above-mentioned English-German differences in communicative preferences as they manifest themselves in the popular science genre. Section 4 then discusses four case studies featuring different linguistic phenomena. Finally, Section 5 gives a summary and some conclusions.

2.   Corpus

All studies presented below were carried out using the project's popular science corpus. This corpus is a unidirectional translation corpus consisting of:

---

1.   The project started in July 1999 and was funded for 12 years by the German Science Foundation (Deutsche Forschungsgemeinschaft, DFG) as part of the Collaborative Research Center on Multilingualism (Sonderforschungsbereich 538 "Mehrsprachigkeit") at the University of Hamburg. We gratefully acknowledge this generous support. Since its inception, Juliane House has been principal investigator of the project. Current research associates are Viktor Becher and Svenja Kranich. In previous project phases, Claudia Böttger, Julia Probst, Nicole Baumgarten und Demet Özçetin were members of the research team.

Table 1. Structure and size of the popular science corpus

	1978–1982	1999–2002
English originals	26 texts	38 texts
	42,497 words	122,866 words
German translations	26 texts	38 texts
	37,830 words	113,420 words
German originals	19 texts	32 texts
	82,480 words	100,648 words

1. English originals
2. Their German translations
3. German originals

All texts in the corpus are popular scientific magazine articles that have appeared in publications such as *Scientific American* or *Spektrum der Wissenschaft* (see Baumgarten 2007 for a more detailed presentation of the corpus). Most importantly, the corpus features two 'time-frames': One part of the texts contained in the corpus were published between 1978 and 1982, while the remaining texts were published between 1999 and 2002. This 'micro-diachronic' structure of the corpus allows us to track diachronic changes in translation habits (English originals → German translations) and monolingual language use (German originals). Table 1 gives a summary of the structure of the corpus and provides details on the size of the individual subcorpora.

As the table shows, the individual corpus parts differ substantially in terms of word count (the total word count being approximately 500,000). This is why we will here limit ourselves to presenting percentages and normalized frequencies in the studies to be discussed.

3. Popular scientific writing: A contrastive perspective on the genre in English and German

In this section, we present some contrastive results on general tendencies in communicative styles in English and German, followed by findings about the way these differences manifest themselves in the genre of popular science.

Overall, the same contrasting tendencies could be observed in different types of English and German discourse, spoken and written. It is crucial, in this context, to firmly base one's observations on detailed qualitative and quantitative studies, in order to avoid creating "scientifically manufactured stereotypes", a tendency that Ehlich (2000: 69) has noted for some contrastive work on styles of scientific discourse (he names e.g. Galtung 1985, Clyne 1987). The observations we present are grounded in substantial contrastive multi-genre research conducted over the past thirty years (summary in House 1996, 2006, 2009). A series of German-English contrastive discourse and pragmatic analyses comparing oral and written discourse in original and translated versions focused on such phenomena as opening and closing phases, discourse structures, discourse strategies and discourse markers, politeness and directness in the realization of speech acts and speech act sequences. These analyses resulted in the postulation of a set of dimensions of culturally determined and empirically established communicative preferences such as preferred foci on the interpersonal versus the ideational meta-function of talk (*sensu* Halliday, see, e.g., Halliday & Matthiessen 2004), and on informational vagueness versus specificity. Concretely, English speakers were found to give preference to more addressee-oriented, implicit and indirect ways of expression and to using more verbal routines, whereas German speakers were found to show a tendency towards a more pronounced content-orientation, explicitness, directness and the use of situation-anchored ad-hoc formulations. Thus, English speakers tended to be more interactional and involved in their communicative style as opposed to the more transactional and detached communicative style found to be preferred in discourse by German speakers.

Contrastive studies on genre conventions in popular science are few, even fewer than studies dealing with professional science communication.[2] While tendencies may be the same (e.g. English texts tend to be more interpersonal than German texts in both text types), one should not neglect the basic communicative differences between popular and professional scientific writing. As far as author-reader interaction is concerned, one can say that in scientific writing for peers, authors have the goal to "give the impression of being very knowledgeable in the field ..., want[ing] to be recognized or accepted as experts" (Cecchetto & Stroińska 1997: 148). For authors of scientific texts for interested laymen, on the other hand, being recognized or accepted as an expert is secondary and only relevant in so far as it promotes the primary, more commercial goal, i.e. producing texts that people enjoy reading (so much that they are willing to pay money for reading them). It is thus essential for the popular science genre that texts are perceived not only as informative, but also as pleasurable reading. Striking the right tone, constructing an author-reader relationship perceived as appropriate by the reader (based on his/her previous communicative experience and genre expectations) may therefore be considered even more important in popular scientific texts than in scientific writing for peers.

Let us now look at the way the differences in communicative preferences between English and German are acted out in popular scientific writing in the two languages. Baumgarten, House & Probst (2001) have found that authors of English popular scientific articles tend to make an effort to establish a symmetrical relationship between author and addressee and to simulate interaction with the reader. The reader is often

---

2.   Contrastive studies of professional scientific communication have been presented e.g. by Clyne (1987, 1991), Taylor & Tingguang (1991), Mauranen (1993), Duszak (1994), Kreutz & Harres (1997), and Fandrych & Graefen (2002).

addressed directly and drawn into the scenes described in the text, as in the following example from the *Scientific American*:

(1) a. **EngOrig:** Suppose you are a doctor in an emergency room and a patient tells you she was raped two hours earlier. She is afraid she may have been exposed to HIV ... Can you in fact do anything to block the virus from replicating and establishing infection?[3]

This opening passage of an article on HIV-infections is translated into German for *Spektrum der Wissenschaft* as follows:

(1) b. **GerTrans:** In der Notfallaufnahme eines Krankenhauses berichtet eine Patientin, sie sei vor zwei Stunden vergewaltigt worden und nun in Sorge, dem AIDS-Erreger ausgesetzt zu sein ... Kann der Arzt überhaupt irgend etwas tun, was eventuell vorhandene Viren hindern würde, sich zu vermehren und sich dauerhaft im Körper einzunisten?
Gloss: 'In the emergency room of a hospital, a patient reports having been raped two hours ago and now being in worry about having been exposed to the Aids virus. Can the doctor do anything at all that would prevent possibly present viruses from replicating and establishing themselves permanently in the body?'

This translation can be understood as governed by the aim to adapt the American English original to the reading habits of the German target audience. Note that changes have been made in particular concerning the degree of addressee-involvement: The German reader is no longer asked to imagine himself or herself one of the agents of the scene presented. Instead, the scene in the hospital is presented in the German version 'from the outside', the addressee not asked to actively engage with what is presented (Baumgarten et al. 2001).

Based on observations such as these, quantitative studies were conducted to verify the presumed tendencies. For this purpose, we have looked at linguistic phenomena associated with the area of author-reader interaction. Thus we have examined the use of personal pronouns and connectives, linguistic means that can be employed to produce more interaction in a text. Furthermore, we have investigated the field of hedging, in particular the use of epistemic modality, since epistemic modal marking can help present opinions brought forward in a text as less definite, thus leaving more room for the addressee's own judgment. These phenomena are commonly associated with writer-reader interaction. They have been investigated, among others, by Hyland (1996, 2002, 2005) and Hunston & Thompson (2001). Other phenomena to do with writer-reader interaction include mood switches (alternations of statements, imperatives, and rhetorical questions), parenthetical

---

3.   All the examples presented in this paper are taken from our project corpus of popular scientific texts described in Section 2.

constructions, in which the writer comment on his/her text, functional sentence perspective, mental processes, discourse markers (Bührig & House 2004, 2007, House 2011) as well as evaluative lexis (see, e.g., Böttger 2007).

As stated above, our basic assumption is that English-German translations in the field of popular science tend to allow more and more imports of conventions and norms from the English source texts, which then even find their way, in some cases, into comparable German, monolingually produced texts. In this section, we will now first look at the results produced by the analysis of the earlier English and German comparable texts in our corpus from the time-frame 1978–1982, to find out which basic contrasts can be established.

First of all, in the domain of textual cohesion,[4] Baumgarten (2007) has analyzed the use of the coordinating conjunctions *and* ~ *und* in sentence-initial position. When used sentence-initially, *And* and *Und* support an informal, interaction-oriented style reminiscent of spoken discourse: Information is presented in an incremental, non-hierarchic way (Fabricius-Hansen 1999) and the semantic-pragmatic relation between two sentences linked by *And/Und* is left underspecified and has to be inferred by the addressee (Posner 1980). As would have been predicted from the above-mentioned general findings, this interactional stylistic device is more typical of the English popular scientific texts: In the 1978–1982 part of the corpus, 3.1 tokens per 10,000 words can be found in the English originals, whereas the German originals only contain 0.9 tokens per 10,000 words.

Becher, House & Kranich (2009) present results on the sentence-initial use of the conjunctions *but* ~ *aber* ~ *doch* in our popular science corpus. This use is interesting for the present purpose because it often simulates interaction between author and reader. A typical example is presented below:

> (2)   Still, for some it may seem disturbing that life, certainly in its physical incarnation, must come to an end. *But* to us, it is remarkable that even with our limited knowledge, we can draw conclusions about such grand issues.

In this example, the sentence-initial *but* encodes the transition from one opinion to another, a rhetorical move that has been called Claim-Response Pattern (Hoey 2001). The author first presents one opinion assigned to an unspecified group of people, which he assumes the reader shares. In the second part, the author moves on to present a counter-position to the widely-held opinion presented before. In this way, an interactional structure reminiscent of interaction in spoken dialogue is created. The use of

---

4.   An interesting study of the importance of explicit cohesive markers in popular science has been presented by Myers (1991). He shows that science writing for specialist audiences can rely on the profound background knowledge of the audience, which helps them to infer relations between statements that might appear completely unrelated to a layperson (similar results are obtained by Koskela 1997). Writers of popular scientific articles, by contrast, need to rely to a much greater extent on the explicit encoding of relations between the states of affairs they present. One means of achieving this is the use of conjunctions (Myers 1991: 22).

sentence-initial concessive conjunctions such as *But, Aber* and *Doch* typically creates such interaction-simulating patterns. As we would expect from the general insights into English-German communicative contrasts, the frequency of these items in the first time-frame of our data is as follows: Sentence-initial *But* occurs much more frequently in the English texts from 1978–1982, with 32.6 tokens per 1,000 sentences, than sentence-initial *Aber* and *Doch* in the German texts of the same time frame. The combined frequency of the latter two conjunctions in the German texts is only 9.0 per 1,000 sentences (Becher et al. 2009: 143).

Baumgarten (2008) has investigated the use of the personal pronouns *we ~ wir.* Her results for the early part of the corpus show clear differences between English and German along the predicted lines: English originals from 1978–1982 contain 27.5 tokens of *we* per 10,000 words, while German originals from this time-frame contain only 17.7 tokens of *wir* per 10,000 words (Baumgarten 2008: 417). The difference can be taken as evidence for the less personal nature of the German texts: the German texts encode the agents of the research process described in the text much less frequently than their English counterparts.

In the functional domain of epistemic modality, we have also found some interesting contrasts between the English and the German originals, which can be linked to the different communicative preferences in the two linguacultures. Broadly speaking, epistemic modal markers serve the purpose of marking that the speaker is not fully certain that the proposition encoded by the clause is true (see, e.g., Palmer 2001: 8, Van der Auwera, Schalley & Nuyts 2005: 201 and Verstraete 2007: 17). In discourse, these items can be used to create a more 'dialogic' text (White 2003), since alternative positions are implicitly acknowledged (see also Kreutz & Harres 1997: 186).

One can distinguish two main motivations for using epistemic modal markers in discourse: The first type expresses content-oriented caution (the author does not have enough information to be sure whether the proposition is true). The second type reflects reader-oriented caution (the author does feel sure that the proposition is true, but uses the modal marker in order to leave more room for other opinions; Hyland 1996). This second type of use can be seen as a hedging device, i.e. an element that allows the speaker to weaken the force of a proposition (Markkanen & Schröder 1997: 7, Mauranen 1997: 115–116). An example of this type is presented below:

(3)   In the past few decades, however, they [viz. biologists] have largely ignored one important property of organisms which, it now seems, *may well* play a significant part.

In this example, the author presents new results which go counter to previous beliefs held by the scientific community. The use of the epistemic modal combination *may well* is probably motivated not only (or not mainly) by the lack of full information about the facts, but also or predominantly by the wish to present a statement that contradicts the opinion of important scientists in a more mitigated way. Since English text conventions tend to make more use of such indirect as well as addressee-oriented strategies (see Section 3), we expected to find overall more epistemic modal markers in the English texts. We assumed that the content-oriented need for caution is the same in the English and German popular scientific texts in our corpus (as they deal largely with very similar topics), but we hypothesized that the reader-oriented use is more typical of English discourse, leading to an overall higher frequency of epistemic modal markers in our English originals.

To test this idea, all linguistic markers that serve the purpose of marking a proposition as only possibly or probably true had to be counted manually, since there are so many different linguistic devices that can fulfill this purpose (e.g. modal verbs such as *may*, modal adverbs such as *presumably*, ad-hoc combinations such as *there is evidence to indicate that* ..., etc.). We thus extracted a mini-corpus of 320 sentences per sub-corpus which made the manual analysis feasible, representing a total of a little more than 85,000 words. The hypothesis was borne out: English originals in the first time-frame exhibit a frequency of 22.8 epistemic modal markers per 10,000 words, while German originals from the same time period contain only 7.1 epistemic modal markers per 10,000 words (Kranich 2011: 91).[5]

A further cross-linguistic difference can be seen in the use of modal markers of high and of low modal strength. Markers of low modal strength present statements as possibly true, markers of high modal strength as probably true (see Kranich 2009, 2011 for more detail). A marker of low modal strength, such as *perhaps*, leaves more room for other opinions than a marker of high modal strength, such as *probably*, which is why markers of low modal strength represent more effective hedges than markers of high modal strength (compare *Perhaps you have made a mistake* vs. *Probably you have made a mistake*). In accordance with our expectations, the proportion of markers of low modal strength in the English texts is much higher than in the German texts: Markers of low modal strength make up for 53.5% of all epistemic markers in English, whereas in the German texts, they only amount to 26.8% (Kranich 2011: 91). Again,

---

5.   This result is in accordance with results obtained by Kreutz & Harres' (1997) small-scale study of academic writing in English and German, where they also found that the German texts in their corpus contained very few hedges. Their result was surprising in so far as they analyzed texts from the same corpus used by Clyne (1991), who stated that the German texts in the corpus contained more hedges than the English texts. However, Clyne extended the concept of hedging to include, in addition to epistemic modal markers, such de-personalizing constructions as impersonal constructions, reflexive constructions and agentless passives, which can be presumed to be much more common in German than in English academic writing (Fabricius-Hansen 2000). Kreutz & Harres (1997: 189) actually note in their detailed analysis of a smaller sample of the texts used by Clyne (1991) that such impersonal constructions as e.g. *kann* + passive do not normally function as hedges in the German texts. This shows that it has an impact on the results of a study how far one extends the rather fuzzy concept of hedging (see also Clemen 1997: 242). This is why we have chosen to concentrate on epistemic modal expressions, which are easier to define and to isolate from a text in a reliable and replicable way.

Table 2. Pragmatic contrasts between English and German original popular scientific texts as seen from the frequency[6] of selected linguistic items (1978–1982)[7]

	Personal Pronoun *we ~ wir*	Sentence-initial *and ~ und*	Sentence-initial *but ~ aber ~ doch*	Epistemic modal markers
English Originals	27.5	3.1	32.6	22.8
German Originals	17.7	0.9	9.0	7.1
Conclusions	English texts are more personal.	English texts simulate spoken interaction more.	English texts simulate spoken interaction more.	English texts are more dialogic.[8]

this confirms the view that English texts tend to be more addressee-oriented, in this case by leaving more room for alternative views.

The contrastive results for the popular scientific texts from 1978–1982 are summarized in Table 2.

4. Popular scientific writing in translation and its influence on the German genre

4.1 The case of *And ~ Und*

In Section 3 we have seen that – as a consequence of English-German differences in communicative conventions – the sentence-initial use of *and* was much more frequent in the first time-frame of our corpus than the sentence-inital use of *und* (see Table 2). This raises the questions of (1.) how English-German translators deal with sentence-intial *and* and *und,* and (2.) whether any diachronic trends are discernible. The following table compares the frequency of *And* in the English original texts with the frequency of *Und* in the English-German translations and shows how frequencies have changed over the investigated time-span (Baumgarten 2007: 153):

---

6.   The frequencies are normalized on the basis of 10,000 words, except the frequencies for *But ~ Aber ~ Doch*, which are normalized on the basis of 1,000 sentences.

7.   Our results were not tested for statistical significance. As we can see in Section 4, the only case where Anglophone influence seems to have occurred is the case of *But/Aber/Doch*. However, it is impossible to prove that the quantitative and qualitative changes in the use of these conjunctions – although remarkable – are actually due to influence from English. Significance testing would not make this situation any better, since statistical tests by themselves cannot prove the existence of an assumed causal link (see Dallal 2007). They can only show that a particular distribution pattern is non-random.

8.   We use the term *dialogic* in the sense of White (2003) and White & Sano (2006).

Table 3. Frequency of sentence-initial *and* and *und* (normalized on the basis of 10,000 words)

	1978–1982	1999–2002
English originals (*And*)	3.1	4.5
German translations (*Und*)	2.3	6.3
German originals (*Und*)	0.9	3.1

The relatively small increase in the use of sentence-initial *and* evidenced in Table 3 "suggests that *And* is already a comparatively stable and established feature of the register". In contrast, the frequency of sentence-initial *und* has almost tripled, which "indicate[s] that the use of *Und* is more of an innovation whose place in the register is not yet fixed" (Baumgarten 2007: 153f). The question now is of course where the "innovation" of sentence-initial *und* comes from: is it an 'import' from the English source texts, or is it simply due to a development internal to the target language genre, a kind of diachronic change in translation norms?

Unfortunately, the results of Baumgarten's study do not allow a definite answer to this question. On the one hand, the figures presented in Table 3 suggest that English-German translators have aligned their use of *Und* to the use of *And*, at least as far as frequency is concerned. On the other hand, translators have clearly overshot the mark, with *Und* being even more frequent than *And* in the second time-frame (6.3 vs. 4.5 occurrences per 10,000 words). This means that translators have inserted *Und* in places where *And* does not appear as a source text trigger. In a qualitative analysis of the translation relation between *And* and *Und*, Baumgarten found that "only about 25% of the English *And*'s are actually translated by a German *Und*." Moreover, "80% of the translational occurrences of *Und* are not motivated by their source texts" (2007: 160f). Thus, it is not clear to what extent English-German translators were actually influenced by the English source texts in their use of sentence-initial *und*.

Turning to the frequency of *Und* in the German originals, we do note a considerable increase in frequency over time (from 0.9 to 3.1 occurrences per 10,000 words) – a possible sign of Anglophone influence. However, as Baumgarten (2007: 154–160) shows, *Und* in the non-translated German texts is used in part for different rhetorical purposes than *And*/*Und* in the English originals and German translations. Thus, "the uses of *And* and *Und* seem to differ altogether too much to be seen as a direct import of an English register feature into the German sister register" (Baumgarten 2007: 166).

4.2   The case of *But ~ Aber ~ Doch*

The results obtained for the concessive conjunctions *but*, *aber* and *doch* in sentence-initial position turned out to be much clearer than those obtained for *And ~ Und*. In Section 3, we have seen that in the corpus texts from the years 1978–1982, *but* was used much more frequently in sentence-initial position than *aber* and *doch* taken together (see Table 2). From this, one should expect that English-German translators applying a cultural filter do not render every instance of *But* as *Aber* or *Doch*, but come up with other translational equivalents more in line with the communicative norms of German. Indeed, Becher et al. (2009) found three principal ways of translating *But* into German in the investigated corpus: an English-German translator may directly render *But* as *Aber* or *Doch* (4), choose a sentence-internal connective such as *jedoch* ('however') instead (5), or drop the conjunction altogether (6). See the following examples:

(4) **EngOrig:** Something must have drained away its [sc. the sun's] angular momentum. *But* what?
  GerTrans: Irgendwann muß sie den Drehimpuls verloren haben. *Aber* wie?
  Gloss: 'At some point it must have lost the angular momentum. *But* how?'

(5) **EngOrig:** *But* that scenario is now thought to contradict observations ...
  GerTrans: Dieses Szenario scheint *jedoch* den Beobachtungen zu widersprechen.
  Gloss: 'This scenario, *however*, seems to contradict the observations.'

(6) **EngOrig:** *But* what caused these calamities in the first place ...?
  GerTrans: Wie kam es zu der erstaunlichen Klima-Instabilität ...?
  Gloss: 'How did the astonishing climate instability come about?'

The English source text sentences in the above examples are characterized by a high degree of interaction: in (4), *But* marks the second part of a Claim–Response pattern (see example (2), above); in (4) and (6), the sentence-initial conjunction marks the Question part of a Question–Answer pattern. The translators of (4) through (6) have dealt very differently with the interactional effect of *But*. While the translator of (4) has fully retained the interactional style of the English original by translating *But* as *Aber*, the translator of (5) has toned down the degree of interactionality by choosing a less colloquial, sentence-internal connective (*jedoch*). Finally, the translator of (6) chose not to use a translational equivalent of *But* at all.

In order to find out how the translation strategies evidenced in the above examples compare in terms of frequency, let us first look at the overall frequency of *But* and *Aber/Doch* in our corpus of English-German translations:

Table 4. Frequency of sentence-initial *but*, *aber* and *doch* (normalized on the basis of 1,000 sentences)

	1978–1982	1999–2002
English originals (*But*)	32.6	32.6
German translations (*Aber, Doch*)	22.7	30.1
German originals (*Aber, Doch*)	9.0	19.8

Table 4 (taken from Becher et al. 2009: 143) leads to a number of interesting observations. First of all, we can see that, like the use of *And*, the sentence-initial use of *But* seems to be a relatively stable feature of the English popular science genre. The sentence-initial use of *aber* and *doch* in the German translations, on the other hand, shows considerable diachronic variation, namely an increase in frequency by 32.5% (from 22.7 to 30.1 occurrences per 1,000 sentences). This increase suggests that "shining-through"[9] (Teich 2003) has become more prominent over time, i.e. English-German translators have increasingly translated *But* as *Aber* or *Doch*, not making use of the alternative translation strategies evidenced in (5) and (6). As Table 5 (taken from Becher et al. 2009: 144) shows, this is indeed the case.

From Table 5, we can see that in the first time-frame, only 26.8% of all occurrences of *But* have been translated as *Aber* or *Doch*, with almost half of all occurrences (46.4%) having been rendered as a (less interactional) sentence-internal connective such as *aber, jedoch* or *allerdings* 'however'. In 17.9% of all cases, *But* does not have a translational equivalent at all in the German target text. These figures show that translators have applied a strong cultural filter in the first time-frame. The second time-frame, however, presents a very different picture. Here, *But → Aber/Doch* has become the new default translation strategy (applied in 47.4% of all cases), and only in 36.2% has a sentence-internal connective been chosen as a translation of *But*. The omission of *But* has become marginal (7.2%). These figures make it clear that the increasing frequency of *Aber* and *Doch* in the English-German translations which we saw in Table 4 is actually due to a marked increase in source language shining-through.

Let us now return to Table 4. The most interesting finding to be gleaned from this table concerns the frequency of *Aber* and *Doch* in the German original texts. We already saw from Table 2 (Section 3) that *But* occurs more than three times more

Table 5. Translations of sentence-initial *but* into German

	1978–1982	1999–2002
But → Aber/Doch	26.8%	47.4%
But → aber, (je)doch, allerdings	46.4%	36.2%
But → <null>	17.9%	7.2%
But → <other>	8.9%	9.2%
Total	100%	100%

---

9. We use the term *shining-through* as a cover term for various interference phenomena relating to the transmission of source language features into the target text in the process of translation. These features may either be typological (i.e. structures not typical of the target language are taken over from the source language) or related to register (i.e. structures or overall frequencies of constructions that are characteristic of a certain register in the source, but not in the target language, are adopted in the translated text) (Teich 2003).

frequently in the English originals than do *Aber* and *Doch* in the German originals (32.6 vs. 9.0 occurrences per 1,000 sentences). We can now see from Table 4 that this English-German usage contrast has considerably diminished over time due to a remarkable increase in frequency of *Aber/Doch* in the German original texts by 119.8% (from 9.0 to 19.8 occurrences per 1,000 words). Comparing this to the frequency of *Aber* and *Doch* in the English-German translations, which has been anomalously high right from the start, we get the impression that the German originals have aligned their use of sentence-initial *aber* and *doch* to the English-German translations over time.

To check the plausibility of this interpretation, a qualitative analysis was carried out in which the use of *Aber* and *Doch* in the German originals was compared with the use of these items in the English-German translations and with the use of *But* in the English originals. The result of the analysis was that *Aber* and *Doch* are used in the German originals for the same purposes as in the translations, which supports our assumption that German popular science authors are influenced by translations from English in producing their texts. See the following examples:

(7) **GerOrig:** Gewiss sind unter den Lockstoffen für bestäubende Insekten auch Monoterpene. *Aber* das kann nur ein Nebeneffekt sein ...
Gloss: 'Certainly, among the attractants of pollinating insects are also monoterpens. But that can only be a side-effect ...'

(8) **GerOrig:** ... eine Folge von sehr vielen Einzelanweisungen ... Erst deren Ausführung in ihrer Gesamtheit erweckt den geschilderten Eindruck. *Aber* wer ist es, der diese Einzelanweisungen ausführt?
Gloss: '... a sequence of very many single orders. Only their execution in their entirety gives rise to the described impression. *But* who is it that carries out these single orders?'

In (7), *Aber* is used as a marker of the Claim–Response pattern, while in (8) the conjunction is used to signal a Question–Answer pattern. As the examples illustrate, German popular science authors tend to use sentence-initial concessive conjunctions for the same purposes as both English authors of popular science texts and the English-German translators of these texts. We take this observation as evidence for our project hypothesis, i.e. for the assumption that authors of German popular scientific texts were influenced by translations from English in their use of sentence-initial *aber* and *doch* as markers of interactionality and spokenness. An interesting question for further research would be whether German authors have only adopted the more frequent use of the conjunctions, or if they have also taken over the translations' rhetorical structure, which would be evident from a generally more frequent use of highly interactional patterns such as Claim–Response and Question–Answer.

4.3   The case of *we ~ wir*

Table 6 shows the frequency of the personal pronoun *we* and its German equivalent *wir* in the investigated corpus (figures taken from Baumgarten 2008: 417).

In the German translations, we can see a similar trend as in *Aber* and *Doch*, the frequency of *wir* increasing in the second time-frame (from 13.2 to 31.0 occurrences per 10,000 words), possibly in an adaptation to the English original texts. Indeed, as Baumgarten (2008: 418) shows, shining-through has increased in the investigated time-span, with a rising number of occurrences of *we* being translated as *wir*, which suggests than English-German translators' application of a cultural filter has decreased.

However, the frequency of *wir* in the German originals does not fit into the picture. First of all, we note that in the first time-frame, the frequency of *wir* in the translations is lower than the frequency of the pronoun in the German originals. Baumgarten explains this as a result of "normalization" (or "conservatism"), i.e. translators' hypothesized "tendency to exaggerate features of the target language and to conform to its typical patterns" (Baker 1996: 183).

But what about the second time-frame? In the texts from 1999–2002, the frequency of *wir*, having risen to 36.3 occurrences per 10,000 words, is even higher than the frequency of *we* in the English originals (33.8). This makes it seem improbable that the German originals have aligned their usage of *wir* to Anglophone conventions, especially since the frequency of *wir* in the German translations, despite the increase noted above, is still lower than the frequency of the pronoun in the German originals. While the figures for *But ~ Aber ~ Doch* (Table 4) suggest that the English-German translations have, as it were, dragged the German originals behind them with respect to their more frequent use of *Aber* and *Doch*, the trend seems to be the other way round in the case of *wir*: It seems that, in this case, the German translations have followed the German originals in their more frequent use of *wir*, not vice versa.

This interpretation of the data is corroborated by additional analyses of the textual functions of *wir* carried out by Baumgarten (2008). For example, Baumgarten classified all occurrences of *we* and *wir* in the corpus according to their referential range. As the following examples illustrate, depending on the context of utterance, the reference of *we*/*wir* may be reader-exclusive (9) or reader-inclusive (10):

Table 6. Frequency of *we* and *wir* (normalized on the basis of 10,000 words)

	1978–1982	1999–2002
Engllish originals (*we*)	27.5	33.8
German translations (*wir*)	13.2	31.0
German originals (*wir*)	17.7	36.3

(9)   With help from state biologists, *we* obtained water samples in 1991 during a kill of about one million Atlantic menhaden in the Pamlico Estuary.

(10)   *We* must also become more proactive in addressing the state of our waterways …

In (9), *we* refers to the author of the magazine article in question and her research group (reader-exclusive reference), while in (10) (taken from the same text) the reference of *we* includes the reader.

What is interesting about the reader-exclusive and reader-inclusive uses of *we* and *wir* is that they are distributed very unevenly across the individual parts of the investigated corpus: while reader-inclusive uses are more frequent than reader-exclusive uses in both the English originals and their German translations, the German originals are characterized by a predominance of reader-exclusive uses, and this tendency holds across the two time-frames. This fundamental difference in *we/wir* usage between English originals and their German translations on the one hand and German originals on the other hand – which does not change in the course of the investigated time-span – suggests that German authors were not inspired by the translations in their diachronically increasing use of *wir*. A possible alternative explanation for German authors' increasing use of *wir* would be a (language- and genre-internal) trend towards more colloquial ways of expression – a hypothesis that lends itself to further investigation including a comparison with German reference corpora.

4.4   The case of epistemic modal markers

The use of epistemic modal markers is, as we have seen in Section 3, another area where there are considerable differences between English and German. The English-German translations exhibit some shining-through in this area, both with regard to the overall frequency of epistemic modal markers and with regard to the proportions of markers of low and high modal strength. The following figure summarizes the findings:

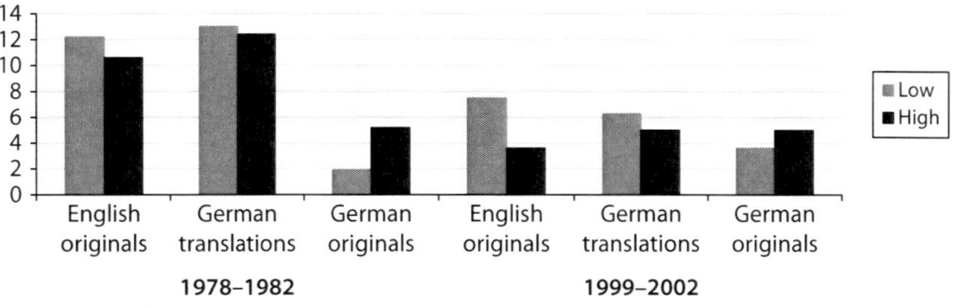

Figure 1.   Epistemic markers of low and high modal strength in the popular science corpus

Figure 1 (taken from Kranich 2011: 92) shows several things: First, one can note that German originals consistently use fewer epistemic modal markers than English originals. At the same time, one can observe a change in genre conventions in the English originals over the two time-frames. English texts of the earlier time-frame make use of these markers to a much greater extent than is the case in the texts in the later time-frame. It will not be possible to explain this difference within the scope of the present article. Let us here instead concentrate on the differences between English and German originals and the English-German translations evidenced by Figure 1.

It is evident that German originals of both time-frames make less use of epistemic modal markers overall and particularly of markers of low modal strength. The translations show two clear effects of 'registerial shining-through' (Teich 2003: 146), i.e. they exhibit frequency distributions more typical of the genre in the source language culture than of the genre in the target language culture. The first shining-through effect is the overall higher frequency. The second shining-through effect lies in the more frequent use of epistemic modal markers of low modal strength (such as *vielleicht* 'maybe', *könnte* 'might') than of markers of high modal strength (such as *wahrscheinlich* 'probably') in the German translations, whereas the distribution is reversed in the German originals.

However, as is also evident from Figure 1, in this respect one can see no trend of increasing adoption of source language features in the translations (which our hypothesis would have predicted). In fact, German translated texts in the first time-frame use over three times as many epistemic modal markers as the German originals, while they only make use of 31% more epistemic modal expressions in the second time-frame.

The same trend is apparent in an investigation of the translations of English modal verbs (Kranich 2011). Investigating the German translations of all English modal verbs with epistemic function, Kranich (2011: 88–91) has shown that translation choices that can be seen as an adaptation to German norms (namely leaving out the modal marker or choosing one of higher modal strength) have in fact become more frequent in the second time-frame. In the domain of epistemic modal marking, Anglophone norms are thus not increasingly adopted in the English-German translations (see also Becher et al. 2009: 130–137).

5. Summary and conclusions

The following table summarizes the findings presented in this paper.

The overview in Table 7 shows that shining-through is a common phenomenon in English-German translations of popular scientific texts. In three of the four phenomena investigated, clear evidence for source-language shining-through was found. Although translators obviously do not take over source language expressions uncritically, but make adaptations (e.g. they sometimes use sentence-internal connectives instead of sentence initial *but*, or translate epistemic modal markers of low modal strength

Table 7. Shining-through and contact-induced changes in translated and non-translated German popular scientific texts

	Personal Pronoun *we ~ wir*	Sentence-initial *and ~ und*	Sentence-initial *but ~ aber ~ doch*	Epistemic modal markers
Shining-through effects in translations	YES	UNCLEAR	YES	YES
Impact on German originals	NO	NO	YES	NO
Conclusions	German original texts become more personal, but change is not due to translations.	German original texts become more interactional, but reason is unclear.	German original texts become more interactional as authors adopt Anglophone usage patterns from translations.	German original texts do not become more dialogic.

with markers of high modal strength), they still make a number of translation choices that lead to features in the translated text which make it different from target language texts produced monolingually. We can therefore conclude that German popular scientific texts translated from English are indeed more interactional than German original texts in this genre.

As far as our other main hypothesis is concerned, namely that German original texts in the genre of popular science will also increasingly adopt Anglophone conventions, we find, however, that the evidence to support this view is not very strong. Only the case-study on the sentence-initial concessive conjunctions (*But, Aber, Doch*) furnishes results that clearly support the hypothesis. In this case, the English-German translations appear indeed to pave the way for an overall change in conventions in the German genre of popular scientific writing, leading to a higher degree of interaction in the original German texts as well. As far as epistemic modal markers are concerned, on the other hand, we see absolutely no evidence that the German original texts adopt a more interpersonal style.

Results with respect to the use of sentence-initial *and ~ und* and the personal pronouns *we ~ wir* are somewhat less clear. The German originals do in fact become more interactional, increasingly using both sentence-initial *und* and the personal pronoun *wir*. However, the functions attributed to these two linguistic items differ remarkably from the functions of English *and* and *we*. English influence on German text conventions via English-German translations is therefore not likely. A more indirect type of Anglophone influence might be a more plausible explanation. Over the last decades, a general trend in English (both British and American) texts towards increased informality and colloquiality, as well as interaction can be observed (Mair 2006). This trend can be linked to general cultural processes, such as the democratization of knowledge and a growing taste for informality in interaction. It seems reasonable to assume that the same overall societal processes are at work in German society as in the UK and the USA. These cultural-societal trends may be influenced by the prestige of Anglophone (particularly US-) culture, so that the trends we see in the German original texts in our corpus might be said to be caused by the presence of the prestigious Anglophone model in a rather indirect way. And it may well be that the effect on German originals shown in our research are simply due to the exposure of German writers to texts written in English, which may be even more important than translated literature from English into German, i.e. it may be English originals, not their German translations which are influencing German writers' language. This may also explain why in some cases the phenomena investigated occur more frequently in the German originals than in the English originals: the German writers may be over-adapting, as it were, to Anglophone norms.

As far as the impact of English-German translations on changes in German genre conventions is concerned, we can only conclude that its role is rather marginal, as it can only be clearly established for one out of four features investigated.

References

Baker, M. 1996. Corpus-based translation studies: The challenges that lie ahead. In *Terminology, LSP and Translation: Studies in Language Engineering in Honour of Juan C. Sager*, ed. H. Somers, 175–186. Amsterdam: John Benjamins.

Baumgarten, N. 2007. Converging conventions? Macrosyntactic conjunction with English *and* and German *und. Text & Talk* 27: 139–170.

Baumgarten, N. 2008. Writer construction in English and German popularized academic discourse: The uses of *we* and *wir. Multilingua* 27: 409–438.

Baumgarten, N., J. House & J. Probst. 2001. *Untersuchungen zum Englischen als 'lingua franca' in verdeckter Übersetzung: Theoretischer Hintergrund, Weiterentwicklung des Analyseverfahrens und erste Ergebnisse* (Arbeiten zur Mehrsprachigkeit 20). Hamburg: Universität Hamburg.

Becher, V., J. House & S. Kranich. 2009. Convergence and divergence through language contact in translation. In *Convergence and Divergence in Language Contact Situations* (Hamburg Studies on Multilingualism 8), eds. K. Braunmüller & J. House, 125–151. Amsterdam: John Benjamins.

Böttger, C. 2007. *Lost in Translation? An Analysis of the Role of English as the Lingua Franca of Multilingual Business Communication*. Hamburg: Kovač.

Bührig, K. & J. House. 2004. Connectivity in translation: Transitions from orality to literacy. In *Multilingual Communication* (Hamburg Studies on Multilingualism 3), eds. J. House & J. Rehbein, 87–114. Amsterdam: John Benjamins.

Bührig, K. & J. House. 2007. Linking constructions in discourse across languages. In *Connectivity in Grammar and Discourse* (Hamburg Studies on Multilingualism 5), eds. J. Rehbein, C. Hohenstein & L. Pietsch, 345–366. Amsterdam: John Benjamins.

Cecchetto, V. & M. Stroińska. 1997. Systems of reference in intellectual discourse: A potential source of intercultural stereotypes. In *Culture and Styles of Academic Discourse*, ed. A. Duszak, 141–154. Berlin: Mouton de Gruyter.

Clemen, G. 1997. The concept of hedging: Origins, approaches and definitions. In *Hedging and Discourse: Approaches to the Analysis of a Pragmatic Phenomenon in Academic Texts*, eds. R. Markkanen & H. Schröder, 235–248. Berlin: Mouton de Gruyter.

Clyne, M. 1987. Cultural differences in the organization of academic texts: English and German. *Journal of Pragmatics* 11: 211–247.

Clyne, M. 1991. The sociocultural dimension: The dilemma of the German-speaking scholar. In *Subject-oriented Texts: Languages for Special Purposes and Text Theory*, ed. H. Schröder, 49–67. Berlin: Mouton de Gruyter.

Dallal, G. E. 2007. *The Little Handbook of Statistical Practice*. Chapter: Cause and effect. <http://www.jerrydallal.com/LHSP/cause.htm> (6 June 2012).

Duszak, A. 1994. Academic discourse and intellectual styles. *Journal of Pragmatics* 21: 291–313.

Ehlich, K. 2000. "Wissenschaftsstile", Wissenschaftssprache und ihre (wissens-)soziologischen Hintergründe. In *Einstellungsforschung in der Soziolinguistik und in den Nachbardisziplinen*, eds. S. Deminger, T. Fögen, J. Scharloth & S. Zwickel, 59–71. Frankfurt: Peter Lang.

Fabricius-Hansen, C. 1999. Information packaging and translation: Aspects of translational sentence splitting (German-English/Norwegian). In *Sprachspezifische Aspekte der Informationsverteilung*, ed. M. Doherty, 175–214. Berlin: Akademie Verlag.

Fabricius-Hansen, C. 2000. *Wissenschaftssprache versus Gemeinsprache aus kontrastiver Sicht*. SPRIKreports 2. <http://www.hf.uio.no/ilos/forskning/prosjekter/sprik/docs/pdf/cfh/cfhansen1.pdf> (6 June 2012).

Fandrych, C. & G. Graefen. 2002. Text commenting devices in German and English academic articles. *Multilingua* 21: 17–43.

Galtung, J. 1985. Struktur, Kultur und intellektueller Stil: Ein vergleichender Essay über sachsonische, teutonische, gallonische und nipponische Wissenschaft. In *Das Fremde und das Eigene*, ed. A. Wierlacher, 151–193. München: Iudicium.

Halliday, M. A. K. & C. Matthiessen. 2004. *An Introduction to Functional Grammar*, 3rd edn. London: Arnold.

Hoey, M. 2001. *Textual Interaction: An Introduction to Written Discourse Analysis*. London: Routledge.

House, J. 1977/1981. *Translation Quality Assessment: A Model for Analysis*, 2nd edn. Tübingen: Narr.

House, J. 1996. Contrastive discourse analysis and misunderstanding: The case of German and English. In *Contrastive Sociolinguistics*, eds. M. Hellinger & U. Ammon, 345–361. Berlin: Mouton de Gruyter.

House, J. 1997. *Translation Quality Assessment: A Model Revisited*. Tübingen: Narr.

House, J. 2006. Communicative styles in English and German. *European Journal of English Studies* 10: 249–267.

House, J. 2009. *Translation*. Oxford: OUP.

House, J. 2010. Overt and covert translation. In *Handbook of Translation Studies*, Vol. 1, eds. Y. Gambier & L. van Doorslaer, 245–247. Amsterdam: John Benjamins.

House, J. 2011. Linking constructions in English and German translated and original texts. In *Multilingual Discourse Production: Diachronic and Synchronic Perspectives*, eds. S. Kranich, V. Becher, S. Höder & J. House, 163–182. Amsterdam: John Benjamins.

Hunston, S. & G. Thompson. 2001. *Evaluation in Text: Authorial Stance and the Construction of Discourse*. Oxford: OUP.

Hyland, K. 1996. Writing without conviction? Hedging in science research articles. *Applied Linguistics* 17: 433–454.

Hyland, K. 2002. Authority and invisibility: Authorial identity in academic writing. *Journal of Pragmatics* 34: 1091–1112.

Hyland, K. 2005. Stance and engagement: A model of interaction in academic discourse. *Discourse Studies* 7: 173–192.

Koskela, M. 1997. Inference in science and popular science. In *Culture and Styles of Academic Discourse*, ed. A. Duszak, 343–357. Berlin: Mouton de Gruyter.

Kranich, S. 2009. Epistemic modality in English popular scientific articles and their German translations. *trans-kom* 2: 26–41.

Kranich, S. 2011. To hedge or not to hedge: The use of epistemic modal expressions in popular science in English texts, English-German translations, and German original texts. *Text & Talk* 31: 77–99.

Kreutz, H. & A. Harres. 1997. Some observations on the distribution and function of hedging in German and English academic writing. In *Culture and Styles of Academic Discourse*, ed. A. Duszak, 181–201. Berlin: Mouton de Gruyter.

Mair, C. 2006. *Twentieth-century English: History, Variation, and Standardization*. Cambridge: CUP.

Markkanen, R. & H. Schröder. 1997. Hedging: A challenge for pragmatics and discourse analysis. In *Hedging and Discourse: Approaches to the Analysis of a Pragmatic Phenomenon in Academic Texts*, eds. R. Markkanen & H. Schröder, 3–18. Berlin: Mouton de Gruyter.

Mauranen, A. 1993. *Cultural Differences in Academic Rhetoric*. Bern: Peter Lang.

Mauranen, A. 1997. Hedging in language revisers' hands. In *Hedging and Discourse: Approaches to the Analysis of a Pragmatic Phenomenon in Academic Texts*, eds. R. Markkanen & H. Schröder, 115–133. Berlin: Mouton de Gruyter.

Myers, G. 1991. Lexical cohesion and specialized knowledge in science and popular science texts. *Discourse Processes* 14: 1–26.

Palmer, F. 2001. *Mood and Modality*. Cambridge: CUP.

Posner, R. 1980. Semantics and pragmatics of sentence connectives in natural language. In *Speech Act Theory and Pragmatics*, eds. J. R. Searle, F. Kiefer & M. Bierwisch, 169–203. Dordrecht: Reidel.

Taylor, G. & C. Tingguang. 1991. Linguistic, cultural, and subcultural issues in contrastive discourse analyses: Anglo-American and Chinese scientific texts. *Applied Linguistics* 12: 319–336.

Teich, E. 2003. *Cross-linguistic Variation in System and Text*. Berlin: Mouton de Gruyter.

Van der Auwera, J., E. Schalley & J. Nuyts. 2005. Epistemic possibility in a Slavonic parallel corpus: A pilot study. In *Modality in Slavonic Languages: New Perspectives*, eds. P. Karlik & B. Hansen, 201–217. München: Sagner.

Verstraete, J. C. 2007. *Rethinking the Coordinate-subordinate Dichotomy: Interpersonal Grammar and the Analysis of Adverbial Clauses in English*. Berlin: Mouton de Gruyter.

White, P. R. R. 2003. Beyond modality and hedging: A dialogic view of the language of intersubjective stance. *TEXT* 23: 259–284.

White, P. R. R. & M. Sano. 2006. Dialogistic positions and anticipated audiences – a framework for stylistic comparisons. In *Pragmatic Markers in Contrast*, eds. K. Aijmer & A. M. Simon-Vandenbergen, 189–214. Amsterdam: Elsevier.

Perception and interpretation of intonational prominence in varieties of South African English*

Sabine Zerbian
University of Potsdam, Germany

Through its intonation an utterance conveys semantic and pragmatic meaning, as e.g. in prosodic focus marking. Languages differ in the use and realization of intonation. Many studies have investigated the production of intonation in learner and contact varieties. The study reports on three experiments that investigate the perception and interpretation of prosodic differences and prominence in contact varieties of South African English. The results show that dominant language background is a significant factor in the perception of intonation and that the interpretation of focus marking through prosodic means is difficult for all multilingual speakers.

Keywords: South African English, prosody, intonation, language contact, focus, perception, interpretation

1. Introduction

Intonation, i.e. the modulation of suprasegmental features of speech such as pitch, duration and intensity, conveys a wealth of semantic and pragmatic information. Languages like English use intonation to differentiate between sentence types (*He got the job.* versus *He got the job?*), to demarcate syntactic units (*The student says | the teacher is crazy.* versus *The student | says the teacher | is crazy*; where | indicate prosodic

---

*   The author wants to thank all participants of the experiments, the School of Languages and Literature Studies at the University of the Witwatersrand, Johannesburg, Steven Fielding and Svenja Schuermann for their help in conducting the study, as well as two anonymous reviewers for their helpful feedback. The research that went into this article was funded by the German Research Foundation (Deutsche Forschungsgemeinschaft, DFG), grant to the Collaborative Research Center on Information Structure (Sonderforschungsbereich 632, Potsdam).

boundaries), and to highlight discourse-new information (*He* BROKE *the car* versus *He broke the* CAR; where capitals indicate a strong accent).

The current article only deals with the last-mentioned function of intonation, namely the highlighting of salient (=focused) information. This function has been considered a prosodic universal by Bolinger (1978). However, research has shown that there are differences in the expression of focus across languages, both in the phonetic and/or phonological realization of prosodic prominence as well as in the function of intonation in general (Ladd 2008, see also Zerbian 2010 for an overview).

Native listeners process sentence accent patterns and their discourse implications rapidly and efficiently (see Cutler, Dahan & Van Donselaar 1997 for a review). But the processing and representation of suprasegmental information in a non-native language is impeded. This has been shown for word accent in French learners of Spanish (Dupoux, Pallier, Sebastian & Mehler 1997) and in bilingual Spanish-French speakers (Dupoux, Peperkamp & Sebastián-Gallés 2010), for focus accent in non-native varieties of English (Pennington & Ellis 2000, Akker & Cutler 2003) and for heritage speakers of *Porteño* Spanish (Feldhausen, Pešková, Kireva & Gabriel 2011). Interestingly, difficulties in processing suprasegmental information can be observed between unrelated languages (e.g. Chinese/English, Pennington & Ellis 2000) and even between closely related languages (e.g. English/Dutch, Akker & Cutler 2003). The complexity of intonation is mirrored in the difficulties of its acquisition in learner varieties (Mennen 2007 for an overview).

This article investigates the perception and interpretation of narrow focus marking by prosodic means in varieties of South African English. South Africa is a multilingual country, which is home to several unrelated languages, such as English, Afrikaans und several Southern Bantu languages. English is the lingua franca in the country, and consequently varieties of South African English have emerged that show linguistic reflexes of the language contact situation (see Sichel-Bazin, Buthke & Meisenburg this volume, Gabriel, Feldhausen & Pešková 2011 and Gut 2005 for other cases of contact intonation).

The article considers both a contact variety (acrolect) and a second language variety (mesolect) in South Africa (see Bickerton 1971 for terminology). There are two reasons why these varieties are considered together: (1) the same mechanisms seem to apply, namely interference from either the first language or the dominant language, (2) in multilingual societies such as South Africa, the transition from second language variety to contact language variety is blurred (Sridhar & Sridhar 1986).

The investigation of narrow focus marking by prosodic means is especially interesting in varieties at the intersection between English and South African Bantu languages, because the South African Bantu languages Northern Sotho and Zulu are reported to not mark focus prosodically, similar to many African languages (Zerbian 2007, Swerts & Zerbian 2010, Zerbian, Genzel & Kügler 2010 for an overview). Furthermore, previous research has shown that Black South African English (the cover term for contact varieties at this intersection, abbreviated as BSAE) differs in its focus intonation, both compared to White South African English (WSAE) and within the variety. Based on perceptual judgments, Swerts & Zerbian (2010) found that mesolect speakers of BSAE do not encode narrow focus in a way which is perceptually equivalent to either acrolect speakers of this variety nor to the control group of speakers of WSAE (see also Lanham 1984). The results are consistent with an active mechanism of interference in the mesolect, parallel to learner varieties.

The current article addresses the question how South African listeners perceive and interpret WSAE focus intonation. This is done by means of three offline experimental tasks which will be presented and discussed in Sections 2–4. In Section 5 the results of the three tasks are summarized and the research question is answered.

2. Task 1: Perception of prosodic differences

2.1 Research question and hypotheses

South African Bantu languages are tone languages, whereas English is a stress language which uses suprasegmental modulation at the sentence level as illustrated in Section 1. Because of the differences in the prosodic system between the languages concerned, a first question is whether speakers of different varieties of South African English perceive intonational differences between utterances as expressed by pitch accents and resulting changes in duration and intensity.

Dupoux et al. (1997: 415) claim that acoustic information is processed the same way across languages, and we would therefore expect that all listeners perform equally on a discrimination task, independent of language background. However, research by Grabe, Rosner, García-Albea & Zhou (2003) and Liang & Van Heuven (2007) equally suggests that speakers of tone languages attend less to intonational differences than speakers of languages that use intonation. The resulting hypothesis is that both monolingual as well as multilingual speakers of South African English are generally able to perceive intonational differences between phrases which differ in pitch accent placement only, with potentially slightly better performance by speakers of WSAE.

2.2 Research design

2.2.1 *Experimental task*

The participants heard a sequence of two English modified noun phrases which constituted a minimal pair in that they only differed in the placement of the pitch accent on either the noun or the modifying adjective. By means of a forced-choice paradigm the listeners' task was to decide if the two phrases they heard were the same or different.

The stimuli were presented by means of Praat's Experiment MFC for simple discrimination experiments (Boersma & Weenink 1992ff). The presentation started with the instructions[1], followed by two examples which illustrated the task. The listeners had to decide for each of the pairs of phrases if they were identical or different and answer by clicking the respective button. There was an initial silence of 0.8 sec, and the two stimuli phrases were separated by a 0.5 sec[2] pause. There was a possibility to take a short break after 25 stimuli. The experiment was self-paced, and the participants could listen to the stimuli twice.

2.2.2   *Stimuli*

The modified noun phrases which served as stimuli in the experimental task were "red cow" and "blue star". The stimuli were selected from a previous production study (Swerts & Zerbian 2010) and stem from ten monolingual speakers of WSAE. The stimuli were judged by two trained listeners to constitute clear cases of pitch accent placement on either the adjective or the noun.

There were 50 stimuli pairs altogether. Each stimuli pair is taken from the same speaker. Of these 50 stimuli pairs, 20 were identical, which means that they were true copies of each other. In these cases, the correct answer would be "They are the same". 21 stimuli pairs differed as to which constituent carried the pitch accent, noun or adjective. In these cases, the correct answer would be "They are different". Finally, 9 stimuli pairs were identical in the accented constituent in that either the noun (N = 5) or the adjective (N = 4) carried the pitch accent, but they were taken from different focus conditions: one phrase of the stimulus pair was taken from a context in which the noun/adjective was *contrasted*, the other phrase was taken from a context in which the noun/adjective was *corrected*. Thus, these phrases were similar in the location of their pitch accent on either noun or adjective but not true copies of each other. There is not one correct answer for these cases as they are not 100% identical, but they are similar in their phonological representation, i.e. which constituent carries the pitch accent. This condition was included to see if listeners' decisions were based on phonetic or phonological similarity.

The stimuli pairings were presented in different randomized orders generated by Praat's Experiment MFC.

2.2.3   *Participants*

The same participants took part in all three tasks reported in the current article. They were students at the University of the Witwatersrand, Johannesburg, and aged between

---

1.   Instructions were: "You will hear two renderings of the same phrase. The phrases always refer to either a "red cow" or a "blue star". Your task is to decide if the two renderings are exactly the same or if they differ in their speech melody and/or rhythm. The differences might be minor. Before the task starts, you will hear one example with and one example without a difference. Click OK if you agree or click replay to hear the example again."

2.   Dupoux et al. (1997) show that the working memory can maintain acoustic information for more than 2 seconds.

19 and 30. The 33 participants were speakers of three different varieties of South African English based on their performance in an English test (Quick Placement Test, QPT) and ethnicity.

Of the participants, eight speakers were white speakers of WSAE with English as their first and only language (8/8) and an average QPT score of 97 (out of 100). Eleven speakers were black speakers of a variety that comprises both the acrolect variety of BSAE (N = 5) and a new variety that does not necessarily reveal its speaker's ethnicity (N = 6; termed postacrolect in Mesthrie 1992: 45). These speakers predominantly gave an African Bantu language as their first language (10/11), and the majority gave English as their sole preferred language (6/11). They had an average QPT score of 89. Acrolectal and postacrolectal speakers are considered together here under the cover term "acrolect" due to the small sample size of each group individually and the fact that they behave parallel in the tasks reported on in this article. Fourteen speakers were black speakers of what can be considered an upper mesolect variety of BSAE. They all reported an African Bantu language as their first language (14/14) and also gave English as or among their preferred languages (8/14), but they scored an average QPT score of 62.

As for the pronunciation features of the participants' speech, the speakers of WSAE and some speakers of the acrolectal variety of South African English shared the features of General South African English. Some speakers of the acrolect and all speakers of the mesolect, on the other hand, showed phonological features reported for BSAE (see Van Rooy 2004), e.g. mergers in vowel quality especially with the high lax vowels and the NURSE vowel, a trilled /r/ (predominantly male speakers, Hartmann & Zerbian 2009), differences in word stress in polysyllabic words (Van Rooy 2002), and general overall rhythm (Coetzee & Wissing 2007). The groups are summarized in Table 1.

2.3   Results

For the data analysis shown in Table 2, the correct or incorrect responses were counted for those 41 stimuli pairs that allowed an unambiguous response as to the two phrases being either identical or different.

Table 1. Indicators of the varieties

Variable	WSAE	Acrolect	Mesolect BSAE
Ethnicity	White	Black	Black
QTP level (average %)	5 (97.13)	5 (88.75)	2–4 (61.64)
Phonological features	General South African English	less to none L1 influence	strong L1 influence
N	8	11	14

Table 2. Correct responses as average raw numbers and percent per variety (max. number of correct responses 41)

Variety	Average correct responses	percent
WSAE	36.1	88.3
Acrolect	35.3	85.9
Mesolect BSAE	31.8	77.4

Table 3. Responses to ambiguous stimuli as average raw numbers and percent per variety (max. number of responses = 9)

Variety	Number of pairs with the same focused constituent which were perceived to be different	Percent
WSAE	8	89
Acrolect	7.5	83
Mesolect BSAE	7.1	77.9

The results show a decrease of correct responses from WSAE to the mesolect of BSAE. A one-factor analysis of variance (ANOVA) revealed an effect of "variety" ($F(2,30) = 5.867$; $p < 0.01$). A (post hoc) Tuckey-Kramer test for samples of unequal size showed a significant difference between the varieties WSAE and Mesolect BSAE ($p<0.05$) and between the varieties Acrolect and Mesolect BSAE ($p<0.05$).

Despite the decrease in correct responses it is important to note that the number of correct responses in all varieties is well beyond chance, which would be 50% because of two possible answers.

The results for the evaluation of the 9 additional stimuli pairs in which the same constituent was accented (either noun or adjective) are presented in Table 3. Note that they were not true copies of each other but have been elicited in differing focus contexts (i.e. corrective and contrastive focus).

The results show that these stimuli were consistently interpreted as different with respect to their intonation by speakers of all varieties. A one-factor analysis of variance (ANOVA) revealed no effect of variety on the responses.

2.4   Discussion

The results of the experiment show that all listeners perceive intonational differences in minimal pairs. This supports the work by Dupoux et al. (1997) cited above, as well as work by Atoye (2005) on the perception of intonational differences in sentences by Nigerian users of English. It should be noted, however, that a significant difference exists between the mesolect variety of BSAE on the one hand and WSAE and the acrolectal variety of South African English on the other hand. In the mesolect, the linguistic influence of the South African Bantu tone language is strongest. This result is therefore in agreement with the work by Grabe et al. (2003) and Liang & Van Heuven (2007) that speakers of a tone language attend less to intonational differences. The higher error rate in mesolect speakers might be a consequence of a difference in parsing, processing or storing suprasegmental information.

The observation that non-identical pairs with the same constituent in focus were judged to be different (see Table 3) seems to suggest that minimal pairs were evaluated on phonetic rather than on phonological grounds.

3.   Task 2: Perception of prominence

3.1   Research question and hypotheses

As mentioned in the introduction, intonation in English has among other things the function of making salient information prosodically prominent. This is not the case in the South African Bantu languages (Zerbian 2007, Swerts & Zerbian 2010), that achieve this by using (morpho-)syntactic means. The next task therefore investigates if speakers of different varieties of South African English associate pitch accent placement (and connected changes in duration and intensity) with prominence.

The hypothesis is that there is a correlation between correct assignment of prominence on the basis of pitch accent and language variety: speakers of WSAE as well as the multilingual speakers of the South African English acrolect will associate intonational features with prominence more reliably than speakers of the mesolect. This is because mesolect BSAE is a variety with greater linguistic influence from the South African Bantu languages. These languages lack prosodic prominence marking, and its acquisition has been shown to be difficult (Mennen 2007).

3.2   Research design and methodology

3.2.1   *Experimental task*
The participants heard an English modified noun phrase which carried a pitch accent on either the noun or the modifying adjective. By means of a forced-choice paradigm the listeners' task was to decide which of the two words in the phrase was more prominent.

The stimuli were presented by means of Praat's Experiment MFC for simple discrimination experiments. The presentation started with the instructions[3], followed by

---

3.   Instructions were: "Now you will hear one phrase, denoting either a "red cow" or a "blue star". Your task is to decide which of the words is the strongest or most salient in the phrase. Click "1st word" if you think that the adjective is the strongest word in the phrase, or click "2nd word" if you think that the noun is the strongest word in the phrase. Only if you cannot decide, click "don't know". Before this task starts, you will hear one example with the 1st word as the

two examples which illustrated the task. The listeners had to decide for each phrase which of the two words was more prominent (referred to as "stronger" or "salient") and click the respective button as a response. The experiment was self-paced, and the participants could listen to the stimuli twice.

3.2.2   *Stimuli*

The modified noun phrases which served as stimuli in the experimental task were either "red cow" or "blue star". The stimuli were selected from a previous production study (Swerts & Zerbian 2010) and stem from 9 white, monolingual students speaking General South African English. They were judged by two trained listeners to constitute clear cases of pitch accent placement on either the adjective or the noun.

There were 20 stimuli altogether. Of these, 9 phrases showed a pitch accent on the adjective. For these cases the appropriate answer is "first word is stronger/more salient". The remaining 11 phrases had a pitch accent on the noun. Here the appropriate answer is "second word is stronger/more salient". The stimuli were presented in randomized order. The same listeners as in 2.2.3 took part in this task.

3.3   Analysis and results

The number of correct responses was counted. Table 4 shows their distribution across varieties.

We find consistent results of around 60% of the responses given correctly. A one-factor analysis of variance (ANOVA) confirmed no effect of variety on the number of correct responses. Again, it needs to be noted all speakers perform above chance, which in the case of three possible answers is at 33.33%. The initial research hypotheses, however, must be rejected.

In analyzing the results it became apparent that participants chose "don't know" as a response on average 12% of the time, with no significant difference between the varieties. Interestingly, though, across all varieties "don't know" was chosen nearly twice

Table 4. Correct responses in prominence judgment

Variety	Correct responses, (max. 20 per speaker, absolute numbers)	N speakers	Average	Percent
WSAE	100	8	12.5	63
Acrolect	134	11	12.2	61
Mesolect BSAE	160	14	11.4	57

strongest word in the phrase and one example with the 2nd word as the strongest word. Click OK if you agree or click replay to hear the example again."

as often when the noun carried a pitch accent (N = 54) than when the adjective carried one (N = 28). This might be indicative of the fact that a pitch accent on an adjective is perceptually much more prominent than on a noun.

3.4   Discussion

The task of judging which constituent in a given phrase or sentence is prominent is widely used in intonation studies. Judgments of linguistically naïve raters seem to provide reliable results with a focus identification rate of e.g. 70–80% in Wu & Xu (2010). Our results, in contrast, suggest a poor performance on prominence identification by listeners of all varieties. This cautions to interpret the results with respect to the research question and calls for reflection on the task instead.

First, with only two words, the phrases were comparatively short. Given that prominence is relative, there might have simply been too little speech material available to listeners to make such a judgment. This is supported by the observation that a phrase with an initial accented adjective was more confidently evaluated with respect to its prominence distribution as opposed to a phrase with an accented noun, which often yielded "don't know". Second, assigning a rather abstract notion of prominence or salience to a constituent is not a trivial task as it addresses metalinguistic knowledge of a listener.

4.   Task 3: Functional interpretation of prominence

4.1   Research question and hypotheses

Listeners have been shown to process prosodic information and its discourse implications (Cutler et al. 1997), e.g. in order to reconstruct a previous discourse (Swerts, Krahmer & Avesani 2002). The third research question therefore asks whether listeners of different varieties of South African English interpret intonational differences expressed by pitch accents and related changes in duration and intensity with respect to the preceding linguistic context.

The hypothesis is that, just as in the previous experimental task, there is a correlation between the correct semantic/pragmatic interpretation of intonational differences and language variety: monolingual as well as the multilingual speakers of the acrolect are expected to interpret intonational features as indicating focus structure more reliably than speakers of the mesolect. This is because mesolect BSAE is a variety with greater linguistic influence from the South African Bantu languages which lack this function of intonation.

4.2   Research design and methodology

4.2.1   *Experimental task*

Modified noun phrases were presented auditorily and the participants' task was to evaluate their functional interpretation in a forced-choice paradigm. The task was to decide what the preceding context of any given phrase was: either a phrase denoting the same object but in a different color or a phrase denoting a different object but in the same colour.

The stimuli were presented by means of Praat's Experiment MFC for simple discrimination experiments. The presentation started with the instructions[4], followed by four examples which illustrated the task. The listeners had to decide for each phrase what the preceding context was and click the respective button as answer. The two different phrases were presented in two separate sets and the answer buttons were adjusted accordingly ("green cow" and "red house" for the target phrase "red cow", and "white star" and "blue bird" for the target phrase "blue star"). The experiment was self-paced, and the participants could listen to the stimuli twice.

4.2.2   *Stimuli*

The experimental stimuli were the same 20 modified noun phrases used in 3.2.2. Again, it is important to note that these phrases were judged to constitute clear cases of pitch accent placement in order to facilitate pragmatic interpretation.

The 10 phrases denoting "red cow" were presented first, followed by a short break, followed by 10 phrases denoting "blue star". This was done in order to minimize confusion regarding different colours and objects. Each block of 10 was presented in randomized order.

For phrases with a pitch accent on the noun, the appropriate answer is that the preceding phrase referred to a different object but in the same colour. For phrases with a pitch accent on the adjective the appropriate answer is that the preceding phrase referred to an identical object but in a different colour. The same participants as in 2.2.3 participated in this task.

4.3   Analysis and results

The data of five participants had to be excluded from further analysis as they had clicked the same response throughout half or even the entire experimental task,

---

4.   Instructions were: "Now you will hear one phrase, denoting either a "red cow" or a "blue star". Your task is to decide which phrase could have preceded the phrase you have just been listening to. It might either be a phrase with the same object but in a different color, or with a different object in the same color. Click the button with the phrase which is more likely to have been the preceding phrase. Only if you cannot decide, click "don't know". Before this task starts, you will be presented with four examples. For the first two examples, we will give you the right answer. Click the button with the correct answer or click replay to hear the example again."

suggesting that the task was not performed as intended. For all other participants, correct confident responses were counted. Where participants have been unsure (and thus clicked "don't know") the answers were not considered and the overall count of possible answers was reduced by these tokens.

The results of correct responses both as raw numbers and as percentages are given in Table 5 per speaker, ordered by variety.

There is a moderate correlation of r = 0.42 between the percent of correct confident responses and English proficiency as measured by the QPT score (p<0.05), suggesting a relation between proficiency level and correct responses.

A comparison of the averages suggests a decrease of correctly interpreted phrases across varieties. A one-factor analysis of variance (ANOVA) reveals that the factor "variety" has indeed an effect on the number of correct responses in this task (F(3,24) = 4.96; p < 0.01). A (post hoc) Tuckey-Kramer test showed a significant difference between the varieties WSAE and mesolect BSAE (p<0.01) and between the varieties WSAE and acrolect (p < 0.05).

It is important to note that only in the case of the speakers of WSAE does the average mean lie above chance (50%). Speakers of all other varieties perform below chance on this task.

4.4   Discussion

A comparable task has been used by Swerts et al. (2002) to show that Dutch listeners are able to reconstruct the preceding context based on prosodic information. The results of the present study suggest that this is also the case for speakers of WSAE, although to a lesser degree. For all multilingual speakers of South African English

Table 5. Correct responses as raw numbers and percent per speaker

Variety: White South African English (overall mean: 13.3 = 68.4%)

Speaker	2	5	7	12	16	26	33			
Correct	14/20	10/20	17/20	16/20	18/19	4/19	14/18			
Correct %	70	50	85	80	95	21	78			

Variety: Acrolect (overall mean: 8.7 = 46.5%)

Speaker	1	3	8	19	30	10	23	28	32	35
Correct	8/20	13/20	8/16	4/13	8/20	12/20	10/19	7/20	7/17	10/20
Correct %	40	65	50	31	40	60	53	35	41	50

Variety: Mesolect Black South African English (overall mean: 7.6 = 40.8%)

Speaker	11	14	18	20	21	22	24	25	29	31	34
Correct	8/20	6/20	7/20	8/16	8/20	8/20	8/20	4/15	7/15	12/20	8/20
Correct %	40	30	35	50	40	40	40	27	47	60	40

performance on this task was below chance. Thus, the interpretation of focus intonation, although a difficult task anyway, is particularly difficult for the multilingual speakers of South African English.

Related studies by Atoye (2005) and Baker (2010) showed comparable results. Nigerian users of English (N = 120) described the intonation of English sentences correctly only in every fourth case and performed particularly poor on those sentences that involved the interpretation of focus intonation (Atoye 2005). Also Mandarin and Korean learners of English had difficulties matching pitch accent location with intended focus in English speech (Baker 2010).

5. Summary

The article set out to address the question how South African listeners perceive and interpret narrow focus marking by prosodic means in General South African English. The experimental tasks showed a significant difference in the perception of intonational differences between mesolect BSAE on the one hand and the other varieties of South African English on the other hand. Mesolect listeners detect intonational differences significantly less often than speakers of the other multilingual or monolingual varieties of South African English considered in this study. This finding is in accordance with the view that the mesolect is influenced considerably by the substrate language, i.e. the South African Bantu languages such as Sotho or Zulu. Given that these languages are tone languages, the influence implies a reduced awareness towards intonational differences.

As for the semantic/pragmatic interpretation of narrow focus marking by intonation, it is interesting to note that the significant difference lies between monolingual speakers of WSAE on the one hand and multilingual speakers on the other hand. Moreover, multilingual speakers assign a correct interpretation of narrow focus marking below chance level. Together these two observations suggest that the semantic/pragmatic interpretation of intonation is more difficult than perception (task 1) and production (Swerts & Zerbian 2010).

Intonation as a carrier of semantic/pragmatic meaning (not to mention attitudinal meaning) is highly relevant in everyday communication. This study contributes results concerning the perception and interpretation of intonation in contact varieties and thereby aims to raise the awareness for this topic in applied areas of linguistics.

References

Akker, E. & A. Cutler. 2003. Prosodic cues to semantic structure in native and nonnative listening. *Bilingualism: Language and Cognition* 6: 81–96.

Atoye, R. O. 2005. Non-native perception and interpretation of English intonation. *Nordic Journal of African Studies* 14: 26–42.

Baker, R. E. 2010. Non-native perception of native English prominence. In *Proceedings of Speech Prosody 2010*, Chicago, IL. <http://speechprosody2010.illinois.edu/papers/100171.pdf> (8 June 2012).

Bickerton, D. 1971. Inherent variability and variable rules. *Foundations of Language* 7: 457–492.

Boersma, P. & D. Weenink. 1992ff. *Praat: Doing Phonetics by Computer* (Computer program). <http://www.praat.org>

Bolinger, D. L. 1978. Intonation across languages. In *Universals of Human Language*, Vol. 2: *Phonology*, ed. J. H. Greenberg, 471–524. Stanford CA: Stanford University Press.

Coetzee, A. W. & D. Wissing. 2007. Global and local durational properties in three varieties of South African English. *The Linguistic Review* 24: 263–290.

Cutler, A., D. Dahan & W. van Donselaar. 1997. Prosody in the comprehension of spoken language: A literature review. *Language and Speech* 40: 141–201.

Dupoux, E., C. Pallier, N Sebastian & J. Mehler. 1997. A destressing "deafness" in French? *Journal of Memory and Language* 36: 406–421.

Dupoux, E., S. Peperkamp & N. Sebastián-Gallés. 2010. Limits on bilingualism revisited: Stress 'deafness' in simultaneous French-Spanish bilinguals. *Cognition* 114: 266–275.

Feldhausen, I., A. Pešková, E. Kireva & C. Gabriel. 2011. Categorical perception of Porteño nuclear accents. In *Proceedings of the 17th International Congress of Phonetic Sciences 2011, Hong Kong, China (ICPhS 17)*, eds. W. Lee & E. Zee, 116–119. Hong Kong: City University of Hong Kong.

Gabriel, C., I. Feldhausen & A. Pešková. 2011. Prosodic phrasing in *Porteño* Spanish. In *Intonational Phrasing in Romance and Germanic: Cross-linguistic and Bilingual Studies* (Hamburg Studies on Multilingualism 10), eds. C. Gabriel & C. Lleó, 153–182. Amsterdam: John Benjamins.

Grabe, E., B. S. Rosner, J. E. García-Albea & X. Zhou. 2003. Perception of English intonation by English, Spanish, and Chinese listeners. *Language and Speech* 46: 375–401.

Gut, U. 2005. Nigerian English prosody. *English World-Wide* 26: 153–177.

Hartmann, D. & S. Zerbian. 2009. Rhoticity in Black South African English: A sociolinguistic study. *Southern African Linguistics and Applied Language Studies* 27: 135–148.

Ladd, R. D. 2008. *Intonational Phonology*, 2nd edn. Cambridge: CUP.

Lanham, L. W. 1984. Stress and intonation and the intelligibility of South African Black English. *African Studies* 43: 217–230.

Liang, J, & V. J. van Heuven. 2007. Chinese tone and intonation perceived by L1 and L2 listeners. In *Tones and Tunes*, Vol. 2: *Experimental Studies in Word and Sentence Prosody*, eds. C. Gussenhoven & T. Riad, 27–61. Berlin: Mouton de Gruyter.

Mennen, I. 2007. Phonological and phonetic influences in non-native intonation. In *Non-native Prosody: Phonetic Description and Teaching Practice*, eds. J. Trouvain & U. Gut, 53–76. Berlin: Mouton de Gruyter.

Mesthrie, R. 1992. *English in Language Shift*. Cambridge: CUP.

Pennington, M. C. & N. C. Ellis. 2000. Cantonese speakers' memory for English sentences with prosodic cues. *The Modern Language Journal* 84: 372–389.

Quick Placement Test. 2004. Oxford: OUP.

Sridhar, K. K. & S. N. Sridhar. 1986. Bridging the paradigm gap: Second language acquisition theory and indigenized varieties of English. *World Englishes* 5: 3–14.

Swerts, M., E. Krahmer & C. Avesani. 2002. Prosodic marking of information status in Dutch and Italian: A comparative analysis. *Journal of Phonetics* 30: 629–654.

Swerts, M. & S. Zerbian. 2010. Intonational differences between L1 and L2 English in South Africa. *Phonetica* 67: 127–146.

Van Rooy, B. 2002. Stress placement in Tswana English: The makings of a coherent system. *World Englishes* 21: 146–160.

Van Rooy, B. 2004. Black South African English: Phonology. In *Handbook of Varieties of English,* Vol. 1: *Phonology,* eds. E. Schneider, K. Burridge, B. Kortmann, R. Mesthrie & C. Upton, 943–952. Berlin: Mouton de Gruyter.

Wu, W. L. & Y. Xu. 2010. Prosodic focus in Hong Kong Cantonese without post-focus compression. In *Proceedings of Speech Prosody 2010*, Chicago IL. <http://speechprosody2010.illinois.edu/papers/100040.pdf> (8 June 2012).

Zerbian, S. 2007. Investigating prosodic focus marking in Northern Sotho. In *Focus Strategies: Evidence from African Languages,* eds. K. Hartmann, E. Aboh & M. Zimmermann, 55–79. Berlin: Mouton de Gruyter.

Zerbian, S. 2010. Recent developments in the typology of intonation. *Linguistics and Language Compass* 4: 874–889.

Zerbian, S., S. Genzel & F. Kügler. 2010. Experimental work on prosodically-marked information structure in selected African languages (Afroasiatic and Niger-Congo). In *Proceedings of Speech Prosody 2010*, Chicago IL. <http://speechprosody2010.illinois.edu/papers/100976.pdf> (8 June 2012).

The prosody of Occitan-French bilinguals

Rafèu Sichel-Bazin[1,2], Carolin Buthke[1] and Trudel Meisenburg[1]
[1]University of Osnabrück, Germany; [2]Universitat Pompeu Fabra,
Barcelona, Spain

Occitan is a threatened Gallo-Romance language in a diglossic contact situation
with French in Southern France. To examine the extent of prosodic interference
we proceeded to a comparative analysis of semi-spontaneous speech recorded
with bilingual speakers in both languages and monolingual northern French
speakers. The higher frequency of schwa syllables gives southern French
rhythmic properties that recall Occitan. Both languages display Accentual
Phrases, a prosodic unit that may contain more than one lexical word but only
one final pitch accent, and an optional initial rise. However, in the bilinguals'
prosody, AP-internal rhythmic prominences denote a tendency to maintain
remainders of Occitan lexical accent in their French, whereas they correspond to
a weakening of word accent in Occitan under French influence.

Keywords: Occitan, French, bilingualism, prosody, intonation, phrasing,
language contact

1. Occitan and French: Two Romance languages in contact

1.1 Occitan and French: The challenge of diglossia

Occitan, spoken mainly in the southern third of France, occupies a central position
within the Romance languages, which all derive from Latin. Together with French,
which is about to supplant it in its ancestral territory, Occitan belongs to the Gallo-
Romance subfamily, but is neighboring with southern Romance branches in the South-
West (Ibero-Romance) and East (Italo-Romance); see Hualde (2003).

While Occitan benefits from legal protection in Spain (Aran Valley, Catalonia)
and in the Italian alpine valleys where it is spoken, it does not have any legal status in
France, where all other languages but French have been banned from official usage
since 1539 (*Ordonnance de Villers-Cotterêts*). This has led to a situation of diglossia
characterized by the coexistence of two languages which fulfill complementary functions within a society: the low variety – in this case, Occitan – is consigned to private

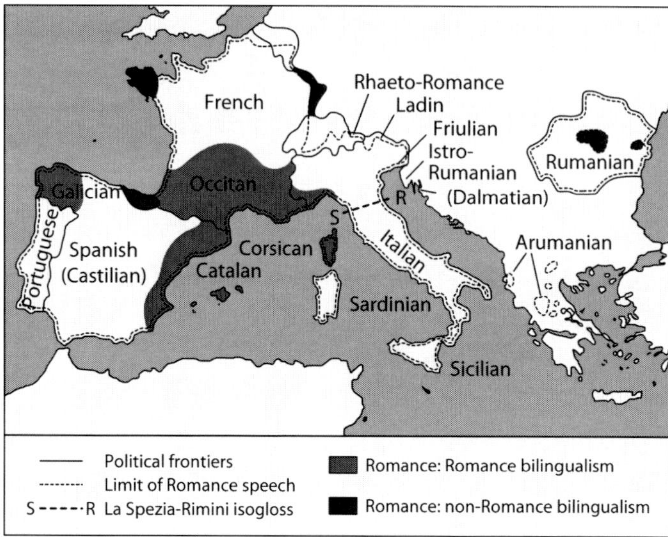

Figure 1. Geographic location of Occitan and French within Romance
(from Green 2009: 165)

uses, whereas the high variety – here, French – is employed in all public and prestigious situations (Ferguson 1959, Lafont 1971a, Meisenburg 1998). In this state of imbalance Occitan became more and more marginalized, and generational transmission finally stopped during the first half of the last century: speaking the local language, labeled as a useless, disturbing *patois*, and prohibited at school, was considered a lack of education impeding social advancement. Today French is the main language, and Occitan continues declining: following estimations from the late 1960's, there were one to two million people (out of the 11.8 million inhabitants of the Occitan territory) who spoke Occitan habitually, another one to two million who used it occasionally, and one million who could be considered as potential speakers, while between six and nine million did not speak it at all (Lafont 1971b: 56–57). Reliable statistics are not available but the situation has not improved since, rather the contrary, and it is still as difficult to clearly define a speaker of Occitan. What is sure is that they are few, dispersed on a large territory, and that their language is highly threatened.

1.2 Implications of the contact between Occitan and French

The diglossic situation in Southern France has entailed that all Occitan speakers are bilingual, and while the close contact between the two languages has led to interference on all linguistic levels, its impact is particularly strong in the phonology, where both segmental and prosodic properties are concerned (Coquillon & Durand 2010, Lonnemann & Meisenburg 2009). On the segmental level, for example, the uvular fricative rhotic has made its appearance in the pronunciation of Occitan speakers, partly replacing apical trill and flap (Durand 2009). In the other direction, nasal vowels – which are not part of the Occitan phonemic inventory – are often (partly) denasalized and followed by a consonantal nasal appendage in southern French (Durand 1988: 29–54, Clairet 2008). Moreover, the neutral vowel schwa, derived from Latin -*a*, has been largely eliminated in standard French, but is usually maintained in the southern varieties (Durand, Slater & Wise 1987: 983–1004, Eychenne 2006, Lonnemann 2005). Here again southern French shows interference with Occitan where the outcome of Latin -*a* is still present, resulting in an increased number of syllables that affects the rhythmic shape of utterances.

At the prosodic level, it has been shown that language contact induces mutual transfer of suprasegmental features, such as pitch accent types and distribution (Romera & Elordieta in press, Colantoni & Gurlekian 2004) or rhythmic properties (Gabriel & Kireva 2012). Focusing on phrasing and its accentual and intonational correlates, this article aims at characterizing prosodic interference in the linguistic systems of Occitan-French bilinguals, in contrast with monolingual speakers of northern French.

2.   Theoretical framework

Prosody can be defined as the set of phenomena involving variations in pitch, temporal organization and intensity during the speech act. Though the speech flow is continuous throughout time, discourse is structured by phrasing in chunks of variable degree of (in-)dependence. Besides by silent pauses, the breaks that separate these prosodic constituents are instantiated by pre-boundary lengthening and/or tonal marking. Moreover, some syllables are perceived as more prominent than others within an utterance; these syllables are said to be accented, and they are usually marked by a clearer segmental articulation as well as by an increase in fundamental frequency (F0), duration and/or intensity (Ladd 2008: 49–55). The distribution of accents in an utterance is subject to rules, which arise from lexical, morphological, syntactic, semantico-pragmatic and/or prosodic constraints (Hayes 1995: 24–61, 367–399). Intonation *stricto sensu* consists in variations in F0, which constitute the pitch contour of utterances. Prosody is the result of the interaction of all these suprasegmental phenomena, used to express both linguistic and paralinguistic information (Ladd 2008).

The different levels of prosodic constituency are modeled in a hierarchy, which aims at being universal. Following Selkirk (1984, 1986) and Nespor & Vogel (1986/2007), this prosodic hierarchy includes the following constituents: Syllable, Foot, Prosodic Word, Clitic Group, Phonological Phrase (PP), Intonation Phrase (IP) and Utterance. While the necessity of all these units continues to be subject to debate, other constituents were introduced to account for the prosody of individual languages. In particular, Beckman & Pierrehumbert's (1986) proposal of the Accentual Phrase

(AP), a prosodic unit that may contain more than one lexical word but displays at most one pitch accent, and of the intermediate phrase (ip), situated in between the AP (or PP) and the IP, constitutes an important contribution, on which we will rely in our study. We will thus consider the relevance of Syllable, Foot, AP, ip and IP in Occitan and French.

Our work is based on the Autosegmental Metrical (AM) model, which was initially developed by Pierrehumbert (1980) in order to describe English intonation and has been adapted to many other languages since. Its precepts have been integrated into the language-specific prosodic transcription systems ToBI (Tone and Break Indices). The AM model basically posits an independent tonal tier with two discrete levels: a high tone (H) and a low tone (L), which associate with the segmental tier on specific landmarks[1]. The overall pitch contour of an utterance is the result of an interpolation between the tonal targets.

Metrically strong syllables are the anchor points for *pitch accents*, which may be monotonal – comprising one tone only (H* or L*) –, or bitonal, that is, composed of two tones (HL*, LH*, H*L or L*H). While the starred tone is always associated with the accented syllable, the preceding or following tone within a bitonal pitch accent is considered a *leading* or *trailing tone* respectively. Out of all these pitch accent types, each language chooses its own inventory and follows specific rules for their distribution and combination. The most important accent in the IP is called *nuclear*; its realization is more marked and it is generally in final position. Non-nuclear accents, which are less important for the expression of meaning, normally display fewer types.

Tones can also associate with the edges of prosodic constituents and are then *boundary tones*: H% or L% at the right edge of an IP, H- or L- at that of an ip. Some languages (for example Catalan) make use of bitonal (LH-, LH%, HL%) or even tritonal (LHL%) boundary tones (Prieto, Aguilar, Mascaró, Torres-Tamarit & Vanrell 2009).

3.   Current approaches to Occitan and French prosody

3.1   Accentuation

Accentuation is the assignment of a prominence to certain syllables by means of variations in F0, duration and/or intensity. At least two different levels are traditionally distinguished: primary and secondary accentuation (Van der Hulst 1999: 72–75).

3.1.1   *Primary accentuation*
Latin had a quantity-sensitive accent, falling always on the penultimate syllable in disyllabic words, and in longer words on the penultimate syllable if it was heavy, otherwise

---

1.   Lowering or raising of a tone with respect to the preceding one may be transcribed by '!' (downstep) and 'ɪ' (upstep).

on the antepenultimate (1a)[2] (Pulgram 1975, Wanner 1979). Loss of vocalic quantity and effects of apocope and syncope led to a lexically defined position for accent in the majority of Romance languages, where it hits one of the last three syllables of the word (Roca 1999), this being the present situation in southern Romance languages (1b). Occitan went one step further in this evolution by giving up antepenultimate accent in the medieval period (Schultz-Gora 1924: 37): the position of lexical accent is either the last or the penultimate syllable of the word (1c) (Meisenburg 2001). French evolution was even more radical. By deleting segmental material following the accented syllable, it showed an intermediate stage with a fixed accent system that allowed only schwa syllables in post-accentual position. So accent location became totally predictable, hitting always the last full vowel of a lexical word (Lahiri, Riad & Jacobs 1999: 392–399). Finally French gave up its lexical accent in favor of a prominence that falls on the last full vowel of a group of words, the *groupe rythmique* or Accentual Phrase (AP) (1d) (Fouché 1959: XLIX–LVII, Astésano 2001). French thus differs from Occitan and the southern Romance languages, on the one hand, in that accent is not lexically contrastive and, on the other hand, in that the domain of primary accentuation is the AP, a unit that may contain more than one lexical word. In southern Romance, on the contrary, the AP does not seem to be relevant since primary accentuation is based on the Prosodic Word.

(1) a. Latin: $[(\sigma)_n \; '\sigma_h \; \sigma]/[(\sigma)_n \; '\sigma \; \sigma_l \; \sigma]/['\sigma \; \sigma]$
    a<u>mī</u>cus *<u>la</u>crima* *<u>ma</u>lum* *<u>mā</u>lum*
    'friend' 'tear' 'evil' 'apple'

  b. Southern Romance (e.g. Catalan): $[(\sigma)_n \; '\sigma \; (\sigma) \; (\sigma)]$
    pa<u>tir</u> *<u>pa</u>ti* *<u>llà</u>grima* *pe<u>ti</u>tes <u>llà</u>grimes*

  c. Occitan: $[(\sigma)_n \; '\sigma \; (\sigma)]$
    pa<u>tir</u> *<u>pa</u>ti* *<u>la</u>grema* *de pi<u>cho</u>nas la<u>gre</u>mas*

  d. French: $[(\sigma)_n \; '\sigma \; (\partial)]_{AP}$
    pâ<u>tir</u> *pa<u>tio</u>* *<u>larme</u>* *de petites <u>larmes</u>*
    'suffer' 'patio' 'tear' 'small tears'

3.1.2 *Secondary accentuation*

Secondary accents are said to be relatively rare in southern Romance languages; in Ibero-Romance, for instance, they are found mainly in particular speech styles such as broadcasting, didactic or public speech (Hualde 2006/2007). French on the contrary is considered to display frequent tonal rises at the beginning of APs (2a)[3]. Originally used to mark insistence, a generalization of these secondary accents has been observed

---

2. σ: syllable; 'σ: accented syllable (in the examples of (1), underlined and in boldface); (σ): facultative syllable; the index *n* marks recursivity; σ_l: light syllable; σ_h: heavy syllable; (∂): potential schwa syllable; AP: Accentual Phrase.

3. $_l\sigma$: secondarily accented syllable (in the examples of (2), underlined and in boldface).

lately (Fouché 1959: LVIII–LXIII, Fónagy 1980, Lyche & Girard 1995, Astésano 2001): usually associated with the first syllable of the first lexical word in the AP, they would have become a mere marker of the left edge of this prosodic constituent (Jun & Fougeron 2000, 2002, Welby 2006, Astésano, Bard & Turk 2007). In Occitan (2b), similar initial rises have been described (Hualde 2003, 2004, Sichel-Bazin 2009) and the question arises whether they may have similar functions as in French.

(2) a. French: $[_{\iota}\sigma\,(\sigma)_n{}'\sigma\,(\partial)]_{AP}$ *de **pe**tites larmes* 'small tears'
     b. Occitan: $[_{\iota}\sigma\,(\sigma)_n{}'\sigma\,(\sigma)]$ *la **ma**ionesa*   'the mayonnaise'

3.2   Intonation and phrasing in the AM model

The first autosegmental approach to French intonation stems from Hirst & Di Cristo (1984); in its most recent version (Di Cristo 2011) prosodic structure is defined regardless of syntax, semantics or pragmatics. Prosodic entities rather derive from the projection of underlying prominences that surface as accents indicating right edges and serving different functions. Organized in a recursive hierarchy, these prosodic constituents start at the lowest level with the *unité tonale* (UT, Tonal Unit), which is characterized by a tonal rise (LH) at its right edge and corresponds to the metrical foot of other approaches (Hayes 1995, Fagyal, Kibbee & Jenkins 2006: 56). The following entity, the *syntagme prosodique* (SP, Prosodic Phrase) is marked by final lengthening and may display tonal bipolarization: while it obligatorily ends in a tonal rise coinciding with the lengthened final syllable, it may begin with another rise at its left edge. The *unité intonative* (UI, Intonation Unit) is marked by a major final lengthening and a final nuclear contour, which can be conclusive or non-conclusive. When the UI is followed by a *segment d'UI* (Segment of Intonation Unit) the two form a *macro-UI*. At the top of the hierarchy, UIs are organized in *périodes* (Periods) and these in *paratons* ((prosodic) paragraphs).

The basic unit of Post's (2000) grammar of French intonation, the Phonological Phrase (PP), is derived from the morpho-syntactic structure: it maps projections of X-bar category heads and is thus defined independently from phonological properties (see Post 2011 for a recent summary). PPs group into Intonation Phrases (IP), which are marked by boundary tones on either side and a nuclear accent on the last full syllable. Further (prenuclear) pitch accents may associate with full final as well as initial syllables of lexical items inside the IP, and an elaborate constraint hierarchy accounts for their optimal distribution.

As for Di Cristo (2011), Jun & Fougeron's (2000, 2002) approach is not syntactically defined. Their basic unit is the Accentual Phrase, the tonal bipolarity of which they formalize by means of an underlying tonal structure LHiLH*, constituted of an initial rise (LHi), and a final pitch accent (LH*), which is accompanied by lengthening. Not all tones of this structure are necessarily realized on the surface: Welby (2006), who describes their different alignment patterns, found the complete LHiLH* in 50% of her data. APs are organized in IPs, which end in an L% or H% boundary tone.

In our study, we basically follow Jun & Fougeron's approach to examine whether Occitan also shows evidence of the AP. In front of Post's model, Jun & Fougeron's has the advantage of being prosodically based, without syntactic constraints on the prosodic constituents, and it is thus directly applicable to transcription. Moreover, it gives a better representation of the difference between final and initial accents than does Di Cristo's. We therefore adopt AP and IP in the sense Jun & Fougeron use them. However, we consider that AP-final accents may display a larger variety than they claim. Moreover, as in Di Cristo's model, we assume that minor prominences may be found at the foot level within the AP (or SP).

Whether a prosodic unit between AP and IP – namely, the intermediate phrase (ip) – is needed in the hierarchy, is an open question for many languages, and different standpoints are in competition. While Post's (2000, 2002) proposal for French does not include the ip, but considers as an IP any maximal syntactic projection when it is marked by final lengthening and a boundary tone, D'Imperio & Michelas (2010) introduce the intermediate phrase to account for the grouping of several APs that belong to the same heavy syntactic constituent. The ip would be marked by a less pronounced final lengthening than in IP-final position and by a boundary tone showing a narrower range but blocking downstep. This is another point that we wanted to check in our analysis, both in French and in Occitan.

As to the prosody of Occitan, very little work has been done so far. Hualde (2003, 2004) draws up an overall view of its intonational organization, in which he distinguishes nuclear configurations associated to different sentence types. While showing that Occitan is close to its southern neighbors in this aspect, he points out that by displaying initial rises it approaches French. Such initial rises as well as a variety of pitch accents were also found in the Occitan data analyzed in Sichel-Bazin (2009) and Meisenburg (2011).

4. Methodology

This study is based on data from a DFG-funded research project on *Intonation in language contact: Occitan and French*, namely on a number of summaries of the Aesop fable *The North Wind and the Sun*. The speakers had to listen to an audio recording of the fable interpreted by a speaker of a dialectal variety similar to theirs[4], and then sum it up in their own words. This enabled us to record short texts (between 20 and 80s), with a similar organization in common lexical items, which facilitates comparisons. Since the corpus we recorded is huge, only the speakers showing the most fluent

---

4.   We want to thank Sèrgi Carles for establishing and performing an Occitan version of *The North Wind and the Sun* (*La Cisampa e lo Solelh*) in the Lengadocian dialect.

productions were retained, so we used a sample of five bilingual speakers from La Cauna/Lacaune (F-81), comparing their Occitan and French versions to the French summaries of four speakers from Lille (F-59) and four from Orléans (F-45), who served as a control group for French varieties without contact with Occitan. The 18 sound files were analyzed in Praat (Boersma & Weenink 1992ff) labeling syllables, tones and prosodic boundaries.

As we will focus on the relevance and potential realization of APs, ips and IPs in our Occitan and French data, it was first necessary to define clear criteria for the detection and classification of prosodic boundaries and prominences. The boundary markers we retained are silent pauses, final lengthening, tonal marking (by a pitch accent, a boundary tone and/or a blocking of downstep), the absence of concatenation or resyllabification and the autonomy of the chunk[5]. Since the data consist of spontaneous speech, no systematic comparable measurements were possible and we had to rely mainly on our perceptive judgments. In this type of data, speakers plan what they want to say while they are summing up the story; this entails frequent pauses and hesitations, speech rate varies along the recordings, and constituents of different length and autonomy appear, being difficult to classify, a fortiori in comparison with read lab speech. Therefore no quantitative analysis was performed.

5.   Results

This section presents the qualitative results of our analysis, aiming at determining the role, realization and internal organization of AP, ip and IP in the spontaneous speech of Occitan and French bilinguals. To better account for possible interference these results are further compared with our findings from monolingual speakers of northern varieties of French.

5.1   Accentual Phrase (AP)

As said in Section 3, the Accentual Phrase (AP) has been defined in French as a prosodic unit that may contain more than one lexical word but displays only one final pitch accent marked by lengthening; additionally it may begin with a tonal rise. Its internal coherence, indicated by generalized resyllabification, is reinforced by tonal bipolarization: initial and final accents mirror Jun & Fougeron's (2000) LHiLH* scheme. Occitan is a word-accent language, like its southern Romance neighbors, but it displays initial tonal rises on syllables that are not lexically accentable, accompanied by a reinforcement of the onset consonant, comparable to the French AP-initial rises. Furthermore we found lexical words realized with hardly any prominence; consequently,

---

5.   To test their autonomy, we extracted the chunks in Praat and determined perceptively whether they sounded as if they could have been produced as such in isolation.

these cannot be considered to be accented but seem to be integrated in prosodically coherent groups of words that recall the French AP. These findings argue in favor of the relevance of the AP in the prosodic hierarchy of Occitan.

5.1.1 *AP-final accents*

The prosodic function of the final accent is to mark the right edge of the AP. It aligns with the last accentable syllable, the head of the AP. Its features include lengthening of the rime, a tonal movement and often an intensity peak. These characteristics are shared by Occitan and French, so no influence of language contact can be found at this level.

Our data display quite a lot of surface variation in the intonation contours: we found different rising, falling and level pitch accents in all three varieties, with different alignment properties. This suggests that, possibly, there is a higher diversity of final pitch accents than what has been described in the literature on French and even on Occitan (see Section 3.2). However, further research is needed to determine whether all these configurations are phonologically contrastive and to which meaning they are associated in both languages. Moreover, the phonetic timing and scaling of each pitch accent category might differ from one variety to the other, and interference phenomena might be found at this level.

5.1.2 *AP-initial accents*

Initial accents are optional tonal rises aligned with one of the first syllables of the AP. Even if they are not very frequent in our corpus, initial accents are present in Occitan as well as in southern and northern French. So, they must be considered as a common feature of the Gallo-Romance group singularizing it within Romance.

The possible features that characterize the initial accent are a tonal rise (L)Hi, an intensity peak and/or a reinforcement of the initial consonant – all enhanced in the case of emphasis. Its prosodic function is to mark the left edge of the AP, and it may be used for pragmatic purposes to highlight the constituent it associates with. It may align with initial syllables of lexical words, but it is also possible to find it on one of the first clitics in the AP. This appears to be more frequent in Occitan than in French. In the Occitan example of Figure 2, for instance, the proclitic pronoun *se* bears an initial rise.

Even though bilingual speakers sometimes accentuate clitics in their French productions (see for instance the first definite article *le* in Figure 5), they seem to maintain quite well this alignment difference between the two languages and to use a pattern in one language and another one in the other: in French, initial accents mainly align with the left edge of the first content word in the AP, whereas they appear to align roughly with the left edge of the whole AP in Occitan.

5.1.3 *Minor prominences within the AP: The role of feet*

The frequent realization of schwa syllables in southern French, which entails a larger quantity of syllables, distinguishes it from northern varieties while approaching it to Occitan. As schwa syllables are quite weak, they contribute to the impression of a more

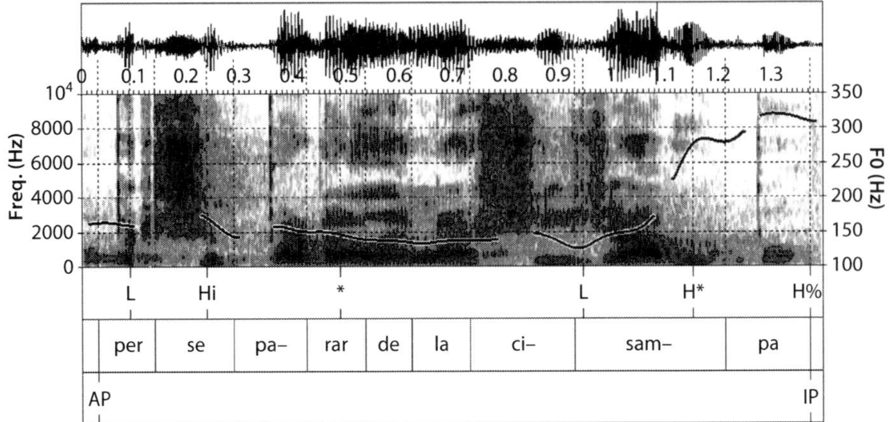

Figure 2. Initial accent on the clitic *se* in the Occitan AP *per se parar de la cisampa* ('in order to protect himself from the wind') (La_oc_AE01)

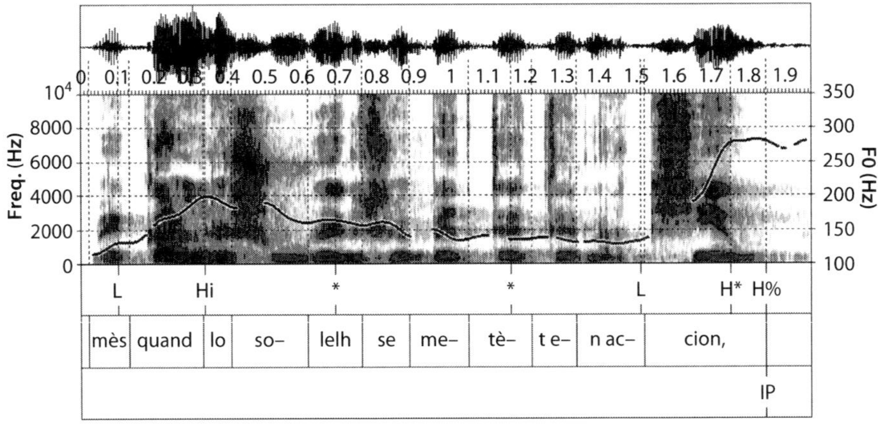

Figure 3. Occitan AP with several lexical items *mès quand lo solelh se metèt en accion* ('but when the sun started up') (La_oc_AE01)

regular alternation between strong and weak syllables in southern French, which again is parallel to Occitan. A similar effect results from the emergence of AP-internal weak prominences. With an increase in F0 and/or intensity, their acoustic correlates are somehow comparable to those of accents, yet being minimized, and as duration does not seem to be involved, they may not be qualified as proper final accents, but rather seem to be reduced to a rhythmic function. Most of the time, they recall the position of lexically accentable syllables within the AP. In Figures 2 and 3 the APs *per se parar de la cisampa* and *mès quand lo solelh se metèt en accion* contain several lexical words;

the accentable syllables *-rar* (Figure 2), *-lelh* and *-tè(t)* (Figure 3) do not bear any primary accent but are marked by merely rhythmic prominences.

As these rhythmic prominences do not mark the head of APs, they must be the head of a prosodic constituent occupying a lower level in the prosodic hierarchy, presumably the foot. Following this hypothesis, the AP would be constituted of feet whose heads consist in different types of syllables: besides those that bear – initial or final – accents, there are the AP-internal syllables that are not completely deaccented, and in long APs even word-internal syllables can serve for this purpose (see for instance the syllable *-sa-* in the word *desabilhèt* in Figure 4). From our observations so far, the heads of AP-internal feet, which align mainly with lexical accent positions, surface more frequently and are marked in a somewhat stronger way in Occitan than in southern French, while they hardly appear in northern French: they thus seem to signal a continuum of word autonomy between these three linguistic varieties. In the bilinguals' prosody, these AP-internal rhythmic prominences denote a tendency to maintain remainders of the Occitan lexical accent in French, whereas in Occitan they correspond to a weakening of the word accent, which might result from French influence.

5.2   Intonation Phrase (IP) and intermediate phrase (ip)

The IP is the highest prosodic constituent, shared by French and Occitan, and it consists of one or more APs[6]. Its head is constituted by the most prominent or *nuclear* accent, which is generally the last one; a major final lengthening and a boundary tone (T%) mark its right edge, often followed by a silent pause. It generally forms a more or less autonomous syntactic and semantic unit.

The example in Figure 4 counts two IPs. The final tonal configuration of the first one consists in a rising nuclear accent (LH*) and a high boundary tone (H%), signaling continuation; the second one is terminative and concludes with a low nuclear accent (L*) and a low boundary tone (L%) that triggers a pitch fall to the baseline of the speaker's tessitura.

As said in Section 3.2, it is not clear if another level in between AP and IP – namely, the intermediate phrase (ip) – is needed. The difference in their surface forms is subtle. On the one hand, both IP and ip are supposed to be marked by final lengthening and a boundary tone blocking downstep. On the other hand, as blocking of downstep is only detectable when the constituents contain more than one AP, and as lengthening marks the AP-final accent as well, ips are also hard to distinguish from APs. Relying on syntactic criteria, APs would be combined into an ip to individualize within the IP the heavy syntactic constituent they belong to. On a semantico-pragmatic basis, an ip alone could never signal finality.

---

6.   However, several IPs may appear to group together at a higher level since downtrend may occur over longer stretches of speech and not all IPs are necessarily followed by a register shift.

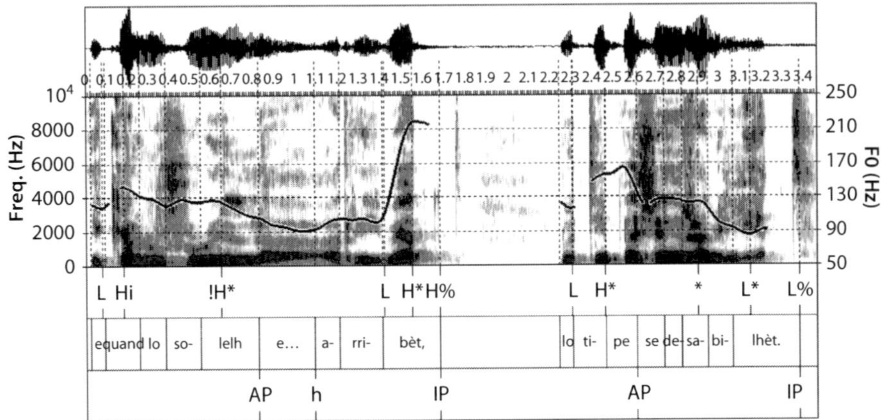

Figure 4. Occitan example of two IPs: *e quand lo solelh arribèt, lo tipe se desabilhèt* ('and when the sun arrived, the guy took his clothes off') (La_oc_AM01)

In all varieties of our corpus we detected prosodic boundaries that we perceived as stronger than those at the end of an AP, but as weaker than those at the end of an IP; theses boundaries might thus define a prosodic unit with an intermediate autonomy. It is marked by a boundary tone, but its realization is less clear than in IP-final position. Such boundary tones are more easily detectable in Occitan and in southern French, as these provide a higher rate of post-accentual syllables serving as anchor points, but they are also present in northern French.

Figure 5 shows a southern French example of such boundaries, for which it is not straightforward to determine whether they should be analyzed as IP- or as ip-final. High boundary tones (annotated H-) align with the final syllables *-leil* and *-se*. The edges of the first two constituents do not correspond with major syntactic boundaries but mark a moment of detention during the speech act that interrupts the speech flow; it indicates that the speaker is planning what she is going to say. The last constituent, however, is syntactically completed, and the final boundary tone (annotated H%) corresponds to a standard continuation rise. While we opted to distinguish ips and IPs in the annotation, the criteria to define these units and to differentiate between them need further adjustment; a more detailed analysis of their acoustic correlates will allow for a better comparison between varieties.

6. Conclusions

The long-lasting diglossic situation in Southern France has led to interference between French and Occitan, two languages that differ on several prosodic aspects. Most notably French has lost its lexical accent in favor of a phrase-final prominence, while

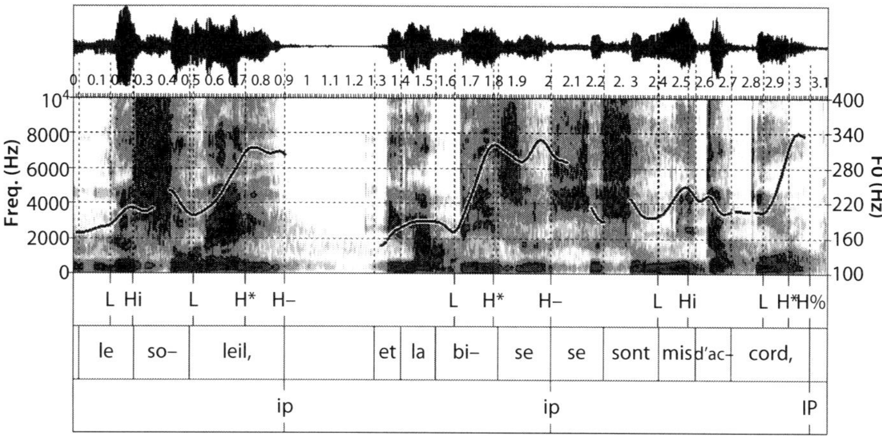

Figure 5. *Le soleil, et la bise se sont d'accord* ('The sun, and the wind found an agreement') (La_fr_AE01)

Occitan still displays a lexically contrastive accent that hits the final or penultimate syllable of a word. But as we have shown, Occitan seems to be on its way to adopt the Accentual Phrase (AP), the characteristic *groupe rythmique* of French prosody. The AP may contain more than one lexical word but displays only one pitch accent aligned with the lengthened last or penultimate syllable of the group. In French as well as in Occitan the AP optionally shows an initial tonal rise whose delimitative function is often associated with a pragmatic one. While this rise is usually aligned with the initial syllable of the first lexical word in northern French, bilingual speakers do not hesitate to associate it with clitics in Occitan, and sometimes even in French.

Lexical accent thus seems to be weakened in Occitan but is not completely given up: we detected slight prominences on lexically accentable syllables within the AP, which we interpret as heads of metrical feet serving for rhythmical purposes. Very rare in northern French, these prominences surface rather regularly in the French of our bilingual speakers too. Another rhythmic characteristic of Occitan results from the persistence of both ultimate and penultimate accentuation in AP-final position. While northern French has erased post-tonic material, southern French realizes underlying schwa syllables in this place, thereby recalling Occitan rhythm.

Quantitative work will have to establish if the observed patterns are systematic, thus allowing to generalize our qualitative results on transfer and change of prosodic characteristics. However, our findings indicate that bilingualism, which has been shown to induce transfer of intonational and rhythmic properties in other contact situations, has led to prosodic interference between Occitan and French, reflected in accentuation and phrasing. To what extent it has affected intonation and rhythm will be the object of further studies.

References

Astésano, C. 2001. *Rythme et accentuation en français: Invariance et variabilité stylistique.* Paris: L'Harmattan.

Astésano, C., E. Bard & A. Turk. 2007. Structural influences on initial accent placement in French. *Language and Speech* 50: 423–446.

Beckman, M. & J. Pierrehumbert. 1986. Intonational structure in Japanese and English. *Phonology Yearbook* 3: 255–309.

Boersma, P. & D. Weenink. 1992ff. *Praat: Doing phonetics by computer* (Computer program). <http://www.praat.org>

Clairet, S. 2008. Une étude aérodynamique de la nasalité vocalique en français méridional. In *Actes des journées d'études sur la parole XXVII.* Avignon, Paper 1677. <http://www.afcp-parole.org/doc/Archives_JEP/2008_XXVIIe_JEP_Avignon/PDF/avignon2008_pdf/JEP/073_jep_1677.pdf> (6 June 2012)

Colantoni, L. & J. Gurlekian. 2004. Convergence and intonation: Historical evidence from Buenos Aires Spanish. *Bilingualism: Language and Cognition* 7: 107–119.

Coquillon, A. & J. Durand. 2010. La France hexagonale méridionale. Introduction: Tendances lourdes du français du midi. In *Normes et variations en français parlé contemporain: ressources pour l'étude du français,* eds. S. Detey, J. Durand, B. Laks & C. Lyche, 185–197. Paris: Ophrys.

D'Imperio, M. & A. Michelas. 2010. Embedded register levels and prosodic phrasing in French. In *Proceedings of Speech Prosody 2010,* Chicago IL. <http://speechprosody2010.illinois.edu/papers/100879.pdf> (6 June 2012).

Di Cristo, A. 2011. Une approche intégrative des relations de l'accentuation au phrasé prosodique du français. *French Language Studies* 21: 73–95.

Durand, J. 1988. Phénomènes de nasalité en français du midi: Phonologie de dépendance et sous-spécification. *Recherches linguistiques* 17: 29–54.

Durand, J. 2009. Essai de panorama phonologique: Les accents du Midi. In *Le français, d'un continent à l'autre: Mélanges offerts à Yves Charles Morin,* eds. L. Baronian & F. Martineau, 123–170. Québec: Presses de l'Université Laval.

Durand, J., C. Slater & H. Wise. 1987. Observations on schwa in southern French. *Linguistics* 25: 983–1004.

Eychenne, J. 2006. *Aspects de la phonologie du schwa dans le français contemporain: Optimalité, visibilité prosodique, gradience.* PhD dissertation, Université de Toulouse-Le Mirail.

Fagyal, Z., D. Kibbee & F. Jenkins. 2006. *French: A Linguistic Introduction.* Cambridge: CUP.

Ferguson, C. 1959. Diglossia. *Word* 15: 325–340.

Fónagy, I. 1980. L'accent français: Accent probabilitaire (dynamique d'un changement prosodique). In *L'accent en français contemporain,* eds. I. Fónagy & P. León, 123–233. Ottawa: Didier.

Fouché, P. 1959. *Traité de prononciation française.* Paris: Klincksieck.

Gabriel, C. & E. Kireva. 2012. Intonation und Rhythmus im spanisch-italienischen Kontakt: Der Fall des *Porteño*-Spanischen. In *Testo e ritmi: Zum Rhythmus in der italienischen Sprache,* eds. M. Selig & E. Schafroth, 131–149. Frankfurt: Peter Lang.

Green, J. 2009. Romance languages. In *The World's Major Languages,* 2nd edn, ed. B. Comrie, 164–170. London: Routledge.

Hayes, B. 1995. *Metrical Stress Theory: Principles and Case Studies*. Chicago IL: The University of Chicago Press.

Hirst, D. & A. di Cristo. 1984. French intonation: A parametric approach. *Die Neueren Sprachen* 83: 554–569.

Hualde, J. I. 2003. Remarks on the diachronic reconstruction of intonational patterns in Romance with special attention to Occitan as a bridge language. *Catalan Journal of Linguistics* 2: 181–205.

Hualde, J. I. 2004. Romance intonation from a comparative and diachronic perspective: Possibilities and limitations. In *Contemporary Approaches to Romance Linguistics*, eds. J. Auger, J. C. Clements & B. Vance, 217–237. Amsterdam: John Benjamins.

Hualde, J. I. 2006/2007. Stress removal and stress addition in Spanish. *Journal of Portuguese Linguistics* 5–6: 59–89.

Jun, S.-A. & C. Fougeron. 2000. A phonological model of French intonation. In *Intonation: Analysis, Modeling, and Technology*, ed. A. Botinis, 209–242. Dordrecht: Kluwer.

Jun, S.-A. & C. Fougeron. 2002. Realizations of accentual phrase in French intonation. *Probus* 14: 147–172.

Ladd, R. D. 2008. *Intonational Phonology*, 2nd edn. Cambridge: CUP.

Lafont, R. 1971a. Un problème de culpabilité sociologique: La diglossie franco-occitane. *Langue française* 9: 93–99.

Lafont, R. 1971b. *Clefs pour l'Occitanie*. Paris: Seghers.

Lahiri, A., T. Riad & H. Jacobs. 1999. Diachronic prosody. In *Word Prosodic Systems in the Languages of Europe*, ed. H. van der Hulst, 335–422. Berlin: Mouton de Gruyter.

Lonnemann, B. 2005. Schwa, Phrase und Akzentuierung im *français du Midi* – eine kontrastive Untersuchung im Rahmen des Projektes *La Phonologie du français contemporain (PFC): usages, variétés et structure*. PhD dissertation, Universität Osnabrück. <http://repositorium.uni-osnabrueck.de/bitstream/urn:nbn:de:gbv:700-2006102523/2/E-Diss606_thesis.pdf > (8 June 2012).

Lonnemann, B. & T. Meisenburg. 2009. Une variété française imprégnée d'occitan (Lacaune/Tarn). In *Phonologie, variation et accents du français*, eds. J. Durand, B. Laks & C. Lyche, 285–306. Paris: Hermès science.

Lyche, C. & F. Girard. 1995. Le mot retrouvé. *Lingua* 95: 205–221.

Meisenburg, T. 1998. Diglossie et variation linguistique: Le cas de l'occitan. In *Toulouse à la croisée des cultures: Actes du Ve Congrès international de l'A.I.E.O. 1996*, eds. J. Gourc & F. Pic, 657–667. Pau: A.I.E.O.

Meisenburg, T. 2001. À propos des caractéristiques prosodiques de l'occitan. In *Le rayonnement de la civilisation occitane à l'aube d'un nouveau millénaire: Actes du 6e Congrès international de l'A.I.E.O.*, ed. G. Kremnitz, 553–560. Wien: Praesens.

Meisenburg, T. 2011. Prosodic phrasing in the spontaneous speech of an Occitan/French bilingual. In *Intonational Phrasing in Romance and Germanic: Cross-linguistic and Bilingual Studies* (Hamburg Studies on Multilingualism 10), eds. C. Gabriel & C. Lleó, 127–151. Amsterdam: John Benjamins.

Nespor, M. & I. Vogel. 1986 (2007). *Prosodic Phonology*. Berlin: Mouton de Gruyter. (Dordrecht: Foris, 1986).

Pierrehumbert, J. 1980. *The Phonology and Phonetics of English Intonation*. PhD dissertation, MIT.

Post, B. 2000. *Tonal and Phrasal Structures in French Intonation*. The Hague: Thesus.

Post, B. 2002. French tonal structures. In *Proceedings of the First International Conference on Speech Prosody*, eds. B. Bel & I. Marlin, 583–586. Aix-en-Provence: SProSIG.

Post, B. 2011. The multi-faceted relation between phrasing and intonation in French. In *Intonational Phrasing in Romance and Germanic: Cross-linguistic and Bilingual Studies* (Hamburg Studies on Multilingualism 10), eds. C. Gabriel & C. Lleó, 43–74. Amsterdam: John Benjamins.

Prieto, P., L. Aguilar, I. Mascaró, F. Torres-Tamarit & M. M. Vanrell. 2009. L'etiquetatge prosòdic Cat_ToBI. *Estudios de Fonética Experimental* XVIII: 287–309.

Pulgram, E. 1975. *Latin-Romance Phonology: Prosodics and Metrics*. München: Fink.

Roca, I. 1999. Stress in the Romance languages. In *Word Prosodic Systems in the Languages of Europe*, ed. H. van der Hulst, 659–811. Berlin: Mouton de Gruyter.

Romera, M. & G. Elordieta. In press. Prosodic accommodation in language contact: Spanish intonation in Majorca. *International Journal of the Sociology of Language*.

Schultz-Gora, O. 1924. *Altprovenzalisches Elementarbuch*, 4. verm. Auflage. Heidelberg: Winter.

Selkirk, E. 1984. *Phonology and Syntax: The Relation between Sound and Structure*. Cambridge MA: The MIT Press.

Selkirk, E. 1986. On derived domains in sentence phonology. *Phonology* 3: 371–405.

Sichel-Bazin, R. 2009. *Leading Tone Alignment in Occitan Disapproval Statements*. MA thesis, Universitat Autònoma de Barcelona. <http://prosodia.upf.edu/home/arxiu/tesis/master/tesina_sichel.pdf> (8 June 2012).

Van der Hulst, H. 1999. Word accent. In *Word Prosodic Systems in the Languages of Europe*, ed. H. van der Hulst, 3–116. Berlin: Mouton de Gruyter.

Wanner, D. 1979. Die Bewahrung der lateinischen Haupttonstelle im Romanischen. *Vox Romanica* 37: 1–36.

Welby, P. 2006. French intonational structure: Evidence from tonal alignment. *Journal of Phonetics* 34: 343–371.

Diachronic prosody of a contact variety

Analyzing *Porteño* Spanish spontaneous speech*

Andrea Pešková[1], Ingo Feldhausen[2,3], Elena Kireva[1]
and Christoph Gabriel[1]
[1]University of Hamburg, Germany; [2]University of Paris 3, Sorbonne
Nouvelle, France; [3] Goethe-University Frankfurt, Germany

This paper presents a micro-diachronic study of the prosody of *Porteño*, the
Spanish variety spoken in Buenos Aires, by comparing spontaneous speech
data collected in 1983 with comparable recordings made in 2008. *Porteño*
Spanish is said to be influenced by Italian due to massive immigration between
1830 and 1950. The question arises of whether the use of "Italian" features in
Porteño prosody has increased or decreased since the shift from Spanish-Italian
bilingualism to prevailing Spanish monolingualism. Tonal and durational
analyses performed on our data reveal that by and large, the presumably "Italian"
characteristics remain unchanged, although some significant differences were
found between the two time periods with respect to the occurrences of certain
pitch accents and boundary tones.

Keywords: Spanish, Italian, *Porteño* Spanish, diachronic prosody, intonation,
pitch accents, boundary tones, speech rhythm, duration

*   This paper is based on the pilot studies presented in Valencia (September 2010) at the *26é
Congrés de Lingüística i Filologia Romàniques* (see Pešková, Feldhausen & Gabriel in press) and
at the *International Conference on Multilingual Individuals and Multilingual Societies* (Hamburg,
October 2010). We are grateful to the participants of these conferences for the fruitful discussions, as well as to two anonymous reviewers for their insightful comments and constructive
criticism. We would also like to express our gratitude to Hugo Kubarth (Karl-Franzens-University Graz, Austria) for kindly supplying us with a corpus of spontaneous speech data, gathered
in Buenos Aires in 1983, to Tomke Brüggemann for her statistical support, and to Audrey
MacDougall for checking and correcting the English of this paper. It goes without saying that all
errors remain ours.

1. Introduction

The field of Romance historical linguistics has benefited considerably from the rich existing philological record of these languages. Since these records consist of written sources, however, they do not provide any reliable information about prosody – perhaps apart from punctuation, which might reflect the division of the stream of speech into smaller chunks. It is especially difficult to draw conclusions from these sources concerning historical developments in prosody and particularly in intonation (see Hualde 2003: 182, 2004: 218). Diachronic studies on prosody thus concentrate mainly on lexical stress and metrical structure (see, e.g., Riad 1998, 2003 on Scandinavian or Lahiri, Riad & Jacobs 1999 on Germanic and Romance) and apply comparative methods. Hualde (2003, 2004) also employs such a method, but in contrast to previous research concentrates on intonational patterns. He coined the term 'diachronic Romance intonology' for this quite under-developed field (Hualde 2004: 218); his purpose was to gain knowledge of proto-Romance intonation. By comparing the intonational systems of contemporary Romance languages, Hualde attempts to identify prosodic features that are common to a number of these languages or peculiar to Romance languages (Hualde 2004: 221). With the help of these data, he begins to reconstruct proto-Romance intonation.

The language considered in this paper is *Porteño* Spanish, the variety spoken in the Argentinean capital of Buenos Aires. We also enter the field of diachronic Romance prosody, but from a different perspective than in the studies described above. Instead of trying to reconstruct the prosodic system of a proto-language or retrace possible historical shifts in lexical stress, we aim to detect alterations in the prosodic system of the variety under investigation by comparing recordings from an earlier period with present day ones.

The paper is structured as follows: In Section 2, the reader is provided with basic information on the historical background of *Porteño* Spanish. Section 3 outlines the prosodic characteristics of this variety, thereby offering a brief description of its tonal and durational properties. In Sections 4 and 5, we then present the methodology used in our study as well as the results of the tonal and durational analyses before discussing them in Section 6. Finally, Section 7 offers some concluding remarks.

2. *Porteño* Spanish: A brief historical overview

The history of the Spanish variety spoken in Buenos Aires, *Porteño*, involves a period of intensive linguistic contact with Italian due to extensive migration, which makes it particularly worth studying from a diachronic point of view: Several linguistic particularities of this variety probably arose as a consequence of this long-lasting contact situation. Between 1830–1950, more than 3.5 million Italians came to the second largest country in South America. 35% of them settled in Buenos Aires and accounted for more than one-third of the urban population in some neighborhoods (Fontanella de Weinberg 1987, Baily 1999, Devoto 2002).[1] The considerable influence of Italian on *Porteño* can hardly be denied and is detectable not only in the lexicon, but also in prosody (Vidal de Battini 1964, Colantoni & Gurlekian 2004, Feldhausen, Gabriel & Pešková 2010, Colantoni 2011, Gabriel, Feldhausen & Pešková 2011). The following citation from *Ficciones* (1944/1991), a collection of short stories written by the Argentinean author Jorge Luis Borges (*1899, †1986), can be considered the first to mention, though not explicitly from a linguistic perspective, the influence of Italian on the phonological system of the Spanish variety spoken in the Rioplatense region: *Recuerdo claramente su voz; la voz pausada, resentida y nasal del orillero antiguo, sin los silbidos italianos de ahora* 'I remember clearly his voice, the deliberate, resentful, nasal voice of the old Eastern Shore man, without the Italianate syllables of today' (Borges 1944/1991: 121; translation by A. Kerrigan, see Borges 1962: 107). In this excerpt, the author describes a fictional Rioplatense speaker at the end of the 19th century. From a literal perspective, the translation of *los silbidos italianos* as 'the Italianate syllables' is not correct, as *silbidos* means 'whistle, hiss' and not 'syllable'. Thus, at first glance, this word might refer to the coronal sibilants [ʃ/ʒ] which form part of the phonological systems of both Rioplatense Spanish and Italian. Due to the fact that an Italian influence can be ruled out here for chronological reasons (see Fontanella de Weinberg 1973, 1987: 55f and Gabriel & Kireva 2012: 133f), it seems more natural to relate the *silbidos italianos* to the pronunciation of the phoneme /s/ by the Italian immigrants, who overtly realized it as a sibilant [s] in pre-consonantal position (e.g. *mosca* 'fly' [mɔs.ka]). Argentinean speakers, in particular those from the more wealthy classes, tended to dissociate themselves from the immigrants by intensifying the *aspiración*, i.e. the realization of pre-consonantal /s/ as a glottal fricative (e.g. *mosca* [mɔh.ka]). Interestingly enough, the aspiration of /s/ before consonants forms part of the cultivated pronunciation of educated speakers of present-day *Porteño* Spanish, while the sibilant realization is regarded as being sociolinguistically inferior (Norma Carricaburo, personal communication). Another possible way of interpreting Borges' characterization of his protagonist's manner of speaking is to attribute it to suprasegmental rather than to segmental properties, as is done implicitly in the English translation (see also Colantoni & Gurlekian 2004). Twenty years after *Ficciones*, the first linguistic observation of the prosody of Buenos

---

1.   The first Italian immigrants who arrived in Argentina came predominantly from the northern provinces of Liguria, Piedmont and Lombardy; after the turn of the century, many settlers also came from the southern parts of the country (e.g. Calabria). The majority of the first immigrants were male agricultural workers and unskilled laborers who came to Argentina to find work. Italian settlers accounted for over one-third of all European immigrants during this period. The strongest Italian influence was registered at the end of 19th and at the beginning of the 20th centuries. For instance, in 1895, Buenos Aires had 663,854 inhabitants, 27% of whom were Italians. In 1914, Italian-born inhabitants represented 20% of the total population of the city. Since then, the number of new Italian immigrants to Buenos Aires has decreased (see Devoto 2002, Baily 1999).

Aires was made in Vidal de Battini's (1964) study on Argentinean Spanish: *Ya es común que los extranjeros comenten como algo sabido que Buenos Aires habla con entonación italiana* 'It is already common to hear foreigners commenting as a fact that Buenos Aires speaks with an Italian intonation' (Vidal de Battini 1964: 144; translation taken from Colantoni & Gurlekian 2004: 107). Even though no recordings or (linguistic) descriptions of the Italian intonation or the intonation of the Spanish spoken in Buenos Aires at the end of the 19th and at the beginning of the 20th century exist, the history of Buenos Aires as well as the various features that *Porteño* shares today with different Italian dialects make it reasonable to attribute the intonational particularities of *Porteño* to contact with Italian. According to Colantoni (2011: 192), "(i) the evidence of the existence of a social bilingualism; (ii) the documented transfer at other linguistic levels (e.g. lexicon); and (iii) the typological similarities in the prosodic systems of Spanish and Italian" clearly speak in favor of such an assumption.

Although the "Italianate syllables" had already been recognized by the middle of the 20th century, not much is known about the details of the evolution of "Italian" features in Buenos Aires Spanish prosody. Colantoni & Gurlekian (2004), following Vidal de Battini (1964), mention that Buenos Aires Spanish "did not differ substantially from Peninsular Spanish" (Colantoni & Gurlekian 2004: 108) in the 19th century, and that new intonation(s) arose at the dawn of the 20th century. In the present study, however, we consider a specific period (the 1980s) and are thus able to make detailed statements concerning what happened before and after the sociolinguistic upgrading of *Porteño* Spanish in the 1980s.[2] This raises the question of whether the frequency of the prosodic features that *Porteño* shares with Italian increases due to this social upgrading or instead decreases as a consequence of the turn to Spanish monolingualism in today's Buenos Aires.[3] As far as we know, the prosody of *Porteño* Spanish has yet to be studied from a diachronic point of view. In the present study, we therefore compare recordings of spontaneous speech from 1983 (Corpus_1983) with comparable data from 2008 (Corpus_2008); see Section 4.1 for more detail. We additionally attempt to widen the temporal distance by selecting older speakers (> 50 years) from the subjects recorded in 1983, while choosing young speakers from 2008 (< 33 years).

The question arises as to whether the speakers recorded in 1983, who stem from the middle/upper social class and acquired *Porteño* in the 1920s and 1930s, would exhibit fewer "Italian" features than the young speakers recorded in 2008, who also come from middle/upper social class backgrounds and acquired *Porteño* between the

---

2.   Further information on this issue is given in the following paragraphs.

3.   Even though present-day Argentina is officially a Spanish-speaking monolingual country, the languages of the immigrants live on in the relevant communities and in certain cultural institutions, where they are still practiced to a certain extent, e.g. in the *Istituto Italiano di Cultura di Buenos Aires*. See Veith (2008) regarding the position of the Italian language in contemporary Argentina; for information about Italian cultural life in Buenos Aires consider Maronese (2009).

1970s and 1990s.[4] The special interest in the social background of the speakers is based on Klee & Lynch (2009: 191), according to whom the change in the prosodic system of *Porteño* Spanish most probably started in the lower social classes before spreading to higher social classes. The variety under discussion, which is today usually considered to be "the" typical Argentinean Spanish, used to be a socially inferior urban vernacular. The particular interest in the two age groups is based in this social upgrading. One important step in this change took place in the 1980s, when typical features of *Porteño* Spanish found acceptance in school education (Lipski 1996, Labraña & Sebastián 2004).[5] Consequently, the Castilian variety was no longer officially considered to be superior to *Porteño* Spanish. The speakers recorded in 1983 went to school long before this upward revaluation, unlike the young Argentineans recorded in 2008, who grew up with a well-established and officially recognized variety. Finally, it should be mentioned that the continual upgrading and increasing social acceptance of *Porteño* Spanish (not only in Buenos Aires but all over in Argentina) also seem to be reflected in the self-evaluations of the speakers. In addition to the Italian influences in the lexicon (Muñoz 2007), it is especially prosody that functions as a marker of identity (see also Kabatek 2005). Signaling *Porteño* identity, it is possible that these "Italian" features could be more likely to be used by the speakers recorded in 2008 than by those recorded in 1983. However, our results show that the "Italian" features in *Porteño* Spanish prosody largely remain unchanged. We will show that the tonal inventory is the same for both time periods and that the slight differences only concern the frequencies of several pitch accents and boundary tones. This overwhelming consistency in the "Italian" features in the two time periods indicates that typical *Porteño* prosody had already been part of the variety long before the 1980s, thus supporting assumptions made by Colantoni & Gurlekian (2004). The sociolinguistic upgrading of *Porteño* Spanish in the 1980s was just one step in the general upgrading of the variety, and we can conclude from our data that prosody did not play a predominant role in this step.

3. "Italian" features and the prosody of *Porteño* Spanish

This section presents basic patterns of contemporary *Porteño* Spanish prosody and highlights the tonal and durational characteristics this variety shares with Italian. In a

---

4. As this paper is not conceived as a sociolinguistic study, the criterion for social class is provisional with respect to its definition. Kubarth (1986: 189), who recorded the older data analyzed in our paper (see Section 4.1), categorized his speakers by their level of education, their profession and their place of domicile. For a more fine-grained sociolinguistic classification including further categories such as sex, the reader is referred to the sociolinguistic studies on *Porteño* by Enbe & Tobin (2008) and Enbe (2009).

5. For instance, the morpho-syntactic phenomenon of *voseo* (i.e. the use of the pronoun of informal address *vos* together with the corresponding verb forms, e.g. *vos querés*; 'you want' instead of *tú quieres*) was officially recognized by *La Academia Argentina de Letras* in 1982. By contrast, it remains a non-standard form in other Spanish-speaking countries (Carricaburo 1999).

first step, we illustrate the tonal inventory of *Porteño* Spanish – pitch accents and boundary tones – as proposed in Feldhausen et al. (2010), Gabriel, Feldhausen, Pešková, Colantoni, Lee, Arana & Labastía (2010), Gabriel et al. (2011), and Gabriel, Pešková, Labastía & Blázquez (in press). In a second step, we point out some durational particularities (i.e. speech rhythm, lengthening effects).

Our description of *Porteño* intonation is compatible with the labeling conditions proposed within the Sp_ToBI system (Beckman, Díaz-Campos, McGory & Morgan 2002, Estebas-Vilaplana & Prieto 2008, Aguilar, De la Mota & Prieto 2009, Prieto & Roseano 2010), which itself is based on the autosegmental-metrical (AM) model of intonation (Pierrehumbert 1980, Ladd 2008). The AM model distinguishes between a phonological representation on the one hand, which consists of underlying tonal targets represented on a tonal tier, and the concrete pitch contour (fundamental frequency, F0) on the other hand, which is produced by the speaker as a result of the phonetic interpolation between the underlying tonal targets. Two types of tonal units are assumed: *pitch accents*, which associate with metrically strong syllables, and *boundary* or *edge tones*, which mark the edge of higher-level prosodic constituents of the Prosodic Hierarchy (Selkirk 1984, Nespor & Vogel 1986/2007) such as the intermediate phrase (ip) or the Intonation Phrase (IP). The relevant tonal targets can be either low (L), high (H) or complex (e.g. HL); the diacritics '*', '-', and '%' used in the ToBI labeling system indicate their association with the syllabic level, the ip level or the IP level, respectively. Figure 1 depicts the association of the tonal targets with different levels of the Prosodic Hierarchy (i.e. syllabic, ip and IP level); the symbol T stands for any possible underlying tonal unit.

In addition to tonal patterns, the prosodic structure of a language is also defined by the degree of juncture between any two adjacent words in the ToBI transcription system (Pitrelli, Beckman & Hirschberg 1994: 123, Jun 2005: 2). A boundary between ips is marked by the numerical break index 3 (BI 3), while a boundary between IPs is marked by break index 4 (BI 4).

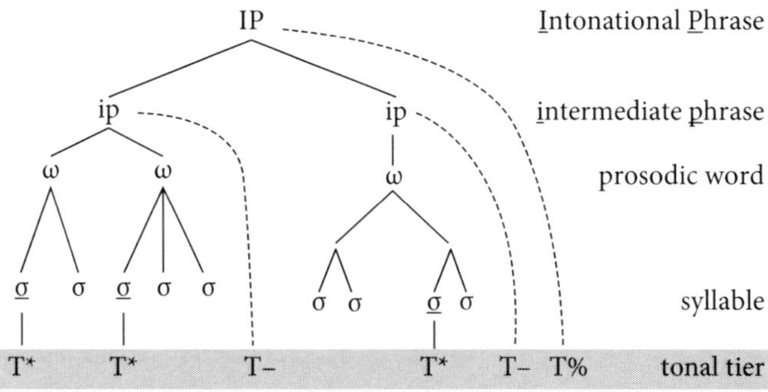

Figure 1. Association of tonal targets with the different levels of the Prosodic Hierarchy

One of the most characteristic features of the intonation of *Porteño* Spanish is the realization of the prenuclear (i.e. non-final) pitch accents as L + H*. This rising tone with the pitch peak located within the limits of the metrically strong syllable reflects the Italian influence (Colantoni & Gurlekian 2004, for Italian see D'Imperio 2001). The realization of the nuclear accent[6] of broad focus declaratives as H + L* or L* (Gabriel et al. 2010) is another common characteristic of Italian and *Porteño* Spanish (Kaisse 2001). These two tonal features also exist in other Spanish varieties; they are used, however, with different pragmatic meanings (Prieto & Roseano 2010). A further important characteristic of *Porteño* Spanish is the existence of the tritonal accent L + H* + L (Gabriel et al. 2010, in press, Feldhausen, Benet & Pešková 2011, Feldhausen, Pešková, Kireva & Gabriel 2011), which is not attested in any other Spanish variety (Prieto & Roseano 2010). The tone is characterized by a rise and fall within the limits of the stressed syllable and occurs predominantly in emphatic and contrastive contexts. A comparable tonal movement is also attested in contrastive contexts in some Italian varieties, e.g. in the dialect spoken in Pisa (see Gili Fivela 2002 and Gili Fivela & D'Imperio 2010).[7]

Turning to boundary tones, HL% is typical of absolute questions (Gabriel et al. 2010). This pattern is also reminiscent of some Italian varieties (see Sorianello 2006 and Savino 2009 for Italian yes-no questions). A further important similarity between Italian and *Porteño* is the phonetic shape of the high boundary tone of break index level 3 (H-). While Peninsular Spanish has a clear preference for the so-called *continuation rise* (CR), a rising F0 movement beginning with the last accented syllable and lasting until the word's end (see Figure 2, panel a), Italian shows a balanced frequency between CR and the so-called *sustained pitch* (SP), a rising F0 movement which maintains its height until the right edge of the word, thus creating a plateau (Figure 2, panel b). In the analysis proposed by Feldhausen et al. (2010), Gabriel et al. (2011), and Pešková, Feldhausen & Gabriel (2011), the label H- is used for the CR, while the SP is labeled as a down-stepped high ip boundary tone, i.e. !H-. The latter studies also show that *Porteño* Spanish patterns with Italian in exhibiting a balanced frequency between CR and SP. For our diachronic study, we concentrate on the pitch accents and boundary tones presented so far.

---

6. The term 'nuclear accent' stems from the British school of intonation and originally referred to the most prominent syllable of an F0 contour (Ladd 2008). In the ToBI transcription system, the nuclear accent is often defined as the "last accent in the intermediate phrase" (Ladd 2008: 133). In the present paper, we follow the ToBI transcription system as outlined by Prieto & Roseano (2010) in differentiating between sentence-final (BI 4) and sentence-internal (BI 3) nuclear accents. Any pitch accent that precedes the nuclear accent of either BI 3 or BI 4 is called a prenuclear accent.

7. Interestingly enough, El Zarka (2011) reports a comparable F0 movement which also expresses contrast and emphasis in Egyptian Arabic.

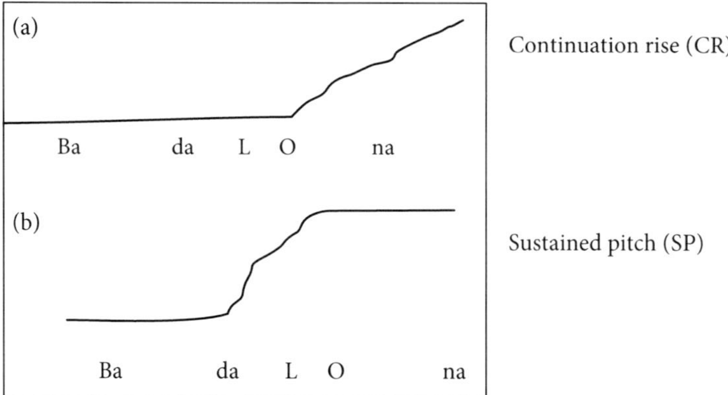

Figure 2. Schematic representation of the continuation rise (CR), panel a, and the sustained pitch (SP), panel b, for the word *Badalona* (place name, city in Catalonia) with penultimate stress; taken from Frota, D'Imperio, Elordieta & Vigário (2007: 135)

In Table 1, we present an overview of the tonal inventory of *Porteño* Spanish (based on laboratory and semi-spontaneous speech; see Feldhausen et al. 2010, Gabriel et al. 2010, 2011, in press, and Pešková et al. 2011). The pitch accents and boundary tones are schematically represented. The grey area corresponds to either the accented syllable (in the case of pitch accents) or the pre-boundary syllables (in the case of boundary tones). The black line illustrates the pitch contour (F0). The combination of a nuclear pitch accent and an IP-edge tone is known as the nuclear configuration (referred to as *tonema* by Navarro Tomás 1944 in his seminal work on Spanish intonation). Different pragmatic meanings are expressed by different nuclear configurations (see Gabriel et al. 2010 for details on Argentinean Spanish).

Given that the prosodic shape of a language or variety is not only characterized by tonal but also by durational properties, we briefly consider the latter in the following. It has been shown in the literature that Italian generally tends to mark stress by considerably lengthening the relevant syllable, while in Spanish such durational effects are used to a lesser extent (Alfano, Savy & Llisterri 2009). Regarding the additional marking of intermediate phrasal (ip) boundaries by means of lengthening effects, it was shown by Frota et al. (2007: 135) that in Italian, pre-boundary lengthening (PBL) was used in 100% of the cases examined, whereas the relevant percentage for Peninsular Spanish only amounted to 40%. Giordano (2008) points out that "duration is ... a reliable acoustic parameter related to prominence in Italian and the increase in its values can be gradually reinforced ..., mainly in case of final lengthening" (Giordano 2008: 349). Regarding the use of lengthening (of the syllable immediately preceding the boundary) as an additional durational cue of intermediate phrasing, Gabriel et al. (2011) state that "*Porteño* tends to more closely resemble the pattern of Peninsular Spanish, with the values for both Spanish varieties being almost identical" (Gabriel et al. 2011: 179).

Table 1. Tonal inventory of *Porteño* Spanish according to Feldhausen et al. (2010), Gabriel et al. (2010, 2011, in press), and Pešková et al. (2011)[8]

Pitch accents

L*		L + H*	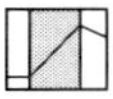	L + ¡H*	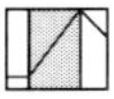	L + >H*	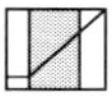
H*		H + L*	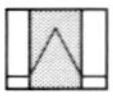	L + H* + L	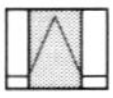		

Boundary tones (BI 3 marked by '-', BI 4 marked by '%')

L-, L%		M-, M%		H-, H%	
HL-, HL%		LH-			

Interestingly enough, the Italian influence appears in the considerable lengthening of the nuclear syllable in both Italian and *Porteño* Spanish. According to Estebas-Vilaplana (2010), "the duration of the nuclear syllable is significantly longer in AS [Argentinean Spanish] than in PS [Peninsular Spanish] indicating that duration seems to be more important than intonation to distinguish between AS and PS declaratives" (Estebas-Vilaplana 2010: 153). While the typical nuclear accent in neutral declarative sentences is L* in both varieties, the lengthening of the nuclear syllable in *Porteño* is said to be the crucial difference between the varieties examined. Such durational effects clearly have an impact on the ratio of vocalic to consonantal material in the speech signal and thus on speech rhythm in general, given that the greater durations of certain syllables are reflected in a higher proportion of vocalic material in the speech signal (%V) as well as in the greater durational variability of vocalic and consonantal intervals. The latter can be expressed in terms of the standard deviation of the relevant intervals (usually abbreviated as $\Delta V/\Delta C$, see Ramus, Nespor & Mehler 1999) or through the variation coefficient VarcoΔV/VarcoΔC (Dellwo & Wagner 2003), for example. It has been shown in comparative studies on speech rhythm that the values for both the proportion of vocalic material (%V) and the variability of V/C intervals are higher for Italian than for (Peninsular) Spanish (e.g. Ramus et al. 1999). Regarding the speech rhythm of *Porteño* Spanish, Toledo (2010: 103) showed on the basis of read speech data that the values for %V are higher in Argentinean Spanish than in all Peninsular Spanish varieties examined in his study (Sevilla, Aragón, Granada, Canary Islands). In two recent pilot studies, Gabriel & Kireva (2012: 141ff) and Benet, Kireva, Pešková &

---

8. One might add that Aguilar et al. (2009) introduced the prenuclear accent labeled as L* + H (realized as a low target in the accented syllable and followed by a rise on the posttonic syllable) and the nuclear accent L + ¡H* (similar to L + H*, but with a wider pitch range) for (Peninsular) Spanish. Neither of these tones is systematically used in Argentinean Spanish (Gabriel et al. 2010); the same holds for the additional boundary tones LM-, LM%, LHL- and LHL% also proposed by Aguilar et al. (2009). The bitonal target LH only occurs as a boundary tone at the intermediate level (BI 3).

Gabriel (in press) also examined the rhythmic properties of *Porteño* Spanish and compared them with those of the L2 Spanish produced by Italian natives. They hypothesized that the speech rhythm of this L2 (Peninsular) Spanish should be comparable to that of *Porteño* as a consequence of transfer from the mother tongue Italian to the target language Spanish. Their results in fact corroborate this hypothesis, showing that *Porteño* and L2 Spanish (produced by speakers of L1 Italian) pattern similarly with respect to speech rhythm and exhibit greater values for both %V and the variability of the V/C intervals.

In the following, we present the comparative analyses performed on the *Porteño* data from two time periods (1983 and 2008), thereby focusing on the tonal and durational similarities between *Porteño* and the contact language Italian discussed in this section. We first concentrate on intonation (Section 4) before turning to durational effects (Section 5).

4.   Tonal analysis

In this section, we begin by describing our methods and data (Subsection 4.1) before presenting the results of the tonal analysis (Subsection 4.2).

4.1   Methodology

We analyzed two corpora consisting of spontaneous speech recorded in different time periods. The data in the first corpus were gathered in 1983 by Hugo Kubarth (Karl-Franzens-University, Graz, Austria), while the data in the second corpus were collected in 2008 by the authors.[9] For both corpora, freely structured interviews were conducted with native speakers of *Porteño* in Buenos Aires.[10] The subjects were asked to tell the interviewer something about a past experience, be it a vacation or memories of Argentina as it was decades ago. Even though the interviewer was still part of the

---

9.   The data form part of the *Hamburg Corpus of Argentinean Spanish* (HaCASpa), available on the internet at http://www1.uni-hamburg.de/exmaralda/files/h9-korpus/public/. HaCASpa is a speech database compiled in 2008–09 within the scope of the research project "The intonation of Spanish in Argentina", funded by the German Research Foundation (Deutsche Forschungsgemeinschaft, DFG) from 2008–2011 as a subproject of the Collaborative Research Center on Multilingualism (Sonderforschungsbereich 538 "Mehrsprachigkeit"), hosted by the University of Hamburg, Germany.

10.   Since we did not conduct the data collection in 1983, it is fair to ask whether the corpora are entirely comparable (as interviews are known to be highly variable and subject to the personalities of the participating interlocutors; Tagliamonte 2006: 48). We nevertheless believe that the two corpora are comparable: Data from both corpora were gathered by means of freely structured interviews that were similar in their purpose and the way in which the subjects told their stories.

conversation, it was mainly the subjects who spoke during the recordings. For the present study, we chose four speakers (three male, one female) born between 1920 and 1932 (Corpus_1983) as well as three speakers (two male, one female) born between 1975 and 1990 (Corpus_2008). All speakers had university degrees or were studying at the time of the recordings.

The data from 2008 were recorded directly as .wav-files using a hard-disk recorder Marantz PMD671 and a Sennheiser microphone ME64. An Uher Report Mono tape recorder was used for the data collection in 1983; the data were recently digitalized. The acoustic analysis was carried out by using Praat (Boersma & Weenink 1992ff). From each interview, randomly selected sequences of 10 to 50 seconds were extracted for the acoustic analysis. Corpus_1983 consists of nine .wav-files with a total length of five minutes, while Corpus_2008 is made up by seven .wav-files with a total duration of four minutes. Only declarative sentences were used for the analysis. We concentrate here on pitch accents and boundary tones of BI 3 and 4; durational effects are considered in Section 5. Example (1) presents a sequence from Corpus_1983 with a duration of 20.7 seconds. The male speaker, born in 1931, recalls old times in Buenos Aires. Figure 3 shows the corresponding pitch contour, which was analyzed and annotated according to the labeling criteria described in Section 3. The tiers contain the following information (from bottom up): (i) orthographic transcription; (ii) stressed syllables; (iii) boundary tones and break indices, and (iv) pitch accents.

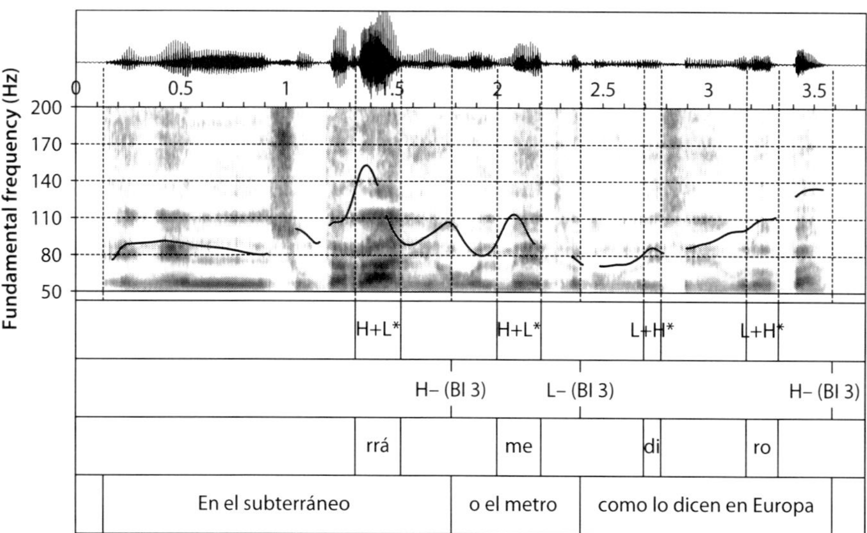

Figure 3. Waveform, spectrogram and F0 trace for the fragment *En el subterráneo o el metro, como lo dicen en Europa* "In the subway or the tube, as they say in Europe" from example (1), male speaker, *Porteño* Spanish, recorded in 1983

(1) *Una de las cosas que yo más extraño es el tranvía. El tranvía daba otro ritmo a la*
ciudad. Era mucho más lento como se desplazaba, uno se sentaba cómodamente,
iba leyendo su diario, eh y veía el paisaje urbano. Veía las calles, tenía tiempo de
ver. En el subterráneo o el metro, como lo dicen en Europa, no se ve nada.
'One of the things that I miss the most is the tram. The tram gave another
rhythm to the city, it was slower how people moved, one sat back reading his
newspaper, eh, and was watching the urban landscape, was watching the
streets, one had time to see. In the subway or the tube, as they say in Europe,
you can't see anything.'

4.2   Results

This section is devoted to the presentation of the results of the tonal analysis. It is
shown that the overall tonal inventory is the same in both time periods, even though
there are several significant differences in the occurrences of certain pitch accents and
boundary tones. Subsection 4.2.1 is devoted to prenuclear pitch accents, while nuclear
pitch accents are discussed in 4.2.2. Detailed information on boundary tones is given
in 4.2.3.

4.2.1   *Prenuclear Accents*

There were a total of 217 prenuclear (i.e. non-final) pitch accents in Corpus_1983 and
201 in Corpus_2008. Seven different tonal realizations exist among them: Two
monotonal accents (L* and H*), four bitonal accents (H + L*, L + H*, L +> H*, and
L* + H), and one tritonal accent (L + H* + L). Table 2 summarizes the absolute numbers and percentages for the detected prenuclear accents.

The most frequent prenuclear pitch accent in both time periods was the rising accent with the F0 peak located at the right edge of the metrically strong syllable (L + H*).
The (slight) difference between 1983 and 2008 (59.5% vs. 64.5%) is not statistically
significant (χ^2-test). The same holds for H*, the realization of which occurs at a

Table 2. Absolute numbers and percentages for prenuclear accents in both corpora

Pitch accents	Corpus_1983		Corpus_2008	
L + H*	129	59.5%	130	64.5%
H + L*	40	18%	11	5.5%
H*	21	10%	32	16%
L +> H*	11	5%	13	6.5%
L*	9	4%	6	3%
L + H* + L	4	2%	4	2%
L* + H	3	1.5%	5	2.5%
Total	217	100%	201	100%

rate of 10% in 1983 and 16% in 2008. The least frequent pitch accents are L*, L* + H, L + > H*, and L + H* + L, with no relevant difference between them in the two time periods. Only the use of the falling accent H + L* shows a (highly) significant difference; it was used less frequently in 2008 than in 1983 (χ^2-test, p < 0.01).

4.2.2 *Nuclear Accents*

In our data, only five different tonal realizations were attested in nuclear position: the two montonal accents L* and H*, two bitonal accents (L + H* and H + L*) and the tritonal accent L + H* + L. Table 3 summarizes the absolute numbers and percentages for the detected nuclear accents.

While all five pitch accents in Corpus_2008 are attested at break index level 3 and 4, not all accents can be found in Corpus_1983. Here, H* was not attested at all, while L + H* appeared only at break index level 3. The most common nuclear accent at break index level 4 was the falling accent H + L*; the difference between the two time periods is not significant (χ^2-test). The same holds for the low accent L*, for which the absolute numbers hardly differ. The only (highly) significant difference at BI 4 was found for L + H* + L. The tritonal pitch accent was clearly used more often in 2008 than in 1983 (χ^2-test, p<0.01).

As for BI 3, several significant differences were determined between the two time periods. Both L + H* and L + H* + L were used more often in 2008 than in 1983 (χ^2-test, p<0.05). H + L*, in turn, was used less often in 2008 than in 1983, with this difference being highly significant (χ^2-test, p<0.01). While the falling accent H + L* used to be the most frequent tone at BI 3 in 1983, the most common tone in 2008 was the rising accent L + H*. Figure 4 illustrates an example of a tritonal pitch accent realization (the symbol '¡' indicates an upstep, i.e. the pitch peak is higher than the previous one).

Table 3. Absolute numbers and percentages for nuclear accents in both corpora

	Pitch accents	Corpus_1983		Corpus_2008	
	L + H*	36	40%	61	70%
	H + L*	50	56%	11	13%
BI 3	L + H* + L	3	3%	11	13%
	L*	1	1%	1	1%
	H*	0	0%	3	3%
	L + H*	0	0%	4	6%
	H + L*	30	73%	35	52%
BI 4	L + H* + L	1	3%	16	24%
	L*	10	24%	9	13%
	H*	0	0%	3	5%

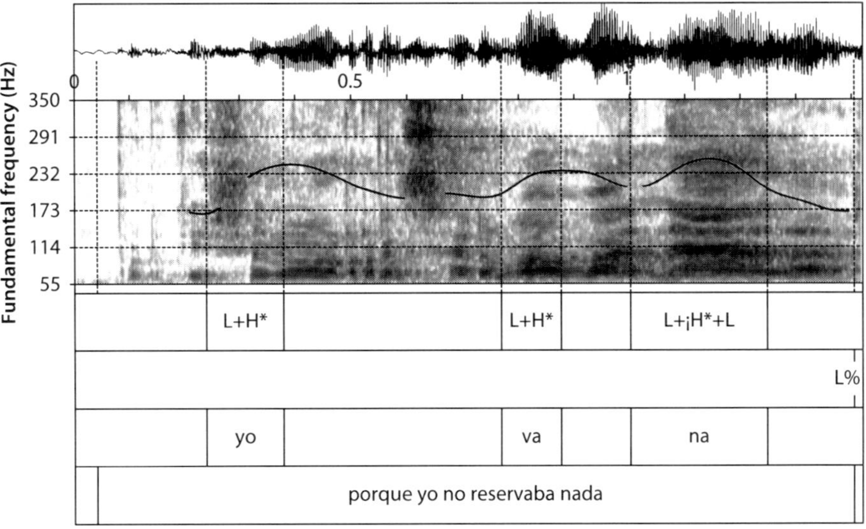

Figure 4. Waveform, spectrogram and F0 trace for the fragment *porque yo no reservaba nada* "because I didn't make any reservation" (Corpus_2008, female speaker) with L + H* + L nuclear accent

4.2.3   *Boundary Tones*

Six different boundary tones were detected in our corpora. Four of them represent ip-boundary tones (L-, LH-, M-, and H-/!H-), while the last tone, L%, represents an IP-boundary tone. Table 4 summarizes the absolute numbers and percentages for the attested boundary tones.

While CR (H-) was more frequent in 1983 than in 2008 (39%, i.e. 35 occurrences vs. 29%, i.e. 25 occurrences; not significant, χ^2-test), SP (!H-) shows the reverse pattern: It was used in 11% of the cases (10 occurrences) in Corpus_1983, but accounts for 28% of the ip-boundaries in Corpus_2008, the difference between the two time periods being significant (χ^2-test, $p<0.05$). The lower percentage for SP in Corpus_1983 is compensated for by the higher occurrence of the mid-boundary tone M-, which is

Table 4. Absolute numbers and percentages for the boundary tones in both corpora

	Boundary Tones	Corpus_1983		Corpus_2008	
	H- (CR)	35	39%	25	29%
	!H- (SP)	10	11%	24	28%
BI 3	M-	16	18%	9	10%
	L-	27	30%	29	33%
	LH-	2	2%	0	0%
BI 4	L%	41	100%	67	100%

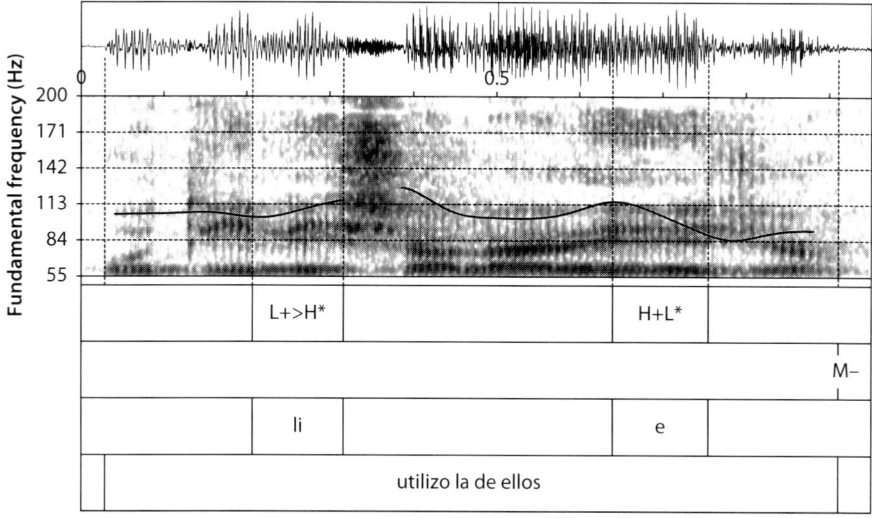

Figure 5. Waveform, spectrogram and F0 trace for the fragment *utilizo la de ellos* "I use theirs" (Corpus_1983, male speaker) with a nuclear accent H + L* and a boundary tone M-

phonetically realized "as a falling movement to a mid tone target or as a mid level plateau when it occurs after a high tone (the mid tone may spread to the left)" (Aguilar et al. 2009). An example of this type of boundary realization is given in Figure 5.

No effect could be found for the difference between the number of L- in the two time periods, however. The bitonal boundary tone LH- was only attested twice in the data collected from one speaker recorded in 1983; we interpret its occurrence as being speaker-specific. Finally, L% represents the only boundary tone at BI 4, which was therefore realized in 100% of the cases (see Table 4). Recall that the data analyzed contain exclusively declaratives, which commonly end in a low target at the right edge of the sentence.

Consider now the combinations of nuclear pitch accents and boundary tones summarized in Table 5. Seen from this angle, the higher percentage for the boundary realization at BI 3 as a mid-tone (M-) in the data from Corpus_1983 is probably due to its frequent combination with the nuclear pitch accent H + L* (as shown in Figure 5).

5.   Durational analysis

The structure of this section follows that of the previous one: We first illustrate the methodology used for this part of the study (Section 5.1) before presenting the results of the durational analysis in Section 5.2.

Table 5. Absolute numbers for the combinations of pitch accents (columns) and boundary tones (rows) in both corpora

Pitch accents Boundary tones	L + H*	H + L*	L + H* + L	L*	H*
BI 3 — H- (CR) 1983/2008	19/24	16/1	0/0	0/0	0/0
!H- (SP) 1983/2008	8/22	2/0	0/0	0/0	0/2
M- 1983/2008	3/8	12/0	0/0	1/0	0/1
L- 1983/2008	5/6	19/10	3/11	0/1	0/1
LH- 1983/2008	1/0	1/0	0/0	0/0	0/0
BI 4 — L% 1983/2008	0/4	30/35	1/16	10/9	0/3

5.1   Methodology

In a first step, we measured the durations of four types of syllables: (1) accented sylla-bles in prenuclear position, (2) accented syllables of paroxytone (e.g. *mesa* 'table') and proparoxytone words (e.g. *rápido* 'rapid') in nuclear position, (3) accented syllables of oxytone words (e.g. *comer* 'eat') in nuclear position, and (4) non-accented syllables in pre-boundary position (i.e. the syllable immediately preceding any boundary of BI 3 or 4). The distinction between types (2) and (3), i.e. between (pro)paroxytone and oxytones in nuclear position, is motivated by the fact that the pre-boundary syllable and the accented syllable coincide in the latter (e.g. the syllable -*mer* in the infinitive *comer*, located immediately before a prosodic boundary). Since two potential triggers of lengthening interact here, this might produce a greater durational effect. In a second step, we concentrated exclusively on the durations of the CV syllables from groups (1) – (4) mentioned above in order to eliminate the effect of different syllable struc-tures (i.e. complexity of syllabic constituents, e.g. CV vs. CCVC).[11] Finally, we tested a possible correlation between the complexity of a given pitch accent (i.e. monotonal vs. tritonal) and the duration of the syllable it associates with by calculating the durations of all nuclear syllables as a function of the surface realization of the nuclear pitch ac-cent. Seen from this angle, the more frequent occurrences of the tritonal pitch accent L + H* + L in Corpus_2008 could be reflected in longer durations of the nuclear syl-lables.[12] The results are presented in the following section.

---

11.   Recall that spontaneous speech data cannot be controlled for the occurrence of different syllable structures as is the case for scripted speech.

12.   Correlations between duration and tonal shape have been attested by Stella, Vanrell, Prieto & Gili Fivela (2011) for Italian and Catalan.

5.2   Results

First we present the results of the measurements performed for the four syllable types mentioned in the previous section. As can be seen in Table 6, the durations of the nuclear syllables in oxytone words are longer (259.536 ms in Corpus_1983; 313.085 ms in Corpus_2008) than those of the nuclear syllables in paroxytone or proparoxytone words (204.655 ms in Data_1983; 229.063 ms in Data_2008).[13] Regarding the comparison between the two time periods, there is a significant difference between Corpus_1983 and Corpus_2008 in prenuclear and nuclear syllables in oxytone words (t-test, $p<0.05$). It should be pointed out in this context that the prenuclear syllables in the data from Corpus_2008 are significantly shorter, while the nuclear syllables in oxytone words are significantly longer. This clearly indicates a reinforcement of the lengthening affecting nuclear and pre-boundary syllables.

Interestingly enough, the accented syllables in prenuclear position are the shortest of all aforementioned syllable types. The durational properties of the four syllable types in both corpora are represented in the hierarchy given in (2), with '>' meaning 'longer in duration than'.

(2)   nuclear σ in oxytone words > nuclear σ in proparoxytone and paroxytone words > pre-boundary σ > prenuclear σ

In general, the comparison of the durations of the different syllable types shows that the lengthening of nuclear syllables plays an important role in both of the periods examined, thereby largely confirming Estebas-Vilaplanas' (2010) findings mentioned in Section 3. Furthermore, the lengthening effect is reinforced in oxytone words, where the immediately following boundary functions as an additional trigger for lengthening.

Table 6. Mean durations and absolute numbers for all syllables of types (1–4), no distinction made according to syllabic complexity

Syllable (σ) Type	Corpus_1983 mean duration in ms (number of σ)	Corpus_2008 mean duration in ms (number of σ)
(1) Prenuclear σ	146.830 ms (212)	128.871 ms (201)
(2) Nuclear σ in (pro)paroxytone words	204.655 ms (90)	229.063 ms (95)
(3) Nuclear σ in oxytone words	259.536 ms (41)	313.085 ms (59)
(4) Pre-boundary σ	197.067 ms (90)	204.611 ms (95)
Total	**179.963 ms (433)**	**190.164 ms (450)**

13. Due to the infrequent occurrence of proparoxytone words in both corpora (less than 1%), we abstained from analyzing possible differences between paroxytone and proparoxytone words.

As already stated in the literature, e.g. by D'Imperio & Rosenthall (1999), Krämer (2009), and White, Payne & Mattys (2009), the lengthening of stressed and phrase-final syllables is also typical of Italian.[14] Our findings for *Porteño* can thus be interpreted as a reflection of contact with Italian varieties.

Regarding the durations of CV syllables, the results from the durational analyses performed on the data from both corpora show exactly the same tendencies as the results obtained from the analysis of all syllable structures. As can be seen in Table 7, CV syllables in prenuclear and pre-boundary position are shorter than nuclear CV syllables in (pro)paroxytone and oxytone words. Once again, the syllables of type (3), i.e. nuclear syllables in oxytone words, exhibit the longest durations in both corpora. Concerning the diachronic evolution of lengthening effects, the comparison between the two time periods points in the same direction, in that once again, prenuclear syllables are shorter and nuclear oxytone syllables are longer in the 2008 data than in the data collected in the earlier epoch. However, only the difference between prenuclear CV syllables is significant (t-test, $p<0.05$), while the numbers of cases are not sufficient to perform a t-test for the CV nuclear syllables in oxytone words.

Finally, we tested the relationship between the durations of accented syllables in nuclear position and the type of pitch accent realization. We found that metrically strong syllables marked by the tritonal accent L + H* + L exhibit longer durations than those bearing less complex tonal units, at least for Corpus_2008 (the syllables bearing a low-high-low target are the longest, especially in oxytone words (413 ms)).[15] The results are given in Table 8.

Table 7. Mean durations and absolute numbers for CV syllables of types (1–4)

Syllable (σ) Type	Corpus_1983 mean duration in ms (number of σ)	Corpus_2008 mean duration in ms (number of σ)
(1) Prenuclear CV σ	144.207 ms (82)	121.817 ms (109)
(2) Nuclear CV σ in (pro)paroxytone words	193.333 ms (48)	212.426 ms (55)
(3) Nuclear CV σ in oxytone words	231.667 ms (12)	286.4 ms (10)
(4) Pre-boundary CV σ	171.429 ms (35)	187.301 ms (67)
Total	168.842 ms (177)	167.560 ms (241)

---

14. White et al. (2009) compare two Italian varieties (Venetian and Sicilian) and show that the durational marking of stressed syllables is used to a greater extent in both Italian dialects than in (Castilian) Spanish. For regional differences in the use of lengthening effects in Italian see Hajek & Stevens (2011).

15. The number of cases is too small to perform a t-test. Our preliminary findings should be tested by analyzing a larger amount of data.

Table 8. Mean durations in ms and absolute numbers for nuclear syllables marked with L + H* + L, H + L*, L + H* and other pitch accent realizations

Nuclear Pitch Accent	Corpus_1983 mean duration in ms (number of σ)	Corpus_2008 mean duration in ms (number of σ)
L + H* + L	210.75 ms (4)	326.824 ms (17)
L + H* + L (oxytone words)	239.00 ms (1)	413.00 ms (9)
H + L*	219.333 ms (57)	208.393 ms (27)
H + L* (oxytone words)	281.000 ms (26)	291.652 ms (22)
L + H*	171.182 ms (22)	221.85 ms (40)
L + H* (oxytone words)	224.5 ms (12)	290.708 ms (24)
other	186.857 ms (7)	136.00 ms (11)
other (oxytone words)	201.00 ms (2)	267.5 ms (4)

6. Discussion

We have shown that the presumably "Italian" features in *Porteño* prosody remained largely unchanged between the two time periods examined. Even though the overall tonal inventory is the same for both epochs, there are some significant differences with respect to the occurrences of single pitch accents and boundary tones. While H + L* is the most frequent nuclear pitch accent at BI 3 in Corpus_1983, the most common pitch accent realization in the data from 2008 is L + H* (see Section 4.2.2). As shown by Frota et al. (2007: 139), the nuclear configuration consisting of an H + L* nuclear pitch accent followed by a rising F0 movement towards the boundary (i.e. H- or M- in our analysis) frequently occurs in Italian, but not in (Peninsular) Spanish. This indicates that, with respect to nuclear configurations, the data from 1983 demonstrate more "Italian" features than the data collected in 2008 (see Section 4.2.3). In addition, we observed a significant difference in the occurrence of !H- (SP) between the time periods; the expected balanced frequency between CR and SP, which is typical of Italian according to Frota et al. (2007) and has also been attested for present-day Porteño Spanish (Feldhausen et al. 2010, Gabriel et al. 2011, Pešková et al. 2011), could only be confirmed for Corpus_2008 (CR/H- 29%, SP/!H- 28%). Seen from this angle, the data collected in 2008 seem to be more "Italianized" than those recorded in the earlier time period. However, the differences in boundary realizations attested between the two epochs could result from the introduction of the mid-boundary tone M- in the present analysis, given that the M- realization may also be interpreted as a variant of SP. Summing up the percentages for M- and !H- for both epochs (i.e. 29% for Corpus_1983, 38% for Corpus_2008), the pictures changes considerably in that the expected balanced frequency between CR and SP cannot be found in either of the corpora. Returning to the results presented by Feldhausen et al. (2010), Gabriel et al. (2011), and Pešková et al. (2011), it must be pointed out that these studies examined phrasing decisions and boundary realizations in controlled laboratory speech (read SVO sentences), while in the present work, we analyzed data from spontaneous speech. Furthermore, our results show that the complex boundary tone LH- was hardly realized in spontaneous speech and only in 1983. However, Feldhausen et al. (2010), Gabriel et al. (2011), and Pešková et al. (2011) show for scripted speech that this boundary tone still occurs in today's *Porteño* Spanish, even though its frequency of use is rather low (7%).

Interestingly enough, we have shown that the use of another tonal feature that can also be traced back to the contact with Italian, namely the use of the tritonal pitch accent L + H* + L, has increased significantly between 1983 and 2008 (see Section 4.2.2). Even though this pitch accent realization has been shown to signal focus and emphasis in the semi-spontaneous data analyzed by Gabriel et al. (2010), it was also found in broad focus declaratives in our spontaneous material. This might be explained by the fact that spontaneous speech usually tends to make more use of linguistic means signaling emphasis than is the case for controlled or semi-spontaneous data.

Comparing the different pitch accent realizations that appear in the two corpora, it is worthwhile pointing out that the increase in the frequency of L + H* + L, the unchanged relevance of L + H* as well as the decrease in H + L* in the *Porteño* Spanish of 2008 indicate that today's *Porteño* has a stronger tendency to place the pitch peak in the middle or at the right margin of the accented syllable. However, the peak is located within the metrically strong syllable (see the grey area in Figure 6) in all three pitch accents and is rarely placed in the post-tonic syllable as is the case for pre-nuclear accents in Peninsular Spanish and several other Spanish varieties (Estebas-Vilaplana & Prieto 2010). Figure 6 gives a schematic representation of the three pitch accent realizations under discussion.

At first glance, the durational analyses also speak in favor of an increase in "Italian" features over time, given that durational effects in the marking of nuclear syllables

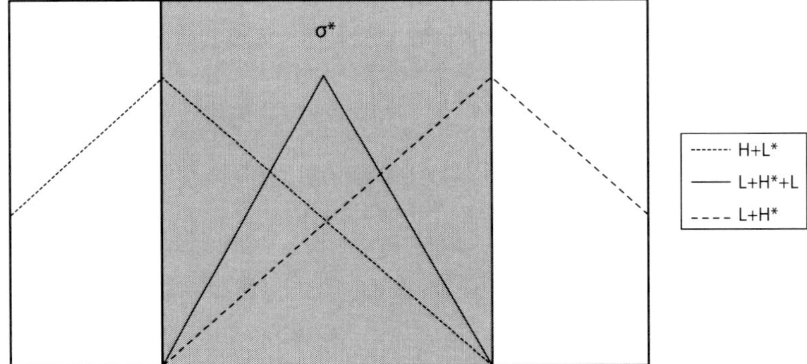

Figure 6. Schematic representation of the three possible realizations of pitch accents with the peak located within the limits of the stressed syllable

occur to a higher extent in the data collected in 2008 than in the older ones. However, when taking only the durations of the CV syllables into account, no statistically significant effect was found for durational marking (see Section 5.2).

All things considered, the overwhelming consistency of "Italian" features in the two groups indicates that typical *Porteño* prosody had already been part of the variety long before the 1980s. The present study thus largely supports previous studies by Vidal de Battini (1964) and Fontanella de Weinberg (1966), who observed as early as in the middle of the 20th century that the intonation of declaratives in Buenos Aires Spanish differed strikingly from that of other Argentinean Spanish varieties. The sociolinguistic upgrading of *Porteño* Spanish in the 1980s was just one step in the general upgrading of the variety, and we can conclude from our data that prosody did not play a major role in this step. It was nevertheless involved with regard to certain shifts in the occurrences of different pitch accents and boundary tones. We therefore conclude that the younger speakers who acquired *Porteño* mainly during or after the period of social upgrading continue to highlight the "Italian" features in their speech – despite Spanish monolingualism.

7.   Concluding remarks

This paper presents a first attempt to compare recorded data of a single language from two different time periods. By using recordings from 1983 and similar ones from 2008, we were able to compare the prosodic patterns of yesterday's and today's *Porteño* Spanish, taking both tonal and durational properties into account. We thus entered the field of diachronic Romance prosody from a micro-diachronic perspective by comparing recordings from two time periods, whereas Hualde (2003, 2004) adopts comparative methods in order to reconstruct earlier stages of Romance languages. The time period we examined, however, was rather short. The lack of speech recordings prior to the invention of appropriate recording devices has also been a limitation. Despite the fact that the time span under investigation embraces only several decades, the present study has shown that such an undertaking can be fruitful: We have demonstrated that the presumably "Italian" features typical of *Porteño* prosody remain largely unchanged and consequently did not play a central role in the social upgrading of the variety during the last 80 to 90 years. We nevertheless demonstrated some shifts in the occurrences of pitch accents and boundary tones between the two epochs investigated in our study. Consequently, we not only describe a recent prosodic development, but also show that such results can be understood within a greater historical picture, in our case the linguistic emergence of today's *Porteño* Spanish.

References

Aguilar, L., C. de la Mota & P. Prieto. 2009. *Sp_ToBI: Training Materials.* <http://prosodia.upf.edu/sp_tobi/en/> (8 June 2012).

Alfano, I., R. Savy & J. Llisterri. 2009. Sulla realtà acustica dell'acento lessicale in italiano ed in spagnolo: La durata vocalica in produzione e percezione. In *La fonetica sperimentale: Metodo e applicazioni. Atti del 4° convegno nazionale AISV (Associazione Italiana di Scienze della Voce)*, eds. L. Romito, V. Galatà & R. Lio, 22–39. Torriana: EDK.

Baily, S. L. 1999. *Immigrants in the Lands of Promise: Italians in Buenos Aires and New York City, 1870 to 1914.* Ithaca NY: Cornell University Press.

Beckman, M. E., M. Díaz-Campos, J. T. McGory & T. A. Morgan. 2002. Intonation across Spanish, in the Tones and Break Indices framework. *Probus* 14: 9–36.

Benet, A., E. Kireva, A. Pešková & C. Gabriel. In press. Transferencia prosódica del italiano al español: El ritmo en el español de Buenos Aires y en el español como L2 de hablantes nativos de italiano. In *Actas del V Congreso Internacional de Fonética Experimental. Cáceres, Extremadura, 25–28 Octubre, 2011*, eds. Y. Congosto Martín, M. L. Montero Curiel & A. Salvador Plans. Universities of Cáceres and Sevilla: Espacio Europeo Educación Superior e Investigación.

Boersma, P. & D. Weenink. 1992ff. *Praat: Doing Phonetics by Computer* (computer program). <http://www.praat.org>

Borges, J. L. 1944/1991. Funes el memorioso. In *Ficciones*, 121–132. Madrid: Alianza (1st edition 1944).

Borges, J. L. 1962. Funes, the memorious. In *Ficciones,* ed. A. Kerrigan, 107–115. New York NY: Grove.

Carricaburo, N. B. 1999. *El voseo en la literatura argentina.* Madrid: Arco Libros.

Colantoni, L. 2011. Broad-focus declaratives in Argentine Spanish contact and non-contact varieties. In *Intonational Phrasing in Romance and Germanic: Cross-linguistic and Bilingual Studies* (Hamburg Studies on Multilingualism 10), eds. C. Gabriel & C. Lleó, 183–212. Amsterdam: John Benjamins.

Colantoni, L. & J. Gurlekian. 2004. Convergence and intonation: Historical evidence from Buenos Aires Spanish. *Bilingualism: Language and Cognition* 7: 107–119.

D'Imperio, M. 2001. Focus and tonal structure in Neapolitan Italian. *Speech Communication* 33: 339–356.

D'Imperio, M. & S. Rosenthall. 1999. Phonetics and phonology of main stress in Italian. *Phonology* 16: 1–28.

Dellwo, V. & P. Wagner. 2003. Relations between language rhythm and speech rate. In *Proceedings of the 15th International Congress of Phonetics Sciences*, eds. M. J. Solé, D. Recasens & J. Romero, 471–474. Barcelona: Futurgraphic.

Devoto, F. 2002. In Argentina. In *Storia dell'emigrazione italiana*, ed. P. Bevilacqua, 25–54. Roma: Donzelli.

El Zarka, D. 2011. Leading, linking, and closing tones and tunes in Egyptian Arabic – what a simple intonation system tells us about the nature of intonation. In *Perspectives on Arabic linguistics: Papers from the annual symposia on Arabic linguistics*, Volume XXII–XXIII: *College Park, Maryland, 2008 and Milwaukee, Wisconsin, 2009* (Current Issues in Linguistic Theory 317), eds. E. Broselow & H. Ouali, 57–74. Amsterdam: John Benjamins.

Enbe, C. 2009. *Buenos Aires Spanish Prosody: Description of Intonation and Rhythm in Normal and Pathological Speech According to the Theory of Phonology as Human Behavior.* Saarbrücken: VDM.

Enbe, C. & Y. Tobin. 2008. Sociolinguistic variation in the prosody of Buenos Aires Spanish according to the theory of phonology as human behavior. In *Selected Proceedings of the 3rd Conference on Laboratory Approaches to Spanish Phonology,* eds. L. Colantoni & J. Steele, 140–154. Somerville MA: Cascadilla Press.

Estebas-Vilaplana, E. 2010. The role of duration in intonational modeling: A comparative study of Peninsular and Argentinean Spanish. *Revista Española de Lingüística Aplicada* 23: 153–173.

Estebas-Vilaplana, E. & P. Prieto. 2008. La notación prosódica en español: Una revisión del Sp_ToBI. *Estudios de Fonética Experimental* 17: 263–283.

Estebas-Vilaplana, E. & P. Prieto. 2010. Castilian Spanish intonation. In *Transcription of Intonation of the Spanish Language,* eds. P. Prieto & P. Roseano, 17–48. München: Lincom.

Feldhausen, I., A. Benet & A. Pešková. 2011. *Prosodische Grenzen in der Spontansprache: Eine Untersuchung zum Zentralkatalanischen und* porteño-*Spanischen* (Arbeiten zur Mehrsprachigkeit 94). Hamburg: Universität Hamburg.

Feldhausen, I., C. Gabriel & A. Pešková. 2010. Prosodic phrasing in Argentinean Spanish: Buenos Aires and Neuquén. In *Proceedings of Speech Prosody 2010,* Chicago IL. <http://speechprosody2010.illinois.edu/papers/100111.pdf> (8 June 2012).

Feldhausen, I., A. Pešková, E. Kireva & C. Gabriel. 2011. Categorical perception of Porteño nuclear accents. In *Proceedings of the 17th International Congress of Phonetic Sciences 2011, Hong Kong, China (ICPhS 17),* eds. W. Lee & E. Zee, 116–119. Hong Kong: City University of Hong Kong.

Fontanella de Weinberg, M. B. 1966. Comparación de dos entonaciones regionales argentinas. *Boletín del Instituto Caro y Cuervo* 21: 17–29.

Fontanella de Weinberg, M. B. 1973. El rehilamiento bonaerense a fines del siglo XVIII. *Thesaurus* 28: 338–343.

Fontanella de Weinberg, M. B. 1987. *El español bonaerense: Cuatro siglos de evolución lingüística (1580–1980).* Buenos Aires: Hachette.

Frota, S., M. d'Imperio, G. Elordieta, P. Prieto & M. Vigário. 2007. The phonetics and phonology of intonational phrasing in Romance. In *Segmental and Prosodic Issues in Romance Phonology* (Current Issues in Linguistic Theory 282), eds. P. Prieto, J. Mascaró & M. J. Solé, 131–153. Amsterdam: John Benjamins.

Gabriel, C., I. Feldhausen & A. Pešková. 2011. Prosodic phrasing in Porteño Spanish. In *Intonational Phrasing in Romance and Germanic: Cross-linguistic and Bilingual Studies* (Hamburg Studies on Multilingualism 10), eds. C. Gabriel & C. Lleó, 153–182. Amsterdam: John Benjamins.

Gabriel, C., I. Feldhausen, A. Pešková, L. Colantoni, S. A. Lee, V. Arana & L. Labastía. 2010. Argentinian Spanish intonation. In *Transcription of Intonation of the Spanish Language,* eds. P. Prieto & P. Roseano, 285–317. München: Lincom.

Gabriel, C. & E. Kireva. 2012. Intonation und Rhythmus im spanisch-italienischen Kontakt: Der Fall des *Porteño*-Spanischen. In *Testo e ritmi: Zum Rhythmus in der italienischen Sprache,* eds. M. Selig & E. Schafroth, 131–149. Frankfurt: Peter Lang.

Gabriel, C., A. Pešková, L. Labastía & B. Blázquez. In press. La entonación en el español de Buenos Aires. In *Perspectivas teóricas y experimentales sobre el español de la Argentina,* eds. L. Colantoni & C. Rodríguez Louro. Frankfurt: Vervuert.

Gili Fivela, B. 2002. Tonal alignment in two Pisa Italian peak accents. In *Proceedings of the First International Conference on Speech Prosody*, eds. B. Bel & I. Marlin, 339–342. Aix-en-Provence: SProSIG.

Gili Fivela, B. & M. d'Imperio. 2010. High peaks versus high plateaux in the identification of two pitch accents in Pisa Italian. In *Proceedings of Speech Prosody 2010*, Chicago, IL. <http://speechprosody2010.illinois.edu/papers/100216.pdf> (6 June 2012).

Giordano, R. 2008. On the phonetics of rhythm of Italian: Patterns of duration in pre-planned and spontaneous speech. In *Proceedings of Speech Prosody 2008, Campinas, Brazil*, eds. P. A. Barbosa, S. Madureira & C. Reis, 247–350. São Paulo: Capes. <http://www.isca-speech.org/archive/sp2008/papers/sp08_347.pdf> (6 June 2012).

Hajek, J. & M. Stevens M. 2011. Vowel duration in stressed position in central and Northern varieties of Standard Italian: A pilot study. In *Proceedings of the 17th International Congress of Phonetic Sciences 2011, Hong Kong, China (ICPhS 17)*, eds. W. Lee & E. Zee, 803–806. Hong Kong: City University of Hong Kong.

Hualde, J. I. 2003. Remarks on the diachronic reconstruction of intonational patterns in Romance with special attention to Occitan as a bridge language. *Catalan Journal of Linguistics* 2: 181–205.

Hualde, J. I. 2004. Romance intonation from a comparative and diachronic perspective: Possibilities and limitations. In *Contemporary Approaches to Romance Linguistics* (Current Issues in Linguistic Theory 258), eds. J. Auger, J. C. Clements & B. Vance, 217–237. Amsterdam: John Benjamins.

Jun, S.-A. 2005. *Prosodic Typology: The Phonology of Intonation and Phrasing*. Oxford: OUP.

Kabatek, J. 2005. Was die Porteños mit ihrer Grundfrequenz ausdrücken wollen. In *Sprache in Iberoamerika*, eds. V. Noll & H. Symeonidis, 261–275. Hamburg: Buske.

Kaisse, E. M. 2001. The long fall: An intonational melody of Argentinean Spanish. In *Features and Interfaces in Romance* (Current Issues in Linguistic Theory 222), eds. J. Herschensohn, E. Mallén & K. Zagona, 148–160. Amsterdam: John Benjamins.

Klee, C. A. & A. Lynch. 2009. *El español en contacto con otras lenguas*. Washington DC: Georgetown University Press.

Krämer, M. 2009. *The Phonology of Italian*. Oxford: OUP.

Kubarth, H. 1986. El idioma como juego social: La conciencia sociolingüística del porteño. *Thesaurus* 41: 187–210.

Labraña, L. & A. Sebastián. 2004. *Lengua y poder: El argentino metropolitano*. Buenos Aires: Comisión para la Preservación del Patrimonio Histórico Cultural.

Ladd, R. D. 2008. *Intonational Phonology*, 2nd edn. Cambridge: CUP.

Lahiri, A., T. Riad & H. Jacobs. 1999. Diachronic prosody. In *Word Prosodic Systems in the Languages of Europe*, ed. H. van der Hulst, 335–422. Berlin: Mouton de Gruyter.

Lipski, J. M. 1996. *El español de América*. Madrid: Cátedra Lingüística.

Maronese, L., ed. 2009. *Buenos Aires italiana*. Buenos Aires: Comisión para la Preservación del Patrimonio Histórico Cultural.

Muñoz, Á. F. 2007. *Bachicha, Cana* und *Chantapufi*: Der italienische Beitrag zur Sprachform am Río de La Plata. In *Von La Quiaca nach Ushuaia*, ed. G. Kremnitz, 129–156. Wien: Praesens.

Navarro Tomás, T. 1944. *Manual de entonación española*. New York NY: Spanish Institute in the United States.

Nespor, M. & I. Vogel. 1986 (2007). *Prosodic phonology*. Berlin: Mouton de Gruyter. (Dordrecht: Foris, 1986).

Pešková, A., I. Feldhausen & C. Gabriel. 2011. Fraseo prosódico en el español Porteño: Evidencia de datos leídos y semi-espontáneos. In *El español rioplatense*, eds. A. di Tullio & R. Kailuweit, 77–102. Frankfurt: Vervuert.

Pešková, A., I. Feldhausen & C. Gabriel. In press. Una perspectiva diacrónica de la entonación bonaerense. In *Actes del 26é Congrés de Lingüística i Filologia Romàniques (València, 6–11 de setembre de 2010)*, eds. E. Casanova Herrero & C. Calvo Rigual. Berlin: Mouton de Gruyter.

Pierrehumbert, J. 1980. *The Phonology and Phonetics of English Intonation.* PhD dissertation, MIT.

Pitrelli, J. F., M. E Beckman & J. Hirschberg. 1994. Evaluation of prosodic transcription labeling reliability in the ToBI framework. In *Proceedings of the Third International Conference on Spoken Language Processing (ICSLP 94)*, Yokohama, Japan, 123–126.

Prieto, P. & P. Roseano, eds. 2010. *Transcription of Intonation of the Spanish Language.* München: Lincom.

Ramus, F., M. Nespor & J. Mehler. 1999. Correlates of linguistic rhythm in the speech signal. *Cognition* 73: 265–292.

Riad, T. 1998. The origin of Scandinavian tone accents. *Diachronica* 15: 63–98.

Riad, T. 2003. Diachrony of the Scandinavian accent typology. In *Development in Prosodic Systems* (Studies in Generative Grammar 58), eds. P. Fikkert & H. Jacobs, 91–144. Berlin: Mouton de Gruyter.

Savino, M. 2009. Where is the rise in Italian yes-no question intonation? A corpus-based study on regional accents. Poster presented at Phonetics and Phonology in Iberia, Las Palmas de Gran Canaria, Spain, 17–19 June 2009.

Selkirk, E. 1984. *Phonology and Syntax: The Relation between Sound and Structure.* Cambridge MA: The MIT Press.

Sorianello, P. 2006. *Prosodia: Modelli e ricerca empirica.* Roma: Carocci.

Stella, A., M. M. Vanrell, P. Prieto & B. Gili-Fivela. 2011. Focus largo e focus contrastivo: Dati articolatori sull'allineamento tonale in italiano e catalano. Poster presented at the 7 convegno AISV (Associazione Italiana di Scienze della Voce), Lecce, Italy, 26–28 January 2011.

Tagliamonte, S. 2006. *Analysing Sociolinguistic Variation.* Cambridge: CUP.

Toledo, G. 2010. Métricas rítmicas en tres dialectos Amper-España. *Estudios filológicos* 45: 93–110.

Veith, D. 2008. *Italienisch am Río de la Plata.* Frankfurt: Peter Lang.

Vidal de Battini, B. E. 1964. *El español de la Argentina.* Buenos Aires: Consejo Nacional de Educación.

White, L., E. Payne & S. L. Mattys. 2009. Rhythmic and prosodic contrast in Venetan and Sicilian Italian. In *Phonetics and Phonology: Interactions and Interrelations* (Current Issues in Linguistic Theory 306), eds. M. Vigário, S. Frota & M. J. Freitas, 137–158. Amsterdam: John Benjamins.

Devoicing of sibilants as a segmental cue to the influence of Spanish onto current Catalan phonology

Ariadna Benet, Susana Cortés and Conxita Lleó
University of Hamburg, Germany

This article presents production data of sibilant segments by Catalan speakers in a Spanish-Catalan bilingual context. Catalan includes voiced sibilants in its sound system, whereas Spanish only has voiceless ones. Subjects come from two areas of Barcelona differing in the degree of presence of Spanish. Based on previous results on vowel production, we predict that Catalan sibilants, especially the voiceless ones, will be less often produced in a target-like manner in the more Spanish-speaking area, and especially in the younger groups (3–5 and 19–23 years old). Our results confirm this prediction for /z/, whereas for the affricate /dʒ/ percentages of target-like production are low in all groups. These results are accounted for by several internal and external linguistic factors.

Keywords: Catalan, Spanish, sibilants, voicing, markedness, complexity, language contact

1. Introduction

The study presented here has been carried out within the research project "Phono-prosodic development of Catalan in its current bilingual context."[1] This project has

---

1.   The project, conducted by Conxita Lleó, belongs to the Collaborative Research Center on Multilingualism (Sonderforschungsbereich 538 "Mehrsprachigkeit"), hosted at the University of Hamburg, Germany. In the first place, we thank the Center and its sponsors, the German Research Foundation (Deutsche Forschungsgemeinschaft, DFG) and the University of Hamburg, for their support. We also thank Anna Schreibweis, Anni Sell, Jorge Vega and Genís Ventura for their essential work transcribing and coding the data. The data collection would not have been possible without the kind collaboration of the subjects from Barcelona; we deeply thank them all. Finally, we thank the editors of this volume, who invited us to participate with the present study. This paper is a revised version of a presentation given at the *International Conference on Multilingual Individuals and Multilingual Societies* (Hamburg, October 2010).

been devoted to examining the production of Catalan phonological segmental categories that do not have equivalent counterparts in the Spanish inventory. Suprasegmental categories involved in intonation, as well as lexical phenomena, such as gender, differing also from Spanish, and lexical loans, have also been included in the project, which has focused on the Catalan spoken in two different areas of Barcelona.

This metropolis, which, according to the Statistics Department of the Barcelona City Council (Departament d'Estadística de l'Ajuntament de Barcelona 2010), has about 1,6 million inhabitants, is the capital of the autonomous region of Catalonia, located in the North East of Spain. Both Catalan and Spanish are official languages, thus bilingualism, with different degrees of dominance of one or the other language, is a very common situation for the majority of speakers. According to the "Statistics on the uses of languages" (Institut d'Estadística de Catalunya 2008), on the question as with which language speakers identify most, 46.5% of the population of Catalonia consider it to be Spanish, 37.2% state it is Catalan and 8.8% give both languages as answer; and 6.4% of the population identify themselves with other languages like Arabic, Romanian and other immigration languages (1% of the answers to the questions were not available). The areas of Barcelona under study differ on the degree of presence of Spanish: Gràcia and Eixample are traditionally Catalan districts located side by side in the city center, whereas Nou Barris is a new district created during the nineteen sixties in the outskirts of the city with the purpose to host thousands of new-comers from the rest of Spain. In fact, according to the Catalan Linguistic Census (Institut d'Estadística de Catalunya 2001), the population from Nou Barris shows one of the lowest percentages of oral and written competence in Catalan, whereas the inhabitants of Gràcia and Eixample are among those with the highest percentages. In our project, speakers are divided into three age groups: children (G1), young adults (G2) and older adults (G3). See Section 2.1 for details.

1.1   Catalan sibilants

Catalan has a complete system of eight sibilants, four voiced and four voiceless: /z/, /ʒ/, /dz/, /dʒ/ vs. /s/, /ʃ/, /ts/ and /tʃ/, respectively. However, in the dialectal variety of central Catalan, especially in Barcelona, phonologists have noted that a process of devoicing of /dʒ/ appeared in the second half of the 20th century. That is, /dʒ/ has been reported to become voiceless [tʃ] in intervocalic position (Veny 1998: 36). Thus, it is reported that in Barcelona words like *rellotge* 'clock' or *metge* 'medical doctor' are produced as [rəˈʎɔtʃə] instead of [rəˈʎɔdʒə], and [ˈmetʃə] instead of [ˈmedʒə]. The devoicing of /z/ has also been pointed out, but this process appears to have been introduced later on, and it occurs in various geographical variants of Eastern Catalan, not only in Barcelona (see Lleó 2006). These two phonemes, /z/ and /dʒ/, are the only ones considered in this article, for the following reasons. They have a very broad distribution, occurring word-initially and word-medially, between vowels, as well as following or preceding a consonant.[2] As far as the other segments are concerned, the phoneme /dz/ is rather infrequent, and it is not found in simple words forming part of young children's vocabularies (see Badia Margarit 1965 for details on the distribution of sibilants). The phoneme /ʒ/ is often produced as an affricate in initial position, and medially after a nasal, which means that several words containing this underlying segment have been added to the words containing underlying /dʒ/ (see list of words in Appendix).

1.2   Research questions

One of the general predictions of the project is that the speakers from Nou Barris will show a Catalan speech production with more Spanish features, due to the more intense contact that they have with this language in comparison to the speakers from Gràcia and Eixample. We consider two types of factor as responsible for the different outcomes: on the one hand, external linguistic factors like education and degree of exposure to each one of the languages in contact; on the other hand, we take into account internal linguistic factors like frequency, markedness, and complexity.[3] Especially the notion of *markedness* constitutes a pre-requisite to determining those areas that are more vulnerable to influence under language contact (Lleó 2006). Here, it is used in the same sense as in Lleó, Cortés & Benet (2008: 188), following Jakobson (1941/1968). Specifically, we consider that marked entities presuppose unmarked ones in a typological, diachronic and acquisition sense. Typologically, unmarked segments appear more frequently than marked ones in the world's languages; moreover, a language is able to contain a marked entity, only if the corresponding unmarked entity is also contained in that same language; thus, diachronically a language will develop a certain marked entity only if it also contains the corresponding unmarked one; and in L1 acquisition, unmarked entities are acquired earlier than marked ones.

Taking this into consideration, the Catalan phonological system is in some respects more marked than the Spanish one. For instance, as far as vowels are concerned: whereas the Spanish system has only five vowels, the Catalan system has eight vowels, exhibiting two opening degrees in the mid vowels as well as schwa, which is typologically a marked vowel (Maddieson 1984, Lleó, Cortés & Benet 2011). The vowels existing in Catalan and not in Spanish, and at the same time implying more markedness, are /ɛ/, /ɔ/ and [ə]. Results on vowel production from this research project (Cortés, Lleó & Benet 2009, Lleó et al. 2008, Lleó, Benet & Cortés 2009) have shown that children (G1) and young adults (G2) in Gràcia have a statistically significantly higher percentage of Catalan target-like production for each of the three vowels than the same age groups in Nou Barris. This was so regardless of the specific language (or languages) spoken at home, especially regardless of the language spoken by the mother.

---

2.   In word-final position, all obstruents are voiceless in Catalan due to the process of syllable final devoicing (see Bonet & Lloret 1998: 103ff).

3.   The notion of complexity will be defined and dealt wih in Section 4.

In this article we focus our attention on the production of the Catalan sibilants /z/ and /dʒ/ in both areas of Barcelona and in the three age groups mentioned. Taking the results of vowel production into account, one plausible hypothesis is that these Catalan sounds, which do not exist in the Spanish phonological system, will be less often produced in a target-like manner in Nou Barris than in Gràcia and Eixample, due to the stronger dominance of Spanish in the first mentioned district. And according to the results on vowels, this difference between both areas will be clearer in the two younger age groups, G1 and G2. By investigating the results on sibilant production, we want to continue the line of research that we applied to vowels, unraveling those Catalan sounds that are more vulnerable to the influence of Spanish, and enlarging our search for the factors explaining such influence.

Summarizing, the goal of this article is to test two hypotheses, namely:

H1   Catalan sounds, which do not exist in the Spanish phonological system, will be less often produced in a target-like manner in Nou Barris than in Gràcia and Eixample.
H2   The difference between these two areas will be larger in both younger age groups, G1 and G2.

The article has the following structure. In the next section, the precise groups of subjects and the method of data collection are described. In Section 3, we present the results of the data production on sibilants. Section 4 discusses the results and answers the questions brought up in this Introduction. Finally, our conclusions are presented in Section 5.

2.   Methodology

2.1   Subjects

The speech of 120 subjects was individually recorded, and relevant utterances were auditorily and acoustically analyzed. The subjects belong to two different areas of Barcelona: a) the districts of Gràcia/Eixample[4] – an area with a low degree of presence of Spanish – and b) Nou Barris – a district with a very high degree of presence of Spanish. The subjects within districts were divided into three age groups:

- G1: children between 3 and 5 years old.
- G2: young adults between 19 and 23 years old.
- G3: adults between 32 and 40 years old.

---

4.   Due to the similarity of results between both districts obtained in preliminary studies and since Gràcia and Eixample are neighboring districts, we consider both of them as one area here, with 20 subjects in each age group as a whole.

Each of the six groups (three age groups and two areas, namely Gràcia/Eixample and Nou Barris) is composed of 20 subjects. In all groups the language of the subject's parents has been kept balanced as far as possible, so that half of the group has a Catalan-speaking mother and the other half a Spanish-speaking mother. The language of the father has also been controlled for, although we have considered the mother's language as the crucial one, assuming that she is the main caretaker in the child's first years. Each group differs as to the amount of Catalan received during socialization and formal education: the subjects in G3 went to school at the end of Franco's dictatorship, when teaching Catalan and instruction in Catalan was forbidden; those in G2 have received their whole compulsory education in Catalan, and G1 are at pre-school level, where the educators speak in Catalan, but at this age children have not yet learned to read or write, so no spelling pronunciation effects are expected to be found in their speech. All subjects participating in the study have been exposed to Catalan from birth, and can thus be considered to be native speakers of Catalan. We tried to balance each group with an equal number of males and females. However, in the oldest group, whose members are the mother or father of the subjects in G1, many more women were interviewed. The purpose of this imbalance was to prioritize analyzing the speech of the mother than that of the father, considering that the mother spends more time with the children in most cases, and thus provides a great deal of input. Table 1 displays the proportion of males and females in each group.

In order to build the groups of children, we contacted several schools in the areas to be investigated. In Gràcia and Eixample, we interviewed children of the state schools CEIP (Centre Públic d'Educació Infantil i Primària 'State School for Infant and Primary Education') Patronat Domènech, CEIP Josep Maria Jujol, CEIP Ramon Llull, CEIP Fort Pienc, and the private school IPSI. In Nou Barris the children attended the state school CEIP Gaudí and the private one Sant Lluís. The teachers chose the children suitable for our study depending on their willingness to talk as well as on their parents' language (and, of course, with previous consent of the parents). Through the teachers we were also able to contact the mother or father of each child to be interviewed in order to plan and perform interviews with them. The latter constituted the G3 groups. As for the G2 subjects, they were contacted through sportclubs, public libraries, language schools and youth associations in their district. All interviews took place in Catalan.

Table 1. Subjects by gender in each age and district group

	G1	G2	G3
Gràcia/Eixample	8 males	8 males	3 males
	12 females	12 females	17 females
Nou Barris	12 males	10 males	5 males
	8 females	10 females	15 females

2.2   Materials and equipment

Elicited words contained the target segments /z/ and /dʒ/ in intervocalic position, in order to avoid spurious phenomena not relevant to the study of sibilant devoicing. In the case of /z/, the position between vowels was selected for the following reasons. In Spanish, the voiced alveolar fricative /z/ does not exist as a phoneme but is traditionally said to occur as an allophone of /s/ before voiced consonants, both word internally and across word boundaries. This is the result of a voice assimilation process, by which a word like *mismo* /ˈmismo/ 'same' is said to be pronounced [ˈmizmo] (Hualde 2005: 159). However, it has been shown that the assimilation is incomplete and gradual, depending on various phonetic and prosodic factors (Romero 1999, Campos Astorkiza 2010). Thus, it is not only the case that the phoneme /z/ does not belong to the Spanish inventory; the segment [z] is hardly present, either, as in the assimilatory contexts, where it was traditionally claimed to appear, voicing is generally not complete (Romero 1999). Anyhow, given the presence of such assimilation process in Spanish, which might give place to [z], the position between vowels seemed to us the clearest one for [z], to exclude the voiced sibilant in Spanish. In the case of [dʒ], the intervocalic position was the clearest one as well, given the various voicing assimilation processes of Catalan clusters. Thus, all target words had the target sibilants between vowels, and none of the target words contained the voiced sibilants before a voiced (or voiceless) consonant. As all subjects were to produce the same set of target words, we chose simple words that could be part of a young children's lexicon (see list of words in Appendix). The audio files were recorded using a Sony ECM-CS1 unidirectional lapel microphone plugged into a portable Hi-MD Walkman MZ-RH10 Sony Mini-Disc recorder.

2.3   Procedure and analysis

Words containing the target segments were elicited by picture naming and by some specific questions for those target words that were not depictable. Each word was expected to be produced only once, thus no repetitions were elicited. Interviews were run individually in the best acoustic conditions available to optimize the acoustic quality of the recordings. The high quality of the recordings allow not only for the auditory but also for the acoustic analysis of the data. The sessions took place in a quiet room at the school, in the institution where the subject was met or at his/her flat. The total recorded data amounts to about 100 hours, 45–60 minutes of interview per speaker. The target words for this specific study on sibilants were extracted out of the whole interview.

Data were auditorily analyzed and transcribed by two native speakers of Catalan with phonetic expertise, a student in linguistics and one of the first two authors. In ambiguous cases, transcriptions were complemented by acoustic measurements, which were carried out by a student in phonetics and the second author. As voicing is the crucial distinctive feature of the segments under study, i.e. the feature to be investigated (given that the voiceless counterparts of sibilants are also part of the Spanish inventory of phonemes), the glottal pulses and the voice report functions in Praat (Boersma & Weenink 1992ff) were used as aiding tools for this analysis. Those few cases that remained unresolved were excluded from further analysis.

3.   Results

The results of the mixed (i.e., auditory and acoustic) analysis of /z/ are shown in Figure 1 and those of /dʒ/ in Figure 2. According to Figure 1, the differences between /z/ production across districts reach significance in the two younger generations, Gràcia/ Eixample always taking the lead with regard to the production percentages of Catalan segments over Nou Barris [(G1: χ^2 (1, N = 40) = 35.374; p < .0001), (G2: χ^2 (1, N = 40) = 37.673; p < .0001)]. As in our previous studies on vowel production (Cortés et al. 2009, Lleó et al. 2008, 2009 and 2011), no significant difference was found across districts in the oldest generation. This is the most homogenous group as far as percentage of target-like production of the segments under study is concerned. These results show the same trend already observed in our just mentioned previous studies on the production of vowels by the same population (see Figure 3, below).

Figure 2 displays no statistically significant differences in the target-like production of the affricate /dʒ/ across districts within age groups. The first thing to be noticed is that the percentages of target-like production for /dʒ/ are in general very low, only reaching 50% and beyond in the case of G2. Another feature to be noticed in relation to the production data of the affricate is the high variability in its output. That is, in the case of /z/, subjects either produced [z] or [s]; however, instead of producing /dʒ/, they produced its voiceless counterpart, [dʃ], and also voiced and voiceless fricatives or approximants, as e.g. [ʃ], [ʒ], [z], [s], [j] or [ð]. As voicing was the main feature of interest in this study, all realizations were divided into voiced or voiceless, and all voiced outputs counted as target-like, provided that they were sibilants, regardless of being fricatives or affricates. Accordingly, productions with the approximant, non-sibilant [j], like the non-target [raˈjɔdja] (for the target [rəˈʎɔdʒə] *rellotge* 'clock') were excluded from the countings.

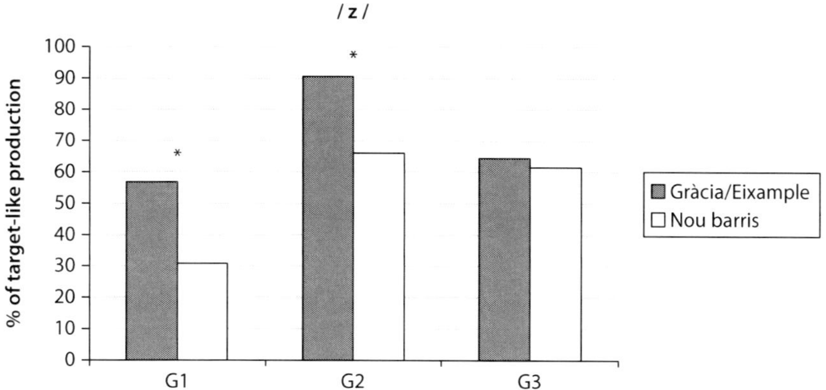

Figure 1. Percentages of /z/ target-like production

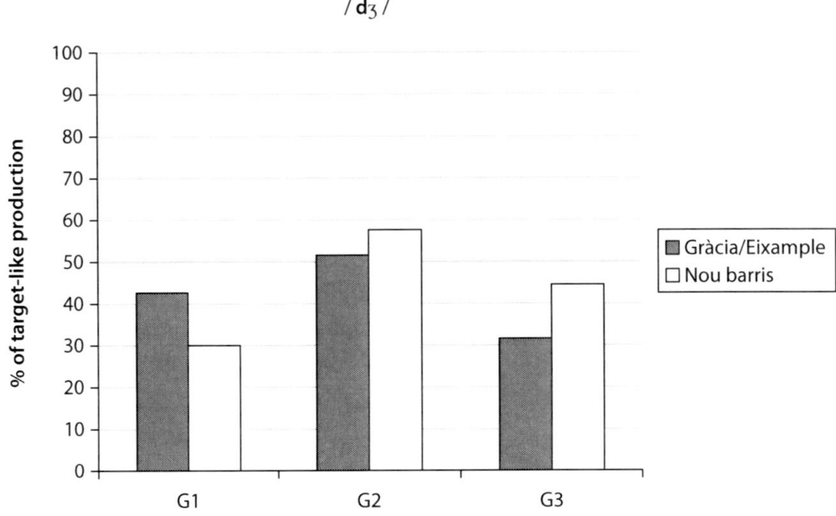

Figure 2. Percentages of /dʒ/ target-like production

When comparing the results of the group production of /z/ with those of /dʒ/ a very clear difference is apparent. Overall, target-like production of the affricate is lower than that of /z/ in most groups, as observed in a comparison of Figure 1 and 2. In the groups of younger adults (G2) and older adults (G3), the production is lower in Gràcia/ Eixample than in Nou Barris, which has never been the case in the data of other segments under study. Nevertheless, differences across districts do not reach significance. Although in terms of percentages, the differences in some cases seem to be large enough, the number of items elicited for the affricate was very small and that is why a difference of 11%, as in G1 in Figure 2, does not reach significance.

4.   Discussion

Results presented in the previous section have shown that the target-like production of /z/ by children (G1) and by young adults (G2) is significantly higher in Gràcia/ Eixample than in Nou Barris. As for older adults (G3), they do not show statistically significant differences between districts. This pattern exactly parallels that of vowel production (as shown in Figure 3), and strongly confirms our two hypotheses: H1 predicted more target-like production in Gràcia/Eixample than in Nou Barris, and H2 expected to find this difference in the two younger generations, G1 and G2. In Figure 3, the results for /ɛ/ are presented (results for the other vowels were very similar and the statistical differences were identical). The results for target-like production of the vowel /ɛ/ also show a statistically significant difference across districts in G1 and G2, Gràcia/Eixample showing much higher values than Nou Barris, whereas the difference of G3 across districts does not reach significance. Something parallel is obviously

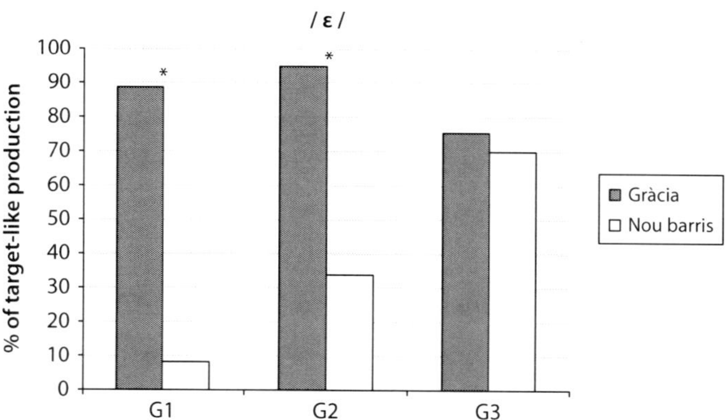

Figure 3. Percentages of /ɛ/ target-like production (from Lleó et al. 2008: 200)

taking place in relation to the production of /z/. This parallelism strongly confirms our hypotheses. That is, for G1 and G2, the dominant language in the district seems to be the key factor for the difference in the production of the Catalan phonemes (both, the vowel /ɛ/, and in the present study, the sibilant /z/): if Spanish is more present in the speaker's social environment, it is more likely that he or she will not produce a voiced sibilant and his/her production will converge with the Spanish one.

One of the conclusions of our results both on vowel and voiced sibilant production is that for children as well as for young adults, the dominant language of the district (for these age groups that mainly means the language at school and its environment) seems to have a stronger influence on their speech production than the input they receive at home. However, the groups of adults (G3) do not display statistical differences for any of the three vowels or sibilants across districts, thus showing that the dominant language in the district does not play a role for them. We assume that their speech production, at least for these segments, is conditioned by the district where they grew up, which generally does not correspond to the district where they live now. The different results obtained in the two areas of Barcelona, Nou Barris on the one hand, and Gràcia/Eixample on the other hand, has been explained by a combination of internal and external linguistic factors in the situation of language contact, which can potentially lead to phonological change (Lleó & Cortés in press).

Additional factors to play a role in the linguistic change may be the marked and complex character of the target Catalan segments. On the one hand, voiced obstruents are more marked than voiceless ones (see, e.g., markedness convention XXI in Chomsky & Halle 1968: 406). In the Introduction, unmarked segments have been typologically defined as those appearing more frequently in the languages of the world. Maddieson (1984)'s survey based on 317 languages offers reliable information on the frequency of segments, which can be interpreted in terms of markedness. From this point of view, we can ascertain that voiced sibilants are more marked than voiceless ones, as e.g. voiceless /s/ occurs in 276 languages (87.1% of languages of the survey), whereas voiced /z/ only occurs in 97 languages (30.6%). The voiceless affricate /tʃ/ appears in 141 languages (44.5%), and the voiced one /dʒ/ in only 80 languages (25.2%).

Moreover, in Catalan, sibilants involve complexity, which we define on the basis of form variation. That is, lexical items involving allomorphy and/or allophony, and thus violating Uniformity, are considered to be complex. Kenstowicz (1997: 139) gives following definition. "Uniform Exponence: a lexical item (stem, affix, word) has the same realization for property P in its various contexts of occurrence". According to this, forms should not change between input and output and should not alternate. This definition applies to the sibilants in the following manner. On the one hand, any sibilant consonant at the end of a word is voiceless in Catalan, as in this language a process of final devoicing applies to all obstruents (see Bonet & Lloret 1998: 103ff). On the other hand, word-final sibilants become voiced through the sandhi process of resyllabification, by which the sibilant preceding a word that begins with a vowel changes from the coda to the onset position of the following syllable, and it concomitantly becomes voiced. For example, the [s] in the article *les* ('the' plural feminine) becomes [z] when the following noun starts with a vowel: *les amigues* /ləs#ə.'mi.ɣəs/ 'the (girl) friends' is thus pronounced [lə.zə.'mi.ɣəs]. The duality of form ([ləs] alternating with [ləz]) resulting from this process of voicing violates Uniformity. The resyllabification of sibilants without voicing, resulting from Spanish influence (Spanish does not have either voiced sibilants nor the sandhi voicing process), has as a concomitant result the avoidance of Uniformity violations.

In order to have an effect, this internal factor of complexity must act together with the external factor of the Spanish dominance in the district. The similar results in both G3 groups can be due to a biographical reason: some of the subjects of this age group were not born in the district where they live now, but they have grown up in another part of the city, where the sociolinguistic context could have been very different from that where they live now.[5] Thus, in G3 the dominant language in the district does not seem to play such a crucial role as in G1 and in G2. At least not anymore, but it might have in the past.

In spite of the overall similarities between the results on /z/ and those on vowels, the G1 results on /z/ are different from those of vowels in one respect: the G1 age group in Gràcia/Eixample reaches a lower target-like production with the sibilant than with the open mid vowels /ɛ/ and /ɔ/. The reason could be developmental: according to Grunwell (1982) for English, children produce [s] at age 3;0 – 3;6, before they produce [z] at ages 3;6 – 4;0 and 4;0 – 4;6. According to Bosch (1987) for Catalan, /s/ is acquired at 4 years and /z/ at 5 years. The children in the group of Gràcia/Eixample have a mean age of 4;5 (and the mean age of the Nou Barris group was 4;10). Thus it is plausible that

---

5.   In the results of the Catalan vowels, G3 mean production was also very similar in both areas, but individual values showed lower target-like production for some of the speakers from Nou Barris and higher for some from Gràcia (Lleó et al. 2008: 205). This is not the case in the individual results of the sibilant /z/.

this voiced sibilant has not been (completely) acquired by some of the younger children yet. In fact, another important observation is that both in Gràcia/Eixample and in Nou Barris, G2 has a higher percentage of target-like production than G1. This result also agrees with those of vowels, as G2 reached higher percentages of target-like vowel production than G1. This difference between the age groups G1 and G2 is also to be attributed to the positive effect of school in Catalan, beside that of media and other social agents.

As for the affricate /dʒ/, the results have shown a different pattern from that of the sibilant /z/ and that of vowels: the target-like production is low overall and there are no significant differences across districts within age groups. The variability of the output forms of the target sound was also quite different from that of the target /z/. While in the case of /z/ the alternative output was always its voiceless counterpart [s], the target /dʒ/ produced a wider variety of answers: the most frequent ones were [tʃ], [ts], [dʃ], [dz], [z], [ʒ] or the target-like [dʒ]. As already mentioned, because voicing was the crucial target feature of our study, when the output was one of the voiced sibilants, it was considered target-like. In spite of this, the results do not reach more than 60% of target-like production (G2 in Nou Barris has the highest percentage with 58%). Several factors could explain these general low results. First, as pointed out in the Introduction, in the dialectal variety of Barcelona, [dʒ] has been reported to become voiceless in intervocalic position (Veny 1998: 36). This happens, for instance, in the word *rellotge* [rəˈʎɔdʒə] 'clock', which was contained in the list of elicited words. Second, although the voiced and voiceless affricates have a contrastive function in Catalan and they can occur in the same context (for instance, in *dutxar* [duˈtʃa] 'to take a shower' vs. *jutjar* [ʒuˈdʒa] 'to judge'), the frequency of the voiced one is not very high (Badia Margarit 1965). Third, the marked character of this voiced affricate can be argued to be a further factor both for the low results and also for the tendency to devoicing in the variety of Barcelona.

A fourth reason for these low results among all groups can be the aforementioned voiced realization resulting from the sandhi process of voicing. Because words containing the target sound /dʒ/ are not numerous in young children's lexica, elicitation of this sound also included combinations of two words, as e.g. *vaig anar* 'I went', the first one ending with the target sound, followed by a word starting with a vowel, or with a voiced consonant, as in *vaig menjar* 'I ate'. The production of such combinations of words involves the process of voicing described above, in this same section. For instance, the auxiliary verb of the past form *vaig* 'I go' ends in an underlyingly voiced fricative: /ˈbaʒ/, as evidenced by certain verb forms, as e.g. [ˈbaʒi] '(I/he/she) go(es)' (Pres. Subj.). This consonant is devoiced and affricated in word final position: [ˈbatʃ] 'I go'. However, if followed by a word beginning with vowel, it becomes voiced: *vaig anar* [ˌbadʒəˈna] 'I went'. According to Nguyen, Wauquier, Lancia & Tuller (2007), the production of segments resulting from sandhi processes in French entails more difficulty than that of a segment in its lexical form because of an added complexity in cognitive processing. Thus, the elicitation of words with target [dʒ] involved a higher degree of complexity, when compared to the elicitation of /z/ (and that of vowels), because the latter phoneme occurs more frequently in lexical items, and could be produced without involving the sandhi process of devoicing. Finally, the high variability in the answers for the target [dʒ] could be related to the general marked character of affricates (see Maddieson 1984).

In view of these results, linguistic external factors like dominant language in the district or education in Catalan do not seem to play a role for the target-like production of the affricate /dʒ/. Instead, complexity and markedness are the decisive factors. However, this is not the same for the sibilant /z/ (and for the vowels), since for this phoneme the dominant language in the district as well as schooling in Catalan can be argued to have a clear effect on the results, which have showed statistically significant differences across groups depending on external linguistic factors. Thus, certain segments may be dispensed with by the bilingual speaker on the basis of internal factors, like markedness and complexity. Only those segments that do not succumb to such internal factors may receive the beneficial effect of external factors, like language dominance in the district, school, media, etc.; see Lleó & Cortés (in press) for an attempt to weigh external factors in the bilingual Catalan-Spanish context.

5. Conclusion

The production of voiced sibilants, /z/ and /dʒ/, by different age groups in Gràcia/ Eixample and Nou Barris has led to two different types of results. On the one hand, the production of /z/ keeps a parallel pattern to that of vowels, showing significant differences across districts in the two youngest generations. This result confirms the initial hypotheses, based on the results on vowel production, namely, that for the youngest generations the factor of the language dominance in the district is the most influential one. On the other hand, the production of /dʒ/ does not show differences across districts, diverging from that of other segments that belong to the Catalan inventory, but not to the Spanish one, namely, the open mid vowels and schwa reported in previous studies stemming from our project. Besides, the indexes of target-like production are considerably lower and the alternative responses to the target segment are much more varied for the affricate than for the fricative. The difficulties in the production of this affricate have been accounted for in terms of markedness, complexity and cognitive processing load. Whereas the production results of this Catalan affricate seem to be conditioned by the internal linguistic factors of markedness and complexity, the results of the fricative /z/ respond to the impact of external linguistic factors like the dominant language of the district.

References

Badia Margarit, A. M. 1965. Problemes de la commutació consonàntica en català. *Boletim de Filologia* 21: 213–335.

Boersma, P. & D. Weenink. 1992ff. *Praat: Doing Phonetics by Computer* (computer program). <http://www.praat.org>

Bonet, E. & M. R. Lloret. 1998. *Fonologia catalana*. Barcelona: Ariel.

Bosch, L. 1987. *Avaluació del desenvolupament fonològic en nens catalanoparlants de 3 a 7 anys.* Barcelona: PPU.

Campos Astorkiza, R. 2010. Voicing assimilation and prosodic structure in Spanish. *Journal of the Acoustical Society of America* 128: 2288.

Chomsky, N. & M. Halle. 1968. *The Sound Pattern of English*. New York NY: Harper & Row.

Cortés, S., C. Lleó & A. Benet. 2009. Gradient merging of vowels in Barcelona Catalan under the influence of Spanish. In *Convergence and Divergence in Language Contact Situations* (Hamburg Studies on Multilingualism 8), eds. K. Braunmüller & J. House, 185–204. Amsterdam: John Benjamins.

Departament d'Estadística de l'Ajuntament de Barcelona. 2010. *Figures of Barcelona: Population.* <http://www.bcn.cat/estadistica/angles/dades/sintesi/images/sintesi1.pdf> (18 June 2012).

Grunwell, P. 1982. *Clinical Phonology*. London: Croom Helm.

Hualde, J. I. 2005. *The Sounds of Spanish*. Cambridge: CUP.

Institut d'Estadística de Catalunya. 2001. *Població segons coneixement del català. Recomptes. Població de 2 anys i més Barcelona. Distribució per districtes.* <http://www.idescat.cat/territ/ BasicTerr?TC=5&V0=8&V1=08019&V3=876&V4=17&ALLINFO=TRUE&PARENT=1& DISTRI=TRUE&CTX=B> (18 June 2005).

Institut d'Estadística de Catalunya. 2008. *Població segons llengua d'identificació Catalunya.* <http://www.idescat.cat/territ/BasicTerr?TC=5&V0=3&V1=3&V3=3171&V4=3173&ALL INFO=TRUE&PARENT=25&CTX=B> (18 June 2012).

Institut d'Estudis Catalans. 2011. *Versió electrònica de la Gramàtica de la llengua catalana.* <http://www.iecat.net/institucio/seccions/filologica/gramatica> (2012).

Jakobson, R. 1941/1968. *Child Language, Aphasia and Phonological Universals* (translated by A. R. Kuler). The Hague: Mouton, 1968. (*Kindersprache, Aphasie und allgemeine Lautgesetze.* Uppsala: Almqvist & Wiksell, 1941).

Kenstowicz, M. 1997. Uniform exponence: Exemplification and extension. In *Selected Phonology Papers from HO-T97* (University of Maryland Working Papers in Linguistics 5), eds. V. Miglio & B. Moren, 139–155. College Park MD: University of Maryland.

Lleó, C. 2006. Fenòmens evolutius i d'ús oral del català des de la finestra psicolingüística de l'adquisició bilingüe. In *Actes del 13è Col·loqui internacional de llengua i literatura catalanes (AILLC)*, eds. S. Martí, M. Cabré, F. Feliu, N. Iglesias & D. Prats, 361–385. Barcelona: Publicacions de l'Abadia de Montserrat.

Lleó, C., A. Benet & S. Cortés. 2009. Límits de la normalització lingüística: Vocals vulnerables en el català de Barcelona. In *Variació, poliglòssia i estàndard* (Biblioteca Catalànica Germànica 7), eds. J. Kabatek & C. D. Pusch, 157–180. Aachen: Shaker.

Lleó, C. & S. Cortés. In press. Modelling the outcome of language contact in the speech of Spanish-German and Spanish-Catalan bilingual children. In *Special Issue on Language Competition and Linguistic Diffusion: Interdisciplinary Models and Case Studies,* eds. J. Kabatek & L. Loureido. *International Journal of the Sociology of Language.*

Lleó, C., S. Cortés & A. Benet. 2008. Contact-induced phonological changes in the Catalan spoken in Barcelona. In *Language Contact and Contact Languages* (Hamburg Studies on Multilingualism 7), eds. P. Siemund & N. Kintana, 185–212. Amsterdam: John Benjamins.

Lleó, C., S. Cortés & A. Benet. 2011. Reanalitzant la vocal neutra barcelonina. In *Noves aproximacions a la fonologia i morfologia del català: Volum d'homenatge a Max W. Wheeler*, eds. M. R. Lloret & C. Pons, 321–351. Alacant: Institut Interuniversitari de Filologia Valenciana.

Maddieson, I. 1984. *Patterns of Sounds*. Cambridge: CUP.

Nguyen, N., S. Wauquier, L. Lancia & B. Tuller. 2007. Detection of liaison consonants in speech processing in French: Experimental data and theoretical implications. In *Segmental and Prosodic Issues in Romance Phonology* (Current Issues in Linguistic Theory 282), eds. P. Prieto, J. Mascaró & M. J. Solé, 3–23. Amsterdam: John Benjamins.

Romero, J. 1999. The effect of voicing assimilation on gestural coordination. In *Proceedings of the 14th International Congress of Phonetic Sciences (ICPhS 99)*, ed. J. J. Ohala, 1793–1796. Berkeley CA: University of California, Department of Linguistics.

Veny, J. 1998. *Els parlars catalans*. Mallorca: Moll.

Appendix

Lists of words containing the target segments /z/ and /dʒ/ elicited from the subjects that participated in the study.

Words with [z]			Words with [dʒ]		
[də'zembrə]	*desembre*	'december'	[ˌmidʒ'diə]	*migdia*	'noon'
[ˌdozu'seʎʃ]	*dos ocells*	'two birds'	[ˌbadʒə'na]	*vaig anar*	'I went'
[əzmur'za]	*esmorzar*	'breakfast'	[ˌbadʒməɲ'ʒa]	*vaig menjar*	'I ate'
['muzikə]	*música*	'music'	[rə'ʎɔdʒə]	*rellotge*	'clock'
[prin'sɛzə]	*princesa*	'princess'			
['rɔzə]	*rosa*	'rose'			
['zebrə]	*zebra*	'zebra'			
['zɛru]	*zero*	'zero'			
['zo]	*zoo*	'zoo'			

PART III

How language is used in multilingual settings

Linguistic practices and policies

Explaining the interpreter's unease

Conflicts and contradictions in bilingual communication in clinical settings

Kristin Bührig[1], Ortrun Kliche[1], Bernd Meyer[2]
and Birte Pawlack[1]
[1]University of Hamburg, Germany; [2]University of Mainz/Germersheim, Germany

This article builds on previous research on ad-hoc interpreting in German hospitals. It discusses the concept of interpreters as "intervenient beings" and its consequences for interpreter training. Although the concept seems to be descriptively adequate, it disregards difficulties of interpreters with their active engagement in communication of others. After discussing two types of active engagement, the article makes suggestions for interpreter training.

Keywords: German, Turkish, Portuguese, community interpreting, doctor-patient communication, interpreter training, discourse analysis

1. Introduction

Research on different types of interpreting has shown that dialogue-interpreters are not just conduits (Reddy 1979) who decode and encode two languages (Weber 1984) when interpreting. Rather, interpreters become involved in the communication process and become co-participants by e.g. coordinating and structuring conversation (Apfelbaum 2004, Bolden 2000, Wadensjö 1998), by changing the illocutionary quality of speech actions (Rehbein 1985), or by explaining technical terms (Angelelli 2003). In fact, they are no longer seen as neutral or invisible, but rather as "intervenient beings" (Maier 2007, Munday 2007) who interact in the communication of others, for example by mediating between discrepant cultural backgrounds (Pöchhacker 2004: 59). In terms of Goffman's well known speaker role categories, they are not only animators ("bod[ies] engaged in acoustic activity"), but also authors that "select the sentiments that are being expressed", or even principals who are "committed to what the words say" (see Goffman 1981: 144). Nowadays, scholars working in the field of translation studies usually consider many of these interventions to be normal and necessary practice in order to enable understanding and to keep the flow of conversation going. Although this view of interpreters (and translators) is widely shared in current research on translation and intercultural communication (House 1981, House & Rehbein 2004, Rehbein 2006), we will discuss this matter with regard to the basic principles of verbal interaction. The reason for this is that the concept of intervention, despite its descriptive power, widely ignores the subjective stance of ad-hoc interpreters towards interventions – how do they feel about intervening in the communication between primary parties?

During the development and evaluation of an interpreter training program for bilingual hospital employees, we interviewed six nurses acting as ad-hoc interpreters about their communicative practice in the context of doctor-patient communication. Interviewees explained that in certain cases, they felt uncomfortable engaging in the communication process; e.g. when acting in place of the doctor or when disrupting the conversation in order to clarify their own questions or to address other difficulties associated with the task. Thus, the focus of this paper lies on what we call "the interpreter's unease" that may result from intervening in certain situations. This unease of ad-hoc interpreters in medical settings seems to be based on the impression that their behavior has in some way negative consequences for the conversation and/ or for themselves. Our question is the source of this unease. We argue that it is not the result of individual characteristics such as weak language abilities or low self-confidence, but is rather caused by communicative challenges that are systematically linked to interpreter-mediated interaction. These challenges are associated with the level of verbal planning that is required of interpreters in different constellations, as well as with the handling of basic communicative principles such as turn-taking and conditional relevance. Two different types of interventions, namely "other-initiated interventions" and "self-initiated interventions", will be identified and analyzed with regard to verbal planning and communicative principles. These two types, which in some way lead interpreters to become involved in the communication, can be identified in excerpts from interviews with ad-hoc interpreters and also on the basis of transcripts of authentic discourse data (Bührig & Meyer 2004).[1] Before we go into the data analysis in Section 3, we shall give some information on our theoretical framework in Section 2.

2. Theoretical background

To understand the communicative challenges that can contribute to an interpreter's unease, it is helpful to look at the constellation of participants in interpreter-mediated

---

1.   The corpus "DiK" can be accessed online at <http://www.corpora.uni-hamburg.de/sfb538/en_overview.html> (16 March 2012). It encompasses about 90 transcripts of audio-recorded doctor-patient communication. Half of the interactions are mediated by ad-hoc-interpreters such as nurses or family members. The languages used are German, Spanish, Turkish and Portuguese.

communication from the perspective of linguistic action theory. The central term that may allow systematic access to the different forms of participation on the part of an interpreter is the concept of "planning" an utterance. In accordance with Miller, Galanter & Pribram (1973) and Austin's (1986) seminal work on the complexity of linguistic action, linguistic action theory (Rehbein 1977, Redder 2008) considers any action that a human performs to be preceded by a "pre-history" and followed by the effects an action has on the hearer, the "post-history". During the history of an action, an interlocutor will develop an utterance-plan, which contains a "focus" (considering what is to be said) and a "scheme" (the way in which something is to be said to a given listener). The object of this planning can range from a single utterance to a complete turn or an entire speech, for instance in planning a presentation etc. Sometimes, the process of planning takes on the character of a collaborative activity, as in the case of collaborative storytelling (see Quasthoff 1980).

In the case of interpreting, planning activities can oscillate between a single and a joint venture: the man or woman in the middle can be involved in the planning activities of the primary parties to different degrees, and they may even employ planning activities that are not at all based on the contributions of co-participants. However, being involved in the primary parties' planning activities involves, among other things, the process of establishing a relation between source language elements and target language elements. By following the original speaker's plan, the interpreter adopts the speaker's focus and looks in the target language for linguistic means that are in some respect equivalent to those expressions the original speaker has chosen.

These mental processes of the interpreter can be understood as "reproducing" a source-language-utterance (Bührig & Rehbein 2000, Bührig 2005). Reproducing is a creative activity that requires an understanding of all formal and functional dimensions of an utterance in the source language, and moreover, its intended effect on the hearer. Thus, in reproducing, the interpreter shares both the role of a listener as well as the role of a speaker whilst performing the given source-language-utterance in the target language. The difference compared to the target-language listener concerns the post-history, i.e. the interpreter is not subject to the effects that the respective utterance may have, in our case the effects that the medical doctor's utterance could have on the patient.

To sum up, the participant status of an interpreter partly depends on the level of verbal planning that becomes necessary in the process of reproducing a source language utterance within the target language. The independent planning of an utterance requires an independent focus-formation, while in the case of adopting the original plan of the speaker, the interpreter only modulates the scheme of the original plan, for example with regard to the grammatical constraints of the target language. Thus, interventions may oscillate between necessary grammatical changes and planning processes in which the interpreter acts more or less autonomously. We shall argue that unease in the context of interpreting is associated especially with situations in which interpreters go through such autonomous planning processes without being equipped with the necessary institutional knowledge or status to do so.

3.   Sources of unease

In the following sections, we will empirically analyse some sources of unease on the basis of data from semi-structured interviews and interpreter-mediated doctor-patient communication. Our aim is to identify and describe situations that systematically lead interpreters to go beyond what is usually expected from them. The interviews were recorded in the context of a project on interpreter training for bilingual nursing staff. The project aimed at developing a training module for nurses who frequently act as ad-hoc interpreters at their workplaces. A group of six nurses participated in the training and gave feedback on their previous experiences as interpreters in the medical context. The transcripts of interpreter-mediated doctor-patient interaction are from an earlier project ad-hoc interpreting in German hospitals.[2]

3.1   Other-initiated interventions

It was discomforting for our interviewees when primary speakers, i.e. the physicians, asked them to perform certain communicative tasks in their place. The nurses told us about situations in which – directly or indirectly – they were asked to carry out rather unpleasant jobs that normally the physicians are responsible for.

The nurse Tanja reported on a conversation in which she was made responsible for addressing the non-compliance of a mother who refused to let her ill child stay in the hospital. The child had burn injuries and was supposed to stay in the hospital so that the wounds would not become infected. Although the pediatrician and surgeons tried to convince the mother to let her child stay, the mother still wanted to take her child home. When the conversation refused to progress beyond this conflict, a surgeon turned to the interpreter. As she explained in the interview, "Well, I was standing between the surgeons, because we were in our examination room. And the pediatrician looks at me and then I say something, because she [the mother] doesn't want to. And the surgeon looks at me again. And/ well, this was really a little bit ((laughs, 1s)) not so nice."

As Tanja reported, the surgeon did not react to the mother's reluctance with any sort of verbal or nonverbal action directed at the mother herself. Instead, he continued to look at the interpreter Tanja as if she were responsible for the situation and expected her to come up with a solution to the stalemate.

Another nurse, Meryem, described a situation in which a doctor asked her to convince an aggressive Turkish-speaking patient to adhere to the hospital rules. The patient had been involved in a stabbing, was injured and had been transported to the hospital. He insisted on keeping a knife in his closet because he felt threatened, and spoke in an aggressive manner to other patients in the same ward: "He [the patient] did not threaten the other patients with his knife or anything, but he directly talked

---

back, in his way, loud, perhaps a little bit aggressive. And it was about me/ about the patient sticking to the rules of conduct for the hospital. I was supposed to make that clear to him. The physician told me to do so."

The only point of reference given to her by the physician was the intended outcome of the conversation, to convince the patient to behave appropriately. In order to be able to follow this instruction, she partly had to complete a planning process of her own. Normally, an interpreter can base his or her translations on the speaker's original utterances. But in the present case, the nurse had no such original draft and was charged with acting in place of the doctor. One could legitimately claim that the task of talking to an aggressive patient is only a borderline case of interpreting. However, she saw herself as the interpreter in this situation. She told us that she was afraid the patient would get the impression that she sided with the doctor and was not merely interpreting. She perceived the position she was put in as very unpleasant and difficult. The only way out of this situation would have been to resist the doctor's request.

In the incident described by Meryem, another phenomenon becomes apparent that needs to be highlighted in the context of "other-initiated interventions". The interviewees stated that they often interpreted in situations when only one of the primary speakers was present. This occurs when, for example, a non-proficient patient has something to ask a doctor who is not present in the given moment. Frequently, the patients then turn to the bilingual nurses who are around more often. The patients ask them their questions, which later, after finding the doctor, will be reproduced in the other language. The doctor then answers the question, which the interpreter remembers and reproduces to the patient when they meet again in the ward. We called this special form of communication *Streckendolmetschen* ('distance interpreting'). Here, the break in the speech situation between doctor and patient is not just based on a language barrier but also on time and space. Distance interpreting, in this way, may generally be considered a specific case of "other-initiated intervention": reception and reproduction of the perceived message no longer take place at the same time, making it difficult to distinguish between message and messenger – the messenger appears to be acting on his or her own account.

Of course, the episodes illustrated by Tanja and Meryem are only the tip of the iceberg. Ad-hoc interpreters change the underlying plan of the original utterance or begin planning autonomously, even in less drastic situations. This can be shown by looking at discourse data.

In the following example (Excerpt 1), we look at a briefing for informed consent in which a patient is prepared for a surgery of his hip joint. The German doctor is a female anaesthesiologist. The patient is a retired Portuguese worker with limited German proficiency. A Portuguese nurse who has lived in Germany for 30 years serves as an ad-hoc interpreter in this conversation; her mother language is Portuguese and she speaks German as a second language. The doctor briefs the patient for anaesthesia and surgery. Then she asks a battery of questions about the patient's medical history in order to fill out the consent form for the anesthesia. In the course of these questions, she asks about his teeth.

Excerpt 1: "May I have a look at your teeth?"
Briefing for informed consent, treatment: surgery of hip joint
Transcript no. 17 from the Corpus "DiK"
DOC: German anaesthesiologist (f), INT: Portuguese nurse (f), PAT: Portuguese patient (m)

101	DOC	Darf ich Ihre Zähne mal sehen?	May I have a look at your teeth?
102	INT	Ehm b/ vá lá mostrar os dentes a ela, se faz favor.	Uhm b/ go ahead and show her your teeth, please.
103	DOC	– Ja, die sind aber katastrophal!	– Oh, they are catastrophic!
104	PAT	É de tanto fumo.	It´s because of smoking so much.
105	PAT	((1s)) Ou keine Ahne.	((1s)) Or keine Ahne[3].
106	DOC	((browses through files 3s)) Sagen Sie ihm bitte, dass wir nicht ausschließen können, dass bei diesen schlechten Zähnen – im Rahmen der Vollnarkose – Zähne abbrechen.	((3s)) Please tell him, that we cannot rule out, that with these bad teeth – during the anaesthesia – teeth break.
107	INT	Disse ehm que o perigo de voc/ como os seus dentes não estão em condições, que tem a, tem a boca – num estado um bocadito/ eh não a condizer com, com o coiso da operação pode acontecer que algum dos dentes que você tem na boca, e que estão assim um bocado podres, – que se partam.	She said uhm that there is the risk of you/ because your teeth are not in a good condition, that you have, have the mouth – in a condition a little bit/ uh not conforming to, to the thing of the surgery, it can happen that some of the teeth you have in your mouth, that are a little bit bad, that they break.

Let us first summarize Excerpt 1. The doctor asks the patient to show his teeth (101) and the interpreter translates the doctor's utterance, whereupon the patient complies. The doctor evaluates the condition of the teeth with an exclamation (103), which is not translated. However, the patient seems to understand what the doctor said because he reacts by giving an excuse in Portuguese (104), which is not interpreted and which he himself subsequently mitigates (105). The doctor then peruses the consent form. It is very likely that she makes a note about the teeth in order to protect herself legally in case teeth are actually broken. Then she asks the nurse to tell the patient that teeth can break during the anaesthesia (106). The interpreter subsequently mitigates the information about the risks in (107).

Our focus for this short passage lies on the last two utterances. After the doctor evaluates the condition of the patient's teeth, she follows the routine plan of telling the patient about the risks. Here, she changes the form of address: she does not address the patient directly as she had during the rest of the previous conversation. Instead, she turns to the interpreter and addresses her directly with a request: "Sagen Sie ihm bitte,

---

3.   'Keine Ahne' stands for the German expression 'keine Ahnung', 'no idea'.

dass ..." ('Please tell him, that ...'). With this shift, she distances herself from the communication, the duty of reproducing the speech action is explicitly passed on to the interpreter. The doctor does not bother to make her utterance less face-threatening by mitigating the drastic evaluation of the patient's teeth. Considering the evaluative stance of her utterance, it seems that she tries to refuse taking any responsibility for the patients' well-being, especially for his teeth, by blaming him for their condition. It is now up to the nurse to formulate the statement appropriately. In doing this, she fails to follow the original plan of the doctor and instead makes some modifications in her own utterance planning. Obviously, this is difficult for her. She reformulates and aborts her utterance several times. However, in the end her translation is less face-threatening than the doctor's original remark. She mitigates the doctor's evaluation of the patient's teeth: *schlechte Zähne* ('bad teeth') turns into *um bocado podres* ('a little bit bad'). Furthermore, she also mitigates the possibility of the risk. Whereas the doctor says that they, the medical authorities, cannot rule out ("nicht ausschließen können") the possibility that teeth may break, the interpreter says that it "could happen" that teeth break ("pode acontecer") by using an impersonal construction. The intervention of mitigating the evaluative statement of the physician and presenting it as a matter of fact rather than a medical judgment linked to an expert was the result of the aggressive and evaluative tone used by the anesthesiologist. In our opinion, it is plausible that the nurse would not have felt obliged to change the original statement if the doctor herself had formulated it more appropriately. The trigger for intervention in Excerpt 1 is obviously more subtle than in the situation with Meryem, who was explicitly requested to convince a difficult patient of something. However, in both incidents presented here, overt or subtle, the ad-hoc interpreters were induced by others to intervene into the interaction.

3.2   Self-initiated interventions

Another source of unease pointed out in the interviews were those situations in which the nurses themselves decided to intervene in the conversation and change or add elements. The ad-hoc interpreter Alicja describes how she feels about this practice: "Because partially I don't know ... if I may, can, should say something in between. ((1,5s)) Should I really just translate what the doctor says, what the patient says? Should I add my two cents?" It seems that Alicja does not know whether she may intervene or whether this may even expected of her. She is torn between different assumptions and lacks guidelines for the extent to which she may or should bring herself into the conversation. In our discourse data, we found incidents of such self-initiated interventions in which ad-hoc interpreters "add their two cents", as Alicja formulated it. The example we look at is from a briefing for informed consent in which a German anaesthesiologist briefs a Portuguese patient for a puncture behind the liver; a Portuguese-speaking nurse interprets for them. In the following excerpt, the doctor informs the patient that because he takes the medicament heparin, he has a higher risk of bleeding. The example shows that such interventions may take place rather unnoticed by other participants, and that they are not without risk for the interpreters.

Excerpt 2: "Inside? No, outside."
Briefing for informed consent, treatment: puncture
Transcript no. 22 from the Corpus 'DiK'
DOC: German anesthesiologist (m, 35), INT: Portuguese nurse (f, 25), PAT: Portuguese patient (m, 40)

52	DOC	– An Risiken – birgt so eine Punktion immer – die Blutung.	– Such a puncture always – bears the risk of bleeding.
53	DOC	– Und zwar insbesondere deshalb, weil Sie ja durch das ähm ((1s)) Heparin, was Sie bis heute morgen bekommen haben, künstlicher Bluter sind.	– And in particular, because with uhm the heparin, that you got until this morning, you are an artificial bleeder.
54	INT	Complicações que pode acontecer: eh durante assim uma/ quando picarem eh pode t/ ter sangue/ pode deitar sangue, – pode perder sangue, como tee/ teve até hoje de manhã – – o medicamento que põe o sangue fino.	Complications that can happen: uh during such a/ when they puncture eh you can h/ have blood/ can put blood/ you can lose blood, because you go/ got this morning a medicament that makes the blood thin.
55	PAT	Pois˙	Yes˙
56	INT	Pode ser que deit/ eh prontos, que continue sangue (a) correr – mais – do que normal.	It can be that bleed/ uh, that it continues to bleed more than normal.
57	PAT	Hmhm˙	Hmhm˙
58	DOC	Deswegen haben wir ...	For this reason we have ...
59	PAT	Para, para dentro?	In/, inside?
60	INT	Não, para fora, para fora.	No, outside, outside.
61	DOC	Deswegen haben wir das Heparin heute ausgestellt, damit – die Blutgerinnung jetzt normal wird.	For this reason we have discontinued the heparin, so that – the blood clotting now gets normal.

The doctor talks about the risks of a bleeding (52), which could be problematic for the patient, since he became an artificial bleeder (53). In the following sections, the nurse interprets the doctor's utterances and expands upon them by explaining the effect of the medicine more explicitly (54, 56); the patient signals that he understands (55, 57). When the doctor wishes to continue with the briefing, the patient interrupts and asks if the possible bleeding would be (on the) "inside" (59). The nurse does not translate his question and answers it herself (60); she states that the bleeding would be on the outside. After this sequence in Portuguese, the doctor continues in German.

By answering the patients' question herself, the nurse carries out an action with an autonomous focus-formation which is not initiated by the doctor or the patient. Rather, her intervention is rooted in the sequential power of the question and in the fact that she believes that she knows the answer. The patient's question causes a "conditional relevance" (Schegloff 1968, 1978), an expectation for a certain type of follow-up utterance, namely an answer. Question (first part) and answer (second part) together form an "adjacency pair" (Schegloff & Sacks 1973: 295). The nurse does what is preferable and expected in dyadic communication and answers the question herself. This procedure does not seem to disturb the conversation, and neither the patient nor the doctor complains. It saved time and the conversation continues without any notable break.

However, this form of intervention may result in severe negative consequences. It might be the case that interpreters overestimate their competence and do not give the right answer, which occurs in the present example. The nurse states that the bleeding would be "on the outside", but actually the risk the doctor is talking about is internal bleeding. Since the nurse did not inform the doctor about the question-answer sequence, he had no chance to adjust his contributions. Furthermore, the hidden intervention makes it more difficult for him to monitor the extent to which the patient understands what he is trying to explain. In light of the potentially negative consequences of such interventions, it is not surprising that interpreters feel uncomfortable with them.

4.   Conclusion: Consequences for ad-hoc interpreter training in hospitals

In our paper, we have discussed different types of interventions on the part of ad-hoc interpreters in interpreter-mediated doctor-patient communication. Our aim was to enhance our understanding of how certain tasks and constellations evoke unease in ad-hoc interpreters with respect to their own performance. The background of the study was a project for the development of an interpreter training program for bilingual hospital employees. The basic approach to this project entails that the training contents should be developed in a bottom-up fashion, from the perspective of the trainees and in accordance with what they themselves perceive as relevant. Therefore, interviews were carried out before the project started to elucidate the perspective and the needs of trainees. One of the topics addressed in these interviews was the unease of ad-hoc interpreters about how and to what degree it is useful or even desirable for them to intervene in the communicative exchange between primary parties. In accordance with previous research, it was clear that interventions in general are necessary to facilitate communication between doctor and patient, and that some of them need to be accepted as a natural part of the interpreters' footing. On the other hand, it also turned out that in certain cases, physicians and nurses themselves overestimated their own abilities in terms of the performance of specific speech actions. These cases range from seemingly simple speech actions such as spontaneously answering a question that seems easy to answer, as in the case of internal or external bleeding, to complex and large communicative projects such as admonishing an aggressive patient for failing to adhere to hospital rules. All incidents have in common that interpreters become involved in the communication without being prepared to do so. A nurse that answers questions about possible risks or convinces a mother to let her baby stay in the hospital is often not necessarily equipped with the relevant knowledge or the institutional status to complete these tasks. However, we do not take such case studies as warning signs indicating a road block. Rather, we use them as examples that serve to mirror communicative practices and which can be reflected on by participants. Thus, within our approach to interpreter training, sources of unease are interesting objects of study because they may tell us something about the hidden conflicts and contradictions in multilingual communication in institutions.

References

Angelelli, C. 2003. The visible co-participant: The interpreter's role in doctor-patient encounters. In *From Topic Boundaries to Omission: New Research on Interpretation*, eds. M. Metzger, S. Collins, V. Dively & R. Shaw, 3–26. Washington DC: Gallaudet University Press.

Apfelbaum, B. 2004. *Gesprächsdynamik in Dolmetsch-Interaktionen*. Radolfzell: Verlag für Gesprächsforschung.

Austin, J. L. 1986. *How to Do Things with Words,* 2nd edn. Oxford: OUP.

Bolden, G. 2000. Toward understanding practices of medical interpreting: Interpreters' involvement in history taking. *Discourse Studies* 4: 387–419.

Bührig, K. 2005. 'Speech action patterns' and 'discourse types'. *Folia Linguistica* 39: 143–171.

Bührig, K. & B. Meyer. 2004. Ad hoc interpreting and achievement of communicative purposes in briefings for informed consent. In *Multilingual Communication* (Hamburg Studies on Multilingualism 3), eds. J. House & J. Rehbein, 43–62. Amsterdam: John Benjamins

Bührig, K. & J. Rehbein. 2000. *Reproduzierendes Handeln: Übersetzen, simultanes und konsekutives Dolmetschen im diskursanalytischen Vergleich* (Arbeiten zur Mehrsprachigkeit 9). Hamburg: Universität Hamburg.

Goffman, E. 1981. Footing. In *Forms of Talk*, ed. E. Goffman, 124–159. Philadelphia PA: University of Pennsylvania Press.

House, J. 1981. *A Model for Translation Quality Assessment,* 2nd edn. Tübingen: Narr.

House, J. & J. Rehbein. 2004. What is multilingual communication? In *Multilingual Communication* (Hamburg Studies on Multilingualism 3), eds. J. House & J. Rehbein, 1–17. Amsterdam: John Benjamins.

Maier, C. 2007. The translator as an intervenient being. In *Translation as Intervention*, ed. J. Munday, 1–17. London: Continuum.

Miller, G. A., E. Galanter & K. H. Pribram. 1973. *Strategien des Handelns: Pläne und Strukturen des Verhaltens.* Stuttgart: Klett.

Munday, J., ed. 2007. *Translation as Intervention.* London: Continuum.

Pöchhacker, F. 2004. *Introducing Interpreting Studies.* London: Routledge.

Quasthoff, U. M. 1980. Gemeinsames Erzählen als Form und Mittel im sozialen Konflikt oder Ein Ehepaar erzählt eine Geschichte. In *Erzählen im Alltag*, ed. K. Ehlich, 109–141. Frankfurt: Suhrkamp.

Redder, A. 2008. Functional pragmatics. In *Interpersonal Communication: Handbook of Applied Linguistics,* Vol. 2, eds. G. Antos & E. Ventola, 133–178. Berlin: Mouton de Gruyter.

Reddy, M. 1979. *The Conduit Metaphor: A Case of Frame Conflict in our Language about Language.* Cambridge: CUP.

Rehbein, J. 1977. *Komplexes Handeln: Elemente zur Handlungstheorie der Sprache*. Stuttgart: Metzler.

Rehbein, J. 1985. Ein ungleiches Paar – Verfahren des Sprachmittelns in der medizinischen Beratung. In *Interkulturelle Kommunikation*, ed. J. Rehbein, 420–448. Tübingen: Narr.

Rehbein, J. 2006. The cultural apparatus: Thoughts on the relationship between language, culture, and society. In *Beyond Misunderstanding: Linguistic Analyses of Intercultural Communication* (Pragmatics & Beyond New Series 144), eds. K. Bührig & J. D. ten Thije, 43–96. Amsterdam: John Benjamins.

Schegloff, E. A. 1968. Sequencing in conversational openings. *American Anthropologist* 70: 1075–1095.

Schegloff, E. A. 1978. On some questions and ambiguities in conversation. In *Current Trends in Text Linguistics*, ed. W. Dressler, 81–102. Berlin: Mouton de Gruyter.

Schegloff, E. A. & H. Sacks. 1973. Opening up closings. *Semiotica* 8: 289–327.

Wadensjö, C. 1998. *Interpreting as Interaction*. London: Longman.

Weber, W. 1984. *Training Translators and Conference Interpreters*. New York NY: Harcourt Brace Jovanovich.

Measuring bilingual accommodation
in Welsh rural pharmacies*

Myfyr Prys, Margaret Deuchar and Gwerfyl Roberts
Bangor University, Wales, UK

This paper introduces a method to address the theoretical and practical question of whether speech accommodation aids compliance in bilingual healthcare settings. It describes a method to measure bilingual speech accommodation in interviews between pharmacists and patients about the use of regularly prescribed medication. The method involves calculating the relative proportion of Welsh and English words in segments of the transcripts and using a formula which we devised to measure how much the speaker changes his or her proportion of Welsh versus English words over time in relation to the proportion being used by the interlocutor. Positive scores indicate convergence, negative scores divergence, and a score of zero indicates neither convergence nor divergence. The findings suggest that speech accommodation is widespread within bilingual clinical encounters and there are complex factors at work that influence the dynamics of the bilingual healthcare consultation. Refining methods for measuring accommodation will shed further light on this phenomenon and offer opportunities for enhancing communication skills training for healthcare professionals.

Keywords: Welsh, English, bilingualism, speech accommodation, healthcare

*   The work presented in this paper was funded by the Pharmacy Practice Development Scheme of the Welsh Assembly Government and was part of the programme of research of the ESRC Centre for Research on Bilingualism in Theory and Practice at Bangor University, Wales, UK. The support of the Economic and Social Research Council (ESRC) and the Welsh Assembly Government is gratefully acknowledged. We also acknowledge the work of all those who were involved in the PILSen project, including Dyfrig Hughes, Llyr Hughes, Fiona Irvine, Steffan Rhys John, Sion Llewelyn, Berwyn Owen, Heledd Owen, Alwyn Rowlands, Rhiannon Whitaker and service users. We are also indebted to Lowri Hadden, Margaret Toye, and to Chris Whitaker for statistical advice.

1.   Introduction

The role of the patient in treatment decision making has increased significantly in recent years. Terms such as 'shared decision-making' and 'concordance' have become commonplace, and refer to consultations in which the healthcare professional and the patient participate as partners to reach an agreement on treatment; drawing on the expertise of the healthcare professional as well as the experiences, beliefs and wishes of the patient (Légaré, Elwyn, Fishbein, Fremont, Frosch, Gagnon, Kenny, Labrecque, Stacey, St-Jacques & Van der Weijden 2008). Early evidence suggests that asking patients about their experiences and concerns can have many positive effects, such as increased knowledge and understanding, adherence to treatment regimes, enhanced satisfaction and improved health outcomes (Stevenson, Cox, Britten & Dundar 2004, Hack, Degner, Watson & Sinha 2006). A key component of concordance is two-way communication whereby patients are offered the information they want and need; and the practitioner listens and responds to them. These processes are enhanced when the communication is tailored to the patient's unique blend of beliefs, understanding and ability to communicate (Audit Commission 1993).

Previous research on patient communication in healthcare settings has suggested that where a clinician uses the preferred language of his or her patients, both clinical outcomes and patient satisfaction are enhanced. For example, Freeman, Rai, Walker, Howie, Heany & Maxwell (2002) provided evidence that patients with a first language other than English derived greater satisfaction if they were able to consult their doctor in their own language, and Fernandez, Schillinger, Grumbach, Rosenthal, Stewart, Wang & Pérez-Stable (2004) demonstrated that Spanish-speaking patients reported a higher level of patient-centred care when their doctors were competent in Spanish. On the other hand, language barriers in healthcare lead to poorer comprehension of care (Cass, Lowell, Christie, Snelling, Flack, Marrnganyin & Brown 2002); less satisfaction (Carrasquillo, Orav, Brennan & Burstin 1999); and poorer adherence to treatment recommendations and follow-up appointments (Sarver & Barker 2000). However, previous studies of this kind describe clinicians making a choice between two or more languages in addressing patients, and have not considered the possibility that the clinician may use both languages simultaneously, as happens in the practice of code-switching. Code-switching will be defined for our purposes as the insertion of words or phrases from one language into sentences from another language. In this chapter we shall discuss how code-switching can be measured in healthcare encounters to approximate to the language choice of the interlocutor, which we shall suggest is a form of speech accommodation.

Our study is set in Wales, UK (see Figure 1 for the location of Wales) where Welsh is the indigenous language and Welsh speakers represent 21% of the overall population (National Assembly for Wales 2003). The last twenty years in Wales have seen the development of political autonomy with significant legislative powers held by a devolved Welsh National Assembly in Cardiff. Welsh is currently considered an official language alongside English, and is supported by legislation facilitating its use in the public

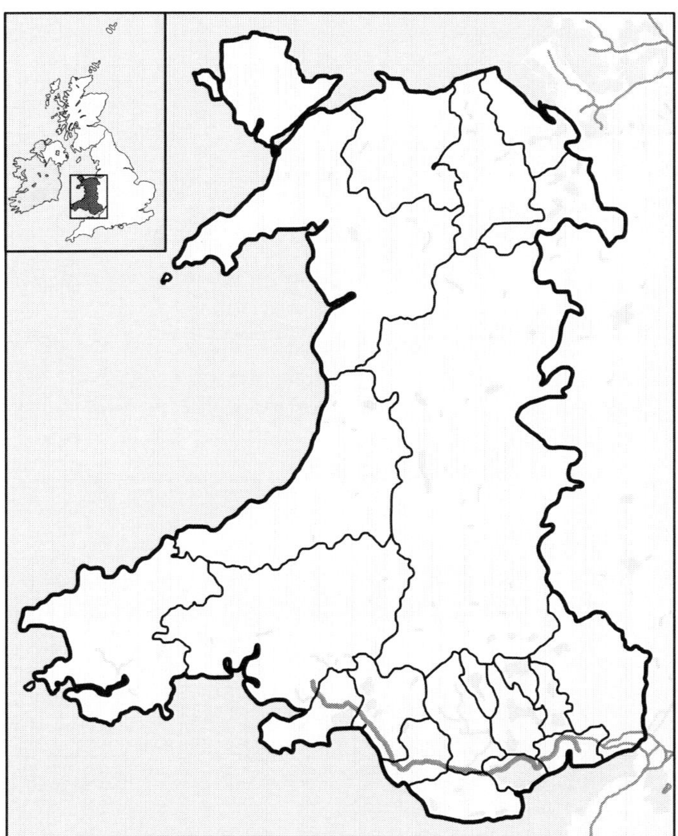

Figure 1. Map illustrating the location of Wales in the UK[1]

sector throughout Wales (although not the private or voluntary sectors). Although Welsh speaking communities are more prevalent in the rural North of the country, there are no areas of the country where Welsh is not spoken (The Office of National Statistics 2001).

In situations of stress and vulnerability, many Welsh speakers feel more comfortable and confident communicating in Welsh or bilingually with healthcare professionals (Misell 2000). Nevertheless, there is a dearth of literature that focuses specifically on code-switching in a bilingual healthcare context and its impact on the health outcomes of patients.

We shall describe a pilot study that sought to relate our measures of speech accommodation to outcome measures relating to medicines use. A practical question guiding this research was whether bilingual speech accommodation might aid compliance in a bilingual healthcare setting. Whilst reporting the full findings of the study is

1.   <http://commons.wikimedia.org/wiki/File:Wales_outline_map_with_UK.png> (15 March 2012, by kind permission of Wikimedia editor Jza84).

beyond the scope of this paper, we shall report on the methods established to measure bilingual speech accommodation and demonstrate the implications for enhancing communication skills training for healthcare professionals.

2. Review of the Literature

Speech accommodation is the phenomenon of modifying one's speech to become more similar (convergence) or less similar (divergence) to the interlocutor. Since an important contribution of this paper will be about how to measure accommodation, we shall review in this section previous work on this topic. Speech accommodation theory stems from the discipline of social psychology and focuses on the effect of the interlocutor on speech. It allows for individual choice (convergence or divergence) and it is based on the social psychological models of similarity-attraction and intergroup distinctiveness. According to Giles & Smith (1979) similarity-attraction relates to the desire to be similar to those of whom one requires approval, while intergroup distinctiveness is involved where the converse holds, i.e. a speaker wishes to dissociate him or herself from someone who belongs to a different group. A number of features of speech may be affected in the process of accommodation (including convergence and divergence) such as phonology, speech rate, turn length and language choice (Giles, Coupland & Coupland 1991).

Since there is a large body of literature on speech accommodation we shall limit ourselves to describing a few examples of relevant studies, in particular on phonology in monolinguals, phonology in second-language learners, language choice in bilinguals (monolingual mode) and language choice in bilinguals (bilingual mode).[2] We shall also review some previous studies on accommodation in healthcare.

Regarding phonology in monolinguals, Coupland (1984) conducted a pioneering study of a travel agent in Cardiff, analysing specific phonological variables in her speech and in that of her clients. His results showed that her speech varied according to the speech of her clients, who came from a range of socioeconomic backgrounds. Figure 2 is reproduced from Figure 4 in Coupland (1984: 63) and shows the results for one of the variables, (t), which could be realised standardly as [t] or alternatively as a tap. As can be seen in Figure 2, her speech approximates closely to that of the clients of all backgrounds except those belonging to the highest social class.

To take an example of a study which also focused on phonology, although this time amongst second-language learners, Bourhis & Giles (1977) compared the speech of two groups of Welsh learners living in South Wales. One group was described as 'integrative' because its members were learning in their own time and were interested in cultural integration while the other group was considered 'instrumental' because its

---

2.   The notions 'monolingual mode' and 'bilingual mode' derive from the work of Grosjean (1998) and will be further explained below.

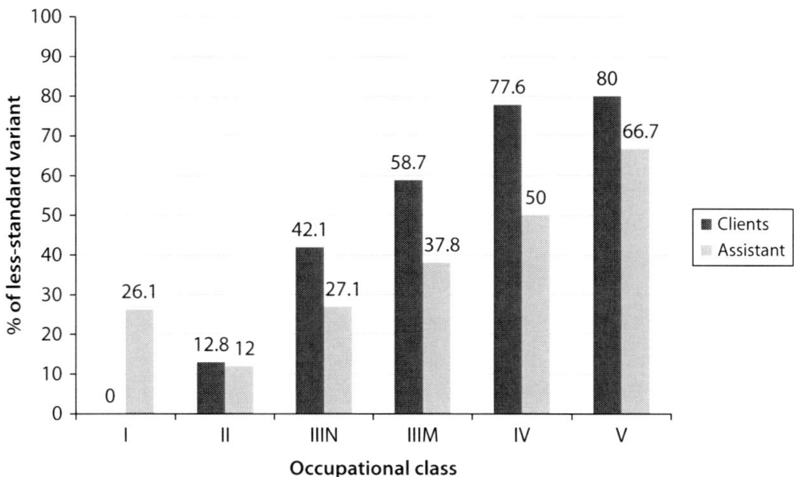

Figure 2. Travel agent's convergence in use of intervocalic (t) variable to five occupational classes of customers (reproduced from Figure 4 in Coupland 1984: 63)

members were learning during company time in order to improve their employment prospects. Both groups listened to a recorded voice in English asking questions to which they were invited to respond. In the first, pre-experimental phase, the participants listened to a speaker with a French Canadian accent and were asked to talk about weekend activities. This was to provide baseline information about their pronunciation. In the second phase, which was a neutral condition, participants were asked questions in Received Pronunciation regarding the best techniques for adult language teaching. There was then a third, nationally-salient phase during which participants heard a statement about the death of the Welsh language and were asked to voice their opinions. Judges then rated the speech of subjects in all three phases on an 11-point scale from a 'mild Welsh' to a 'broad Welsh' accent. The results showed that the integrative group diverged from the stimulus pronunciation in the third phase whereas the instrumental group converged somewhat in the second phase and even more in the third phase. These results can be seen to match both the models of similarity-attraction and intergroup distinctiveness outlined above. As the authors say, "The instrumental group, arguably perceiving the situation more as an inter-individual encounter, tended to reduce the accent differences between themselves and the speaker, whereas the integrative group, perceiving the situation more in intergroup terms, tended to emphasise such differences" (Bourhis & Giles 1977: 128).The latter type of divergent accommodation has been linked to intergroup interactions, particularly as a mechanism of increasing in-group solidarity (Tajfel 1974). In interactions which are considered inter-individual rather than inter-group, such as healthcare consultations, convergence strategies are considered more typical (Giles et al. 1991).

While the studies by Coupland (1984) and Bourhis & Giles (1977) dealt with accommodation within a single language (English in both cases), Sachdev & Giles (2004) introduce the notion of bilingual accommodation, which has to do with language choices made by bilingual speakers which are, in turn, influenced by the language choices of their interlocutors. The authors argue that "a focus on bilingual (as opposed to monolingual) contexts has contributed significantly to the development of accommodation theory from the very beginning" (Sachdev & Giles 2004: 370). An example of the type of study of bilingual accommodation which they have in mind is that by Moise & Bourhis (1994). These authors examined the language strategies used by Francophones and Anglophones in Québec when approached on the street by a researcher seeking directions either in English or French. The researcher noted whether or not the speakers (Francophones and Anglophones) switched languages to match that of the interlocutor. The results showed that 63% of the Anglophones answered in French to a French enquiry while 86% of the Francophones responded in English to an English enquiry. This suggests that, in the public domain, Francophones are more likely to converge to the language choice of the interlocutor than Anglophones. This form of convergence is associated with a direct language switch, where participants either accommodate completely or maintain hold of their language and offer no accommodation at all, This position is most likely to occur when bilinguals are in monolingual mode (Grosjean 1998), where they are interacting only with monolinguals of one or other of the languages they speak. At this point, for the bilingual, one language is activated and the other deactivated.

The bilingual mode (Grosjean 1998), on the other hand, is addressed in a study by Finlayson, Calteaux & Myres-Scotton (1998) who suggest that code-switching "is a means of accommodation or 'meeting each other halfway'". To illustrate this the authors quote an utterance by one of their South African participants which they translate as follows: "It will happen that when I speak Sotho to accommodate that which I hear in Sotho, I'll say in Sotho and she/he too will say in Zulu – whereby we'll meet each other halfway, we'll understand each other because I'll replace Zulu words where she/he does not understand and she/he'll do the same" (Finlayson et al. 1998: 396). It is interesting to note that this view of code-switching is not far removed from the idea proposed by Sachdev & Giles (2004: 370) that code-switching is "partial accommodation". There have nevertheless been few studies, to our knowledge, particularly in the healthcare context, that have quantified partial accommodation of this kind, and our aim with this study is to fill that gap.

We now survey briefly previous work on speech accommodation in health care settings. Bourhis, Roth & MacQueen (1989) used a survey to examine doctors', student nurses' and patients' perceptions of their use of 'medical' and 'everyday' language in their interactions with one another. While the doctors reported converging to the 'everyday' language of their patients, the patients and student nurses did not perceive them as converging. Patients, on the other hand, reported attempting to converge to the medical language of health professionals. The student nurses were perceived as converging to the 'everyday' language of patients by all groups. 'Medical' language was seen as a source of problems for patients whilst 'everyday' language was deemed to improve their understanding.

While the study by Bourhis et al. (1989) suggested that doctors failed to accommodate sufficiently to patients, Street (1991) argues that over-accommodation (where speakers converge excessively towards the interlocutor) can occur when doctors underestimate the ability of patients to understand, for example, medical terms, and use simplified terms such as 'bellyache' and 'tummy'. Brown & Draper (2003) describe how over-accommodation is particularly evident in the context of the care of older adults and how this fosters dependence and lowered self-esteem.

Finally, we review one study (Bourhis & Giles 1976) which investigated the role of accommodation in gaining compliance, a relevant issue for the present study, which fulfils both the requirements of a naturalistic setting outside the classroom and that of involving bilingual respondents. The subjects for their study in Cardiff, Wales, were people in different theatre audiences who were asked over the loudspeaker system at the beginning of the interval to help plan future programmes by completing questionnaire forms in the foyer and returning them to the box office. The announcement was presented in four matched-guises, one per evening: (1) standard Received Pronunciation (RP), (2) broad South Welsh-accented English, (3) mild South Welsh-accented English, and (4) standard non-localized Welsh. There were two kinds of audience: monolingual English speakers and Welsh-English bilinguals. The behavioural reactions of the two kinds of audience were measured as the ratio between completed questionnaires and tickets sold. No difference in response to the RP and mildly Welsh-accented English was found amongst the mainly monolingual audience, and the broader-accented English resulted in a significantly lower number of questionnaires being completed. The bilingual theatregoers, however, were significantly more responsive to the request in the Welsh language than to those voiced in the three English guises. This suggests that speech accommodation influences compliance amongst bilingual speakers. Nevertheless, effective methods for measuring speech accommodation are slow to emerge from the literature and the extent to which accommodation maximises compliance in healthcare communication is largely unknown.

3. Measuring accommodation

In the early period of accommodation research, most studies relied primarily upon evaluations as a source of evidence of accommodation (Giles et al. 1991). Thakerar, Giles & Cheshire (1982) formulated a distinction between psychological accommodation and linguistic accommodation (later termed 'objective accommodation' by Giles et al. 1991). Psychological accommodation is described as the belief of an individual that they are either converging or diverging from the speech of their interlocutor, while linguistic accommodation refers to the objectively measurable speech behaviour of the speaker. Recent studies have focused increasingly on the objective element of accommodation, thus enhancing the rigour of enquiry.

A study carried out by Niederhoffer & Pennebaker (2002) used the text analysis computer programme LIWC to analyse chat room conversations for evidence of linguistic style matching. The programme counted linguistic markers of synchrony for each turn of the conversation, allowing the researchers to observe converging usage of word types by both participants. The researchers observed that speaker accommodation is based on previous turns: "What person A says at Time 1 influences what person B says at Time 1. But what person B says at Time 1 also directly influences what person A says (in response) at Time 2" (Niederhoffer & Pennebaker 2002: 347). In order to analyse this effect, the study used two sets of correlations, with a correlation between speaker A and B at the same time point, then a correlation between speaker A at the current time point and speaker B at the previous time point.

Lewis (2003) attempted to measure interlocutor influences on females' pitch in conversations. Pitch was measured in three ways, median pitch, standard deviation of pitch and 80% pitch range; and the extent of correlation between pairs of speakers was assessed. Correlations were measured in two different ways, one using normalized scores based on averages in separate minutes of the conversations, and the other using a delta measure based on differences between scores from consecutive minutes.

Positive correlations were the predominant pattern. This is interpreted by the author as indicating the importance of positive politeness strategies, and can also be said to indicate a tendency for these speakers towards convergence in general.

Our first attempt to develop our own method of measuring accommodation took place in early 2009 in the form of a small pre-pilot study. The data analysed were taken from the Siarad corpus (<http://tinyurl.com/6yyuapm>, 16 March 2012) funded by the UK Arts and Humanities Research Council (AHRC) which consists of approximately 40 hours of transcribed Welsh – English bilingual conversations between acquaintances. Conversations were recorded at informal settings of the participants' choosing, ranging from homes to outdoor festivals.

Although the Siarad corpus conversations do not exhibit the power asymmetry of pharmacist-patient interactions, they do provide an easily accessible data set which is already glossed and coded. Six files were randomly selected from the corpus and segmented into 6 x 5 minute intervals. Analyses relied upon the coding of all words in the corpus as either Welsh, English or ambiguous (@cy, @en and @s:cy&en respectively). The FREQ function of CLAN was then used in order to determine the frequency of English words in each 5 minute segment of the recording. As in the Niederhoffer & Pennebaker (2002) study mentioned above, accommodation over time was considered a crucial factor in measuring the degree of accommodation between speakers. A formula was developed which calculated both the variation in frequency of the speaker's English word use from one segment to the next, and the variation with respect to the interlocutor's usage of English from the previous turn. The formula below provides the basis for our present research study.

Accommodation =

$$\frac{\text{PEng for speaker during time period N} - \text{PEng for speaker during time period (N + 1)}}{\text{PEng for speaker during time period N} - \text{PEng for interlocutor during time period N}}$$

(where 'PEng' = 'Percentage of English words out of total[3] of English + Welsh words').

The formula represents the fact that the difference between a speaker's score for the proportion of English words in their speech during a specific time period and the subsequent one is divided by the difference between the speaker's and the interlocutor's score during the first time period. The denominator in the formula represents the measurement of the difference between the scores of the speaker and interlocutor during a specific time period, while the numerator represents the change in the scores of the speaker from that specific time period to the next. The amount of change in the speaker's scores is divided by the difference between the scores of the speaker and the interlocutor to determine how much of the difference or distance between the speaker and the interlocutors' scores has been covered by the change in the speaker's score. From the speaker's point of view, it is as if he/she notes how far he/she is from the interlocutor during a specific period in time, and then decides how close to approximate the interlocutor during the next period. In other words, using discrete measures, the formula allows us to estimate the degree to which the speaker has accommodated his or her speech style to that of the interlocutor and vice versa from one time period to the next.

Applying our method to pharmacist-patient communication

The six month study centred on two community pharmacies in rural North Wales, UK, where the Medicines Use Review (MUR) community pharmacy service was introduced in 2006 to improve patient knowledge, concordance and use of medicines through a standard patient-pharmacist consultation (Department of Health 2006). Patients with long-term conditions who may be taking multiple medicines are invited to consult their community pharmacist for an MUR appointment. Adopting a standardised, systematic approach, the pharmacist assesses any problems with current medication and its administration and discusses general issues on maintaining a healthy lifestyle, including diet and fitness.

Following ethical approval by the local research ethics committee, forty bilingual (Welsh/English) patients eligible for a MUR were invited to be allocated to a bilingual or English language consultation with one pharmacist in each location (Pharmacists A and B) during June 2009. Pharmacists A and B exchanged pharmacies for the purpose of the study, in order to reduce bias and ensure that outcomes were not influenced by previously established relationships. In order to ensure that the data would be as

---

3.   The total excludes words which are ambiguous between English and Welsh.

naturalistic as possible, each consultation was audio-recorded by the pharmacist himself in a private area of the pharmacy, with no other participants present. Although participants may have been affected in their language choice to some extent by the recording process, our focus on accommodation means that we are interested in how their language choice changes within the same speech event relative to that of their interlocutor. Validated outcome measures relating to medicines use were administered at day one and month one post MUR. These were correlated against measures of speech accommodation derived from the corpus linguistic analysis.

On entering the study, patients were invited to consent to the digital audio-recording of the MUR. Participants were assured that the information provided during the consultation remained confidential and that the data would be strictly anonymous. The audio-recordings were transcribed verbatim and subject to corpus linguistic analysis techniques, as outlined below. The results provided finely detailed analyses of the MUR discourse and quantitative measures in relation to speech accommodation.

The transcription of the recorded participant-pharmacist interviews involved the use of a machine-readable transcription system known as CHAT, which is part of CLAN (see <http://childes.psy.cmu.edu/clan>, 16 March 2012). Each word in the transcription was tagged with a language marker indicating whether the word was Welsh or English, or ambiguous between the two. For a word to be classified as ambiguous it had to appear in both the Welsh and the English dictionaries[4] and to have a similar pronunciation. This is true, for example of the word pronounced [ʃɒp]: This appears as *shop* in the English dictionary and as *siop* in the Welsh dictionary, but in both languages it means 'shop' and is pronounced in the same way. Once the transcriptions were completed, they were then divided into six equal segments for analysis. The CLAN FREQ programme was used to calculate the number of English and Welsh words in each segment. The proportion of English versus Welsh words was then calculated. For each segment except the first (which was taken as a baseline for the next segment), the accommodation (convergence versus divergence) of each speaker to the interlocutor was calculated using the formula outlined previously.

The formula measures how much the speaker changes his or her proportion of English versus Welsh words over time in relation to the proportion being used by the interlocutor. Positive scores indicate convergence (where '1' represents exact convergence on the interlocutor's percentage of English in the previous segment), negative scores divergence, and a score of zero indicates neither convergence nor divergence. Using the scores for each segment for each speaker, it was possible to calculate the average degree of accommodation by that speaker over the entire conversation, and to compare this with the accommodation of the interlocutor. It was also possible to plot

---

4. The three Welsh dictionaries used were *Geiriadur Prifysgol Cymru* (Thomas 1950–2002), *Geiriadur yr Academi* (Griffiths & Glyn 1995) and *Cysgair* (Canolfan Bedwyr 2004). The English dictionary used was the Oxford English dictionary (Soanes & Stevenson 2004).

the scores for each segment for both the speaker and the interlocutor and to show graphically the accommodation by speaker and interlocutor.

4. Results

Nineteen MUR interviews were recorded where the language use was predominantly Welsh (ten interviews by Pharmacist A and nine by Pharmacist B). This paper focuses on the ten recordings made by Pharmacist A. The language convergence of the patient to pharmacist and pharmacist to patient was measured during each consultation, according to the formula outlined above.

For example, Pharmacist A's accommodation to participant 113 was measured by calculating the English word frequency differences from one segment to the next, which was then divided by the difference between Pharmacist A's and 113's English word frequency during the first segment. Similarly, Participant 113's accommodation to Pharmacist A score was calculated adopting the same formula. By following the graph in Figure 3 of a consultation between Pharmacist A and participant 113, the methodological process can be understood in detail.

Each segment of the conversation provides the baseline for calculating accommodation in the next segment. For example, the accommodation score for Pharmacist A in segment 2 is calculated with reference to his and the interlocutor's scores in segment 1 as follows: (2%–4%)/(2%–3%) = 2 (see Tables 1 and 2 for values). In this formula the numerator represents how much the speaker's score has changed during segment 2 as compared with segment 1 and the denominator represents the distance between the scores of the speaker and the interlocutor during segment 1. This distance provides a

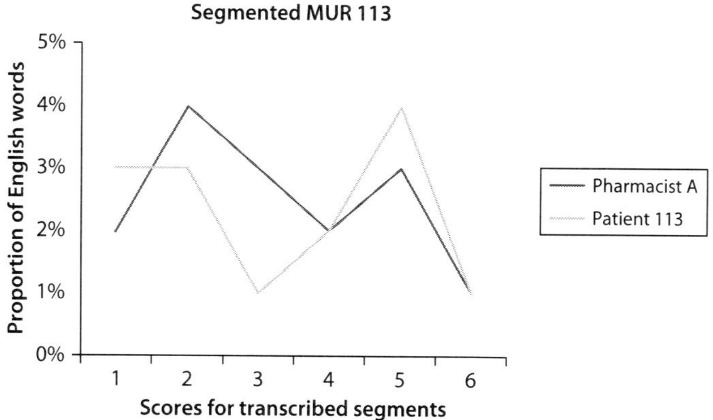

Figure 3. English word frequencies for both pharmacist A and participant 113 during six equal segments of the MUR

baseline to measure the accommodation of the speaker in segment 2. The accommodation score of 2 indicates that the pharmacist has not only converged on the patient's score from the previous turn, but has gone beyond this to the same extent again, giving him a score of 2. The accommodation score for patient 113 in the same period (segment 2) is 0, as the patient has maintained their own score from one turn to next.

In segment 3 the pharmacist again converges towards the speech of the patient in segment 2, but this time reproduces exactly the proportion of English used by the interlocutor in segment 2 (3%) giving him an accommodation score of 1. In the same segment 3, however, the patient decreases her use of English, moving away from the high proportion of English (4%) used by the pharmacist in segment 2. Her score is thus a divergent −2.

It should be noted that zero sometimes occurs as the value for either the numerator or the denominator. If zero is the value for the nominator then this indicates that the speaker's scores during two adjacent segments were identical and hence no change has taken place from one segment to the next. No change of course means no accommodation, and an accommodation score of 0, whatever the value of the denominator might be.

If zero occurs as the value for the denominator then this indicates that the speaker and the interlocutor's scores were identical in the segment providing the baseline for the measurement of accommodation in the next segment. This means that no convergence by the speaker towards the interlocutor is possible in the next segment. However, divergence (from both the speaker's and the interlocutor's identical scores) is clearly possible. In this case the value in the numerator is used to represent the divergent score, but the percentage score is converted into an accommodation score through multiplying by 100, and if positive, transformed into a negative number to capture the divergence. We can illustrate the process using the score for Pharmacist A in segment 5. If we were to apply the original formula (2%–3%)/ (2%–2%) or: −1%/0, we would get a denominator of zero. But if we multiply the numerator of −1% by a hundred we arrive at an accommodation score of −1. This method allows us to use the measurement scale to justify the value, leading to consistency with other scores.

Average accommodation scores were calculated across all five segments for each speaker in the corpus. These averages represent whether the predominant tendency for a speaker is to either converge or diverge in relation to the code switching frequency of their interlocutor. Figure 4 compares average accommodation scores for Pharmacist A and his patients in each MUR consultation. Pairs of adjacent bars allow comparison of the scores of the pharmacist and patient in each interview. The predominant tendency for the pharmacist was that of convergence, although there is some variation within this pattern. Pharmacist A has predominantly convergent averages in eight out of ten of the recordings, and also converges more than the patient in eight of the ten recordings. The tendency for patients however was more divergent than convergent, with six out of ten of the patients mostly diverging during recordings, although some patients do have convergent average scores of up to 1.

Table 1. Proportion of English words during six segments of the MUR interview between Pharmacist A and Participant 113

Segment	Pharmacist A English word frequency[5]	Participant 113 English word frequency
1	2%	3%
2	4%	3%
3	3%	1%
4	2%	2%
5	3%	4%
6	1%	1%

Table 2. Accommodation scores for Pharmacist A and Participant 113 in segments 2–6 of the MUR interview

Segment	Pharmacist A Accommodation to Participant 113	Participant 113 Accommodation to Pharmacist A
2	2	0
3	1	−2
4	0.5	0.5
5	−1	−2
6	−2	3

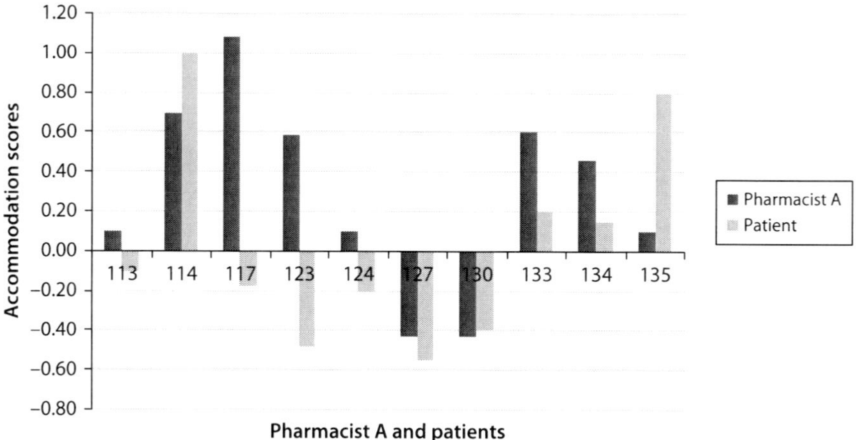

Figure 4. Average Accommodation scores for interviews between Pharmacist A and patients

---

5.   The scores have been rounded to the nearest round number in order to avoid exaggerating minor differences between speakers.

5.   Discussion

The method that we have developed for measuring and interpreting accommodation has proved broadly successful. By using a formula that allows us to calculate the variation in English word usage over time and in relation to that of the interlocutor, we are able to represent accommodation as a phenomenon that is both sequential and dynamic. The overall results display a disparity in accommodation strategies between the pharmacist and his patients. While the pharmacist in general converges on the interlocutor's use of code-switching in previous segments, the patients are almost equally divided between those who tend to converge and those who diverge. It may be possible to ascribe this difference to a variety of factors, including the degree of motivation a speaker has to converge, interpersonal affinity between speakers and a speaker's linguistic and perceptual ability. An accommodation score close to '1' presumably requires a speaker to be consistently paying close attention to the output of the interlocutor, as well as to be able to recall the degree of code-switching used over a relatively lengthy period of time. The pharmacist's superior performance could partly be explained by the fact that he has received training in interpersonal communication, which includes the development of active listening skills (NCP Plus 2007). Maintaining attention is also presumably easier if the speaker is highly motivated to do so, and we do have evidence that the pharmacist is likely to be more motivated in this regard than the patients. In an interview conducted as part of an ethnography following the project, the pharmacist explicitly stated that he would consider tailoring his use of code-switching to that of the patient as an essential communication strategy. The pharmacist thus has a consistent, personally professed motivation to engage in a strategy of reciprocation and convergence, while the patients may have varying levels of ability and readiness to do so. Discrepancies in this pattern, particularly in the divergent scores held by the pharmacist for MURs 127 and 130, could be related to the differences in the degree of interpersonal affinity established between the pharmacist and patient during each consultation. Another possibility with interesting implications is that the pharmacist is reciprocating divergent behaviour by the patients as well as convergence, although further research would be required to establish whether or not this is the case. The implications of such a finding, if proved significant, would be useful for the future training of pharmacists, who could be taught to respond with convergence even when their patients are diverging.

A further study will involve the transcription of the dataset relating to Pharmacist B, which includes an additional nine MUR consultations. This will allow for a comparison between both pharmacists, which could provide an opportunity to test the hypothesis that the practitioners are more likely to converge than the patients due to greater motivation and skills to attend to interlocutor speech patterns. An extended study will also permit the adoption of a broader multi modal analytical approach, including further ethnographic work with the pharmacists and more qualitative approaches to analysing the corpus data.

6.   Conclusion

In this paper we have provided a method for calculating speech accommodation in bilingual settings where speakers are using both languages within the same sentence while making choices at the lexical level. This approach can easily be applied to other bilingual data provided that the transcriptions mark the language membership of each lexical item. We are confident that these and other results using the method will have important implications for communication skills training in healthcare. Our aim is for our work to facilitate language-appropriate practice in the bilingual context and for the new evidence from our work to inform the delivery of healthcare education that is sensitive to the needs of bilingual service users and cognisant of the language skill requirements of a bilingual workforce.

References

Audit Commission. 1993. *What seems to be the matter? Communication between hospitals and patients.* London: HMSO.

Bourhis, R. Y. & H. Giles. 1976. The language of cooperation in Wales: A field study. *Language Sciences* 42: 13–16.

Bourhis, R. Y. & H. Giles. 1977. The language of intergroup distinctiveness. In *Language, Ethnicity and Intergroup Relations,* ed. H. Giles, 119–135. London: Academic Press.

Bourhis, R. Y., S. Roth & G. MacQueen. 1989. Communication in the hospital setting: A survey of medical and everyday language use amongst patients, nurses and doctors. *Social Science and Medicine* 28: 339–346.

Brown, A. & P. Draper. 2003. Accommodative speech and terms of endearment: Elements of a language mode often experienced by older adults. *Journal of Advanced Nursing* 41: 15–21.

Canolfan Bedwyr. 2004. *Cysgair: The English and Welsh Dictionary for Windows.* Bangor: Bangor University.

Carrasquillo, O., E. Orav, T. Brennan & H. Burstin. 1999. Impact of language barriers on patient satisfaction in an emergency department. *Journal of General Internal Medicine* 14: 82–87.

Cass, A., A. Lowell, M. Christie, P. Snelling, M. Flack, B. Marrnganyin & I. Brown. 2002. Sharing the true stories: Improving communication between aboriginal patients and healthcare workers. *Medical Journal of Australia* 177: 466–470.

Coupland, N. 1984. Accommodation at work: Some phonological data and their implications. *International Journal of the Sociology of Language* 46: 49–70.

Department of Health. 2006. *The Pharmaceutical Services: Advanced and Enhanced Services (England). Amendment Directions.* <http://www.dh.gov.uk/en/Publicationsandstatistics/Publications/PublicationsLegislation/DH_130135> (6 June 2012).

Fernandez, A., K. Schillinger, A. Grumbach, A. Rosenthal, F. Stewart, F. Wang & E. Pérez-Stable. 2004. Physician language ability and cultural competence: An exploratory study of communication with Spanish-speaking patients. *Journal of General Internal Medicine* 19: 167–174.

Finlayson, R., K. Calteaux & C. Myers-Scotton. 1998. Orderly mixing and accommodation in South African codeswitching. *Journal of Sociolinguistics* 2: 395–420.

Freeman, G., H. Rai, J. Walker, D. Howie, D. Heaney & M. Maxwell. 2002. Non-English speakers consulting with the GP in their own language: A cross-sectional survey. *British Journal of General Practice* 52: 36–38.

Giles, H., N. Coupland & J. Coupland. 1991. Accommodation theory: Communication, context and consequence. In *Contexts of Accommodation,* eds. J. Coupland, N. Coupland & H. Giles, 1–68. Cambridge: CUP.

Giles, H. & P. M. Smith. 1979. Speech markers in social interaction. In *Social markers in speech*, eds. K. R. Scherer & H. Giles, 343–381. Cambridge: CUP.

Griffiths, B. & D. G. Glyn. 1995. *Geiriadur yr Academi.* Cardiff: University of Wales Press.

Grosjean, F. 1998. Studying bilinguals: Methodological and conceptual issues. *Bilingualism: Language and Cognition* 1: 131–149.

Hack, T., L. Degner, P. Watson & L. Sinha. 2006. Do patients benefit from participating in medical decision making? Longitudinal follow-up of women with breast cancer. *Psycho-Oncology* 15: 9–19.

Légaré, F., G. Elwyn, M. Fishbein, P. Fremont, D. Frosch, M. Gagnon, D. Kenny, M. Labrecque, D. Stacey, S. St-Jacques & T. van der Weijden. 2008. Translating shared decision-making into health care clinical practices: Proof of concepts. *Implementation Science* 3. <doi:10.1186/1748-5908-3-2>

Lewis, J. 2003. *Social Influences on Female Speakers' Pitch.* PhD dissertation, University of California at Berkeley.

Misell, A. 2000. *Welsh in the Health Service: The Scope, Nature and Adequacy of Welsh Language Provision.* Cardiff: Welsh Consumer Council.

Moïse, L. C. & R. Y. Bourhis. 1994. Langage et ethnicité: Communication interculturelle à Montréal, 1977–1991. *Canadian Ethnic Studies* 26: 86–107.

National Assembly for Wales. 2003. *National Statistics.* Cardiff: National Assembly for Wales.

Niederhoffer, K. & J. Pennebaker. 2002. Linguistic style matching in social interaction. *Journal of Language and Social Psychology* 21: 337–360.

NPC Plus. 2007. *A Competency Framework for Shared Decision-making with Patients: Achieving Concordance for Taking Medicines.* Keele: NCP Plus.

Sachdev, I. & H. Giles. 2004. Bilingual accommodation. In *The Handbook of Bilingualism*, eds. T. K. Bhatia & W. C. Ritchie, 353–378. Oxford: Blackwell.

Sarver, J. & D. Barker. 2000. Effect of language barriers on follow-up appointments after an emergency department visit. *Journal of General Internal Medicine* 15: 256–264.

Soanes, C. & A. Stevenson. 2004. *Concise Oxford English Dictionary*, 11th edn. Oxford: OUP.

Stevenson, F., K. Cox, N. Britten & Y. Dundar. 2004. A systematic review of the research on communication between patients and health care professionals about medicines: The consequences for concordance. *Health Expectations* 7: 235–245.

Street, R. 1991. Accommodation in medical consultations. In *Contexts of Accommodation: Developments in Applied Sociolinguistics*, eds. H. Giles, J. Coupland & N. Coupland, 131–156. Cambridge: CUP.

Tajfel, H. 1974. Social identity and intergroup behaviour. *Social Science Information* 13: 65–93.

Thakerar, J. N., H. Giles & J. Cheshire. 1982. Psychological and linguistic parameters of speech accommodation theory. In *Advances in the Social Psychology of Language*, eds. C. Fraser & K. R. Scherer, 205–255.

The Office of National Statistics. 2001. *Census 2001: Report on the Welsh language.* <http://www.ons.gov.uk/ons/rel/census/census-2001-report-on-the-welsh-language/report-on-the-welsh-language/report-on-the-welsh-language-.pdf> (3 July 2012).

Thomas, R. J., ed. 1950–2002. *Geiriadur Prifysgol Cymru.* University of Wales. <http://www.cymru.ac.uk/geiriadur/gpc_pdfs.htm> (16 March 2012).

Becoming bilingual in a multilingual context

A snapshot view of L2 competences in South Tyrol

Chiara Vettori, Katrin Wisniewski and Andrea Abel
European Academy of Bolzano/Bozen, Italy

In this contribution we present the results of an extensive linguistic and psycho-social survey we conducted on a representative sample of Italian and German-speaking high school pupils in multilingual South Tyrol (Italy). The aim of the project was to describe their L2 competences (Italian/German) according to the CEFR levels and to find out extra-linguistic factors that exercise an influence on the L2 competence levels of the students. In this article, we focus in particular on L2 motivation and orientations, explaining the role they play in this peculiar context. Furthermore, we comment on the results of the language tests in the light of these extra-linguistic findings, trying to point out some key elements that might help to promote bilingualism in South Tyrol.

Keywords: German, Italian, second language acquisition, CEFR L2 proficiency levels, L2 learning motivation, L2 learning orientations

1. Introduction

The educational system in multilingual South Tyrol is strongly concerned with the instruction of the second language (Abel, Stuflesser & Voltmer 2007, Voltmer 2007, ASTAT 2006a, 2006b) with the aim of fostering bilingualism in individuals. Nevertheless, the ability and also the willingness to participate in life using the L2 are generally considered to be alarmingly low so that South Tyrol results de facto divided into separate linguistic sub-groups rather than representing a truly multilingual society (Baur 2000, ASTAT 2006a, 2006b). In spite of the many complaints about the supposedly insufficient L2 proficiency of both Italian and German speaking South Tyroleans, until recently only small-scale projects have engaged in its assessment (e.g. Vettori 2005), often using self-evaluation methods (i.e. ASTAT 2006a, 2006b).

With the project KOLIPSI, the European Academy of Bolzano/Bozen (EURAC) and the Department of Cognitive Science and Educational Sciences at the University of Trento (DiSCof) conducted an extensive analysis of communicative/interactive L2 writing of approximately 1200 South Tyrolean pupils. Partly also speaking abilities were tested. Given the particular and contradictory social context described, we also concentrated on the sociolinguistic and socio-psychological factors influencing L2 proficiency levels. This in order to achieve a possibly accurate picture of linguistically and extra-linguistically meaningful parameters from which to draw useful inputs for a conscious language and education policy.

2. Background

2.1   South Tyrol between historical and language concerns

The Autonomous Province of Bolzano/Bozen – South Tyrol (for short South Tyrol), once part of the Austrian-Hungarian Empire, belongs to Italy since 1919. It hosts the largest German-speaking community in Italy. According to the most recent census carried out in the year 2001, it makes up 69.38% of the entire local population. 26.30% are Italian speakers[1] who mainly live in the towns. German speakers live both in the towns and, in larger part, in the countryside. The possibility of "spontaneous" contacts between the two language groups therefore mostly occurs in the towns.

From a linguistic and cultural point of view, South Tyrol is strongly characterised by the meeting of the Italian and the Austrian-German worlds. This is the result of South Tyrol's annexation to Italy after World War I, which happened by no means voluntarily. During the fascist years (1923–1939), a strong Italianization aimed at fostering the immigration of Italian speakers and, above all, at banning the use of the German language (see Autonome Provinz Bozen-Südtirol 2004, Alcock 2001, 1970). In the battle for the safeguard of their civil and cultural rights that took place afterwards, German-speaking South Tyroleans obtained two important achievements: in 1946 the signature of the Paris Treaty between Austria and Italy and in 1972 the Second Autonomy Statute, which contain the most important provisions regarding language rights such as linguistic equality, the Ethnic Proportions Decree, the Declaration as to Linguistic Origin and the bilingualism examination. In the Autonomy Statute, the German language is declared equal to the Italian language (Article 99) and "German-speaking citizens of the Province of Bolzano/Bozen have the right to use their own language in relations with the judicial offices and with the bodies and offices of the public administration ..." (Article 100, see Autonome Provinz Bozen-Südtirol 2006). Children are educated in their mother tongue by mother tongue teachers and attend schools that are separated for each linguistic group; second language (L2) learning, Italian or German respectively, is compulsory in both primary and secondary schools.

---

1.   As well as 4.32% of Ladin speakers. For practical reasons, the Ladin language could not be covered in the KOLIPSI project and it will not be taken into consideration within this contribution.

The principle of ethnic proportion reflects the fact that the positions in public offices are occupied according to the numerical strength of the language groups living in South Tyrol. This in turn is determined via the census carried out every ten years. In that occasion each citizen must declare to which of the three language groups he/she belongs to.

To guarantee that everyone can use his/her mother tongue when dealing with public offices, in 1976 the bilingualism examination was introduced as a pre-condition for recruitment into the public service. The examination, consisting of a written and an oral test, should test the candidates' bilingual proficiency. It must be taken in both languages, i.e. German and Italian, in one of four levels of difficulty (from D to A) according to the professional position desired (see Voltmer 2007, Autonome Provinz Bozen-Südtirol 2004, Abel, Vettori & Forer forthcoming).

2.2   Language proficiency in South Tyrol

The education system in South Tyrol is strongly concerned with second language instruction. From the first to the thirteenth school grade (age 6 to 19) L2 learning is compulsory and comprises more than 2000 hours for both German and Italian-speaking pupils (see Egger 2001: 163). Moreover, it is also promoted by a range of special measures such as language courses, study trips, partnerships with German/Italian-speaking schools and experiments of subject teaching in L2. However, despite the considerable resources invested and the many initiatives, L2 proficiency of South Tyroleans is widely believed to be inadequate. Findings of previous investigations regarding L2 competences as well as the results of the bilingualism examination all point at a relatively low L2 proficiency of the South Tyrolean population (see Putzer 1997a, 1997b, Deflorian 1997, Vettori 2005, CENSIS 1997, ASTAT 2006a, 2006b). The data from the bilingualism examination sessions in 2009 show that only half of the candidates passed the examination at the highest level (A), while only 22.3% of those who took the second highest level (B) examination succeeded (ASTAT 2010). Furthermore, according to the *language barometer* (ASTAT 2006a, 2006b), a study carried out in 2004 on a representative sample for the whole South Tyrolean population (adults aged 19 and above), 40% of the Italian-speaking community state that they can only say a few words of German. Only 5.1% of the German-speakers state the same regarding Italian. As a matter of fact, most recurrent complaints and negative evaluations refer to the L2 skills of the Italian-speaking community rather than those of the German-speaking one.

Neither the efforts of the education system nor the physical proximity of the two groups seem therefore sufficient to produce the multilingual society one would expect in such circumstances; on the contrary, literature and observers of local everyday life (see Egger 2001, Lanthaler 2006) speak of separate linguistic sub-groups, which do not get in contact with each other and where "the language of the other is learned as if the other lived in a far away, unreachable country" (Baur 2000: 300). [2] This is a well known phenomenon in regions where different linguistic groups live together and where bilingualism and interculturality are not per se given and do not normally develop on a large scale, as it is the case in Switzerland and in the region on the border between Germany and Denmark (Baur, Mezzalira & Pichler 2008: 35). The same happens also in Canada where, after twelve years of French learning, English-speaking pupils are not sufficiently competent to speak in their L2 with French-speaking Canadians (Baker 2006: 224).

It is evident that becoming bilingual in South Tyrol – and not just there – involves a series of factors that exceed the mere educational and didactic dimension and that embrace diverse sociolinguistic and psycho-social issues such as attitudes, prejudices, contact and speaking habits, motivation, etc.

3.   Some linguistic and socio-psychological insights

3.1   The KOLIPSI project

In the absence of large scale empirical studies regarding the L2 proficiency of South Tyrolean pupils, EURAC and DiSCoF carried out the project "KOLIPSI. *South Tyrolean pupils and the second language: a linguistic and socio-psychological investigation*" (see Abel, Vettori & Wisniewski forthcoming). The concept of L2 communicative language competence on which the project is based relates to the Common European Framework of Reference (CEFR) definition (Trim, North & Coste 2001: 9–13)[3]: The CEFR follows an action-oriented approach that views "users and learners of a language primarily as 'social agents', i.e. members of society who have tasks (not exclusively language-related) to accomplish in a given set of circumstances, in a specific environment and within a particular field of action" (Trim et al. 2001: 9). The aim of the project was twofold: first of all, in the specifically language related part we aimed at describing the L2 competences (Italian/German) for a representative sample of pupils of secondary schools according to the CEFR levels. To that end, we applied various data collection methods in order to elaborate a competence profile for

---

2.   Own translation from Baur (2000: 300): "Anstatt die Sprache der anderen in direktem Kontakt mit den anderen zu lernen, wird die Sprache von den sprechenden Menschen getrennt und so gelernt, als gäbe es die anderen gar nicht, so als lebten sie in einem fernen unerreichbaren Land."

3.   This comes quite close to Bachman & Palmer's (1996) conceptualization of "communicative language ability" (for a detailed comparison see Schneider & North 2000). Bachman & Palmer (1996) focus on language use in test situations as expression of L2 communicative language ability (CLA). Their model has been used for the definition of the test construct, as the Bachman & Palmer's widely accepted model is a lot more specific and explicit than the CEFR terminology, especially in language testing. Furthermore, communicative ability model components have been partly confirmed by empirical studies.

interactive and productive communicative activities that, for the first time in this context, were directly related to the CEFR. Secondly, in the sociolinguistic and psycho-social part, we aimed at finding out extra-linguistic factors that may exercise an influence on the L2 competence levels of the students. In consideration of the status quo described above and given that no survey had tried to read the South Tyroleans' L2 proficiency in the light of the many extra linguistic factors involved before[4], we spent great efforts in investigating these aspects with qualitative and quantitative survey techniques.

Data were collected for a representative sample of around 1200 17–18 year old randomly selected pupils in the fourth grade of all secondary schools[5] in the Province (school year 2007/2008). The demographical distribution of the local language groups was roughly maintained (69% German, 29% Italian speakers (ASTAT 2006a, 2006b) versus 77.6% German, 22.4% Italian speakers in the KOLIPSI project).

3.2   KOLIPSI: Linguistic data collection methods and language tests

In the language-related part of the project, a written classroom test served as pre-test for estimating the students' achievement levels, which were found to be mostly at the levels B1/B2 of the CEFR. The second language test was the written part of the South Tyrolean bilingualism examination. During the official test, candidates have to answer questions about an Italian text in German and the other way round. In the KOLIPSI project, for practical reasons, pupils only had to answer questions in their L2 about a text in their L1 (level B)[6]. The decision to include this examination in the survey derives from the awareness of the crucial importance that the bilingualism examination holds for the working life in South Tyrol and with the aim of producing data of special interest to the local reality. At the core of the linguistic part, though, lied the KOLIPSI writing test, which was developed ad hoc at the EURAC in collaboration with the Herder Institute in Leipzig. The results of this test will be presented in this paper. It aimed at assessing the productive and interactive writing competences for different aspects of the L2 according to CEFR reference levels. Linguistic, socio-linguistic, and pragmatic aspects

---

4.   The last extensive study about the L2 proficiency of both German- and Italian-speaking middle and high school pupils (Putzer 1997a, 1997b, Deflorian 1997) has never been published nor put in relation to the survey of L2 learning motivations and contact habits that had been carried out in parallel on the same test sample (Baur 1996).

5.   The Italian secondary school system comprises two paths to the school leaving exam (called *esame di maturità/Reifeprüfung*) that allows pupils to access university. Students can either attend different kinds of academic high school (called *Liceo/Gymnasium*) or a technical high school (called *Istituto tecnico/Fachoberschule, Lehranstalt*); both types of school last five years. As a consequence, the pupils who participated in the KOLIPSI project were tested one year before taking their school-leaving examination.

6.   For details see <http://www.provinz.bz.it/zdp/themen/wer-wie-wo-wann.asp> (8 June 2012)

(see Wisniewski 2009) were analysed. In a parallel approach, a sub-sample of 100 participants was tested for oral communicative and interactive language abilities.[7]

The test consisted in writing an e-mail based on a picture story and a letter to a friend. The range of competences targeted for these tasks lay around B1/B2.[8] However, since we were aware that not all performances would lie within this range, the adjacent upper and lower levels (i.e. A2 and C1) were also foreseen in the assessment, in order to gain a comprehensive picture of the linguistic abilities of the target group.

For practicality reasons, only a sub-sample of 100 pupils[9] who had mostly also taken the writing test could participate in the KOLIPSI speaking test. The sample was carefully chosen to take a closer look at the important assumption that the availability of L2 contact would enhance L2 competence. The sample is too small to draw generalizing conclusions regarding the complete population and a restricted range of statistical procedures can be employed here. The speaking test consisted of a short warm-up, after which a picture-prompted monologue task was to be solved. In a second (dialogic) task, the candidate was to choose between two topics that had shown to be adequate in the pretesting phase.

Quality management was of major importance in the construction, administration and evaluation of the KOLIPSI language tests. The relevant research literature (e.g. Bachman & Palmer 1996), the AERA, APA & NCME (1999) standards and the quality recommendations of the Association of Language Testers in Europe (ALTE 2001) were fundamental. Quantitative and qualitative evidence was gathered in order to describe and guarantee validity, reliability, authenticity and practicality (see Bachman & Palmer 1996, Kane 2001). For instance, our trained raters' judgments (double-blind ratings for each test were collected, in both the speaking and the writing test) were examined for falsifying tendencies (such as varying severity). With the help of multi-faceted Rasch analyses fair averages could be calculated for the pupils' overall L2 performance as well as for single rating criteria used (e.g. grammar, vocabulary, coherence; see Hesse & Römisch forthcoming).

3.3   Results of the KOLIPSI project: Language-related part

The results of the German- and Italian-speaking pupils in the KOLIPSI writing test are displayed in Figures 1 and 2.[10]

---

7.   Wisniewski's work has been funded by ESF and Federal State of Saxony.

8.   For a description of the respective tasks see Abel et al. forthcoming.

9.   50 Italian native speakers and 50 German native speakers were chosen; half of each group came from a mainly L2-speaking environment, the other half lived in an environment where their mother tongue was the main language of communication (Bolzano/Bozen and Bressanone/ Brixen). A variety of possibly influencing factors were considered (age, school marks, school biography, age of first contact with L2 and others).

10.   The results (German vs. Italian pupils) should not be directly compared for reasons of statistical coherence.

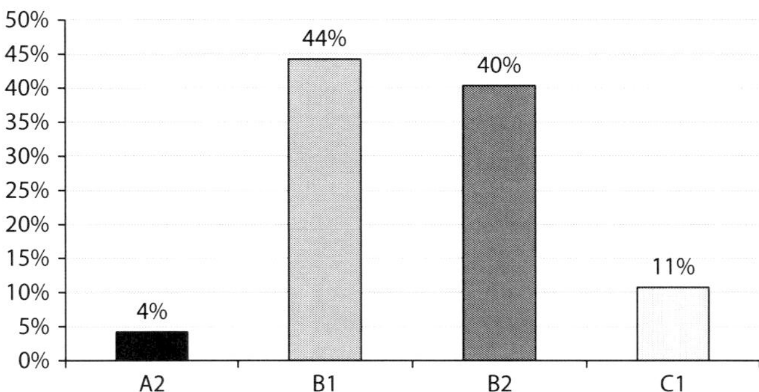

Figure 1. KOLIPSI writing test (%) with Italian as L2 (A2 = lower – C1 = higher level of proficiency). Extreme cases (levels A1 and C2) were excluded from the diagram

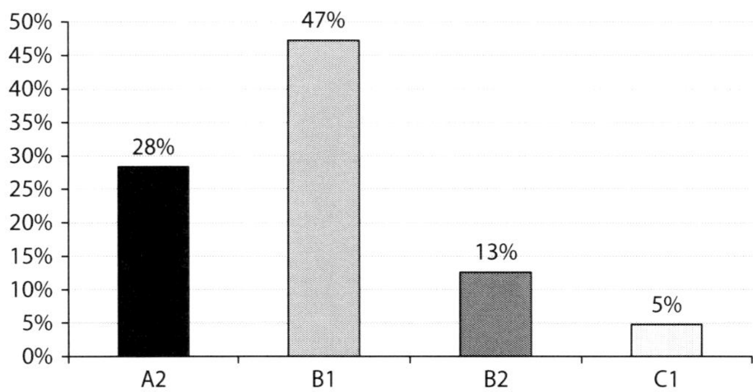

Figure 2. KOLIPSI writing test (%) with German as L2 (A2 = lower – C1 = higher level of proficiency)

Learners of Italian very often reach level B1 of the CEFR (44%), but many achieve B2 (40%). A remarkably low number of students performs at levels below B1 (4%), and more than a tenth of the sample is at level C1 (11%; speakers that declared to feel "bilingual" were excluded from this calculation). Compared to that, learners of German seem to have more difficulties in writing in their L2: while almost one third remains at level A2 (28%), most Italian native speakers achieve a B1 (47%), with a small group of pupils performing better than that (13% B2, 5% C1).

Among a number of possible factors that influence these results, the type of school attended turned out to play a particularly important role (see Figures 3 and 4).

The diagrams show remarkable differences between school types for both language groups, but especially for Italian speakers. For almost half of our sample attending an Italian technical high school coincides with L2 competences below the threshold level B1, while in the academic secondary schools this share amounts to only 15%. Those attending Italian academic secondary schools have hardly any problems in achieving at least a B1 level (78%).

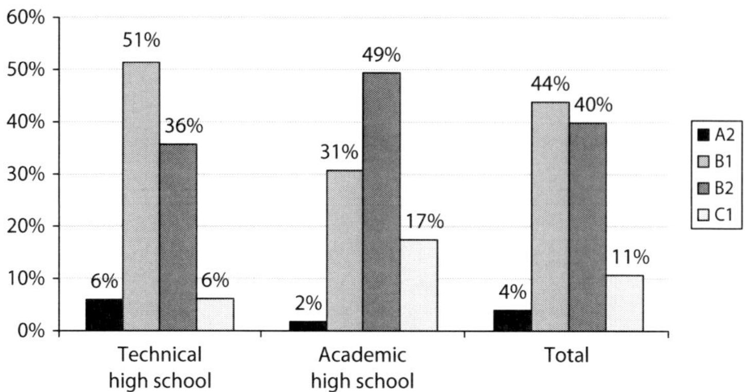

Figure 3. KOLIPSI writing test (%) according to school type (Italian as L2)

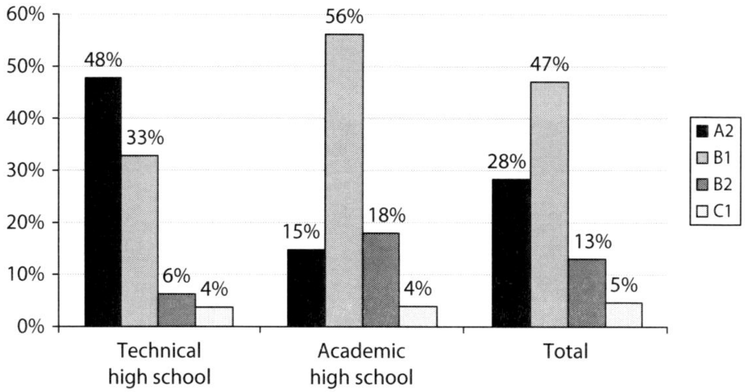

Figure 4. KOLIPSI writing test (%) according to school type (German as L2)

Differences at German schools show the same tendencies, but in a less marked way, although pupils at C1 level are to be found a lot more often at academic secondary schools (17% compared to 6% at technical secondary schools). For German-speaking pupils some robust context factors for L2 competence seem to be school type, gender, but also the language environment (the more Italian is spoken, the higher the performance). For Italian-speaking pupils it is above all the school type that influences language performance.[11]

---

11.   Results of regression analyses (questionnaire study, see below). Factors taken into consideration were: gender, language environment, school type. As to "language environment", we made a distinction between Italian vs. German speaking majority in the pupils home town (over 60%, respectively). Further statistical details and aspects (e.g. socio economic status, mother tongue, sense of belonging to a German, Italian, Ladin, bilingual or other group) can be found in the forthcoming publication of the KOLIPSI project (see Abel et al. forthcoming).

The results of the KOLIPSI speaking test seem to confirm the tendency that for German native South Tyrolean pupils it is easier to learn Italian than the other way round (Figure 5): 42% achieve a B2, 10% even a C1, whereas learners of German mostly get a B1 level (56%), and there are no ratings above B2 to be found. On the other hand (Figure 6), a third of the Italian native speakers achieves a B2 (35.4%), and the number of very weak learners does not differ very much between the groups (learners of Italian/German below B1: 6%/8.3%).[12] Even though for statistical reasons it cannot be considered appropriate to directly compare results from the writing and the speaking test, it is indeed interesting to see that the distribution of CEFR levels among pupils who learn Italian are almost identical in both tests. On the contrary, for the learners of German the oral test appears to be somewhat easier (speaking/writing for German as L2: A2: 8.3%/28%/; B1: 56.3%/47%; B2: 17%/35.4%).

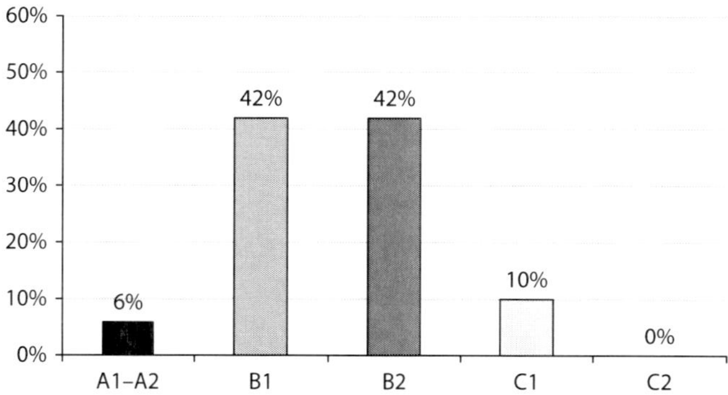

Figure 5. KOLIPSI speaking test (in %; Italian as L2)

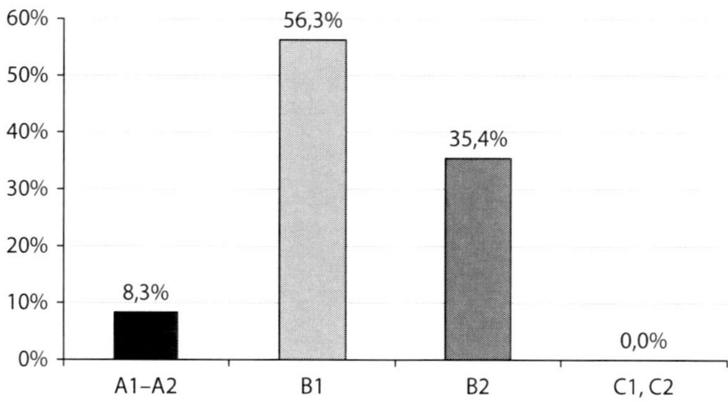

Figure 6. KOLIPSI speaking test (in %; German as L2)

---

12. For methodological reasons, extreme values calculated with the multi-faceted Rasch analysis are less reliable than the values in the centre of the scale.

Furthermore, test results seem to support the quite obvious assumption of higher L2 competences in more L2-affected environments. Pupils who learn Italian and live in an environment where mostly Italian is spoken (i.e. Bolzano/Bozen) performed better in the speaking test. 70% of them achieve level B2 or higher, compared to only 40% of those living in a context where more German is spoken (i.e. Bressanone/Brixen). Pupils learning German also achieve remarkably better results in their speaking tests if they attend school and live in an environment characterised by dominant use of the L2 (i.e. Bressanone/Brixen): 64% of them achieve a B2, and no one performs below B1. In Bolzano/Bozen, B2 performances drop to 34%, and 8% of candidates were even below B1. While these findings seem to suggest that the language environment plays a more decisive role in supporting the spoken rather than the written language competences (where the school type seems to be a particularly strong context factor), the results have to be interpreted with extreme caution because of the small size and the particular composition of the oral test sample (which was not randomly selected but strictly hypothesis-driven, see above).

3.4 KOLIPSI: Socio-psychological and sociolinguistic data collection methods – focus on motivation

To collect the socio-psychological data, we employed different qualitative and quantitative methods. We conducted interviews with key figures from South Tyrolean life and focus groups with fourth grade high school pupils to gather some first, interesting stimuli and issues (see Forer, Paladino, Vettori & Abel 2008) we then investigated through an extensive questionnaire study that involved the pupils we tested on their language competence, but also their parents and L2 teachers. The topics we addressed ranged from the demographic, cultural and social characteristics of the target population to self- and external evaluation of L2 skills, L2 use, L2 confidence, L2 learning motivation, attitudes towards the language groups, linguistic identity, relative deprivation, ethnolinguistic vitality etc.[13] In the present contribution we will focus on the pupils' L2 learning motivation, which has been a major research topic since Lambert and Gardner's studies in the 70's and which is said to be "a key, if not the key, to successful language learning" (High Level Group on Multilingualism 2007: 9).

Gardner (2007: 10) defines L2 learning motivation as something "more complex than merely wanting to learn the language" and a synthesis of three elements: the effort spent to learn the language, the desire to learn it and the positive attitude toward the task itself. Strictly connected to motivation are the so-called orientations that, in Gardner's theory, "help arouse motivation and direct it towards a set of goals" (Dörnyei 2001: 49) and that can be labelled as either *integrative* or *instrumental*. In the first case, the L2 learner has a positive disposition towards the L2 group and he/she desires to

---

13. For a more detailed description of the contents of the questionnaire see Abel et al. forthcoming.

communicate with it and even to become similar to its valued members; in the second, he/she thinks merely of the pragmatic gains of L2 proficiency, for example for his/her working life, without having any interest in socializing with the language community (Masgoret & Gardner 2003: 129). Both motivation and orientations correlate with L2 competences, that is they are both in relationship with L2 proficiency, but it is motivation that correlates higher and that exerts a direct effect on L2 learning achievement (Masgoret & Gardner 2003: 123–124).[14] This last specification is particularly interesting for the South Tyrolean context, therefore we selected the pupils in the sample who answered the questions about their L2 learning motivation and orientations and put them in relationship to their results in the KOLIPSI language test. The purpose was to gain a picture of the motivational dynamics that develop in such a bilingual setting and to see to what extent they play a role in the L2 learning process.[15]

3.5   Results of the KOLIPSI project: Psycho-social part

The subsample we analyzed is representative of the original sample and consists of 734 pupils, 80.7% of whom are German speaking and 19.3% Italian speaking.[16] Their test scores reflect the tendency already described (see Section 3.3). After calculating an aggregate index[17] for motivation and for integrative and instrumental orientation[18], we looked for the possible correlations between the three indexes and the pupils' L2 proficiency. In both groups L2 proficiency correlates positively with motivation and with integrative orientation but not with instrumental orientation.[19] This means that, although the vast majority of the sample states that studying the L2 is important for

---

14.   Correlation is a statistical measurement of the relationship between two variables. Two variables are positively correlated if high values of one are likely to be associated with high values of the other. They are negatively correlated if high values of one are likely to be associated with low values of the other. Correlation does not imply causation.

15.   For a more detailed analysis see Vettori forthcoming.

16.   39.2% of them are male and 60.8% female; 57.3% attend a technical high school and 46.3% an academic high school.

17.   An aggregate index is based on the average values of the chosen indicators.

18.   We employed items inspired by the Attitude/Motivation Test Battery by Gardner (1985) such as: I am very motivated to learn German/Italian; If L2 were not a compulsory school subject, I would choose to learn it anyway; When I am in L2 class, I enjoy it/I feel bored; Studying German/Italian can be important to me because it will allow me to communicate better with the L2 group; Studying German/Italian can be important to me to get a job in the Public Administration etc. (see Vettori forthcoming).

19.   Motivation [r(592, TED) = .278**, p < .001, r(142, ITA) = .328**, p < .001], integrative orientation [r(590, TED) = .163**, p < .001; r(140, ITA) = .330**, p < .001], instrumental orientation [r(585, TED) = .051, p = .216, r(140, ITA) = .077, p = .367].

pragmatic reasons, it is not this type of goals that play a primary role in the virtuous circle that helps pupils achieving good L2 results.

Moreover, dividing the two groups on the basis of their motivation and levels of integrative orientation grades (into highly and poorly motivated and highly and poorly integrative oriented pupils) confirmed that those who are highly motivated and highly integratively oriented also have better language skills than the others. A slight difference can be seen between German and Italian-speaking pupils: the former have better L2 proficiency if they are highly motivated (Figure 7 as compared to Figure 8), while the latter show better competence levels if they have higher integrative orientation (Figure 9 as compared to Figure 10), although their motivation and integrative orientation seem to have almost the same strength in their relationship with L2 competence.

Gardner observes that "one might profess an integrative orientation in language study but still may or may not be motivated to learn the language" (Masgoret & Gardner 2003: 129). The data just presented suggest that in Italian-speaking South Tyroleans integrative orientation and motivation are closely connected to each other and that the integrative goal plays a major role in arousing and sustaining their L2 learning motivation.

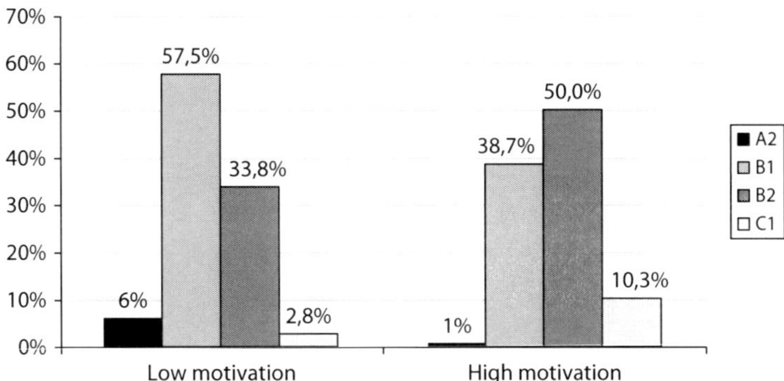

Figure 7. German speaking pupils, L2 proficiency and motivation degree

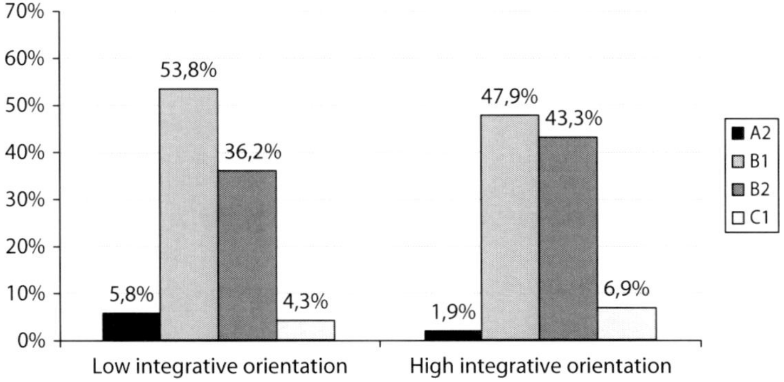

Figure 8. German speaking pupils, L2 proficiency and integrative orientation degree

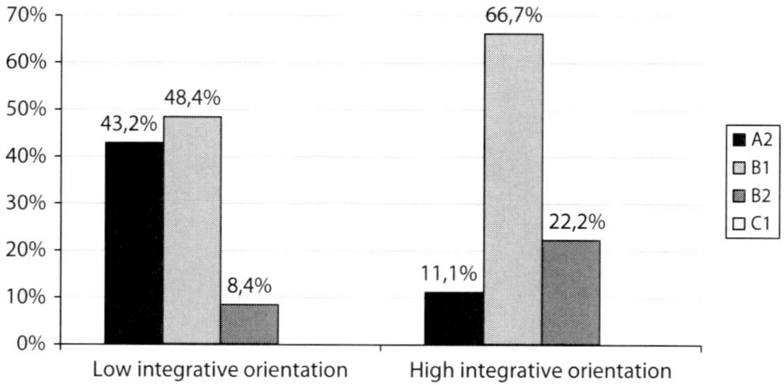

Figure 9. Italian speaking pupils, L2 proficiency and integrative orientation degree

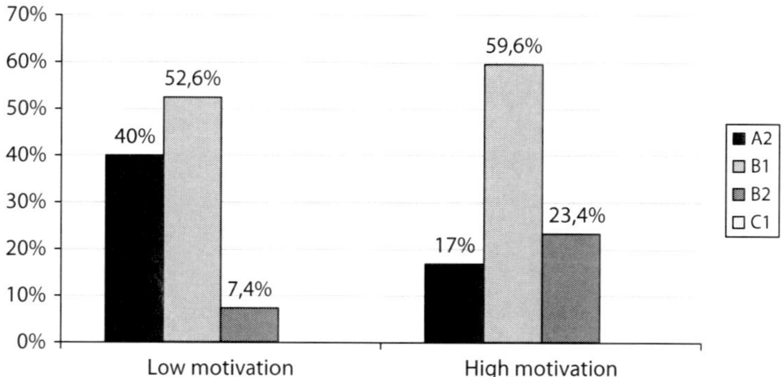

Figure 10. Italian speaking pupils, L2 proficiency and motivation degree

In the definition of motivation itself, the effort made on L2 learning finds its place between desire and attitudes and it is exactly in the effort dimension that one of the most important differences between the two South Tyrolean communities becomes clear. Besides school work, neither German nor Italian-speaking pupils spend much effort in reading books or newspapers/magazines, in watching TV/films or in listening to the radio in their L2 (Figure 11).

On the contrary, in intergroup communication 4/5 of German-speaking pupils (85.98%) address their interlocutors in their L2, while 69% of the Italian-speaking ones choose their L1. The same happens in the closest relationship they have with people of the L2 community: even in such a context, Italian-speakers tend to speak Italian (67.4%) and German-speakers tend to speak Italian, too (78.88%).

This habit seems to have little to do with motivation and integrative orientation. It is true that almost all highly motivated German-speaking pupils (95.6%) speak in their L2, while the percentage decreases among less motivated ones (78.9%) and that highly

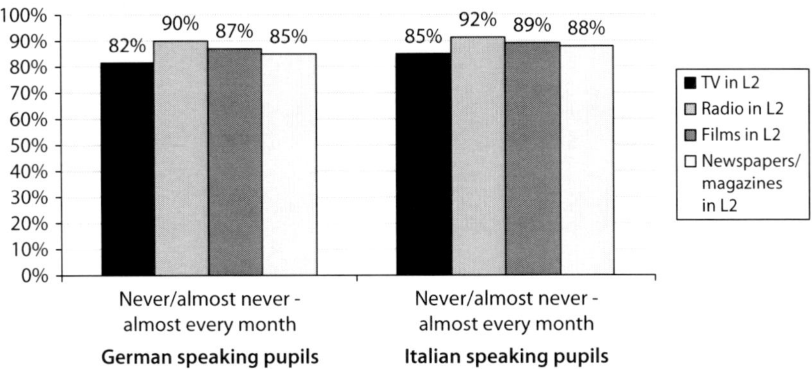

Figure 11. Activities in L2, comparison between German and Italian speaking pupils

integratively oriented Italian speaking pupils are more willing to speak in their L2 (11.1% state that they *speak more German than Italian/always German* and 22.2% that they *speak German and Italian in equal amounts* versus 2.1% and 12.6% respectively among the less integratively oriented pupils)[20]. However, these numbers suggest that communicative habits in South Tyrol have little to do with motivational issues but rather that they root into South Tyrol's history itself. As a matter of fact, after the annexation by Italy, the Italian language was imposed on the German-speaking South Tyrolean community and, over the decades, it has conquered a stable position in its everyday language repertoire. The same has not yet happened in the Italian-speaking community, which started to ask for better L2 teaching programs after the introduction of the bilingualism examination as a pre-condition for recruitment into the public service in 1976 (DPR 752/1976). This also meant an ever-increasing importance of the German language in all economic sectors. Nevertheless, strong requests are still being voiced, but they risk to burden school with excessive expectations. The Italian speaking community, in fact, tends to consider school as the only occasion where the L2 can be acquired (see Giudiceandrea 2006: 23–37). Nobody can deny that school plays a crucial role in L2 learning, but one would expect that the opportunities to learn the L2 in such a bilingual context were not confined to school walls. On the contrary, the ever-recurrent debate about L2 teaching[21] and the emphasizing of the importance of good L2 proficiency for their future job by parents and teachers, move pupils away from the idea that a language should serve principally as a means of getting in touch with the L2 group, thus emptying the integrative goals of their meaning. Moreover, this tendency to look at the L2 as a "tool for the future" backs Italian-speaking pupils'

---

20. Only 45 pupils out of 142 are highly integratively oriented, so that 11.1% and 22.2% represent 15 respondents belonging to this group.

21. The claim for immersion teaching programs by the Italian community becomes more and more pressing (see Baur & Mezzalira, Pichler 2008).

tendency of avoiding L2 use in intergroup communication; this has negative repercussions on motivation itself as it closes off "a whole dimension of motivational experience that is crucial to autonomous language learning – that is, the experience of *language use*, and all the positive motivational repercussions, self-perceptions and intrinsic rewards that using the language can bring" (Ushioda 1996: 31). It cannot be left out, however, that the German speakers' widespread use of dialect variants represent an obstacle to communication for the vast majority of Italian speakers (Abel et al. forthcoming, Abel & Stuflesser 2009, Abel 2007, Riehl 2007) and that – ironically enough – their promptness in speaking Italian could have a further demotivating impact on Italian speakers, who do not see the necessity to commit themselves to speaking their L2 with people who master Italian better than they master German.[22]

Results thus strongly suggest that the dynamics which develop around intergroup contacts and intergroup communication habits in South Tyrol are extremely complex and bring many assumptions, prejudices and consequences with them which tend to freeze the situation.

4. Conclusions

The KOLIPSI project has highlighted many aspects crucial in South Tyrolean bilingualism from both the linguistic and psycho-social perspective. Even though we had to disregard many other factors related to L2 learning, e.g. attitude shaping, language habits etc. that were analyzed in the project (such as the widespread use of the German dialect, direct and indirect contact patterns, relative deprivation feelings, parents'/peers' influence), some of the most striking results we found have been discussed in this contribution. First of all, school type appears to be the strongest predictor of L2 proficiency in South Tyrol. As a matter of fact, in both communities pupils attending a technical high school achieve L2 competences that are clearly below the ones observed in academic high schools. It will be utmost interesting to further investigate the attitudes, beliefs and habits of the two groups of students as well as the L2 programs applied, in order to propose an explanation of the phenomenon and possible suggestions for improving the situation at technical schools. In addition, the data support the belief that it is the Italian-speaking community who has more difficulties in L2 learning in South Tyrol, as one third of the KOLIPSI target group still shows elementary L2 competences (A2). Regarding this result, we also showed how linguistic aspects go hand in hand with psycho-social ones, in particular with the orientation/motivation issue that seems to play an important role, in particular for the Italian speaking group. Motivation correlates positively with L2 proficiency of both German and Italian-speaking pupils but, in the latter case, integrative orientation seems to have a slightly higher

---

22. 81.6% of the Italian pupils who speak Italian in intergroup communication state that German-speaking South Tyroleans master Italian better than they master German.

correlation with L2 competence than motivation. This result hints at the fundamental role integrative goals seem to play in arousing and sustaining motivation among Italian-speaking pupils and on which society and school should build on. On the contrary, instrumental orientation does not correlate with L2 skills, showing that, in the South Tyrolean context, stressing the pragmatic benefits of mastering the L2 does not contribute to improving the pupils' competences at all. Nonetheless, both school and society rhetorically tend to focus exclusively on the importance that a good L2 mastery has for the pupils' future professional career, neglecting in a sense both the mere presence of the L2 community and the need and pleasure to get in touch with it. If this does not change things much for German-speaking pupils, as the vast majority of them normally speak Italian in intergroup communication, it does matter for the Italian-speaking ones who tend to constantly rely on their L1.

In order to improve their L2 competences, the availability of contact occasions between language groups ought to be enhanced along with the promotion of new communication routines where Italian speakers try to speak German and where German speakers are less eager to speak Italian. By showing positive cooperative multilingual communication examples[23], media and various social initiatives, involving not only the education system, but also family and friendship networks etc., could help to gradually introduce this new model of intergroup communication.

References

Abel, A. 2007. Die Südtiroler SchülerInnen und die Zweitsprache: Eine linguistische und sozialpsychologische Untersuchung (Werkstattbericht). *Linguistik Online* 32: 4–14.

Abel, A. & M. Stuflesser. 2009. Language-Bridges-Interviewstudie zum Zusammenspiel von Überzeugungen, Erfahrungen und Sprachenlernen: Methodenfragen und Ergebnisauswertung. In *Sprachvermittlung in Europa. Beiträge der Angewanden Linguistik zum Dialog zwischen Wissenschaft und Gesellschaft*, eds. E. Werlen & F. Tissot, 75–87. Baltmannsweiler: Schneider Hohengehren.

Abel, A., M. Stuflesser & L. Voltmer, eds. 2007. *Aspects of multilingualism in European border regions: Insights and views from Alsace, Eastern Macedonia and Thrace, the Lublin Voivodeship and South Tyrol*. Bolzano/Bozen: Eurac.

Abel, A., C. Vettori & D. Forer. Forthcoming. Learning the neighbour's language: The many challenges in achieving a real multilingual society. The case of second language acquisition in the minority-majority context of South Tyrol. In *European Yearbook of Minority Issues*, Vol. 9, eds. European Centre for Minority Issues & European Academy Bolzano/Bozen. Leiden: Brill.

Abel, A., C. Vettori & K. Wisniewski, eds. Forthcoming. *KOLIPSI. Die Südtiroler SchülerInnen und die Zweitsprache: Eine linguistische und sozialpsychologische Untersuchung*. Bolzano/Bozen: Eurac.

---

23. See, e.g., Lüdi (1996: 240): monolingual vs. multilingual mode.

AERA, APA & NCME (American Educational Research Association, American Psychological Association & National Council on Measurement in Education). 1999. *Standards for educational and psychological testing*. Washington DC: AERA.

Alcock, A. 1970. *The History of the South Tyrol Question*. PhD dissertation, University of Geneva.

Alcock, A. 2001. *The South Tyrol Autonomy: A Short Introduction*. County Londonderry, Bolzano/Bozen. <http://www.provinz.bz.it/lpa/themen/publikationen.asp?&somepubl_action=300&somepubl_image_id=1899> (6 June 2012).

ALTE (Association of Language Testers in Europe Principles of Good Practice). 2001. *Principles of good practice for ALTE examinations*. <http://www.testdaf.de/institut/pdf/ALTE/ALTE_good_practice.pdf> (3 July 2012).

ASTAT (Landesinstitut für Statistik, Autonome Provinz Bozen-Südtirol), ed. 2006a. *Südtiroler Sprachbarometer 2004*. Bolzano/Bozen: Autonome Provinz Bozen-Südtirol, Landesinstitut für Statistik.

ASTAT (Landesinstitut für Statistik, Autonome Provinz Bozen-Südtirol), ed. 2006b. *Ausländische Schulbevölkerung in Südtirol*. Bolzano/Bozen: Autonome Provinz Bozen-Südtirol, Landesinstitut für Statistik.

ASTAT, ed. 2010. *Zwei- und Dreisprachigkeitsprüfungen/Esami di bi- e trilinguismo* (ASTAT Info 05.02). Bolzano/Bozen: Autonome Provinz Bozen-Südtirol, Landesinstitut für Statistik.

Autonome Provinz Bozen Südtirol, ed. 2004. *Südtirol-Handbuch*, 23. Auflage. Bolzano/Bozen: Landespresseamt.

Autonome Provinz Bozen-Südtirol, ed. 2006. *Das neue Autonomiestatut*. Bolzano/Bozen: Landespresseamt.

Bachman, L. & A. Palmer. 1996. *Language Testing in Practice*. Oxford: OUP.

Baker, C. 2006. *Foundations of Bilingual Education and Bilingualism*, 4th edn. Clevedon: Multilingual Matters.

Baur, S. 1996. *Relazione complessiva sulla ricerca 'Motivazione e contatti': Condizioni di base dell'apprendimento della seconda lingua in Alto Adige*. Ms, Freie Universität Bozen.

Baur, S. 2000. *Die Tücken der Nähe: Kommunikation und Kooperation in Mehrheits-/Minderheitssituationen*. Meran: Alpha Beta.

Baur, S., G. Mezzalira & W. Pichler. 2008. *La lingua degli altri: Aspetti della politica linguistica e scolastica in Alto Adige-Südtirol dal 1945 ad oggi*. Milano: Angeli.

CENSIS (Centro studi nazionali investimenti sociali) & Autonome Provinz Bozen-Südtirol, eds. 1997. *Identität und Mobilität der drei Sprachgruppen: Abschließender Bericht*. Roma: Centro Studi Investimenti Sociali.

Deflorian, F. 1997. *Considerazioni riassuntive sui risultati delle prove nella comprensione scritta e orale, nella produzione scritta e nella produzione orale della lingua seconda degli alunni delle ultime classi della scuola elementare, media e superiore in lingua tedesca*. Ms, Provincia Autonoma di Bolzano/Bozen, Ufficio Bilinguismo.

Dörnyei, Z. 2001. *Teaching and Researching Motivation*. Harlow: Longman.

DPR 752/1976. *Dekret des Präsidenten der Republik vom 26. Juli 1976 (Nr. 752 1): Durchführungsbestimmungen zum Sonderstatut der Region Trentino-Südtirol auf dem Sachgebiet des Proporzes in den staatlichen Ämtern in der Provinz Bozen und der Kenntnis der beiden Sprachen im öffentlichen Dienst*. <http://www.provinz.bz.it/praesidium/0101/verletzungen/downloads/DPR%20752%201976%20dt.pdf> (6 June 2012).

Egger, K. 2001. *Sprachlandschaft im Wandel: Südtirol auf dem Weg zur Mehrsprachigkeit; soziolinguistische und psycholinguistische Aspekte der Ein- und Mehrsprachigkeit*. Bozen: Athesia.

Forer, D., M. P. Paladino, C. Vettori & A. Abel. 2008. Il bilinguismo in Alto Adige: Percezioni, osservazioni e opinioni su una questione quanto mai aperta. *Il Cristallo* L1: 49–62.

Gardner, R. C. 1985. The attitude/motivation test battery: Technical report. <http://publish.uwo.ca/~gardner/docs/AMTBmanual.pdf> (8 June 2012)

Gardner, R. C. 2007. Motivation and second language acquisition. *Porta Linguarum* 8: 9–20.

Giudiceandrea, L. 2006. *Spaesati: Italiani in Südtirol.* Bolzano/Bozen: Raetia.

Hesse, H. & S. Römisch. Forthcoming. Zur Einschätzung von Sprachleistungen auf der Grundlage des GERS: Ein IRT-Modell. In *KOLIPSI. Die Südtiroler SchülerInnen und die Zweitsprache: Eine linguistische und sozialpsychologische Untersuchung*, eds. A. Abel, C. Vettori & K. Wisniewski. Bolzano/Bozen: Eurac.

High Level Group on Multilingualism. 2007. *Final report.* <http://ec.europa.eu/education/policies/lang/doc/multireport_en.pdf> (8 June 2012).

Kane, M. T. 2001. Current concerns in validity theory. *Journal of Educational Measurement* 38: 319–342.

Lanthaler, F. 2006. Die Vielschichtigkeit des Deutschen in Südtirol. In *Mehrsprachigkeit in Europa: Erfahrungen, Bedürfnisse, Gute Praxis, Atti del convegno (Bolzano, 24–26 agosto 2006)*, eds. A. Abel, M. Stuflesser & M. Putz, 371–380. Bolzano/Bozen: Eurac.

Lüdi, G. 1996. Mehrsprachigkeit. In *Kontaktlinguistik: Ein internationales Handbuch zeitgenössischer Forschung*, 1. Halbband, eds. H. Goebl, P. H. Nelde, Z. Starý & W. Wölck, 233–245. Berlin: Mouton de Gruyter.

Masgoret, A. M. & R. C. Gardner. 2003. Attitude, motivation, and second language learning: A meta-analysis of studies conducted by Gardner and associates. *Language Learning* 53: 123–163.

Putzer, O. 1997a. *Zusammenfassende Analyse und Ergebnisse der schriftlichen Sprachfertigkeiten an den italienischen Oberschulen, Mittelschulen und Grundschulen.* Ms, Provincia Autonoma di Bolzano/Bozen, Ufficio Bilinguismo.

Putzer, O. 1997b. *Zusammenfassende Analyse und Ergebnisse der mündlichen Sprachfertigkeiten an den italienischen Oberschulen, Mittelschulen und Grundschulen.* Ms, Provincia Autonoma di Bolzano/Bozen, Ufficio Bilinguismo.

Riehl, C. M. 2007. Varietätengebrauch und Varietätenkontakt in Südtirol und Ostbelgien. *Linguistik Online* 32: 105–177.

Schneider, G. & B. North. 2000. *Sprachen können – was heisst das? Skalen zur Beschreibung, Beurteilung und Selbstbeurteilung von fremdsprachlicher Kommunikationsfähigkeit.* Chur: Rüegger.

Trim, J., B. North & B. Coste. 2001. *Common European framework of reference for languages (CEFR).* <http://www.coe.int/t/dg4/linguistic/Source/Framework_EN.pdf> (6 June 2012).

Ushioda, E. 1996. *The Role of Motivation.* Dublin: Authentik.

Vettori, C. 2005. *La competenza del tedesco degli studenti italofoni di scuola media inferiore e superiore di Bolzano e Trento: Confronto e valutazione.* PhD dissertation, University of Modena and Reggio Emilia.

Vettori, C. Forthcoming. L'apprendimento della seconda lingua in Alto Adige: orientamenti e motivazione. Contesto e criticità. In *KOLIPSI. Die Südtiroler SchülerInnen und die Zweitsprache: Eine linguistische und sozialpsychologische Untersuchung*, eds. A. Abel, C. Vettori & K. Wisniewski. Bolzano/Bozen: Eurac.

Voltmer, L. 2007. Languages in South Tyrol: Historical and legal aspects. In *Aspects of Multilingualism in European Border Regions: Insights and Views from Alsace, Eastern Macedonia and Thrace, the Lublin Voivodeship and South Tyrol*, eds. A. Abel, M. Stuflesser & L. Voltmer, 201–220. Bolzano/Bozen: Eurac.

Wisniewski, K. 2009. La conoscenza della seconda lingua nel contesto multilingue dell'Alto Adige: Un confronto fra attività comunicative orali e scritte con particolare attenzione alla competenza pragmatica. In *Atti del 9° Congresso dell'Associazione Italiana di Linguistica Applicata (AItLA): Oralità/scrittura. In memoria di Giorgio Raimondo Cardona*, eds. C. Consani, C. Furiassi, G. Francesca & C. Perta, 283–303. Perugia: Guerra Edizioni.

List of contributors

Abel, Andrea
andrea.abel@eurac.edu

Akpınar, Deniz
deniz.akpinar@yahoo.de

Becher, Viktor
vibe@fastmail.fm

Benet, Ariadna
ariadna.benet@gmail.com
Universität Osnabrück
Fachbereich 7 (Sprach- und Literaturwis-
senschaft) – Romanistik
Altes Kreishaus
Neuer Graben 40
49074 Osnabrück
Germany

Bianchi, Giulia
giulia.bianchi@uni-hamburg.de

Braunmüller, Kurt
braunmueller@uni-hamburg.de
Universität Hamburg
Institut für Germanistik I -Skandinavistik
Von-Melle-Park 6
20146 Hamburg
Germany

Brehmer, Bernhard
bernhard.brehmer@uni-hamburg.de
Universität Hamburg
Institut für Slavistik
Von-Melle-Park 6
20146 Hamburg
Germany

Bührig, Kristin
buehrig@pragmatiknetz.de
Universität Hamburg
Institut für Germanistik I
Von-Melle-Park 6
20146 Hamburg
Germany

Buthke, Carolin
caro.buthke@gmx.de

Carroll, Susanne Elizabeth
susanne.carroll@ucalgary.ca
Language Research Centre
University of Calgary
2500 University Dr. N.W.
Calgary, AB, T2N 1N4
Canada

Cortés, Susana
cortes.susana@gmail.com

Czachór, Agnieszka
agnieszka.czachor@uni-hamburg.de

Deuchar, Margaret
m.deuchar@bangor.ac.uk

Elsig, Martin
martin_elsig@msn.com
Goethe Universität Frankfurt am Main
Institut für Romanische Sprachen und
Literaturen
Grüneburgplatz 1
60629 Frankfurt am Main
Germany

Feldhausen, Ingo
ingo.feldhausen@gmx.de

Festman, Julia
festman@uni-potsdam.de
Universität Potsdam
Potsdam Research Institute for
Multilingualism
Haus 2
Campus Golm
Karl-Liebknecht-Str. 24–25
14476 Potsdam
Germany

Gabriel, Christoph
christoph.gabriel@uni-hamburg.de
Universität Hamburg
Institut für Romanistik
Von-Melle-Park 6
20146 Hamburg
Germany

Gagarina, Natalia
gagarina@zas.gwz-berlin.de
Zentrum für Allgemeine Sprachwissenschaft
Schützenstr. 18
10117 Berlin
Germany

Haenni Hoti, Andrea U.
andrea.haenni@phz.ch
Pädagogische Hochschule Zentralschweiz
Institut für Schule und Heterogenität
Töpferstrasse 10
6004 Luzern
Switzerland

Heinzmann, Sybille
sybille.heinzmann@phz.ch

Heycock, Caroline
heycock@ling.ed.ac.uk
University of English Language

School of Philosophy, Psychology and
Language Sciences
Dugald Stewart Building
3 Charles Street
Edinburgh
EH8 9AD
United Kingdom

Höder, Steffen
dr@steffenhoeder.de
Christian-Albrechts-Universität zu Kiel
Institut für Skandinavistik, Frisistik und
Allgemeine Sprachwissenschaft
Christian-Albrechts-Platz 4
24098 Kiel
Germany

House, Juliane
jhouse@fastmail.fm

Kireva, Elena
elena_kireva2004@yahoo.de

Kliche, Ortrun
ortrun.kliche@uni-hamburg.de

Kranich, Svenja
svenjakranich@googlemail.com
UHH

Kupisch, Tanja
tanja.kupisch@rom.lu.se
Universität Hamburg
Institut für Romanistik
Von-Melle-Park 6
20146 Hamburg
Germany

Lleó, Conxita
lleo@uni-hamburg.de
Universität Hamburg
Institut für Romanistik
Von-Melle-Park 6
20146 Hamburg
Germany

Meisenburg, Trudel
tmeisenb@uos.de
Universität Osnabrück
Fachbereich 7 (Sprach- und
Literaturwissenschaft) – Romanistik
Altes Kreishaus
Neuer Graben 40
49074 Osnabrück
Germany

Meyer, Bernd
meyerb@uni-mainz.de

Pawlack, Birte
birte@pawlack.de

Pérez-Leroux, Ana
at.perez.leroux@utoronto.ca

Pešková, Andrea
andrea.peskova@uni-hamburg.de
Universität Hamburg
Institut für Romanistik
Von-Melle-Park 6
20146 Hamburg
Germany

Petersen, Hjalmar P.
hjalmar@setur.fo

Pierantozzi, Cristina
cripierantozzi@yahoo.it

Pirvulescu, Mihaela
ma.pirvulescu@utoronto.ca
University of Toronto
Department of Language Studies
3359 Mississauga Road North
North Building, Room 238
Mississauga, ON, L5L 1C6
Canada

Prys, Myfyr
elsa03@bangor.ac.uk
ESRC Centre for Research on Bilingualism
in Theory and Practice
Bangor University
College Road
Bangor, Gwynedd
LL57 2DG
Wales
United Kingdom

Ringblom, Natasha
natasha.ringblom@slav.su.se
Stockholm University
Russian (Department of Slavic Languages)
Universitetsvägen 10 E, plan 6
106 91 Stockholm
Sweden

Roberge, Yves
yves.roberge@utoronto.ca

Roberts, Gwerfyl
gwerfyl.w.roberts@bangor.ac.uk

Rothweiler, Monika
rothweil@uni-bremen.de

Schönenberger, Manuela
iris.schoenenberger@uni-oldenburg.de
Carl von Ossietzky Universität
Oldenburg
Institut für Anglistik/Amerikanistik
Fakultät 3: Sprach- und Kulturwissen-
schaften
Postfach 2503
26111 Oldenburg
Germany

Sichel-Bazin, Rafèu
rsichelb@uos.de
Universität Osnabrück
Fachbereich 7 (Sprach- und Literaturwis-
senschaft) – Romanistik
Altes Kreishaus
Neuer Graben 40
49074 Osnabrück
Germany

Sterner, Franziska
franziska.sterner@uni-hamburg.de

Stöhr, Antje
antje.stoehr@yahoo.de

Strik, Nelleke
nelleke.strik@dal.ca
Dalhousie University
Department of French
Marion McCain Arts & Social Sciences
Building, room 3130
6135 University Avenue
PO Box 15000
Halifax, Nova Scotia
Canada B3H 4R2

Szabó, Csilla-Anna
csilla.wilhelm@germanistik.uni-giessen.
de
Justus-Liebig-Universität Gießen
FB 05 Sprache, Literatur, Kultur
Otto-Behaghel-Str. 10C
35394 Gießen
Germany

Vettori, Chiara
chiara.vettori@eurac.edu
Institute for Specialised Communication
and Multilingualism
Viale Druso 1
39100 Bolzano
Italy

Wisniewski, Katrin
katrin.wisniewski@eurac.edu

Żaba, Aleksandra
aleksandra.zaba@uni-hamburg.de

Zerbian, Sabine
sabine.zerbian@gmail.com
Universität Potsdam
Department Linguistik
Haus 14/35
Karl-Liebknecht-Straße 24–25
14476 Potsdam
Germany

Name index

Subject index